Lonely Planet Publications
Melbourne I Oakland I London I Paris

D1385735

Duncan Garwood &
Kristin Kimball

Rome

The Top Five

1 Roman Forum
The beating heart of ancient Rome (p72)

2 Capitoline Hill
Perhaps the most elegant public space in the world (p80)

3 Colosseum
The symbol of the Eternal City (p76)

4 St Peter's Basilica
An awesome spectacle whatever your faith (p128)

5 Trastevere
One of Rome's most charming areas (p108)

Contents

Published by Lonely Planet Publications Pty Ltd
ABN 36 005 607 983

Australia Head Office, Locked Bag 1, Footscray
Victoria 3001 ☎ 03 8379 8000, fax 03 8379 8111
talk2us@lonelyplanet.com.au

USA 150 Linden St, Oakland, CA 94607
☎ 510 893 8555, toll free 800 275 8555
fax 510 893 8572, info@lonelyplanet.com

UK 72–82 Rosebery Ave, Clerkenwell, London,
EC1R 4RW ☎ 020 7841 9000, fax 020 7841 9001
go@lonelyplanet.co.uk

France 1 rue du Dahomey, 75011 Paris
☎ 01 55 25 33 00, fax 01 55 25 33 01
bip@lonelyplanet.fr, www.lonelyplanet.fr

© Lonely Planet 2004
Photographs © Martin Moos and as listed on p285,
2004

The Authors

DUNCAN GARWOOD

Duncan currently lives in the wine-rich hills overlooking Rome, dividing his time between writing and teaching the English language to, among others, Miss World contestants. Prior to this, he spent two years in the southern port town of Bari. His first, and nearly last, taste of travelling came with a trip to India and Nepal where an inescapably intimate encounter with a pig almost put paid to any further travel. University and a spell in corporate journalism followed, but writing about sewerage couldn't match the exotic lures of the Puglian capital which claimed him in 1997.

KRISTIN KIMBALL

Kristin Kimball fell in love with Italian art and culture at an impressionable age, and was hooked for life. This is her second book on Rome. She's also written on scuba diving in Key West and the volcano of Montserrat for *Travel + Leisure* magazine. When not travelling, she writes, edits and teaches in Upstate New York, where she lives with her wily hound, beloved hens, a hive of honeybees and one wingnut farmer.

CONTRIBUTING AUTHORS

MATTHEW EVANS
The Food & Drink chapter was based on Lonely Planet's *World Food Italy* by Matthew Evans. A chef before becoming a food writer and restaurant critic, Matthew is currently chief restaurant reviewer for the *Sydney Morning Herald* and co-editor of the *Sydney Morning Herald Good Food Guide*.

WENDY OWEN
Wendy fell hopelessly in love with Italy and stayed for over seven years. After a glorious time as a freelance journalist, TV researcher and sometime English teacher, she completed an honours degree in Fine Art before joining Lonely Planet's editorial team. The Excursions chapter is based on Wendy's research.

RICHARD WATKINS
Richard studied ancient history at Cardiff University, before continuing his interest in all things ancient and Roman at Oxford University, with a penchant for late-Roman paganism. For this book Richard wrote the History chapter.

PHOTOGRAPHER
MARTIN MOOS
Born in Zürich, Switzerland, Martin got the obvious banking degree before escaping onto the travellers' trail with his Nikon gear in 1986. Seven years in Northeast Asia have provided oodles of motives for an in-depth learning by doing. He is presently based again in Zürich, together with his wife and two children, cramped by mountains of slides…

Introducing Rome

Rome is the real thing. So many of its legendary sights are the original article that to see them is often to fulfil a lifelong dream. And it's this that raises the goose pimples: the feeling that the city really is as old as its seven hills, that in Rome time and beauty are measured on an altogether grander scale.

But to label this bewitching, chaotic, exhausting and romantic city an open-air museum is to deny it much of its character. Take the Colosseum, for example. To look up in awe, ignoring the hive of activity that's taking place all around you – the hustlers hawking their overpriced tat, the gladiators with their crocodile grins and plastic swords – is to overlook the minutiae of everyday Roman life. Romans don't deny their heritage, nor do they seek to set it on a pedestal, they simply accept it and get on with the onerous task of earning their daily crust.

For Rome, more than for most cities, this has always been the central dilemma of city life: how to maintain its priceless heritage while improving the lot of its cheerfully cynical inhabitants. Certainly the Jubilee-inspired efforts of recent years have made a difference. Transport has been boosted, new museums have been opened and old ones renovated, and the long-awaited music auditorium has opened to universal praise – improvements which even the most begrudging of Romans would acknowledge. To say, however, that Rome has never had it so good would be to overstate the case. It hasn't re-found the heady days of *la dolce vita*, but it is looking good and it is feeling better than it has for a long time.

In a country of unparalleled beauty, both natural and architectural, Rome remains the jewel in the crown. In no other city can you see so much in such a short space of time and yet merely scratch the surface. Strip away one layer of history and another appears in its place – often quite literally. The city you see on the surface tells quite a tale, but not the whole story. About 4m below ground level there exists another world, with traces of other settlements deeper still. St Peter's Basilica stands on the site of an earlier basilica, built by Emperor Constantine in the 4th century AD over the necropolis where St Peter is believed to have been buried. Castel Sant'Angelo was the tomb of Emperor Hadrian before it was converted into a fortress. The form of Piazza Navona suggests a hippodrome and, in fact, it was built on the ruins of the Emperor Domitian's stadium.

In Rome every period has left a mark. In fact, from the time when it was *caput mundi* (centre of the world), through the development of Christianity to the present day – a period of more than 2500 years – Rome has become an unsurpassed anthropological and archaeological archive of Western culture. And it's enough to wander the streets to see this. The art of Michelangelo, the sculptures of Bernini, the ivy-clad *palazzi* lining cobbled streets, the perfectly formed piazzas – Rome is all this. Nothing is hidden, it's all there waiting for you, much as it has been for hundreds of years.

But what you see in Rome is not everything. What you eat also counts – pizzas bubbling with tomato and mozzarella, the thin crust just beginning to blacken in the heat of the burning wood; pasta cooked *al dente* and seasoned with nothing more than black pepper and pecorino cheese; the freshly baked croissant that tastes so good with cappuccino, served just the warm side of hot. These simple staples are an integral part of any Roman holiday.

Rome is a hugely popular year-round tourist destination, but the summer months can be steaming. In particular, July and August are usually unpleasantly hot, making sightseeing a considerable physical challenge. However, it's in precisely these months that you'll find the city at its least chaotic and most festive as festivals turn much of the city centre into a vast open-air stage. Traditionally, the best times to visit are spring and autumn. Spring sees the city's flora burst into life, while autumn witnesses the city reawakening after its August torpor.

Lowdown

Population 2,546,000
Population over 65 458,425
Population under 13 303,070
Time zone Central European Time (GMT + 1 hour)
Churches 900
Museums 92
Public toilets 40
Symbol The wolf

DUNCAN'S TOP ROME DAY

I'm staying in the Borgo, just outside the Vatican. It's a quiet area, at least at night, and one that captures the Rome of my imagination. It's also perfect for an early morning visit to St Peter's. I get there with the larks and am treated to an amazing light display as columns of May sunshine stream into the near empty basilica. Breaking the spell I decide to head into town on foot. Crossing the bridge by Castel Sant'Angelo, I hit Corso Vittorio Emanuele II, but decide at a certain point to veer off and check out the second-hand shops along Via del Governo Vecchio.

A quick mid-morning coffee at Piazza Navona and it's off to Largo Argentina where I pick up the tram for Trastevere and lunch. It's a long lunch with just a little wine which needs to be walked off. No problem. I head up Via Garibaldi to the Gianicolo and the most spectacular view in, and of, town. Once there I have to make a decision. If the match starts at 8.30pm, what time shall I leave for the stadium? Tonight it's the Rome derby and I have tickets.

Duncan Garwood

My Essential Rome

- **St Peter's Basilica (p128)** – in particular Michelangelo's La Pietà
- **Piazza Santa Maria in Trastevere (p109)**
- **Terme di Caracalla (p114)**
- **Museo e Galleria Borghese (p125)**
- **Piazzale Giuseppe Garibaldi (p111)** – the view from Gianicolo Hill

City Life

City Life

ROME TODAY

Images of life in Rome – Gregory Peck and Audrey Hepburn hurtling round on a moped, a voluptuous Anita Ekberg cavorting in the Trevi Fountain – unfortunately bear little resemblance to the modern reality of this two-faced city. It is true that well-dressed Romeos still buzz around the city on Vespas, riding with the type of skill that can only be innate. It's also true that Romans like to cut a figure and wouldn't dream of venturing out in anything less than their finest threads. Where film and life tend to diverge, however, is suburban Rome, the Rome as experienced by virtually no tourist and almost every inhabitant. It's a Rome of sprawling housing blocks, of hugely popular out-of-town shopping malls, of groups of identically dressed teenagers comparing mobile phones; it's a city embracing the global brand culture. You only have to check out the Saturday afternoon shopping frenzy to see that 21st-century consumerism is alive and well in the Eternal City.

But while the lure of the label is nothing new – think Vespa and Valentino, Fendi and Ferrari – the mall is. Where before small neighbourhood shops provided most necessities (Italians include swanky threads as necessities), now it's all supermarkets, megastores and continuous opening hours. And while this change has been welcomed by many, particularly the younger generations, others are sceptical, bemoaning the demise of the old ways.

Romans love to grumble and have a stock list of subjects. Topping the chart is the lament that the city authorities don't give a monkey's about the suburbs as long as the tourists are happy in the centre. The much hallowed city-wide cleanup for the Holy Jubilee in 2000 did wonders for the historic *palazzi* and museums of tourist itineraries, but little for the nuts and bolts of suburban infrastructure. Not a new issue, it's something that left-wing Walter Veltroni has been seeking to address since he succeeded Francesco Rutelli as mayor in 2001. He brought with him a list of worthy projects for the 'burbs, including a planned €1,800 million investment package specifically for the outskirts. And there have been improvements – a library here, a car park there – but still the folk wait for the big money to arrive.

And still they wait for public transport to improve. Rome's desperately inadequate metro struggles to cope with a daily demand that is already well over operating limits while buses battle their way through traffic and streets made impenetrable by cars double parked. Add to this the occasional strike and you have a recipe for chaos. Lucky then that Romans love to drive. Head into the centre on a Saturday night and you'll witness traffic jams worthy of a Monday rush hour. Where are they all going, you ask. Probably nowhere, aimless cruising being a favourite Saturday night pastime. Besides, no young Roman would be seen dead arriving at the disco in anything other than a car – *Sei matto? Are you mad?*

Hot Conversation Topics

- I reckon this government's going to fall within the next six months.
- OK, we've got the Auditorium now, so I guess that means we'll start getting some decent big-name concerts?
- The Underground works in London, so I don't see why we can't get ours to work. And when are they going to put in a proper air-conditioning system?
- Let's have a look. My sister's boyfriend's got one the same, except he's got his tattooed on his left shoulder.
- Rents are really getting out of hand. You can't get a room in the centre for less than €500 these days.
- I hate having to wear a helmet. I only use my scooter in town.
- Will Lazio ever beat Roma in a derby game?

CITY CALENDAR

Rome's calendar bursts with events ranging from colourful traditional celebrations with a religious and/or historical flavour, through to festivals of the performing arts, including opera, music and theatre.

Summer is definitely the best time to visit if you want to catch the best of the festivals. The Estate Romana festival which runs from June to September sponsors literally hundreds of events, many of which are staged in spectacular outdoor settings. But the fun doesn't end with the onset of autumn as the Romaeuropa festival (dance, theatre and opera) simply takes over.

For music and film festival listings see the Entertainment chapter p176; for a list of public holidays see p267.

Autumn is regarded as high season in Rome; the weather is cooler and better suited to pounding the streets. In summer daytime temperatures can soar, but the evenings are long and, if you know where to go, lively. However, be warned: in August many small businesses, including some restaurants and hotels, simply down tools until September. This can be frustrating but is unlikely to change, so get used to the idea.

February
CARNEVALE

Children in fancy dress parade the streets – favourite costumes include Zorro for the boys and Snow White for the girls – and throw confetti over each other. Adults eat *bigné* (profiteroles) and *fritelle* (fried pastries).

March/April
FESTA DELLA PRIMAVERA
Piazza di Spagna; metro Spagna

The Spanish Steps are filled with thousands of azaleas – a perfect photo occasion.

SETTIMANA DEI BENI CULTURALI
☎ 06 589 98 44; www.beniculturali.it

A bonanza of free culture. Public museums and galleries open free of charge and free guided tours aim to get Italians (and foreigners) back into their heritage.

April
NATALE DI ROMA
21 April; Campidoglio; bus to Piazza Venezia

The Eternal City explodes with joy on her birthday. Founded in 753 BC, Rome was 2756 in 2003. Bands and standard bearers perform in Piazza del Campidoglio as fireworks go off all around.

May
PRIMO MAGGIO
1 May; Piazza San Giovanni; metro San Giovanni

Rome's biggest open-air rock concert attracts top international names and thousands of fans from all over the country. May Day is the workers' holiday and until recently public transport didn't run on 1 May with comically predictable chaos.

Posters advertising Roman rock concerts

July
FESTA DI NOANTRI
Last two weeks of the month; Piazza Santa Maria in Trastevere; tram to Viale Trastevere

Fireworks and festivities fill Trastevere's streets for two hot summer weeks. There are plenty of stalls and residents noisily drink local wine and eat *porchetta* (roasted suckling pig, stuffed with herbs and cooked on the spit).

ROME PRIDE
www.mariomieli.it (Italian only) for information

An annual festival celebrating gay rights and culture.

August
FERRAGOSTO
15 August
The Festival of the Assumption is celebrated with almost total shutdown. Everything closes, and the only thing served in the few restaurants still open is the traditional Ferragosto dish of *pollo con peperoni* (chicken with capsicum).

September
VIA DELL'ORSO CRAFT FAIR
Piazza Navona; bus to Corso Rinascimento
Artisans in and around this characteristic street near Piazza Navona open their studios and workshops to browsers and buyers.

October/November
VIA DEI CORONARI MOSTRA-MERCATO
Piazza Navona; bus to Corso Rinascimento
This famous antiques street just off Piazza Navona opens its doors and displays its wares.

December/January
PIAZZA NAVONA CHRISTMAS FAIR
Early Dec-6 Jan; Piazza Navona; bus to Corso Rinascimento
Depending on how you look at them, the stalls and souvenirs that take over the piazza are either great fun or one big eyesore. But, like a bad case of herpes, they keep coming back.

PRESEPI
Churches around Rome set up their nativity scenes. The mother of all *presepi* is in Piazza San Pietro in front of the Basilica. You can't miss it.

Festival Fun

Estate Romana Every year from June to September this festival turns Rome into a giant stage. Events range from book fairs to opera to poetry recitals.
Romaeuropa Rome's autumn arts festival (September to November) brings top artists to the capital with dance, theatre and opera the main ingredients.
Feast of Sts Peter and Paul Every Italian city has a patron saint but Rome has two. The two saints are celebrated in religious services and with a street fair and fireworks on 29 June.
Carnevale If you're around in the week before Lent expect to be assailed by little people in costume.
¡Fiesta! The sights, sounds and rhythms of Latin America hit Rome's suburbs. You can eat Argentinian steak, dance the samba and buy Andean pipe music. It's held on the race track on Via Appia from mid-June to September.

CULTURE

IDENTITY

Romans present two faces to the visitor: one the charming smiler for whom nothing is too much trouble, the other the unhelpful, indifferent oaf for whom everything is too much trouble. So what is the true Roman like?

The common perception that all Italians are as spontaneous as they are laid-back is a misconception. They *can* be spontaneous and they *can* be laid-back. But Romans in particular can also be completely conformist and inflexible.

Conformity comes out in the way they dress. In winter in particular, the men wear a uniform – albeit an elegant one with more than a passing resemblance to an English country squire – think well-cut sports jacket, casual trousers, shirt and tie, topped by a Barbour-style waxed jacket.

It also comes out in the way they behave. For Italians in general, and Romans are no exception, looks count, and *la bella figura* (which roughly translates as making a good impression) is everything. Few Italians drink much alcohol, it being difficult to remain cool if you're drunk, and overt drunkenness – especially if you are a woman – is *really* frowned upon.

Pride also informs much of the typical Roman character. Subject to *campanilismo* (literally, an attachment to the local bell tower) as much as their neighbours, Romans are first and foremost Roman and only then Italian. This naturally engenders a deep-rooted pride which, in the case of the Romans, some would say slips over into arrogance. In fact, the Romans are often presented as a lazy, smug lot, happy to live off the fat of other people's work.

Inroads into the Old Order

Rome is synonymous with Catholicism. The Pope lives in the centre of town (OK, technically it's the Vatican) and every year millions come to Italy just to catch a glimpse of the octogenarian pontiff.

The year 2000 witnessed a particularly spectacular influx, as more than 16 million poured into the city for the Holy Jubilee celebrations. These culminated in a mega-concert held in the city outskirts, attended by some two million young papal fans. Judged a success by everyone, the message was clear: world Catholicism is thriving. But what of religion in Italy?

The role of religion in modern Italian life often appears to be more a matter of form than serious belief. But form counts in Italy and first communions, church weddings and religious feast days are an integral part of life. Church attendance stands at about 35%, compared with 70% after the war, yet 84% of Italians consider themselves Catholic.

Of the non-Catholics in Italy, it's the Muslims who are making the furthest inroads. Boosted by immigration – 36.5% of immigrants are Muslim – there are now anywhere between 580,000 and 700,000 Muslims in Italy, making Islam Italy's second religion. Most have settled in the industrial north, but there is a community in Rome, based around the city mosque which was inaugurated in 1995.

The issue of immigration is one that divides Italy. Some say it's essential to maintain population growth (without immigration Italy's population would be decreasing), others that it's an open invitation for criminals to enter the country. However, the upper hand is held firmly by the anti-immigration lobby. Parliament recently passed a much debated law – the Bossi-Fini law, after the two authors, Umberto Bossi of the *Lega Nord* (Northern League) and Gianfranco Fini of the post-Fascist *Alleanza Nazionale* (National Alliance) – according to which an immigrant can enter the country only with a valid work contract. Once the contract period is over, the right to stay in Italy is automatically revoked. Critics note that the exception made of home-helps conveniently allows the rich to keep their army of formerly clandestine servants.

Partly envy, partly racism – in the case of Umberto Bossi's Lega Nord (Northern League) chanting *Roma, Roma, Padrone, Ladrona* (Rome, Rome, Boss, Thief), most definitely racism – this anti-Rome feeling is fuelled by the fact that for many Rome is synonymous with the state. And the state means taxes. The fact that services and welfare benefits are woefully inadequate and that Italian politicians are among the highest paid in Europe, despite average salaries well below those of England, France and Germany, merely adds salt to the wounds. Is it not also a well-known fact, inquire Rome bashers, that the bloated state bureaucracy is vastly overstaffed by underqualified relatives of former workers?

Miracle Worker or Madman?

In November 2002 a controversial Roman doctor announced that he had successfully implanted three women with cloned human embryos and that the first baby was due in January 2003. The world's scientific community was not amused, furiously condemning the news as nothing more than self-publicity. The fact that no baby ever appeared and that no names were ever released seemed to support their case. But with Professor Severino Antinori you can never be quite sure.

The 58-year-old Roman embryologist has been provoking admiration and animosity ever since he first came to the world's notice in 1994. A renowned expert in in-vitro fertilisation, it was to Antinori that a certain Rosana Della Cortes turned when she decided, at the age of 63, she wanted a baby. The assisted pregnancy that followed was successful and Mrs Cortes earned her place in the record books as the oldest woman ever to give birth.

To his happy army of mums Antinori is a saint, to others he's a madman who wants to imitate Hitler. For his part, he claims to want nothing more than to help childless couples. It's for this reason, he says, that he's switched his attention to cloning.

Human cloning is outlawed by European law but the good doctor has gone on record to say that if necessary he'll work on a boat in international waters. The technology, he says, exists, and he can see no medical or ethical reason why he shouldn't use it.

A devout Catholic, Professor Severino Antinori is a man who knows his mind.

This resentment all points towards Rome and the people who work there, the Romans. Their response, however, is typical – 'what do I care?' You see, the Romans know they live in the centre of the world and if the rest of Italy doesn't like it, well, tough, that's their problem.

LIFESTYLE

Many people say of Rome that it's the largest town in Italy. What they mean is that it lacks the cosmopolitan air that characterises so many of Europe's capitals and even, to an extent, some of northern Italy's industrial centres. Milan, for example, is regarded as a much more European city than Rome will ever be. This is partly explained through geography and partly through business. Milan is the commercial and financial capital of Italy, Rome the political and banking centre.

Much professional life in the capital is, in fact, centred around the machinery of government. The huge civil-service structure has long been the city's major employer, providing jobs for an army of less than dedicated bureaucrats. The pace, naturally, is slow and although things are changing as younger managers are brought in, the pace remains less than electric. Just so with Roman life, which can either be delightfully relaxed or absolutely maddening, depending on your mood.

Locals catch up on Piazza Navona (p89)

In Rome, as in all of Italy, the one institution on which people continue to depend is the family. It is still the rule rather than the exception for young Italians to stay at home until they marry although modern attitudes are beginning to erode the traditions. This is especially true in Rome and Milan where many young people (particularly students from regional Italy) are forced to live away from home. But necessity is one thing, choice another.

Traditionally, young Italians claim they can't leave home because they can't afford it – rents are universally high and unemployment is a problem. True enough, but these reasons don't totally convince. Cynics suggest it's a quid pro quo arrangement with parents booking a comfortable retirement courtesy of their children and the kids there to enjoy life before work, marriage and parenthood. Italy's highest appeals court seemed to sustain this in April 2002 when it ruled that a Neapolitan doctor continue to pay for his son. The son in question was a law graduate in his mid-thirties, had a trust fund of US$220,000 and had previously rejected more than one job offer. Other people say that Italian families simply like living together.

The Italian family is, however, shrinking. Nearly half of all families are ruled by a single child, childless couples are no longer the exception and in 2000 the divorce rate hit 39%, meaning an increase in single-parent families. The church is not impressed.

The power of the church might not be what it once was, but it still counts, especially on social issues. Generously, the Vatican is never afraid to help when it feels Italians need a little moral guidance. It's not surprising therefore to hear the Pope reminding married couples that it's their duty to procreate. A sentiment much endorsed by politicians, who for their part worry that the world's lowest birth rate threatens the future tax returns necessary for paying the country's pensions.

Italian women, it would seem, are increasingly choosing a career over children. Italy's maternity allowances are generous but still women, who today constitute 37.5% of the workforce, prefer to limit themselves to a single child at most. Italy's army of grandparents berate their children for this, grumbling that the younger generation simply won't make the sacrifices necessary to bring up kids. Certainly the 'we can't afford children' argument seems difficult to sustain as although average disposable incomes for Italian families are still lower than those in other parts of Europe, they are on the rise. According to the Centre for Economic and Business Research, the average disposable income for an Italian family in 2002 was €24,640 (compared to €35,270 in the UK and €32,757 in France).

Despite these changes, Italy remains a country of conservative mores. While, for example, cohabiting among unmarried couples is becoming more widespread and homosexuality is well tolerated in Rome, the idea of gay marriages has most politicians choking on their cappuccinos.

Latin Lovers & Mummies' Boys

The rough charm of the unshaven Italian Lothario is an inescapable image. The truth is perhaps a little less alluring.

According to figures published in 2003 by Istat (Istituto Centrale di Statistica), the country's main statistics body, Italian men actually constitute an *esercito di mammoni* (army of mummies' boys). If you believe the figures, 67.9% of single Italian men remain at home with mum (and dad) up to the age of 34 at least. And even after the big move, one in three continue to see *la mamma* every day.

Not surprisingly this is not always appreciated by Italian wives. In fact, nagging mothers-in-law are the direct cause of about 30% of all marriage breakdowns and in March 2003 the Italian Supreme Court granted a woman from L'Aquila a divorce on the grounds of an invasive mother-in-law. Perhaps this shrewish relative would have benefited from the course for prospective mothers-in-law set up by an enterprising lawyer from Reggio Emilia. Lessons focused on the tricky art of how *not* to tell your daughter-in-law she shouldn't work, can't cook and doesn't know the first thing about bringing up your grandchild.

The chances of the marriage taking place at all are also looking grim. Research carried out by the Italian Institute of Andrology reveals that many young Italian men are struggling to live up to the stereotype of the Latin lover. Around 18% of 18 to 30-year-olds admitted to having no sex life at all, with a further 20% stating that they suffered serious problems in sexual performance, blaming it on work stress and fatigue. But things picked up in the older age group, with 75% of men between the ages of 60 and 70 claiming that they had a happy sex life.

So if it's a Latin lover you're after, find one of pensionable age...or go to Spain.

FASHION

To a Roman, young or old, being different is not something aspired to. In fact, fitting in is everything. The uniformity of taste is total. When, for example, the craze for tattoos and piercing swept in from America via MTV and Eminem, Roman teenagers couldn't leap onto the bandwagon quickly enough. Body art, most commonly in the form of a discreet shoulder design or a lower-back wing spread, hit Rome's young flesh like a plague of ink. It was a short-lived craze that was symptomatic of Roman fashion, both high and street. Romans are no innovators, they follow. The trendsetters look abroad and copy the foreign modes of the moment, the rest follow them first, each other second. For the cutting Italian edge, head north to Milan.

However, unoriginal as styles may be, clothes are invariably of a high quality, outfits well thought out and perfectly proper. It's rare to see a Roman fashion disaster. Italians seem to have an innate sense of what works well for them and they'll stick with that. Conservatism and elegance are the order of the day, even when that involves the figure-hugging styles so beloved of Italian womenfolk. Skintight hipsters and miniskirts may be sexy but they no longer shock, they've become mainstream.

The two major names in the world of Roman fashion are Valentino Garavani, best known by his Christian name, and Laura Biagiotti. When Valentino set up his *alta moda* in 1959, his clientele included Jackie Kennedy, Sophia Loren and Audrey Hepburn. While his couture collections, featuring spectacular evening gowns, have always been inaccessible to all but the wealthiest of customers, his ready-to-wear lines for both men and women, introduced in the 1970s, have become staples of the fashionable set. Laura Biagiotti, however, is known for her luxurious knitwear and sumptuous silk separates, often in cream and white. Something of a philanthropist, Biagiotti has funded many restoration projects in Rome.

Rome's major fashion event is the Alta Moda spectacle, staged every July in Piazza di Spagna. Covered by national television, it offers a glitzy occasion for Rome's designers to showcase their latest collections.

Me & My Mobile

Mobile phones might be everywhere, but in Italy they seem to be, well, more everywhere. In fact, with subscription rates forecast to hit 90% by 2004, Italians are among the best connected people in the world.

Mobile phones are the one truly universal accessory that *no* self-respecting Roman could possibly be without. Many people have two, one for business, one for pleasure; grandparents use them to call their children; and teenagers organise their Saturday nights with them. You can't escape them. And the fact is they're as much about fashion as Armani suits or Prada handbags.

Coming in a myriad of shapes, sizes and colours they arouse an interest way beyond their function. It's not uncommon to see groups of excitable adolescents spending an entire evening comparing models, trying out new ring tunes – the Mission Impossible soundtrack is a Rome favourite – and generally enthusing on the subject.

But what lies behind this craze? Certainly slick marketing has ruthlessly played on the Italians' love of fashionable gizmos but maybe the answer lies closer to home. A survey carried out in July 2003 revealed that 56% of nine to 10-year-olds owned a mobile phone. Of these, four out of 10 had received them from their parents and of calls made, more than 40% were to parents. Statistics would thus seem to suggest that once again it's a case of the long arm of *la mamma*. The survey also showed that of the children without a mobile phone, 100% wanted one.

SPORT

In Rome, as in Italy, sport means football. With the right satellite dish it would now be possible to spend all and every weekend between October and May watching footy on the box. This, of course, is exactly what the TV execs who lord it over football would like you to do. No other sport in Italy enjoys anything like the saturation coverage given *il calcio* (football). Formula One comes the closest but even then only when Ferrari are winning.

Il calcio to an Italian is all about passion, fashion (check out the centre forward's latest tattoo) and controversy; it's one of the great forces in national life. Parliamentary fights have even been known to break out over refereeing decisions. To experience this fervour, at times bordering on the pathological, get to a big match. Spirits can run wild and although outbreaks of violence have been on the increase, games are generally safe.

Predictably enough, Serie A (Italy's premier league) is dominated by an elite group of *squadre* (teams) from the north. Among the leading teams, well known to football fans everywhere, are Juventus (based in Turin) who won their 27th league title in 2003, Inter Milan and AC Milan.

Rome's two teams, AS Roma and Lazio, play in Serie A, at the Stadio Olimpico in the Foro Italico, north of the city centre. Both are considered big guns, winning titles in 2000 (Lazio) and 2001 (Roma). However, the Roman holiday was short-lived and honours quickly returned north.

Lazio's championship in 2000 broke a 26-year drought and was met with manic celebrations throughout the city, at least by the light-blue half. Representing the climax of Lazio's brief *tour de force* – they had already won the European Cup Winners' Cup in 1999 – it was the club's finest moment. Basking in the glory were team coach Sven Goran Eriksson (now England manager) and club president Sergio Cragnotti. However, it wasn't to last and the club, currently managed by ex-player Roberto Mancini, is now struggling to emerge from a crisis caused by the collapse of ex-president Cragnotti's business empire.

Roma is coached in strict military style by Fabio Capello who, having steered the club to victory in the 2001 championship, spent a period as idol of the *giallorossi* (literally, yellow and reds, but meaning Roma's fans or players). Celebrations following Roma's championship were, if anything, more extravagant than those staged by the Lazio lot the year before, culminating in a mass concert at the Circo Massimo. But, like their city rivals, Roma's glory was to be short-lived. The 2002–03 season was fairly disastrous, with star player Francesco Totti spending much of the season injured and club president Franco Sensi publicly arguing with his manager.

Other sports followed, to a greater or lesser degree in the capital, are basketball out at the Palazzo dello Sport in EUR, rugby at the Stadio Flaminio and, in May, tennis at the Italian Open Foro Italico. For further details see p199.

MEDIA

Any discussion of the media in Italy inevitably revolves around Silvio Berlusconi (see the boxed text, p16), who dominates the media as much as he does Italian politics. But his power base is Milan, not the capital. Still, if Silvio doesn't like the mountain, move the mountain to Milan. Which is exactly what's been happening as the government starts to break up the Rome stronghold of state broadcaster RAI. Under recent pressure from Bossi's northern cohorts, the government has decided to relocate RAI's second national channel to the Lombard capital – a move that didn't go unnoticed, despite a strangely muted press coverage.

Milan is also the publishing capital of Italy. Rome's publishing houses tend to be smaller, often family-run, affairs which cannot compete in the same markets as the commercial monsters from Milan. They therefore tend to aim at specialised markets, such as the academic university sector, or to rely on government contracts.

La Repubblica and *Il Messaggero* are the two major newspapers produced in the capital, along with the highly popular sports daily, *Corriere dello Sport*.

For more information, see p271.

Curva Sud or Curva Nord?

Rivals Roma and Lazio share the same stadium, the same city and very little else. Competition between the two is fierce with loyalties divided down predictably political lines; Lazio attracts right-wing support, Roma left-wing.

Lazio's fans traditionally come from the provincial towns outside Rome although recent success has seen this boosted by *tifosi* (fans) from the city's wealthy middle class. Enjoying less than brilliant press, they have an unfortunate (but deserved) reputation for racist abuse of opposition players.

Roma's supporters, known as *romanisti*, are historically from the working class, from Rome's Jewish community and from Trastevere and Testaccio.

The great rivalry between the teams can often spill over into other facets of life, sometimes comically. For example, when the then Lazio president Cragnotti (who also owned Rome's central dairy) spent a record sum on Italian striker Cristian Vieri in August 1998 and increased the price of milk later in the same week, *romanisti* all over the city boycotted their morning cappuccino in protest!

So, if you go to the Stadio Olimpico, make sure you get it right – Roma fans flock to the Curva Sud (southern stand) while Lazio supporters stand in the Curva Nord (northern stand).

For more details on the clubs, visit online at www.asromacalcio.it (Italian only) and www.sslazio.it.

LANGUAGE

One of the many results of Italy's disunited history is the profusion of local dialects. So, while villagers in Alto Adige natter away in their home tongue, the visitor from Puglia looks on with total bewilderment. Similarly, the Neapolitans speak a language as foreign to the Milanese as dim sum.

Rome does not have a specific dialect but what it does have is *romanaccia*, a rough version of modern Italian. Understandable to most Italians, it's more like a heavy accent than a separate language.

English is the most commonly spoken foreign language, although many Italians (especially those working in the tourism industry) speak French, German and Spanish. See the Language chapter (p279) for some practical hints.

ECONOMY & COSTS

Tourism generates 12% of Rome's economy with the rest largely coming from banking, fashion, insurance, printing and publishing. The Comune di Roma (City of Rome) itself is one of the biggest employers while many Romans working in the private sector are self-employed. Unemployment in Rome stands at around 11.2%.

The mainstays of the city's budget are the annual 'garbage tax' paid by residents (a form of municipal tax) and its share of taxes paid to the national government. Rome receives a fairly low share of the tax pool compared to other cities; just €150 per resident while Naples and Milan receive €524 and €232, respectively.

But is Rome an expensive town? Certainly not the most expensive in Italy – that dubious honour usually goes to Venice – but neither is it particularly cheap, at least not from a visitor's point of view. Obviously, accommodation is going to be your biggest outlay, costing anywhere between €50 for a double room in a bargain two-star hotel to €400 in a city centre four-star. Food costs also vary tremendously. A sit-down pizza with a beer might cost around €15, while a full meal at a renowned restaurant could set you back anything from €20 to €70. Museums generally cost between €6 to €10, but many are free to the under-18s and over-60s with discounts generally available to students. Public transport is fairly cheap with a day pass costing €3.10. See p258 for further transport details.

If you want to do a spot of shopping you'll find that Rome is not as cheap as you might have wished. Yes, there are bargains to be had but much of the designer ware on sale around Piazza di Spagna is still very expensive. Shoes and leather gear, likewise. High quality certainly but cheap no.

How Much Is A...?

Double room in a three-star hotel – around €150
Cappuccino & croissant (breakfast) – €1.30
½ litre of mineral water – anywhere between €0.40 and €2
Slice of takeaway pizza – €1.50
Beer – €1 in the supermarket, €5 and upwards in a city centre pub
Single metro ticket – €0.77
City-centre taxi ride – €5 to €15
One hour's parking (streetside) – €1
Ticket to the Colosseum – €8
24-exposure camera film – €4.50

GOVERNMENT & POLITICS

Italian life is political to degrees that foreigners find difficult to comprehend. Nothing happens here without speculation as to the dark political motives behind it. Controversy theorising is a national pastime which never fails to set passions boiling and voices rising. Rome excels at this, being the heart of political Italy.

The top man in Rome is the *sindaco* (mayor), Walter Veltroni, who heads the city's municipal government up on the Capitoline, the seat of city government since the late 11th century. Elected in 2001 by a public vote, he leads his appointed *giunta*, a group of councillors called *assessori* who hold ministerial positions as heads of municipal departments. The *assessori* are appointed from the *consiglio comunale*, a body of elected officials much like a parliament.

A Helping Hand

Silvio Berlusconi is the world's 45th richest person, a media mogul supreme who just happens to be Italy's prime minister and a man who repeatedly claims not to see why his hold over much of the country's media should be a problem. Others are not so sure, pointing out that having a head of government control, either directly or indirectly, up to 90% of the nation's TV output is not ideal in a democracy.

There are seven main TV channels in Italy of which the three state channels (RAI) and the three belonging to Mediaset, a Berlusconi company, enjoy almost total hegemony. Obviously, Mediaset is blatantly pro-Berlusconi but the question of RAI's neutrality depends on your political viewpoint. The right wing say it's objective, the left wing counter that it's pro-Berlusconi.

Still, some facts speak for themselves. On an official trip to Bulgaria in 2002, Berlusconi accused two RAI journalists and a comedian of making criminal use of the state broadcaster in the run up to the 2001 election. Their crimes had been to criticise the great man on national television, thereby abusing RAI's neutral position. 'I'm not interfering', Berlusconi said, 'simply putting the record straight'. To date none of the three has worked on television again.

Berlusconi also owns the country's biggest publishing house, advertising agency and film production and distribution company. His wife and brother have a daily newspaper each.

A member of the Democratici di Sinistra (DS democracy of the left) party, Veltroni has spent much time and effort encouraging tourism and working for an increased foreign business presence in Rome; many see these measures as an effort to counter the government's desire to diminish Rome's considerable political clout.

A parliamentary republic, Italy is headed by a president, who appoints the prime minister. The parliament consists of two houses – a Senate and a Chamber of Deputies – both with equal legislative power.

The president resides in the Palazzo del Quirinale, on Rome's Quirinal Hill, the Chamber of Deputies sits in the Palazzo di Montecitorio, just off Via del Corso, and the Senate sits in the Palazzo Madama, near Piazza Navona.

Italy's notoriously complex electoral system generally forces the formation of unstable coalition governments. At the time of writing, for example, Prime Minister Berlusconi was struggling to hold together his fractious right-wing government.

The president of the Lazio regional council is Francesco Storace from the far-right Alleanza Nazionale (National Alliance) party.

ENVIRONMENT

CLIMATE

Spring and autumn are the best times to visit Rome, when the weather is warm and generally sunny. In September it is often still warm enough to head for the beach and well into October you'll be able to sit comfortably at an outside table while drinking your cappuccino. In a good year, mild weather can continue right up to December, punctuated by occasional days of icy winds that blow in from northern Europe. However, in a bad year you might strike heavy rain in October.

July and August are generally extremely hot, with temperatures often reaching as high as 37°C for days on end, making sightseeing unpleasant, particularly if you are travelling with children. Romans desert their city in droves, heading for the beaches or mountains, which means that tourists (and the few remaining residents) can enjoy light traffic and semideserted footpaths.

From November to February the weather can be unpredictable, with heavy rain, particularly in November, and icy winds. However, even when it's chilly in January and February you'll often find blue skies and sunshine.

Rome's sunniest months are May, June and July; its hottest months are June, July and August; its coldest are December, January and February; and the wettest are October, November and December.

THE LAND

The Comune di Roma covers an expanse of roughly 150,000 hectares, of which 37% is built-up urban area, 15% is parkland and 48% is under agricultural use.

Rome's best-known geographical features are its seven hills: the Palatine (Palatino), Capitoline (Campidoglio), Aventine (Aventino), Caelian (Celio), Esquiline (Esquilino), Viminal (Viminale) and Quirinal (Quirinale). Two other hills, the Gianicolo, which rises above Trastevere, and the Pincio, above Piazza del Popolo, were never actually part of the ancient city.

Statue of Romulus and Remus suckling on a she-wolf

Top Five Political Books

To bone up on Italy's political past and present you could do worse than these books:

- *A History of Contemporary Italy*, Paul Ginsburg (1990) – a well-written book that will help Italophiles place the country's modern society in perspective.
- *Modern Italy: A Political History*, Denis Mack Smith (1997) – the title tells all. Mack Smith is widely regarded as the leading authority on Italian politics writing in English.
- *The New Italians*, Charles Richards (1995) – British journalist Richards takes you through the murky backstage of modern Italian life. Packed with surprising revelations, not all of them bad, it's a fascinating eye-opener.
- *Italy – The Unfinished Revolution*, Matt Frei (2001) – the BBC's former Rome correspondent catalogues the changes Italian society has undergone in the past decade.
- *The Dark Heart of Italy*, Tobias Jones (2003) – a scathing study of the Berlusconi phenomenon, this fierce critique caused a scandal in Italy. What does he know, critics said. Quite a lot, really.

The Gianicolo is, in fact, a good vantage point from which to survey Rome's geography. From there it is possible to identify each of the seven hills, although two of them – the Viminal and Quirinal – are swallowed up by the city sprawl and seem not much more than gentle slopes. From here you can see how the River Tiber winds through town, a handy reference for navigating your way around the city centre.

The Tiber, which has its source in the Apennines north of Arezzo (in Tuscany) and runs into the sea at Ostia, is subject to sudden flooding. Until the late 19th century this caused significant problems for the areas bordering the river, including Trastevere. There were 46 devastating floods on record up to 1870. The problem was solved in 1900 by raising the level of the river's embankments. It is still possible to see markers around Trastevere denoting the water level reached by various floods. The ancient Romans built a major sea port, Ostia Antica, at the mouth of the Tiber but the harbour silted up long ago. Today the area is Rome's closest beach resort, known as Lido di Ostia.

In ancient times the city covered what is now called the *centro storico* (historic centre) and was enclosed by defensive walls built in two periods – the first, the Servian Wall in 378 BC; the second, the Aurelian Wall between AD 271 and 275.

Modern Rome is divided into 22 *rioni*, 35 *quartieri* and six *suburbi*. The *rioni*, which are all in or near the city centre, trace their origins back to the regions of the city of the Roman Republic. The regions evolved into *rioni* during the Middle Ages and by the late 16th century there were 14. Another eight were declared in 1921. Based on what might be called neighbourhoods, some retain a strong sense of history and tradition, notably Monti, the area incorporating the Esquiline, Viminal and Caelian; Borgo, next to St Peter's and the Vatican; and Trastevere, bordered by the Gianicolo hill and the Tiber.

GREEN ROME

Rome is famous for its ludicrous traffic and not without reason. Its traffic problems are appalling and the air pollution caused by vehicles idling in traffic jams choking! Efforts have increased in recent years to steer the traffic away from the city's historic centre and its main monuments, and only holders of special permits are allowed to drive in certain restricted areas of the centre. However, many of the city's most important monuments, the Colosseum included, remain at risk from pollution.

At the same time, things have improved. A massive cleanup and restoration effort led by the Comune di Roma has seen many of Rome's historic churches and palaces emerging from behind scaffolding with their facades finally cleaned of the dirt and grime built up over centuries.

Rome's former mayor Francesco Rutelli oversaw a huge public works program, mainly concentrated on improving roads, public transport and other infrastructure. Works are still under way to create an integrated railway network, to further develop the subway and tramlines and to create plans for traffic and pedestrian areas.

But this is Rome and things are never simple. The major problem for the authorities is, and has always been, how to modernise the city while preserving its extraordinary historical, architectural and artistic heritage. In this difficult task the Comune has regularly fallen foul of the Sovrintendenza dei Beni Culturali, the body responsible for protecting and maintaining the city's art and architectural patrimony. Over the years, many public works projects have been halted or delayed by the Sovrintendenza when it was discovered that they could have interfered with monuments.

Parks & Green Spaces

Rome has an extensive network of parks, many of which were the former private gardens and parklands of the city's nobility. According to figures provided by the Comune di Roma, 64% of the territory of the Comune is 'green', although this includes agricultural land as well as parkland.

As most of these parks were designed and planted according to the fashion of the relevant periods, they generally contain a wide variety of exotic species – plants indigenous to the city were rarely considered fashionable.

But long before the nobles started to plant their spectacular gardens, the Etruscans and ancient Romans had been chopping down trees, trampling the native vegetation and importing exotic species. The stone pine *(pino domestico)*, considered a symbol of the city, was in fact imported, probably by the Etruscans, from the Middle East and botanists debate whether or not it should be considered indigenous to Rome.

Despite thousands of years of interference, Rome manages to maintain almost 1300 native plants. Typical trees include about 10 species of oak *(quercia)*, including the holm oak *(leccio)* and the cork oak *(sughera)*, both of which grow spontaneously in small forests in the Roman countryside.

Rome's archaeological sites provide an ideal environment for the caper *(cappero)*. This plant, which usually grows only in the hot, dry climate of the country's south, has found ideal conditions in the rocks of Rome's ruined monuments. In spring, the caper forms cascading, puffy bushes, which in June become masses of pink flowers. You will see them growing in areas including the Palatine, the Terme di Caracalla (Baths of Caracalla), the Aurelian Wall and on the Ponte Rotto near the Isola Tiberina.

Rome's parks provide a place to play

Rome's botanic gardens *(orto botanico)* are at the base of the Gianicolo in Trastevere, at Largo Cristina Svezia. Originally part of the grounds of the Palazzo Corsini, the gardens were handed over to the University of Rome in 1883. There are more than 7000 plant species from around the world in the gardens and the collection of orchids is particularly notable.

Animals

The animals you are most likely to observe in Rome are cats, dogs and perhaps the odd rat, although you might be lucky to spot a squirrel or fox in one of Rome's numerous parks. However, in the green areas and even while walking around the city streets, you can observe a surprising variety of birdlife. More than 100 different types of bird life are said to nest in Rome's parks and rooftops, including kingfishers, kites, woodpeckers, kestrels, barn owls and horned owls. You'll have no trouble spotting robins, sparrows, finches, tits, swallows and seagulls, as well as ducks, moorhens and swans on lakes. Some of the lakes in Rome's parks are also occasional refuges for cormorants and grey herons.

Fellini's Felines

While animal rights are not a major consideration for the average Roman, the welfare of the city's 150,000 strong stray cat population is a fascinating exception.

The strays are often well fed and contented, thanks to the army of women who leave them leftover pasta on street corners. But not always. A cat's life is a hard life and many of Rome's felines finish up severely the worse for wear, often savaged in fights or hit by cars. And where do you go if you're a mauled cat with no friends? The answer is the Torre Argentina Cat Sanctuary.

Located, as the name would suggest, in the historic piazza, it's staffed by an army of international volunteers who work valiantly to look after their 250 resident cats, as well as any others who might limp in. Funded by the goodwill of Rome's cat lovers, as well as donations from the Anglo-Italian Society for the Protection of Animals, it's an operation that knows the value of publicity. Hence the success of the Cat Pride parade which, in February 2003, drew more than 6000 people to the streets of Rome.

The cats also have friends in high places as the introduction of an extraordinarily humane law in 1988 demonstrated. Under the terms of the law, Rome's stray cats are guaranteed the right to live where they're born – meaning that locals can't chase them away, whatever problems they cause.

For more information about the Torre Argentina Cat Sanctuary go online at www.romancats.de.

URBAN PLANNING & DEVELOPMENT

While most city planners struggle with the thorny issue of housing an ever-increasing population, Rome's authorities face another challenge: how to stem the flow of people leaving the city. Deterred by rising house prices and rents, pollution and dire services, many people, particularly young couples, are choosing to move out of town. This, however, is not a uniquely Roman issue – in 2001, Italian cities of over 100,000 inhabitants registered a 7.8% decrease in population. It's a national trend that currently looks set to continue.

Arts & Architecture

Arts & Architecture

Since ancient times Italy has been a fertile ground for artistic creativity. The Romans, admittedly fine architects and engineers, nevertheless did little more than follow the lead of their predecessors the Etruscans and the Greeks. Before the Roman Empire slowly slid into chaos, the artists and architects of the peninsula and its far-flung possessions had scaled enormous heights, leaving behind remarkable testimony to their power and diligence in Rome.

ARCHITECTURE

PRE-ROMAN

There are archaeological and architectural remains dating back to the 4th millennium BC in Italy, but the earliest well-preserved Italian architecture dates from the 1st millennium BC. It comes from three cultures: Latin and Roman culture in Lazio; Etruscan culture, from what is now northern Lazio and southern Tuscany; and the culture of Magna Grecia, in southern Italy and Sicily, where city states were founded in the 8th and 7th centuries BC by Greek colonists.

> ### Top 10 Notable Buildings & Monuments
> - Basilica di San Clemente (p97)
> - Basilica di San Giovanni in Laterano (p116)
> - Colosseum (p76)
> - Fontana dei Quattro Fiumi (p90)
> - Palatine (p78)
> - Pantheon (p88)
> - Roman Forum (p72)
> - Spanish Steps (p100)
> - St Peter's Basilica (p128)
> - Trevi Fountain (p105)

Like the Greeks, the early Romans built temples of stone. Whereas the Greek temples had steps and colonnades on all sides, the Roman variety had a high podium with steps and columns only at the front, forming a deep porch. The Romans also favoured fluted Ionic columns with volute capitals and Corinthian columns with acanthus leaf capitals (rather than the Greek Doric columns with cushionlike capitals). Examples still standing today in Rome include the Republican Tempio di Ercole Vincitore (see p115) and the Tempio di Portunus (see 115) by the Tiber near Piazza della Bocca della Verità and, though not so well preserved, the temples in the Area Sacra di Largo Argentina (see p87).

ROMAN

The Romans' great achievement was in perfecting existing construction techniques and putting these skills to use in the service of the Republic and later the Empire. For example, they learnt how to build roads and bridges from the Etruscans, and used these skills to create aqueducts and arches on a grandiose scale, the likes of which had never been seen before.

From the 1st century BC the Romans, using volcanic sand, made a quick-curing, strong concrete for vaults, arches and domes. It was used in Rome to roof vast areas such as the Pantheon (see p88), which was until the 20th century the largest poured concrete dome in existence. Huge vaults covered the hot baths and other rooms in complexes such as the Terme di Caracalla (see p114) built in AD 217.

Marble was a popular building material in both Republican and Imperial Rome and was used from the 2nd century BC. As Rome's power grew, new buildings were needed to reflect the city's status in the Mediterranean world. The Romans developed complexes used for commercial and political activities, such as Foro di Traiano (Trajan's Forum) and Mercati di Traiano (Trajan's Markets; see p71). Building projects became increasingly ambitious. Artistic concerns took second place to size and impressive engineering, evident in structures such as the huge Terme di Diocleziano (see p103), built in AD 298.

In the 4th century an ambitious building program financed by Constantine saw the erection of several places of worship, most of which followed the basilican style of late antiquity, although little remains of the original buildings. A notable exception is the domed baptistry of San Giovanni in Laterano (see p116), built by Constantine between 315 and 324 and remodelled into its present octagonal shape in the 5th century.

MIDDLE AGES

Early-medieval architecture in Italy (around 600 to 1050) involved mainly the construction and decoration of Christian churches and monasteries, much of which took place outside Rome, notably in Ravenna. Among the most important churches in Rome of this period were Santa Maria in Cosmedin (see p115), built in the 8th century, and the 9th-century Santa Prassede (see p99).

The basilican style survived into the so-called Romanesque period (11th to 13th centuries), which saw a revival of buildings whose size and structure resembled those of the Roman Empire.

Late-medieval Gothic architecture, influenced by northern European styles of pointed arches and vaults, never took off in Rome the way it did in northern Italy. The city's only Gothic church is the Chiesa di Santa Maria sopra Minerva (see p88).

RENAISSANCE

Almost all the artistic and architectural activity of the early Renaissance was in Tuscany and Venice. However, with the revival of the papacy, Rome was on course to take over the limelight. The 15th-century popes saw that the best way to ensure political power was to rebuild the city, and the leading artistic and architectural masters were summoned to Rome. The Venetian Paul II (1464–71) commissioned many works including Palazzo Venezia (see p82), Rome's first great Renaissance *palazzo* (palace), built in 1455 when he was still a cardinal and enlarged when he became pope in 1464.

Top Five Books

- *Inside Rome: Discovering Rome's Classic Interiors*, Joe Friedman (1998)
- *Roman Architecture*, Frank Sear (1983)
- *Roman Art & Architecture*, Mortimer Wheeler (1985)
- *Roman Builders: A Study in Architectural Process*, Rabun Taylor (2003)
- *Rome: An Oxford Archaeological Guide*, Amanda Claridge (1998)

The pontificate of Julius II (1503–13) marks the true beginning of the high Renaissance in Rome.

Domes, vaults and arches and the model of classical Rome provide the key to Renaissance architecture. The first such buildings were by Donato Bramante (1441–1514), who had already made a name for himself in Milan when he arrived in Rome. Impressed by the ruins of ancient Rome, he created a refined classicism that embodied the concerns of the Renaissance more fully than any previous architecture. Bramante's respect for the ancients and understanding of Renaissance ideals can be seen in his Tempietto (1502; see p111), next to the Chiesa di San Pietro in Montorio on the Gianicolo, and in the perfectly proportioned cloister (1504) of the Chiesa di Santa Maria della Pace (see p92) near Piazza Navona. The circular Tempietto, surrounded by 16 Doric columns, was the first building to depend entirely on the proportions of the classical orders and the most sophisticated attempt that had yet been made to combine the highest ideals of faith and art in order to create a perfect temple.

In 1506, Bramante was commissioned by Julius II to start work on St Peter's Basilica (see p128), the reconstruction of which under Nicholas V had virtually ground to a halt 50 years earlier. Bramante died in 1514, at which time the four central piers and the arches of the dome had been completed.

St Peter's Basilica occupied most of the other notable architects of the high Renaissance including Raphael (1483–1520), Giuliano da Sangallo (1443–1517), Baldassarre Peruzzi (1481–1537) and Antonio da Sangallo the Younger (1483–1546). Commissioned by Paul III, Michelangelo Buonarroti (1475–1564) took over the task and created the magnificent light-filled dome, 42m wide, based on Brunelleschi's design for the Duomo cupola in Florence.

COUNTER-REFORMATION

During the period of Counter-Reformation both art and architecture were entirely at the service of the Church. A costly building program was begun, largely under the direction of the Jesuits, to create massive and impressive churches to attract and overawe worshippers.

Giacomo della Porta (1539–1602) was the leading architect of the age and the last of the Renaissance tradition. He designed the Mannerist facade of the main Jesuit church in Rome, the Gesù (1568–75; see p87). In a move away from the style of earlier Renaissance churches, the facade has pronounced architectural elements that create a contrast between surfaces and a play of light and shade. Della Porta also worked on the construction of St Peter's Basilica (see p128) and designed the Palazzo della Sapienza (see p91), which was the seat of Rome's university until 1935.

The end of the 16th century and the papacy of Sixtus V (1585–90) marked the beginning of major urban planning schemes as the city became a symbol of the resurgent Church.

Ceiling of the Chiesa di San Luigi dei Francesi (p92)

Domenico Fontana (1543–1607) and other architects created a network of major thoroughfares to connect previously disparate parts of the sprawling medieval city and erected obelisks at various vantage points. Fontana also designed the large-scale but uninspiring Palazzo Laterano (1607; see p117) next to the Basilica di San Giovanni in Laterano.

In his design for the facade of Chiesa di Santa Susanna (1603; see p105), Fontana's nephew Carlo Maderno (1556–1629) created his masterpiece, which was regarded as a forerunner of baroque.

BAROQUE

The two great artistic figures of 17th-century Rome are the architect Francesco Borromini (1599–1667) from Lombardy and the Neapolitan-born architect and sculptor Gian Lorenzo Bernini (1598–1680).

No other architect before or since has had such an impact on a city as Bernini did on Rome. His patron was the Barberini pope, Urban VIII, who appointed him as the official architect of St Peter's from 1629. Bernini designed towers for Carlo Maderno's facade (which were structurally problematic and later demolished) and the *baldacchino* (altar canopy) above St Peter's grave, for which ancient bronze was stripped from such places as the Pantheon.

Under Urban VIII's patronage, Bernini had an opportunity, afforded to no other man before or since, to transform the face of the city, and his churches, palaces, piazzas and fountains are Roman landmarks to this day. However, things soured for a short time on the death of Urban VIII in 1644 and the accession of Innocent X, who wanted as little contact as possible with the favoured artists and architects of his detested predecessor. Instead he turned to Borromini, Alessandro Algardi (1598–1654) and Girolamo and Carlo Rainaldi.

The son of an architect and well-versed in stone masonry and construction techniques, Borromini created buildings involving complex shapes and exotic geometry. Distinctive features of his designs were windows, often oval-shaped and positioned for maximum illumination. His most memorable works are Chiesa di San Carlo alle Quattro Fontane (1634; see p104), which has an oval-shaped interior, and Chiesa di Sant'Ivo alla Sapienza (see p91), which combines a unique arrangement of convex and concave surfaces and is topped by an innovative spiral campanile.

Stories abound about the rivalry between Bernini and Borromini. Certainly, the latter was envious of Bernini's early success. Bernini came back into favour with his magnificent design for the Fontana dei Quattro Fiumi (1651; see p90) in the centre of Piazza Navona, opposite Borromini's Chiesa di Sant'Agnese in Agone. It is said that Bernini's figure of the Nile is holding up his arm to shield his eyes from the sight of Borromini's church. In fact the fountain was built several years before the church so the story, while engaging, doesn't stand up. What is true is that together they were the dominating architectural forces of the baroque period.

Like Michelangelo, Bernini thought of himself first and foremost as a sculptor, and his best-known works fall somewhere between sculpture and architecture. He was responsible for the setting for the throne and tombs for Urban VIII and Alexander VII in St Peter's Basilica and the magnificent sweeping colonnade in Piazza San Pietro (1656–67; see p127) as well as the church of Sant'Andrea al Quirinale (1658; see p105). His most endearing works include the small obelisk set on the back of an elephant in Piazza della Minerva (p87), near the Pantheon, and the angels set on the parapets of the Ponte Sant'Angelo (see p138) over the Tiber.

LATE 17TH TO 20TH CENTURY

The Spanish Steps (Scalinata di Spagna; see p100), built between 1723 and 1726 by Francesco de Sanctis, provided a focal point for the many Grand Tourists (European elites) who came to rediscover Rome's classical past. The rococo Piazza Sant'Ignazio (see p95) designed by Filippo Raguzzini (1680–1771) in 1728, with its curved facades, gives Sant'Ignazio, Rome's second Jesuit church, a theatrical setting.

Carlo Fontana (1634–1714), the most popular architect at the tail end of the baroque era, designed various palaces and churches.

The baroque love of grand gesture continued with the Trevi Fountain (see p105), one of the city's most exuberant and enduringly popular monuments. It was designed in 1732 by Nicola Salvi (1697–1751) and completed three decades later.

The beginning of modern architecture in Italy is epitomised by the late-19th-century shopping galleries with their iron and glass roofs in Milan, Naples, Genoa and Turin. However, this fashion never quite made it to Rome, which instead received the massive white-marble monument – the so-called 'wedding cake' or 'typewriter' – to Victor Emmanuel II built between 1885 and 1911 (see p82). Its enormous colonnade alludes to ancient precedents.

There was still time for flights of fancy, such as the wonderfully frivolous Art-Nouveau *palazzi* of Coppede (see p124), northeast of the city centre near Via Salaria, before Mussolini and the Fascist era made its architectural mark with grandiose building schemes, such as the Foro Italico sports centre (see p122) at the foot of Monte Mario (1928–31) and Esposizione Universale di Roma (EUR; see p121), a complete district on the outskirts of Rome that has a classicising, axial monumentality, massive statues and underutilised museums.

Other than rather hideous and anonymous apartment buildings in the outer suburbs of the city, Rome has seen little new architecture in the second half of the 20th century. Exceptions are the Stadio Flaminio built for the 1960 Olympics, the Stadio Olimpico (see p123) also built for the Olympics and revamped for the 1990 World Cup, the mosque in the Parioli area, designed by Paolo Portoghesi, and the new auditorium north of the city centre designed by Renzo Piano.

Two projects by the American architects Richard Meier & Partners are currently under way. One of these is a church officially known as Dio Padre Misericordioso (God the Merciful Father) in Tor Tre Teste, a suburb east of the city centre. The spectacular church was destined to be the symbol of the Holy Year 2000 and *should* have been consecrated during Rome's Jubilee celebrations. Administrative and technical problems delayed the construction and it is now due for completion in 2004.

Years of mainly bureaucratic and political obstacles have delayed another project by Richard Meier, who was commissioned by Rome's mayor Francesco Rutelli in 1995 to build a new museum complex for the Ara Pacis (see p93) in Piazza Augusto Imperatore. Rutelli had a vision for Rome, along the lines of Barcelona or London, which included an important contemporary building in the heart of the ancient city. Due for completion in autumn 2003, the Ara Pacis museum will be the first new building in Rome's historic centre in 60 years.

Dio Padre Misericordioso church (p25)

VISUAL ARTS

ETRUSCAN

Most evidence of Etruscan art has come from their tombs, richly furnished with carved stone sarcophagi, fabulous gold jewellery, ceramic and bronze statues and utilitarian objects, as well as frescoes, fine examples of which are displayed in the Villa Giulia (see p127). The Etruscan artists learned Greek artistic techniques and transformed them into a unique style of their own.

They were famous for metalwork such as the bronze *Lupa Capitolina* (Capitoline Wolf; see p81) in the Capitoline Museums, though such a large piece is a rarity. The made-to-measure figures of Romulus and Remus were added during the Renaissance. Most of the surviving Etruscan pieces are small figurines and household items, such as engraved mirrors. The techniques used to make the amazingly intricate filigree work, which decorates Etruscan gold jewellery, were only rediscovered in the 20th century.

ROMAN

The Romans used painting and mosaic work, both legacies from the Etruscans and Greeks, to decorate houses and palaces from at least the 1st century BC. Although little decoration of this type survives, there are some magnificent examples in the Museo Nazionale Romano collection at Palazzo Massimo alle Terme (see p101).

Roman wall-paintings, including those of the catacombs (see p118), were in true fresco technique with water-based pigments applied to wet plaster. The frescoes represent four styles: the first imitates stonework; the second creates illusions of architectural settings and dates to the last century BC; the

Top 10 Museums & Galleries

- Capitoline Museums (p81)
- Centrale Montemartini (p121)
- Galleria Colonna (p101)
- Galleria Doria Pamphilj (p94)
- Galleria Nazionale d'Arte Moderna (p125)
- Museo e Galleria Borghese (p125)
- Museo Nazionale Etrusco di Villa Giulia (p127)
- Palazzo Altemps (p90)
- Palazzo Massimo alle Terme (p101)
- Vatican Museums (p132)

third has a pattern of delicate architectural tracery combined with imitations of panel paintings; and the fourth, from the mid-1st century, combines features of the second and third styles and is the most common. Later frescoes, found at Ostia Antica and in the catacombs, tend towards simpler decoration and are often on a white background.

During the periods of both the Republic and the Empire, sculpture was very much at the service of the Roman state (and the emperor), and more than any other art form provides a compelling record of the city's history.

The first 'Roman' sculptures were actually made by Greek artists or were copies of imported classical Greek works. An exception was Roman portrait sculpture, derived from the Etruscans who aimed for naturalism and the honest representation of the subject. A popular form of sculpture for the Romans was to have statues made of themselves in the guise of Greek gods or heroes. However, the most interesting Roman sculpture is that of the 1st and 2nd centuries AD, which commemorates the city's history and its citizens.

The Emperor Augustus (r 27 BC–14 AD) was an expert at exploiting the possibilities of sculpture as a propaganda tool. One of the most important works of Roman sculpture is the Ara Pacis Augustae (Altar of Augustan Peace; consecrated 9 BC), made to celebrate the peace that he had brought to the Empire – and established at home. The reliefs, exemplified by clarity and classical restraint, mark the point at which Roman art gained its own identity. The Prima Porta statue of Augustus himself, now in the Vatican Museums (see p132), is another masterpiece of intricate symbolism combined with idealised portraiture.

In the 3rd and 4th centuries there was little public sculpture, although a notable exception is the 4th-century statue of Constantine, a 10m colossus, which stood at his basilica in the Roman Forum. Pieces of it (namely the head, a hand and a foot) are now in the Capitoline Museums (see p81).

CHRISTIAN

The early-Christian period saw an almost total rejection of sculpture, except for carved decoration on sarcophagi. The 5th-century carved-wood panels depicting scenes of the Passion of Christ on the doors of the Basilica di Santa Sabina (see p113) are a significant but rare exception. Mosaic work instead came to the fore.

At first, black-and-white mosaic cubes were used for floors; later coloured stones were employed. By the 4th century glass tesserae were used to splendid effect in the apses of the early Christian churches of Rome, including Santa Costanza, Santa Pudenziana, Santi Cosma e Damiano and the Basilica di Santa Maria Maggiore.

During the 5th and 6th centuries the only art permitted was Christian art, which changed little in style but broadened its subject matter, including scenes from the Old Testament and the Passion of Christ. The tradition of mosaic decoration of churches continued from the 7th to the 9th century in Chiesa di Santa Prassede and the Basilica di Santa Cecilia in Trastevere, and the influence of Byzantine mosaic artists who created images against a gold background became more widespread.

MIDDLE AGES

Local artists were employed to decorate churches and palaces when Rome started building again in the 12th century. The most famous decorative artists of the day were the Cosmati, a single family of artisans whose title eventually became a name for a whole school. They revolutionised the already well-established art of mosaic by reusing fragments of coloured glass from the ruins of ancient Rome. They also sliced up ancient columns of coloured marble and other precious stones into circular slabs, which were used to create intricate patterned pavements, altars, paschal candlesticks, pulpits and other decoration. Their work is referred to as 'Cosmati' or 'Cosmatiesque' and can be found in churches all over Rome. Two of the best surviving examples are San Giovanni in Laterano and San Paolo Fuori-le-Mura.

RENAISSANCE

The main artistic activity of the early Renaissance took place in Florence, Siena and Venice. However, painting flourished once again as Rome was rebuilt after the 15th-century restoration of the papacy.

Between 1481 and 1483 some of the country's greatest painters were employed by Sixtus IV to decorate the walls in his newly rebuilt Sistine Chapel (see p135) in the Vatican. The frescoes of the lives of Moses and Christ and portraits of popes were done by Perugino (1446–1523), Sandro Botticelli (1444–1510), Domenico Ghirlandaio (1449–94), Cosimo Rosselli (1439–1507) and Luca Signorelli (c 1441–1523). These artists were assisted by members of their workshops, including Pinturicchio (1454–1513), who subsequently frescoed the Borgia apartments (see p135) between 1492 and 1494, Piero di Cosimo (1462–1521) and Bartolomeo della Gatta (1448–1502).

The decoration of the official apartments of Pope Julius II (the *Stanze di Raffaello* or Raphael Rooms; see p135) marked the beginning of the brilliant Roman career of

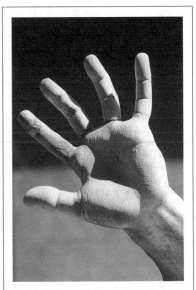

Hand detail of a statue on Fontana dei Quattro Fiumi (p90)

Urbino-born Raphael (Raffaello Sanzio, 1483–1520), who arrived from Florence in 1508. In true Renaissance spirit, he absorbed the manner of classical Rome and became the most influential painter of his time.

The greatest achievement of the period was by Raphael's contemporary, Michelangelo Buonarroti (1475–1564) on the Sistine Chapel ceiling (1508–12). It is the most moving and original combination of art and faith in Renaissance Rome, and one of the greatest artistic achievements of all time – by an artist who didn't think of himself as a painter. Thirty years later, after the 1527 sack of Rome, Michelangelo returned to the Vatican to adorn the altar wall of the Sistine Chapel with *The Last Judgement* (1535–1541).

COUNTER-REFORMATION

Both painting and sculpture hit a low point in the late 16th century, although there were some highlights at the very end of the century. Annibale Carracci (1560–1609) left his mark on Rome with magnificent frescoes (1597–1603) of mythological subjects in the Palazzo Farnese (see p84), and the technically proficient, if uninspiring, Cavalier d'Arpino (1568–1640) designed the mosaics covering the inside of St Peter's dome.

The arrival of Michelangelo Merisi da Caravaggio (1573–1610) heralded a move away from the confines of the high Renaissance towards a new naturalism. In Caravaggio's case, his naturalism was often regarded as being just a little too 'real' and his paintings were often rejected. However, his innovative sense of light and shade and supreme draughting ability meant that he was courted by contemporary collectors who wanted to cash in on his talent, and was an influential figure for centuries.

BAROQUE

In Rome, baroque meant one thing: Gian Lorenzo Bernini (1598–1680). A visit to the Museo e Galleria Borghese (see p125), which houses many of Bernini's early and best works, gives a clear idea of the sculptor's astounding talent.

On the Caravaggio Trail

Much of the information that scholars have gathered about Caravaggio's time in Rome has been gleaned from police records. Trouble with the law was a fact of daily life for the artist.

He arrived in Rome around 1590 where he gained a reputation for wandering around the streets of the historic centre, from Campo de' Fiori to the Pantheon, brandishing (and sometimes using) a long sword. One of his girlfriends was a prostitute who worked in Piazza Navona and he was arrested on several occasions, once for launching a tray laden with artichokes at a waiter in a restaurant and another time for throwing rocks at the windows of his former landlady's house.

He was, however, fortunate to meet a number of influential churchmen who recognised his artistic genius, provided him with lodgings and introduced him to important dealers and collectors.

He fled Rome in 1606 after a ball game in Campo de' Fiori during which he killed his opponent, and spent four years on the run in Naples, Malta and Sicily. He died in Porto Ercole in Tuscany at the age of 36.

Caravaggio's paintings were controversial. He used peasants, beggars and prostitutes as his models, which gave the Madonnas and saints of his paintings a realism that was not always well received. On several occasions he had to repaint commissions for churches because the subjects were deemed to be too lifelike: saints would *not* have had such dirty feet.

Several of these rejected works were bought by intuitive private collectors, including Cardinal Scipione Borghese. Borghese is said to have used his influence in the Church (he was a nephew of Pope Paul V) to persuade several religious confraternities, who had commissioned Caravaggio works, to reject the completed paintings for being too 'realistic'. Caravaggio would then be constrained to produce a more acceptable version of the same subject, enabling Scipione to buy the offending work, soon to be considered a masterpiece, at a bargain price.

Caravaggio's work dots Rome. The *Madonna dei Pellegrini* (Madonna of the Pilgrims) in Chiesa di Sant'Agostino (see p225) is regarded as one of his most alluring works and features a superbly serene Madonna surrounded by scruffy pilgrims. Two saintly masterpieces in Chiesa di Santa Maria del Popolo (see p89) show the *Conversione di San Paolo* (Conversion of St Paul), a daring composition dominated by the rear end of a horse, below which the saint is sprawled; and the *Crocifissione di San Pietro* (Crucifixion of St Peter), which uses dramatic foreshortened figures and depicts the moment when St Peter is tied upside down on the cross.

The Museo e Galleria Borghese (see p125) contains six paintings including the *Ragazzo con Canestro di Frutta* (Boy with a Basket of Fruit), the *Bacchino Malato* (Sick Bacchus) and the famous *Madonna dei Palafrenieri*, commissioned for a chapel in St Peter's but snapped up by Scipione.

The dramatic *Davide con la Testa di Golia* (David with Goliath's Head) and *San Giovanni Battista*, showing a young St John the Baptist, were apparently given to Scipione by the artist in exchange for clemency from Pope Paul V for the murder he committed in 1606. Another *San Giovanni Battista* is in the Pinacoteca of the Capitoline Museums (see p81). The Galleria Nazionale d'Arte Antica (see p107) at Palazzo Barberini has a striking *Narcissus* and a gruesome *Giuditta e Oloferne* (Judith and Holofernes). Caravaggio's *Deposizione nel sepolcro* (Descent from the Cross) is in the Pinacoteca of the Vatican Museums (see p132).

Bernini could do things with marble that no-one before or since has managed. He could make the cold hard stone appear to be soft flesh and a solid static figure seem to be dynamic. Not only was he a virtuoso carver but he also took risks using the marble blocks, breaking all sorts of unwritten sculptors' rules about wasting expensive stone by creating an outflung limb or a figure that genuinely appears to be in motion.

Baroque sensibilities gave a new importance to exaggerated poses, cascading drapery and primacy of emotions and Bernini was an unequalled master. His were not sculptures but rather theatrical and emotional spectacles set in stone that unfolded before the viewers' eyes. His *David*, *Rape of Persephone* and *Apollo and Daphne*, all in the Museo e Galleria Borghese, and *The Ecstasy of St Teresa* in Santa Maria della Vittoria (see p104) are cases in point.

Bologna-born Alessandro Algardi (1595–1654) was one of the few sculptors in Rome not totally overshadowed by Bernini, his great rival. His white-marble monument to Pope Leo XI (1650) is in St Peter's (see p128).

Michelangelo's ceiling frescoes inspired a fashion that continued well into the 17th century. Pietro da Cortona (1596–1669) was one of the most sought-after decorators of baroque Rome. His fresco on the ceiling of the Salone Grande in Palazzo Barberini (see p107), begun in 1632, paved the way for numerous other commissions including the ceiling frescoes in Chiesa Nuova (see p90). Many painters tried, but failed, to match his talent.

THE 18TH TO 20TH CENTURY

By the 18th century, Rome's artistic heyday was over; the attention of the many foreign artists who settled in Rome turned to the antique. The widely disseminated etchings of the city and its ancient ruins by Giovanni Battista Piranesi attracted Grand Tourists and artists alike. The Swiss-born Angelica Kauffmann was just one example of a foreign artist who settled in the Eternal City and produced proficient, if ordinary, academic art.

The neoclassicism of the late 18th and early 19th centuries was a reaction to the excesses of baroque and a response to the renewed interest in the classical world, sparked by the excavations of Pompeii and Herculaneum.

The neoclassical style was best represented by Antonio Canova (1757–1822), an accomplished modeller, whose work is often devoid of obvious emotion. His most famous piece is a daring sculpture of Paolina Bonaparte Borghese as a reclining *Venere Vincitrice* in the Museo e Galleria Borghese (see p125). Her diaphanous drapery leaves little to the imagination and is typical of the mildly erotic sculptures for which Canova became known.

The Sicilian-born sculptor Mario Rutelli (1859–1941), great-grandfather of Rome's former mayor, left his mark on the city with a series of fountains, monuments and mainly academic equestrian statues, including that of Anita Garibaldi on the Gianicolo. One of his most visible and delightful works is the theatrical Fontana delle Naiadi (1901) in Piazza della Repubblica (see p103).

Painting and sculpture since Italian unification in 1870 are most readily found in the Galleria Nazionale d'Arte Moderna (see p125). The late 19th century saw the emergence of Italian postimpressionism with the *Macchiaioli* school ('*macchia*' means 'stain' or 'spot'), who produced a version of pointillism using thousands of dots of pure colour to build up the picture, and Italian Symbolists.

The Italian Futurists were inspired by the characteristics of urbanism and industry and by the idea of progress. Umberto Boccioni (1882–1916) and Giacomo Balla (1871–1958) aligned themselves with the futurist manifesto (1909) of writer Emilio Marinetti, whereas their contemporary Carlo Carrà (1881–1966) had much in common with Cubists such as Pablo Picasso. Giorgio Morandi (1890–1964) consistently depicted bottles and jars as forms rather than objects, while the surrealist Giorgio De Chirico (1888–1978) painted visionary empty streetscapes with disconcertingly juxtaposed objects and elements, which often incorporated allusions to classical antiquity.

Galleria Nazionale d'Arte Moderna (p125)

Giacomo Manzù (1908–91) revived the Italian religious tradition. His best-known work is a bronze door (to the left of the central Holy Door) in St Peter's Basilica, which he was awarded after a competition in 1949.

Important post-WWII and contemporary artists include Burri, Colla, Manzoni, Pascali and the Transavanguardia, whose exponents such as Enzo Cucchi, Francesco Clemente (born 1952), Mimmo Paladino and Sandro Chia (born 1946) have gained success both in Italy and abroad.

LITERATURE

LATIN OF THE REPUBLIC

Marcus Tullius Cicero (106–143 BC) stands out as the pre-eminent prose author of the Roman Republic. A 'new man' without consuls in his family tree, Cicero won his way to the consulship of 63 BC through his brilliance as a barrister. As well as his philosophical works, he tidied up many of his notable speeches for publication, and his secretary later published many of his letters to family and friends. Fancying himself as the senior statesman, Cicero took the young Octavian under his wing and attacked Mark Antony in a series of 14 speeches, the *Philippics*. These soon proved fatal when Octavian changed sides and joined Mark Antony, who then demanded – and got – Cicero's head.

GOLDEN-AGE LATIN

This era centred around the reign of Augustus. With the *Aeneid*, Virgil (70–19 BC) transformed the various Aeneas legends into the great foundation myth of Rome. This blend of legend, history and moral instruction immediately became a school text, and remained one for the next 1700-odd years. The *Aeneid* acquired such an aura that a popular method of fortune-telling involved interpreting the significance of a randomly selected passage – the same process used by some with the Bible.

SILVER-AGE LATIN

As Roman society began to change over the century, so too did the Latin language and the people who used it. While Livy, Virgil's contemporary, had written the history of Rome's glorious past, Tacitus (c 56–116) viewed more recent history with a decidedly colder eye.

Emperors also left their versions of history, often following the example set by Julius Caesar's war *Commentaries*. As well as his autobiography, the scholarly Claudius produced volumes of Etruscan, Carthaginian and Augustan history. Agrippina, Nero's mother, wrote her autobiography. All of these are unfortunately lost but the philosophical *Meditations* of Marcus Aurelius (161–180) have survived.

VULGATE BIBLE

Pope Damasus (333–384) made the first concerted effort to Christianise Roman culture. As part of his program, he commissioned his secretary, Eusebius Hieronymous (St Jerome), to render the Bible in elegant but accessible Latin. The Vulgate Bible has been used ever since.

MIDDLE AGES

From before the final collapse of Rome till the Middle Ages, creative literary production declined, kept barely alive in Western Europe by clerics and scholars who debated theology, wrote histories and handbooks of rhetoric, translated or interpreted classical literature and used Latin as their lingua franca. The 12th-century *Mirabilia Romae* were effectively the first guidebooks to the monuments of the ancient city.

Although 13th-century popes wrote great books, instructive sermons and issued laws and official acts, the removal of the papacy to Avignon in 1309 meant that 14th-century literary activity in Rome was less noteworthy. Throughout the Italian peninsula, Latin had already ceased to be a living language. Florence was the most productive centre and the period was marked by the production of literature in Italian, in the highly influential work of Dante, Boccaccio and Petrarch (Francesco Petrarca).

Dante (1265–1321) was probably the greatest figure in Italian literature. His *Divina Commedia* (Divine Comedy) is an allegorical masterpiece that takes his protagonist on a search for God through hell, purgatory and paradise.

Even more influential than Dante was the Tuscan humanist Petrarch (1304–74). Petrarch was the most important Latinist of his day and was crowned poet laureate in Rome in 1341 after earning a reputation throughout Europe as a classical scholar. He had sought to win recognition through his Latin writings but in fact the reverse happened. His lyrical works in the Tuscan vernacular, such as his epic poem *Africa*, and the sonnets of *Il Canzoniere*, have had a permanent influence on Italian poetry.

The humanist movement that swept Italy and Europe in the 14th and 15th centuries put Rome in the spotlight. After centuries of religion-dominated writing, scholars and intellectuals became more interested in the secular aspects of antiquity, and the idea of classical Rome began to play a crucial role in the evolution of western culture.

Flavio Biondo (1392–1463) was a disciple of Petrarch and the founder of modern archaeology. His *Decades*, a history of Christendom from the fall of Rome to the 1440s, was effectively the first history of the Middle Ages.

Lorenzo Valla (1407–57) was the greatest Roman humanist. He bravely challenged Church administration and was sceptical about various aspects of papal primacy. He also produced a humanist commentary on the New Testament, pioneering a new critical attitude to the text – at times he was branded a heretic because of his philosophy. He was renowned for his vigorous mind, sharp tongue and expert command of Latin (exhibited in his *Elegantiae linguae Latinae*) to which few of his contemporaries could aspire.

RENAISSANCE

By the end of the 15th century, Rome was a cultural capital of Europe due to the papal and ecclesiastical patronage of artists, architects and a multitude of Latinists. However, the most significant 14th- and 15th-century literary activity actually took place outside Rome.

In the 16th century, the qualities inherent in the Petrarchan and Neo-Platonic tradition became more pronounced. Although better known as a painter, sculptor and architect, Michelangelo Buonarroti (1475–1564) was also one of the great poets of the time. At an early age, in the Florentine court of Lorenzo de' Medici, he was exposed to Neo-Platonist writers and began writing poetry. His most outstanding works were composed in Rome during the last 20 years of his life and are regarded as the finest Italian poems since Petrarch and Dante.

His writing was not actually published until 1623, when his great-nephew released a slightly edited version of the poems, suppressing the fact that many of them were written for Tommaso Cavalieri (a young man Michelangelo fell in love with in 1532) and explored the dilemma of a homosexual whose moral beliefs conflict with his sexuality. It was mistakenly thought for several centuries that they were love poems for the Roman noblewoman Vittoria Colonna.

Vittoria Colonna (1490–1549) was a member of the noble Roman Colonna family. She spent much of her early life on Ischia, an island in the Bay of Naples, but visited Rome regularly. Her unusual intellectual abilities won her a considerable reputation and she formed friendships with many outstanding writers, reformers and religious figures. Her poetry – skilful but not strikingly original – was written in the Petrarchan and Neo-Platonic style. Her friendship with Michelangelo was truly 'Platonic', marked by frequent exchanges of philosophical sonnets and letters. Michelangelo was at her bedside when she died in 1549.

Giorgio Vasari's *Vite dei Più Eccellenti Pittori* (Lives of the Artists; 1550, republished 1568), a treatise on the lives of his artist predecessors and contemporaries, remains one of the most informative works of Renaissance art history. Vasari was a contemporary of Michelangelo and spent several years in Rome as chief architect of St Peter's (to which he was appointed in succession to Michelangelo).

The sculptor and goldsmith Benvenuto Cellini (1500–71) began his autobiography, *Vita*, in 1558. A native of Florence, Cellini spent many years in Rome working for eminent ecclesiastical figures including Popes Clement VII and Paul III. In his writing, Cellini used an uninhibited spoken manner, which was unparalleled for several centuries. The story reaches its dramatic climax with the 1527 sack of Rome and the author's escape in 1538 from Castel Sant'Angelo (see p138), where he had been imprisoned.

Censorship became institutionalised under Paul IV with the 1554 publication of the Index of Prohibited Books. The publication of the list, which concerned itself not only with faith but also morals, was accompanied by public book-burnings and many printers were forced to flee the city.

Giordano Bruno (1548–1600) was one of the earliest champions of freedom of speech and thought. His fiery temperament brought him into conflict with one form of Counter-Reformation establishment after another. Originally a Dominican priest, his interests included natural magic, cosmology and astrology – one of his assertions was that the earth was not the centre of the universe, a belief that Galileo was also forced to renounce. Among the orthodox Church doctrines that he questioned was the notion of the Immaculate Conception. He spent many years in exile outside Italy, returning only in 1591. In 1600, after an eight year trial, he was branded a heretic and burned at the stake in Campo de' Fiori (see p83). In 1603 all Bruno's books were placed on the Index of Prohibited Books.

The absence of free speech in Counter-Reformation Rome is one explanation for the lack of significant literature from that period; anything the Church and State disapproved of was suppressed. But in 17th-century Rome an 'underground' literary form emerged, in the posting of anonymous satirical writings or *pasquinades* (named after the first person identified as having written one), which criticised the Church and authoritative figures. One of the most popular places for such notices to be left was on the torso of a Roman statue, near Piazza Navona (in a small square today known as Piazza Pasquino; see p91). The epigrams were usually posted in the dark of night and then gleefully circulated around town the following day.

THE 18TH CENTURY

Rome soon became a hotbed for many 18th-century historians and Grand Tourists from northern Europe. Edward Gibbon penned his influential *The History of the Decline & Fall of the Roman Empire* between 1776 and 1778. Johann Wolfgang von Goethe, already a celebrated poet when he arrived in Rome in 1786, found the city an inspiration for his literary and artistic travails. His *Italian Journey* captures better than any other text the elation of the northern travellers as they discovered the ruins of ancient Rome and the colours of the modern city.

Rome was also a magnet for the English Romantics. Keats, Byron, Shelley, Mary Shelley and other writers all spent time in the city. Byron claimed Rome as the city of his soul even though he visited it only fleetingly. John Keats came to Rome in 1821 in the hope that it would cure his ill health but he died of tuberculosis in his lodgings at the foot of the Spanish Steps after only a few months in the city.

THE 19TH CENTURY

Italy's home-grown Romantic, Giacomo Leopardi (1798–1837), was less inspired by the wonders of Rome than his northern counterparts and spent only a few months in Rome from 1822 to 1823.

The American author Nathaniel Hawthorne lived in Italy between 1857 and 1859. *The Marble Faun* (1860) recreates his impressions of Rome in a narrative context. In 1869 Henry James made the first of 14 trips to Italy, which inspired his enduringly popular classic, *The Portrait of a Lady* (1881) and his book of essays, *Italian Hours* (1909).

Romans are particularly proud of their most famous local poets, Gioacchino Belli (1791–1863), Carlo Alberto Salustri (1871–1950), better known as Trilussa, and Cesare Pascarella (1858–1940), who all wrote in Roman dialect.

Belli started his career with conventional and undistinguished verse but found the medium for his expression in the crude and colourful dialect of the Roman people, making use of its puns and obscenities. He was a savage satirist and outspoken in his attacks on all classes and institutions. Belli also often painted vulgar caricatures of important Risorgimento figures.

THE 20TH CENTURY

Gabriele D'Annunzio (1863–1938) is the most flamboyant Italian literary figure of the turn of the 20th century and into the modern era. Born in Pescara, D'Annunzio settled in Rome in 1881. An ardent nationalist, his virulent poetry was perhaps not of the highest quality, but his voice was a prestigious tool for Mussolini's Fascists.

Italy's richest contribution to modern literature has been in the novel and short story, and two of the most popular figures were closely tied to the capital.

Alberto Moravia (1907–90) grew up in the residential area east of the Villa Borghese. He describes Rome and its people in his prolific novels, such as *La Romana* (The Woman of Rome; 1949), which conveys the detail and sharp sense of social decay that make his storytelling so compelling. The alienated individual and the emptiness of Fascist and bourgeois society are common themes in his writing. *Racconti Romani* (Roman Tales; 1954) and *Nuovi Raconti Romani* (New Roman Tales; 1960) offer amusing sketches of the lives of Roman characters including plumbers, servants and hoodlums.

The novels of Elsa Morante (1912–85) are characterised by a subtle psychological appraisal of her characters and can be seen as a personal cry of pity for the sufferings of individuals and society. Her 1974 novel *La Storia* follows the fortunes of a half-Jewish woman in occupied Rome.

Pier Paolo Pasolini (1922–75) moved to Rome in 1950 in the wake of a sex scandal in his native Friuli. Rome gave him an opportunity to explore both his homosexuality and different ways of writing. His first novel, *Ragazzi di Vita* (1955), explores the violent, linguistically explosive and sordid world of the dilapidated suburbs of Rome, in which theft, card-sharping, prostitution and murder are commonplace. These were subjects Pasolini returned to in later works such as *Una Vita Violenta* (1956) and in many of his (often controversial) films.

Rome is a continual source of inspiration for foreign writers. It is becoming increasingly fashionable for many contemporary novelists to use ancient and modern Rome as a backdrop for their stories.

CINEMA

Rome has always played a major role in Italian cinema, both as a subject and as a production centre. Born in Torino in 1904, the Italian film industry originally made an impression with silent spectaculars. By 1930 it was virtually bankrupt and Mussolini began moves to nationalise the industry. These culminated in 1940, when Rome's version of Hollywood, Cinecittà, was ceded to the State. Set up in 1937, this huge complex was fitted out with the latest in film equipment. Half the nation's production took place here – 85 pictures in 1940 alone – and in its glory days it was labelled 'Hollywood on the Tiber'.

> ### Top Five Films
>
> - *Roma Città Aperta* (Rome Open City; 1945) – directed by Roberto Rossellini
> - *Ladri di Biciclette* (Bicycle Thieves; 1948) – directed by Vittorio de Sica
> - *Roman Holiday* (1953) – directed by William Wyler
> - *La Dolce Vita* (1960) – directed by Federico Fellini
> - *Caro Diario* (Dear Diary; 1994) – directed by Nanni Moretti

Abandoned later in the war, Cinecittà only went timidly back into action in 1948, although its absence had not bothered the early neorealist directors. In 1950 an American team arrived to make *Quo Vadis?*, and for the rest of the '50s, film-makers from Italy and abroad moved in to use the site's huge lots.

Major American productions at Cinecittà included William Wyler's *Ben Hur* (1959) with Charlton Heston, Stanley Kubrick's *Spartacus* (1960) starring Kirk Douglas, and Joseph Mankiewicz's *Cleopatra* (1963) with Elizabeth Taylor and Richard Burton. By the early 1960s, however, this symbol of Italian cinema had again begun to wane as location shooting became more common. The main moneymakers for the Italian film industry in the 1960s and '70s were Sergio Leone's 'spaghetti westerns' shot near Viterbo.

In the three years following the close of hostilities in Europe, Roberto Rossellini (1906–77) produced a trio of neorealist masterpieces. The first and most famous of these was *Roma Città Aperta* (Rome Open City; 1945), set in German-occupied Rome and starring Anna Magnani. It was filmed in the working-class district of Via Prenestina east of the city centre. For many cinephiles the film marks the true beginning of neorealism, uniting a simplicity and sincerity peculiar to Italian film-making; often heart-rending without ever descending into the bathos to which so many Hollywood products fall victim.

Vittorio de Sica (1901–74) kept the neorealist ball rolling in 1948 with another classic set in Rome, *Ladri di Biciclette* (Bicycle Thieves), the story of a man's frustrated fight to earn a crust and keep his family afloat. It was filmed in the outskirts of the city where the ugly purpose-built suburbs meet the countryside.

Federico Fellini (1920–94) took the creative baton from the masters of neorealism and carried it into the following decades. Some of his best-known films were set in Rome, his adopted home (he lived for many years in Via Margutta). His disquieting style demands more of audiences, abandoning realistic shots for pointed images at once laden with humour, pathos and double-meaning – all cleverly capturing not only the Rome of the day, but the human foibles of his protagonists. Fellini's greatest international hit was *La Dolce Vita* (1960), starring Marcello Mastroianni and Anita Ekberg, with memorable scenes set in the Trevi Fountain (for which a Cinecittà set was actually used) and Via Veneto. *Roma* (1972) could almost be described as a surreal and poetic documentary about Rome. It satirised the Church and used relatively unpicturesque parts of Rome as a backdrop, including the Grand Raccordo Anulare, the city's motorway ring road.

Pier Paolo Pasolini (1922–75) used his local neighbourhood, Pietralata, in his films and books. Homosexual, Catholic and Marxist, Pasolini's films reflect his ideological and sexual tendencies and are a unique portrayal of Rome's urban wasteland. In his earlier work he was preoccupied with the condition of the subproletariat in films like *Accattone* (1961), set in the forgotten suburbs of Rome, and *Teorema* (1968). Later he became obsessed with human decay and death as reflected in *Il Decamerone*, *I Racconti di Canterbury* and *Il Fiore delle Mille e Una Notte*. Pasolini was murdered in mysterious circumstances in 1975.

Nanni Moretti (born 1953), who first came to the silver screen in the late 1970s, has proved to be a highly individualistic actor-director. *Caro Diario* (Dear Diary), his whimsical, self-indulgent, autobiographical three-part film, won the prize for best director at Cannes in 1994. A major part of the film involved a camera recording Moretti driving through the streets of Rome on a Vespa. His ninth feature, *La Stanza del Figlio* (The Son's Room), won him the Palme d'Or at Cannes in 2001.

A wonderful homage to film-making is *Nuovo Cinema Paradiso* (1988), by Giuseppe Tornatore (born 1956). Tornatore was back in 1995 with *L'Uomo delle Stelle* (The Starmaker), the story of a fraud touring around Sicily and peddling hopes of a screen career in Cinecittà, in 2000 with *La Leggenda del 1900* and again in 2001 with *Malèna*.

According to recent reports, the glory days of Italian cinema are back and the future for Cinecittà looks rosy with increased private investment in state-of-the-art digital technology and special effects equipment. There has also been a revival of interest in ancient Rome by leading Hollywood directors.

Rome has starred in many movies. Who can forget Audrey Hepburn and Gregory Peck causing havoc around the streets of Rome in the 1953 romantic comedy *Roman Holiday*? Other memorable movies with Rome as subject or backdrop include the famous *Three Coins in the Fountain* (1955).

Rome, the movie star, has had a busy time in recent years. Anthony Minghella depicted Rome at its most beautiful in *The Talented Mr Ripley* (1999), starring Matt Damon,

Gwyneth Paltrow, Cate Blanchett and Jude Law. And the buildings of ancient Rome (albeit generated by computer) were on show in Ridley Scott's box-office smash *Gladiator* (2000).

MUSIC

The Italians have played a pivotal role in the history of music: they invented the system of musical notation in use today; a 16th-century Venetian printed the first musical scores with movable type; Cremona produced immortal violins; and Italy is the birthplace of the piano.

CHORAL MUSIC

Not surprisingly, the medieval and Renaissance popes had a strong influence on music in Rome. The Church was by far the most stable employer for talented musicians, and individual popes established the great musical institutions, many of which have survived. It is unlikely that Gregory I actually had any hand in creating the liturgical music known as Gregorian chant, but this certainly provided the basis for the uniform liturgical music still in use. Sixtus IV greatly increased the status of the papal choir, not the least by having a new chapel commissioned – the Sistine Chapel (see p135).

The greatest musicians of the day served as papal choirmasters, including Giovanni Pierluigi da Palestrina (c 1525–94) and Domenico Scarlatti (1685–1757). Girolamo Frescobaldi (1583–1643), admired by the young JS Bach, was twice an organist at St Peter's Basilica.

The papal choirs, originally composed of priests, were closed to women, and the high parts were originally taken by men singing in falsetto. The *falsetti* were gradually supplanted by *castrati*, boys surgically castrated before puberty to preserve their high voices for life. Although castration was punishable by excommunication, the Sistine Chapel and other papal choirs contained *castrati* as early as 1588; the last known *castrato*, Alessandro Moreschi (1858–1922), had been a member of the Sistine Chapel choir. Moreschi even made a primitive recording in 1903, the very year that Pius X banned *castrati* from the papal choirs. Boy sopranos were introduced in the 1950s.

As well as liturgical singing, *castrati*, whose unique voices combined a female register with the lung power of a man, were also in demand for the operatic stage and are known to have taken female roles even before Sixtus V, worried about society's morals, banned women from performing in public. The *castrati* were the pop stars of their day, with voices described as 'the singing of angels'.

The Sistine Chapel choir now consists of 20 men and 30 to 40 boys. It is regarded as the pope's personal choir and accompanies him whenever he celebrates a papal mass (which is three or four times a month). The choir also sings at any festivities on the church calendar, such as beatifications, canonisations, funerals and papal anniversaries.

Musician entertaining café crowds on Campo de' Fiori (p83)

In 1585 Sixtus V formally established the Accademia di Santa Cecilia, originally called the Congregazione dei Musici di Roma and formed as a support organisation (perhaps even an early trade union) for papal musicians. From its 17th-century role in musical education and the publication of sacred music, it developed a teaching function (Arcangelo Corelli was an early maestro of the instrumental section in 1700), and in 1839 it reinvented itself as an academy with wider cultural and academic goals – including even the admission of women! It is today one of the most highly respected conservatories in the world, with its own orchestra and chorus.

Ottorino Respighi (1879–1936) came to Rome from Bologna as Professor of Composition at the Accademia di Santa Cecilia and later served as its director. His works include three sets of tone poems evoking various features of his adopted city: *Pini di Roma* (Pines of Rome), *Fontane di Roma* (Fountains of Rome) and *Feste Romane* (Roman Festivals).

Outside the Vatican precinct, music publishing came to Rome soon after its birth in Venice. Music was printed in Rome from 1510 and Roman music publication was the first to replace movable type with copperplate engraving.

OPERA

Ballet and opera developed in Rome as they did in Florence and Venice – out of the lavish musical entertainment that diverted the nobility. The Barberini were particularly noted for the extravagance of their 17th-century spectacles, held either in their new palace at Piazza Barberini (see p106) or in the Cardinal's residence in the Palazzo della Cancelleria (see p83).

The melodramatic story of Giacomo Puccini's opera *Tosca* (1900) is set entirely in Rome during Napoleonic occupation. Puccini researched tirelessly for his opera, ensuring that all references to historic figures, places and events were exact. The first act takes place in the Chiesa di Sant'Andrea della Valle, the second in Palazzo Farnese and the final act is set at Castel Sant'Angelo, from which Tosca jumps to her death. Neither the diva Floria Tosca nor her revolutionary lover Mario Cavaradossi existed, but the villainous police chief, Baron Scarpia, may well have been based on Baron Sciarpa, a Bourbon officer. In 1992 an Emmy Award–winning television broadcast was made of the opera (starring Catherine Malfitano and Placido Domingo), shot on location and at the precise times specified by the libretto.

Tenor Luciano Pavarotti (born 1935) is still the best known of Italy's opera singers, though these days he is well past his prime. The remarkable blind tenor Andrea Bocelli (born 1958) has taken his superb voice to the pop charts and some see him as Pavarotti's natural successor. Bocelli's *Con Te, Partirò* ('I'll Go With You') was a huge hit in 1998 and he has since given concerts around the world, even if his voice is not in the calibre of Pavarotti.

Other current operatic talents include home-grown mezzo-soprano superstar Cecilia Bartoli, Barbara Frittoli, Cecilia Gasdia, Anna Caterina Antonacci, Luciana Serra, Sonia Ganassi, Ruggero Raimondi, Renato Bruson, Ferruccio Furlanetto and Giuseppe Sabbatini, many of whom regularly sing in Rome.

CONTEMPORARY MUSIC

Modern musicians are not as famous as their illustrious predecessors. Part of the reason lies in the importance singers attach to their lyrics. Singer-songwriters like Francesco de Gregori, Fabrizio De Andrè and Pino Daniele simply don't translate well into English. Seventies idol Lucio Battisti tried to break into the American market but his soft, syrupy material just didn't cut it, while rockers Vasco Rossi, Ligabue and Irene Grandi fill home stadiums but offer international audiences nothing new.

Zucchero (Adelmo Fornaciari) is a phenomenon on the Italian music scene. Starting out as a session musician with the likes of Joe Cocker, he has aimed at both the Italian and international markets as few other Italians have, earning many sour grapes along the way. Lots of his songs are sung in Italian *and* English.

Zucchero is one of only few who have enjoyed success outside of Italy; Eros Ramazzotti is another Italian artist who has made a small dent on the international pop scene.

But still home-grown talent thrives. Rappers Jovanotti and 99 Posse bang out songs with enviable energy, Carmen Consoli woos with her silky Sicilian voice and DJs scratch and mix with the best of them. DJ Robert Miles (real name Roberto Concina) may have found success abroad but his musical schooling was pure Italian.

THEATRE & DANCE

The junior member of Italy's arts family, theatre and dance flourish without startling; in Rome performances tend to be quite conservative.

Italy's most famous playwright is Sicilian Luigi Pirandello (1867–1936). With such classics as *Sei Personaggi in Cerca d'Autore* (Six Characters in Search of an Author), he earned the 1934 Nobel Prize for Literature and influenced a whole generation of European writers.

On the contemporary scene, Nobel prizewinner Dario Fo (born 1926) has been writing, directing and performing since the 1950s. His work is laced with political and social critique and has proved popular on London's West End. Hits have included *Morte Accidentale di un Anarchico* (Accidental Death of an Anarchist), *Non si Paga, Non si paga* (Can't Pay, Won't Pay) and *Mistero Buffo*.

Dacia Maraini (born 1936) is one of Italy's most important feminist writers. She continues to work as a journalist while her all-women theatre company Teatro della Maddalena stage her 30-plus plays. Some of these, including the 1978 *Dialogo di una Prostituta con un suo Cliente* (Dialogue of a Prostitute with Client), have played abroad.

Dance is something that most Italians prefer to do rather than watch. Carla Fracci (born 1936) enjoyed a long dancing career with, among others, the Royal Ballet in England and the American Ballet Theatre, while Alessandra Ferri (born 1963) is today regarded as one of the world's premier ballerinas.

Food & Drink

Food & Drink

The experience of eating in Italy is not portable. While the food can be bottled and exported, the culture and importance of eating aren't things you can grasp without a visit to Italy itself; and where better to start than Rome? To eat with passion here isn't the preserve of the well off or well heeled: food and its enjoyment are embedded in the psyche of the people. Unlike many English-speaking nations, eating well isn't something to be done occasionally, it's something you do at least twice a day.

HISTORY

The ancient empire, with all its cultural, artistic and academic wealth, fell into the doldrums with the arrival of the so-called barbarians. But agricultural practices continued as they always had: sheep were farmed, the artichoke flourished and wheat and *farro* (an ancient grain still in use today) continued to be sown.

There has always been an underclass in Rome. At times, even in the heyday of the Empire, up to a third of the inhabitants of the Eternal City were given a bread ration to prevent them from starving to death. Impoverished Romans used to sit by while the mon-eyed aristocrats lived off the proverbial fattened calves. Sitting in *osterie* (neighbourhood inns) near the abattoirs, they watched as all the beasts' innards (the *quinto quarto*, the fifth quarter) were chucked out, and worked out how to cook them. How else can you explain dishes like *pajata*, made with the entrails of very young veal calves, considered a delicacy since they contain the mother's congealed milk? Most of what is now considered *cucina romana* (Roman cuisine) developed from these *osterie*, especially those near the abattoirs in Testaccio and Trastevere. There are still restaurants opposite where the abattoirs once were, producing dishes from the parts of animals that the wealthy didn't want, and Testaccio is still known as *the* place to go for an authentic Roman dining experience.

Roman food is not all offal, but a lot of it is. When you see the word *coratella* in a dish, it implies that you'll be eating lights (lungs), kidneys and the heart. Often these dishes are cooked with *carciofi*, the wonderful artichoke that in Rome is rounder, fleshier and better-tasting than virtually anywhere in the country. It cuts the richness of the offal and leaves the palate refreshed if not cleansed. At other times tomato is used with offal, and the expression 'in umido', while normally meaning cooked in a broth, in Lazio tends to mean cooked in a broth scented with tomato. Offal eaters shouldn't miss the opportunity to try *coda* (oxtail) or *trippa* (tripe) here, where they are done best.

Poverty also led to the judicious use of other ingredients. Pork is commonly used, but sparingly. *Spaghetti alla carbonara* is the classic pasta dish, with a gorgeous, barely-there sauce of egg, cheese and *guanciale* (cured pig's cheek) or, more commonly now, pancetta

---

Top Five Foodie Reads

- *Around the Roman Table*, Patrick Faas (2003) – more fun than instruction, this book details the peculiar culinary habits of the ancient Romans. Anyone for stuffed dormice?
- *Roman Cookery: Ancient Recipes for Modern Kitchens*, Mark Grant (1998) – everyday dishes rather than the exotic banquets of the elite.
- *Rome for all Seasons*, Diane Seed (1996) – seasonal recipes from the celebrated culinary author and cookery-school host (see p264).
- *In a Roman Kitchen: Timeless Recipes from the Eternal City*, Jo Bettoja (2003) – a delightful collection of Rome's signature dishes.
- *Italian Wines: A Guide to the World of Italian Wine for Experts & Wine Lovers*, Gambero Rosso (Ed) – Slow Food's annually updated guide is an excellent resource with region-by-region profiles of producers and their wines.

(cured bacon). Small amounts of prosciutto (ham) and sage are used to spark up the veal dish *saltimbocca*, while even the humble chicken broth is given a lift by the judicious use of Parmesan and whisked egg to make the soup *stracciatella*.

Deep frying, which has its origins in Jewish cooking, is another important feature of Roman cuisine. Deep-fried fillets of *baccalà* (salted cod), *fiori di zucca* (zucchini flowers) stuffed with mozzarella and anchovies, and *carciofi alla giudia* (artichokes) are a must on any Roman gastronomic itinerary, whether they be eaten as a snack, as a prelude to a pizza or as a course in themselves.

Rome was built on the Via Salaria, the salt road, where traders set up camp on the banks of the Tiber. You get the impression that they love salt, even today, by the amounts used, which can be quite excessive, even in comparison with other Italian regions. If you aren't used to it, be prepared for a lip-smacking, water-drinking few days when you first arrive.

CULTURE

ETIQUETTE

Just as an Italian at our table would make few faux pas, so too most Westerners at an Italian table get it right. We simply aren't that different. That's the good news. The bad news is that what constitutes 'good manners' alters – as it does everywhere – depending not only on whom you're with, but where you are eating. But the *really* good news is that Italians are so hospitable that they will forgive virtually anything you do unwittingly.

HOW ROMANS EAT

Romans rarely eat a sit-down *colazione* (breakfast). They tend to drink a cappuccino, usually *tiepido* (warm) with a *cornetto* (croissant) or other type of pastry while standing at a bar.

Pranzo (lunch) is traditionally the main meal of the day, and many shops and businesses close for three to four hours every afternoon to accommodate the meal and siesta which is supposed to follow.

A full meal will consist of antipasto, a light starter. Next comes the *primo piatto* (first plate) – a pasta or risotto – followed by the *secondo piatto* of meat or fish. Romans often then eat an *insalata* (salad) or *contorno* (vegetable side dish) and round off the meal with fruit, or occasionally with a sweet, and *caffè*, often at a bar on the way back to work.

The evening meal *(cena)* is traditionally a simpler affair, but habits are changing because of the inconvenience of travelling home for lunch every day.

Dos & Don'ts

- *Buongiorno* or *Buonasera* is the basic greeting in any bar or restaurant.
- Italians dress with impeccable style at most meals, so brush up when eating out.
- When eating pasta, any bits hanging down should be bitten through rather than slurped up. You'll probably never be offered a spoon to eat your pasta with as this practice is considered to be quite rude.
- If you are lucky enough to eat in an Italian home, remember that generosity at a meal is a sign of hospitality so refuse at your own peril! You can, and should, *fare la scarpetta* (make a shoe) with your bread and wipe plates clean of sauces – a sign you've really enjoyed the meal and one that won't go unnoticed.

STAPLES & SPECIALITIES

Antipasto

Antipasto dishes (starters) in Rome are particularly good and many restaurants allow you to make your own mixed selection from a buffet. It varies from bruschetta (a type of garlic bread with various toppings) to fried vegetables or *prosciutto e melone* (cured ham wrapped around melon).

Smoked Out

Apparently there's a law in Italy requiring all restaurants to provide a nonsmoking area. We say 'apparently' because you'll be hard-pressed to find a nonsmoking section except in the most expensive of *ristoranti* (restaurants). Smoking is a way of life – locals will puff energetically on cigarettes and cigars just as your meal hits the table. As a visitor there's nothing you can do about it except request nonsmoking when you book. Don't be surprised, however, if you receive a total blank in response.

Primo Piatto

While risotto is often on offer, the ubiquitous choice is pasta. Traditional Roman pasta dishes include *spaghetti alla carbonara* (with egg, Parmesan cheese and pancetta) and *all'amatriciana* (with tomato sauce, pancetta and a touch of chilli), which originates from Amatrice, a town east of Rome. *Penne all'arrabbiata* (literally 'angry' pasta) has a tomato and chilli sauce.

Another favourite is *spaghetti al cacio e pepe*, a deceptively simple dish of piping-hot pasta topped with freshly grated *pecorino Romano* cheese, ground black pepper and a dash of olive oil. It appears on many Roman menus, traditionally in the more humble *osterie* and trattorie, although in recent years there has been a fashion in more upmarket eateries for this and other dishes of the *cucina povera* (literally 'poor cooking') school. *Spaghetti alla gricia* is similar but with the addition of pancetta. It comes from the town of Griciano in northern Lazio.

Although pasta with seafood sauces hails from southern Italy, many Roman restaurants serve delicious *spaghetti alle vongole* (with clams) – best on Tuesday or Friday when the seafood is guaranteed to be really fresh.

In many Roman restaurants, Thursday is the day for gnocchi (dumplings). The traditional Roman recipe uses semolina flour and makes quite heavy gnocchi, usually served with a tomato or meat *ragù* (sauce).

Nonsqueamish eaters might want to try *pasta pajata*, made with veal calf intestines. But if you don't fancy that then try the hearty and warming *pasta e lenticchie* (pasta with lentils) – but be prepared for the postmeal anaesthetic effect!

Freshly grated cheese is the magic ingredient for most pasta (although don't try adding it to a seafood sauce unless you want to receive some really strange looks and comments). Parmesan *(parmigiano)* is the most widely used, particularly in the north. Look for the name 'Parmigiano Reggiano' on the rind to ensure you're getting the genuine article because there is also the similar, but lower-quality, *grana padano*. In and around Rome there is a tendency to use the sharp and slightly salty sheep's milk *pecorino*.

Secondo Piatto

For your second course, meat dishes to look out for are *saltimbocca alla Romana*, veal topped with a slice of *prosciutto crudo* (cured ham), white wine and sage, and *abbacchio al forno*, lamb roasted with rosemary and garlic. In recent years fish has become an important item on the menus of Rome's better eateries; more often than not it's grilled whole and then filleted by the waiter at the table. It is, however, more expensive than any other main course.

Insalati & Contorno

Try these vegetable dishes: *carciofi alla Romana*, artichokes stuffed with mint or parsley and garlic; a salad of curly *puntarelle* (Catalonian chicory) tossed in a garlic, olive oil and anchovy dressing; and, in spring, freshly shelled *fave* (broad beans) served with a slice of *pecorino Romano*, the most famous *pecorino* (sheep's milk) cheese.

DRINKS

Nonalcoholic Drinks

COFFEE

The first-time visitor to Rome is likely to be confused by the many ways in which the locals consume their caffeine. An espresso is a small amount of very strong black coffee. It is also referred to simply as *un caffè*. You can ask for a *doppio espresso*, which means double the amount, or a *caffè lungo* (translated as a slightly diluted espresso). If you want a long black coffee (as in a weaker, watered-down version), ask for a *caffè Americano*.

A *caffè corretto* is an espresso with a dash of grappa or some other spirit and a *macchiato* ('stained' coffee) is espresso with a dash of milk. You can ask for a *macchiato caldo* (with a dot of hot, foamed milk) or *freddo* with a spot of cold milk. On the other hand, *latte macchiato* is warmed milk stained with a spot of coffee. *Caffè freddo* is a long glass of cold, black, sweetened coffee. If you want it without sugar, ask for *caffè freddo amaro*. *Gran caffè* is a wonderful, almost bubbly, coffee made by beating the first drops of espresso and several teaspoons of sugar into a frothy paste, then adding the coffee on top.

Then, of course, there is the cappuccino, coffee with hot, frothy milk. If you want it without froth, ask for a *cappuccino senza schiuma*. Italians tend to drink cappuccino only with breakfast and during the morning. They never drink it after meals – 'How can you put all that hot milk on a full stomach?' – or in the evening and, if you order one after dinner, don't be surprised if the waiter asks you two or three times, just to make sure that they heard correctly.

You will also find it hard to convince bartenders to make your cappuccino hot rather than lukewarm. Ask for it *ben caldo*, *molto caldo* or *bollente* (boiling) and wait for the same 'tut-tut' response that you got when you ordered a cappuccino after dinner.

Milky coffee variations include *caffè latte*, a milkier version of the cappuccino with less froth. In summer the *cappuccino freddo*, a type of iced coffee, is popular.

TEA

Italians don't drink a lot of tea *(tè)* and generally only do so in the late afternoon, when they might take a cup with a few *pasticcini* (small cakes). You can order tea in bars, although it will usually arrive in the form of a cup of warm water extracted from the espresso machine (with a strange smell and sometimes a slightly rotten taste) with an accompanying tea bag. If this doesn't suit your taste, ask for the water *bollente* (boiling).

FRUIT JUICES & NECTARS

Most bars will make you a freshly squeezed fruit juice, known as a *spremuta* for around €1.50 to €3. Orange juice, *spremuta di arancia*, is the most common, but you can also get *spremuta di limone* (lemon juice) and *spremuta di pompelmo* (grapefruit). Bars also sell small glass bottles of thick, sweet fruit juices *(succhi di frutta)* in flavours including apricot *(albicocca)*, peach *(pesca)* and pear *(pera)*.

GRANITA & GRATTACHECCA

Refreshingly cool *granita* is a drink made of crushed ice with fresh lemon or other fruit juices, or with coffee topped with whipped cream. A slightly different kind of ice drink, and uniquely Roman, is *grattachecca*, ice grated off a huge block and flavoured with syrups or juices. There used to be *grattachecca* kiosks all over Rome but now there is only a handful left (including two in Testaccio, one on the Trastevere side of the Isola Tiberina and one on the Lungotevere near Ponte Umberto I, north of Piazza Navona).

WATER

Rome's water is among the cleanest in Italy and you can drink the water from any of the ubiquitous street fountains. Most of these run continuously and have a small hole in the

Travel Your Tastebuds

For an authentic Roman dining experience you shouldn't miss:

Carciofi Try the *carciofi alla romana* (artichokes stuffed Roman style), or *alla giudia* (deep-fried whole).

Pajata Surprisingly delicious veal entrails roasted or tossed through penne or rigatoni.

Saltimbocca alla romana The name of this veal dish means to 'jump in the mouth'.

Gelati Some of the best ice cream in the world is to be found in Rome.

spout to facilitate drinking; just hold your finger over the bottom of the spout and a jet of water will emerge higher up. The water is ice-cold year-round, which is especially refreshing in summer.

The water does contain relatively high levels of calcium and many Romans prefer to drink bottled mineral water *(acqua minerale)*. This is either sparkling *(frizzante* or *gasata)* or still *(naturale)* and you will be asked in restaurants and bars which you prefer. If you want a glass of tap water, ask for *acqua dal rubinetto*, although simply asking for *acqua semplice* will suffice.

Alcoholic Drinks
WINE

Wine *(vino)* is an essential accompaniment to any meal. Italians are very proud of their wines and find it hard to believe that anyone else could produce wines as good as theirs. Many Italians drink alcohol only with meals and the foreign custom of going out for a drink is still considered unusual although, in some parts of Italy (mainly the north), it is common to see men starting their day with a grappa (a very strong clear grape spirit) for breakfast and continuing to consume strong drinks throughout the day.

There are four main classifications of wine – DOC *(Denominazione di Origine Controllata)*, DOCG *(Denominazione di Origine Controllata e Garantita)*, IGT *(Indicazione Geografica Tipica)* and *vino da tavola* (table wine) – which will be marked on the label.

Frascati wine bottles

A DOC wine is produced subject to certain specifications, although the label does not certify quality. DOCG is subject to the same requirements as normal DOC but it is also tested by government inspectors for quality. IGT is a relatively recent term introduced to cover wines from quality regions that use grapes or are of a style that falls outside of the DOC and DOCG classifications. Table wines can vary considerably in quality; some are very good and others best avoided.

Although some excellent wines are produced in Italy, most trattorie stock only a limited selection of bottled wines and generally only cheaper varieties. Most people tend to order the house wine *(vino della casa* or *vino sfuso)* or the local wine *(vino locale)* when they go out to dine.

The styles of wine vary throughout the country. While many wine buffs would argue that Rome and the Lazio region are poor relations as far as Italian wine production is concerned, some good white wines are produced in the Castelli Romani area (southeast of the city, see p242), notably Frascati Superiore. You can taste local and not-so-local wine in many of Rome's *enoteche* (specialist wine shops). Torre Ercolana from Anagni is an opulent local red.

BEER

The main local labels are Peroni, Dreher, Nastro Azzuro and Moretti, all very drinkable and cheaper than the imported varieties. If you want a local beer, ask for a *birra nazionale*, which will be either in a bottle or *alla spina* (on tap). Italy also imports beers from throughout Europe and the rest of the world.

SPIRITS

Before dinner, Italians might drink a Campari and soda or a fruit cocktail (usually pre-prepared and often without alcohol – *analcolico*). After dinner try a shot of grappa or an *amaro*, a dark liqueur prepared from herbs. If you prefer a sweeter liqueur, try an almond-flavoured amaretto, a sweet aniseed *sambucca* or, in the hotter months, a chilled *limoncello*.

CELEBRATIONS

Italy celebrates an unprecedented number of festivals, many of them coming from the region's pagan past.

People on the peninsula have always celebrated a harvest, some god or other, a wedding, a birth, or just whatever. And when Christianity arrived, they simply put their new God as the figurehead. Most of these festivals were wild affairs, such as the Saturnalia festival in Roman times, where a week of drunken revelry in honour of the god of disorder was marked by a pig sacrifice at the start and a human sacrifice at the end. Celebrations these days are more sedate affairs by comparison. But they can still be amazing. The biggest times for festivals these days centre around *Natale* (Christmas), *Pasqua* (Easter) and *Carnevale* (the period leading up to Ash Wednesday, the first day of Lent).

The classic way to celebrate any feast day is to precede it with a day of eating *magro* (lean) because the feast day is usually a day of overindulgence. While just about every festival has some kind of food involved, many of them are only about food. The general rule is that a *sagra* (feasting festival) will offer food (although you'll normally be expected to pay), and at a *festa* (festival or celebration) you may have to bring your own.

WHERE TO EAT & DRINK

Eateries are divided into several categories. A *tavola calda* (literally 'hot table') usually offers cheap, pre-prepared pasta, meat and vegetable dishes in a self-service style. A *rosticceria* usually offers cooked meats but often has a larger selection of takeaway food. A *pizzeria* will of course serve pizza, but usually also a full menu including antipasto, pasta, meat and vegetable dishes. An *enoteca* is a specialist wine shop which also serves wine by the glass (or bottle), light snacks (such as cheeses or cold meats) and often a couple of hot dishes. An *osteria* is likely to be either a wine bar offering a small selection of dishes or a small trattoria. A trattoria is a cheaper version of a *ristorante* (restaurant), which in turn has a wider selection of dishes and a higher standard of service. The problem is that many of the establishments that are in fact restaurants call themselves trattorie or *osterie* for reasons best known to themselves. It is advisable to check the menu, usually posted by the door, for prices.

Don't judge the quality of a *ristorante* or trattoria by its appearance. You are likely to eat your most memorable meal at a place with plastic tablecloths in a tiny back street, on a dingy square or on a back road in the country.

And don't panic if you find yourself in a trattoria which has no printed menu: they are often the ones which offer outstanding, authentic food and have menus that change daily to accommodate the availability of fresh produce. Just hope that the waiter will patiently explain the dishes and cost.

After lunch and dinner, you might like to head for the nearest *gelateria* (ice-cream parlour) to round off the meal with some excellent *gelati*, followed by a *digestivo* (after-dinner liqueur) at a bar.

A Snail's Pace

Fast food as a concept doesn't sit easily with Italians, and it was here in 1986 that the first organised, politically active group decided to tackle the issue head on. Symbolised by a snail, the Slow Food movement now has chapters in 48 countries and over 77,000 members. It promotes good food and wine to be consumed (slowly, of course) in good company, and champions traditional cuisine and sustainable agricultural practices. Every two years the movement publishes *Osterie d'Italia*, which rates what they believe to be the top restaurants in the country. You'll spot them by the Slow Food sticker proudly displayed outside. For more information check out www.slowfood.com.

For a light lunch or a snack, most bars serve *tramezzini* (sandwiches) and *panini* (rolls), which cost €1 to €3 taken at the bar (*al banco*). Another option is to go to one of the many *alimentari* (delicatessens) and ask them to make a *panino* with the filling (usually cold meats and cheeses) of your choice. At a *pasticceria* you can buy pastries, cakes and biscuits. Bakeries (*forni*), numerous in the Campo de' Fiori area, are another good choice for a cheap snack. Try a piece of *pizza bianca*, a flat bread resembling focaccia, which costs from around €1 per slice.

During summer these areas are lively and atmospheric, with most establishments offering outside tables. Restaurants usually open for lunch from noon to 3pm but many are not keen to take orders after 2.30pm. In the evening, restaurants open from about 7.30pm, though they will often open earlier in tourist areas. If you want to be sure of finding a table (especially if you want one outside), either drop into the restaurant during the day and make a booking or arrive before 8.30pm. Many restaurants close during part of August.

Coperto

Most disputes visitors find themselves in when visiting a restaurant in Italy concern the *pane e coperto*. This is the charge you incur just for sitting down for a meal in most restaurants. Basically it's a set, nominal charge you're going to have to pay regardless of what you eat. *Coperto* means 'cover' and doesn't necessarily include *servizio*, the service charge. While we all know that things such as bread and linen cost money, it would seem logical to include them as overheads in the prices of dishes. But that's simply not the way it's done and you won't change it by arguing that you didn't eat the bread or order any *copertos*.

Vegetarians & Vegans

Rome is not great for vegies although there are a few dedicated meat-free places, and there's an abundance of antipasti, suitable pasta dishes for primi, along with plenty of insalati (salads), contorni (vegetable sides) and pizzas. Your only problem may be a lack of variety; because Roman cuisine is so seasonal you'll find that most trattorie serve the same dishes although this is a bonus in autumn when truffles and other fungi abound.

Be mindful of hidden ingredients not mentioned on the menu – for example, steer clear of anything that's been stuffed (like zucchini flowers) or check that it's *senza carne o pesce* (without meat or fish) – and note that vegetarian to many Italians means you don't eat red meat. Look for the word *magro* (thin or lean) on menus, which usually means that the dish is meatless.

Vegans are in for a much tougher time. Cheese is used universally, so you have to say *'senza formaggio'* (without cheese) as a matter of course. Also remember that pasta fresca, which may also turn up in soups, is made with eggs.

Children

You'll be hard-pressed to find a children's menu in most Italian restaurants. It's not that kids aren't welcome but because, more than just about anywhere, they are. Local children are treated very much as adults and are taken out to dinner from a very tender age. You'll often see families order a *mezzo piatto* ('half-plate') off the menu for the smaller guests. Virtually all restaurants are perfectly comfortable tailoring a dish to meet your kid's tastes.

High chairs are available in many restaurants, but you're safest to bring one along as some restaurants don't supply them. While children are often taken out, and the owner's kids may be seen scrambling about the room, it's expected that kids be well behaved, and disciplined if they are not. For more information on travelling with your little ones, see p264.

Quick Eats

Fast food is becoming increasingly popular in Rome: you'll find the usual global suspects throughout the city. But seriously, why would you bother when you can pick up a delicious slice of pizza from one of the many *pizza a taglio* or *pizza rustica* outlets.

History

HISTORY *by Richard Watkins*

THE RECENT PAST
1980S & 1990S

Italy enjoyed significant economic growth throughout the 1980s, during which it became one of the world's leading economic powers.

Socialist Bettino Craxi held the premiership from 1983 to 1989, a period characterised by high-level corruption. He fled the country in 1993 after being implicated in the Tangentopoli national bribery scandal (see the boxed text below). Convicted *in absentia* on corruption charges, he remains in self-imposed exile in Tunisia.

The 1990s heralded a new period of economic and political crisis. High unemployment and inflation, combined with a huge national debt and an extremely unstable lira, led the government to introduce Draconian measures to revive the economy.

In 1993 Francesco Rutelli – at that stage nominally part of the Verdi (Green Party) – became the first mayor of Rome to be directly elected by the inhabitants of the city. The suave, media-savvy Rutelli set about cleaning up the city, targeting transport, pollution and protection of cultural patrimony.

The 1994 national election was won by a new right-wing coalition known as the Polo per le Libertà (Freedom Alliance), whose members included the newly formed Forza Italia, the Neo-Fascist Alleanza Nazionale (National Alliance) and the secessionist Lega Nord (Northern League). Its leader, billionaire media-magnate Silvio Berlusconi, who had entered politics only three months before the elections, was appointed prime minister (PM). After a turbulent nine months in power, Berlusconi's volatile coalition government collapsed.

In the ensuing chaos, President Scalfaro appointed an interim government which ran the show until the 1996 elections. By that time, there was a clear division of the parties into two main groups: *centro-destra* (centre-right) and *centro-sinistra* (centre-left).

It was the centre-left Ulivo coalition, led by Romano Prodi, which claimed a landslide victory at the 1996 elections. Prodi's government drastically reduced public spending and introduced new taxes, enabling Italy to join the single currency as planned.

In 1998 Prodi lost a vote in parliament and was replaced as PM by Massimo D'Alema, of the Partito Democratico della Sinistra (PDS). Thus Italy gained its first former-communist prime minister.

Tangentopoli

The Tangentopoli (literally 'kickback cities') scandal broke in Milan in early 1992 when a functionary of the Partito Socialista Italiano (Italian Socialist Party) was arrested on charges of accepting bribes in exchange for public works contracts. Led by Milanese magistrate Antonio di Pietro, dubbed the 'reluctant hero', investigations known as Mani Pulite (clean hands) eventually implicated thousands of politicians, public officials and businesspeople.

Charges ranged from bribery, making illicit political payments and receiving kickbacks to blatant thievery. Typically, few ordinary Italians were surprised that many politicians, at all levels of government, were entrenched in this corrupt system that affected the whole country.

TIMELINE	753 BC	715-673	509
	Legendary foundation of Rome by Romulus	Numa Pompilius becomes first Etruscan king of Rome	Expulsion of monarchy; Lucius Junius Brutus founds Republic

THE 21ST CENTURY

The 2001 elections saw Silvio Berlusconi (leader of the centre-right coalition and Italy's richest man) become the country's 59th postwar prime minister, despite the fact that he was still under investigation for bribery and tax fraud. Berlusconi owns the three main commercial TV networks and now controls the state-run entities. In recent years his increasing influence over the Italian media has caused alarm. In 2002 two popular news-readers on the state-run RAI channel were dismissed after criticising Berlusconi, while arguments over press censorship continue as news stories unpalatable to the government are pulled. Avoiding the injunction against public office–holders owning broadcasting licences, Berlusconi has placed members of his family in charge of his media interests and has attempted to install his own nominees in key positions.

Meanwhile, the Italian PM's lack of tact has continued to enliven the European political scene. After assuming the six-month presidency of the EU in 2003, he likened one German politician to a Nazi concentration camp commander, prompting the German chancellor to cancel his holiday in Italy. Love him or loathe him, Berlusconi's never boring.

FROM THE BEGINNING

THE FOUNDATIONS

Rome's precise origins are lost in the proverbial mists of time, but it is generally agreed that they lay in a group of Etruscan, Latin and Sabine settlements on the Palatine, Esquiline and Quirinal Hills. Ancient Romans dated their city's foundation to 21 April 753 BC, and indeed archaeological discoveries have confirmed the existence of a settlement on the Palatine dating from the 8th century BC, while traces from the 9th century BC have been unearthed in the Foro di Cesare.

However, it is the legend of Romulus and Remus that prevails. According to this legend, the twin sons of Rhea Silvia (a Latin princess) and the war god Mars were raised by a she-wolf after being abandoned on the banks of the River Tiber. The myth says Romulus killed his brother during a battle over who should govern, and then established the city of Rome on the Palatine, making himself the first king. Later he disappeared, poetically taken up by the gods or, more prosaically, secretly murdered by senators.

The next seven kings of Rome were elected from the ranks of the nobles. Most notably, Numa Pompilius is credited with installing the state religion and the Etruscan Servius Tullius built the first walls around the city-state, establishing the basic organisation of the political and military system. The last king, Tarquinius Superbus (Tarquin the Proud), was expelled from Rome after his son raped a nobleman's wife. The Etruscan royal house was overthrown and the Roman Republic was born.

THE REPUBLIC

In government, the Romans combined the best of all the known systems. At the top were the two consuls, who were also the alternating commanders-in-chief; next came the Senate, to which all higher magistrates, including the consuls, belonged; while almost all political offices were up for election. To keep the magistrates in check, all offices were changed annually; re-election was originally forbidden, then later allowed only after a 10-year gap. No man was permitted to stand for high office until he had progressed through the sequence of junior posts, and all magistracies were held jointly. The exception was the dictator, appointed for six months during periods of crisis.

390	264	142	82
Sack of Rome by Gauls	First gladiatorial show in Rome	First stone bridge over River Tiber	Cornelius Sulla becomes dictator

The Romans also developed a unique system for dealing with the other peoples in the region. Defeated city-states were not taken over but became allies. Allowed to retain their own government and lands, they were required to provide troops to serve alongside Roman soldiers in future wars. This naturally increased Rome's military strength, and the protection offered by the Roman hegemony induced many cities to become allies voluntarily.

The civic structure also expanded. In 450 BC, the existing laws were codified as the Law of the Twelve Tables, which remained in force for the next 1000 years. Construction of the Via Appia began in 312 BC and in 244 BC the road was extended to the eastern port of Brindisi.

However, Rome itself was still vulnerable. In 390 BC, Gauls swept down from the north and besieged the city. The populace retreated to the Capitoline, which was saved on one occasion when Juno's sacred geese alerted the defenders to a nocturnal attack. The invaders were finally bought off with a massive bribe.

The Teatro di Marcello (p115)

The other Mediterranean power during this period was Carthage, a kingdom of Phoenician origin in North Africa. The power-politics of the day inevitably led to conflict, and the First Punic War (264–241 BC) eventually handed Rome the territories of Sicily and Sardinia.

The Carthaginians weren't out of the picture yet, though, and in 218 BC war flared up again. This time Rome faced its most dangerous adversary to date, Hannibal, who daringly led his army into Italy over the Alps.

The Romans suffered major defeats at Lake Trasimeno in 217 BC, and at Cannae in the following year. With Hannibal entrenched in Italy, the Roman military commander Publius Cornelius Scipio attacked Africa itself in 204 BC, forcing the Carthaginians to recall Hannibal to defend their own capital. Scipio defeated Hannibal at Zama in 202 BC and Carthage fell to Rome.

The ensuing Macedonian Wars saw Roman power extend into the wealthy Hellenistic east, and a series of 'client kingdoms' were established, favourable to Roman interests.

FROM REPUBLIC TO EMPIRE

Roman politics was polarised into two factions, linked as much by marriage as by policies: the Optimates (conservatives), who upheld the primacy of the Senate; and the Populares (populists), who preferred to take their bills before the people's assemblies. This split caused civil conflict between the supporters of Marius, a Populare, and Sulla, an Optimate.

Sulla twice threatened to invade Rome and in 82 BC the Senate gave in to his demands and he was voted dictator for the extraordinary period of 10 years.

In 71 BC the fabulously wealthy Marcus Licinius Crassus finally mopped up the dramatic slave rebellion led by the gladiator Spartacus, which had been raging through Italy for two years. At its conclusion, 6000 slaves were crucified along the Via Appia.

73-71	44	27	9
Revolt of Spartacus	Caesar assassinated	Pantheon built	Ara Pacis dedicated

Nero Rules

Adopted by Emperor Claudius at the age of 10, Lucius Domitius Ahenobarbus – later known as Nero – was only 17 when the old man died, and he found himself proclaimed his successor. His early popularity, though, soon evaporated along with his hold on sanity, as he spent his time singing and playing the lyre in public, and, according to Suetonius, practising 'every kind of obscenity', including serial rape of both men and women. He was even said to have prowled the streets of Rome at night, attacking drunks and burgling houses, then selling his loot at a market in the palace the next day. His wastefulness, too, was legendary; his Domus Aurea (Golden House), of which only a small section survives today, was built on a scale only a megalomaniac could have conceived. Decorated with gold, ivory and precious stones, its entrance hall contained a 120-foot statue of the emperor, with a mile-long corridor leading off it, while in the dining room, guests would be showered with perfume from sprinklers in the ceiling as they ate. The complex even included vineyards, woodland and a lake.

Although Nero was in Anzio when the great fire of Rome broke out in AD 64, rumour quickly spread that he was responsible. One tale was that he callously used the burning city as a backdrop for a recital on the fall of Troy; even worse was the rumour that he had actually started the fire, in order to build a vast new city called Neropolis. The pleasure with which he used a large amount of the ruined city for his new palace, the Domus Aurea, hardly helped calm popular feeling.

Unnerved, Nero looked for scapegoats, and chose the early-Christian community, for whom the rest of the population had little understanding and no sympathy. Some were thrown to wild animals in the circus, and others, in perverse retribution for arson, were burned alive as human torches.

St Peter and St Paul are said to have been martyred during this period. Peter was crucified (upside down at his own request so as not to imitate the death of Jesus too closely) near Nero's racetrack in the Vatican, and Paul, a Roman citizen, was given the privilege of decapitation.

In the culture of fear he generated, no-one was safe; he finally had his mother assassinated, after convoluted plans to poison her and to drown her by sinking her ship failed. With revolt spreading among the provincial governors, the Senate declared Nero a public enemy in AD 68 and he committed suicide while on the run, supposedly with the last words, '*Qualis artifex pereo!*' (What an artist dies with me!).

Crassus and Pompey, a protege of Sulla, together campaigned (and bribed) their way to the consulships of 70 BC.

In 59 BC Julius Caesar was running for consulship, and made a deal with Crassus and Pompey in return for their electoral and financial support. The three men became known as the First Triumvirate and their pact was reinforced by Pompey's marriage to Caesar's daughter, Julia. The First Triumvirate was renewed in 56 BC, and with Caesar's electoral support, Crassus and Pompey shared another consulship in 55 BC. The alliance was shaken, however, when Julia died in 54 BC and Crassus was heavily defeated and killed in Parthia the following year.

Pompey became increasingly influenced by the Optimates, who wanted to impeach Caesar for irregularities in Gaul, causing civil war when Caesar crossed into Italy with his army of devoted veterans in 49 BC. Pompey's main force was defeated by Caesar at Pharsalus a year later and Pompey himself was assassinated in Egypt.

Caesar returned to Rome in 47 BC and began to institute reforms, overhauling both the calendar and the Senate. Of his extensive building program, the Curia (Senate House) and the Basilica Guilia remain. Initially declared dictator for one year, Caesar had this extended to 10 years and then, in 44 BC, was proclaimed dictator for life. This accumulation of power fatally alienated even those who had initially supported him, and Caesar was assassinated in the portico of the Teatro di Pompeo on the Ides of March (15 March) 44 BC.

Caesar's lieutenant, Marcus Antonius (Mark Antony), took command of the city, aided by the troops under the command of Lepidus. Caesar's will had declared the adoption of

AD 14	48	59	64
Death of Augustus	Claudius holds games to celebrate Rome's 800th anniversary	Murder of Agrippina, Nero's mother; Nero makes his stage debut	Great Fire of Rome

his 18-year-old great-nephew, Octavian, as his son and heir. Octavian, then studying in Greece, returned to Rome to claim his inheritance. First siding with Caesar's assassins against Antony, he then switched sides and fought with Antony against Brutus and Cassius who were defeated at Philippi. The orator Cicero, who had attacked Antony in a series of speeches, became a victim of the political bloodshed that followed.

Civil war broke out between Octavian and Antony, with the latter finally being defeated at Actium.

THE EMPIRE

Octavian was left the sole ruler of the Roman world, but, remembering Caesar's fate, trod very carefully. In 27 BC, he officially surrendered his extraordinary powers to the Senate, which promptly gave most of them back, making him the first emperor of Rome and voting him the unique title of Augustus. As emperor (27 BC–AD 14), he avoided the more obvious trappings of monarchy, maintaining at least the superficial structure of Republican government.

The new era of political stability also saw a flourishing of the arts, with the likes of Virgil, Ovid, Horace and Tibullus contributing to what later generations of Romans wistfully regarded as a golden age. Augustus encouraged the visual arts, restored existing buildings and commissioned many new ones, including the Ara Pacis (Altar of Peace) explicitly to commemorate his achievement. His boast that 'he found Rome in brick, and left it in marble' was no exaggeration.

His successor, Tiberius (AD 14–37), ruled with the merciless savagery that became a hallmark of the Julio-Claudian dynasty, and his death, most likely murder, at his villa in Capri brought cheering crowds onto the streets of Rome. Little did they know how much worse things were about to become. The brief reign of Caligula (AD 37–41) was characterised by excessive brutality and depravity, with incest, torture, murder and rape among the young emperor's daily diversions. His infamous acts of sheer lunacy included making his horse a senator and ordering his soldiers to collect seashells. Such erratic behaviour led to his timely assassination at the age of 29.

In the chaos following Caligula's death, the Senate set out to restore the Republic, but the Imperial Praetorian Guard had other ideas. Discovering Caligula's bumbling uncle Claudius hiding behind a curtain in the palace, they carted the terrified 50-year-old off to their camp and declared him emperor. Despite this ignominious beginning to his reign, Claudius proved to be a conscientious ruler. He extended the port facilities at Ostia and constructed a new aqueduct, the Acqua Claudia, to service Rome's growing population. He also strengthened Rome's hold on Britain, first invaded by Caesar.

Probably poisoned in AD 58 by his ambitious wife, Agrippina, Claudius was succeeded by Nero, her 17-year-old son by a previous marriage (see the boxed text, p51).

In the 'Year of the Four Emperors' that followed Nero's death, Galba, Otho and Vitellius came and went in quick and bloody succession, and stability was only restored when Vespasian, a hard-nosed general, took command. A practical man, Vespasian (AD 69–79) constructed a huge amphitheatre (the Colosseum) in the grounds of Nero's demolished Domus Aurea. Vespasian's dry wit and generous nature endeared him to Rome and helped restore the severely tarnished image of the emperorship. Like Augustus and Claudius before him, he knew he would be accorded divine honours after his death, and as he lay dying proclaimed 'Alas, I fear I am becoming a god!'

The short-lived Flavian dynasty died with Vespasian's sons, Titus (AD 79–81) and the ruthless Domitian (AD 81–96), who greatly extended the palace complex on the Palatine.

Trajan (98–117), an experienced general, presided over the greatest period of expansion the empire had seen, and initiated a period of great prosperity and stability at home. His victories over the Dacians are depicted in meticulous detail on the column erected in his

67	69	80	174
St Peter and St Paul martyred	Year of the Four Emperors	Dedication of the Colosseum	*Meditations* of Marcus Aurelius

forum, which also contained his multistorey market, a triumph of Roman architecture that survives in remarkable condition.

Hadrian (117–138), a prodigious traveller and keen architect, remodelled the Pantheon and built an extensive villa at Tivoli, outside Rome. By 100, the city of Rome had over 1.5 million inhabitants and all the trappings of the capital of an empire, its wealth obvious in the marble temples, public baths, theatres, circuses and libraries.

The reigns of Antonius Pius (138–161) and the philosopher-emperor Marcus Aurelius (161–180) were stable, but the latter ominously spent 14 years fighting northern invaders. A slow decline began with the disturbed gladiator-emperor Commodus (180–192) and with his assassination chaos ensued, before the dictatorial Septimius Severus (193–211) restored order temporarily.

The Mysteries of Mithras

Oriental cults had always appealed to the Romans; the Egyptian deities Isis and Serapis had long enjoyed mass followings in the city and, indeed, elsewhere in the empire. One of the most influential and widespread of these eastern deities was Mithras, a heroic saviour-god of vaguely Persian origin, worshipped by his male-only devotees in subterranean temples (*mithraea*) such as that beneath the present church of San Clemente (see p97).

The central image of the cult was the bull slaying scene *(tauroctony)*, which took pride of place in every *mithraeum*, and showed the young god sacrificing a bull, from whose blood and semen grew all life on earth. Watching above are the Sun god and Moon goddess, while either side of Mithras stand the two torchbearers, Cautes and Cautopates, who represent day and night, spring and autumn or light and darkness. The god's other companions include a raven, dog, snake and scorpion. This scene, whether painted or carved, is remarkably consistent, and its complex astrological symbolism continues to fuel scholarly debate.

The strict, hierarchical cult was especially favoured by soldiers – altars to the god have been found as far afield as Hadrian's Wall in northern England – and was closely identified with the Sun god *Sol Invictus*. It was a private, secretive cult, not supported by state funds or public temples, and was organized by groups of wealthy individuals, including the emperor Commodus, who is said to have accidentally killed a fellow worshipper during an initiation ceremony.

All classes of society, even slaves, could become *fratres* (brothers), while the temple head, the *Pater* (Father), was normally a man of some standing who had contributed significant finances to the temple's upkeep. Unfortunately, no written Mithraist documents survive, and much of what we know of this deeply philosophical 'mystery religion' comes from archaeology. At Ostia, the mosaic floor of one *mithraeum* survives in surprisingly good order, decorated with ritual symbols connected with the seven 'ranks' of initiates into the cult, from the lowest, *Corax* (Raven), to the ultimate grade of *Pater* (Father). One of the best-preserved temples, though, is found below the church of Sánta Prisca (see p112). The cultic statues and paintings here were vandalised by early Christians; you can still see the axe marks in the frescoes. Mithraism, in fact, was particularly reviled by the Christians, who saw this monotheistic, salvationist religion, with its rites of baptism and communion, as a diabolical mockery of their own church.

Mithraism was at the height of its popularity during the 3rd and 4th centuries AD, a period of social, cultural and intellectual turmoil, when monotheistic philosophies were gaining ground with educated pagans; there were as many as two thousand Mithraic temples in Rome alone, of which around forty survive in various states of preservation today.

For more information on Mithraism, try David Ulansey's *The Origins of the Mithraic Mysteries: Cosmology & Salvation in the Ancient World*.

Severus was jointly succeeded by his sons, Caracalla and Geta, with Caracalla predictably organising the assassination of his sibling. Caracalla's building program included his monumental public baths, but his cruel rule lead to his own murder in 217. What followed was one of the bleakest periods in Roman history, a period of civil war, anarchy, and economic decline, with more than 20 emperors violently battling over a fragmenting empire. The situation was

285	313	361-3	370
East and West division of Empire	Christianity legalised	Revival of paganism under Julian the Apostate	Sorcery trials in Rome

rescued by Diocletian (284–305), who established a new administrative system, known as the Tetrarchy, splitting the empire into eastern and western halves, with himself controlling the rich east and Maximian, based in Milan, in charge of the shaky west. Rome's days as *caput mundi* (centre of the world) were numbered.

DECLINE & FALL

In 305 Maximian and Diocletian abdicated simultaneously, leaving the Empire to Constantius in the west and Galerius in the east. A four-way tug-of-war ensued until, in 312, Constantine (Constantius' son) faced Maxentius, his last rival, just outside Rome. After claiming to have seen a vision of the Christian cross and the message 'with this sign you will conquer', Constantine prevailed at the Battle of Ponte Milvio. The new emperor declared Christianity the state religion and in 313 granted the Edict of Milan, which enshrined religious freedom in law. Constantine himself, however, was a devotee of the Sun god Sol Invictus, only converting to Christianity on his deathbed.

Constantine's ambitious building program included churches such as St Peter's Basilica and San Lorenzo Fuori-le-Mura, the Basilica di Costantino in the Roman Forum and his triumphal arch, the Arco di Costantino. However, in 330 he dedicated the new city of Constantinople, which from then on was the principal residence of the Imperial court.

The division of the Roman Empire was formalised after the death of Emperor Theodosius I in 395. One of his sons, Honorius, ruled the crumbling Western Empire from Milan, while his other son, Arcadius, ruled the East.

The sack of Rome by the Goths in 410 marked the beginning of the end for the ancient city. In 440 only the intervention of Pope Leo I persuaded Attila the Hun not to attack Rome, while 15 years later it was thoroughly plundered by the Vandals. The Eastern Empire had its own problems to contend with, while the Western emperors in Milan were too weak and overstretched to defend the Eternal City.

In 476, the year traditionally recognised as the end of the Western Empire, the last emperor, Romulus Augustulus, was deposed. Gothic rule in Italy reached its zenith with the Ostrogothic emperor Theodoric (493–526), who established his court in Ravenna. By 500 the aqueducts feeding into Rome had been deliberately cut by invaders or had been looted for the lead piping; the swamps created by the leaking water were to last until the 20th century.

MEDIEVAL ROME

In 590 Gregory I became pope and set the pattern of Church administration, which was to guide Catholic services and rituals throughout history. Gregory oversaw the Christianisation of Britain, improved conditions for slaves, provided free bread in Rome and repaired Italy's extensive network of aqueducts, as well as leaving an enormous volume of writing on which much Catholic dogma was subsequently based.

After Gregory's death, Rome was threatened first by waves of barbarians and then, from the mid-7th century, by Islamic armies that swept through the Mediterranean world.

Pepin, the Merovingian king, offered to conquer Lombard territory for Pope Stephen II in return for papal recognition of the legitimacy of his dynasty. The relationship between the Church and the Frankish kings was further cemented when Leo III crowned Pepin's son Charlemagne as emperor during Christmas Mass at St Peter's in 800.

In 962 the Saxon Otto I was crowned emperor in Rome and formally founded the Holy Roman Empire, a vast but loose agglomeration of lands that survived, at least in name, until 1806.

The campaign of Hildebrand (later to become Pope Gregory VII) to bring the world under the rule of Christianity was, in reality, a struggle for power between Church and

455	476	754	800
Vandals sack Rome	Romulus Augustulus deposed; end of the Western Roman Empire	Papal States created	Charlemagne crowned Holy Roman Emperor

State. The papacy, based in Rome, and the Holy Roman Empire, with its power base north of the Alps, were compelled to agree in order to reconstruct the political and cultural unity lost with the fall of the Western Roman Empire. The two powers were in perennial conflict and the consequences of this dual leadership dominated Rome throughout the Middle Ages.

The 11th and 12th centuries saw arguments over temporal and spiritual power rage unabated. Rome was the battleground over which popes fought antipopes and supporters of the papacy attacked supporters of the emperor. Norman troops under Robert Guiscard sacked the city in 1084.

Rome's aristocratic families continued to engage in battles for the papacy but a new force of Roman society, composed of artisans, traders and professionals, was developing. Organised into guilds, they demanded the establishment of a Republic and in 1188 Pope Clement III recognised the city as a commune with rights to appoint senators and a prefect. A proportion

The view from the lower floors of the Colosseum (p76)

(p76)

of papal income was set aside for maintenance in the city and in exchange the senators recognised the pope's temporal powers. With stability restored, the popes turned their attention to the city's material improvement, including building a fortified mansion on the site of the present Vatican, the Tor de' Conti (near the Foro di Nerva).

In 1300 Pope Boniface VIII proclaimed the first Holy (Jubilee) Year, with the promise of a full pardon for those who made the pilgrimage to St Peter's and San Giovanni in Laterano. It is said that there were 200,000 pilgrims in Rome at any one time during that year. Boniface also used his power to continue his family feud with the Colonna clan. When he was preparing to excommunicate King Philip of France, the Colonna family helped French forces to break into the papal palace at Anagni and threaten the life of the pope. Boniface died a month later and the next eight popes based themselves in Avignon.

During this period, goats and cows grazed on the Capitoline and in the Roman Forum, and the population fell dramatically. The city became a battleground for the struggles between the powerful Orsini and Colonna families. The ruling families challenged the papacy's ongoing claim to be temporal rulers of Rome and the papal state began to fall apart.

After the failed attempt of Cola di Rienzo, a popular leader, to wrest control of Rome from the nobility in 1347, Cardinal Egidio d'Albornoz managed to restore the Papal State, enabling Pope Gregory XI to return to Rome in 1377. When he found a ruined and almost deserted city, Gregory transferred the papal residence from the Lateran Palace to the Vatican. When Gregory died shortly after, Roman cardinals tried to consolidate their power by electing the controversial Urban VI as pope. Rival cardinals elected a second 'antipope', Clement VII, who set up his claim in Avignon, initiating the Great Schism, which continued until 1417.

1300	1309-77	1471	1500
First Jubilee Year proclaimed	Papacy based in Avignon	Capitoline Museum and Sistine Chapel founded	Pietà sculpted by Michelangelo

RENAISSANCE & COUNTER-REFORMATION

The election of Nicholas V as pope in 1447 marked the beginning of a new era for Rome, at the time when the Renaissance was flowering in Florence. The prestige of the papacy was restored under such popes as Sixtus IV, who built the Sistine Chapel. The artists Donatello, Botticelli and Fra Angelico lived and worked in Rome at this time.

In 1471 Sixtus IV effectively created one of the oldest museums in the world, the Capitoline Museum, when he handed over to the people of Rome a selection of bronzes. At the beginning of the 16th century, Pope Julius II opened Via del Corso and Via Giulia and in 1506 ordered that the old St Peter's Basilica be demolished, commissioning Bramante to build a new church. In 1508 Raphael started painting the rooms in the Vatican known today as the Stanze di Raffaello (Raphael Rooms), and Michelangelo began work on the Sistine Chapel vaults.

Rome had 100,000 inhabitants at the height of the Renaissance and was the major centre for Italian political and cultural life. Pope Julius II was succeeded by the Medici Pope, Leo X, and the Roman Curia (Papal Court) became the meeting place for learned men such as Baldassar Castiglione and Ludovico Ariosto.

But the papacy was also deeply involved in the power struggles that kept Europe in turmoil. In 1527 Pope Clement VII, another Medici, was forced to take refuge in Castel Sant'Angelo when the troops of Charles V of Spain sacked Rome – an event that is said to have deeply influenced Michelangelo's vision of *The Last Judgment*, which he began for Clement VII only two years later.

Rome owes much of its present splendour to 16th-century popes Paul III and Sixtus V, who altered the urban plan, opening up straight avenues, raising obelisks and laying out grand piazzas. In 1538 Paul III asked Michelangelo to lay out the Piazza del Campidoglio, which included the placement of the bronze statue of the Emperor Marcus Aurelius in its centre. Under Sixtus V, the dome of St Peter's was completed.

By the third decade of the 16th century, the broad-minded curiosity of the Renaissance had begun to give way to the intolerance of the Catholic Counter-Reformation.

The transition was epitomised by the reign of Pope Paul III (1534–49), who allowed the establishment of Ignatius Loyola's order of the Jesuits (Society of Jesus) and the organisation in 1542 of the Holy Office. This was the ruthless final court of appeal in the trials that began to gather momentum with the increased activities of the Inquisition (1232–1820), the judicial arm of the Church whose aim was to discover and suppress heresy.

Pope Paul III's opposition to Protestantism and his purging of clerical abuse, as he saw it, resulted in a widespread campaign of torture and fear. In 1559 the Church published the *Index Librorum Prohibitorum*, the Index of Prohibited Books, and the Roman

Statue at the top of the Cordonata di Michelangelo (p80)

1508	1547	1721	1762
Sistine Chapel frescoes begun	Michelangelo appointed architect of St Peter's	Bonnie Prince Charlie born in Rome	Trevi Fountain completed

Church's determination to regain papal supremacy over the Protestant churches set the stage for the persecution of intellectuals and freethinkers.

Galileo Galilei (1564–1642) was forced by the Church to renounce his assertion of the Copernican astronomical system, which held that the earth moved round the sun rather than the reverse. He was summoned by the Inquisition to Rome in 1632 and exiled to Florence for the rest of his life.

This was also a time of architectural splendour. The Chiesa del Gesù was the prototype of Rome's great Counter-Reformation churches, built to attract huge congregations. In the 17th century, under the popes and grand families of Rome, the theatrical exuberance of the Baroque found masterful interpreters in Bernini and Borromini. The designs of Piazzas Navona and San Pietro, and the sculptures in Rome's churches and museums confirm Bernini's genius as both architect and artist.

NAPOLEON TO RISORGIMENTO

The Papal States, covering a swathe of central Italy and ruled by the popes in Rome, constituted a strategic prize that Napoleon set out to win as he made his bid for power in Europe. In 1796 he forced a humiliating armistice on Pope Pius VI and, in 1805, Napoleon crowned himself king of Italy (later naming his infant son king of Rome). Three years later he demanded the abdication of the pope, annexing Rome.

Goethe's 1816 account of his travels in Italy, *Italian Journey*, opened the way for a flow of literary and artistic visitors to Rome, including Byron, Shelley and Keats, and it became the principal destination for cultivated travellers on the Grand Tour.

After Napoleon's defeat, action to unify Italy under a modern Roman Republic took the form of revolt in 1849. Giuseppe Mazzini and Giuseppe Garibaldi led an assault on Rome that failed miserably, but the Risorgimento (Resurgence) movement proved irresistible. At the head of a band of militia, Garibaldi took Sicily and Naples. In 1861 the Kingdom of Italy was declared and Victor Emmanuel II was proclaimed king. However, the French-backed pope remained sovereign of Rome.

In 1870 the French were busy defending themselves from the Prussians, thus enabling Italian troops to breach Rome's city walls at Porta Pia. At last Rome was capital of the newly united Kingdom of Italy. The city was soon transformed by a scandal-ridden building boom, land speculation and an influx of bureaucrats, politicians and labourers.

FASCISM & WWII

In 1922, a year after winning 35 of the 135 seats in parliament, Mussolini's Fascists staged the March on Rome, obliging King Victor Emmanuel III to invite Mussolini to form a government. Following a violent campaign, the Fascists won the subsequent national elections and by the end of 1925 Mussolini had expelled opposition parties from parliament, gained control of the press and trade unions and reduced the voting public by two-thirds.

In 1929 Mussolini and Pope Pius XI signed the Lateran Treaty, whereby Catholicism was declared the sole religion of Italy and the Città del Vaticano was recognised as an independent state.

With the intent of glorifying Rome's imperial past, Mussolini's regime initiated radical, often destructive, public works. Via dei Fori Imperiali and Via della Conciliazione were laid out, parks were opened at the Colle Oppio and Villa Celimontana, the Imperial Fora and the temples at Largo Argentina were excavated, and the monumental Foro Italico sports complex and the Esposizione Universale di Roma (EUR) district were built. Dreams of imperial glory also led Mussolini to invade Abyssinia (present-day Ethiopia) in 1935 and to form the Rome-Berlin Axis with Hitler in 1936. In 1940, from the balcony of Palazzo

1797	1819	1870	1929
Napoleon captures Rome	Shelley writes *Prometheus Unbound* in Rome	Victor Emmanuel II enters Rome; unification of Italy	Mussolini and Pius XI sign Lateran Treaty

Top Five Books

- *The Twelve Caesars*, Suetonius (c 120) – classic and colourful account of the lives of Rome's rulers from Julius Caesar to Domitian, by the 2nd-century historian.
- *The Oxford History of the Roman World*, John Boardman, Jasper Griffin and Oswyn Murray (Eds, 2001) – fascinating collection of essays on various aspects of the ancient Roman world, including literature, arts and politics, by leading Oxford historians.
- *Rome: The Biography of a City*, Christopher Hibbert (1998) – an overview of the city's history from its distant origins to the 20th century.
- *The Later Roman Empire*, Averil Cameron (1993) – a scholarly and highly readable account of this crucial period in Roman history.
- *The Popes: Histories and Secrets*, Claudio Rendina (2002) – an intriguing look at the influence of the papacy both on Roman and world history, through potted biographies of the 264 pontiffs from St Peter to John Paul II.

Venezia, Mussolini announced Italy's entry into WWII to a vast, cheering crowd. These were dark days for Italy, as the totalitarian regime committed atrocities such as the deportation of many members of the city's Jewish community to Nazi death camps. Although there were many acts of individual heroism, the official silence from the Vatican during the Holocaust continues to be controversial.

One of the worst atrocities of WWII in Italy occurred in Rome. In March 1944, partisans killed 32 German military police in Via Rasella. In reprisal, the Germans rounded up 335 people who had no connection with the incident, and shot them at the Fosse Ardeatine, just outside the city. A monument was constructed at the site.

In a 1946 referendum the Italian people voted to abolish the monarchy and adopt a republican form of government. Immediately after the war there was a series of three coalition governments, dominated by the newly formed Democrazia Cristiana Party (Christian Democrats), which remained the most powerful party in subsequent coalition governments until the '80s.

Rome was the scene in 1953 of the signing of the Treaty of Rome, which established the European Economic Community and laid the groundwork for the present European Union.

In the late 1960s university students in Rome rose up in protest, ostensibly against poor conditions in universities, but in reality against what they saw as a moribund political order. The movement threw up many small revolutionary groups.

Terrorism now began to overshadow this turbulent era of protest and change, most notoriously during the so-called Anni di Piombo (Years of the Bullet) from 1973 to 1980. The highest profile victim was former prime minister Aldo Moro, who was kidnapped and murdered in 1978. He had been moving towards a compromise that would have allowed the Communist Party to become part of a coalition government.

1960	1990	2001
Olympic Games; Fellini makes *La Dolce Vita*	World Cup held in Rome	Berlusconi becomes prime minister

1 Caravaggio's *Saint Matthew and the Angel in the Chiesa di San Luigi dei Francesi (p92)* 2 *The Cordonata (designed by Michelangelo) leading to the Piazza del Campidoglio on the Capitoline Hill (p80)* 3 *The home of many of Rome's exquisite art treasures – the Museo e Galleria Borghese (p125)* 4 *The impressive frescoed ceiling of the Galleria delle Carte Geografiche (Map Museum) at the Vatican Museums (p135)*

1 The awe-inspiring Pantheon and portico in Piazza della Rotonda (p88) 2 A pigeon takes a break atop the head of a statue on Fontana del Moro in Piazza Navona (p90) 3 The imposing fortress of Castel Sant'Angelo (p138) 4 Crowds of tourists on a cobbled path behind the Arco di Settimio Severo in the Roman Forum (p73)

1 The unforgettable Trevi Fountain, created by Nicola Salvi (p105) *2* The ruins of imperial residences on the Palatine Hill seen from the Aventine Hill, above Circo Massimo (p78) *3* Looking down on the garden courtyard ruins of Domus Augustana on the Palatine (p78) *4* A bronze statue of St Paul sits atop the intricately decorated Colonna Antonina in Piazza Colonna (p95)

1 A lion fountain in the magnificently restored Piazza del Popolo (p89) 2 A restored fountain in the centre of the lively Piazza Santa Maria in Trastevere (p109) 3 The Barcaccia ('old tub') fountain at the base of the Spanish Steps was the last work of Pietro Bernini (p100) 4 Bernini's figure atop the Fontana dei Quattro Fiumi, supposedly shielding his eyes from the sight of Borromini's church on the other side of Piazza Navona (p90)

1 Café crowds soak up the sun on the Campo de' Fiori (p83) *2* An ornate statue with dragon lantern outside the splendid Palazzo Barberini (p106) *3* Visitors make their approach to St Peter's Basilica across the cobbled Piazza San Pietro at dusk (p128) *4* Pigeons enjoy a cool-down from the Roman heat in a fountain outside Basilica di Santa Maria Maggiore (p98)

1 The massive Basilica di San Giovanni in Laterano, the first Christian basilica built in the city (p116) 2 The impressively detailed apse mosaic in the Basilica di Santa Cecilia in Trastevere (p108) 3 Close-up of the facade of Basilica di Santa Maria Maggiore, one of Rome's four patriarchal basilicas (p98) 4 Locals and tourists congregate on the Spanish Steps, one of Rome's favourite meeting spots (p100)

1 Tourists and locals congregate on the steps of the Basilica di Santa Maria Maggiore (p98)
2 & 3 Floor mosaics in Basilica di San Giovanni in Laterano (p116)

1 *Ancient pottery in the gardens of Terme di Diocleziano (Diocletian's baths) (p102)* 2 *Detail of a statue in the garden behind the Museo e Galleria Borghese (p125)* 3 *Peacocks adorn two statues in the garden of the Vatican Museums (p132)* 4 *A pavilion at Orti Farnesiani in the Palatine, one of Europe's earliest botanic gardens (p80)*

Neighbourhoods

Neighbourhoods

Rome is as densely packed with treasures as it is with visitors. They're overhead, underfoot and around every corner. It would be very un-Italian, however, to get stressed out by the sheer volume of must-sees. Unless you have several years, it's impossible to see everything. The best thing is to treat Rome like a gorgeous smorgasbord, and choose among the delicacies according to time, interest and energy levels. Stop for a *caffè* or *gelato* when map fatigue threatens to cramp your neck in a downward position.

The historic centre of Rome is small, and most of the major attractions are packed within the city walls. However, there are a number of sights further afield that are well worth the extra effort to visit, including the catacombs dotted along the Appia Antica. Most of these locations are easily reached by metro, bus or tram (for information on Rome's public transport system see p260).

Be flexible with your sightseeing, as unpredictability is a fact of life in Rome. It's not unusual to find that churches, museums or

Egyptian obelisk on the Piazza del Popolo (p89)

archaeological sites on your well-planned itinerary are closed when you get there. This could be due to any number of factors, from ongoing excavations to lack of personnel.

Museum admission is generally free for those aged under 18 or over 65 and there are usually discounts for students and those aged under 26. The prices here indicate full admission.

Most churches request you dress appropriately when entering, covering your shoulders and in some cases your knees. A shawl or scarf will do.

After a thorough and costly revamp completed in 2000, the extensive collection of priceless antiquities that make up the Museo Nazionale Romano are now split among Palazzo Massimo alle Terme (diagonally across Piazza dei Cinquecento), Palazzo Altemps (near Piazza Navona), the Museo Palatino (on the Palatine), the Crypta Balbi (near Largo di Torre Argentina) as well as the Terme di Diocleziano. A seven-day ticket (€20) gives admission to all six museums as well as to the Colosseum, Terme di Caracalla, Mausoleo di Cecilia Metella and the Villa dei Quintili. A visit to all the sites gives you an idea of just how vast and rich the Museo Nazionale Romano collection is. If you don't have time to fit all these in, toss a coin into the Trevi Fountain and tradition says you will return to Rome.

ITINERARIES

One Day

Visit the Sistine Chapel, the Vatican Museums and St Peter's Basilica in the morning, and then catch your breath over a leisurely lunch around Piazza Navona. Pass by the Pantheon before exploring the Roman Forum and Colosseum in the afternoon. Make a night of it in lively and atmospheric Trastevere.

Top Five for Kids

- Capuchin Cemetery (p106)
- Dome of St Peter's (p131)
- Bioparco (p124)
- Colosseum (p76)
- Explora – Museo dei Bambini di Roma (p124)

Three Days

Add a morning at the market in Campo de' Fiori and the Capitoline Museums. Let the ancient wonders at Palazzo Massimo alle Terme captivate you, before plumbing Rome's multilayered history at the San Clemente Basilica. Wander through Villa Borghese and visit the magnificent, and hopefully prebooked, Galleria Borghese. Spruce up your wardrobe at the swish designer stores around Via Condotti and spend your evenings on a *passeggiata* (stroll) – with *gelato* – from Piazza di Spagna to the Trevi Fountain. Check out 'Il Campo' for fun after dark, or stay out far later than you should in Testaccio.

One Week

After you've seen the greatest hits, take some wanders outside the walls. Appia Antica and the Catacombs deserve a day – make that a Sunday. Check out the Via Salaria on an architectural tour. Read poetry in the Cimitero Acattolico. Spend an evening tracking the artists and student radicals in San Loreno, and treat yourself to a fabulous meal.

ORGANISED TOURS

BUS TOURS

ATAC operates two special buses for tourists. The air-conditioned 110 leaves from the bus terminus in front of Stazione Termini every half-hour from 9am to 8pm daily. Commentary is provided in English, Italian and several other languages. The tour takes three hours and the bus stops at Piazza del Popolo, Piazza San Pietro, Piazza del Campidoglio, Circo Massimo and the Colosseum. Tickets cost €12.91 if you want to get on and off the bus, and €7.75 for a straight run that takes 2½ hours.

The Archeobus hits the major archaeological sites and leaves from Piazza Venezia from 9am to 5pm. Tickets cost €7.75 and the trip takes three hours.

Buy the special ATAC tickets from the information booth on stand C at the terminus.

Green Line Tours (Map pp314–16; ☎ 06 482 74 80; info@greenlinetours.com; Via Farini 5a), near Piazza Esquilino, operates various tours including classical, Imperial and Christian Rome. The night-time tour of illuminated Rome gives you a different perspective on the city. Each tour costs €18 and up.

WALKING & CYCLING TOURS

Through Eternity (☎ 06 700 93 36; www.througheternity.com) gives highly entertaining tours led by enthusiastic 'storytellers' who are passionate about their subject and make Rome come alive. Twilight tours (€20) of Renaissance and baroque Rome show the city in arguably its best light, and 'Feast of Bacchus' wine-sampling tours combine aesthetic and gastronomic pleasures. They offer a 10% discount for booking online.

Enjoy Rome (Map pp314–16; ☎ 06 493 82 724; www.enjoyrome.com; Via Marghera 8a) organises tours of the major sights for groups of 15 to 25 people most days of the week. Their client base is fairly young and the tours are peppy. The tour lasts three hours and tickets cost €10 to €25. Enjoy Rome also organises bicycle tours, which last 3½ hours and include bike and helmet rental.

> ### Top Five Ancient Rome
> - Capitoline Museums (p81)
> - View from Il Vittoriano (p82)
> - Colosseum (p76)
> - Roman Forum (p72)
> - Michelangelo's Cordonata (p80)

Scala Reale (☎ 06 474 56 73; www.scalareale.org) is a nonprofit cultural organisation run by an American-Italian couple who organise (by prior arrangement – get in touch before you go) sophisticated themed walks in small groups with knowledgeable guides. Bike and scooter tours can also be arranged. At €30 to €50, the tours are a bit pricier than other walks, but well worth it. **ContextRome** (www.contextrome.com) is a new venture affiliated with Scala Reale that offers orientation chats with experts living in Rome, among other specialised services.

ANCIENT ROME

Eating p155; Shopping p204; Sleeping p223

This busy nugget at the geographical centre of the modern city contains the grand, mummified heart of Rome's past. From the oxbow curve of the Tiber River that cradled Romulus and Remus to the heights of the Capitoline and Palatine, landscape and history are visibly bound together here – in particular, the history of Roman governance. In the remains of the Forum, ghosts of the Senators wander the ruins, looking for the lost riches of the Republic. To the east, the great Colosseum, leviathan emblem of the Empire's domestic policy of bread and circuses for the masses, is as eternal as Rome itself. Moving through the ages but hardly moving at all, the monarchist spirit of Italian unification is seared into the landscape in the form of the shining white Vittoriano monument. At its feet is Palazzo Venezia, where, mere decades later, Mussolini plotted Fascist domination; at its back, Piazza del Campidoglio, where history circles around to grab the tail of the present, for the Capitoline, true heart of the Republic, is the current seat of Rome's municipal government. Flowing through and around and over these treasures is the ubiquitous Roman traffic: compact minis honking at sexy girls and boys perched on *motorino*, helmets askew, miraculously missing the nuns in the crosswalks; and the big dodgy touts dressed up as gladiators, soliciting the myriad tourists from every continent, whose faces are glued to maps and guidebooks just like this one. With everyone going somewhere, this is hardly a restful section of Rome. It's a neighbourhood to tackle when your energy levels and tolerance for chaos are high, or to take bit by bit, since your travels through the city will inevitably bring you through this, its centre, more than once.

Transport

Bus 64 or 40 from Termini or the Vatican; 63 or 95 from Piazza Barberini

THE FORUMS & AROUND

In ancient Rome, a forum was a shopping mall, city hall and civic centre all rolled into one. The original Roman Forum got too small around 46 BC, and many emperors built new ones in the centuries that followed, naming them, of course, after themselves. These were grand public spaces, richly decorated and grandly scaled. As much as they were for the use of the people, they were testaments to the power of their leaders.

It's hard to overstate the impact of the forums on western architecture. As the Roman Republic was a template for governance, the forums were prototypes for the buildings and public spaces that followed. When Christianity came along, the great churches were simply adaptations of the design of Roman basilicas. Even today, architecture borrows from or reacts to the forums.

The originals, however, haven't survived intact. Keep in mind that much of the enjoyment to be had from visiting these ruins will depend on the limits of your own imagination. Without any context or history, the forums are just big piles of rocks. Fans of ruins know they give up their secrets to those who come prepared (or those who tag along with a tour guide).

IMPERIAL FORUMS Map pp314–16

☎ 06 679 00 48, 06 678 94 87; www.capitolium.org; Via dei Fori Imperiali; admission €7 (includes admission to Foro di Traiano); ☾ 9am-7pm Tue-Sun; bus to Via dei Fori Imperiali

The **Imperial Forums** (Fori Imperiali) of Trajan, Caesar, Nerva and Augustus were built between 42 BC and AD 112, as the demands of the Empire exceeded the limits of the existing forums. In 1933 Mussolini's thoroughfare from Piazza Venezia to the Colosseum was built over the Imperial Forums, and their excavation is recent and ongoing. A new visitor centre provides historical info on the area and organises tours of the individual forums (with chaperone and audio guide).

The most extensively excavated was the last forum to be built: **Foro di Traiano** (Trajan's Forum). It dates from the beginning of the 2nd century AD and was a vast complex even by modern standards, measuring 300m by 185m. It was comprised of Basilica Ulpia (in ancient Rome, 'basilica' was the general term for a hall used for the court of justice and public assembly), not one but *two* libraries for the bookish citizenry (one Greek, one Latin), a temple, a triumphal arch, and the **Colonna di Traiano** (Trajan's Column), erected to mark the victories of Trajan over the Dacians. Trajan's ashes were placed in a golden urn at the base of the column, but the urn (and all traces of Trajan himself) disappeared during one of the barbarian sacks of Rome. The column was restored in 1980. It's decorated with a spiral of reliefs depicting the battles against Dacian armies, who lived in modern-day Romania. It's considered among the finest existing examples of ancient sculpture. A golden statue of Trajan used to top the column, but it was lost during the Middle Ages and replaced with a statue of St Peter.

Tempio di Venere e Roma and Chiesa di Santa Francesca Romana in the Roman Forum (p75)

Other than the column, obvious traces of the forum are as scarce as Trajan's ashes. The only clearly visible artefacts are some pillars from the basilica, which was the largest in Rome.

Mercati di Traiano (Trajan's Markets) are much better preserved. They are the ancient equivalent of today's ubiquitous shopping malls, only much grander. Built in semicircles three levels high, they sold everything from oil, spices and vegetables to flowers and silks. If you pay the admission fee, you can see how grand the high

vaulted roofs are, and you get a spectacular view across to the Roman Forum to boot.

Roma Gratis

The following sights won't burn a hole in your pocket – they're free!
- Pantheon (p88)
- St Peter's Basilica (p128)
- Roman Forum (p72)
- Vatican Museums (last Sunday of the month; p132)
- Rome's Parks

The red-brick tower above the market building, the Torre delle Milizie (Militia Tower), was built in the 13th century for defence purposes.

There is a delightful walkway beneath the loggia of the 12th-century **Casa dei Cavalieri di Rodi** (Ancient Seat of the Knights of St John of Jerusalem), which is between the Foro di Traiano and the Foro di Augusto, and accessible from either Via dei Fori Imperiali or Piazza del Grillo. The building itself, which contains a beautiful chapel, is open only by appointment.

Augustus ordered the **Foro di Augusto** (Forum of Augustus) to be built in 42 BC but it was not completed and dedicated until 40 years later. Three columns of a temple dedicated to Mars the Avenger are still standing and others have been reconstructed from fragments, but over half the original area is now covered by Via dei Fori Imperiali. The 30m-high wall behind the Foro di Augusto was built to protect the area from the fires that frequently swept through the area known as the Suburra.

Next to the Foro di Augusto is the **Foro di Nerva**, much of which is also covered by Via dei Fori Imperiali. Part of a temple dedicated to Minerva still remains on the site. The temple was still standing in the 17th century when Pope Paul V had it pulled down to provide marble for the Fontana dell'Acqua Paola on the Gianicolo. The Foro di Nerva connected the Foro di Augusto to the **Foro di Vespasiano**, also known as the Forum of Peace, which was built in AD 70 by Vespasian. A large hall was converted in the 6th century into a church, the Basilica di SS Cosma e Damiano (see p75).

Across the Via dei Fori Imperiali is the **Foro di Cesare** (Caesar's Forum), built by Julius Caesar at the foot of the Capitoline. It is not open to the public but can be viewed from Via dei Fori Imperiali. Caesar claimed the goddess Venus in his family tree and his forum included a temple to her as Venus Genetrix – Venus the Ancestor. All that remains today are three columns on a platform. Trajan made various additions to the forum, including the Basilica Argentaria, a financial exchange, some shops and a heated public lavatory.

Open Only on Request

Several archaeological sites in Rome are open to the public only on request. To gain entry to a closed site, you should send a fax or letter well in advance of your trip to the Ufficio Monumenti Antichi e Scavi del Comune di Roma (fax 06 689 21 15; Via del Portico d'Ottavia 29, 00186 Rome).

You should state the dates of your stay in Rome, the monuments you want to see and how many people are in the party. Letters and faxes can be written in any major western language. The office will then write back to you (probably in Italian) with possible dates and times, and the cost of the visit. A further confirmation from you might also be required. If you do not get a response, try harassing the folks at ☎ 06 671 03 819 during office hours. If you don't manage to organise a special visit in advance of your trip, all is not lost. Archaeological sights are opened periodically by the authorities, so you might strike it lucky. Tourist information booths can provide details.

Following Via di San Pietro in Carcere you come to the ancient **Carcere Mamertino** (Mamertine Prison; Map pp314–6), where condemned prisoners were garrotted. It is believed St Peter was held here prior to his trial and that he created a miraculous stream of water to baptise his jailers and his fellow prisoners. The site was later consecrated and is now the church of San Pietro in Carcere.

ROMAN FORUM Map pp314–16
☎ 06 399 67 700; entrances at Largo Romolo e Remo 5-6, Piazza di Santa Maria Nova 53 & Via di Monte Tarpeo; admission free; ☼ 9am-1 hr before dusk; metro Colosseo

Before you go poking around the ruins of the Roman Forum, perch yourself on the ledge behind the Capitoline, and look over the whole site. This was the stage across which all the key figures of the Republic wandered. It is the oldest of the ancient forums, growing over the course of 900 years, as the Republic itself grew. In the beginning, it was a swamp and burial ground, drained by the Etruscans in the 7th century BC for use as a public space – first shops and temples, later gleaming white-marble law courts, offices, temples and

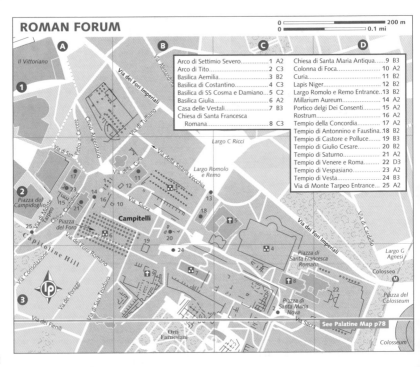

ROMAN FORUM

Arco di Settimio Severo............1 A2	Chiesa di Santa Maria Antiqua......9 B3
Arco di Tito................................2 C3	Colonna di Foca.........................10 A2
Basilica Aemilia.........................3 B2	Curia..11 B2
Basilica di Costantino...............4 C3	Lapis Niger................................12 B2
Basilica di SS Cosma e Damiano...5 C2	Largo Romolo e Remo Entrance..13 B2
Basilica Giulia...........................6 A2	Millarium Aureum......................14 A2
Casa delle Vestali.....................7 B3	Portico delgi Dei Consenti.........15 A2
Chiesa di Santa Francesca	Rostrum.....................................16 A2
Romana.............................8 C3	Tempio della Concordia.............17 A2
	Tempio di Antonnino e Faustina..18 B2
	Tempio di Castore e Polluce.......19 B3
	Tempio di Giulio Cesare.............20 B2
	Tempio di Saturno......................21 A2
	Tempio di Venere e Roma...........22 D3
	Tempio di Vespasiano................23 A2
	Tempio di Vesta.........................24 B3
	Via di Monte Tarpeo Entrance....25 A2

See Palatine Map p78

the other trappings of ancient prosperity. Its importance declined along with the Roman Empire after the 4th century AD, and the temples, monuments and buildings constructed by successive emperors and senators fell into ruin, eventually leading to the spaces being used as pasture land.

In the Middle Ages the area was used as a pasture, the Campo Vaccino (literally 'cow field'), and the ruins were extensively plundered for building materials. Note that it was the Romans, not invading barbarians, who dismantled the ancient city brick by brick in order to build their own palaces, churches and monuments.

With renewed appreciation of all things classical during the Renaissance, the Forum provided inspiration for artists and architects. The area was systematically excavated in the 18th and 19th centuries and excavations are still continuing today. You can watch archaeological teams at work in several locations.

From your vantage point, you can get an overview to guide you through the confusing tangle below. The cobbled and ceremonial Via Sacra (Sacred Way) runs to the **Arco di Settimio Severo** (Arch of Septimius Severus) to your left, built in 203 in honour of the eponymous emperor and his two sons, Caracalla and Geta, to celebrate the Roman victory over the Parthians (modern-day Iran). The centre panel depicts defeated Parthians led away in chains. The dedication on it is the largest to survive from antiquity. After Caracalla murdered his brother, he had the inscription altered so that the bragging words *optimis fortissimisque principibus* (which translate roughly as 'Caracalla Rulz!') covered Geta's name. If you look closely at the fourth line of the inscription, you can see the original lettering. Near here, the **Millarium Aureum** (Golden Milestone) marked Rome's geographical heart, from which the distance of the road to Rome was measured.

To your right are the remains of the **Rostrum**, or public oratory, where Shakespeare's Mark Antony asked friends, Romans and countrymen to lend him their ears after Caesar's assassination. At that time, it was decorated with the bows of defeated ships.

Next to it are the foundations of the **Basilica Giulia**, the law court built by Julius Caesar in 55 BC.

Behind it was the **Casa delle Vestali**, home of the Vestal virgins, whose job it was to keep the sacred flame kindled (see the boxed text, p75).

The arches of Basilica di San Clemente (p97)

At the far end of the Forum, leading to the Colosseum, is the **Arco di Tito** (Arch of Titus), built in AD 81 in honour of the victories of Titus against the Jews.

Now that you have the big picture, take a wander down to the ruins themselves for a closer look.

If you enter from Via dei Fori Imperiali at the Largo Romolo e Remo Entrance heading southwest, to your left is the **Tempio di Antonino e Faustina**, erected in AD 141 by Antonius Pius as a memorial to his wife, Empress Faustina. The temple was transformed into a church in the 8th century, so the soaring Corinthian columns now frame **Chiesa di San Lorenzo in Miranda**, a perfect example of Roman religious recycling.

To your right are the remains of the **Basilica Aemilia**, built in 179 BC. The basilica was to Rome's lawyers what the Colosseum was to its gladiators – their own special battleground. For evidence the Romans were a litigious bunch, note the basilica's dimensions: the building was 100m long, its facade an imposing two-storey portico lined with shops. Destroyed and rebuilt several times, the basilica was completely ravaged for its precious marble during the Renaissance.

The **Via Sacra**, which you saw from the Capitoline Hill, traverses the Forum from northwest to southeast, and runs in front of the basilica. Continuing along Via Sacra in the direction of the Capitoline, you will reach the **Curia**. It was the meeting place of the Roman Senate, rebuilt successively by Julius Caesar, Augustus, Domitian and Diocletian. It too was converted into a church in the Middle Ages, but the church was dismantled and the Curia restored in the 1930s to the form it had under Diocletian in the 3rd century AD. The bronze doors are copies – the Roman originals were borrowed by Borromini to hang on San Giovanni in Laterano (p96).

In front of the Curia is the **Lapis Niger**, a piece of black marble, which covered a sacred area. According to legend, the tomb of Romulus was beneath it. Down a flight of stairs (rarely open to the public), under the Lapis Niger, is the oldest-known Latin inscription, dating from the 6th century BC.

Southwest across the Via Sacra lies the **Tempio di Saturno** (Temple of Saturn), inaugurated in 497 BC and one of the most important temples in ancient Rome. It was used as the city's treasury and during Caesar's rule contained 13 tonnes of gold, 114 tonnes of silver and 30 million *sestertii* (Roman silver coins). Eight granite columns are all that remain. Behind the temple and backing onto the Capitoline are (roughly from north to south) the ruins of the **Tempio della Concordia** (Temple of Concord), the three remaining columns of the **Tempio di Vespasiano** (Temple of Vespasian) and the **Portico degli Dei Consenti**, of which 12 columns remain (five are restorations). The remains of the **Basilica Giulia**, which you spotted from above, are just across from Basilica Aemilia, at what is known as Piazza del Foro. The square was the site of the original forum, which served as the main meeting place during the Republican era.

The **Colonna di Foca** (Column of Phocus), which stands in the square and dates from AD 608, was the last monument erected in the Forum. It honoured the Byzantine emperor Phocus who donated the Pantheon to the Church. At the southeastern end of the square is the **Tempio di Giulio Cesare** (Temple of Julius Caesar), which was erected by Augustus in 29 BC on the site where Caesar's body was cremated after Brutus betrayed him.

Back towards the Palatine is the **Tempio di Castore e Polluce** (Temple of Castor and Pollux; also known as the Tempio dei Dioscuri), built in 489 BC to mark the defeat of the Etruscan Tarquins and in honour of the Heavenly Twins, or Dioscuri, who miraculously appeared to deliver tidings of a victory. Three elegant Corinthian columns from the temple, which served at times as a banking hall and also housed the city's weights and measures office,

survive today. The temple was restored during the 1980s.

In the area south of the temple is the **Chiesa di Santa Maria Antiqua**, the oldest Christian church in the Forum. Inside the church are some early Christian frescoes. This area, including the church, has been closed to the public since 1992.

Just off the Via Sacra is the **Casa delle Vestali** (House of the Vestal Virgins), home of the virgins who tended the sacred flame in the adjoining **Tempio di Vesta**.

The next major monument is the vast **Basilica di Costantino**, also known as the Basilica di Massenzio. Maxentius initiated work on the basilica and it was finished in AD 315 by Constantine. Its impressive design provided inspiration for Renaissance architects,

Decorated walls in the Basilica di San Giovanni in Laterano (p116)

possibly including Michelangelo, who is said to have studied its construction when he was designing the dome for St Peter's. The basilica was the largest building in the Forum, covering an area of approximately 100m by 65m, and was used for business and the administration of justice. The three massive barrel-vaulted aisles that remain today were used as law courts. One of the basilica's original columns now stands in Piazza Santa Maria Maggiore. A colossal statue of Constantine was unearthed at the site in 1487. Pieces of this statue are on display in the courtyard of the Palazzo dei Conservatori in the Capitoline Museums (see p121).

The **Arco di Tito** (Arch of Titus), at the Colosseum-end of the Forum, was built in AD 81 in honour of the victories of the future emperor Titus against the Jewish rebels in Jerusalem. Titus is represented with Victory personified on one of the reliefs on the inside of the arch; the spoils of Jerusalem are paraded in a triumphal procession on the other. Along with the Arco di Costantino (see p76), this arch was incorporated into a fortress by the Frangipani family in the Middle Ages.

BASILICA DI SS COSMA E DAMIANO

Map pp314–16
Via dei Fori Imperiali; ☺ 9am-1pm & 3-7pm; metro Colosseo

Just southeast of the Largo Romolo e Remo entrance to the Roman Forum, this small 6th-century basilica is dedicated to the twin doctors St Cosmas and St Damian, who healed both the rich and the poor without accepting money for it. They were martyred (on the third try – the docs would neither drown nor burn) in 287.

The church once incorporated a large hall, which formed part of the Foro di Vespasiano. The delightful 6th-century mosaics, located in the apse, were restored in 1989 and are among the most beautiful in Rome. The central figure of Christ against a deep-blue background is flanked by St Peter and St Paul (in white robes), who are presenting St Cosmas and St Damian to him. On the far left is St Felix, holding up a model of the church, and on the right is St Theodore. Below this scene is a frieze of the Lamb of God (representing Christ) and his flock of 12 lambs (representing the 12 Apostles). These mosaics were copied in several Roman churches, especially during the 9th century. Make sure you have plenty of spare change on you as this is possibly the stingiest mosaic lighting system in Rome: your clanking coin buys only the briefest of glimpses of these stunning mosaics.

Children in particular will love the Neapolitan *presepio* (nativity scene) in a room off the cloisters, which places the birth of Jesus among Neapolitan folk going about their daily business. Dotted around the finely crafted wooden and terracotta figures are animals, a chestnut vendor, fruit seller, grape harvester, soldier and an innkeeper. It can be viewed from 9.30am to 12.30pm and 3pm to 6.30pm (a donation of €1 is requested).

Like a Vestal Virgin

They came from patrician families, six physically perfect girls between the ages of six and 10 chosen by lottery to serve Vesta, daughter of Saturn, goddess of hearth and household. There were 10 years of training, wherein they'd learn their duties, which included tending the sacred fire of Vesta that burned in the inner chamber of the goddess's temple and was regarded as the hearth fire of Rome itself. Then, there were 10 years of service, during which they were treated as deified beauty queens, appearing at public ceremonies, participating in harvest festivals and taking the seats of honour at dinner parties and spectacles at the Colosseum. After their term of active service, there would be a final decade as teachers, passing the knowledge on to the next generation of vestals-in-training. At the end of these 30 years, vestals were free to marry. There would have been plenty of hopeful suitors, even at the elderly age of 40, because it was considered a great honour to marry a former vestal virgin. Still, most retired virgins chose to stay on in the House of the Virgins.

The wellbeing of the state was thought to depend on the cult of Vesta, and in particular on the vestals' virginity. While they were held in the highest esteem and received all privileges, punishment for dereliction of their duties was severe. Virgins who let the flame go out were severely beaten. A vestal accused of breaking her vow of chastity was buried alive on the reasoning that if she were innocent, Vesta herself would rescue her. The man involved was taken outside the city walls and clubbed to death. The vestals left the Atrium Vestai when non-Christian cults were outlawed, in the late 4th century, and their home was converted to government office space.

CHIESA DI SANTA FRANCESCA ROMANA Map pp314–16

Piazza di Santa Francesca Romana; ☺ 9.30am-noon & 3-5pm; metro Colosseo

Past the Basilica di Costantino there is a small stairway leading to the Chiesa di Santa Francesca Romana. Built in the 9th century over an earlier oratory, the church (also known as Santa Maria Nova) incorporates part of the **Tempio di Venere e Roma** (Temple of Venus and Rome). It has a lovely Romanesque bell tower.

There is a 12th-century mosaic of the Madonna and child and saints in the apse, as well as a 7th-century painting of the Madonna and child above the high altar. During restoration works in 1949, another painting of the Madonna and child was discovered beneath the 7th-century work. Dating from the early 5th century and probably taken from the Chiesa di

Santa Maria Antiqua in the Roman Forum, this precious painting is now in the sacristy which you can enter if the sacristan is around.

Francesca Romana is the patron saint of motorists. On 9 March (her feast day) taxi drivers park their vehicles close to the church to be blessed. Her mummified body, wrapped in a white diaphanous cloth, holding a book and wearing rather modern-looking, black-leather slippers, is in a chapel under the altar (steps lead down from both sides).

Two flagstones in the south wall of the church are said to hold the knee prints of St Peter. Their story is particularly colourful. In St Peter's day, a wizard named Simon Magus was showing off his powers by flying above the Forum. Peter knelt to pray that God would humble Simon Magus, thereby creating the imprints in the stone. His prayer was answered, and how: the wizard dropped from the sky to his death.

PALATINE TO THE COLOSSEUM

ARCO DI COSTANTINO Map pp320–1
Via di San Gregorio VII; metro Colosseo
This arch was built in AD 312 to commemorate Constantine's victory over his rival Maxentius at the Battle of the Milvian Bridge (near the present-day Zona Olimpica, northwest of the Villa Borghese). Although an impressive Roman memorial, the arch is evidence of how Rome had by then fallen on hard times; the great sculptors' studios had closed and the arch was largely cobbled together with fragments pinched from other sculptures. The lower stonework dates from Domitian's reign (AD 81–96); the eight large medallions depicting hunting scenes are Hadrianic (AD 117–138). Four enormous reliefs on the inside of the central archway and the sides of the arch depict Trajan's battle against the Dacians. Removed from the Foro di Traiano, these reliefs are believed to be by the same sculptor who carved the Colonna di Traiano. Incorporated into the Frangipani family's fortress in the Middle Ages, the arch was 'liberated' in 1804. Major restoration work was completed in 1987.

CIRCO MASSIMO Map pp320–1
Via del Circo Massimo; metro Circo Massimo
In its heyday, it was Rome's largest stadium, where some 200,000 spectators would gather in wooden stands to watch chariots race around a 600m track decorated with statues and columns. Races were run anticlockwise around the track, the greatest excitement coming when the chariots had to negotiate the tight turns at each end. In 46 BC, Julius Caesar recreated battles for his amusement, using prisoners of war as his expendable actors. Augustus erected the obelisk of Ramses II in 10 BC; the obelisk now stands in Piazza del Popolo. The fire of AD 64 that destroyed much of Rome is thought to have started in the stadium's wooden stands. It was rebuilt by Trajan in about 100 to hold 250,000 spectators. It was then expanded by Caracalla and restored by Constantine, who gave it a second obelisk, that of Tutmosis III, which was later moved to Piazza San Giovanni in Laterano. The Circo remained in use until 549. Unfortunately, it is Rome's most sadly neglected ancient site, without much to see: a trace of ruins and a litter-strewn dog park.

COLOSSEUM Map pp320–1
☎ 06 399 67 700; Piazza del Colosseo; admission €8, includes Palatine; ☼ 9am-1 hr before dusk; metro Colosseo
Catching sight of the Colosseum for the first time is like seeing a celebrity in the flesh. It is *the* symbol of the Eternal City, where the blood-thirsty Roman populace was kept entertained and war-ready with gory battles pitting gladiators against wild animals, slaves and anybody else deemed expendable.

The amphitheatre, inaugurated in AD 80, was built on the grounds of Nero's private ode to conspicuous consumption, the Domus Aurea. The ruling class's idea of governance was to keep the populous fat with bread and happy with the state-sponsored spectacle happening here. The Colosseum could hold more than 50,000 spectators seated on one of three levels depending on their status and gender. Knights sat in the lowest tier, wealthy citizens in the middle and the populace in the highest. Women (except for vestal virgins) were relegated to the nosebleed sections. The podium, a broad terrace in front of the tiers, was reserved for emperors, senators and other VIPs. To celebrate victory over the Dacians, Trajan held games here that lasted 117 days, during which 9000 gladiators and 10,000 beasts fought to the death. Gladiators were professional and sometimes spared for putting up a good fight, but no such luck for slaves, prisoners or animals.

The outer walls of the Colosseum have three levels of arches, articulated by columns topped by capitals of the Ionic (at the bottom), Doric and Corinthian (at the top) orders. The external walls were covered in travertine, and marble statues once filled the niches on the second and third storeys. The upper level, punctuated by windows and slender Corinthian pilasters, had supports for 240 masts, which held up a canvas awning over the arena to shield spectators from sun and rain. The 80 entrance arches allowed spectators to enter and be seated in a matter of minutes.

The interior of the Colosseum was divided into three parts: the arena, the cavea and the podium. The arena originally had a wooden floor covered in sand to prevent the combatants from slipping and to soak up the blood spilt there. It could also be flooded for mock sea battles. Trapdoors led down to the underground chambers and passageways beneath the arena floor, which can be clearly seen today. Animals in cages and sets for the various battles were hoisted onto the arena by a complicated system of pulleys.

With the fall of the Empire, the Colosseum was abandoned and gradually became overgrown. Exotic plants grew there for centuries: seeds had inadvertently been transported from Africa and Asia with the wild beasts that appeared in the arena (including crocodiles, bears, lions, tigers, elephants, rhinos, hippos, camels and giraffes). In the Middle Ages the Colosseum became a fortress, occupied by two of the city's warrior families: the Frangipani and the Annibaldi. Its reputation as a symbol of Rome, the Eternal City, also dates to the Middle Ages, with Bede writing that: 'While the Colosseum stands, Rome shall stand, but when the Colosseum falls, Rome shall fall – and when Rome falls, the world will end'.

Damaged several times by earthquakes, it was later used as a quarry for travertine and marble for the Palazzo Venezia, Palazzo Barberini and Palazzo Cancelleria among other buildings. Pollution and the vibrations caused by traffic and the metro have also taken their toll. Restoration works have periodically been carried out, the latest starting in 1992 but suspended in 2000. Despite this it remains an evocative spot to explore while imagining yourself in the latest Hollywood sword-and-sandals epic, giving Russell Crowe a run for his money.

DOMUS AUREA Map pp314–16

☎ 06 399 67 700; Viale della Domus Aurea; admission €5, audioguide €2; ☺ 9am-8pm Wed-Mon (to 5pm Oct-Mar), visits only in accompanied groups, reservations recommended; metro Colosseo

The megalomaniac emperor Nero didn't do things by halves. His massive Domus Aurea

(Golden House), built after the fire of AD 64, extended over the Palatine, Oppian and Caelian Hills. The gold leaf that covered the facade gave the palace its name and the banqueting halls, nymphaeums, baths and terraces were decorated with frescoes and mosaics, a few of which remain. The extensive grounds had vineyards, game and an artificial lake.

Nero didn't have long to enjoy his palace. After his death in 68, his successors were quick to remove all trace of his excesses, razing much of the Domus Aurea to the ground. Vespasian drained the lake and built the Colosseum in its place, Domitian built his palace on the Palatine, and Trajan constructed a baths complex on top of the Oppian ruins using the Domus Aurea as a foundation. Archaeologists have spent 25 years excavating this area.

Many of the original loggias and halls were walled in when Trajan's baths were built and the light that filtered through the Domus Aurea was completely lost. It's quite confusing trying to identify parts of the original complex and the later baths. Among the scant fresco remnants are mythical creatures, flowers, fruit, vines and human figures staring out of illusionary windows. The best preserved of them illustrate scenes from Homer's *Iliad* where Achilles is disguised as a woman on the island of Skyros. The octagonal room at the end of the tour has been identified as the circular dining room described by the ancient writer Suetonius, where Nero sang and played the lyre on a revolving stage.

Nero was a great pillager and had hundreds of Greek bronzes and marble copies of Greek statues placed in his palace. Among them were the *Galata Morente* and *Galata Suicida* (now in the Capitoline Museums, see p81, and Palazzo Altemps, see p90, respectively), which were displayed in the octagonal room of the Domus Aurea. The *Laocoön* (a statue of the Trojan priest and his two sons), now in the Vatican Museums, is also thought to have once been in the Domus Aurea.

The baths and underlying ruins were abandoned by the 6th century. During the Renaissance, artists (including Ghirlandaio, Perugino and Raphael) lowered themselves into the ruins in order to study the frescoed grottos (which gave us the word 'grotesque'). Some left their own graffiti – not quite 'Pinturicchio woz 'ere', but not far off – and all copied motifs from the Domus Aurea frescoes in their work in the Vatican and other parts of Rome.

Excavations of the Domus Aurea and the Colle Oppio are well under way, and archaeologists expect major discoveries in the area.

PALATINE Map pp320–1

☎ 06 399 67 700; entrances at Via di San Gregorio 30 & Piazza di Santa Maria Nova 53; admission €8, includes Museo Palatino & Colosseum; ☾ 9am-1 hr before dusk (museum closes 1 hr earlier); metro Colosseo

Palatine Hill (Palatino) is the founding place of Rome, where the mythical she-wolf nursed Remus and Romulus and where the first actual evidence of human habitation was discovered in the form of 9th-century-BC Iron Age huts. It offers some of the most spectacular views of ancient Rome. As the most central of Rome's seven hills – and because it was close to, but above, the riffraff of the Roman Forum – this hill was the most desirable place to live during the Republican and Imperial eras. Augustus was born on the Palatine and lived there throughout his life, although his residences were modest compared to the more extravagant rulers who came after him: Tiberius, Nero, the Flavians and Septimius Severus. Their dwellings were the source of the English word 'palace' and eventually merged into one monolithic complex.

Like most of the Forum, the temples and palaces of the Palatine fell into ruin in the Middle Ages and a few churches, monasteries and castles were built over the remains. During the Renaissance, wealthy families established their gardens on the hill, notably Cardinal Alessandro Farnese.

The largest part of the Palatine as it appears today is covered by ruins of a vast complex built for Emperor Domitian, which served as the main imperial palace for 300 years. This was an ambitious project to create an official imperial palace, the Domus Flavia (the emperor's private residence), the Domus Augustana and a stadium. The complex was designed by the architect Rabirius, who levelled a crest of land, the Palatium, on the steep eastern side of the Palatine, and filled in the depression between it and the next crest, the Germalus, demolishing or burying many Republican-era houses in the process. Some of these buried buildings have since been unearthed, and excavations are continuing.

On entering from the Roman Forum, take the path straight ahead past a grassy area on the right, to the ruins of the **Domus Augustana**. The path from the entrance at Via di San Gregorio leads to the same place. The Domus Augustana was built on two levels, with rooms leading off a *peristilio* (peristyle or garden courtyard) on each floor. You can't get down to the lower level, but from above you can see

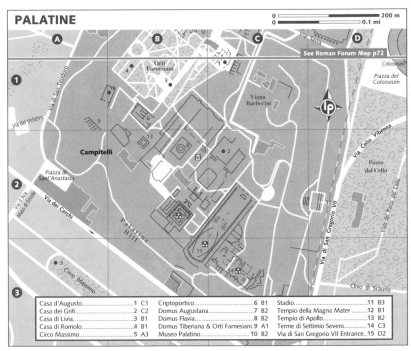

Casa d'Augusto.............................1 C1	Criptoportico.................................6 B1	Stadio..11 B3
Casa dei Grifi...............................2 C2	Domus Augustana........................7 B2	Tempio della Magna Mater.........12 B1
Casa di Livia................................3 B1	Domus Flavia................................8 B2	Tempio di Apollo........................13 B2
Casa di Romolo............................4 B1	Domus Tiberiana & Orti Farnesiani..9 A1	Terme di Settimio Severo............14 C3
Circo Massimo..............................5 A3	Museo Palatino...........................10 B2	Via di San Gregorio VII Entrance..15 D2

the basin of a fountain and beyond it rooms which were paved with coloured marble. The palace had an elaborate two-storey colonnaded facade to the south overlooking Circo Massimo (from where you get the clearest indication of the grand scale of the complex).

Southeast of the Domus Augustana is the **Stadio** (stadium) probably used by the emperors for private games and events. An oval recess in the eastern wall is thought to have served as the emperor's private viewing area. Next to the *stadio* are the scant remains of baths built by Septimius Severus, the **Terme di Settimio Severo**. Considerable engineering skill was required to build this complex on an extension of the southernmost point of the Palatine. It was supported by enormous arched substructures, best seen from Circo Massimo.

The **Museo Palatino** is the big white building (a former convent) located between the Domus Augustana and the Domus Flavia. It was established in the 1860s and houses artworks and artefacts found on the Palatine. For the past century, the most important of the excavated pieces from the Palatine were kept in the Museo Nazionale Romano. Some objects remain in the Museo Nazionale Romano collection (including stuccoes from the Palatine criptoportico or underground tunnel) but many were transferred to the restored Museo Palatino in 1998. Admission is included in your ticket for entry to the Palatine. Note that the museum closes one hour earlier than the Palatine itself.

The ground floor illustrates the history of the hill from its origins to the Republican age. In Sale (Halls) I, II and III there are pots, eating and cooking utensils from the Palaeolithic Age to the Bronze Age as well as models of how the Iron Age huts and tombs might have appeared. Sala IV contains artefacts from the Archaic and Republican Ages (6th to the 1st century BC) including an altar to a pagan god and ceramic masks.

On the 1st floor, the entrance hall contains statuary that decorated the various imperial palaces on the Palatine. On display in Sala V are artefacts from the Augustan period (27 BC–AD 14) including reliefs and black marble statues from the **Tempio di Apollo**, which was located next to the Casa d'Augusto. Sala VI contains objects pertaining to Nero's reign (AD 54–68), including remnants of decorative frescoes. Sculpted heads and busts dating from the 1st to the 4th century AD can be seen in Sale VII and VIII.

Northwest of the Museo Palatino is the **Domus Flavia**, which was connected to the Domus Augustana. The palace comprised three large halls to the north, the central one of which was the emperor's throne room, and a large banqueting hall or triclinium *(triclinio imperiale)* to the south, which was paved in coloured marble that can still be seen. The triclinium looked out onto an oval fountain, the remains of which are still clearly visible. Domitian was terrified of being assassinated and had the peristyle of the Domus Flavia lined with shiny marble slabs so that, from whichever room he was in, he could see who was approaching. Nonetheless he ended up being murdered in his bedroom, possibly with the connivance of his wife. The Domus Flavia was constructed over earlier edifices. One of these, which can sometimes be visited (ask at the Palatine entrance), is the **Casa dei Grifi** (House of the Griffins), so called because of a stucco relief of two griffins in one of the rooms. It is the oldest building on the Palatine and dates from the late 2nd or 1st century BC. It was excavated in the 18th century.

Tourists cycling through the Domus Augustana (p78)

Among the best-preserved buildings on the Palatine is the **Casa di Livia**, north of the Domus Flavia. It is well below current ground level and is reached by steps down to a mosaic-covered courtyard. Livia, the wife of Augustus, owned this house and a larger villa at Prima Porta to the north of Rome (see p101). The Casa di Livia contains a forecourt or atrium leading onto what were once reception rooms. The walls of the house were decorated with frescoes – of mythological scenes, landscapes, fruits and flowers – some of which can still be seen, although they have been detached from the walls for preservation purposes. In front of the Casa di Livia is the **Casa d'Augusto**, Augustus' own residence – the two constructions were most likely part of the same complex. Both are being restored and have been closed to the public for several years, though they can sometimes be visited by appointment; ask at the entrance to the Palatine.

Next to the Casa d'Augusto is the **Casa di Romolo** (House of Romulus) where, it is thought, the twin brothers Romulus and Remus were brought up after their discovery by the shepherd Faustulus. Excavations in the 1940s revealed evidence of supports for wattle and daub huts dating from the 9th century BC. The **Tempio della Magna Mater** is just south of the huts. Also known as the Tempio di Cibele, it was built in 204 BC to house a black stone connected with the Asiatic goddess of fertility, Cybele.

South of the Casa di Livia is the **criptoportico**, a 128m tunnel built by Nero to connect his Domus Aurea with the imperial palaces on the Palatine. Unfortunately you can't walk into it. The tunnel had windows on one side which provided light and ventilation. Elaborate stucco decorations once lined part of the criptoportico but these have been replaced by copies. The originals are in the Museo Nazionale Romano. A second tunnel was later added to link it with the Domus Flavia.

The area west of the criptoportico was once the **Domus Tiberiana**, Tiberius' palace, which Gaius Caligula extended further north towards the Roman Forum. Today, it is the site of the **Orti Farnesiani**. Cardinal Alessandro Farnese, a grandson of Pope Paul III, bought the ruins of Tiberius' palace in the mid-16th century. He had the ruins filled in and asked the acclaimed and fashionable architect Vignola to design a garden for him. One of Europe's earliest botanic gardens, it contained a number of plant species that had never before been planted in Italy. The garden originally extended from the Forum up terraced levels connected with steps. Today there are various paths, rose gardens and shady parasol pines and it's a great place for a picnic. Twin pavilions stand at the northern end of the garden, from where the view over the Forum and the rest of Rome is breathtaking.

CAPITOLINE

PIAZZA DEL CAMPIDOGLIO Map p314–16

bus to Piazza Venezia

Climbing the **Cordonata di Michelangelo** fills even the most footsore traveller with a sense of grace. Michelangelo's ramp, opening gently as it ascends the **Capitoline Hill**, conveys pedestrians from bustling Piazza d'Aracoeli to the serene height of the Renaissance **Piazza del Campidoglio**.

Three palaces border the harmonious Renaissance piazza: the **Palazzo Nuovo** to the left, the **Palazzo Senatorio** straight ahead, and the **Palazzo dei Conservatori** to the right. Michelangelo authored their serious facades. He designed the piazza's pavement, too, but its installation was delayed for 400 years.

In the days of the Empire, this hill, whose name is derived from the Latin *caput*, or head, was site of the temple of Juno Moneta (now covered by the church of Santa Maria in Aracoeli) which housed the mint. Juno Moneta gave us the English word 'money'.

The piazza's statuary come from different eras and locales. Two ancient Egyptian granite lions guard the base of the *cordonata*, spitting water into the breeze. At the top reside a pair of statues rescued from the Ghetto in the 16th century: Castor and Pollux, the twin offspring of Leda and a seductive swan (who was actually Jupiter in disguise). The twins are called the saviours of Rome because they appeared during a grim point of the Battle of Lake Regillus to tell Romans all would be well. Their divine half-sister, Minerva, who emerged full-grown out of Jupiter's head, is the subject of the fountain at the base of the Palazzo Senatorio's double staircase. On either side of her are colossal statues representing the Tiber (on the right) and the Nile (on the left).

In the middle of the square is a copy of one of the only ancient equestrian bronzes to survive the Dark Ages. It is Marcus Aurelius, the great 2nd-century emperor and stoic who came closest to embodying Plato's famous dictum: 'States will never be happy until rulers become philosophers or philosophers become rulers'. The statue was saved from recycling only because early Christians mistook him for their hero, Emperor Constantine. The restored original is behind glass in Palazzo Nuovo.

The **Palazzo Senatorio** is the seat of the municipal government. It is open to the public 9am to 4pm on Sunday. Admission is free but identification is required.

Neighbourhoods – Ancient Rome

CAPITOLINE MUSEUMS Map pp314–16

☎ 06 399 67 800; www.museicapitolini.org; Piazza del Campidoglio 1; admission €6.20 (€7.80 when there's an exhibition on); ☼ 9am-8pm (last tickets 7pm) Tue-Sun; bus to Piazza Venezia

The world's oldest public museums, occupying two palaces on Michelangelo's delightful piazza, were founded in 1471 when Pope Sixtus IV donated a few bronze sculptures to the city. Subsequent popes followed suit as the city expanded and more ancient statues were unearthed. The museums now house some of the finest treasures of ancient Rome, with an emphasis on sculpture. The work is presented to stunning visual effect. One ticket buys entry to both Palazzo Nuovo and its neighbour across the square, Palazzo dei Conservatori.

Palazzo Nuovo is rich with important sculpture. It houses the *Venere Capitolina* (Capitoline Venus) in Room 3, the epitome of classical grace. Room 5 houses busts of the great philosophers, poets and politicians. The *Galata Morente* (Dying Gaul) in Room 8, a Roman copy of a 3rd-century-BC Greek work, captures the essence of defeat in the anguished pose of a fallen warrior. Note the bushy moustache that marks the Gaul as a barbarian. The *Satiro Ridente* (Laughing Satyr) in Room 7, crafted of red marble and holding a bunch of grapes, is the title character of Nathaniel Hawthorne's *The Marble Faun*.

Stairs to the lower-ground floor lead to a tunnel between Palazzo Nuovo and Palazzo dei Conservatori. A connecting passage leads to the **Tabularium** of Palazzo Senatorio, ancient Rome's hall of records, built in 78 BC. It was used as a salt deposit and prison in the Middle Ages.

The **Palazzo dei Conservatori** houses more sculpture, and its 2nd-floor *pinacoteca* (picture gallery) includes some important paintings.

The disarming remains of a colossal statue of Constantine – a mammoth head, hand and foot – reside in the inner court of the ground floor. In its original form Constantine was 12m high, seated, with his index finger pointing at the sky to represent his direct connection with God.

The famous bronze *Lupa Capitolina* (Capitoline Wolf) has her own room, the Sala Della Lupe, as befits the wet nurse of the founders of Rome. The wolf was crafted by Etruscans around 500 BC. Surprisingly, the nursing boys, Romulus and Remus, weren't added until the Renaissance.

The Sinai, in Room 3, is an expressive 1st-century-BC crowd pleaser – a young boy plucking a thorn from his foot

The **Pinacoteca** on the 2nd floor contains a wealth of work by heavy hitters such as Titian, Tintoretto, Reni, Rubens and Van Dyck. Caravaggio's sensual young *San Giovanni Battista* has his arm looped over the head of a ram, creating speculation the subject was not St John at all, but the Old Testament Isaac. Compare this mature painting in high chiaroscuro to the sly fortune-teller beside it, a piece from his earlier days, before his darks were so dark, his light so dramatic.

Many of the sculptures from the Palazzo dei Conservatori, including pieces which have rarely or never been on display before, have been transferred to a former thermoelectric plant in Via Ostiense, south of the city centre (see Capitoline Museums at Centrale Montemartini, p121).

ROMAN INSULA Map pp311–13

Piazza d'Aracoeli; bus to Piazza Venezia

At the bottom of the Capitoline, next to the staircase leading up to Santa Maria in Aracoeli, are the ruins of a Roman apartment block or *insula*. Apparently, a good, cheap studio was as scarce in ancient Rome as modern Tokyo or New York: the ruins reveal cramped and squalid conditions.

CHIESA DI SANTA MARIA IN ARACOELI Map pp314–16

Piazza d'Aracoeli; ☼ 6.30am-noon & 3.30-6pm; bus to Piazza Venezia

A dramatic 14th-century staircase leads from Piazza d'Aracoeli to the church of Santa Maria in Aracoeli, near Piazza del Campidoglio at the highest point of Capitoline Hill. Dating from the 7th century, this church like other ancient Roman structures has been rebuilt over the years. The latest redesign came in the 13th century, for Franciscans began but never completed a Romanesque facade. The first chapel of the southern aisle holds a fresco by 15th-century great Pinturicchio, known for his attention to detail.

Built on the site where legend says the Tiburtine Sybil told Caesar Augustus of the coming birth of Christ, this church has a strong association with the nativity and is very lively at Christmas time. It is home to a beloved statue of the baby Jesus, said to have been carved of wood from the garden of Gethsemane, the scene of Christ's agony. The statue was believed to heal the sick, and was taken to the bedsides of ill parishioners. The original was stolen in 1994, but the replica is as venerated as the original. A Christmas procession of Romany people delivers him to his crèche each year.

PIAZZA VENEZIA

IL VITTORIANO Map pp314–16

☎ 06 699 17 18; Piazza Venezia; admission free;
☽ 10am-1 hr before dusk Tue-Sun; bus to Piazza Venezia

Romans say Il Vittoriano is the best address in the city: it's the only place from which you can't see the monstrous structure itself. The popular complaints encompass its marble (too white), its placement (it disrupts the view of the Capitoline) and its form (described deprecatingly as 'the typewriter' and 'the wedding cake'). The best use of the much-maligned confection may well be to stand upon it. From the portico, you can see Piazza del Popolo and St Peter's to the north, and the Roman Forum to the south. The monument was begun in 1885 to commemorate Italian unification and honour Victor Emmanuel II, the first king of united Italy and subject of the Vittoriano's gargantuan equestrian statue. The eternal flame commemorates the Unknown Soldier. The **Museo del Risorgimento**, located in the thick-walled undercarriage of the Vittoriano, hosts temporary exhibitions and relics from the years leading up to Italian unification. The entrance is on Via di San Pietro in Carcere.

PALAZZO VENEZIA/MUSEO DEL PALAZZO DI VENEZIA Map pp311–13

☎ 06 69 99 41; Via del Plebiscito 118; admission €4;
☽ 8.30am-7.30pm Tue-Sun; bus to Piazza Venezia

On the western side of Piazza Venezia is the first great Renaissance palace in Rome, which was partially constructed with materials scavenged from the Colosseum. It was built for the Venetian cardinal Pietro Barbo, who later became Pope Paul II. Work began on the square in 1455 but bits were added until the 16th century. Mussolini used it as his official residence and made some of his famous speeches from the balcony. The best way to see the interior is to visit the oft-overlooked **Museo del Palazzo di Venezia**, which has an excellent collection of Byzantine and early Renaissance art, ranging from jewellery and ceramics to pastel portraits (an entire room of them) and arms.

Since Rome is chock-full of relics, check out the exquisite 14th- and 15th-century Tuscan reliquaries, decorated with delicate images of the Madonna and saints. The care that went into creating these pieces reflects the value put on the objects within. Of note, too, is the small, delightful 14th-century picture of the chorus of angels by Paolo Veneziano.

Among the best paintings are Guercino's sad *San Pietro*, Carlo Maratta's *Cleopatra*, which clothes the Egyptian queen in a 17th-century gown, and Orazio Borgianni's *Cristo Deposto* (The Deposition of Christ), a prostrate and foreshortened Christ painted with the feet in the foreground.

While gazing at all the goodies on the walls, don't forget to look up. The painted, coffered ceilings ought not to be missed.

The museum also hosts temporary exhibitions, often of important contemporary artists. Parts of the museum were closed for restoration at the time of writing.

BASILICA DI SAN MARCO Map pp311–13

Piazza di San Marco; ☽ 7am-1pm & 4-7pm;
bus to Piazza Venezia

Actually part of the Palazzo Venezia, but facing onto Piazza di San Marco, the **Basilica di San Marco** was founded in the 4th century in honour of St Mark the Evangelist. After undergoing several major transformations over the centuries, the church has a Renaissance facade, a Romanesque bell tower and a largely baroque interior. The main attraction is the 9th-century mosaic in the apse, which depicts Christ with saints and Pope Gregory IV.

CENTRO STORICO

Eating p156; Shopping p204; Sleeping p223

Of all the styles and movements of art and architecture that have found purchase on Roman soil through the millennia, the baroque is dominant. Prolific Bernini sewed it into the landscape like the Johnny Appleseed of plaster and stone; his works in this area of the city alone would have taken a mere mortal a lifetime. His great rival Borromini turned out fewer projects but notched up the already feverish energy of the style, morphing flat planes into undulating waves of convex-meets-concave, and putting the idea of movement into that most staid of structural elements, the wall. Rome's *centro storico* (historic centre) contains some of the best work of the baroque period, and the area seems to exude some

of its theatrical spirit. Here, even the streets curve gently so the facades, like vain ladies in an opera box, may each be seen. Luckily, there are some elements to counterbalance all that flamboyance. Campo de' Fiori's morning market adds an earthiness to the neighbourhood, and the Pantheon, with its cool classical proportions, anchors it architecturally.

CAMPO DE' FIORI & AROUND
Map pp311–13

'Il Campo' is a major focus of Roman life; by day it's a fruit and vegetable market packed with browsing mamas and their shopping baskets, while at night it fills with local and foreign revellers. Towering over them all is Darth Vader lookalike Giordano Bruno, who was burned at the stake here for heresy in 1600. Caravaggio went on the run after killing a man who had the nerve to beat him at tennis on this piazza.

Many of the streets near Campo de' Fiori are named after the artisans who traditionally occupied them, like Via dei Cappellari (hatters), Via dei Baullari (trunk makers) and Via dei Chiavari (key makers). Via dei Giubonnari (jacket makers) is still a popular street for clothing shops.

MUSEO BARRACCO DI SCULTURA ANTICA Map pp311–13
☎ 06 688 06 848; cnr Via dei Baullari & Corso Vittorio Emanuele II; admission €2.58; ☼ 9am-7pm Tue-Sat, until 1.30pm Sun

If you're into the sculpture of early Mediterranean cultures, you'll love this charming museum which houses exquisite Greek, Etruscan, Roman, Assyrian, Cypriot and Egyptian works donated to the state by Baron Giovanni Barracco in 1902. It's housed in a small palace known as the Piccolo Farnesina, built for a French clergyman, Thomas Le Roy, in 1523. Underneath the museum are remains of what is said to be a Roman fish shop, complete with counter and a water trough (ask for access). Fresco fragments found there are displayed on the ground floor.

MUSEO DI ROMA Map pp311–13
☎ 06 820 77 304; Piazza di San Pantaleo; admission €6.20, weekend guided tours in English & Italian €3.10 weekends; ☼ 9am-7pm Tue-Sun; bus to Corso Vittorio Emanuele II

The 18th-century **Palazzo Braschi**, built by Cosimo

Transport
Bus 40, 64 along Corso Vittorio Emanuele II; 116, 30, 70, 81, 87 along Corso de Rinascimento; 40, 64 to Largo di Torre Argentina
Tram 8 to Largo di Torre Argentina
Metro Flaminio

Morelli, houses the recently reopened **Museo di Roma**, dedicated to the history and life of Rome from the Middle Ages to the present day. A sizable collection of landscapes illustrates the evolution of famous Roman vistas through the centuries. Ippolito Caffi's pictures from the 1840s are particularly fine. There are enough portraits of popes to last you a lifetime. Many of the exhibits came from buildings that have since been demolished. The interior decoration of the *palazzo* is at least as interesting as the exhibits. The Chinese Room, decorated in the mid-18th century, shows how crazy Europe was at that time for all things from the East.

PALAZZO DELLA CANCELLERIA
Map pp311–13
☎ 06 698 93 491; Piazza della Cancelleria; bus to Corso Vittorio Emanuele II

This impressive late-15th-century Renaissance palace was built for Cardinal Raffaele Riario, a gambling man who got on the wrong side of the powerful Florentine Medici clan and had his home confiscated by the Vatican when one of their number, Leo X, became pope. It once housed the Papal Chancellery and is still Vatican property. It is thought that Bramante designed the double loggia in the magnificent interior courtyard. Recent excavations beneath the palace have revealed ruins of one of the most important early-Christian churches in Rome, the Basilica di San Lorenzo in Damaso, which was finally demolished in the 15th century to make way for a new church (of the same name) and the palace into which it is incorporated. The palace and its ruins are open only by appointment.

PALAZZO SPADA/GALLERIA SPADA
Map pp311–13
☎ 06 687 48 93; www.galleriaborghese.it/spada/en/einfo.htm; Piazza Capo di Ferro 13; admission €5; ☼ 8.30am-7.30pm Tue-Sat, closes 6.30pm Sun; bus to Largo di Torre Argentina

This stunning *palazzo* is a rare example of Mannerism in Rome, built in 1540 and restored by Borromini a century later. The building now houses the Italian Council of State and the **Galleria Spada**. In Room I, *The Slave of Ripa Grande*, cautiously attributed to Reni, highlights the almost reptilian neck of a tired-looking slave, both withered and muscled. Room II's *Portrait of a Musician*, attributed to Titian, smoulders with sexiness, the curve of his violin echoing the curl of manuscript tucked under his gloved hand. Room III contains two fascinating 17th-century globes by the Dutch cartographer Wilhelm Blaeu, and a daring, seductive *Saint Lucy* by Francesco Furini. But the Palazzo's highlight is Borromini's ingenious colonnade in the courtyard, built as an entertainment for Cardinal Bernadino Spada. It appears to be a long colonnade leading to a hedge and large statue, but it's only 10m long, and the statue comes up to a man's hip. If your eye can't believe it, join the guide who takes visitors to view it for fifteen minutes every hour on the half-hour. On close inspection, the 'hedges' are made of stone: Borromini didn't trust the gar-

One of the twin fountains in Piazza Farnese

deners to clip the real things precisely enough. In his original design, a trompe l'oeil of more columns on the back wall extended the illusion. The tiny statue was a modern addition. It may be possible to view the perspective through the library window in the courtyard of Palazzo Spada, but an up close and personal look requires a ticket to the gallery.

PIAZZA FARNESE/PALAZZO FARNESE
Map pp311–13
Palazzo not open to the public; bus to Corso Vittorio Emanuele II

Open and quiet compared to its bustling neighbour, Campo de' Fiori, Piazza Farnese's focal point is its grand **Palazzo Farnese**, the 'king of palaces'. Begun by Antonio da Sangallo, continued by Michelangelo and finished by Giacomo della Porta, the Palazzo is now the **French Embassy**. Inside are superb frescoes by Annibale Caracci, said by some to rival the Sistine Chapel but sadly off limits to visitors. Cleaning of the facade in 1999 revealed interesting polychrome brickwork that no-one ever knew was there.

The twin fountains in the square were enormous granite baths taken from the Terme di Caracalla.

CHIESA DI SAN CARLO AI CATINARI
Map pp311–13
Via dei Giubbonari; 🕐 **7.30am-noon & 4.30-7pm; bus to Corso Vittorio Emanuele II**

This 17th-century church and its exquisite dome were designed by Rosato Rasati for Cardinal Carlo Borromeo. 'Catinari' refers to the bowl makers whose shops dotted the neighbourhood. Inside, there are altarpieces by Pietro da Cortona and Guido Reni. Don't miss the richly decorated crucifix on the sacristy altar.

CHIESA DI SANT'ANDREA DELLA VALLE Map pp311–13
Corso Vittorio Emanuele II; 🕐 **7.30am-noon & 4.30-7.30pm; bus to Corso Vittorio Emanuele II**

The church's dome is the second-highest in Rome after that of St Peter's, and was designed by Carlo Maderno. The interior decoration is scaled to match. Mattia Preti's supersized frescoes across the apse depict St Andrew's martyrdom. Domenichino's frescoes above the apse play off those of his rival Lanfranco in the dome. Competition between the artists was fierce, especially when they were working at the same time, and legend has it that Domenichino once took a saw to Lanfranco's scaffold.

The first act of Puccini's *Tosca* is set here, with its hero, appropriately, painting a portrait of the Madonna.

GHETTO
There have been Jews in Rome since a wave of immigration in the 2nd century BC, making Rome Europe's longest surviving

Jewish community. At one point, there were as many as 13 synagogues in the city, but Titus' victory in Jerusalem in AD 70 changed the status of Jews from citizen to slave (Jewish slaves were the labour force that built the Colosseum). In the 2nd century AD, Romans tended to confuse Jews with the despised monotheistic Christians, making them targets for persecution. In subsequent centuries, everything depended on who was in charge, with rights limited under some governments, nonexistent under others. Things took a turn for the worse with a papal bull in 1555 that forced confinement in the Jewish Ghetto, marking the beginning of a period of official intolerance which lasted, off and on, into the 20th century. Ironically, confinement in the Ghetto meant that Jewish cultural and religious identity survived intact in Rome.

Via del Portico d'Ottavia is the centre of what remains of the Jewish Ghetto. The tightly packed buildings on the northern side of the street incorporate the remains of old Roman and medieval buildings. The house at No 1 (on the corner of Piazza Costaguti) dates from 1468 and the facade is decorated with pieces of ancient-Roman sculpture including a fragment from a sarcophagus. At street level, in a tiny unmarked shop, an all-female bakery produces traditional Jewish breads, pastries and cakes.

FONTANA DELLE TARTARUGHE
Map pp311–13
Piazza Mattei; bus to Largo di Torre Argentina
This most enchanting fountain depicts four boys gently hoisting tortoises up into a bowl of water. Taddeo Landini apparently created it in a single night in 1585, on behalf of the Duke of Mattei who had gambled his fortune away and was on the verge of losing his fiancée in the process. His father-in-law was suitably impressed and the Duke got the girl. However, the fountain owes its charm to Bernini who added the tortoises in 1658.

MUSEO D'ARTE EBRAICA pp308–10
☎ 06 684 00 66; Lungotevere dei Cenci; admission €5.20; ⏰ 9.30am-4.30pm Mon-Thu (until 7.30pm Apr-Sep), 9.30am-1.30pm Fri, 9.30am-12.30pm Sun; bus to Largo di Torre Argentina
The historical, cultural and artistic heritage of Rome's Jewish community is chronicled in this small museum, which is part of the city's main synagogue (and can be visited on the same ticket). It presents harrowing reminders of the hardships experienced by Europe's oldest Jewish community.

PALAZZO CENCI Map pp320–1
Vicolo dei Cenci; closed to the public; tram to Via Arenula
The largest *palazzo* in the area is decorated by elaborate stucco work around small balconies. The palace belonged to the family of the ill-fated Beatrice Cenci, who was abused by her tyrannical father; she eventually killed him and was subsequently beheaded. Shelley based his tragedy *The Cenci* on the family and a portrait of her by Guido Reni is one of the most famous works in the Galleria Nazionale d'Arte Antica in Palazzo Barberini (see p106).

PORTICO D'OTTAVIA Map p308–10
Via del Portico d'Ottavia; bus to Teatro di Marcello
These evocative remains – a few columns and a fragmented pediment that the neighbourhood has casually enveloped – were originally the entrance to an enormous square colonnade enclosing temples, libraries and shops erected in 146 BC and then rebuilt by Augustus in 23 BC. The original builder was called Octavius, and Augustus kept the name since it happened to honour his sister Octavia.

The visible remains are a fraction of the original vast rectangular portico, supported by 300 columns. Measuring 132m by 119m, the complex included temples dedicated to Juno and Jupiter (the latter was the first temple in Rome to be built entirely of marble), a Latin and a Greek library, and numerous magnificent statues and works of art. By the Middle Ages the Roman structure had already been sacked for its marble and been pulled down.

From the Middle Ages until the end of the 19th century, the portico formed part of the city's main fish market. Recent excavations have uncovered the remains of a small fishmonger's stand, complete with a bench for displaying the wares, clam shells and a stone basin in which the fish were washed. On one of the brick pillars outside the church a stone plaque states that the fish sellers had to give city officials the head *usque ad primas pinnas inclusive* (up to and including the first fin) of any fish longer than the plaque itself. Fish heads, and particularly those of the sturgeon that lived in the Tiber at the time, were prized for soup.

In AD 755, part of the original colonnade was incorporated into the facade of **Chiesa di Sant'Angelo in Pescheria**. To the right of the portico you will notice the stucco facade of the 17th-century oratory of **Sant'Andrea dei Pescivendoli** (1689).

ISOLA TIBERINA Map pp317–19

The world's smallest inhabited island – artist Joseph Kosuth is one of the two residents – has been linked with healing since the 3rd century BC, when the Romans adopted the Greek god of healing Aesculapius as their own and erected a temple to him here. Today the island is home to Fatebenefratelli hospital.

According to some ancient writers the island was formed by the grain stores thrown into the river after the expulsion of the Tarquins from the city. Another version states that a Greek ship ran aground at this spot and was later surrounded by a travertine wall. In its shape, the island still resembles a ship but it is in fact made of volcanic rock.

PONTE CESTIO & PONTE FABRICIO
Map pp317–19
bus to Lungotevere dei Pierleoni

The **Ponte Cestio**, built in 46 BC, connects the island to Trastevere. It was rebuilt in the late

---

The Tragedy of the Cenci

In the church of San Pietro in Montorio, at the base of the altar, there is a stone slab marked with a cross and the single word *Orate*: Pray. Here lies the body of Beatrice Cenci, whose story is more sensationally tragic than any Italian opera, or any contemporary soap opera for that matter.

Beatrice was the unfortunate daughter of an evil man, Francesco Cenci. By the time he married and had seven children, Francesco's cruelty and lawlessness were common knowledge, but his enormous fortune bought him out of trouble with the law. When his first wife and mother of the children died, he married Lucrecia Petroni, a celebrated beauty.

Francesco hated his children and gave them nothing of his enormous fortune. Of the seven, two were killed, and four of the remaining five escaped Francesco's clutches: the boys through lawsuits that granted them some of the money Francesco denied them, and one daughter through a marriage arranged against Francesco's will by the reigning pope. Francesco focused all his ire on the remaining daughter Beatrice, who was the youngest and most beautiful. Her portrait, attributed to Guido Reni, hangs in the Galleria Nazionale d'Arte Antica in the Palazzo Barberini (see p106), showing a sweet-faced young girl with soft eyes and dark blonde hair.

Francesco locked Beatrice in a room of his palace when she was about 13 and refused to let her out. He abused and raped her, and forced her to sleep with her equally abused stepmother, Lucrecia.

A few years later, Francesco was obliged to leave home for several months. In his absense, Beatrice and Lucrecia tried to get a request for mercy to the pope, but Francesco had paid off the papal courtiers. During this same time, Beatrice's brother introduced her to a handsome young priest, with whom she fell in love. When Francesco returned, the priest asked for Beatrice's hand in marriage, and was denied.

In despair and with nothing to lose, Beatrice and Lucrecia began to plot Francesco's murder. With the help of Beatrice's brother and her ex-lover the priest, they planned to orchestrate a fake kidnapping that was supposed to end in Francesco's death. It failed. Then, the family hired two hitmen to kill Francesco in his sleep. When they chickened out, Beatrice threatened to kill him herself. The two shamed assassins, accompanied by Beatrice and Lucrecia, returned to Francesco's bedroom, and killed him by driving long nails into his eyes and throat.

Francesco's death created suspicion almost immediately. When one of the hired hit men was arrested and tortured, he sang like a bird, and the whole Cenci family was arrested. There followed a series of awful tortures. Lucrecia gave in immediately and confessed, but Beatrice wouldn't admit anything. The judge ordered her to be stripped and then hung from her hands, which were tied behind her back. She still would not confess. They tied weights to her feet, and dislocated her shoulders, and she still wouldn't confess. Finally, the rest of the family begged the judge to let her down and begged her to confess. When she did, the pope sentenced the family to be dragged to death by horses through the streets of Rome. The public, on to the story by this time, was outraged, and two skilled lawyers were sent to argue for clemency. For a while, it looked like they all would be pardoned, but just then another young Roman nobleman murdered his rich father, and while the two cases were unrelated, it appeared to the pope there was a rash of patricides within the aristocracy, and he felt obliged to put a stop to it. Lucrecia and Beatrice, along with Beatrice's brother, were once again sentenced to death, this time by decapitation.

Then as now, a story as full of pathos and drama as this one couldn't fail to find an audience. When the guillotine was erected on Ponte Sant'Angelo (see p138), a giant crowd gathered. According to Alexander Dumas' account of the execution, bleachers were erected for the event, and shortly became so packed they collapsed, killing several people. The whole bloody spectacle took three hours under a scorching September sun, and several more people died from heatstroke.

At her request, Beatrice was interred near Raphael's brilliant *Transfiguration*, which, in her day, decorated San Pietro in Montorio. Today, it hangs in the Vatican Museums (see p132).

19th century. What remains of the **Ponte Rotto** (Broken Bridge), Rome's first stone bridge, is visible on the south side. Most of the bridge was swept away in a terrible flood in 1598. From the Ghetto, you cross the **Ponte Fabricio** which was built in 62 BC and is Rome's oldest standing bridge.

CHIESA DI SAN BARTOLOMEO
Map pp317–19
Isola Tiberina; bus to Lungotevere dei Pierleoni
The recently restored **Chiesa di San Bartolomeo** was built in the 10th century on the ruins of a Roman temple. It has a Romanesque bell tower and a marble wellhead, believed to have been built over the same spring which provided healing waters for the temple. The church has suffered damage from floods several times. Floating mills were a feature of the Tiber near the Isola Tiberina (and upstream to the Ponte Sisto) from the 6th to the 19th century.

PANTHEON & AROUND
AREA SACRA DI LARGO ARGENTINA
Map pp311–13
Largo di Torre Argentina; ☒ closed to public; bus or tram to Largo di Torre Argentina
Surrounded by a busy bus and tram junction, the remains of these four Republic-era temples were revealed during construction work in the 1920s, close to the spot where Julius Caesar was slain. It is now home to hundreds of stray cats, and you can visit the ruins on a free guided tour organised by the volunteers at the cat sanctuary (see the boxed text, p88) each Sunday.

MUSEO NAZIONALE ROMANO:
CRYPTA BALBI Map pp311–13
☎ 06 481 55 76; Via delle Botteghe Oscure 31; admission €4; ☒ 9am-7.45pm Tue-Sun; bus to Largo di Torre Argentina
The newest seat of the Museo Nazionale Romano collection illustrates – almost better than any other museum in Rome – the city's multilayered history. The museum is based around the ruins of medieval and Renaissance structures built on top of a grand Roman portico and theatre, the Theatre of Balbus, which was constructed between 19 and 13 BC.

Many of the artefacts on display – including vividly coloured and decorated ceramics whose designs are still used today – were excavated in the immediate area; the rest (including most of the exhibits on the 2nd floor) come from the Museo Nazionale Romano's vast and valuable collection.

ELEFANTINO Map pp311–13
Piazza della Minerva; bus to Largo di Torre Argentina
You can't but love this monument of a 6th-century-BC Egyptian obelisk being carried on the back of a white-marble elephant sculpted by Ercole Ferrata to Bernini's design. The obelisk was found in the cloister of Santa Maria Sopra Minerva and erected here by Pope Alexander VII. The elephant, representing strength and wisdom, was meant to symbolise those virtues that sustained Christian faith.

The monument was unveiled in 1667, the result of many consultations between Bernini and Pope Alexander, whose reign it was intended to glorify. The pope composed the inscription on its base, which states: 'You who see here the figures of wise Egypt carved on a column carried by an elephant, the strongest of animals, understand it is the proof of a robust mind to sustain solid wisdom'.

CHIESA DEL GESÙ Map pp311–13
☎ 06 69 70 01; Piazza del Gesù; ☒ 6am-12.30pm & 4-7.15pm; bus to Piazza Venezia
Rome's first Jesuit church, built between 1568 and 1575, is the epitome of Counter-Reformation architecture and reflected the 'shock and awe' tactics of the time; the idea was to attract worshippers with breathtaking splendour and then involve them as closely as possible in the ecclesiastical proceedings. It influenced a trend in western architecture and became the standard for other churches around Italy.

The Spanish soldier Ignatius Loyola was wounded in battle in 1521, came to Rome in 1537, and founded the Jesuits in 1540. The order trained missionaries and teachers and sent them all over the world. Loyola is buried in the Cappella di Sant'Ignazio in the northern transept in an opulent marble and bronze tomb with columns encrusted with lapis lazuli. The tomb, which doubles as an altar, was made by Andrea Pozzo and other artists and is topped by a representation of the Trinity with a terrestrial globe which is in fact the largest solid piece of lapis lazuli in the world. The marble sculpture to the right of the tomb represents *Religion Triumphing over Heresy*, which just about sums up what the Jesuits were all about.

Giacomo Barozzi da Vignola, a pupil of Michelangelo and an important architect of the transition period between the Renaissance and the baroque, designed the elaborate interior. His contemporary Giacomo della Porta designed the facade. The project was financed by Alessandro Farnese, who was subsequently regarded as being the owner of the three most beautiful things in Rome – his family palace, his daughter and the church of the Gesù.

The extraordinary fresco on the vault, depicting the *Triumph of the Name of Jesus*, is by Giovanni Battista Gaulli (known as Il Baciccia). The wonderfully foreshortened figures appear to tumble from the vault onto the coffered ceiling. Baciccia also painted the frescoes inside the cupola and designed the church's stucco decoration.

St Ignatius' rooms, where he lived for 12 years, are to the right of the church. They have been restored and display paintings and memorabilia, including a masterful trompe l'oeil perspective by Andrea Pozzo.

PANTHEON Map pp311–13
Piazza della Rotonda; admission free; 🕙 8.30am-7.30pm Mon-Sat, 9am-5.30pm Sun & holidays; bus to Largo di Torre Argentina

Having withstood the rigors and fashions of almost two millennia, the Pantheon is the best-preserved ancient Roman building and one of those sights that gets more profound every time you visit. Come before you visit the Roman Forum, to experience a living contemporary of those ruins. The Pantheon has been in constant use since it was built.

Dedicated to 'all the gods', the Pantheon gets its name from the Greek words *pan* (all) and *theos* (god). General Marcus Agrippa built an earlier temple here in 27 BC and, although Hadrian constructed this version around AD 120, Marcus is credited on the facade's inscription.

Its dramatic, imposing exterior with 16 Corinthian columns (each a single piece of stone) and a triangular pediment was supposedly designed to hide the dome. The plan was to fill unsuspecting visitors with a sense of awe when they entered and, after all this time, the plan's still working; it's the kind of place that inspires people to become architects. The extraordinary dome is a perfect semisphere (the diameter is exactly equal to the interior height of 43.3m) and considered the most important achievement of ancient Roman architecture. Light is provided by a 9m *oculus* (round widow), which was also meant as a symbolic connection between the temple and the gods. If you're in the neighbourhood during a rainstorm, take shelter here and watch the water gushing down in a perfect circle, before draining away through

almost invisible holes the Romans drilled in the marble floor. Clear days are nearly as dramatic: the *oculus* lets in a slanting column of pure light.

The weight of the dome, which thins as it rises, is supported by brick arches embedded in the structure of the walls; these are evident from the exterior. Rivets and holes in the brickwork indicate where the original marble veneer panels have been removed. Michelangelo copied the design for the dome of St Peter's, figuring if the structure stood for the ancients, it would stand for him.

Colosseum Kitty

Postcard images of cats reclining amid ancient ruins belie the sorry state of Rome's feline population. Many Romans are backward when it comes to animal welfare, refusing to get their pets sterilised and abandoning unwanted kittens. *Gattari* (cat ladies) have always tried tending to the strays but a dedicated and international band of volunteers has established a sanctuary for hundreds of sick, abandoned and stray moggies in the Largo Argentina archaeological site. You're welcome to visit the **Cat Sanctuary** (☎ 06 687 21 33; www.romancats.com), where thousands of strays are fed, sterilised and vaccinated each year without a red cent from the authorities. Pinch your nose, and give 'Wood' a cuddle from us.

Because it was consecrated as a church in 606, the building was spared the Christian neglect that left other structures to crumble – although it wasn't entirely safe even then. The temple has been consistently plundered and damaged. The gilded-bronze roof tiles were removed by an emperor of the Eastern empire and, in the 17th century, the Barberini pope, Urban VIII, allowed Bernini to melt down the bronze ceiling of the portico for the *baldacchino* (canopy) over the main altar of St Peter's (plus 80 cannons for Castel Sant'Angelo). Thankfully, they left the original Roman bronze doors.

The Italian kings Victor Emmanuel II and Umberto I are buried here. Monarchist geezers like to leave them wreaths. Raphael is buried along the left wall, closer to the altar.

CHIESA DI SANTA MARIA SOPRA MINERVA Map pp311–13
Piazza della Minerva; 🕙 7am-7pm; bus to Largo di Torre Argentina

The resting place of the headless body of

St Catherine is one of the few Gothic-style churches in Rome. It's built on the site of an ancient temple of Minerva, goddess of wisdom and war. The Latin inscriptions on the 13th-century exterior are flood markers. The oldest reads: 'In the year of the Lord 1422 on the day of Saint Andrew the water of the Tiber rose as far as to the top of this stone, in the time of the Pope Martin V, his sixth year'.

The apse fresco in the Chiesa di Santa Maria della Vittoria (p104)

Inside, superb late-15th-century frescoes by Filippino Lippi in the Cappella Carafa (the last chapel in the southern transept) depict events in the life of St Thomas Aquinas. The central *Annunciation* also shows St Thomas Aquinas presenting Cardinal Olivieri Carafa to the Virgin. Left of the high altar is Michelangelo's statue of *Christ Bearing the Cross*, completed around 1520 (although the bronze drapery was added later). As Michelangelos go, it's nobody's favourite, but still outstrips the work of mere mortals. An altarpiece of the *Madonna and Child* in the second chapel in the northern transept is attributed to Fra Angelico, the Dominican friar and painter, who is also buried in the church.

St Catherine's body lies under the high altar. The tombs of two Medici popes, Leo X and Clement VII, are in the apse. The church was heavily restored in the Gothic style in the 19th century, when the rose windows were added and the vault painted with overly vibrant colours.

PIAZZA DEL POPOLO Map pp304–5
metro Flaminio

This magnificently restored piazza, at the northern gateway to the city, was laid out in 1538 and redesigned in neoclassical style by Giuseppe Valadier in 1823. Carlo Rainaldi designed the seemingly twin baroque churches, **Chiesa di Santa Maria dei Miracoli** and **Chiesa di Santa Maria in Montesanto**, in the 17th century. Bernini did a number on the actual gate itself, in honour of Queen Christina of Sweden's defection to Catholicism. In the square's centre is an **obelisk** brought by Augustus from Heliopolis, in ancient Egypt, and moved to the square from the Circo Massimo in the mid-16th century. To the east is a ramp leading up to the **Pincio**, a hill which affords a stunning view of the city. Via di Ripetta, Via del Corso and Via del Babuino converge here, forming a trident.

CHIESA DI SANTA MARIA DEL POPOLO Map ppp304–4
Piazza del Popolo; ☯ 7am-noon & 4-7pm; metro Flaminio

The first chapel was built here in 1099 to exorcise the ghost of Nero, who was secretly buried on this spot and whose malicious spirit was supposed to haunt the area. Transformed into this church in the 15th century, it is now a who's who of artistic treasures. Bramante designed the apse, which contains the tombs of Cardinal Ascanio Sforza and Cardinal Girolamo Basso della Rovere. Pinturicchio painted the lunette frescoes and the *Adoration* above the altar in the first chapel to the right of the entrance. Raphael began decorating the Chigi Chapel, second on the left. He died and it was left unfinished until Bernini completed it more than 100 years later. It contains a mosaic of a kneeling skeleton, to remind the living of the inevitable end. For the Cerasi Chapel (to the left of the altar), Caravaggio provided two of the most spectacular paintings in Rome, depicting the *Conversion of St Paul* (in which the lovingly rendered horse steals the show) and the pulls-no-punches *Crucifixion of St Peter*.

PIAZZA NAVONA & AROUND
PIAZZA NAVONA Map pp311–13
bus to Corso del Rinascimento

This vast piazza provides a dramatic baroque backdrop for the drama of living Roman-style.

It's filled from dawn until well after dusk with busking musicians, grumpy old men, enterprising fortune-tellers, devious pickpockets, *gelato*-licking tourists and the ubiquitous pigeons. It is laid out on the ruins of a very different public space, an arena built by Domitian in AD 86, fragments of which can still be seen under glass at its northern end. This was the scene of more brutal Roman spectator sports: jousting, javelin and an annual mock naval battle, for which the piazza was flooded. (The name 'Navona' is a corruption of the Greek word 'agon', meaning public games.) It was paved over in the 15th century and reigned as the city's main market for almost 300 years.

The square's boisterous energy focuses on Bernini's **Fontana dei Quattro Fiumi**, completed in 1651 and depicting the Nile, Ganges, Danube and Rio Plata Rivers, which represented the then-known four continents of the world. Bernini had to bring all his estimable forces to bear to get the commission, as he was out of favour with the commissioning pope, Innocent X. An apocryphal story says Bernini's figure shades his eyes from the Chiesa di Sant'Agnese in Agone, designed by his bitter rival, Borromini. It's not true: the fountain was competed before the church was built. The gesture actually indicates that the source of the river was unknown at the time.

The **Fontana del Moro** at the southern end of square was designed by Giacomo della Porta in 1576. Bernini added the Moor holding a dolphin in the mid-17th century. The surrounding Tritons are 19th-century copies. The 19th-century **Fontana del Nettuno** at the northern end depicts Neptune fighting with a sea monster, surrounded by sea nymphs.

In the centre of the square facing the Fontana dei Quattro Fiumi is the **Chiesa di Sant'Agnese in Agone**; its concave facade is pure Borromini: stately, calculated, yet vibrantly theatrical. The crafty trompe l'oeil interior makes the apses appear to be the same size. The church honours the virgin St Agnes, whose hair instantly grew to cover her body when her persecutors stripped her in public. Her preternaturally small skull resides here.

The largest building in the square is the elegant **Palazzo Pamphilj**, built between 1644 and 1650 by Girolamo Rainaldi and Borromini for Giovanni Battista Pamphilj when he became Pope Innocent X. It was later occupied by his domineering sister-in-law, Olimpia Maidalchini, who like other members of the pope's family received enormous riches and favours during his pontificate. It is now the Brazilian Embassy.

CHIESA NUOVA Map pp311–13
Via della Chiesa Nuova; bus to Corso Vittorio Emanuele II
'Nuova' in the Eternal City has a pretty loose meaning. This 'new' church replaced Santa Maria in Vallicella in 1575, built for the personable Filippo Neri, who ministered to Rome's sick and poor. Legend says Neri found Barocci's painting of the *Presentation of the Virgin in the Temple* (in the northern transept) so uplifting, he levitated beneath the altar as he prayed in front of it. Gilding, fancy marbles and frescoes weren't added until after Neri's death. Rubens contributed the paintings over the high altar, and Pietro da Cortona, known for his luminous, springlike palate, decorated the dome, tribune and nave. Neri died in 1595, was canonised in 1622 and is buried beneath the altar in a chapel to the left of the apse. He and his posse of plain-speaking priests invented the oratory as a form of worship through music. Next to the church is Borromini's **Oratorio dei Filippini**. Behind it is his **Torre dell'Orologio**, a clock tower built to decorate one corner of the convent attached to the church. Note the play between concave and convex surfaces. That's Borromini having fun. The Madonna below is by Pietro da Cortona.

MUSEO NAZIONALE ROMANO: PALAZZO ALTEMPS Map pp308–10
☎ 06 399 67 700; www.pierreci.it/13ing.htm; Piazza Sant'Apollinare 46; admission €5; ☻ 9am-7.45pm Tue-Sun, ticket office closes 6.45pm; bus to Corso del Rinascimento
Part of the state's stock of ancient treasures is housed in this restored Renaissance palace. (The rest of the national collection of ancient treasures is split among the Palazzo Massimo, see p101, Crypta Balbi, see p87, and the Terme di Diocleziano, see p102.)

It was largely the prestigious collection of Cardinal Ludovico Ludovisi, a nephew of Pope Gregory XV and a ravenous collector of the ancient sculpture that was being unearthed and sold off on an almost daily basis in the building boom of Counter-Reformation Rome. He took advantage of his wealth and position to build up one of the most extensive and celebrated private collections of all time. Much of the excavated sculpture was damaged in some way, so he employed leading sculptors like Bernini to repair them and 'enhance' the ones that didn't fit his taste. At the time, neither collectors nor their artists-for-hire blinked at the thought of replacing a missing limb with one that had been found elsewhere or sculpting a new 17th-century head to stick on top of a headless torso.

The booty was displayed in the gardens of Ludovisi's palace in the present-day Via Veneto area, among follies, mazes, orchards and formal gardens that attracted travellers from all over Europe for two centuries. One of the most interesting things about Palazzo Altemps is that the sculptures are displayed in a way that is very similar to common 16th-century exhibition criteria, so you get a good idea of how a Renaissance palace and collection would have looked.

Prize exhibits (untouched by the baroque fixers) include the 5th-century carved-marble *Ludovisi Throne,* discovered at the end of the 19th century in the grounds of the Villa Ludovisi. Note the beguiling girl musicians on the side reliefs. Most scholars believe that the throne came from one of the Greek colonies in Italy, though its authenticity is still a subject of debate. It shares a room with two colossal heads, one of which is the goddess Juno and dates from around 600 BC. The wall frieze (about half of which remains) depicts the 10 plagues of Egypt and the Exodus. Equally impressive is the sculptural group *Galata Suicida,* a dramatic depiction of a Gaul knifing himself to death over a dead woman. It's gloriously melodramatic and the creator clearly revelled in the gory details. This is a marble copy of a 230 BC bronze, probably commissioned by Julius Caesar.

Baroque frescoes throughout the building not only provide a decorative backdrop for the ancient sculpture but are fascinating exhibits in themselves. The walls of the Sala delle Prospettive Dipinte (on the 1st floor) are decorated with landscapes and hunting scenes seen through trompe l'oeil windows. These frescoes were painted in the 16th century for Cardinal Altemps. The Sala della Piattaia, once the palace's main reception room, has a superb 15th-century fresco by Melozzo da Forlì of a cupboard displaying gifts received by Girolamo Riario and Caterina Sforza on the occasion of their wedding.

The Egyptian collection from the Museo Nazionale Romano is housed here, too, along with the Mattei collection, formerly at Villa Celimontana (once the Mattei family estate). However, the Ludovisi Boncompagni collection forms the main body of the exhibits.

PALAZZO DEL BANCO DI SANTO SPIRITO Map pp308–10
Via del Banco di Santo Spirito; bus to Corso Vittorio Emanuele II
The early-16th-century Palazzo del Banco di Santo Spirito at the end of the street was designed by Antonio Sangallo the Younger and was the mint of Papal Rome. The facade of the building resembles a Roman triumphal arch and the two statues crowning it represent Charity and Thrift.

PALAZZO DELLA SAPIENZA & CHIESA DI SANT'IVO ALLA SAPIENZA
Map pp311–13
☎ 06 686 49 87; Corso del Rinascimento 40;
🕙 10am-1pm Sat, 9am-noon Sun; bus to Corso del Rinascimento
Until 1935 the **Palazzo della Sapienza** housed Rome's university, La Sapienza, which was founded by Pope Boniface VIII in 1303. Giacomo della Porta designed the Renaissance facade. The building now houses the state archives. Borromini designed a library in the palace as well as its courtyard which has porticoes on three sides. The fourth side is occupied by the tiny **Chiesa di Sant'Ivo alla Sapienza**, a Borromini masterpiece that must be experienced, preferably repeatedly, as photographs do not do it justice. In it, Borromini solved the problem of where to place a priest in a round space by basing the floor plan on a six pointed star.

The walls alternate between being convex and concave, and the bell tower is crowned by a distinctive twisted spiral. Note the limited opening hours.

PALAZZO MADAMA Map pp311–13
☎ 06 6 70 61; www.senato.it (Italian only); Corso Rinascimento; 🕙 free guided tour at regular intervals from 10am-6pm on 1st Sat of month; bus to Corso del Rinascimento
The 16th-century **Palazzo Madama** was originally the Rome residence of the Medici family. It was enlarged in the 17th century when the baroque facade was added together with the decorative frieze of cherubs and bunches of fruit. The building is named after 'Madama' Margaret of Parma, the illegitimate daughter of Charles V, who lived here from 1559 to 1567. It has been the seat of the Senate, the upper house of the Italian parliament, since 1871.

PASQUINO Map pp311–13
Piazza Pasquino; bus to Corso Vittorio Emanuele II
This weather-and-time-beaten sculpture (once much admired by Bernini) is Rome's most famous 'talking statue'. During the 16th century – when there were no safe outlets for dissent – a Vatican tailor named Pasquino began sticking notes to it with satirical verses

lampooning the church and aristocracy. Others joined in and pretty soon there were talking statues having conversations all over town. Even today, Romans still leave messages to express their discontent through the stone lips of Pasquino. The messages left on the statue (and other similar statues around the city) are known as pasquinade.

CHIESA DI SAN LUIGI DEI FRANCESI

Map pp311–13

Piazza di San Luigi dei Francesi; 🕑 **8.30am-12.30pm & 3.30-7pm; bus to Corso del Rinascimento**

The opulent interior of this 16th-century French national church is completely upstaged by its art: three astounding canvases by Caravaggio, known as the St Matthew cycle. *The Calling of Saint Mathew*, *Martyrdom of Saint Matthew* and *Saint Matthew and the Angel* stress the utter humanity of the saint, and highlight Caravaggio's dramatic use of colour, light and narrative. Unlike his canvases that hang in crowded galleries, these can be enjoyed in relative solitude, and for free. Domenichino's 17th-century frescoes featuring St Cecilia, second chapel on the right, are also well worth a look, though they're overdue for restoration. St Cecilia is also depicted in the altarpiece by Guido Reni, which is in fact a copy of a work by Raphael.

The tombs hold eminent French citizens – artists, cardinals and soldiers – who spent time in Rome, including the 17th-century French landscape painter Claude Lorrain.

CHIESA DI SANTA MARIA DELLA PACE Map pp311–13

☎ **06 688 09 036; Via della Pace;** 🕑 **Church 8am-noon & 4.30-7.30pm Tue-Sat, 9am-1pm Sun; Chiostro 10am-1.30pm & 3.30-7pm (during exhibitions only); bus to Corso del Rinascimento**

The undulating baroque facades are by Pietro da Cortona, but the quiet, Renaissance cloister was authored by Bramante and is one of his masterpieces. The combination is heavenly counterpoint: the facade foments religious fervour, while the cloister encourages meditation. The first chapel on the southern side contains frescoes by Raphael representing the future-savvy sibyls listening to their angels. These were painted for the banker Agostino Chigi in 1514. The first chapel on the northern side is decorated with frescoes by Baldassare Peruzzi who also did *The Presentation in the Temple* to the right of the high altar.

CHIESA DI SANT'AGOSTINO Map pp308–10

Piazza di Sant'Agostino; 🕑 **8am-noon & 4-7.30pm; bus to Corso del Rinascimento**

This 15th-century church contains two outstanding artworks: Raphael's fresco of Isaiah on the third column in the nave, which shows the influence of Michelangelo (both artists were working in the Vatican at the time); and Caravaggio's *Madonna of the Pilgrims*, so stark that it was rejected by the church that commissioned it. Note Caravaggio's palate. The two beggars are painted in warm, dirty, human tones, while the Madonna and child appear ethereal in cool whites, their otherworldly flesh aglow.

Pasquino statue (p91)

VIA DEI CORONARI Map pp311–13

This street runs westwards from the north end of Piazza Navona towards Via del Banco di Santo Spirito. It follows the course of an ancient Roman road that ran in a straight line from the area of Piazza Colonna to the Tiber and was a popular thoroughfare for pilgrims. The rosary-bead sellers *(coronari)* who once lined the street have been replaced by antique shops, though many of the original buildings remain.

VIA DEL GOVERNO VECCHIO

Map pp311–13

The narrow Via del Governo Vecchio was once part of the papal thoroughfare from the Palazzo Laterano in San Giovanni to St Peter's. It takes its name from the 15th-century Palazzo del Governo Vecchio (also known as the Palazzo Nardini) at No 39, which was the seat of the papal government in the 17th and 18th centuries. Bramante is thought to have lived in the palace opposite (No 123). Former workshops that lined the street have been converted into shops selling second-hand goods such as leather jackets, old linens, lace, watches, clocks and antique furniture. See Shopping (p204) for more details.

VIA DEL CORSO

Beginning in 1466, this straight and flashy street was transformed, once a year, into a chaotic track for festive pre-Lent races between Piazza del Popolo and Piazza Venezia. There were donkey races and lady-of-the-evening races, but the seasonal climax was the contest among riderless horses wired on stimulants and worked into a panic with a barrage of fireworks at the starting line. The Roman taste for spectacle dies hard – the tradition continued until the late 19th century, and gave the street its name. Today, swank shops line Il Corso, and the spectacle is limited to what's provided by the gorgeous young men and women cruising by on *motorino*. Traffic near Piazza del Popolo is (mostly) halted in the evenings after 6pm.

ARA PACIS AUGUSTAE Map pp308–10

☎ 06 688 06 848, 06 360 03 471; Piazza Augusto Imperatore; admission free; ☒ closed at time of writing, call for information; bus to Piazza Augusto Imperatore

The marble reliefs of this 1st-century-BC 'altar of peace' commemorate the victories of Augustus and represent the first distinctive Roman sculptural work. That it is on display here – behind a glass case – is testament to the skill and determination of the archaeologists who over the last century have pieced it together from fragments. A new Richard Meier–designed exhibition space, the first modern building to be constructed in decades, was due to open in autumn 2003.

CASA DI GOETHE Map pp304–5

☎ 06 326 50 412; www.casadigoethe.it; Via del Corso 18; admission €3; ☒ 10am-6pm Wed-Mon; metro Flaminio

The Via del Corso apartment where Johann Wolfgang von Goethe lived between 1786 and 1788 was a gathering place for German

artists and intellectuals. It was transformed into a quiet museum in 1997, housing documents relating to Goethe's Italian sojourn and some interesting drawings and etchings of him – the best, by his friend JHW Tischbein, shows Goethe leaning out the window to watch the action on Il Corso, like any procrastinating writer. Goethe composed part of his *Italian Journey* here. With advance permission, hard-core Goethe fans can use the library full of first editions.

COLLEGIO ROMANO Map pp311–13

Piazza del Collegio Romano; bus to Piazza Venezia

Until 1870, this Jesuit college educated many future popes, including Urban VIII, Innocent X,

Clement IX, Clement X, Innocent XII, Clement XI, Innocent XIII and Clement XII. Dominating the northern side of Piazza del Collegio Romano, the building is now used partly by the national heritage ministry.

PALAZZO DI MONTECITORIO

Map pp308–10

☎ 06 6 76 01; www.senato.it (Italian only); Piazza di Montecitorio; admission free; ☽ 10am-5.30pm 1st Sun of month; bus to Via del Corso

Built in 1650 by Bernini although greatly modified since, this has been the parliament of Italy's lower house since 1871. It was expanded by Carlo Fontana in the late 17th century and given a larger facade by Art-Nouveau architect Ernesto Basile in 1918.

A new-look square was unveiled in 1998 which returned to Bernini's plan of a gently sloping ramp up to the entrance of the building articulated by three radiating semicircles.

The **obelisk** in the centre of the square was brought to Rome from Heliopolis in Egypt by Augustus to celebrate his victory over Cleopatra VII and her ally Mark Antony in 30 BC. It was originally set up in the area known as Campus Martius and served as part of a huge sundial. It was excavated from an area north of the square and erected on its present site in 1792.

Reliefs on the Colonna di Traiano (p71)

PALAZZO DORIA PAMPHILJ Map pp311–13

☎ 06 679 73 23; Piazza del Collegio Romano 2; admission €7.30; ☽ 10am-5pm Fri-Wed; bus to Piazza Venezia

For a change of pace from the usual museum routine, head to this magnificent *palazzo* where one of the finest private art collections in Rome is hung just as it was in the 18th century. Along with several masterpieces, sumptuous period rooms and galleries, a highlight here is the wonderful audio tour. It provides an intimate insight into one of Rome's great families, headed now by half-Irish siblings, one of whom narrates the tour.

The history of the family is too complex to cover here but it's useful to know that their heyday came during the papacy of one of their own, Innocent X, and their cosy relationship led to the word 'nepotism'. Some 400 paintings are spread throughout the stunningly restored *palazzo* although the most interesting pieces are found in the elaborate galleries themselves, **Galleria Doria Pamphilj**. Among the big names are Raphael, Tintoretto, Brueghel and Titian who chips in with four works including the powerful *Salome* holding the head of John the Baptist. Side by side are two outstanding early works by Caravaggio, *Rest During the Flight into Egypt* and *Penitent Magdalen*, where the artist used the same model for the Virgin and the prostitute.

But the collection's most precious and famous work is the Velázquez portrait of an implacable *Pope Innocent X*, who grumbled that the depiction was 'too real'. In the same room is Bernini's bust of Innocent X and it's fascinating to see how two great artists could interpret the same subject so differently.

The private apartments of the *palazzo*, the nucleus of which is from the 15th century, are due to open by 2004 when this little gem will dazzle even more.

MAUSOLEO DI AUGUSTO Map pp308–10

bus to Piazza Augusto Imperatore

What was once one of the most imposing monuments in ancient Rome is now an unkempt mound of earth, overgrown with weeds and covered with litter. Built in 28 BC, the mausoleum was the tomb of Augustus and his descendants. Nerva was the last to be interred here, in AD 98. It served as a fortress in the Middle Ages and was later used as a vineyard, a private garden and a travertine supply for new buildings. The mausoleum was excavated and restored in the 1920s, not long before the Fascist-era buildings went up on three sides of the surrounding square. The city council has as yet unrealised plans to turn the mausoleum and square into an important urban space.

PIAZZA COLONNA Map pp308–10
bus to Largo Chigi

You could while away hours – and eventually topple over backwards – gazing at the vivid, spiralling reliefs on the 30m **Colonna Antonina** that gives the piazza its name. Inspired by Colonna di Traiano, which is almost a century older, it was erected in AD 180 to commemorate Marcus Aurelius' victories in battle. In 1589 Marcus was replaced on the top of the column with a bronze statue of St Paul. The carved reliefs on the lower part represent the war between 169 and 173 against the Germanic tribes; those on the upper part commemorate the war against the Sarmatians between 174 and 176. For those who want to spare their necks, there are casts of the reliefs in the Museo della Civiltà Romana in EUR (see p121).

Palazzo Chigi on the northern side of the square is the prime minister's official residence. The building was started in the 16th century by Matteo di Castello and finished in the 17th century by Felice della Greca.

South of Piazza Colonna in Piazza di Pietra is the **Tempio di Adriano** (Map pp311–13). You might pass this sight and wonder where the 11 huge Corinthian columns fit in to Rome's ancient history. They're all that remain of a 2nd-century temple dedicated to Hadrian and are embedded in what used to be the Roman stock exchange.

PIAZZA SANT'IGNAZIO Map pp311–13
bus to Via del Corso

This small, harmonious square by Filippo Raguzzini, built during the transition between baroque and rococo, is the most theatrical of all Rome's many flashy piazze. It uses wildly undulating surfaces to create the illusion of a larger space, and just about begs you to look at it. Unkind commentators have called it frivolous, but we find it delightful. The picturesque and elegant buildings opposite the church of Sant'Ignazio house the *carabinieri* who specialise in art theft. Some of their unclaimed pieces are on display near the door – a 'hot' lost and found.

CHIESA DI SAN LORENZO IN LUCINA
Map pp308–10
Piazza San Lorenzo in Lucina; 🕑 **9am-noon & 4.30-7.30pm, ruins open 4.30pm last Sat of month; bus to Largo Chigi**

In a city full of old churches, this is one of the oldest, dating from the 5th century, and built on an even older site sacred to Juno. It was rebuilt to its current form in the 12th century. Six ancient Ionic columns support a long portico, and the church has a pretty Romanesque bell tower. The simple facade hides an elaborate interior totally overhauled in the 17th century, when numerous side chapels were added. Guido Reni's *Crucifixion* is positioned above the main altar, and there is a fine portrait bust by Bernini in the stucco Cappella Fonseca, the fourth chapel on the southern side. The French painter Nicholas Poussin, who died in 1655, is buried in the church.

CHIESA DI SANT'IGNAZIO DI LOYOLA
Map pp320–1
Piazza Sant'Ignazio; 🕑 **7.30am-12.30pm & 3-7pm; bus to Via del Corso**

The second Jesuit church of Rome occupies the northeastern corner of the Collegio Romano building (take Via di Sant'Ignazio from Piazza del Collegio Romano) and rivals the Gesù for opulence and splendour. The church was commissioned by Cardinal Ludovico Ludovisi and built by the Jesuit mathematician and architect Orazio Grassi. The sumptuous interior is covered with paintings, stucco, coloured marble and gilt. Paintings in the nave show the Jesuit fathers doing missionary work.

A masterpiece by Andrea Pozzo (1642–1709) shows the *Triumph of St Ignatius*, but his trompe l'oeil ceiling perspective is what everyone comes to see. His ingenious scheme makes the walls appear to extend beyond their limits, and an illusionary dome painted on canvas covers the area where the real thing should have been. It looks best viewed from a small yellow spot on the floor of the nave.

VIA GIULIA Map pp311–13

Running parallel to the Tiber, Via Giulia was designed by Donato Bramante for Pope Julius II, who wanted a new approach road to St Peter's. It is lined with Renaissance palaces, antique shops and art galleries.

At its southern end, near Ponte Sisto, is the **Fontana del Mascherone**, a baroque fountain made by combining two ancient pieces of sculpture: a grotesque mask and a stone basin. Just beyond it and spanning the road is the **Arco Farnese**, from which ivy tendrils hang like stalactites. Built to a design by Michelangelo, the arch was intended to be part of a bridge across the Tiber connecting the Palazzo Farnese and its gardens with the Villa Farnesina on the opposite side of the river. Note the two giant falcon heads which glare at each other across the doorway of the **Palazzo Falconieri** (Via Giulia 1), which houses the Hungarian Academy. Borromini had a hand in the enlargement and decoration of the building.

To the left, in Via di Sant'Eligio, is **Chiesa di Sant'Eligio degli Orefici**, the 16th-century goldsmiths' church, which was designed by Raphael. Further along on the right is **Palazzo Ricci**, famous for the 16th-century frescoes on its facade. Beyond the ruined church of San Filippo Neri are the **Carceri Nuove** (Map pp308–10), built in 1655 and used as a prison until the 19th century when they were replaced by the Regina Coeli prison on the other side of the Tiber.

There are several massive Renaissance palaces with elaborate facade decoration at the northern end of Via Giulia. This area is sometimes known as the Quartiere Fiorentino because of the Florentine colony that at one time inhabited the area.

CHIESA DI SAN GIOVANNI BATTISTA DEI FIORENTINI Map pp308–10

Via Acciaioli 2; ☺ 9am-1pm & 4-7pm; bus to Corso Vittorio Emanuele II

Many Florentine artists and architects contributed to the construction and decoration of the Chiesa di San Giovanni Battista dei Fiorentini – not surprising, since construction took over a century. Jacopo Sansovino won a competition for its design, which was executed by Antonio Sangallo the younger and Giacomo della Porta. Carlo Maderno completed the elongated cupola (a Roman landmark) in 1614. Of note inside are the sculptures on the high altar by Antonio Raggi representing the baptism of Christ. The altar is by Borromini, who arranged, on his deathbed, to be entombed here, despite the fact that he committed suicide (see the boxed text, p93). The church's restored 17th-century organ gets played at the noon Mass on Sunday.

EAST OF VIA DEL CORSO

Eating p164; Shopping p211; Sleeping p227

This slice of Rome is full of ghosts. The Romantics haunt the Spanish Steps, while the faded glory of Via Veneto is the province of forgotten movie stars. Outside the city walls, the vast cemetery of San Lorenzo holds the everyday dead, while the neighbourhood church, San Lorenzo Fuori-le-Mura, was resurrected from the ruins of its earlier incarnation, destroyed by allied bombs in 1943. Among all these traces of the past a lively, diverse, multicultural present thrives.

ESQUILINE Map pp314–16

The Esquiline Hill (Esquilino) is the largest and highest of Rome's seven hills. It stretches from the Colosseum to Stazione Termini, encompassing Via Cavour (a major traffic artery between Stazione Termini and Via dei Fori Imperiali), the Basilica di Santa Maria Maggiore, the market square of Piazza Vittorio Emanuele II and the Oppian Hill. The Esquiline originally had four summits. In ancient times the lower slope of the western summit, the Suburra, was occupied by crowded slums while the area between Via Cavour and the Colle Oppio was a fashionable residential district for wealthier citizens. Much of the hill was covered with vineyards and gardens, many of which remained until the late 19th century, when they were dug up to make way for grandiose apartment blocks.

Today, the Esquiline is the most multicultural area of Rome and home to thousands of immigrants. It is also popular with young artists enticed, like young artists everywhere, by low rents and spacious lofts.

Transport

Bus 85, 87, 117, 186, 810, 850 to Labicana; 40, 64, 70 to Piazza della Repubblica; 40, 64 to Piazza Venezia; 116, 117, 119 to Piazza di San Silvestro; 16, 75 to Piazza Santa Maria Maggiore
Tram 3 along Labicana; 5, 14 to Piazza Santa Maria Maggiore
Metro Barberini, Termini, Repubblica, Colosseo, Cavour, Spagna

The western side of the Esquiline is known as Rione Monti (or simply Monti) and includes some of Rome's most famous smaller churches.

Top Five East of Via del Corso

- Spanish Steps (p100)
- Palazzo Barberini (p106)
- Trevi Fountain (p105)
- Basilica di San Clemente (below)
- Basilica di Santa Maria Maggiore (p98)

PIAZZA VITTORIO EMANUELE II
Map pp314–16

Within the square are the ruins of the **Trofei di Mario**, once a fountain at the end of an aqueduct. The square itself hosts ethnic food and cultural festivals throughout the year and an outdoor film festival in the summer (see p198).

In the northern corner of the square is the **Chiesa di Sant'Eusebio**, which was founded in the 4th century and rebuilt twice in the 18th. Each year, worshippers of the four-legged variety – dogs, cats and even horses – attend the annual blessing of the animals, held on the saint's day (17 January) of their protector, St Anthony the Abbot.

The square used to be the scene of Rome's largest and most boisterous food market, but the action has moved indoors, to the nearby **Nuovo Mercato Esquilino** at Via Principe Amedeo. It's a multiculti riot of African, Asian and Italian food and products, but keep an eye on your wallet or handbag as it is also a popular spot for pickpockets.

BASILICA DI SAN CLEMENTE Map pp320–1
Via San Giovanni in Laterano; admission to the lower levels €3; ⏰ 9am-12.30pm & 3-6pm, from 10am Sun; metro Colosseo

For a fascinating dip into Roman history, visit this 12th-century basilica built over a 4th-century church, which, in turn was built over a 1st-century Roman house containing a 2nd-century temple to the Pagan god Mithras (an early rival to Christ). In time, perhaps, you might be able to visit the Republican-era foundations that are believed to lie beneath the house.

As soon as you enter, head to the courtyard through the right door and re-enter the way the architect intended. From here the 12th-century mosaic in the apse is even more stunning – it depicts the Triumph of the Cross and combines saintly figures and

pastoral scenes. Masolino decorated the chapel of St Catherine, between the doors, possibly with the help of his brilliant student Masaccio. Frescoes recount scenes from the life of the saint who was eventually strapped to a wheel and tortured to death (after going through all that she was honoured by having a firework named after her). Note the Schola Cantorum, a marble choir screen dating from the 6th century which was originally in the older church below. It is decorated with panels of white and coloured marble and the early-Christian symbols of the fish, the dove and the vine. The high marble pulpit on the left, together with the beautiful Paschal candlestick decorated with Cosmati mosaics, was added when the new church was built. High pulpits, common in medieval churches, were probably designed so that the priest could read from illuminated manuscripts in the form of scrolls and, as he read, the congregation could see the pictures. The floor is paved with intricate patterns of coloured marble.

Although the 4th-century church was virtually destroyed by Norman invaders in 1084 you can still trace the lines of the original building and study faded 11th-century frescoes illustrating the life and many miracles of St Clement. According to legend, Pope Clement (who, it is believed, was born Jewish) was banished to the Crimea and forced to work in the mines. His preaching among the other prisoners caused the Romans to bind him to an anchor and throw him into the Black Sea. The water receded sometime later, revealing a miraculous tomb containing Clement's body. Thereafter, the tomb would be revealed once a year, when the waters miraculously receded. One year, a child was swept away by the returning tide, but was found alive and well in the tomb the next year.

Descend another level and you'll find yourself treading an ancient Roman lane leading to a 1st-century house and the Temple of Mithras, containing an altar with a sculpted relief of Mithras slaying the primordial bull (the blood from which he used to fertilise the world). Don't be alarmed by the sound of running water down here: it's an underground river flowing through a Republican-era drain.

CHIESA DI SAN MARTINO AI MONTI
Map pp314–16
Viale del Monte Oppio 28; ⏰ 7.30am-noon & 4.30-6.30pm; metro Cavour

Third-century Christians worshipped here, in the home of a Roman named Equitius. In the

4th century, after Christianity was legalised, a church was constructed and subsequently rebuilt in the 6th and 9th centuries and then completely transformed by Filippo Gagliardi in the 1650s. The sacristan can show you the remains of Equitius' house, beneath the church. The 24 Corinthian columns in the nave are all that remain of the 6th-century building. Of note are Gagliardi's frescoes of the Basilica di San Giovanni in Laterano before it was rebuilt in the mid-17th century by Borromini; and St Peter's Basilica before it assumed its present appearance in the 16th century at the hands of Bramante, Raphael, Michelangelo, Maderno and others. There are also frescoes from 1651 by the half-French, half-Italian Gaspard Dughet, who was famous for the naturalism of his landscapes.

BASILICA DI SAN PIETRO IN VINCOLI

Map pp314–16

Piazza San Pietro in Vincoli; 7am-12.30pm & 3.30-7pm; metro Cavour

Pilgrims and art lovers alike flock to this 5th-century church, built specially to house the chains that were supposed to have bound St Peter while he was imprisoned in the Mamertine (see p72). The chains were sent to Constantinople before returning to Rome as relics. They arrived in two pieces, and when they were reunited they miraculously joined together.

The art lovers, armed with cameras, are looking for a glimpse of Michelangelo's unfinished tomb of Pope Julius II, where statues of Leah and Rachel flank a commanding Moses. Yes, those are horns on his head, and Michelangelo got the idea from the mistranslation of a biblical passage. Where the original said that rays of light issued from Moses' face, the translator wrote 'horns'. Michelangelo was aware of the mistake, but he gave his Moses horns anyway. We don't know why, but they give Moses, with his luxurious flowing hair, a look more devilish than saintly. Some 40 other figures were planned for the tomb but Michelangelo was otherwise engaged in the Sistine Chapel and never had time to finish them. In the end, Pope Julius was buried in St Peter's without the great tomb he had envisioned and the unfinished sculptures, which were to have adorned it, are in the Louvre (Paris) and the Galleria dell'Accademia (Florence).

BASILICA DI SANTA MARIA MAGGIORE Map pp314–16

Piazza Santa Maria Maggiore; 7am-6.30pm; bus to Santa Maria Maggiore

One of Rome's four patriarchal basilicas (the others being St Peter's, San Giovanni in Later-ano and San Paolo Fuori-le-Mura), Santa Maria Maggiore was built on the highest point of the Esquiline in the 5th century, during Pope Sixtus III's era. According to legend, in 352 Pope Liberius had a dream in which he was instructed by the Virgin Mary to build a church in the exact place where he found snow. When, on the following morning (5 August – the middle of a hot Roman summer), snow fell on the Esquiline, he obeyed. The original church was called Santa Maria della Neve. Each year on 5 August there is a service in the basilica, during which white petals are released from the ceiling to commemorate the miracle.

Its main facade was added in the 18th century, preserving the 13th-century **mosaics** of the earlier facade. These are beautifully illuminated at night. The interior is baroque and the bell tower Romanesque.

The basilican form of the vast interior, a nave and two aisles, remains intact and the most notable feature is the cycle of mosaics, dating from the 5th century, which decorate the triumphal arch and nave, some of which are so high up that they are difficult to see (a pair of binoculars or a telephoto lens would be useful). They are the most important mosaics of this period in Rome and depict biblical scenes, in particular events in the lives of Abraham, Jacob and Isaac (to the left), and Moses and Joshua (to the right). Scenes from the life of Christ decorate the triumphal arch. The central image in the apse, signed by Jacopo Torriti, dates from the 13th century and represents the coronation of the Virgin. The Virgin is seated on the same throne as Christ and it is thought that the artist was influenced by the mosaics of the same scene in Santa Maria in Trastevere. Further scenes of the life of the Virgin are below.

The **baldacchino** over the high altar is elaborately decorated with gilt cherubs. The altar itself is a porphyry sarcophagus, which is said to contain the relics of St Matthew and other martyrs. Steps lead down to the Confessio where a reliquary preserves a fragment of baby Jesus' crib. Note the Cosmati pavement of the nave and aisles, dating from the 12th century. The sumptuously decorated **Cappella Sistina** (not to be confused with the Sistine Chapel in St Peter's), last on the right, was built by Domenico Fontana in the 16th century and contains the tombs of Popes Sixtus V and Pius V. Opposite is the **Cappella Borghese** (or Cappella Paolina), also full of elaborate decoration, erected in the 17th century by Pope Paul V. The *Madonna and Child* panel above the altar, surrounded by lapis lazuli and agate, is believed to date from the 12th to the 13th century.

CHIESA DI SANTA PRASSEDE

Map pp314–16

Via Santa Prassede 9a; ⏰ 7.30am-noon & 4-6.30pm; bus to Piazza Santa Maria Maggiore

Pope Paschal I had mosaic artists brought from Byzantium (later Constantinople) to decorate the church he built in the 9th century. The resulting jewel-coloured mosaics – on the triumphal arch, apse and in the diminutive Cappella di San Zenone – are breathtaking and not to be missed. The church is dedicated to Praxedes, the sister of Pudentiana.

The naturalism evident in earlier mosaics from the late-classical period has been replaced here with a marked Christian symbolism. On the first triumphal arch, angels guard the door to the New Jerusalem. On the underside of both arches are beautifully worked garlands of lilies and foliage. The apse mosaics are slightly blocked from view by the baroque *baldacchino*. Climb up the red marble steps for a better view if you need to. Christ is flanked by St Peter, St Pudentiana and St Zeno (on the right) and St Paul, St Praxedes and Paschal on the left. All the figures have golden halos except for the figure of Paschal, whose head is shadowed by a green square or nimbus, indicating that he was still alive at the time the mosaic was done (but expected to be on a fast track to sainthood). Below are the Lamb of God and the faithful flock.

The small **Cappella di San Zenone** in the southern aisle was built by Paschal as a mausoleum for his mother. The mosaics on the outside show distinctive Roman faces representing the Virgin and Child, Praxedes, Pudentiana and other saints (inner group) and Christ and the Apostles. Enter the chapel and you feel like part of the mosaic. It is unlikely that you will get much closer to mosaic decoration anywhere in Rome, and you can really appreciate the skill of the artists. A small mosaic in the altar niche depicts the Virgin and Child with St Praxedes and St Pudentiana; in the vault is Christ with four angels; on the inside of the doorway are St Peter and St Paul supporting the throne; and on the left, facing the altar, are St Praxedes, St Pudentiana and St Agnes. The fragment of marble in the glass case on the right is thought to be a piece of the column to which Christ was tied when he was scourged.

If you can tear your eyes away from the mosaics, have a look at the other features of the church, such as the trompe l'oeil frescoes in the nave, which are the work of various artists and were completed in the 16th century. The architrave of the nave is made up of ancient Roman fragments, some with inscriptions. The floor is paved in coloured marble. A large round porphyry disc surrounded by an inscription, located in the nave near the main door, marks the spot where Praxedes is thought to have hidden the bones of Christian martyrs.

CHIESA DI SANTA PUDENZIANA

Map pp314–16

Via Urbana 160; ⏰ 8am-6.30pm; metro Cavour

The magnificent 4th-century apse mosaic here is the oldest of its kind in Rome. An enthroned Christ is flanked by two female figures who are crowning St Peter and St Paul; on either side of them are the Apostles as Roman senators dressed in togas. You can only see 10 out of the original 12 Apostles, because barbaric 16th-century restoration chopped off two of them and amputated the legs of the others.

The church is dedicated to Pudentiana, the daughter of a Roman senator, who is said to have given hospitality to St Peter on the site that is now occupied by the church. Most of the facade was added in the 19th century although elements from the earlier buildings, such as the delicately carved frieze and medallions dating from the 11th century, were retained. The Romanesque arched windows and the bell tower date from the 12th century.

CHIESA DI SS QUATTRO CORONATI

Map pp320–1

Via dei Santissimi Quattro Coronati 20; ⏰ 8am-noon & 4-6pm; bus or tram to Labicana

The four crowned saints to whom this fortified medieval convent is dedicated were four Christian sculptors killed for refusing to make a statue of a pagan god. The squat bell tower dates from the 9th century. Note the extremely well-preserved 13th-century frescoes of St Sylvester and Constantine in the **Cappella di San Silvestro**. There is also a pretty early-13th-century cloister and garden off the northern aisle (ring the bell for admission).

PIAZZA DI SPAGNA & AROUND

COLONNA DELL'IMMACOLATA

Map pp314–16

Piazza Mignanelli; metro Spagna

To the right of the Spanish Steps, in Piazza Mignanelli, is the Colonna dell'Immacolata, crowned with a statue of the Virgin Mary. On 8 December each year, local firefighters climb up a ladder to place a wreath on the arm of the Virgin Mary. Many moons ago, a more nimble Pope John Paul II did the honours.

KEATS-SHELLEY HOUSE Map pp314–16

☎ 06 678 42 35; www.keats-shelley-house.org; Piazza di Spagna 26; admission €2.60; ⏰ 9am-1pm & 2.30-5.30pm Mon-Fri; metro Spagna

The melodramatic Romantics were drawn to Italy, where little good befell them. John Keats came to Rome in 1820, desperately hoping the Italian climate would improve his failing health. He lived his last agonising months in this house to the right of the Spanish Steps, and died here in February 1821 at the age of 25. Shelley drowned off the coast of Tuscany in a particularly desperate period of his life. The house is a small museum that's crammed with memorabilia of the two great poets plus Mary Shelley, Lord Byron and the other Romantics who spent time in the neighbourhood.

PIAZZA DI SPAGNA Map pp308–10

metro Spagna

This exquisite piazza, and especially the famous **Spanish Steps** (Scalinata di Spagna), has acted as a magnet for foreigners since the 18th century when so many Grand Tourists descended on the area that it came to be known as the *ghetto de l'inglesi* (English ghetto).

Built in 1725 with French money – but designed by a Spaniard and named after the Spanish Embassy nearby – the elegant steps were built to connect the piazza with the eminent folk who lived above it. During the 18th century, the most beautiful men and women used to gather here hoping to be chosen as artists' models. They, of course, became a separate attraction and, ever since, the steps have become a superlative spot for a sit-and-stare (or pester and proposition in the case of Rome's suburban youth).

The **Barcaccia** (loosely translated as 'the old tub') is the unusual fountain at the foot of the steps and was the last work of Pietro Bernini, father of the more famous Gian Lorenzo.

Opposite the steps is Via Condotti, the swishest shopping strip in the city. Each April a fashion show is held in and around the piazza, and the tourists are replaced on the steps with a blaze of pink azaleas.

While the steps might look like the perfect spot for a picnic, don't get too excited: theoretically you're not allowed to eat while sitting here. The municipal police who patrol the area can be quite strict and transgressors can be fined.

PINCIO Map pp304–5

metro Spagna

The Viale Trinità dei Monti at the top of the Spanish Steps leads to the Pincio, named after the Pinci family who owned it in the 4th century. (If you can't manage the steps there's a lift to the top outside the Piazza di Spagna metro station.) Don't miss the view from here of St Peter's Basilica. Giuseppe Valadier designed the shady gardens (which adjoin Villa Borghese) in the early 19th century. Go for a stroll and follow in the footsteps of Keats, Strauss, Gandhi and – if you take short steps – Mussolini.

Pincio is also accessible from Piazza del Popolo (see p89).

VILLA MEDICI Map pp306–7

☎ 06 6 76 11; www.villamedici.it (French only); Viale Trinità dei Monti 1; ⏰ open for events; metro Spagna

One of Rome's best pieces of real estate with one of the city's best views, the palace was built for Cardinal Ricci da Montepulciano in 1540. Ferdinando dei Medici bought it in 1576 and it remained his family's property until Napoleon acquired it in 1801, when the French Academy was transferred here. The academy was founded in 1666 to provide talented French artists, writers and musicians – *Prix de Rome* winners – with an opportunity to study and absorb Rome's enormous classical heritage.

A good way to get inside the building is by seeing one of the regular art exhibitions that are held there. Guided tours of the villa's spectacular gardens are conducted intermittently; call for information.

QUIRINAL TO THE TREVI FOUNTAIN

CHIESA DI SAN BERNARDO ALLE TERME Map pp314–16

Piazza San Bernardo; metro Repubblica

The late-16th-century church was built into the ruins of a circular tower that had been part of the Terme di Diocleziano. Like the Pantheon, the church has a dome with a small *oculus* (round window) at the top to illuminate the interior.

FONTANA DELL'ACQUA FELICE

Map pp314–16
cnr Via XX Settembre & Via Vittorio Emanuele Orlando; metro Repubblica

This is also known as the Moses Fountain because of the huge figure of Moses in its central niche. It was designed by Domenico Fontana and finished in 1586 to mark the terminus of the Acqua Felice aqueduct, which carried clean water to this part of the city for the first time. The water may still be relatively clean but the statues, which are suffering from pollution caused by passing traffic, are filthy.

GALLERIA COLONNA Map pp314–16

☎ 06 678 43 50; www.galleriacolonna.it; admission €7; ☽ 9am-1pm Sat only, closed Aug; bus to Piazza Venezia

This gallery, open only on Saturday morning, holds one of the city's most important private art collections. The entrance is at Via della Pilotta 17, a pretty street spanned by four arches which connect the **Palazzo Colonna** to its gardens. The vestibule, at the top of the stairs, leads into the **Sala della Colonna Bellica** lined with fine portraits of Colonna family members and others. In the centre of the room is a carved *colonna* (column) of red marble dating from the 16th century. Steps lead down to the lavishly gilded **Salone** – don't trip over the cannon ball which became lodged there during the 1849 siege of Rome.

The treasures are spread under a loud and lovely ceiling painted by Sebastiano Ricci. Among the artists competing for your attention are Salvator Rosa, Guido Reni and Guercino, but it's Annibale Carracci's charming *The Bean Eater* that you remember best. In the next room, a chair is kept ready (turned to the wall) in case of a papal visit.

MUSEO NAZIONALE ROMANO: PALAZZO MASSIMO ALLE TERME

Map pp314–16
☎ 06 399 67 700; entrance at Largo di Villa Peretti 1; admission €6; ☽ 9am-7.45pm Tue-Sun; metro Repubblica, bus to Piazza della Repubblica

The **Palazzo Massimo alle Terme**, part of the **Museo Nazionale Romano** collection boasts some of the best examples of Roman art in the city. It took 16 years to transform the 19th-century building, a former Jesuit college, into a museum. It is one of Rome's best – light-filled, spacious and blissfully air-conditioned in summer.

The ground and 1st floors are devoted to sculpture and statuary dating from the end of

The Palazzo Massimo alle Terme

the Republican age (2nd to 1st centuries BC) to the late-Imperial era (4th century AD). Some original 5th-century-BC Greek sculptures are dotted among the numerous Roman copies of Greek originals and the portraits of emperors and their families and of eminent citizens.

One of the first pieces you see as you enter is *Minerva*, a huge polychrome statue of the goddess made of alabaster, white marble and black basalt. The face is a modern plaster cast taken from another statue of Minerva. The statue, possibly inspired by early Greek artists working on the Italian peninsula, was found at the bottom of the Aventine, and probably formed part of a temple to Minerva on the hill.

An airy courtyard is surrounded by three long galleries containing portrait busts, off which are rooms arranged thematically. The first two contain funerary reliefs, portrait busts and statues of emperors, statesmen and their families. These were commissioned works and represented the ruling classes as they wanted to be depicted. Realism had little to do with these idealised statues, which were carved at a time when self-glorification was the order of the day.

An anonymous Republican general (in Sala I) depicted in heroic nudity, semidraped with his armour next to him, shows evidence of Greek sculpting techniques and dates from the 1st century BC. A full-length portrait of Augustus (in Sala V) depicts him as Pontifex Maximus

(Chief Priest), his head covered with a fold of his toga. A portrait head of Augustus' wife Livia, with her distinctive braided hairdo, is one of many images of the emperor's wife which had a strong influence on private portraiture of the period.

Terracottas, reconstructed from various fragments found in the area of the Domus Tiberiana on the Palatine in the 1980s, are on display in Sala VI. Sala VII contains a superb original Greek sculpture, dating from the 5th century BC, of a young woman trying to extract an arrow from her back. The statue, along with other Greek originals, was found in the Horti Sallustiani (now the Via Veneto area), which belonged to Julius Caesar and was later the estate of the Roman historian Sallust. In the 17th century, it was also where Ludovico Ludovisi housed his magnificent collection of ancient statuary, which is now part of the Museo Nazionale Romano.

Sculptures from the time of the Flavian emperors (late 1st to 4th century AD) demonstrate various iconographic trends in official Roman art. Among the highlights (Sala V) are pieces that come from Nero's residence at Anzio (two full length statues) and a wonderfully naturalistic image of a voluptuous *Afrodite* crouching down, a Roman copy of a Greek original from the Villa Adriana at Tivoli.

The badly damaged *Apollo del Tevere* in Sala VI shows what too long in polluted water can do to marble; this piece was discovered in the banks of the Tiber during the embankment process in the late 19th century. In the same room are the *Discobolus Lancellotti* and the *Discobolus di Castelporziano*, two marble statues of a discus thrower copied from one of the most famous of all Greek bronzes.

The highlight of Palazzo Massimo is the collection of Roman paintings and mosaics displayed on the 2nd floor. Many of these rare pieces have been out of public view for decades and have undergone extensive restoration. Thoughtfully installed in their new home, these examples of Roman interior decoration positively sparkle.

Among the most beautiful are the frescoes (in Sala II) from the Villa Livia, a house that belonged to the wife of Augustus. The villa, located on the Via Flaminia north of Rome, was excavated in the 19th century. The frescoes were removed from the villa in 1951 and transferred to the Museo Nazionale Romano. The room in which they were originally painted was half underground and covered by a barrel vault decorated with stuccoes and reliefs

(unfortunately only a small part of this vault decoration has survived and is too delicate to exhibit). It was probably a summer *triclinium*, a large living and dining area protected from the heat, and has been recreated in Palazzo Massimo in a specially constructed gallery space. The frescoes, which totally surround you, depict an illusionary garden with all the plants in full bloom, regardless of the season. There are tall cypresses, pines and oak trees, shrubs and bushes of oleander, myrtle and laurel, and fruit trees abundant with ripe pomegranates and quinces. The style dates from between 20 and 10 BC.

Frescoes from an ancient-Roman villa, found in the grounds of Villa Farnesina, are on display in Galleria II and Sale III, IV and V. The villa was discovered and excavated in the 19th century during the embankment of the Tiber. Dating from around 20 BC, these frescoes are among the most important surviving examples of Roman painting. It is thought that the villa belonged to an important figure close to Augustus' circle. The substantial fragments illustrate clearly the style and taste of the period. There is a great variety of decoration: landscapes, narrative friezes that have an almost Egyptian appearance, and illusionary architectural elements such as columns, cornices and vases.

The museum also boasts a stunning collection of inlaid marble and mosaics, including (in Sala VII) the surviving wall mosaics from a *nymphaeum* at Nero's villa in Anzio. In the basement is an extensive display of ancient and medieval coins, including a collection donated to the state by King Victor Emmanuel II.

MUSEO NAZIONALE ROMANO: TERME DI DIOCLEZIANO Map pp314–16

☎ 06 399 67 700; Viale Enrico de Nicola 78; admission €5; ☾ 9am-7.45pm Tue-Sun; metro Repubblica or Termini

The portion of the Museo Nazionale Romano treasures housed here is relatively small compared to other venues but the real draw is the ruins of the baths themselves. **Terme di Diocleziano** (Diocletian's baths) – built at the turn of the 3rd century – were the largest in ancient Rome and could accommodate 3000 people at a time. The *caldarium* (hot room) extended into what is now Piazza della Repubblica. After the aqueduct which fed the baths was destroyed by invaders in about AD 536, the complex fell into disrepair.

Designed by Michelangelo, the **Chiesa di Santa Maria degli Angeli** incorporates what was the great central hall and *tepidarium* (lukewarm room) of the original baths. During the following centuries his work was drastically changed and little evidence of his design, apart from the great vaulted ceiling, remains. An interesting feature of the church is a double meridian in the transept, one tracing the polar star and the other telling the precise time of the sun's zenith, visible at midday (solar time). The church is open 7.30am to 6.30pm. Through the sacristy is an entrance to a stairway leading to the upper terraces of the ruins. A plaque near the stairway records the traditional belief that the baths were built by thousands of Christian slaves.

The **cloister** was for many years attributed to Michelangelo but this is unlikely – it was built in 1565, a year after his death. In the centre is a 17th-century fountain surrounded by cypress trees, one of which dates from the same period. There are also huge statues of animals' heads, thought to have come from the Foro di Traiano. Lining the cloister are ruins of columns and capitals, friezes, sarcophagi and (mostly headless) statues.

The modern and airy ground-floor and 1st-floor galleries contain a display of epigraphs with informative panels in English and Italian on their production and place in history. A large collection of vases, amphorae and household objects in terracotta and bronze are also on display. Among the highlights are three stunning terracotta statues of seated female figures that were found in the Ariccia area southeast of Rome. The extensive 2nd-floor galleries contain artefacts (mainly burial objects such as jewellery and domestic items) from Italian protohistory – 11th to 6th century BC – when communities in the Lazio region evolved from tribal structures towards the beginning of city states. There are also galleries devoted to much more recent ethnographic objects from the Pacific Islands.

PIAZZA DELLA REPUBBLICA Map pp314–16
metro Repubblica
Symbolising the transition from ancient to modern Rome, this piazza follows the line of the semicircular *exedra* (benched portico) of the ancient bath complex that stood here (see p102). The fountain in its centre, the **Fontana delle Naiadi**, was designed by Mario Rutelli and features a central figure of Glaucus wrestling a fish, surrounded by four naiads or water nymphs. When the fountain is shooting the right way the nymphs really do look like they are frolicking in the water. The scantily clad figures caused a furore when they were first put in place in 1901. The models for the curvaceous nymphs were two sisters, well-known musical stars of their day. It is said that in their old age the sisters visited the fountain daily and that once a year the sculptor would travel from his native Sicily to take them out to dinner.

PALAZZO COLONNA Map pp314–16
Piazza dei Santissimi Apostoli; bus to Piazza Venezia
It was begun in the 15th century for Pope Martin V (who lived here from 1424 until his death in 1431), although most of the building dates from the 18th century. It is still occupied by members of the Colonna family. The private gardens behind the palace, on the site of a 3rd-century Temple of Serapis, rise in terraces to the grounds of the Palazzo del Quirinale. The *palazzo* houses one of the city's most important private art collections, but is open only on Saturday morning (see Galleria Colonna, p101).

PALAZZO DELLE ESPOSIZIONI
Map pp314–16
☎ 06 474 59 03; www.palaexpo.com (Italian only);
✆ closed for renovation; bus to Via Nazionale
This vast 19th-century building is Rome's most prominent cultural centre and has made a name for itself with a vibrant program of multimedia events, art exhibitions, performances and cinemas. It once housed the Communist Party and was used as a mess for allied servicemen. It also served as a polling station and as a public loo. At the time of writing it was closed again for major renovation with plans to reopen in 2004.

PALAZZO MUTI Map pp314–16
Piazza dei Santissimi Apostoli; bus to Piazza Venezia
At the end of the square is the baroque **Palazzo Muti** which was given to James Stuart, the Old Pretender, in 1719 by Pope Clement XI.

PALAZZO ODELSCALCHI Map pp314–16
Piazza dei Santissimi Apostoli; bus to Piazza Venezia
The facade of the building opposite Santi Apostoli church, **Palazzo Odelscalchi**, was designed by Bernini in 1664.

PIAZZA DEL QUIRINALE Map pp314–16
bus to Via Nazionale
The Quirinal Hill (Quirinale) is the highest of Rome's seven hills. At its summit is the **Palazzo del Quirinale**, in the square of the same name, the official residence of the president of the republic.

PALAZZO DEL QUIRINALE Map pp314–16

☎ 06 469 92 568; Piazza del Quirinale; admission €5.16; ☺ 8.30am-12.30pm Sun (unless there are official receptions); bus to Via Nazionale

This immense *palazzo* served as the papal summer residence for almost three centuries until the keys were handed over, begrudgingly and staring down the barrel of a gun, to Italy's new king in 1870 and then to the president of the Republic in 1946. Domenico Fontana designed the main facade, Carlo Maderno the chapel, and Bernini was responsible for the long wing that runs the length of Via del Quirinale. The **obelisk** in the centre of the square was moved here from the Mausoleo di Augusto in 1786. It is flanked by large statues of the Dioscuri, Castor and Pollux, which are Imperial Roman copies of 5th-century-BC Greek originals. Changing of the (two) guards takes place at 3pm Monday to Saturday and 4pm Sunday. The *palazzo* is open to the public on Sunday morning, when there is a free concert series at 11am in the chapel.

PIAZZA DEI SANTISSIMI APOSTOLI
Map pp314–16
bus to Piazza Venezia

The long, thin Piazza dei Santissimi Apostoli runs off Via Cesare Battisti, east of Piazza Venezia. It is a popular place for political demonstrations.

CHIESA DI SAN CARLO ALLE QUATTRO FONTANE Map pp314–16

Via del Quirinale; ☺ 10am-1pm & 3-4pm Mon-Fri, 10am-1pm Sat, 11am-1pm Sun; bus to Via Nazionale

Completed in 1641, this is the first church Borromini designed in Rome, and one of his great masterpieces. The elegant curves of the facade, the play of convex and concave surfaces inside and the dome illuminated by hidden windows ingeniously transform this tiny space.

The church stands at the intersection known as **Quattro Fontane**, after the late-16th-century fountains at its four corners which represent Fidelity, Strength and the Rivers Aniene and Tiber. From the intersection you can see Porta Pia and the obelisks of the Quirinal, Trinità dei Monti and the Esquiline.

CHIESA DI SANTA MARIA DELLA VITTORIA Map pp314–16

☎ 06 482 61 90; Via XX Settembre 17; metro Repubblica

This modest church is most famous for Bernini's highly theatrical and sexually charged

sculpture, the *Ecstasy of St Teresa*, in the last chapel on the left. The saint is in rapture as a teasing angel pierces her repeatedly with a golden arrow. The spectators along the wall include Cardinal Federico Cornaro, for whom the chapel was built. Whatever Teresa's up to, it's a stunning work, bathed in soft natural light filtering through a concealed window. Go in the afternoon for the most stunning effect. Below is a gilded-bronze relief of the Last Supper. The second chapel on the left as you enter the church contains an altarpiece by Domenichino, *La Madonna che Porge il Bambino a San Francesco*, depicting the Madonna showing the baby Jesus to St Francis. The late-19th-century apse fresco commemorates the victory of a Catholic army over Protestant forces in Prague in 1620.

CHIESA DI SANT'ANDREA AL QUIRINALE Map pp314–16

☎ 06 489 03 187; Via del Quirinale 29; ☺ 9am-noon & 4-7pm Mon-Fri, 9am-noon Sat; bus to Via Nazionale

This church is considered one of Bernini's masterpieces. In his old age he liked to come and enjoy it himself. He designed it with an elliptical floor plan and with a series of chapels opening onto the central area. The interior is decorated with polychrome marble, stucco and gilding. Note the cherubs that decorate the lantern of the dome. After hiking through some of the supersized basilicas in Rome, the smaller scale feels intimate.

CHIESA DI SANTA SUSANNA
Map pp314–16
Via XX Settembre 15; metro Repubblica

The Catholic church of the American community in Rome. Dating from the 4th century, the church was rebuilt several times. The impressive facade was added by Carlo Maderno in 1603 and is considered his masterpiece.

CHIESA DI SANTI APOSTOLI Map pp314–16

Piazza dei Santissimi Apostoli; ☺ 7am-noon & 4-7pm; bus to Piazza Venezia

Originally built in the 6th century and dedicated to the Apostles James and Philip (whose relics are in the crypt), the church was enlarged in the 15th and 16th centuries and then rebuilt in the early 18th century by Carlo and Francesco Fontana who were responsible for the baroque interior. The unusual facade with Renaissance arches dates from the early

16th century. The church contains the tomb of Pope Clement XIV by Antonio Canova.

ST PAUL'S WITHIN-THE-WALLS
Map pp314–16
cnr Via Nazionale & Via Napoli; metro Repubblica
This American Episcopal church is famous for its magnificent mosaics designed by the 19th-century Birmingham-born Edward Burne-Jones. In his representation of The Church on Earth, Burne-Jones followed the Renaissance tradition of employing the faces of his famous contemporaries in his portraits. St Ambrose (on the extreme right of the centre group) got JP Morgan's face, and General Garibaldi and Abraham Lincoln (wearing a green tunic) are among the warriors.

TREVI FOUNTAIN Map pp314–16
bus to Piazza di San Silvestro
Rome's largest and most famous fountain, Fontana di Trevi, was completed by Nicola Salvi in 1762, and famously graced 200 years later by Marcello Mastroianni and Anita Ekberg (spilling out of a black strapless gown) in Fellini's *La Dolce Vita*. It takes up most of the piazza, appears to meld into the *palazzo*, and depicts Neptune's chariot being led by Tritons with seahorses – one wild, one docile – representing the moods of the sea. Trevi refers to the three roads *(tre vie)* that converged here.

Water for the fountain is supplied by one of Rome's earliest aqueducts. Work to clean the fountain and its water supply was completed in 1991, but the effects of pollution have already dulled the brilliant white of the clean marble.

The famous custom is to throw a coin into the fountain (over your shoulder while facing away) to ensure you return to Rome. For a second coin you can make a sure you'll fall in love with an Italian. The third coin will have you marrying him or her. The terraces around the fountain are always packed with tourists throwing coins and, on average, €118,785 is recovered from the basin each year (see the boxed text, p106).

TEATRO DELL'OPERA DI ROMA
Map pp314–16
Piazza B Gigli 1; bus to via Nazionale
The Fascist-era exterior hides a richly decorated 19th-century interior of plush red-velvet seats, gilded stucco and a glittering chandelier in the centre of the auditorium (see p198).

VIA NAZIONALE Map pp314–16
This busy shopping street and traffic thoroughfare connects Piazza della Repubblica to the Quirinal and Piazza Venezia.

Via Condotti Map p210
metro Spagna
If you're hunting for the source of the river of chic Romans flowing past you, look no further. Via Condotti is it, the city's most elegant shopping street. Gucci, Bulgari and Armani are here, attracting the people who love and wear them. Two centuries ago, it was stylish in a very different way: the street belonged to the writers and the musicians who'd meet at the famous **Caffè Greco** (No 86).

Other top shopping streets in the area include Via Frattina, Via della Croce and Via delle Carrozze (see Shopping, p211, for more details). Another exclusive shopping street is **Via del Babuino**, which runs off Piazza di Spagna towards Piazza del Popolo. The pretty **Via Margutta** (parallel to Via del Babuino; Map pp304–5) is lined with art galleries and antique shops. The Italian film director Federico Fellini lived in Via Margutta for many years.

VIA VITTORIO VENETO & PIAZZA BARBERINI Map pp314–16
metro Barberini
Through the 1960s, this was the street that

The Trevi Fountain

Penny Wise

If the pickpockets don't relieve you of it first, throw a coin into the Trevi Fountain and legend has it that you'll someday return to Rome. Virtually every visitor tosses a coin (or two if the photo didn't work the first time), which adds up to a pretty penny in the pool.

The cache ostensibly goes to the Catholic charity Caritas, but there was uproar in 2002 when the press revealed that a homeless, mentally unstable man who went by the name 'D'Artagnan' had been conducting dawn raids of the fountain. For more than 30 years, he used magnets and a rake to bag up to €1000 a day in myriad currencies.

For some time, it was not clear he was breaking any laws. The high court had ruled in 1994 that taking coins from Rome's fountains was as legal as tossing them in. Moreover, D'Artagnan was the Robin Hood of the Trevi: he claimed he gave his loot away to other homeless and needy people. He owned nothing of value and didn't seem to be holding on to the money he collected.

But a 1999 law, aimed mostly at cheeky foreign students on drunken rampages, prohibited swimming or wading in the city's fountains, and imposed a hefty €500 fine on trespassers. (Note the international 'do not swim' icon now posted at Rome's most tempting decorative pools.) The police fined D'Artagnan several times and were ignored. Conversion to the euro put a much bigger damper on his scheme – his magnet was useless on them. But when the press got a hold of the story in 2002, the public was outraged and police took D'Artagnan more seriously, banning him from the fountain. The self-proclaimed certifiably insane man slashed at his own stomach with a razor in protest, and threatened to slash his wrists if the police continued to harass him.

put the *dolce* in Rome's *vita* – off-duty film stars could avail themselves of the paparazzi's cameras from dusk until dawn. But the atmosphere of Fellini's Rome is long dead, and the street today is little more than a thoroughfare for traffic to and from the centre. The US embassy in the late-19th-century Palazzo Margherita takes up a sizable chunk of the street. You can still pay through the nose for a meal or a coffee in one of the glass-enclosed restaurants if you want, but the premium's a waste here. Go to Piazza Navona instead.

CAPUCHIN CEMETERY/CHIESA DI SANTA MARIA DELLA CONCEZIONE

☎ 06 487 11 85; Via Vittorio Veneto 27; admission by donation; ☼ 9am-noon & 3-6pm; metro Barberini

Long after all the rest of Rome's interiors run together in the memory, visitors vividly recall the particulars of these bizarre and macabre chapels, where the decorative elements are all made of human bones. Between 1528 and 1870, the brown-clad Capuchin monks adorned this cemetery with the dried remains of their departed brothers. The message is appropriately pious: 'What you are now we used to be, what we are now you will be'. The effect is rather sensational. There is an arch crafted from hundreds of skulls, vertebrae used as fleurs-de-lis, and light fixtures made of limb bones. The monks who

guard the cemetery request a 'compulsory' donation, so have some small notes handy.

The **Chiesa di Santa Maria della Concezione**, above the cemetery, contains a gorgeous *St Michael* by Reni (in the first chapel to the right of the door) and Pietro da Cortona's *St Paul's Sight Being Restored* (first chapel on the left).

PIAZZA BARBERINI Map pp314–16
metro Barberini

The Barberini family was not only for a time Rome's most powerful, but it had the coolest heraldic crest: three bees in flight. In and around Piazza Barberini, there are swarms of the iconic bees. Best, perhaps, are those in Bernini's charming **Fontana delle Api** (Fountain of the Bees) in the northwestern corner of the square. Bernini also crafted the spectacular **Fontana del Tritone** (Triton Fountain) in the traffic-swamped centre of the piazza. Triton, with an enviable washboard stomach, blows a stream of water from a conch shell. He is seated in a large scallop shell that is supported by four dolphins.

PALAZZO BARBERINI/GALLERIA NAZIONALE D'ARTE ANTICA

☎ 06 481 45 91; www.galleriaborghese.it; entrance at Via Barberini 18; admission €6; ☼ 9am-7pm Tue-Sat, 9am-8pm Sun; metro Barberini

There's hardly a 17th-century genius who *didn't* leave his mark on the splendid palace created for the Barberini pope, Urban VIII. Carlo Maderno was the original architect, and the facade is a variation on Raphael's design. The two great rivals of the baroque face off on the staircases (the round one on the right is Borromini, the square one on the left, Bernini). Borromini also worked his perspective juju on the windows on the upper story, which seem from a distance to be the same size as those on the floor below, but in fact are significantly smaller. Pietro da Cortona is responsible for the grand vault fresco, *Trionfo della Divina Provvidenza* (Triumph of Divine Providence), on the first floor of the palace.

The palace houses part of the **Galleria Nazionale d'Arte Antica**, an invaluable collection that's strongest in paintings of the 16th and 17th centuries. The collection is arranged chronologically. Famous pieces include Raphael's *La Fornarina*, a beguiling portrait of a woman widely believed to be his lover. (She's been tentatively identified as Margherita Lut, daughter of a baker. She entered a convent immediately following Raphael's death.) Cool down with the chaste and ethereal *Annunziazione* by Filippo Lippi, who loosed all his virtuosity on the wings of the angel at the left, before confronting Guido Reni's *Portrait of Beatrice Cenci*. The lurid story of Beatrice's tragedy has been told by Stendhal and Dumas, and immortalised by Shelley in his play, *The Cenci* (for more details of Beatrice Cenci see the boxed text, p86).

Two paintings by Bernini, a portrait of Urban VIII and *Davide con la Testa di Golia*, depicting David with the head of Goliath, show that his skill lay in sculpture and architecture rather than painting. There are two paintings by Caravaggio, *Judith e Holfernes*, a gruesome masterpiece of theatrical lighting, and *Narcissus*. A recent addition to the collection is Jacopo Zucchi's *Il Bagno di Betsabea* (Bathsheba's Bath). Dating from the late 1580s, this piece was lost after WWII, found in Paris, bought by an American museum and returned to Italy in 1998.

BEYOND THE CITY WALLS

San Lorenzo

Young artists and students from La Sapienza University have created a hipster Renaissance in this neighbourhood just northeast of Termini. It's always been a radical neighbourhood. In the 1920s, San Lorenzo's working class took to the streets against the Fascists. Take bus No 71 from Piazza di San Silvestro or No 492 from Piazza Venezia or Stazione Termini.

CIMITERO DI CAMPO VERANO
Map pp302–3
Piazzale del Verano; bus or tram to Piazzale del Verano
The city's largest cemetery was designed by Giuseppe Valadier between 1807 and 1812. From the 1830s to the 1980s virtually all Catholics who died in Rome (with the exception of popes, cardinals and royalty) were buried here. Today, the main cemetery and crematorium is located north of Rome at Prima Porta. Campo Verano gets particularly crowded with people and flowers on *I Morti* (All Souls' Day), 2 November, when thousands of Romans flock to visit their dear departed and the Pope says a special Mass.

BASILICA DI SAN LORENZO FUORI-LE-MURA Map pp302–3
Piazzale del Verano 3; ☾ 7.30am-noon & 4-6.30pm; bus or tram to Piazzale del Verano
In the heart of San Lorenzo you'll find one of Rome's seven pilgrimage churches, dedicated to the martyred St Lawrence, who was slowly cooked to death face down over a bed of coals for distributing some of the church's funds to the people instead of the Roman government. The original structure was erected by Constantine in the 4th century over St Lawrence's burial place, but it was rebuilt in 579 by Pope Pelagius II. Alterations in the 8th through to the 13th century included the incorporation of a nearby 5th-century church by knocking the two buildings into one. The nave, portico and much of the decoration date from the 13th century. San Lorenzo was the only church in Rome to suffer serious damage during WWII.

Inside, a Cosmati floor and 13th-century frescos are the must-see highlights. The remains of St Lawrence and St Stephen are in the church crypt beneath the high altar. A pretty barrel-vaulted cloister contains inscriptions and sarcophagi and leads to the **Catacombe di Santa Ciriaca** where St Lawrence was initially buried (ask the sacristan for admission).

TRASTEVERE

Eating p167; Shopping p217; Sleeping p234

Native Romans may rightly claim they are an endangered species in the city-at-large, but not in Trastevere, where a pocket of old timers keeps the old traditions alive. The name comes from *trans Tiberim* (across the Tiber), and the settlement at Trastevere was, in early time, separate from Rome. Though it was soon swallowed up by urban growth, this notion of separation has survived. Trastevere residents still regard themselves as *noantri*, or 'we others'. These most venerable Romans live cheek-by-jowl with

the newest arrivals, for Trastevere is a magnet for foreign students and residents, attracted by the chic trattorie, picturesque streets, and numerous bars that cater to their tastes.

Neighbourhoods – Trastevere

CHIESA DI SAN FRANCESCO D'ASSISI A RIPA Map pp317–19

Piazza San Francesco d'Assisi 88; ⏲ 7.30am-noon & 4-7pm; bus or tram to Viale di Trastevere

St Francis of Assisi stayed on the site of this 17th-century church when he visited in the 13th century. They've preserved the rock the saint used as a pillow, but much more interesting is Bernini's *Ecstasy of Beata Ludovica Albertoni*, in the fourth chapel on the left. The more famous *Ecstasy of St Teresa* has nothing on her.

BASILICA DI SANTA CECILIA IN TRASTEVERE Map pp317–19

Piazza di Santa Cecilia; admission to ruins & fresco €2; ⏲ church 9.30am-12.30pm, 3.45-6.30pm; fresco 10am-noon Tue & Thu, 11.30am-12.30pm Sun (after Mass); bus or tram to Viale di Trastevere

This 9th-century church was built over the house of St Cecilia, on the spot where she was (eventually) martyred in 230. Cecilia was the Christian wife of Valerian, a Roman patrician. Despite her marriage, she kept her vow of chastity and her husband was so impressed by her faith that he too converted. Valerian was martyred for this act; Cecilia was arrested while burying his body and was subsequently martyred too. Her murderers first tried to scald her to death by locking her in the *caldarium* (hot room) of the baths in her own house. She emerged unscathed and was then beheaded, but the executioner did such a bad job that she took three days to die. Legend has it that she sang as she was dying and, for this reason, she became the patron saint of music and musicians. When her tomb was opened in 1599, the body was miraculously intact and sketched by Stefano Maderno for the exquisite sculpture beneath the altar. His inscription reads: 'Behold the body

of the most holy virgin Cecilia, whom I myself saw lying incorrupt in her tomb. I have in this marble expressed for thee the same saint in the very same posture of body'. There are also ruins of a Roman building to visit below the church, and some precious fragments of a 13th-century Pietro Cavallini fresco.

Transport

Bus H to Viale di Trastevere; 23, 280 to Lungotevere; 44 to Giacinlo Carini
Tram 8 to Viale di Trastevere

An 18th-century facade leads into a pretty courtyard and then to the portico, decorated with colourful 12th-century mosaic medallions, and to the baroque facade of the church itself. The impressive mosaic in the apse was executed in 870 and features Christ giving a blessing. To his right are St Peter, St Valerian (husband of St Cecilia) and St Cecilia. To his left are St Paul, St Agatha and St Paschal. The holy cities are depicted underneath. The *baldacchino* over the main altar was carved by Arnolfo di Cambio.

In the right-hand nave the **Cappella del Caldarium** marks the spot where the saint was allegedly tortured with steam for three days before being martyred. There are two works by Guido Reni here.

Of great interest are the excavations of Roman houses, one of which was perhaps the house of St Cecilia, underneath the church. These ruins are accessible from the room at the end of the left aisle as you enter the church. Note the large room with deep basins in the floor, thought to have been a tannery, the remains of black-and-white mosaic paving and the elaborate crypt which was decorated in the 19th century in Byzantine style.

There is a superb 13th-century fresco of *The Last Judgement* by Pietro Cavallini in the nun's choir, entered through the convent. The fresco used to be the inside facade of the old church. It was boarded up for many years and only rediscovered around 1900, hence its excellent state of preservation and amazingly rich colours and clear details.

CHIESA DI SAN CRISOGONO Map pp317–19
Piazza Sonnino; 🕙 **7-11.30am & 4-7.30pm; bus or tram to Viale di Trastevere**

Beneath this building on busy Viale di Trastevere are the remains of an early-Christian church dating from the 5th century, which was itself built on a *titulus*, a private house used for secret Christian worship.

PIAZZA SANTA MARIA IN TRASTEVERE Map pp317–19
bus or tram to Viale di Trastevere

Trastevere is prime people-watching territory, and this piazza is the heart of the district. By day, it's peopled by mums with strollers, chatting locals and guidebook-toting tourists. By night, it's the domain of foreign students getting their first taste of *la dolce vita*, young Romans looking for a good time and the odd homeless person looking for a bed. It's worth paying extra for a cappuccino or an *aperitivo* to sit down at one of the bars in the square. You'll enjoy not only a great view but also the passing people parade.

The fountain in the centre of the square is of Roman origin and was restored by Carlo Fontana in 1692. An ancient legend says that on the day that Christ was born a miraculous fountain of pure oil sprang from the ground in this area and flowed for a whole day down to the Tiber. **Via della Fonte d'Olio**, a small street leading off the northern side of the square, commemorates this event.

BASILICA DI SANTA MARIA IN TRASTEVERE Map pp317–19
Piazza Santa Maria in Trastevere; 🕙 **7am-8pm (but inconsistent); bus or tram to Viale di Trastevere**

This is likely the oldest place of worship dedicated to the Virgin in Rome. Tradition has it that the church was established by Pope Calixtus in the early 3rd century AD and subsequently rebuilt by Julius I in 337. The present structure was built in 1138 by Innocent II and features a Romanesque facade, with a stunning 12th-century mosaic of the Virgin feeding the baby Jesus flanked by 10 women holding lamps. Two tiny figures kneeling at the Virgin's feet were probably donors to the church. At the top of the Romanesque bell tower (whose bells ring every 15 minutes) is a small mosaic of the Virgin. The portico, embedded with fragments of ancient and medieval sculpture, inscriptions and sarcophagi, was added by Carlo Fontana in 1702.

The impressive interior features 21 irregular ancient Roman columns with Ionian and Corinthian capitals, some of which come from the Terme di Caracalla. The wooden ceiling was designed in 1617 by Domenichino, who painted the central panel depicting the Assumption of the Virgin. The mosaics in the apse and on the triumphal arch date from 1140 and are absolutely stunning. At the top of the triumphal arch are the symbols and names of the four Evangelists. On either side are Isaiah and Jeremiah, each with an image of a caged bird representing Christ imprisoned by the sins of humankind. At the top of the apse are the signs of the zodiac, beneath which is a splendid mosaic against a gold background of the Christ and the Virgin enthroned. They are flanked by various saints and, on the far left, Pope Innocent II holding a model of the church. Note the richly patterned and detailed robes of the Virgin. Below this is a series of six mosaics by Pietro Cavallini (c 1291) illustrating the life of the Virgin.

On the right of the altar is a beautiful Cosmati Paschal candlestick placed, it is said, on the exact spot of the miraculous fountain of oil. The small chapel on the left of the altar, the **Cappella Altemps**, is decorated with frescoes and stuccoes (1588). A Byzantine painting of the Madonna and angels, dating from the 8th century or earlier, was once the altarpiece and is now substituted by a photograph. The badly deteriorated original is displayed in a room to the left.

CHIESA DI SANTA MARIA DELLA SCALA Map pp308–10
Piazza Santa Maria della Scala 23; 🕙 **7am-12.30pm & 3.30-7pm; bus to Lungotevere Farnesina**

The recently restored **Chiesa di Santa Maria della Scala** dates from a great building boom at the turn of the 17th century. The exterior is modest, but the interior is gloriously baroque. Next door, the historic **Farmacia di Santa Maria della Scala** is still run by monks from the adjacent monastery. If it's open, go in and have a look.

PORTA SETTIMIANO Map pp308–10

bus to Lungotevere della Farnesina

Passing through the city walls at **Porta Settimiano**, you reach the long, straight Via della Lungara, built by Pope Julius II to connect the area of the Borgo (near the Vatican) to Trastevere, and Palazzo Corsini, the Orto Botanico and Villa Farnesina (right).

From Porta Settimiano, Via di Santa Dorotea leads to Piazza Trilussa and **Ponte Sisto**, a footbridge over the river that connects Trastevere to Via Giulia and the Campo de' Fiori area. The bridge was built during the pontificate of Sixtus IV (1471–84) to replace the ancient Pons Janiculensis.

PALAZZO CORSINI & GALLERIA NAZIONALE D'ARTE ANTICA Map pp308–10

☎ 06 688 02 323; www.galleriaborghese.it/corsini/en; admission at Via della Lungara 10; admission €4; ☽ 8.30am-7.30pm Tue-Sun; bus or tram to Viale di Trastevere

The large white **Palazzo Corsini** has housed some honoured guests. Michelangelo stayed there, as did Erasmus and Bramante. Queen Christina of Sweden, who had fled her native country after becoming a Catholic, died there in 1689, and Napoleon's mother Letizia took up residency in 1800. Today, the celebrities it houses are purely artistic: half of the National Art Collection, poorer than the Barberini half, perhaps, but boasting some major masterpieces. Highlights of the collection (mainly 16th- and 17th-century works) are Van Dyck's superb *Madonna della Paglia* (Madonna of the Straw) in Room 1 and Murillo's *Madonna and Child* in Room 2. The paintings of the Bologna school in Room 7 stand out, including Guido Reni's richly coloured *St Jerome* and melancholy *Salome*, Giovanni Lanfranco's touching *St Peter Healing St Agatha* and a haunting *Ecce Homo* by Guercino. The galleries are decorated with trompe l'oeil frescoes that are worth the visit on their own.

ORTO BOTANICO Map pp308–10

☎ 06 686 41 93; Largo Cristina di Svezia 24; admission €2.20; ☽ Mon-Sat 9am-6.30pm (to 5.30pm Oct-Mar); bus to Lungotevere della Farnesina

Formerly the private grounds of **Palazzo Corsini**, this botanic garden has over 7000 species including some of the rarest plants in Europe. There is an avenue of palms, Mediterranean succulents, a rock garden of mountain flowers, a cactus collection and even a star-shaped area with plants (not the cactuses) labelled in Braille.

VILLA FARNESINA Map pp308–10

☎ 06 688 01 767; Via della Lungara 230; admission €4.50; ☽ 9am-1pm Mon-Sat; bus to Lungotevere della Farnesina

Fans of Raphael make a beeline for this delightful villa, decorated with frescoes by the Renaissance painter and his pupils. It was created for the wealthy banker Agostino Chigi, and was the first suburban villa of the 16th century. (Villas are simply *palazzi* built outside the city walls.) It now has plenty of neighbours, but when it was built it stood alone on the banks of the Tiber, and must have been a profound statement on the power of its owner. The ceiling of the Sala di Galatea is painted with the stars as they were at the time of Chigi's birth.

The Triumph of Galatea in the room of the same name and the *Cupid and Psyche* in the loggia are outstanding. The building itself was built in the early 16th century by the Sienese architect Baldassarre Peruzzi, who also chipped in with a superb illusionary perspective of a colonnade and panorama of Rome. The building also houses the **Gabinetto Nazionale delle Stampe** (National Print Collection), part of the Istituto Nazionale per la Grafica, which can be consulted by scholars with permission.

Top Five Trastevere

- Basilica di Santa Maria in Trastevere mosaics (p109)
- Palazzo Corsini (left)
- View from the Gianicolo (p111)
- Piazza Santa Maria in Trastevere at night (109)
- Bernini's Ecstasy of Beata Ludovica Albertoni in San Francesco d'Assisi a Ripa (p108)

BEYOND THE CITY WALLS

FONTANA DELL'ACQUA PAOLA

Map pp317–19

Via Garibaldi; bus to Giacinto Carini

This massive fountain was built in 1612 for Pope Paul V to celebrate the restoration of a 2nd-century aqueduct. It incorporates marble pillaged from the Roman Forum. Four of the fountain's six pink-stone columns came from the facade of the old St Peter's Basilica. The large granite basin was added by Carlo Fontana in 1690.

GIANICOLO Map pp308–10
bus to Lungotevere Gianicolense

The Gianicolo Hill rises behind Trastevere and stretches to St Peter's Basilica. In 1849 it was the scene of one of the fiercest battles in the struggle for Italian unity, when a makeshift but brave army commanded by Giuseppe Garibaldi defended Rome against French troops sent to restore papal rule. Garibaldi is commemorated by a **monument** erected at the peak of the hill. His Brazilian-born wife, Anita, is also commemorated on the Gianicolo with an **equestrian monument** by Mario Rutelli (about 200m away, towards St Peter's) completed in 1932. The statue was presented to the city of Rome by the Brazilian government and shows Anita Garibaldi mounted on a rearing horse, holding a baby in her left arm and brandishing a pistol in her right. High relief sculptures depicting Anita Garibaldi's heroic activities during her husband's campaign are at the base of the monument.

On a clear day the panoramic view from **Piazzale Giuseppe Garibaldi** is breathtaking. This is also a top spot to take the kids if they need a change of scene. Just off the Piazzale, there's a merry-go-round and pony rides, and a puppet show on most Sundays. In the square there is a small bar. Take bus No 870 from Via Paola at the end of Corso Vittorio Emanuele where it meets the Lungotevere, or walk up the steps from Via Mameli in Trastevere.

TEMPIETTO DI BRAMANTE & CHIESA DI SAN PIETRO IN MONTORIO
Map pp317–19

☎ 06 581 39 40; Piazza San Pietro in Montorio; ⏰ 9.30am-12.30pm & 4-6pm May-Oct, 9.30am-12.30pm & 2-4pm Nov-Apr; bus to via Giacinto Carini

Bramante's circular **Tempietto**, next to the church of **San Pietro in Montorio**, was built to mark what was once believed to be the site of St Peter's crucifixion. The little temple is a Renaissance masterpiece of classical proportion and elegance, and was used as a model by numerous architects in the 16th century (see p149).

VILLA DORIA PAMPHILJ Map pp302–3
bus to via Giacinto Carini

If the pace of Rome gets to you, recuperate beside a baroque fountain, under a parasol pine or walking along picturesque walkways in Rome's largest park, laid out by Alessandro Algardi in the mid-16th century.

Once an enormous private estate – its perimeter measures 9km – the park was laid out around 1650 for Prince Camillo Pamphilj, a nephew of Innocent X. At its centre is the superb **Casino del Belrespiro**, also designed by Algardi, surrounded by manicured formal gardens and citrus trees. The casino was acquired by the state in the late 1950s and is now used for official government functions.

The surrounding grounds were acquired by the city authorities between 1965 and 1971 and turned into a park. It opens sunrise to sunset.

Neighbourhoods – Southern Rome

SOUTHERN ROME
Eating p171; Shopping p217; Sleeping p235

The southern quadrant of the city has some of Rome's greatest hits, as well as some delicious lesser-known spots. When the city gets too much rise above it all on the Aventine and Caelian Hills. Testaccio is a smaller bump in the landscape – its *monte* is man-made and only accessible by permission. The clubs and restaurants dug into it offer delights of a different sort entirely. Try to cram the obligatory visit to the Bocca della Verità in here somewhere, too.

Transport

Bus 75, 81, 117, 175, 673, 810 to Piazza del Colosseo; 81, 160 to Via del Circo Massimo; 23, 44, 81, 204, 280, 620 to Via dei Cerchi; 63, 630, 780 to Teatro di Marcello; 218, 360 to Porta San Sebastiano; 105 to Porta Maggiore; 16, 81, 85, 87, 186 to San Giovanni; 117 to Via Navicella

Tram 3 to San Giovanni; 3, 5, 14, 19 to Porta Maggiore

Metro San Giovanni, Colosseo, Circo Massimo, Piramide

AVENTINE

This peaceful hill south of Circo Massimo offers stunning views of St Peter's, while the Aventine gardens and quiet residential streets are pretty sights in their own right. Clivo dei Publicii and Via di Valle Murcia are the approaches with the most character. Along the way, you will pass the **Roseto Comunale**, a beautiful public rose garden, open when the roses are in bloom in May and June.

CIMITERO ACATTOLICO PER GLI STRANIERI Map pp317–19

entrance at Via Caio Cestio 5, off Via Nicola Zabaglia, ring bell for entrance; 9am-6pm Tue-Sun (to 5pm Oct-Mar); metro Piramide

The shady 'non-Catholic cemetery for foreigners', packed with the Protestant dead and patrolled by friendly resident cats, is a compelling place for a long wander. The 19th-century Brits were drawn here. Percy Bysshe Shelley wrote: 'It might make one in love with death to think that one should be buried in so sweet a place'. And so he was – or at least, parts of him, eventually. His body was cremated (he drowned off the coast of Viareggio in 1822) but apparently his heart did not burn right away, and his friend Trelawny snatched it from the flames (they were a melodramatic bunch, those Romantics). It was given to his wife, Mary Shelley, and wasn't interred in Rome until after her death in 1851.

Shelley's contemporary and fellow poet John Keats was a Roman for only a matter of months before he died of consumption in his apartment near the Spanish Steps in 1821. His lovely tomb bears the inscription: 'Here lies one whose name was writ in water'.

PARCO SAVELLO Map pp317–19

Via di Santa Sabina; dawn to dusk; bus to Via del Circo Massimo

Romans love this small, quiet park, where the orange trees are the stars. The crushed fruit smells sweet underfoot, and the leafy path leads to a panoramic view of the city.

PIAZZA DEI CAVALIERI DI MALTA & PRIORATO DI CAVALIERI DI MALTA

Map pp317–19
metro Circo Massimo (plus a walk)

This peaceful little square – with Cyprus trees and few people – takes its name from the Knights of Malta, which has its priory here.

Look through the **keyhole** of its door for one of the most splendid and charming views in the whole of Rome: a neat avenue of trees perfectly framing St Peter's Basilica.

The Knights of Malta was founded in the 12th century in Rhodes and later in Malta to assist pilgrims en route to the Holy Land. The villa is the residence of the grand master of the Knights of Malta and served as the order's embassies to Italy and the Vatican. It is surrounded by a radiant garden with laurel hedges and palm trees.

PIRAMIDE DI CAIO CESTIO Map pp317–19

metro Piramide

Gaius Cestius, a 1st-century-BC magistrate, built this brick and marble tomb for himself in the Egyptian style. The sight of its incongruous planes and angles is jarring amidst all of Rome's curves. In the 3rd century AD the builders of the Aurelian Wall found it in their path and simply incorporated it into the fortification near Porta San Paolo. The surrounding area is known as Piramide.

Top Five Southern Rome

- View from keyhole of Priorato di Malta (below)
- Capitoline Museums at Centrale Montemartini (p121)
- Basilica di San Giovanni in Laterano (p116)
- Pilgrims on the Scala Santa (p117)
- Bocca della Verità (p114)

CHIESA DI SAN SABA Map pp320–1

Via di San Saba; 7am-noon & 4-6.30pm; metro Piramide

This picturesque church dates from the 10th century, although it has been substantially rebuilt. Cosmati marble work from the 13th century decorates the main door and floor. The portico contains a number of sculptural and intricately carved Roman sarcophagi. Above the portico is a loggia which was added in the 16th century.

SANTA MARIA DEL PRIORATO

Map pp317–19
metro Circo Massimo (plus a walk)

It's a shame that this masterpiece of the 18th century, the priory of the Knights of Malta, is so rarely open to the public. If you happen to pass on a day that it is, don't miss your opportunity. It's the only architectural work by Giovanni Battista Piranesi, famous for his etchings and engravings of Roman ruins and architectural elements, real and imaginary. His more fantastic work, of impossible structures that led nowhere, influenced the surrealists of the 20th century. Entering **Santa Maria del Priorato** is like walking into one of his exquisite pictures.

CHIESA DI SANTA PRISCA Map pp320–1
Piazza Santa Prisca; ☺ 8am-noon & 4.30-7.30pm; metro Circo Massimo

The church dates from the 4th century AD, but the Mithraic shrine beneath (accessible only by special permission – see the boxed text, p72) is far older. Mithras was a god popular at the same time Christianity was spreading across the planet, particularly among soldiers, as the teachings emphasised loyalty, bravery and redemption through blood. The mysterious graffiti here read: 'You redeemed us by shedding the eternal blood' and 'Sweet are the livers of the birds, but worry reigns'.

BASILICA DI SANTA SABINA Map pp317–19
Piazza Pietro d'Illiria; ☺ 6.30am-12.45pm & 3.30-7pm; metro Circo Massimo (plus a walk)

Despite some careless 20th-century renovation, this is a darn good example of an ancient Roman church. It was founded in 422 by Peter of Illyria, and the carved cypress-wood doors (among other elements) are the 5th-century originals. Standing in the portico, the doors are to the far left and feature 18 carved panels depicting biblical scenes. The crucifixion scene here is one of the oldest in existence. It depicts Jesus and the two thieves but, interestingly, not their crosses. It's a bit difficult to make out the subjects in the dusky portico, but clear photographs of the doors are posted near the entrance.

The church was added to in the 9th century and again in 1216, just before it was given to the newly founded Dominican order. The three naves in the solemn interior are separated by 24 Corinthian columns made (strangely enough for the period) specifically for the occasion. They are Rome's first example of columns that supported arches rather than the horizontal beams called architraves. Above and to the sides of the arches there is a red and green frieze in *opus sectile* – that is, made of marble cut to shape, as opposed to mosaic, which is composed of pieces of marble of the same size and shape. Light streams into the interior of the church from high nave windows added in the 9th century. Windows are covered in sheets of crystallised gypsum, a detail authentic to the 9th century. Also dating from the 9th century are the carved choir, pulpit and bishop's throne. The fresco in the apse was painted in the 19th century. The meditative 13th-century cloister was recently restored and can be visited for a €1 donation.

The Bocca della Verità (p114)

CAELIAN

The Caelian Hill is the place to go when you need a break from Rome's bumper-to-*motorino* traffic, but don't want to miss out on edifying sights. In Imperial times, the hill was home to many wealthy citizens and a few unlucky animals – a zoo here housed the wild fodder for the Colosseum battles nearby. Today, there are more leafy green spots in the Caelian than other places in Rome. The best area for a picnic is the park around stately **Villa Celimontana** (as long as it isn't overrun by wedding parties having photographs taken – common on Saturdays). The villa, once private property of the Mattei family, now houses the Italian Geographical Society.

The big white building on the corner of Viale delle Terme di Caracalla and Piazza di Porta Capena at the park's southwest corner once housed Mussolini's Ministry of Italian Africa. The Axum obelisk in front of it was taken from Ethiopia as war booty. The building now belongs to the

Food and Agriculture Organisation of the United Nations.

CHIESA DI SS GIOVANNI E PAOLO

Map pp320–1

Piazza di SS Giovanni e Paolo 13; ☺ 8.30am-noon & 3.30-6.30pm; metro Colosseo or Circo Massimo

This 4th-century church is dedicated to Saints John and Paul, Romans who had served Constantine II and were beheaded by his anti-Christian successor, Julian, for refusing to serve in his court. The church was built over their houses. A beautiful 13th-century fresco of Christ with the Apostles is in a small room by the altar. It is usually locked but you can ask the sacristan to let you in. The arches in the square are the remains of 3rd-century Roman shops.

CHIESA DI SAN GREGORIO MAGNO

Map pp320–1

Piazza di San Gregorio; ☺ chapels 9.30am-12.30pm Tue-Sun; metro Circo Massimo

This 8th-century church was built in honour of Pope Gregory I (the Great) on the site where he dispatched St Augustine to convert the British to Christianity. The church was remodelled in the baroque style in the 17th century. The atrium, designed by Giovanni Battista Soria, contains tombs of prominent Englishmen including Sir Edward Carne, an envoy of Henry VIII and Mary I. One of his missions was to obtain a papal annulment of the king's marriage to Catherine of Aragon. He died in 1561.

The church's interior was given a baroque make-over in the 18th century by Francesco Ferrari. The **Cappella di San Gregorio**, at the end of the right aisle, contains a stately 1st-century-BC marble throne believed to have been St Gregory's. A gate to the left of the church leads to three small chapels among cypress trees. On the right, the **Cappella di Santa Silvia** (dedicated to Gregory the Great's mother) contains a fresco of angels by Guido Reni. The central chapel, the **Cappella di Sant'Andrea**, contains a painting by Domenichino of the flagellation of St Andrew and Guido Reni's depiction of St Andrew on his way to martyrdom. Giovanni Lanfranco's fresco on the inside of the entrance depicts St Silvia and St Gregory. The altarpiece, by Pomarancio, features the Madonna with St Andrew and St Gregory. The third chapel is dedicated to St Barbara, and along with a statue of St Gregory, contains frescoes illustrating St Augustine's mission.

CHIESA DI SANTA BALBINA

Map pp320–1

Piazza Santa Balbina; metro Circo Massimo

One of the oldest churches in Rome, dating from the 4th century. A notable feature is the fine Cosmati tomb of Stefanus de Surdis, which dates from the early 14th century. The church was extensively restored in the 1930s when 1st-century-AD Roman mosaics found in other parts of the city were installed there.

CHIESA DI SANTO STEFANO ROTONDO

Map pp320–1

☎ 06 704 93 717; Via di Santo Stefano Rotondo 7; ☺ 1.50-4.20pm Mon, 9am-1pm & 1.50-4.20pm Tue-Sat, 9am-noon 2nd Sun of each summer month; bus to Via della Navicella

In form, this small, simple circular church, built in the 5th century, is among the most soothing and meditative in Rome. The decoration, however, is rather startling: a cycle of 34 frescoes depicting the various ways in which saints were martyred. About them, Charles Dickens wrote: 'Such a panorama of horror and butchery no man could imagine in his sleep, though he were to eat a whole pig, raw, for supper'.

TERME DI CARACALLA

Map pp320–1

☎ 06 575 86 26; Via delle Terme di Caracalla 52; admission €4.20; ☺ 9am-4.30pm Tue-Sun; metro Circo Massimo

To the ancients, baths were more than a place for a quick *schvitz*. These, with room for 1600 and covering 10 hectares, would have met with approval from the most fastidious spa-goer. They included richly decorated saunalike hot rooms, a lukewarm *tepidarium*, and a swimming pool, as well as gymnasiums, libraries, shops and gardens. Excavations of the baths in the 16th and 17th centuries unearthed important sculptures and statues from the site, which found their way into the Farnese family collection. Two enormous basins now serve as twin fountains in Piazza Farnese. Begun by Antonius Caracalla, who gave them his name, and inaugurated in AD 217, the baths were used for 300 years until the Goth invaders whacked the plumbing.

FORUM BOARIUM & AROUND

BOCCA DELLA VERITÀ & CHIESA DI SANTA MARIA IN COSMEDIN

Map pp317–19

Piazza Bocca della Verità 18; ☺ church 10am-1pm & 3-7pm, portico 9am-7pm; bus to Via dei Cerchi

Probably the longest queue you'll join in Rome

will be to stick your hand in the cover of an ancient drain. The famous 'Mouth of Truth' (**Bocca della Verità**) is a large disk in the shape of a mask and legend says that if you put your right hand in it while telling a lie, it will be bitten off. Word is that priests used to put scorpions in there to perpetuate the myth. Fans of the film *Roman Holiday* will know it from when Gregory Peck ad-libs losing his hand and draws shrieks of unscripted terror from Audrey Hepburn.

The mouth lives on the portico of one of the finest medieval churches in Rome. Two earlier structures that stood on the site – an arcaded colonnade that was part of an Imperial-era market inspector's office, and the walls from a 7th-century Christian welfare centre – were incorporated by Pope Hadrian I in the 8th century. The church was further altered in the 12th century when the seven-storey bell tower and medieval portico were added. The church's interior, including the beautiful floor, high altar and *schola cantorum* (choir), was decorated with Cosmati inlaid coloured marble. There are 12th-century frescoes in the aisles, inside the nave arches and scant remains high up on the nave walls. An 8th-century mosaic fragment is preserved in the souvenir shop.

FORUM BOARIUM Map pp317–19
Piazza Bocca della Verità; bus to Via dei Cerchi
Opposite Santa Maria in Cosmedin are two tiny Roman temples dating from the Republican era, both of which have been recently restored: the round **Tempio di Ercole Vincitore** and the **Tempio di Portunus**. The temples were consecrated as churches in the Middle Ages and stand in an area once known as the Forum Boarium (cattle market), which existed even before the Roman Forum. The Forum Boarium later became an important commercial centre and had its own port on the Tiber. To its north are the ruins of the **Casa dei Crescenzi**, a former tower fortress transformed into a mansion in the 11th century by the powerful Crescenzi family. It is one of the few medieval Roman houses to have survived.

Off Piazza Bocca della Verità, towards the Palatine in Via del Velabro, is the **Arco di Giano** (Arch of Janus), a four-sided Roman arch which once covered a crossroads. In ancient times, cattle dealers used it to shelter from sun and rain. Beyond the arch, on the northern side of the street, is the medieval **Chiesa di San Giorgio in Velabro**. The church's portico, which dates from the 7th century, has been rebuilt after it was completely destroyed by a Mafia bomb attack in 1993. The convent beside the church was also damaged and has been restored.

CHIESA DI SAN NICOLA IN CARCERE
Map pp308–10
cnr Via Petroselli & Via del Foro Olitorio; ☽ 7am-noon & 4-7pm; bus to Via del Teatro di Marcello
This church was built in the 11th century on the site of the Republican-era vegetable and oil market, and marble columns from temples that once stood there were used in the church's facade and interior. If the sacristan is available and you're not squeamish about poking around in the dark, ask to check out the basement. The foundations from the temples are visible, as are some unidentified human remains.

CHIESA DI SAN TEODORO Map pp320–1
Via di San Teodoro; ☽ closed for restoration; bus to Via dei Cerchi
A church was built on this site in the 6th century on the ruins of warehouses that stood between the Roman Forum and the Tiber. The present church dates from the mid-15th century and was built by Pope Nicholas V, but the breathtaking mosaic in the apse has survived from an earlier building. The church was restored in 1704 by Carlo Fontana working under the commission of Pope Clement XI. Fontana designed the double stairway that leads down from street level to a courtyard, in the centre of which is an altar from a pagan temple. At the time of writing, the church was closed to the public for restoration.

TEATRO DI MARCELLO Map pp308–10
Via del Teatro di Marcello; bus to Teatro di Marcello
Continuing north along Via del Teatro di Marcello, you come to the **Teatro di Marcello**, planned by Julius Caesar and built around 13 BC by Augustus. Architect Baldassarre Peruzzi built a Renaissance palace on the two arcaded storeys.

PORTA SAN SEBASTIANO
Via di Porta San Sebastiano runs from Piazzale Numa Pompilio in front of the Terme di Caracalla to the beginning of Via Appia Antica (see p118). Behind the high stone walls are luxurious private villas and gardens, and on the eastern side, a small public park.

MUSEO DELLE MURA Map pp302–3
☎ 06 704 75 284; Via di Porta San Sebastiano; admission €2.60; ☽ 9am-7pm (closed Mon & 5pm Sun Apr-Oct); bus to Via di Porta San Sebastiano
If you were the kind of kid who liked walking along the top of walls, or still do in our

case, check out this little museum housed in the best-preserved gate of the Aurelian City Wall. There are artefacts pertaining to Roman construction methods and, most merrily, the opportunity to walk along a substantial stretch of the wall and get a wonderful soldier's eye view of the Appia Antica.

SAN GIOVANNI

MUSEO NAZIONALE DEGLI STRUMENTI MUSICALI Map pp302–3
☎ 06 701 47 96; admission €2.58; 🕒 9am-1.30pm Tue-Sat; metro San Giovanni

If gorgeous musical instruments hold an attraction for you, don't miss this little-visited museum. It's home to a collection begun by opera singer Evan Gorga, and contains over 800 fine pieces, including a rare triple-stringed harp.

PORTA MAGGIORE Map pp302–3
Piazza di Porta Maggiore; bus to Porta Maggiore

Via Eleniana leads northwards from Santa Croce to the **Porta Maggiore**, also known as the Porta Prenestina, a gateway to ancient Rome built by Claudius in AD 52. The main southbound roads, Via Prenestina and Via Labicana, passed beneath the gateway and ruts made by carriage wheels can still be seen in the basalt flagstones under the arches. The arch supported two aqueducts – the Acqua Claudia and the Acqua Aniene Nuova – one on top of the other. It was later incorporated into the Aurelian Walls of the city.

Just outside the gate is a rather pretentious travertine monument, the **Sepolcro di M Virgilio Eurisace**. Commonly known as the Baker's Tomb, it was built in around 30 BC by the widow of the baker Vergilius Eurysaces in memory of her husband. The tomb is decor-

ated with reliefs depicting the industrious baker at work, and the monument itself is in the shape of an enormous bread oven.

BASILICA DI SAN GIOVANNI IN LATERANO Map pp320–1
Piazza di San Giovanni in Laterano; admission to the cloister €2; 🕒 cloister 9am-5pm (to 6pm Apr-Oct), baptistry 9am-1pm & 3.30-7.30pm (but irregular); metro San Giovanni, bus or tram to Piazza di San Giovanni in Laterano

Founded by Constantine in the early 4th century, this was the first Christian basilica built in the city. While St Peter's trumps it in scale and grandeur, it is still the Cathedral of Rome, and the pope's seat as Rome's bishop. It has been substantially rebuilt and renovated through the ages, and the combination of styles adds up to a delightful church, packed with interesting features.

The original structure, built alongside an imperial palace donated by Constantine in 313, simply refigured the elements of the Imperial Roman basilica (aisles, nave, apse, colonnade) to meet the demands of Christian rituals. In form and style, this was the prototype for the rest of the early Christian basilicas in Rome. Originally, it paired a plain exterior with a highly decorated interior that incorporated lavish and colourful materials.

Alessandro Galilei designed the mid-18th-century facade, surmounted by leviathan statues of the apostles who appear ready to lift pilgrims to heaven. This disciplined, serious example of late baroque classicism, executed on a colossal scale, was meant to convey the authority and infinite power of the Church. The astounding bronze main doors were moved here by Borromini from the Curia in the Roman Forum. The door to

Teatro di Marcello
This theatre was originally planned by Julius Caesar but remained unfinished at the time of his assassination in 44 BC. Augustus then inherited the project and named it after Marcellus, his nephew, who had died prematurely in 23 BC. By 17 BC, the theatre was in use but it was not formally dedicated for a further four to six years.

Capable of holding over 20,000 people, seated according to social status, the Teatro di Marcello was the most important of Rome's three ancient theatres.

It was restored on many occasions following fires and earthquakes, until it finally fell into disuse and became a quarry for building material. In AD 365 the theatre was partially demolished and the stone used to restore the nearby Ponte Cestio.

The Perleone family converted it into a fortress during the 11th and 12th centuries, and in the 16th century Baldassarre Peruzzi converted the fortress into a luxurious palace for the Savelli family, preserving the original form of the theatre. In 1712 the palace was inherited by the Orsini family who partly restored the theatre.

The theatre and the ruins at its base can only be visited by request.

the right of the main entrance is opened only during Holy Years.

Borromini had updated the interior a century earlier, creating a baroque space. His fingerprint is on the pillars in the nave and the sculptural frames around the funerary monuments in the aisles: he placed his trademark oval window above each one. As you wander around, stop to admire the marvellous mosaic floors, inlaid in the 15th century with marble salvaged from derelict Roman churches. Behind the first pillar on the right is a fragment of a Giotto fresco. While admiring it, cock your ear towards the next pillar, where a monument to Pope Sylvester II is said to sweat and emit the sound of creaking bones when the death of a pope is imminent.

A Gothic **baldacchino** towers above the papal altar. The grilled midsection contains relics of the heads of Saints Peter and Paul. A double staircase leads to the **confessio** below, which houses pieces of what's supposed to be St Peter's wooden altar table, used by 1st- to 4th-century popes.

The Vassalletto family built the beautiful 13th-century Cosmati-style **cloister**. The columns were once entirely covered with inlaid marble mosaics, remains of which can still be seen. On the western side, there's a marble slab supported by four columns, which Christians in the Middle Ages believed represented the height of Christ.

A second entrance into the basilica, the **northern facade**, faces onto Piazza di San Giovanni in Laterano. The two-tiered portico, built by Domenico Fontana in 1586, was damaged by a bomb attack in 1993 and has recently been restored. On the right of the north facade is Constantine's **baptistry**, which, like the church itself, was the prototype for baptistries that followed. Sixtus III gave it its present octagonal shape. A green basalt font rests in its centre, beneath a dome decorated with modern copies of frescoes by Andrea Sacchi. The outer walls are decorated by 17th-century frescoes. It is surrounded by several chapels with magnificent mosaic decorations.

The **Palazzo Lateran** which adjoins the basilica was home to the papal court before it skipped off to Avignon in the 14th century. It was largely destroyed by fire in 1308 and most of what remained was demolished in the 16th century. The present building houses the Rome Vicariate and offices of the diocese of Rome.

CHIESA DI SANTA CROCE IN GERUSALEMME Map pp302–3

☎ 06 701 47 69; Piazza di Santa Croce in Gerusalemme 12; ☷ 6.30am-12.30pm & 3.30-7.30pm; metro San Giovanni

This pilgrimage church was founded in 320 by St Helena, Constantine's mother, who went to Jerusalem and brought back Christian relics, including a piece of Christ's cross and thorns from his crown, as souvenirs. The bell tower was added in 1144, the facade and oval vestibule in 1744. The frescoes in the apse date from the 15th century and represent the legends of the Cross. The relics are housed in a chapel at the end of the northern aisle.

Next to the church are the columns and bricked-up arches of **Anfiteatro Castrense**, a 3rd-century-BC amphitheatre. Once part of an imperial palace on the site, it was used for those pleasant Roman pastimes such as animal baiting.

SCALA SANTA & SANCTA SANCTORUM Map pp320–1

☎ 06 704 94 619; Piazza di Porta San Giovanni; ☷ Scala Santa 6.15am-noon & 3.30-6.45pm Apr-Sep, 6.15am-noon & 3-6.15pm Oct-Mar, Sancta Sanctorum 10.30-11.30am & 3-4pm Tue, Thu & Sat; metro San Giovanni, bus or tram to Piazza di Porta San Giovanni

These 28 steps – purported to be from Pontius Pilate's house and trod by Christ himself – are so holy that believers climb them on their knees. To protect them, the steps are covered with wooden boards. The steps are said to occasionally bleed through the slats. Indulgence is granted to believers who climb on Fridays in Lent. In 1510, one Martin Luther reached halfway before exasperation hit and he walked back down again. He went home to Germany and caused something of a stir.

The sacred staircase (and the two less sacred ones to the left and right) lead to the Holy of Holies, the **Sancta Sanctorum**, once the pope's private chapel. It used to house numerous relics, but they have been moved to the Vatican. The silver-panelled altarpiece, originally a painting of Christ said to have been done by St Luke and an angel, has been restored and repainted so many times that it bears no resemblance to how it once appeared. The vaulted ceiling above it is covered with 13th-century mosaics. The Cosmati marble work on the floor is particularly fine and the lower walls are also adorned with marble. Above are 13th-century frescoes (by the artists who frescoed the stairwells) of the Apostles and saints, separated by swirling Gothic columns and, higher still, frescoes clearly illustrating the various ways that martyrs met their deaths.

TESTACCIO Map pp317–19

Situated southwest of the Aventine, between Via Marmorata and the River Tiber, Testaccio was the river port of ancient Rome from the 2nd century BC to the 3rd century AD. Supplies of wine, oil and grain were transported from Roman colonies to the city via Ostia and the Tiber. The containers used for these goods – huge terracotta amphorae and other pots – were emptied of their contents and then dumped. At first the pots were just tossed into the river, but when the Tiber became almost unnavigable as a consequence, the pots were smashed to pieces and stacked methodically in a pile which over time grew into a large hill, the Monte Testaccio.

The word Testaccio comes from the Latin *testae*, meaning potsherds. In the Middle Ages the area was the scene of jousts and particularly vicious carnival games, when pigs, bulls and other animals were packed into carts and sent flying down the 45m hill. Those animals that survived the journey were slaughtered anyway and eaten.

Most of the area is now occupied by low-cost housing that went up after Italian unification to house workers for the new capital city. Although it is off the regular sightseeing trail, Testaccio is a good place to visit if you want to try that most Roman of Roman culinary specialities: offal (for more details on where to go, see the Eating chapter, p171). There is an excellent morning market from Monday to Saturday selling fruit, vegetables, herbs, flowers and (rather incongruously) cheap shoes.

The area around Monte Testaccio and the former slaughterhouse gets busy after dark (see p175) with some of the bars and clubs in this region occupying caves carved out of the artificial hill (check out the neatly stacked amphora pieces that are still clearly visible). Monte Testaccio itself can only be visited on request (see the boxed text, p72, for details).

BEYOND THE CITY WALLS
Via Appia Antica & the Catacombs Map pp302–3

Known to ancient Romans as the *regina viarum* (queen of roads), the Via Appia Antica (Appian Way) once ran all the way from the walls of Rome to Brindisi, on the Adriatic coast. The name comes from the original builder, Appius Claudius Caecus, who crafted the first 90km section of the road in 312 BC. That stretch was revolutionary in its day because it was almost perfectly straight – the ancient equivalent of an autostrada. Some stretches of the original road still exist, and are best seen on a Sunday, when Via Appia Antica closes to nonlocal traffic. While not exactly a car-free zone, you can walk or bike in relative peace for several kilometres from Porta Viadi San Sebastiano. A newly made-over park, Parco della Caffarella-Parco dell'Appia Antica, encompasses some of the prettiest open land near Rome.

If that's not enough to get you outside of the walls, the catacombs ought to be. Ancient Rome, who burned their dead, banned burials within the city walls, so the early Christians dug some 300km of tunnels through the soft tufa rock beneath the roads leading out of the city. They wrapped their dearly departed in white sheets and placed them in rectangular niches carved into the tunnel walls, and then entombed them with simple marble slabs. The underground chambers doubled as clandestine meeting places where Christians could practise their dissident faith and store important relics. When marauding Barbarians began ransacking the catacombs in the 5th century, the popes gathered up the relics, including the heads of Saints Peter and Paul. The catacombs were abandoned and largely forgotten until a 16th-century farmer stuck his hoe into a 'world of the dead'. Three major catacombs (San Callisto, San Sebastiano and Santa Domitilla) are available for guided exploration.

BASILICA & CATACOMBE DI SAN SEBASTIANO Map pp302–3

☎ 06 788 70 35; Via Appia Antica 136 (just past the main entrance to Catacombe di San Callisto); admission €5; ☷ 8.30am-noon & 2.30-5.30pm (to 5pm in winter) Mon-Sat, closed mid-Nov–mid-Dec; bus to Via Appia Antica

The basilica was built in the 4th century over the catacombs, which were used as a safe haven for the remains of St Peter and St Paul during the reign of Vespasian, who repressed and persecuted Christians. Originally known as the *Memoria Apostolorum* (Memory of the Apostles), the basilica was dedicated to St Sebastian after he was martyred and buried here in the late 3rd century.

Preserved in the **Capella delle Reliquie**, in the right-hand nave of the basilica, is one of the arrows used to kill the saint and the column to which he was tied.

The **Catacombe di San Sebastiano** were the first catacombs to be so called, the name deriving from the Greek *kata* (near) and *kymbas* (cavity), because they were located near a cave. Subsequently, this term was extended to all the other underground burial sites. Over the centuries this catacomb was one of only three to remain open and receive pilgrims. For this reason the first of its three levels is now almost completely destroyed. The public can see the 2nd floor, including areas with frescoes, stucco-work and epigraphs. There are also three perfectly preserved mausoleums and a plastered wall with hundreds of invocations to the Apostles Peter and Paul, engraved by worshippers in the 3rd and 4th centuries.

CATACOMBE DI SAN CALLISTO

Map pp302–3

☎ 06 513 01 580; Via Appia Antica 110; admission €5; ☺ 8.30am-noon & 2.30-5.30pm (5pm in winter) Thu-Tue, closed late Jan-late Feb; bus to Via Appia Antica

These catacombs are the largest, most famous and most touristed tombs. The martyred patron of music, St Cecilia, was buried here (although her body was moved to the Basilica di Santa Cecilia in Trastevere). Founded at the end of the 2nd century on private land, these catacombs became the official cemetery of the newly established Roman Church. Fifty martyrs from the period of Christian persecution and 16 of the first popes, themselves mostly martyrs, are buried here. The catacombs are named after Pope Calixtus I, who was killed in Trastevere in 222 while saying Mass. He had been responsible for the catacombs for 20 years. They cover an area of 15 hectares and 20km of tunnels have been explored to date. Archaeologists have found the sepulchres of some 500,000 people, as well as Greek and Latin inscriptions and frescoes.

CATACOMBE DI SANTA DOMITILLA

Map pp302–3

☎ 06 513 39 56; Via delle Sette Chiese 283; admission €5; ☺ 8.30am-noon & 2.30-5pm Wed-Mon, closed late Dec-late Jan; bus to Via Appia Antica

Among the largest and oldest catacombs in Rome, they were established on the private burial ground of Flavia Domitilla, a niece of Domitian. They contain Christian wall paintings and the underground **Chiesa di SS Nereus e Achilleus**.

CIRCO DI MASSENZIO Map pp302–3

☎ 06 780 13 24; Via Appia Antica 153; admission €2.60; ☺ 9am-5pm Tue-Sun; bus to Via Appia Antica

Built by Maxentius in the early 4th century, this is the best preserved of Rome's ancient racetracks. You can still make out the starting stalls used for chariot races, which were set at an oblique angle so all the chariots would cover the same distance before reaching the beginning of the low wall in the centre. The wall, 1000 Roman feet or 296m in length, consisted of a channel formed by a series of basins. These contained sculptures and tabernacles on columns displaying the seven eggs and the seven dolphins that represented the seven laps that had to be completed to cover a distance of three Roman miles (approximately 4km). The centre was dominated by the obelisk of Domitian, brought here from Campo Marzio and later removed to Bernini's fountain in Piazza Navona on the order of Pope Innocent X in 1650. Maxentius was challenged and killed by Constantine at the battle of Ponte Milvio in 312. It's unlikely the circus was completed before he died, so for all his effort, he never actually saw a chariot race there.

Above the circus are the unexcavated ruins of Maxentius' imperial residence, most of which are still covered in vegetation. In front of the circus is the **Tomba di Romolo** (Tomb of Romulus), built by Maxentius for his young son Romulus. It stands on a circular base measuring 33m in diameter. It was crowned with a large dome and had a rectangular portico similar to the Pantheon. The monument was surrounded on all sides by an imposing colonnade measuring 107m by 121m, in part still visible. In the 19th century the tomb was incorporated into a country villa. The tomb was closed for renovation at the time of writing.

CHIESA DEL DOMINE QUO VADIS?

Map pp302–3

Via Appia Antica; ☺ 7am-7pm; bus to Via Appia Antica

This church marks the place where St Peter, hightailing it out of Rome to avoid Nero's wrath, had a vision of Christ walking toward the city. Peter asked: 'Domine, quo vadis?' – 'Lord, where are you going?'. When Jesus

The Catacombs

The catacombs are underground corridors and passageways that were built as communal burial grounds. The best known are the Christian catacombs along the Via Appia Antica, although there are Jewish and pagan ones too. Scholars are divided as to whether the catacombs were also clandestine meeting places for early Christians, as well as useful places for secreting important relics.

The choice of underground graves was probably influenced by contemporary practices (such as using **columbariums**) and also by practical and economic concerns. Catacombs were often established in areas where there were existing quarries or underground passages: the soft volcanic earth of the Roman countryside enabled the Christians to dig to a depth of 20m or so. They maximised on the land donated by wealthy members of the Christian community by digging on numerous levels, retaining for security purposes only a few entrances.

During the periods of persecution, many martyrs were buried beside the fathers of the Church and the first popes. Many Christians followed suit, wanting to be buried in the same place as the martyrs. Consequently, an increasingly unethical property trade in tombs developed, until Gregory I issued a decree in 597 abolishing the sale of graves. However, Christians had already started to abandon the catacombs as early as 313, when Constantine issued the Milan decree of religious tolerance.

Increasingly, Christians opted to bury their dead near the churches and basilicas that were being built, often above pagan temples. This became common practice under Theodosius, who made Christianity the state religion in 394. The catacombs became sanctuaries for remembering the martyrs buried there.

In about 800 the increasingly frequent incursions by invaders necessitated the removal of the saintly bodies of the martyrs and the first popes to the basilicas inside the city walls. The catacombs were thus left abandoned and eventually many were forgotten and filled up with earth. In the Middle Ages only three catacombs were known about, and those of San Sebastiano were the most frequented as a place of pilgrimage, since they had earlier been the burial place of St Peter and St Paul.

The Catacombe di Priscilla on Via Salaria were discovered by chance at the end of the 16th century, following the collapse of a tufa quarry. From that time on, groups of curious aristocrats began to lower themselves into the dark underground passages on a regular basis, often risking losing themselves permanently in the underground labyrinths. From the mid-19th century onwards passionate scholars of Christian archaeology began a program of scientific research and more than 30 catacombs in the Rome area have been uncovered.

---

replied that he was going to Rome to be crucified again, Peter took the hint and returned to the city, where he was arrested and martyred. In the centre of the aisle, there are two holy footprints supposed to have been made by Christ's image.

MAUSOLEO DI CECILIA METELLA
Map pp302–3

☎ 06 399 67 700; admission €2; ☸ 9am until 1 hr before dusk; bus to Via Appia Antica

Money talked in Roman times, and Cecilia Metella's fabulously wealthy father-in-law Marcus Crassus made sure she was buried in style. Cylindrical in shape and 11m high and roughly 30m in diameter, the mausoleum encloses an interesting burial chamber, now roofless. The walls are made of travertine and decorated with a lovely sculpted frieze featuring Gaelic shields, ox skulls and festoons. The Ghibelline battlements were added in the Middle Ages. Because of its location, the mausoleum was turned into a keep for the 14th-century castle built by the Caetani (medieval ruling family)

astride the road to extract money, rather like a modern motorway tollbooth.

Not far past the tomb is a section of the actual ancient road, excavated in the mid-19th century. It is very picturesque, lined with fragments of ancient tombs.

MAUSOLEO DELLE FOSSE ARDEATINE
Map pp302–3

☎ 06 513 67 42; admission free; ☸ 8.15am-5pm Mon-Fri; bus to Via Appia Antica

A rare modern monument around the historic Appian Way, this moving mausoleum honours 335 random prisoners (including 75 Jews) who were brought to these caves and executed by the Nazis during WWII, in reprisal for the killing of 32 German military police by Roman partisans. The Germans used mines to explode sections of the caves and bury the bodies. After the war, the bodies were exhumed, identified and reburied in a mass grave at the site, now marked by a huge concrete slab and sculptures.

The massacre still angers and distresses many Italians. The German SS commander,

Erich Priebke, who has admitted to killing at least two of the victims himself, was tried and convicted in 1996.

EUR

Mussolini ordered the construction of this satellite city about 5km south of Rome for the Esposizione Universale di Roma, an international exhibition to have been held in 1942. Work was suspended with the outbreak of war and the exhibition was never held, though its acronym gave the area its name, and most of the building was completed in the 1950s. Fans of Fascist architecture (you know who you are) will want to have a good look at the Palazzo della Civiltà del Lavoro (Palace of the Workers), a square building with arched windows, also known as the 'Square Colosseum'. EUR is accessible via Metro Linea B.

MUSEO DELLE ARTI E TRADIZIONI POPOLARI

☎ 06 592 61 48; Piazza Marconi 8; admission €4.13;
🕑 9am-2pm Tue-Sat, 9am-1pm Sun; metro EUR

Count this museum of folk art and rural tradition among Rome's sleeper attractions. It's a heck of a lot more interesting than it sounds. The collection includes agricultural and artisan tools, clothing, musical instruments and a room full of carnival costumes and artefacts.

MUSEO DELLA CIVILTÀ ROMANA

☎ 06 592 61 35; Piazza G Agnelli 10; admission €6.20;
🕑 9am-7pm Tue-Sat, 9am-2pm Sun; metro EUR

A giant model of 4th-century Rome is the highlight of this suburban museum, established by Mussolini in 1937 to glorify Imperial Rome. There are detailed models of the main buildings, an absorbing cross section of the Colosseum and casts of the reliefs on the Colonna di Traiano (see p71) which will save you a lot of neck ache trying to examine the real thing.

MUSEO NAZIONALE PREISTORICO ETNOGRAFICO LUIGI PIGORINI

☎ 06 54 95 21; Viale Lincoln 1; admission €4.13;
🕑 9am-2pm Tue-Sat, 9am-1pm Sun; metro EUR

If you're mad about world prehistoric artefacts (human bones, mammoth tusks, shells etc), this is your place. If not, give it a miss.

Ostiense & San Paolo

About 500m outside the city walls, heading along Via Ostiense away from the centre, are (on the left) the Mercati Generali (Map pp312–3), Rome's wholesale food markets.

CAPITOLINE MUSEUMS AT
CENTRALE MONTEMARTINI Map pp302–3

☎ 06 399 67 800; Via Ostiense 106; admission €6.20;
🕑 9am-8pm Tue-Sun; bus No 23 (or walk) from metro Piramide

This former power station became the home of many pieces from the Capitoline Museums in 1997, at the beginning of a major renovation. It was supposed to be a temporary arrangement, but visitors responded so favourably to the delicious *frisson* that comes from placing ancient sculpture in an industrial setting that this former power plant has become a permanent gallery. The move has given the Capitoline Museums' curators an opportunity to research the collection, display sculptures and mosaics which have been hidden for decades in Capitoline storage vaults, and to exhibit related pieces together, in context.

Metal stairs lead up to the Sala Macchina, painted a garish blue, where antiquities dating from the late-Republican period to the height of the Empire share the exhibition space with two mammoth 7500HP diesel engines. Of note are several Roman copies of original Greek works, including a number of statues of *Athena* (grouped together), a black-basalt statue of *Orantes* (recently identified as being a portrait of Agrippina, the niece of Claudius), and heads of divinities and statues from the pediment of the Tempio di Apollo Soianus, a temple that once stood near the Teatro di Marcello. These statues depict a battle between Greeks and Amazons and were originally coloured. There are also sculptures found on the Capitoline, in the Area Sacra di Largo Argentina and near the Teatro di Pompeo (in the Campo de' Fiori area).

On the ground floor, beyond the entrance, is the Sala Colonne where the oldest pieces in the collection – sculpture and ceramics dating from the 7th century BC – are displayed. These include Etruscan and Greek pieces as well as discoveries from a necropolis on the Esquiline.

The Sala Caldaia, painted a wonderfully sickly hospital green, has the highlights of the collection set against the backdrop of a giant furnace. Many pieces were excavated from imperial and patrician villas and gardens, and represent the taste of the emperors and nobility. The magnificent floor mosaic of hunting scenes has rarely been exhibited. It was found during excavations near the Porta Maggiore.

Two of the most beautiful pieces are statues of young girls: the *Fanciulla Seduta* sitting with her elbow resting on her knee, and *Musa Polimnia* leaning on a pedestal and gazing dreamily into the distance. At the far end of the room, flanked by two attendants and against the backdrop of a giant furnace, is the milky-white *Venus Esquilina* from the 1st century BC, discovered on the Esquiline in 1874.

BASILICA DI SAN PAOLO FUORI-LE-MURA Map pp302–3
Via Ostiense 186; 🕑 **7.30am-6.30pm, cloisters closed 1-3pm; metro San Paolo**
Constantine built a basilica on the site of St Paul's burial in the 4th century which was, until the construction of the present-day St Peter's Basilica, the largest church in the world. The original and additions were destroyed by fire in 1823, so the current building is mostly a faithful reconstruction.

The triumphal arch was part of the former church; its 5th-century mosaics of Christ with angels, St Peter and St Paul and symbols of the Evangelists have been heavily restored. On the other side of the arch are mosaics by Pietro Cavallini. The mosaics in the apse were done by Venetian artists and show the figures of Christ with St Peter, St Andrew, St Paul and St Luke. The 13th-century marble canopy over the high altar was designed by Arnolfo di Cambio together with another artist, possibly Pietro Cavallini. The paintings between the windows of the nave show the life of St Paul. Below are mosaic portraits of all the popes from St Peter to John Paul II.

The **cloisters** of the adjacent Benedictine abbey, a real treasure, were not damaged by the fire. They are masterpieces of Cosmati mosaic work, perhaps the most beautiful example of their kind in Rome. The octagonal and spiral columns supporting the elaborate arcade are arranged in pairs and are inlaid with colourful mosaics. The sacristy contains other objects from the old church, including four fresco portraits of past popes.

NORTHERN ROME

Eating p173; Shopping p217; Sleeping p235
The northern part of the city is less packed with monuments and must-sees than other sections of Rome. Villa Borghese is a perennial delight, and its Galleria and gardens shouldn't be missed.

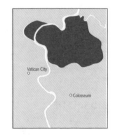

PONTE MILVIO & FORO ITALICO

PONTE MILVIO Map pp302–3
This bridge was the scene of one of the great events in Rome's history: Constantine's defeat of Maxentius in AD 312 when he threw him off the bridge into the Tiber below. **Ponte Milvio** dates from 109 BC and was built to carry the old Via Flaminia over the river. Nicholas V added the watchtowers in the 15th century. Pius VII commissioned Giuseppe Valadier to build the triumphal arch at its entrance. Garibaldi's troops blew up the bridge in 1849 to stop the advancing French soldiers, and it was rebuilt in 1850 by Pius IX. Today, it's just a pretty footbridge, with a colourful market on its northern side (see the boxed text on p153).

FORO ITALICO Map pp302–3
Viale dei Gladiatori 31; bus or tram to Piazza Mancini
About 600m from Ponte Milvio, at the foot of

Transport
Bus 280 to Piazza Mancini; 36, 60, 84, 90 to Via Nomentana
Tram 3, 19 to Viale delle Belle Arti; 2 to Piazza Mancini
Metro Bologna, Flaminio

Monte Mario, is the **Foro Italico**, an ambitious project for a sports centre built under the Fascist regime between 1928 and 1931. It was Mussolini's attempt at a modern form of Imperial-Roman architecture. A 17m-high marble obelisk inscribed with the words 'Mussolini Dux' greets arrivals at the complex. If you like Fascist architecture, it's worth a visit.

STADIO OLIMPICO Map pp302–3
Viale dello Stadio Olimpico; bus or tram to Piazza Mancini

The **Stadio Olimpico** is the largest stadium in the complex, seating 100,000. It was built in 1960 for the Olympic Games and rebuilt in 1990 for the World Cup. It is home to Rome's two teams, Roma and Lazio (see p199 for further details).

Porta Pia & Via Nomentana

Porta Pia, built beside the ruins of the ancient Porta Nomentana, was Michelangelo's last architectural work, commissioned by Pius IV in 1561. The ugly modern building just inside the city walls is the British Embassy. Opposite it is the Villa Paolina, the residence of Napoleon's sister Paolina Bonaparte from 1816 to 1824. It's now the French Embassy to the Holy See. Bus Nos 36 and 90 from Stazione Termini and bus No 62 from Piazza Venezia and Piazza Barberini take you to Porta Pia and the tree-lined Via Nomentana, which heads northeastwards out of the city.

Red Brigade

The Red Brigade, the most famous faction of the Italian radical left, emerged on the political scene in the 1970s in a hail of gunfire. Ideologically, they were Marxist-Leninist, advocating class warfare and revolution. Stylistically, they favoured long, handwritten notes explaining their actions. Their targets included businesspeople, establishment organisations and government. Their most infamous act was the kidnapping and murder of former Prime Minister Aldo Moro. They held him for two months before dumping his body in the middle of Rome. Brigade leaders were put on trail in the 1970s, amidst high tension. The trials took place in the fortresslike Palestra di Scherma in Piazza del Foro, designed for the 1936 Olympics.

VILLA TORLONIA PARK Map pp302–3
metro Bologna & bus 62 or walk

This splendid spread, 1km from Porta Pia, once belonged to the family of Prince Giovanni Torlonia, a banker and landowner. His large neoclassical villa on Via Nomentana was built by Giuseppe Valadier in 1806. Mussolini often stayed with his mistress at Palazzo Venezia, but this was his actual residence, and his wife and children lived here from the mid 1920s until 1943. The villa was occupied by Allied troops after WWII, then abandoned. In 1978 the estate was expropriated by the city council as a public park. A restoration program is under way to bring the park and its buildings back to their former glory.

CASINA DELLE CIVETTE Map pp302–3
☎ 06 442 50 072; admission €2.58; ☼ 9am-7pm Tue-Sun Apr-Sep, 9am-5pm Tue-Sun Oct-Mar

One of the most interesting buildings in Villa Torlonia Park is the **Casina delle Civette**. The house was built between 1840 and 1930 and is an eclectic combination of a Swiss cottage, a turreted Gothic castle and an Arts-and-Crafts farmhouse decorated in Art-Nouveau style. Already in an advanced state of abandon, it was gutted by a fire in 1991. It was reopened as a museum in 1997 after a lengthy and detailed restoration. The museum is dedicated to stained glass and contains the house's original windows, including work done between 1908 and 1930 by leading Italian decorative artist Duilio Cambelotti. There are also over 100 designs and sketches for stained glass, decorative tiles, elaborate parquetry floors and woodwork.

BASILICA DI SANT'AGNESE FUORI-LE-MURA & CHIESA DI SANTA COSTANZA Map pp302–3
☎ 06 861 08 40; Via Nomentana 349; basilica admission free, catacombs €4.20; ☼ 9am-noon Mon-Sat, 4-6pm Tue-Sun; bus to Via Nomentana

The apse of the **Sant'Agnese**, built by Constantine, has a beautiful 7th-century mosaic depicting the martyrdom of St Agnes, who is buried in the eerily atmospheric catacombs below. According to tradition, having rejected the advances of one of Diocletian's courtiers, the 13-year-old Agnes was exposed naked in the Stadium of Domitian. Miraculously, her hair grew to preserve her modesty. She was then burnt at the stake but was untouched by the flames. Eventually, she was beheaded. Her relics are preserved beneath the high altar.

In the same complex, across the convent courtyard, is the circular **Chiesa di Santa Costanza**, built as a mausoleum for Constantine's daughters and decorated with the oldest surviving Christian mosaics. The pretty circular building has a dome supported by 12 pairs of granite columns. The covered walkway that runs outside of the arches has a barrel-vaulted ceiling covered with beautiful 4th-century mosaics of fruit, flowers, vines, animals and geometric figures. There were once mosaics in the dome – said to be even more astounding than those

Neighbourhoods – Northern Rome

in the ambulatory – but these were destroyed by Paul V in 1622. The original porphyry sarcophagi of Constantia and Helena were moved to the Vatican in 1790 and are on display in the Vatican Museums.

VIA SALARIA

This old Roman road, once used to transport salt (sale), is now the heart of a busy residential and shopping district northeast of the town centre. Close to where Via Salaria crosses Viale Regina Margherita, there's a crop of exuberant Art-Nouveau buildings that sprung up after World War II. The area, Coppede, is named for the architect who designed several of the eccentric buildings around Piazza Mincio. Beloved as they are today, they were much maligned in their day, and Coppede killed himself in despair.

Take bus No 56 from Trastevere, Piazza Venezia and Piazza Barberini. Bus No 319 from Stazione Termini runs along Via Tagliamento, which crosses Via Salaria.

Top Five Northern Rome

- Galleria Borghese (p125)
- Giardino del Lago in Villa Borghese (right)
- Galleria Nazionale d'Arte Moderna (p125)
- Art-Nouveau buildings on Piazza Mincio (above)
- Catacombe di Priscilla (below)

CATACOMBE DI PRISCILLA Map pp302–3
☎ 06 862 06 272; Via Salaria 430; admission €4.13; ⏰ 8.30am-noon & 2.30-5pm Tue-Sun

The **Catacombe di Priscilla**, southeast of Villa Ada along Via Nomentana, were originally part of the estate of the patrician Acilii family in the 1st century AD. They were greatly expanded in the 3rd and 4th centuries and became a popular 'society' burial ground – with appropriate upmarket decoration, quite a lot of which has survived. Several popes were buried in the catacombs between 309 and 555. A funerary chapel known as the **Cappella Greca** is thought to have been part of the criptoportico from the Acilii Villa. It retains good stucco decoration and well-preserved late-3rd-century frescoes of biblical scenes.

VILLA ADA Map pp302–3
bus to Piazza Ungheria

Green **Villa Ada Park** is a favourite among joggers. The paths thread among ponds and

lakes. For the more sedentary, there are sloping lawns and shady areas for a picnic any time of year. The villa was once the private residence of Victor Emmanuel III, but it is now the Egyptian Embassy.

VILLA BORGHESE Map pp304–5

entrances at Porta Pinciana, Piazzale Flaminio & Pincio; ⏰ dawn-dusk; bus to Piazzale Flaminio, metro Flaminio

Taking papal nepotism to its extremes, Pope Paul V granted his nephew Scipione the title of cardinal and gave him a sizable chunk of Rome, just outside the Aurelian Walls. There, between 1605 and 1614, Scipione built his casino to house his enormous collection of paintings and sculpture (now the Museo e Galleria Borghese) and had the grounds laid out by leading landscape designers such as Jacob More from Edinburgh. It's now Rome's most popular park, and a haven for many a traffic-weary visitor.

The park is divided into different areas by avenues of trees, hedged walks, planted flowerbeds, gravel paths and named roads. The reserved, English-style **Giardino del Lago** (Map p304–5) in the centre of the park was laid out in the late 18th century. Equestrian events are held in May in **Piazza di Siena**, an amphitheatre built around 1792. The park is dotted with sculptures of various periods, although many of these are not the real thing. The city authorities have been systematically removing the originals for several years and replacing them with resin copies. The originals will eventually be put on display in a museum in the park.

BIOPARCO Map pp306–7
☎ 06 321 65 64; www.bioparco.it (Italian only); Viale del Giardino del Zoologico 20; adult/child €8/6; ⏰ 9.30am-6pm (to 5pm Nov-Mar); metro Flaminio, bus or tram to Bioparco

Although still rather sad and gloomy, the enclosures at this zoo are improving, and there are two hundred species of animals to keep the youngsters engaged. Exotic animals are being phased out and eventually only animals compatible with the ecosystem and climate of central Italy will remain. There are kids' activities on weekends and during school holidays.

EXPLORA – MUSEO DEI BAMBINI DI ROMA Map pp304–5
☎ 06 361 37 76; www.mdbr.it/inglese/index.asp; Via Flaminia 82; adult/child €5/6 (under 3 free);

🕐 visits last for 1¾ hrs & start at 9.30am, 11.30am, 3pm & 5pm Tue-Fri, 10am, noon, 3pm & 5pm Sat & Sun; metro Flaminio

This wonderful new nonprofit museum – in the wrought-iron-and-glass shell of a former tram depot – consists of a miniature play town where children up to the age of 12 can indulge in the ultimate game of grown-ups. With everything from a hospital outpatients' department to a television studio, it's a hands-on, feet-on, full-on experience that your nippers will love. *And* it runs on solar power.

GALLERIA NAZIONALE D'ARTE MODERNA Map pp304–5

☎ 06 32 29 81; www.gnam.arti.beniculturali.it; Viale delle Belle Arti 131; admission €6.50; 🕐 8.30am-7.30pm Tue-Sun; bus to Viale delle Belle Arti

Most people don't come to Rome to look at *modern* art, but art wonks will need to make a stop here, if only to brag later that they've seen the comprehensive collection of works by the *macchiaioli* ('dabbers', the late 19th-century Italian version of the Impressionists). Best of these pictures is Raffaello Sernesi's *Roofs in Sunlight*, which makes poetry of Mediterranean light. Italian futurists are in the house (Boccioni, Balla) as well as a highly respectable international contingent: Degas, Cezanne, Kandinsky, Mondrian, Henry Moore and Cy Twombly, among others. The wing to the left of the entrance has been transformed into a sculpture gallery. Dynamic white marble, such as Canova's majestic *Ercole* (Hercules), contrast dramatically against walls painted in rich, solid colours.

The *belle époque* palace on the edge of Villa Borghese park was built for the 1911 Rome International Exhibition. Extensive renovations have returned it to its former glory. Original architectural elements, like decorative friezes and columns, are restored, and long-closed wings are open.

MUSEO CANONICA Map pp306–7

☎ 06 884 22 79; Viale Pietro Canonica 2; admission €2.60; 🕐 9am-7pm Tue-Sat, 9am-1.30pm Sun; bus to Viale delle Belle Arti

Sculptor and musician Pietro Canonica lived in this delightful villa in Villa Borghese for almost 30 years before his death in 1959. You can wander through the sculpture collection (mostly Canonica's own work), private apartment and studio.

MUSEO E GALLERIA BORGHESE

Map pp306–7

☎ 06 32 81 01; www.ticketeria.it ; Piazzale del Museo Borghese; admission €8.50 (admission every 2 hrs, book in advance by phone or online); 🕐 9am-7pm Tue-Sun; bus to Via Pinciana, tram to Viale delle Belle Arti

Hailed as the 'queen of all private collections', this gallery reflects the exquisite taste of Cardinal Scipione Borghese, the most passionate and knowledgeable art connoisseur of his time, and a man who wasn't afraid to use his papal connections to get the pieces he wanted. He had a keen appreciation for the antique but also patronised his contemporaries including the Caracci, Caravaggio and Gian Lorenzo Bernini. He stopped at nothing to add to his treasures; he had the fashionable painter Cavaliere d'Arpino flung into jail in order to confiscate his canvases, and had Domenichino arrested, to force him to surrender his painting of *The Hunt of Diana*.

Scipione's house, the Casino Borghese, surrounded by formal gardens and parkland, was a private treasure chest where he entertained lavishly. The collection and the building in which it was housed attracted illustrious visitors through the centuries, and both were augmented by the cardinal's heirs. In the late 18th century, Scipione's descendant Prince Marcantonio Borghese had the casino redecorated in a neoclassical style with elaborate gilding, faux-marble finishes and trompe l'oeil frescoes, which is how it appears today. The Mannerist nude figures and cheeky cherubs surrounded by ornate garlands of golden acanthus leaves are at times over the top. However, not all of the original art collection remains. Much of the antique statuary was carted off to the Louvre under the orders of Napoleon, whose sister Paolina was married to Marcantonio's son Camillo. Other pieces were sold off over time.

The entire collection and the mansion were acquired by the Italian State in 1902, but it was badly neglected. Structural problems in the building became evident in the 1940s. In 1983 part of a ceiling fresco by Giovanni Lanfranco crashed to the ground. In 1984 the gallery had to be shut down. After 13 years of restoration, it reopened in 1997.

The **Museo Borghese** (the ground-floor rooms) contains some important classical statuary. In the Salone are intricate floor mosaics of fighting gladiators dating from the 4th century AD and a *Satiro Combattente* (Fighting Satyr) from the 2nd century AD (restored by Bernini). High on the wall opposite the entrance is a gravity-defying bas-relief, *Marco Curzio a Cavallo*, of a horse and rider falling into the void of the room, which was created by Pietro Bernini (Gian Lorenzo Bernini's father) by combining ancient fragments and modern pieces. Throughout the ground-floor rooms there are full-length representations and busts of Roman gods, emperors and public figures. In Sala V, a 1st-century-AD *Ermafrodito* (Sleeping Hermaphrodite), a Roman copy of a Greek original, faces a wall so you can't see the evidence. She/he lies on a rather comfortable looking bed carved by Bernini.

A daring sculpture by Antonio Canova of Paolina Bonaparte Borghese as a reclining *Venere Vincitrice* (Venus Victorius) in Sala I is one of the most famous works in the collection. Her diaphanous drapery leaves little to the imagination and in its day the statue was considered outrageous and provocative. Paolina Borghese had quite a reputation, and tales abounded of her grand habits, her many lovers and her sometimes shocking behaviour. When asked how she could have posed almost naked she apparently pointed out that it was not cold.

Bernini's spectacular carvings – flamboyant depictions of pagan myths – are the stars of the ground-floor museum. Cardinal Scipione Borghese was one of Bernini's earliest patrons. The sculptor's precocious talent is evident in works such as *Il Ratto di Proserpina* (The Rape of Proserpine) in Sala IV, where Pluto's hand presses into Proserpine's solid marble thigh and in his *Davide* (Sala II), grim-faced and muscular, thought to be a self-portrait produced around 1624. In Sala III, Bernini's stunning, swirling *Apollo e Dafne* depicts the exact moment when the nymph is transformed into a laurel tree, her fingers becoming leaves, her toes turning into tree roots, while Apollo watches helplessly.

Other pieces by Bernini include an early work, *Enea e Anchise* (Aeneas and Anchises), which shows the sculptor's slight lack of confidence in depicting movement and *La Verità* (Truth), a rather strange later work done between 1645 and 1652, monumental in character but showing little of the mastery evident in his other significant pieces.

In Sala VIII, a 2nd-century-AD *Satiro Danzante* (Dancing Satyr), a Roman copy of an earlier Greek work, is surrounded by six paintings by Caravaggio. The luscious *Ragazzo con Canestro di Frutta* (Boy with a Basket of Fruit) and the *Bacco Malato* (Sick Bacchus), a self-portrait by Caravaggio painted when he was suffering from malaria, are early works completed between 1593 and 1595, not long

after his arrival in Rome. Both include magnificent representations of still life. The *Madonna dei Palafrenieri*, also known as the Madonna of the Serpent, was commissioned in 1605 by the Confraternity of the Palafrenieri (footmen) for their chapel in St Peter's Basilica. This is one of Caravaggio's masterpieces and to our eyes it is a wonderfully naturalistic work. However, its uninhibited realism was incompatible with early-17th-century ecclesiastical sensibilities and, after being rejected by the Palafrenieri, it was snapped up by Scipione. The other works depict *San Girolamo*, *San Giovanni Battista* (a young St John the Baptist) and *Davide con la Testa di Golia*, a dramatic image where Goliath's severed head is said to be a self-portrait. See the boxed text on p29.

The paintings in the **Galleria Borghese** on the 1st floor, representing the flowering of

Etruscan-style roof ornament in the gardens of the Museo Nazionale Etrusco di Villa Giulia (p127)

the Tuscan, Venetian, Umbrian and northern European schools, are testimony to Scipione's connoisseur's eye. In Sala IX are Raphael's *La Deposizione di Cristo* (Descent from the Cross) dated 1507 and his earlier portraits *Ritratto d'uomo* (1502) and *Dama con Liocorno*, a beautiful woman holding a mythological animal, painted in 1506. In the same room are the superb *Adorazione del Bambino* by Fra Bartolomeo and Perugino's *Madonna con Bambino*. Correggio's rather erotic *Danae* – perhaps an early version of soft porn – is in Sala X. In Sala XX it is interesting to compare Titian's early masterpiece *Amor Sacro e Amor Profano* (Sacred and Profane Love) with his later and less powerful work *Venere che Benda Amore* (Venus Blinding Cupid). There are also pieces by Giovanni Bellini, Giorgione, Veronese, Botticelli, Guercino, Domenichino, Antonello da Messina, Rubens and Cranach, to name a few.

MUSEO NAZIONALE ETRUSCO DI VILLA GIULIA Map pp304–5

☎ 06 322 65 71, for reservations 06 3 28 10; Piazzale di Villa Giulia 9; admission €4.13; ☼ 9am-7pm Tue-Sat, 9am-2pm Sun; metro Flaminio

If you're at all interested in Etruscan artefacts, you'll lose your mind here at Italy's finest collection of pre-Roman treasures, bilingually labelled and considerably presented in the 16th-century pleasure palace of Pope Julius III. Many of the collection's pieces were found in tombs at sites throughout Lazio. If you plan to visit Etruscan sites near Rome (see the Excursions chapter, p239), a visit to the museum before setting out will give you some context.

Lazio Vignola designed most of the building and gardens although a series of architects, including Michelangelo, chipped in before getting on the wrong side of the irascible pope. It has pretty frescoed loggias and a much-imitated *nymphaeum*.

There are thousands of exhibits on show, including domestic utensils, terracotta vases, chests, extraordinary bronze figurines, black bucchero tableware (decorated with geometrical patterns and carved figures), bronze mirrors, engraved wares, personal items such a hairclips, and even the remains of a horse-drawn chariot. Most of the items come from Etruscan burial tombs, one of which has been reconstructed for our benefit.

The Etruscans could work miracles with mud. If your attention will only run to a couple of pieces, look no further than the terracotta statue of *Apollo* and the *Sarcotago degli Sposi* tomb, both made in the 6th century BC. The finely sculpted sarcophagus was made not for royals, but for a regular husband and wife, and is adorned with a sculpture of the happy couple reclining on its lid. This is a good example of the creative heights the Etruscans reached, and which took the Romans several centuries to match. It has been restored several times, most recently in 1998 when a cleaner knocked Mrs Etruscan's arm off.

There is also a dazzling display of sophisticated Etruscan (and later period) jewellery and gemstones.

VATICAN CITY & BORGO

Eating p173; Shopping p218; Sleeping p236

The world's smallest sovereign state is home to the world's largest church: the incomparable St. Peter's. From a religious point of view, there are few places on earth so holy. From a secular point of view, the sheer density of artistic riches here is, well, heavenly. In 1929 Mussolini gave the pope full sovereignty over what is now the Città del Vaticano (Vatican City), as well as the basilicas of San Giovanni in Laterano, Santa Maria Maggiore, San Paolo Fuori-le-Mura, and certain other church-related buildings. Vatican City has its own postal service, currency, newspaper, radio station and train station (now used only for freight). It also has its own army of Swiss Guards, responsible for the pope's personal security. The corps was established in 1506 by Julius II to defend the Papal States against invading armies. The guards still wear the traditional eye-catching red, yellow and blue uniform and brandish unwieldy 15th-century pikes.

Make sure you dress appropriately the day you visit Vatican City. No shorts, no tank tops, no miniskirts, no kidding. The guards at St Peter's will turn away visitors with bare knees or shoulders, regardless of gender.

Transport

Bus 40, 62, 64, 81, 492
Metro Ottaviano

PIAZZA SAN PIETRO Map pp308–10

metro to Ottaviano, bus to Piazza del Risorgimento

Bernini's square is considered one of the world's great public spaces, laid out in the 17th century as a place for the Christians of the world to come together. It's an immense oval 'keyhole' bounded by four rows of Doric columns that first curve around in an embracing pair of semicircles, then straighten to literally funnel believers into the basilica. Bernini described the colonnade as representing 'the motherly arms of the church'. She's one big mama – the scale dazzles, measuring 198m across the long axis. Bernini perched 140 saints on top of the columns, witnesses to the crowds who gather here, pilgrim and tourist alike.

Bernini intended viewers to approach the square through the close and winding streets of the neighbourhood, after crossing the Tiber via his Ponte Sant'Angelo because, true to the spirit of the baroque, one's first view of the dazzling open space was meant to shock and awe. That effect is ruined by Mussolini's straight, wide Via della Conciliazione, so to experience it as Bernini intended, enter from the side. Bernini's original plan included another stretch of columns that would have closed the gap between the two semiovals, increasing the sense of surprise.

The **obelisk** at the heart of the square was brought to Rome by Gaius Caligula from Heliopolis in Egypt. Nero used it as a turning post for the chariot races in his circus. When you stand on the dark paving stones between the obelisk and either of the fountains, the colonnade on that side appears to have only one row of columns.

On Sunday the pope makes his regular address and recites the Angelus at noon from the building to the right of the square. His office is on the top floor, the second window from the right. At Christmas, a huge nativity scene is erected in the centre of the square.

ST PETER'S BASILICA Map pp308–10

☎ 06 698 81 662; www.vatican.va; Piazza San Pietro; basilica admission free, dome with/without lift €5/4; ◷ basilica 7am-6pm (Apr-Sep to 7pm), dome 7am-4.45pm (Apr-Sep to 5.45pm); dress appropriately, cover your knees and shoulders; metro Ottaviano, bus to Piazza del Risorgimento

No matter what your faith, the great basilica amazes. At first, it's only big, and then, as the eye comprehends its scale, it is astounding. It

is comprised, inside and out, of the products of artistic geniuses at the top of their game.

The first basilica was consecrated on the site of Nero's Circo Vaticano, where Christians, including St Peter, had been martyred between AD 64 and 67. St Peter was buried in an anonymous grave next to the wall of the circus, and his fellow Christians built a humble wall to mark the site. When the stadium was abandoned in 160, a small monument was erected to the saint. In the early 4th century, Constantine ordered construction of a basilica on the sight of the tomb, and it was consecrated in 326.

More than a thousand years later, the church had fallen into a state of disrepair. In the mid-15th century, Pope Nicholas V took a stab at reconstruction, but it wasn't until Pope Julius II employed Bramante in 1506 that serious work began. Bramante envisioned a Greek cross plan with a central dome and four smaller domes. He oversaw the demolition of much of the old basilica, and attracted criticism for the unnecessary destruction of many of its precious artworks, including Byzantine mosaics and frescoes.

It took more than 150 years to complete the basilica, involving the contributions of Bramante, Raphael, Antonio da Sangallo, Michelangelo, Giacomo della Porta and Carlo Maderno. It is generally held that St Peter's owes the most to Michelangelo, who took over the project in 1547 at the age of 72 and was responsible for the design of the dome. He died before the church was completed. The facade and portico were designed by Carlo Maderno, who took over the project after Michelangelo's death. He was instructed to lengthen the nave towards the square, effectively altering Bramante's original Greek cross plan to a Latin cross.

The cavernous interior, decorated by Bernini and Giacomo della Porta, can hold up to 60,000 people. It contains a vast number of incredible treasures. The **red-porphyry disk** on the floor just inside the main door marks the spot

---

Top Five Vatican City

- Sistine Chapel (p135)
- Michelangelo's *Pietà* (p130)
- Stanze di Raffaello (p135)
- View from the Dome of St Peter's (p131)
- Bernini's Baldacchino (p129)

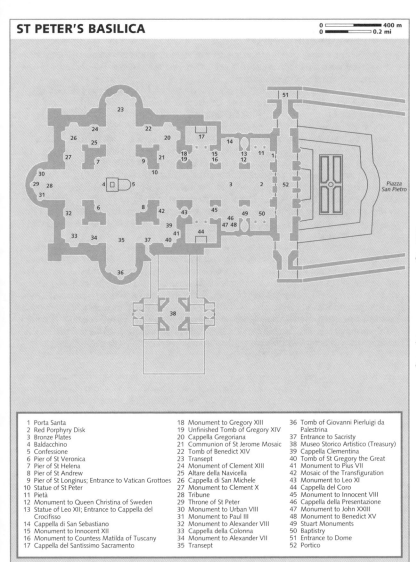

ST PETER'S BASILICA

1 Porta Santa
2 Red Porphyry Disk
3 Bronze Plates
4 Baldacchino
5 Confessione
6 Pier of St Veronica
7 Pier of St Helena
8 Pier of St Andrew
9 Pier of St Longinus; Entrance to Vatican Grottoes
10 Statue of St Peter
11 Pietà
12 Monument to Queen Christina of Sweden
13 Statue of Leo XII; Entrance to Cappella del Crocifisso
14 Cappella di San Sebastiano
15 Monument to Innocent XII
16 Monument to Countess Matilda of Tuscany
17 Cappella del Santissimo Sacramento
18 Monument to Gregory XIII
19 Unfinished Tomb of Gregory XIV
20 Cappella Gregoriana
21 Communion of St Jerome Mosaic
22 Tomb of Benedict XIV
23 Transept
24 Monument of Clement XIII
25 Altare della Navicella
26 Cappella di San Michele
27 Monument to Clement X
28 Tribune
29 Throne of St Peter
30 Monument to Urban VIII
31 Monument to Paul III
32 Monument to Alexander VIII
33 Cappella della Colonna
34 Monument to Alexander VII
35 Transept
36 Tomb of Giovanni Pierluigi da Palestrina
37 Entrance to Sacristy
38 Museo Storico Artistico (Treasury)
39 Cappella Clementina
40 Tomb of St Gregory the Great
41 Monument to Pius VII
42 Mosaic of the Transfiguration
43 Monument to Leo XI
44 Cappella del Coro
45 Monument to Innocent VIII
46 Cappella della Presentazione
47 Monument to John XXIII
48 Monument to Benedict XV
49 Stuart Monuments
50 Baptistry
51 Entrance to Dome
52 Portico

where Charlemagne and later Holy Roman emperors were crowned by the pope. **Bronze plates** in the marble floor of the central aisle indicate the respective sizes of the 14 next-largest churches in the world.

Bernini's baroque **baldacchino** stands 29m high in the centre of the church and is an extraordinary work of art. The bronze used to make it was taken from the roof of the Pantheon. The high altar, at which only the pope

can serve, stands over the site of St Peter's grave. The **Confessione** in front of it, built by Carlo Maderno, is encircled with perpetually burning lamps.

Michelangelo's **dome**, a majestic architectural masterpiece, soars 119m above the high altar. The solid stone **piers** supporting the dome have niches and balconies designed by Bernini. Each pier is named after the saint whose colossal statue stands in its niches – St

Waiting for the White Smoke

Pope John Paul II has been in frail health for some time, and there has been protracted speculation about his possible successor, with bookmakers offering odds on possible future incumbents, and the world's media poised to descend on Rome for the conclave of cardinals which elects a new pope.

The conclave is made up a maximum of 120 cardinals, none of whom may be over 80. They are locked up inside the Vatican, usually in the Sistine Chapel, with no communication to the outside world, until a new pope is chosen through a series of secret ballots. The place chosen is locked both inside and out and it includes rooms for the cardinals and their assistants. The result of the vote is indicated to the outside world by the colour of the smoke which issues from a vent above the Sistine Chapel (black smoke indicates no decision has been made; white smoke indicates a new pope has been elected).

What are the requirements for the Roman Catholic Church's top job? There is a list of unwritten prerequisites. The candidate needs to be well known in the Curia, the papal court and government of the Roman Catholic Church. He must have a reputation as a theologian and must have written prominent Vatican documents. He must also have worked in one of the Church's international organisations. In addition, the candidate must be in good health (to avoid a repeat of John Paul I's month-long papacy); he should be neither too young (there's a feeling that John Paul II's papacy has been too long) nor too old; and he must be media-friendly and capable of projecting a charismatic image. On top of all that, candidates must never appear actually to be campaigning for the job. As one saying goes: 'He who goes into a conclave a *papabile* comes out a cardinal'.

One possible contender is the charismatic and clever Nigerian Cardinal Francis Arinze, 68, a popular figure who has been in charge of the Church's ecumenical relations, with Islam in particular, since 1985. Just as John Paul II has dealt with Communism during his papacy, perhaps Arinze will be the one to be able to handle the Church's relations with other religions in the next century. The media-savvy Arinze is also fiercely orthodox on hot-button Church topics, including his opposition to abortion, female priests and contraception. But is the Catholic world ready for a black African pope? Arinze would not be the first – that honour was taken by Gelasius I who reigned from 492 to 496 – but the excitement and media attention that greeted the first mention of him as a possible candidate in the early 1990s has probably not worked in his favour.

Only one thing is sure. When Pope John Paul II dies and a group of men in red hats get together to elect his successor, the reverberations will be felt around the world, and Rome once again will be the focus of the world's attention.

Longinus (by Bernini), St Helena, St Veronica and St Andrew. The balconies above are decorated with reliefs depicting the Reliquie Maggiori (Major Relics): the lance of St Longinus, which he used to pierce Christ's side; the cloth of St Veronica, which bears a miraculous portrait of Christ; and a piece of the True Cross, collected by St Helena, the mother of Constantine.

To the right as you face the high altar, at the base of the Pier of St Longinus, is a famous **bronze statue of St Peter**, believed to be a 13th-century work by Arnolfo di Cambio. The statue's right foot has been worn smooth and flat by the strokes of pilgrims, who patiently queue to touch it. The statue is dressed in papal robes on the Feast Day of St Peter and St Paul, 29 June.

Michelangelo's devastating **Pietà** is at the beginning of the right aisle just inside the **Porta Santa** (Holy Door). It was sculpted when he was only 25 years old and is the only work to carry his signature (on the sash across the breast of the Madonna). It is now protected by bulletproof glass after having been attacked in 1972 by a hammer-wielding vandal.

Beyond the Pietà is the **Cappella del Santissimo Sacramento**. The iron grille separating the chapel from the rest of the basilica was designed by Borromini. Above the altar is a gilt bronze ciborium by Bernini (modelled on Bramante's Tempietto at San Pietro in Montorio) and behind it an altarpiece, *The Trinity*, by Pietro da Cortona.

At the back of the Pier of St Longinus is a large **mosaic** of the Communion of St Jerome, after Domenichino. From a distance the medium is unclear and this vast artwork looks very like a canvas. The **Cappella Gregoriana** opposite was built by Gregory XIII from designs by Michelangelo. Part of a marble column from the old basilica was placed here in 1578; the painting on it, the *Madonna del Soccorso*, can still be made out.

Two notable artworks in the **transept** right of the main entrance are the **monument of Clement XIII** by Canova, and the bright and garish **Altare della Navicella** mosaic of Christ Walking on the Waters, after Lanfranco. Of the three mosaics in the **Cappella di San Michele**, the Santa Petronilla after Guercino (a massive canvas of the subject is in the Capitoline Museums) is most impressive.

The **Throne of St Peter** by Bernini (1665) in the **Tribune** cannot fail to catch your eye. The huge gilded-bronze throne is supported by statues of St Augustine, St Ambrose, St Athanasius and St John Chrysostom. Its wooden seat, inlaid with ivory, is thought to have been St Peter's chair.

In a very modernist composition, rays of light shine from the figure of a dove (representing the Holy Spirit) towards a halo of flying angels. To the right of the throne is Bernini's monument to Urban VIII, where the pope is flanked by the figures of Charity and Justice. The design is clearly influenced by Michelangelo's Medici tombs in Florence.

The **Cappella della Colonna**, in the northern aisle, is decorated with figures of angels with garlands of flowers. Above the tomb of St Leo the Great is a particularly fine relief (1650) by the baroque sculptor Alessandro Algardi. Opposite it, under the next arch, is Bernini's last work in the basilica, the **monument to Alexander VII**, in which the sculptor has made heavy red marble resemble soft velvet.

The cupola of the **Cappella Clementina** is decorated with mosaics, after Pomarancio. The chapel is named after Clement VIII (died 1605) who had Giacomo della Porta decorate it for the Jubilee of 1600. Beneath the altar is the **tomb of St Gregory the Great** (died 604), and above it a mosaic representing the **Miracle of St Gregory** after Andrea Sacchi. To the left of the altar is a classical **monument to Pope Pius VII** by Thorvaldsen, whose work at the time was strongly influenced by Canova.

Particularly charming is the **monument to Leo XI** by Alessandro Algardi in the next aisle arch. Beyond it, the richly decorated **Cappella del Coro** shows what happens if you go mad with gilt. Giovanni Battista Ricci carried out the work in the chapel following designs by Giacomo della Porta; Bernini designed the elegant choir stalls. The chapel is usually locked but it's worth sticking your nose through the gate to get a good look. The **monument to Innocent VIII** by Antonio Pollaiuolo (in the next aisle arch) is a re-creation of a monument from the old basilica.

The **Cappella della Presentazione** contains two of the most modern works in the whole basilica. On the right of the altar is a **monument to John XXIII** by Emilio Greco and on the left is a **monument to Benedict XV** by Pietro Canonica. Under the next arch are the so-called **Stuart monuments**. On the right is the monument to Clementina Sobieska, wife of James Stuart, by Filippo Barigioni, and on the left is Canova's superb monument to the last Stuarts. The simple sculpture has two angels flanking a door, and busts of the Old and Young Pretenders and of Henry Cardinal York.

DOME Map p129

St Peter's Basilica; access with/without lift €5/4; ☽ **8am-6pm Apr-Sept, 8am-5pm Oct-Mar**
You can't beat the view of the city from the dome of St Peter's, some 111m up. A small lift takes you halfway but it's still a long climb to the top. The ticket office is to the far right of the basilica, and there are often long queues. It is well worth the effort but bear in mind it is a long and tiring climb and not to be recommended for those who suffer from claustrophobia or vertigo.

GIARDINI DEL VATICANO Map pp308–10

☎ **06 698 84 466; €8.78 (by special appointment only);** ☽ **walking tours Mon, Tue & Thu-Sat Mar-Oct, less frequent Nov-Feb**
The **Giardini del Vaticano** (Vatican Gardens) contain fortifications, grottoes, monuments and fountains dating from the 9th century to the present day, as well as a heliport and manicured gardens in various styles tended by 30 full-time gardeners. There's a formal Italian garden, a flower-filled French parterre and a naturalistic English wood. There is even a kitchen garden which provides produce for the pontifical household, although tour groups don't get close enough to check out the papal tomatoes.

Tickets must be booked in advance by calling the Ufficio Visite Guidate dei Musei Vaticani. It's advisable to book well before your visit.

The Face in the Baldacchino

The frieze on Bernini's *baldacchino* contains a hidden narrative that begins at the pillar to the left, if your back is facing the entrance. A woman's face carved into the frieze of each pillar, at about eye level, seems to express the increasing agony of childbirth as you walk clockwise around the baldacchino. On the final pillar, her face is replaced by that of a smiling baby.

MUSEO STORICO ARTISTICO (TREASURY) Map p129

St Peter's Basilica; admission €4.13; ☽ **9am-6pm Apr-Sep (to 5pm Oct-Mar)**
The sacristy entrance leads to the **Museo Storico Artistico** (Treasury) which has sacred relics and priceless artefacts. Highlights include: a tabernacle by Donatello; the Colonna Santa, a 4th-century Byzantine column from the earlier church; the 6th-century Crux Vaticana, made of bronze and beset with jewels – a gift of the emperor Justinian II; and the massive bronze tomb of Sixtus IV by Pollaiuolo.

TOMB OF ST PETER
by appointment only (details below)

The excavations beneath St Peter's, which began in 1940, have uncovered part of the original church, an early-Christian cemetery and Roman tombs. Archaeologists believe they have also found the tomb of St Peter; the site of the empty tomb is marked by a shrine and a wall plastered with red. Nearby is another wall, scrawled with the graffiti of pilgrims; in 1942 the bones of an elderly, strongly built man were found in a box placed in a niche behind this wall. In 1976, after many years of forensic examination, Paul VI declared the bones to be those of St Peter. John Paul II had some of the relics transferred to his hospital room when he was recovering from the 1981 assassination attempt. The bones were then returned to the tomb and are kept in hermetically sealed Perspex cases designed by NASA.

The excavations can be visited only by appointment, which can be made by writing to the **Ufficio Scavi** (☎ 06 698 85 318, fax 06 698 85 518). The office opens 9am to 5pm Monday to Friday.

VATICAN GROTTOES
entrance inside St Peter's Basilica; ⏰ 7am-6pm Apr-Sep, 7am-5pm Sep-Mar

The entrance to the **Sacre Grotte Vaticane** (Vatican Grottoes), the resting place of numerous popes, is tucked inconspicuously next to the Pier of St Longinus (one of four piers supporting the arches at the base of Michelangelo's cupola) to the right as you approach the papal altar. The tombs of many early popes were moved here from the old St Peter's Basilica, and recent popes, including John XXIII, Paul VI and John Paul I, are buried here.

VATICAN MUSEUMS Map pp308–10
☎ 06 698 84 947; www.vatican.va; Viale del Vaticano; admission €10, free last Sun of month; ⏰ 8.45am-1.45pm Mon-Sat Nov-Feb, 8.45am-4.45pm Mon-Fri, closes 1.45pm Sat Mar-Oct (last tickets sold 75 mins before close), 9am-1.45pm last Sun of month only year-round (last admissions 1½ hrs before close); bus to Piazza del Risorgimento, metro Ottaviano

From Piazza San Pietro, follow the wall of the Vatican north to the museums' entrance. It's a good ten-minute hike.

The museums are gargantuan, and contain enough papal treasure to turn heads for weeks. You will need several hours to see

even the highlights of the museum. One visit is probably not enough to appreciate everything.

To make navigating the hallways and galleries easier, the museum has plotted four itineraries which range from a quick dash through the greatest hits to a comprehensive tour that will take about five hours. The Sistine Chapel comes toward the end of each itinerary, and is regularly as crowded as a mall at Christmas time. If you get to the museum at opening time, and sprint directly to the chapel, you might have a semiprivate quarter hour with the ceiling before doubling back to the Quattro Cancelli to pick up one of the itineraries.

The *Guide to the Vatican Museums and City*, on sale at the museums, is a worthwhile investment. You can also hire CD audio guides which provide a commentary for what you are seeing.

The buildings that house the Vatican Museums, known collectively as the Palazzo Apostolico Vaticano, cover an area of 5.5 hectares. Their construction has been a work in progress since the 5th century. Each gallery contains priceless treasures, but if you want to skim the cream of the collection without wearing yourself out, get to the Stanza di Raffaello, the Pinacoteca, the Galleria delle Carte Geografiche and, of course, the Sistine Chapel. Unless they're of particular interest, you can speed walk through the Museo Gregorio Profano, Museo Pio-Cristiano and Museo Missionario-Etnologio.

Papal Audiences

On Wednesday the pope meets his flock. To be present at an audience, write in advance to the Prefettura della Casa Pontificia, 00120 Città del Vaticano (fax 06 698 85 863), requesting the date you'd like to attend. If you're already in Rome, call into the Prefettura (open 9am-1pm Mon-Fri) through the bronze doors under the colonnade to the right of St Peter's.

Check the Vatican website or call to confirm opening times, as the schedule is revised periodically.

The museums are well equipped for disabled visitors; there are four suggested itineraries, several lifts and specially fitted toilets. Ask for a folder at the ticket window or information desk or call in advance on ☎ 06 698 84 341. Wheelchairs can be reserved. Parents with young children can take strollers into the museums.

MUSEO GREGORIANO PROFANO

Sculpture found in the Baths of Caracalla was hauled here, and now stands shoulder to shoulder with other classical statuary. Greek pieces date from the 5th and 4th centuries BC, and Roman sculpture comes from the 1st to the 3rd century AD.

MUSEO PIO-CRISTIANO

The **Museo Pio-Cristiano** contains early-Christian antiquities, including inscriptions and sculpture from catacombs and basilicas, and sarcophagi decorated with carved reliefs of biblical scenes. The collection was founded by Pius IX in 1854. Both these collections were formerly kept in the Palazzo Laterano and were moved to the Vatican in 1970.

PINACOTECA

Among the relatively small number of pictures here is a mother lode of masterpieces. The popes' picture gallery was founded by Pius XI and houses a magnificent collection of paintings dating from the 11th to the 19th century. Napoleon hijacked a number of them in 1797, but they were returned to Rome in 1815. They are hung in chronological order and include works by Fra Angelico, Filippo Lippi, Benozzo Gozzoli, Federico Barocci, Guido Reni, Guercino, Nicholas Poussin, Van Dyck and Pietro da Cortona.

There are several works by Raphael, who has a room to himself, including the *Madonna di Foligno*, originally kept in the church of Santa Maria in Aracoeli, and his last painting, the magnificent *La Trasfigurazione*, which was nearly complete when he died in 1520. Other highlights of the collection include Giotto's *Polittico Stefaneschi* (Stefaneschi triptych), which was originally an altarpiece in the sacristy of St Peter's, Giovanni Bellini's *Pietà*, Leonardo's unfinished *San Gerolamo* and Caravaggio's *Deposizione*.

MUSEO MISSIONARIO-ETNOLOGICO

Missionaries brought back many of these ethnological and anthropological artefacts from Africa, the Americas, Asia and the Middle East.

MUSEO GREGORIANO EGIZIO

Pope Gregory XVI founded the Egyptian museum in 1839 to hold pieces taken from Egypt during Roman times. The collection is small but fascinating, including the **Trono di Rameses II**, part of a statue of the seated king. Room II contains painted wooden **sarcophagi** dating from around

1000 BC, whose colours are unbelievably fresh and rich. The two **mummies** are big hits with macabre-minded small fry. One is totally bandaged. The other has its blackened hands and feet exposed, and you can see the henna-treated hair and a hole where the mummy's left eye should have been; the eye was probably removed so that the brain could be extracted before mummification. There are also two carved-marble sarcophagi from the 6th century BC. Room III has Egyptian-style Roman sculptures, which were used as decoration at the Villa Adriana in Tivoli (see p244).

The rooms were decorated in the 19th century in Egyptian style and have decorative details such as cornice friezes with inscriptions in hieroglyphics, and midnight-blue ceilings peppered with gold stars.

MUSEO CHIARAMONTI

Hundreds of marble statues of gods, playful cherubs and Roman patricians line the corridor. The hairstyles are more dramatic than your mama's beehive. Near the end of the **Museo Chiaramonti**, off to the right is the **Braccio Nuovo** (new wing). It contains important works, including a famous statue of Augustus and a statue depicting the Nile as a reclining god with 16 babies (supposedly representing the number of cubits the Nile rose when in flood) playing on him.

Visible through a gate at the end of the Museo Chiaramonti is the **Galleria Lapidaria**, which only opens to scholars on request. It contains over 3000 Christian and Roman inscriptions, mounted into the walls of the gallery. The Christian inscriptions are on the right side and the classical ones on the left.

MUSEO PIO-CLEMENTINO

This museum is in the belvedere and accessible through the Egyptian Museum or from the Cortile della Pigna. Entering through the square vestibule, you come to the Gabinetto dell'Apoxyomenos, which contains a 1st-century-AD Roman statue found in Trastevere in 1849. The statue depicts an athlete towelling himself off and is actually a copy of a bronze original thought to date from around 320 BC.

In the elegant **Cortile Ottagono** (Octagonal Courtyard), which forms part of the gallery, are several important ancient statues, bas-reliefs and sarcophagi. To the left as you enter, in a niche in the corner, is the famous *Apollo Belvedere*, a 2nd-century Roman copy in marble of a 4th-century-BC Greek bronze, considered one of the great masterpieces of classical sculpture.

Also on the left is an impressive statue of a river god (Tigris). Beyond it is another notable piece, the *Laocoön*, depicting a Trojan priest of Apollo and his two sons in mortal struggle with two sea serpents. When discovered in 1506 on the Esquiline (Michelangelo was said to have been present), the sculpture was recognised from descriptions by the Roman writer Pliny the Elder and purchased by Pope Julius II.

Back inside the Belvedere is the **Sala degli Animali**, filled with sculptures of all sorts of creatures. The floors of both sides of the gallery contain magnificent mosaics dating from the 4th century AD. Don't miss the delightful crab (made from rare green-porphyry stone) at the far end of the room on the right. Facing it, mounted on the wall, is a charming mosaic showing a cat with ducks and fruit. There are also two small mosaic landscapes which came from the Villa Adriana. Beyond the Sala degli Animali are the **Galleria delle Statue**, with several important classical pieces, the **Sala delle Buste**, which contains portrait busts of important Roman emperors and political figures, and the **Gabinetto delle Maschere**, which is named after the floor mosaics of theatrical masks; there are several interesting pieces in this room including two statues of Venus and a group representing the three Graces.

In the **Sala delle Muse** (Room of the Muses) is the *Torso Belvedere*, a Greek sculpture of the 1st century BC, which was found in the Campo de' Fiori during the time of Pope Julius II – it was much admired by Michelangelo and other Renaissance artists. The next room, the round **Sala Rotonda**, built by Michelangelo Simonetti in 1780, was inspired by the Pantheon. It contains a number of colossal statues including the gilded-bronze figure of *Ercole* (Hercules). The ancient mosaic on the floor, featuring sea monsters and battles between Greeks and centaurs, is quite exquisite. The enormous basin in the centre of the room was found at the site of Nero's Domus Aurea and is made out of a single piece of red-porphyry stone.

In the **Sala a Croce Greca** (Greek Cross Room) are the porphyry stone sarcophagi of Constantine's daughter, Constantia, and his mother, St Helena. These were originally in the Mausoleo di Santa Constanza in Via Nomentana.

MUSEO GREGORIANO ETRUSCO

On the upper level of the Belvedere, off the Simonetti staircase, is the **Museo Gregoriano Etrusco** (Etruscan Museum), which contains artefacts from Etruscan tombs of southern Etruria. Of particular interest are those in Room II from the Regolini-Galassi tomb, discovered in 1836 south of Cerveteri. Those buried in the tomb included a princess, and among the finds on display are gold jewellery and a funeral carriage, with a bronze bed and funeral couch, dating from the 7th century BC. The Etruscan rooms were refurbished and expanded in 1996. The exhibits are arranged by subject matter so it is easy to compare pieces.

The **Sala dei Bronzi** has the *Marte di Todi* (Mars of Todi), a full-length bronze statue of a warrior dating from the 4th century BC, as well as bronze figurines, statuettes of young boys, armour, hand mirrors and candelabra. Beyond it, the **Sala delle Pietre** displays sarcophagi and statues in volcanic stone such as tufa and *peperino*, which were favoured by the Etruscans as they were soft and easy to carve, then hardened over time. The **Sala degli Ori** is devoted to beautifully displayed Etruscan jewellery.

The **Sala delle Terracotte** displays terracotta pieces, including some wonderfully expressive portrait heads. Don't miss the bust of an elderly woman. The Etruscan Museum also incorporates a collection of Greek vases and Roman antiquities, a highlight of which is a vase, signed by the Greek artist Exekias and decorated with an image of Achilles and Ajax playing draughts, dating from around 530 BC. Magnificent views of Rome can be had from the last room at the end of the wing. From here you can also get a glimpse down the full drop of Bramante's spiral staircase which was designed so that horses could be ridden up it. The stairway was built for Julius II inside a square tower which was at one time the entrance to the Belvedere.

GALLERIA DEI CANDELABRI

Originally an open loggia, the **Galleria dei Candelabri** (Gallery of the Candelabra) is packed with classical sculpture including several elegantly carved marble candelabra which give the room its name. In the middle section of the long gallery, note the fragments of Roman frescoes and the vividly coloured still-life mosaics. Further on is a charming sculpture of a boy strangling a goose and opposite it a flute player.

GALLERIA DEGLI ARAZZI

You have to walk through the **Galleria degli Arazzi** (Tapestry Gallery) to get to the Sistine Chapel, and it is worth a brief look. The tapestries on the left (opposite the windows) date from the 16th century. They were designed by students of Raphael and woven in the Brussels workshop of Pieter van Aeist. Note the intricate details of flowers and foliage in the penultimate tapestry showing Christ appearing to Mary Magdalen. The tapestries on the right date from the 17th century and were woven by the Barberini workshop.

GALLERIA DELLE CARTE GEOGRAFICHE

Even if you're mid-sprint to the Sistine Chapel, this colourful gallery deserves a close look. Covered from one end to the other with fascinating topographical maps, the **Galleria delle Carte Geografiche** (Map Gallery) contains 40 topographical maps painted between 1580 and 1583 for Pope Gregory XIII based on cartoons by Ignazio Danti, one of the leading cartographers of his day. The ceiling frescoes, representing the lives of saints and the history of the Church, are related geographically to the maps below them.

Next to the Map Gallery is the **Appartamento di San Pio V**, containing some interesting Flemish tapestries, and the **Sala Sobieski**, named after the enormous 19th-century canvas on its northern wall (depicting the victory of the Polish King John III Sobieski over the Turks in 1683). These rooms lead into the magnificent Stanze di Raffaello.

STANZE DI RAFFAELLO

The so-called 'Raphael Rooms' were the private apartments of Pope Julius II. Raphael painted the Stanza della Segnatura and the Stanza d'Eliodoro, while the Stanza dell'Incendio was painted by his students to his designs and the ceiling was painted by his master, Perugino.

The far room, the **Sala di Costantino**, was decorated by Raphael's students with some of the works based on his designs. Off this room is the Sala dei Chiaroscuri and the Cappella di Niccolo V. The **Sala dei Chiaroscuri** was decorated in the 16th century and used for ceremonial purposes. Raphael designed the ceiling which, along with the chiaroscuro figures on the walls, was executed by his students. A small door leads to the tiny **Cappella di Niccolo V** which was Pope Nicholas V's private chapel. The superb frescoes were painted by Fra Angelico around 1450 and depict the lives of St Stephen (upper cycle) and St Lawrence (lower level).

Back in the Stanze di Raffaello you enter the **Stanza d'Eliodoro**. Raphael's fine **Cacciata d'Eliodoro** (Expulsion of Heliodorus from the Temple), on the main wall (to the right as you enter from the Sala dei Chiaroscuri), depicts Julius' military victory over foreign powers. To the left is *Mass of Bolsena*, showing Julius II paying homage to the relic of a 13th-century miracle at Orvieto. Next is *Leone X ferma l'invasione di Attila* (Leo X Repulsing Attila) by Raphael and his school, and on the fourth wall is *Liberazione di San Pietro* (Liberation of St Peter), which depicts St Peter being freed from prison but is actually an allusion to Pope Leo's imprisonment after the Battle of Ravenna (also the metaphorical subject of the Attila fresco).

In the **Stanza della Segnatura** is another masterpiece by Raphael and perhaps his best-known work: **La Scuola d'Atene** (The School of Athens), featuring philosophers and scholars gathered around Plato and Aristotle. The lone figure in front of the steps is believed to be a portrait of Michelangelo, who was painting the Sistine Chapel at the time. The figure of Plato (pointing to the sky) is said to be a portrait of Leonardo da Vinci. In the lower right, the figure of Euclide (bent over and drawing with a compass) is Bramante. Raphael included a self-portrait at the lower right of the fresco (second figure from right). Opposite is *La Disputa del Sacramento* (Dispute over the Holy Sacrament), also by Raphael.

From Raphael's rooms, go down the stairs to the **Appartamento Borgia**, but only to see the ceiling in the first room, decorated with frescoes by Bernardino Pinturicchio. The Vatican collection of modern religious art was installed in the Borgia apartments in 1973 but it's really only worth visiting if religious paintings are your thing.

SISTINE CHAPEL

This is the room from which the sequestered papal conclave sends up its decisive smoke (see the boxed text, p130), and it contains the most famous works of art in the world: Michelangelo's wonderful frescoes of the *Genesis* (Creation) on the barrel-vaulted ceiling, and the *Giudizio Universale* (Last Judgement) on the end wall. Commissioned in the early 16th century, both have been restored to their original technicolour glory. The ceiling was unveiled after a 10-year restoration project in 1990 and work on *The Last Judgement* was completed in 1994. Michelangelo's colours surprised many scholars and art historians, who hadn't imagined such a rich, vibrant palate lurked under the centuries of soot and grime.

Michelangelo was commissioned by Pope Julius II to paint the ceiling and, although very reluctant to take on the job (he never considered himself a painter), he started work on it in 1508. The complex and grand composition which Michelangelo devised to cover the 800

Michelangelo in Rome

Michelangelo Buonarroti was born in Caprese near Arrezzo in Tuscany in 1475, the son of a Tuscan magistrate. He was a moody and solitary figure, easily offended and irritated. The true Renaissance man, he was a supremely talented architect and painter, but he regarded himself as a sculptor above all else.

It was as a sculptor that Michelangelo achieved his early recognition. One of his greatest early carvings is the *Pietà* in St Peter's Basilica which he completed when he was 25.

Michelangelo came to work in Rome for Pope Julius II who wanted a grand marble tomb which would surpass any funerary monument that had ever been built. Michelangelo was dispatched to the marble quarries of Carrara in northern Tuscany (which still provide stone for sculptors today) and spent eight months selecting and excavating suitable marble blocks which, when brought to Rome, reportedly filled half of Piazza San Pietro.

Although the tomb preoccupied Michelangelo throughout his working life, it was never completed and Julius II lies in an unadorned grave in St Peter's. The original design included 40 statues. The famous figure of Moses as well as statues of Leah and Rachel are in the Basilica di San Pietro in Vincoli. Two of the slaves are now in the Louvre (Paris) and several famous unfinished slaves are in the Accademia (Florence).

Despite claiming to be a reluctant painter, Michelangelo's single greatest artistic achievement – and one of the most awe-inspiring acts of individual creativity in the history of the visual arts – is the ceiling of the Sistine Chapel, painted between 1508 and 1512.

Michelangelo never wanted the commission (also from Julius II) and the project was problematic from the outset. First the artist rejected the scaffolding that Bramante had built for him; then he considered his assistants so incompetent that he dismissed them all, scraped off their work, and ended up painting the entire ceiling by himself. The artist was pushed to his physical and emotional limits, and was continually harassed by the pope and his court, who wanted the job finished.

Michelangelo returned to Rome aged 59 at the request of Pope Clement VII to paint *The Last Judgement* on the altar wall of the Sistine Chapel. Once again he accepted the commission against his will, preferring to continue sculpting figures for Julius II's tomb which he did secretly while he prepared cartoons for the chapel.

On Clement VII's death, his successor Paul III was determined to have Michelangelo working exclusively for him and have the Sistine Chapel completed; in 1535 he appointed Michelangelo as chief architect, sculptor and painter to the Vatican, and the artist started working on *The Last Judgement*, which was unveiled in 1541 and claimed by some as surpassing not only the other masters who had decorated the chapel walls but also his own ceiling frescoes.

Paul III then commissioned Michelangelo to create a new central square for the city on the Capitoline and design a grand approach to it. The work was not finished until the mid-17th century but successive architects closely followed the original plans.

Michelangelo's design for the upper storey of the Palazzo Farnese was also realised posthumously, when Giacomo della Porta completed the building, and his design for the city gateway at Porta Pia was finished a year after his death.

The artist spent his last years working – unhappily – on St Peter's Basilica; he felt that it was a penance from God. He disapproved of the plans that had been drawn up by Antonio da Sangallo the Younger before his death, claiming that they deprived the basilica of light, and argued with Sangallo's assistants who wanted to retain their master's designs. Instead Michelangelo created the magnificent light-filled dome, based on Brunelleschi's design for the Duomo cupola in Florence, and a stately facade.

In his old age he was said to work with the same strength and concentration as he had as a younger man. He continued to direct the work until his death on 18 February 1564. He was buried in the Chiesa dei Santi Apostoli although his remains were later moved to Florence. The dome and facade of St Peter's were completed to his designs by Vignola, Giacomo della Porta and Carlo Fontana.

sq metres of ceiling took him four years to complete. He worked on scaffolding which the restorers believe was inserted into holes under the windows. The restorers also learned much about the way in which the artist worked and how his painting skill developed as he progressed through the great project.

Vasari records Michelangelo's suffering and frustration, as well as his problems with an impatient Pope Julius and the fact that he did the work almost entirely alone, after dismissing in disgust the Florentine masters he had gathered to help him.

Looking towards *The Last Judgement*, the scenes down the middle of the ceiling represent nine scenes from the book of Genesis: Division of Day from Night; Creation of the Sun, Moon and Planets; Creation of the Heavens; Separation of Land from Sea; Creation of Adam; Creation of Eve; Temptation and Expulsion of Adam and Eve from the Garden of Eden; Noah's sacrifice; the Flood; the Drunkenness of Noah.

You can track Michelangelo's development as a painter through his ceiling frescoes. He actually worked in reverse order, starting with the *Drunkenness of Noah* (which is fairly stiff and formal) and working back to the *Creation of the Sun, Moon and Planets* and the *Division of Day from Night* (both of which demonstrate the artist at the peak of his powers).

Probably the most famous scene is the image of the *Creation of Adam*, where God points his index figure at Adam, bringing him to life. God's swirling red cape surrounds a group of people, said to represent the generations to come. In the *Temptation and Expulsion of Adam and Eve from the Garden of Eden*, Adam and Eve are shown (on the left) tasting the forbidden fruit, with Satan represented by a snake with the body of a woman coiled around a tree. On the right, Adam and Eve are expelled from Eden by the red-robed, sword-wielding Angel of the Lord.

The main scenes are framed by the *Ignudi*, athletic male nudes, with which Michelangelo celebrates the male figure. Next to them, on the lower curved part of the vault, separated by trompe l'oeil cornices, are large figures of Hebrew Prophets and pagan Sibyls. These muscular, powerful figures – especially the Delphic and Libyan Sibyls – are among the most striking and dramatic images on the ceiling. The bulky arms on the androgynous Cumaean Sibyl are a caseload of steroids short of feminine, and most scholars believe that Michelangelo modelled all his female figures on men. In the lunettes, found over the windows, are the ancestors of Christ.

Michelangelo was commissioned by Clement VII to paint *The Last Judgement* 24 years after he worked on the ceiling (the pope died shortly afterwards and the work was executed under Paul III). Two frescoes by Perugino were destroyed to make way for the new painting, which caused great controversy in its day, and the entire wall had to be replastered, so that it tilted inwards, to avoid dust settling on it.

The painting was done between 1535 and 1541. It is considered to be the masterpiece of Michelangelo's mature years, but the artist's finely honed technical proficiency takes second place against the exuberance of the composition. The painting depicts the souls of the dead being torn from their graves

to face the wrath of God. The subject was chosen by Paul III as a warning to Catholics to toe the line of their faith in the turmoil of the Reformation then sweeping Europe. It is a dynamic, emotional composition, said to reflect Michelangelo's own tormented attitude to his faith.

Criticism of its dramatic, swirling mass of predominantly naked bodies was summarily dismissed by Michelangelo, who depicted one of his greatest critics, Paul III's master of ceremonies, as Minos with donkey's ears. Michelangelo also includes a self-portrait on the shroud held by St Bartholomew, to the right of Christ.

As with the Creation, *The Last Judgement* was blackened by candle smoke and incense, but it was also damaged by poor restorations and by the addition of clothes to cover some of the nude figures. One of Michelangelo's students, Daniele da Volterra, was commissioned by Pius IV to do the cover-up job.

The walls of the chapel were painted by famous Renaissance artists including Botticelli, Domenico Ghirlandaio, Pinturicchio and Luca Signorelli. The restoration of these paintings was completed in 2000. Even if you find it hard to drag your attention away from Michelangelo's frescoes, take time to appreciate these paintings, which were produced in the late 15th century and depict events in the life of Moses (to the left looking at *The Last Judgement*) and Christ (to the right). Anywhere else in the world, these frescoes would be the prime exhibits. As it is, many visitors to the Sistine Chapel hardly give them a second glance, focusing all their attention on Michelangelo's work.

The first parts of each cycle, the Finding of Moses and the Birth of Christ, were the Perugino frescoes destroyed to make way for *The Last Judgement*. The second fresco on the right, depicting the *Tentazione di Cristo* (Temptations of Christ) and the *Purificazione del Lebbroso* (Cleansing of the Leper), by Botticelli is particularly beautiful. Note the typical Botticelli maiden in diaphanous dress in the foreground.

In the fifth fresco on the left, which depicts the Punishment of the Rebels, Botticelli uses the Arco di Costantino as a backdrop for the action and includes a self-portrait (the figure in black behind Moses on the far right). Ghirlandaio's *Vocazione di Pietro e Andrea* (Calling of Peter and Andrew), the third fresco on the right, includes among the crowd of onlookers portraits of prominent contemporary figures. Perugino's *Consegna delle Chiavi* (Christ Giving the Keys to St Peter), the fifth fresco on the right, is a superbly composed cityscape which also includes a self-portrait (the fifth figure from the right).

VATICAN LIBRARY Map pp308–10

Returning to the Quattro Cancelli area from the Sistine Chapel, you pass through the splendid frescoed halls of the **Biblioteca Apostolica Vaticana** (Vatican Library), which was founded by Nicholas V in 1450. The library contains over 1.5 million volumes including illuminated manuscripts, early printed books, prints and drawings, and coins. Selected items from the collection are displayed in the **Salone Sistino**, which has particularly beautiful frescoes on the ceiling and walls. If you haven't run out of time and energy by now, make sure you take a moment to stop and look.

BORGO

The area between the Vatican and the Tiber is known as the **Borgo**. Not much is left of the medieval (and earlier) buildings, as Mussolini had the area virtually razed to the ground to make way for Via della Conciliazione. On the Lungotevere, beside Castel Sant'Angelo is the huge **Palazzo di Giustizia** built between 1889 and 1910. It houses the national law courts.

CASTEL SANT'ANGELO Map pp308–10

☎ 06 681 91 11; Lungotevere Castello; admission €5; ⏱ 9am-8pm (last admission 7pm) Tue-Sun

This imposing round hunk has served to guard both the living and the dead. Built as a mausoleum for Hadrian, it was converted into a fortress for the popes in the 6th century AD. During a wave of plague around that time, Pope Gregory the Great saw a phantom angel hovering over the building, and re-christened the fortress Sant'Angelo. It was linked to the Vatican palaces in 1277 by a wall and passageway, allowing the popes to hightail it to the fortress in times of danger. During the 16th-century sacking of Rome by Emperor Charles V, hundreds of people lived in the fortress for months.

The bar built into the battlements has good snacks and a unique peep-hole view of Rome's rooftops.

PONTE SANT'ANGELO

Hadrian built the Ponte Sant'Angelo across the Tiber in 136 to provide an approach to his mausoleum, but it was Bernini who managed to bring it to life. His angels (executed by his students) line up along the bridge's sides, holding the instruments of Christ's passion. As the traditional pilgrimage approach to St Peters, these are the figures who have greeted the myriad faithful for generations.

Walking Tours

Walking Tours

Buses are crowded, taxis too fast and Vespas can get you killed. But fear not, Rome shows its best side to those who view it from the ground: not at a dash, but a stroll.

AN INTRODUCTORY STROLL THROUGH CENTRO STORICO

If you've never been to Rome, or have limited time, this quick and dirty tour of the greatest hits of the *centro storico* is a place to start.

Begin in Piazza di Trevi, at the iconic **Trevi Fountain 1** (p105). Legend has it that during construction a busybody barber criticised the project from the balcony of his shop on the right side of the square. Architect Nicola Salvi got the last laugh – he blocked the barber's sign and his view with a giant ornament on the balustrade, in the shape of a traditional barber's soap pot. Toss a coin over your shoulder into the fountain, then take Via de Crociferi and cross Via del Corso to the **Colonna Antonina 2** (p95). Mussolini used to give speeches from the balcony of **Palazzo Chigi 3** (p95). Veer left along Via Canova Antonina, heading through narrow, pedestrianised streets. Turn left and right and follow Via dei Pastini until you reach the busy

Walk Facts

Start Piazza di Trevi
End Piazza Farnese
Distance 2.5km
Duration 2 hours
Transport Buses 52, 53, 61, 63, 116, 119 or others along Via del Corso and Via del Tritone

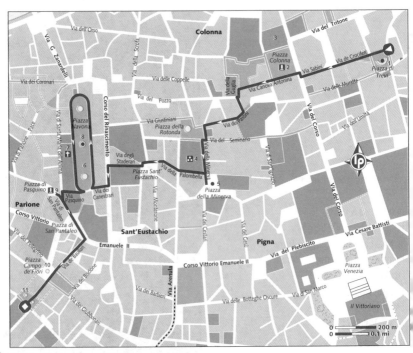

Piazza della Rotonda, where the awe-inspiring **Pantheon 4** (p88) will introduce itself. Mosey along its eastern flank to Bernini's cute **Elefantino 5** (p87), then take Via della Palombella behind the Pantheon to Piazza Sant'Eustachio and possibly the best coffee you'll ever have at the café of the same name. With a spring in your step, follow Via degli Staderari, jag a quick left on Corso del Rinascimento and then right into the brilliantly baroque **Piazza Navona 6** (p89). Duck into Borromini's **Chiesa di Sant'Agnese in Agone 7** (p90) first, then take a lap around the vast square. You can have a restful sit here and check Bernini's **Fontana dei Quattro Fiumi 8** (p90) off your list of must-sees before taking Via Pasquino to **Pasquino 9** (p91), the mutilated 'talking statue'. Turn left and cross the busy Corso Vittorio Emanuele II to Via de'Baullari and the beating heart of modern Roman life, **Campo de' Fiori 10** (p83). What, no Renaissance? Take any of the narrow streets on the far side of Il Campo – will Michelangelo's **Palazzo Farnese 11** (p84) suffice?

Snack van in front of the Trinità dei Monti at the top of the Spanish Steps (p143)

APPIA ANTICA & THE CATACOMBS

This route takes you away from the congested bustle of the city centre into a vestige of the 19th-century terracotta landscape that inspired writers from Keats to Goethe. It requires minimal navigation, perfect for the day you wake up tired of walking around with your face in a map; if you want to speed up the process, consider biking. The café at the intersection of Via Appia Antica and Via Cecilia Metella, right at the beginning of the route, hires bikes by the hour, and the Parco Regionale Dell'Appia Antica (www.parcoappiantica.org), about halfway through the walk, rents them on Sundays only. Whether walking or pedalling, Sunday is best, when traffic (which can be heavy) is halted on Appia Antica from 9.30am to 7pm.

Bus 660 drops you off on Via Cecilia Metella, about 200 well-signposted metres from the intersection with Via Appia Antica, where there is a section of the actual ancient road, excavated in the mid-19th century. The action begins right after the antique paving ends, with a double-header: the imposing **Mausoleo di Cecilia Metella 1** (p120), built for the daughter of Quintus Metellus Creticus, which was incorporated into the castle of the Caetani family in the early 14th century and, on the other side of the road, the roofless ruin of the **Chiesa di San Nicola a Capo di Bove 2**, a rare example of Gothic architecture in Rome. Not much further along Via Appia Antica, you'll reach the archaeological area of **Villa di Massenzio 3**. The area encompasses the **Tomba di Romolo 4** (p119), closed for renovation at the time of writing; the **Circo di Massenzio 5** (p119) and the remains of Maxentius' imperial palace are open.

Just under 200m along will bring you to the entrance to the **Basilica & Catacombe di San Sebastiano 6** (p119), built in the 4th century on the spot where the bodies of the apostles Peter and Paul were buried, before being transferred to the respective basilicas built in their honour. Here, a lovely paved path for visitors to the **Catacombe di San Callisto 7** (p119) branches off to the left. The path (open from 8am to 6.30pm Thursday to Tuesday, 8am to 5.30pm in winter) follows a ridge between fields dotted with tombs and old country residences. Unless you're doing the walk on a Sunday, take this route rather than chancing the fast-moving traffic on Via Appia Antica, which has no sidewalks.

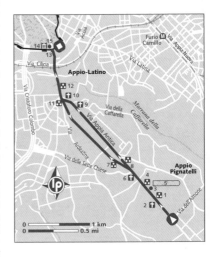

If you choose not to follow the private road and instead continue along Via Appia Antica, you will see the **Jewish catacombs 8** of Vigna Rondanini (accessible only with permission from the Comunitá Ebraica in Rome) – there is no sign indicating the catacombs from the road. There is another entrance to the Catacombe di San Callisto, and the run-down, 16th-century **Cappella del Cardinale Reginald Pole 9** with a circular base leaning against a country house at the corner of Via della Caffarella. The chapel stands on the site where in 1539 the cardinal escaped death at the hands of Henry VIII's hired assassins.

The paved path intersects with Via Ardeatina and Via Appia Antica. There, on Appia Antica, the **Chiesa del Domine Quo Vadis? 10** stands on the spot where Jesus appeared to St Peter who was fleeing Rome to escape persecution by Nero. In the centre isle just inside the door, there's a small square stone said to bear Jesus' footprints. On the Ardeatina side of the intersection, **Catacombe di Priscilla 11** (p124) is hidden from view by the restaurant at No 68, but you can see it from a gate near the intersection or from the car park behind the restaurant. The tomb was used by the Caetani family in the 13th century as the base for a military tower. Just past the restaurant on your right, you can see (over to the left) the remains of the **Tomba di Geta 12**, and above them a 16th-century house. As you continue, the Parco dell'Appia Antica information booth is on your left.

You now have a hike of about 700m, past gorgeous gated houses and their gardens, to the city wall at **Porta San Sebastiano 13** (p116). This is the largest and most-majestic entrance in the walls and houses the very interesting **Museo delle Mura 14**. The museum visit includes the panoramic view of Via Appia Antica from one of the towers and, after restorations going on at the time of writing are complete, a walk along the battlements as far as Porta Ardeatina and Sangallo's 16th-century bastions.

The area inside the museum door is covered by the **Arco di Druso 15**, a simple arch supporting the Antonius aqueduct, a branch of the Acqua Marcia aqueduct, that passed overhead at this point on its way to the Terme di Caracalla.

When Via Appia Antica crosses the city wall, it becomes Via di PS Sebastiano. From here, you could continue to Piazza Numa Pompilio and Terme di Caracalla, or jump on the 118 bus, which takes you to the Piramide stop on the metro.

Walk Facts

Start Intersection of Via Appia Antica and Via Cecilia Metella
End Porta San Sebastiano
Distance 3.5km
Duration 3 hours
Transport Metro Linea A to Colli Albani, then bus 660 to its final stop

AMBLE THROUGH VILLA BORGHESE

The queen of Rome's parks, at the northern edge of the city, is large enough to be free of crowds and green enough to clear the lungs of the street-level carbon monoxide. Since nothing goes together like parks and picnics, this is a fun lunch walk if you shop for your supplies before setting out.

Begin by climbing the grand, sweeping **Spanish Steps 1** (p100), designed by Francesco De Sanctis in 1723, at the height of the tremulous rococo. They (and the square below) aren't Spanish at all, but were named for the Spanish Embassy nearby. **Trinità dei Monti 2** hulks over the top of the steps. Take a right along Via Sistina and left into Via Francesco Crispi. You'll skirt the **Aurelian Wall 3** to your left, before

ducking through the gate and into **Villa Borghese 4** (p124). Designed for Cardinal Scipione Borghese in 1605, its original sculpture was by Pietro Bernini, the father of the more-famous Gian Lorenzo. The pathways are deliciously shaded. Go right along Viale del

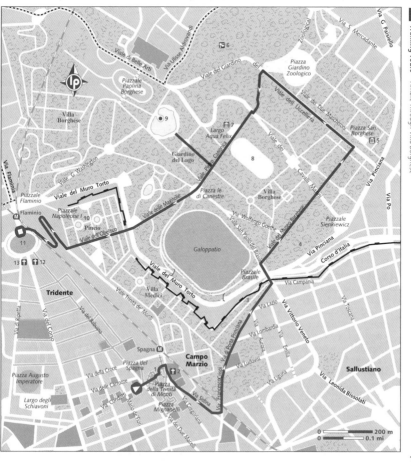

Museo Borghese and you'll reach the stunning **Galleria Borghese 5** (p125) and its gardens. A left here will bring you to the sculpted gates of **Bioparco 6** (p124). Cross-country down a small track, through a dip, and **Museo Canonica 7** (p125) appears on your right. **Piazza di Siena 8** (p124), an 18th-century amphitheatre now used for equestrian events, is on your left. Carrying on along Viale Pietro Canonica, when you see the **Tempio di Esculapio 9** in the distance to your right, follow it to a pretty lake. Your landmark island temple is by the 18th-century architect Antonio Asprucci, and depicts the god of health. Recharged and ready to be reintroduced to Rome, return to the main thoroughfare and carry on through Viale delle Magnolie until you reach the balcony of the **Pincio 10** (p100), with breathtaking views of St Peter's Basilica and **Piazza del Popolo 11** (p89) below. Descend the steps and walk to the centre of the vast oval, where a 3000-year-old Egyptian obelisk that once decorated the Circus Maximus is surrounded by steps. Have a seat here, looking toward the twin churches of **Santa Maria di Montesanto 12** (left) and **Santa Maria dei Miracoli 13** (right). Have a contest to see who can find the structural differences between the churches – loser buys your post-walk drinks. The Flaminio metro stop is your ticket out of the neighbourhood.

THE HEART OF ROME: LARGO DI TORRE ARGENTINA, THROUGH THE GHETTO TO PIAZZA DEL CAMPIDOGLIO

This is a short route through the heart of Rome, an area dense with important monuments, where Renaissance buildings and the impressive ruins of classical antiquity coexist. It explores the courtyards of patrician palaces and the narrow streets of one of the city's more characteristic areas. You end up at Michelangelo's beautiful Piazza del Campidoglio with a breathtaking view over the Roman Forum.

Start on the southern side of **Largo di Torre Argentina 1** and archaeological zone, where Via delle Botteghe Oscure meets Via Florida. Cross Piazza della Enciclopedia Italiana, skirting the elegant **Palazzo Mattei di Paganica 2**, built in 1541, which now houses the Istituto per l'Enciclopedia Italiana. This area was called L'isola dei Mattei (Mattei Island) in the mid-16th century, because the patrician Mattei family had five palaces here.

If you cross Piazza Paganica and follow Via Paganica you come to the charming **Piazza Mattei 3** with its elegant **Fontana delle Tartarughe 4** (p85). In the square at No 10 is the 16th-century **Palazzo Costaguti 5** and at Nos 17 to 19 **Palazzo di Giacomo Mattei 6**. The building on the right has a beautiful 15th-century courtyard with a staircase and an open gallery.

Go left along Via dei Funari and enter the **Palazzo Mattei di Giove 7** at No 3. Built by Carlo Maderno in 1598, today it houses the Centro Italiano di Studi Americani (Italian Centre for American Studies); sections are open to the public.

Head back to Piazza Mattei take Via della Reginella, lined with artisan workshops, framers and bookshops. The street is a reminder

Walk Facts

Start Largo di Torre Argentina
End Capitoline Hill
Distance 1.8km
Duration 1½ hours
Transport Bus 40 or 64 to Largo di Torre Argentina

of what the old Jewish-Ghetto area once looked like. A few paces to the right along Via del Portico d'Ottavia brings you to the curious **Casa di Lorenzo Manilio 8** at No 1. There are fragments of Roman sculpture set into the wall, including a relief depicting a lion killing a deer.

Keeping Casa di Lorenzo Manilio on your left, walk down Via del Portico d'Ottavia until you reach the remains of an entrance to the **Portico d'Ottavia 9** (p85). In AD 755, the portico was remodelled to incorporate **Chiesa di Sant'Angelo in Pescheria 10** (p85). A medieval fish market, established in the portico, was operational until the end of the 19th century.

Beyond the portico at Via del Portico d'Ottavia 29 is the 14th-century **Casa dei Valati 11**, housing the city's cultural department. Unusually for this area, the building stands in isolation, since the surrounding buildings were demolished in 1927 during the restoration of the Teatro di Marcello at the rear.

A narrow passage to the left of the portico opens onto Via della Tribuna di Campitelli. Go round the back of the church and then bear right at a water fountain until you come to a dead end. From this isolated spot you get a view of the arches of the **Teatro di Marcello 12** (p115). Only 12 of the original 41 arches, made of large travertine blocks, remain. You can also see the three marble columns with Corinthian capitals and beams of the Tempio di Apollo Sosiano, dedicated in 431 BC and rebuilt in 34 BC.

Retrace your steps out of the dead-end street, and take Via della Tribuna di Campitelli to the right. On the corner, at No 23, there is a house incorporating a medieval portico with granite columns and Ionian capitals. After a short walk you'll come to **Piazza Campitelli 13**. On the northeastern and western sides of the square stand a row of fine palaces belonging to five noble families: the Gaetani-Lovatelli family at Via Tribuna Campitelli 16; Patrizi-Clementi family at Via Cavaletti 2 (16th century); Cavaletti family at Piazza Campitelli 1 (16th century); Albertoni family (early 17th century); and Capizucchi family (late 16th century).

On the other side of the square, the **Chiesa di Santa Maria in Campitelli 14** was built by Carlo Rainaldi and is a masterpiece of late-baroque style, with a fine travertine facade. The church was built in 1662 to honour the Virgin Mary, who was believed to have halted the plague of 1656. Inside, on the main altar, there is an image in silver leaf and enamel of the miraculous Madonna.

To the left of the church there is a pretty fountain designed in 1589 by Giacomo della Porta. The 17th-century facade of the building at No 6 was designed by the architect Flaminio Ponzio and once adorned his house near the Roman Forum. It was rebuilt here after the house was demolished in 1933, when the area was cleared to make way for the Via dei Fori Imperiali.

Slightly further along on Via Montanara is the **Chiesa di Santa Rita da Cascia 15**, now deconsecrated. It was built by Carlo Fontana in 1665 at the foot of the nearby Scalinata dell'Aracoeli and rebuilt on this spot in 1940 to allow for an urban revamp. Take Via Capizucchi to the left off the square. This takes you through deserted narrow streets into Piazza Capizucchi, and then to the left into Piazza Margana with the **Torre dei Margani 16**. Together with the surrounding buildings, the tower looks like a fortified medieval residence. Set in the wall is an ancient column with an Ionic capital. In the door next to it are large pieces of cornice from buildings of the late Empire.

Turn right into Via Margana and then right again into the darkness of Vicolo Margana. Go under an arch and take a left on Via Tribuna di Tor de'Specchi; here at No 3 there is a medieval tower. Just further on is the chaotic Piazza d'Aracoeli and **Cordonata di Michelangelo 17** (p80), the monumental flight of steps designed by Michelangelo, which lead up to the **Capitoline 18** (p80).

The cordonata is guarded at the bottom by two Egyptian basalt lions (turned into fountains in 1588) and almost touches the older staircase on the left, which leads up to

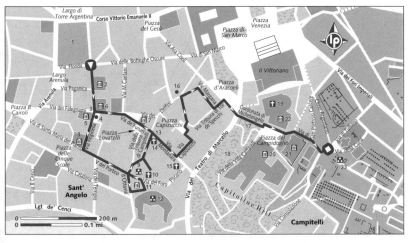

Chiesa di Santa Maria in Aracoeli 19 (p81), also accessible from the Capitoline. Once at the top of the cordonata, bask in the beauty of Michelangelo's square. It is bordered by the **Palazzo dei Conservatori 20** (p81) on the southern side, the **Palazzo Senatorio 21** (p80) at the rear, and the **Palazzo Nuovo 22** (p81) on the northern side. In its centre stands a copy of an original bronze equestrian statue of Marcus Aurelius.

Take the road going downhill to the right of the Palazzo Senatorio. This brings you to a (usually) crowded terrace overlooking the ancient Roman Forum and the Colosseum against the backdrop of the city and the Colli Albani – definitely one of the best views in Rome.

The route ends here. However, if you want to visit the **Roman Forum 23** (p72), there is an entrance to the right of the terrace at Via di Monte Tarpeo.

TRAVERSING TRASTEVERE

This is a walk to do slowly, through the labyrinthine streets of Trastevere, pausing to take in a picturesque Roman tableau or to watch the gaggles of roving foreign students.

Begin across the river from Trastevere, at **Ponte Fabricio 1** (p86), and walk across tiny **Isola Tiberina 2** (p85). The **Ospedale Fatebenefratelli 3** is on the upstream (west) side of the island, while **Chiesa di San Bartolomeo 4** (p87) is downstream. Cross to the Trastevere side of the river on **Ponte Cestio 5** (p86), then cross the road and head just upstream to turn left into **Piazza in Piscinula 6.** On the side closest to the river is **Palazzo Mattei 7**, which is a medieval building dating from 1300 and restored in 1926. On the opposite side of the square you can see the smallest bell tower in Rome.

From Via Lungarina, head south to Via dei Salumi. Follow this street to the left (east) and turn right at Via dei Vascellari, which leads to Piazza di Santa Cecilia, home of **Basilica di Santa Cecilia in Trastevere 8** (p108). This basilica contains many artistic treasures and is worth visiting. From here, go into the adjacent Piazza dei Mercanti, and take Via Santa Maria in Cappella to the left. You will soon find a courtyard containing the small, run-down **Chiesa di Santa Maria in Cappella 9**, which has a lovely Romanesque bell tower with two orders of mullioned windows

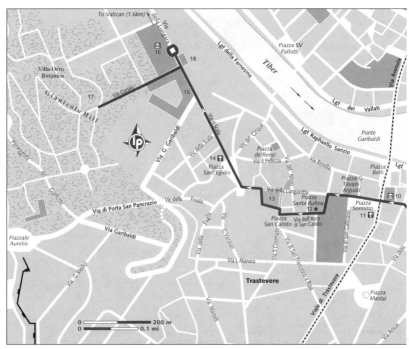

dating from the 12th century. Turn left into Via Jandolo, which becomes Via dei Genovesi, and turn right into the narrow Vicolo dell'Atleta, so named because of the 1844 discovery here of a Greek statue, the *Atleta* (athlete), now in the Vatican Museums. The medieval building at No 14 is the oldest synagogue in Rome.

Take a left on Via dei Salumi and follow it all the way back to Via della Lungaretta, where you'll take another left. Just ahead on the right, you'll pass the **Casa di Dante 10**, a 13th-century towered stronghold that once belonged to the patrician Anguillara family and is now a centre for Dante studies.

Walk Facts

Start Ponte Fabricio
End Villa Farnesina
Distance 2km
Duration 2 hours
Transport Bus 63 to Lgt dei Pierleoni

On the other side of Viale di Trastevere, pop into Piazza Sonnino. Across from the information booth is the **Chiesa di San Crisogono 11** (p109), a baroque reconstruction of a medieval church dating from 1123.

Follow Via della Lungaretta to Piazza Santa Rufina. From here you can see the graceful 12th-century Romanesque **bell tower 12** of the Chiesa di SS Rufina e Seconda inside the convent of the same name. Head south to Via dell'Arco di San Calisto, passing under an arch. Don't miss the tiny medieval house at No 42. Said to be the smallest house in Rome, it has an external staircase and is decorated with a small painted figure of the Madonna. It will lead you to Piazza San Calisto, a great place to pause for refreshment. Head north from here to the adjacent **Piazza Santa Maria in Trastevere 13** (p109), the heart of this lively neighbourhood and one of Rome's most-picturesque squares.

Head northwest out of the square through Piazza Sant'Egidio to Via della Scala. The church of **Santa Maria della Scala 14** (p110) will be on your left. The 17th-century church and adjacent Carmelite monastery has a *speziaria* (pharmacy) dating from the 17th century. In the 18th century, it supplied medicine to the popes. Today it carries the usual preparations plus some antique Carmelite concoctions. The monks here are renowned for having commissioned, and then rejected, Caravaggio's *Il Transito della Vergine* (Transition of the Virgin), now in the Louvre (Paris).

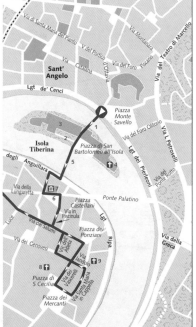

Five blocks further along, and moving out of Trastevere, you'll walk through **Porta Settimiano 15** (p110), a 16th-century reconstruction of an ancient gate in the Aurelian Wall, adorned with battlements. Take a detour down Via Corsini on the left. It runs alongside the 18th-century **Palazzo Corsini 16** (p110) to Rome's **Orto Botanico 17** (botanical gardens, p110), founded in the 19th century in the former gardens of the palace. The gardens are noted for their collections of Mediterranean succulents and tropical species and are an ideal place for a rest.

Back on Via della Lungara, walk the length of Palazzo Corsini. Opposite is the early-16th-century **Villa Farnesina 18** (p110), one of the first examples of a single-standing residence, surrounded by gardens and featuring frescoes by Raphael and others.

If you still have some juice, you could keep walking north until you hit the Vatican. If you're all done in, the 116 bus across Ponte G Mazzini will take you back into the *centro storico*.

ROMANTIC VIEWS OF ROME: THE GIANICOLO TO THE AVENTINE

The Romantics loved a good view. Even poor Keats, dying of consumption, managed to haul himself out of bed and climb the hills of Rome to look out over its rooftops. Keep that in mind as you huff up and down the Gianicolo Hill, across the Tiber, and up the Aventine Hill. This one can knock the stuffing out of you.

Begin in **Piazzale Giuseppe Garibaldi 1**, which sits like a terrace on top of the 17th-century bastions of the Gianicolo, 82m above sea level. The bronze equestrian statue of General Garibaldi faces the city of Rome. His back is turned on St Peter's as a reminder of the battles fought by the general against the papacy and the Bourbon rulers of Naples, which led to the unification of Italy in 1870. You, however, may turn and look, for this is a marvellous panorama. On a clear day, the domes, palaces and *campanili* (bell towers)

Walk Facts

Start Piazzale Giuseppe Garibaldi
End Piazzale Ugo La Malfa
Distance 3.5km
Duration 3 hours
Transport Bus 870 to Piazzale Giuseppe Garibaldi from Via Paola, near Ponte Principe Amedeo Savoia Aosta

of baroque Rome stand out against the foothills of the Apennines.

To your right as you are looking out over the panorama, the *passeggiata del Gianicolo* (Gianicolo walk) divides in two. Take the path to the left, which descends between tall trees, and pass the 17th-century Villa Aurelio (now part of the American Academy in Rome) on your right to emerge into the semicircular square in front of the **Fontana dell'Acqua Paola 2** (p111), from where there is another famed view of Rome. The fountain is known locally as the *Fontanone del Gianicolo* (big fountain of the Gianicolo) because of its monumental form, inspired by

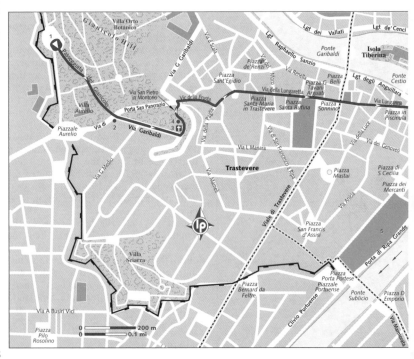

the triumphal arches of ancient Rome. The spot is frequented by Roman newlyweds and their photographers.

Go down Via Garibaldi until you reach the nearby **Chiesa di San Pietro in Montorio 3** (p111), built in the 9th century on the spot believed to have been the site where St Peter was crucified upside down. As you're facing the church's elegant Renaissance facade with its Gothic rose window, a gate to your right leads into the modest cloister of the adjoining convent and the famous **Tempietto di Bramante 4** (p111), built around 1502 and used as a model by numerous architects in the early 16th century.

A gate to the left as you leave the cloister leads to Via San Pietro in Montorio, a flight of steps lined with the stations of the cross. Take a right on Vicolo della Frusta and cut straight through the heart of Trastevere. On the opposite side of Piazza Santa Maria in Trastevere, pick up Via della Lungaretta, and follow it through Piazza Sonnino to Piazza Castellani and the Tiber.

As you cross the bridge, enjoy the view of the city. On the left you can see the square dome of the synagogue and the large dome of St Peter's Basilica in the distance. On the right, you can see the leafy heights of the Aventine and the long 17th- to 18th-century facade of the former **Ospizio Apostolico di San Michele a Ripa 5** on the Trastevere side of the river. This now houses the Ministero per i Beni Culturali e Ambientali (Ministry for Culture and the Environment).

Once across the bridge, turn right into the busy Lungotevere Aventino and follow the river for about 200m. On the other side of the road, just past the traffic lights of Via della Greca, a flight of steps called Clivo di Rocca Savella leads up onto the Aventine Hill through the walls of a 10th-century fortress. At the top, a narrow footpath leads to one of our favourite spots in Rome, the **Parco Savello 6** (p112), where there is a terrace looking over the Gianicolo and the historic centre. The benches, surrounded by fragrant squashed fruit, are a fine place for a mid-walk rest. Exiting from the opposite side of the park you will reach the 5th-century **Basilica di Santa Sabina 7** (p113), one of the most important early-Christian basilicas in Rome.

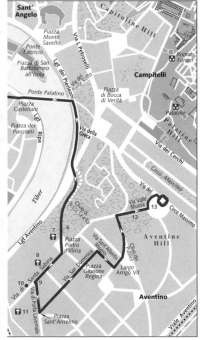

Turning right into Via di Santa Sabina, you'll pass another panoramic garden and will come to the **Santi Bonifacio ed Alessio 8**, a medieval church rebuilt on numerous occasions and almost completely restored in 1750.

Further along Via di Santa Sabina is the **Piazza dei Cavalieri di Malta 9** (p112), designed by Piranesi, famous for his etchings of Rome, in 1734 for the Order of the Knights of Malta. Now, for the climax view of the walk, peer through the keyhole in the door that leads to the splendid gardens (accessible only on special occasions) of the **Priorato di Cavalieri di Malta 10** (p112), the headquarters of the order.

From the square, take Via di Porta Lavernale, passing the **Chiesa di Sant'Anselmo 11**, a 20th-century church in Romanesque-Lombard style, to reach Piazza Sant'Anselmo. Here, turn left into Via San Domenico and follow it until you get to Piazza Giunone Regina. Go past the three arches of a sober Fascist-period building, turn right into Via Sant'Alberto Magno and you come to Largo Arrigo VII. Turn left out of Largo Arrigo on the far side, passing beneath the pine trees in the gardens, and descend to the left along Clivo dei Publicii. Turn right into Via Valle Murcia, which passes through the city **Roseto**

149

Ponte Cestio crossing the River Tiber to Isola Tiberina (p146)

Comunale 12 (rose garden; p112), open to the public in May and June when the flowers are in bloom. A short distance further is **Piazzale Ugo La Malfa** 13, the site of a monument to Giuseppe Mazzini, another father of Italian unity.

At the end of the route, turn right out of Piazzale Ugo La Malfa and follow the road downhill to reach the Circo Massimo stop on the Metro Linea B. Alternatively, a number of buses serve Piazzale Ugo La Malfa, including bus No 81 going to the Colosseum and San Giovanni in Laterano. On the other side of Circo Massimo on Via dei Cerchi the same bus goes towards Piazza Venezia, Piazza Navona and the Vatican.

Eating

Eating

To a Roman, as to most Italians, eating out is one of life's essential pleasures, but it's a pleasure to be taken seriously. It's not the Italian way to step into the first trattoria that you pass. Instead choices must be selected, merits discussed and finally a decision taken on the grounds of food and atmosphere. Romans want to eat well but they also want to do so in convivial surroundings.

There is, therefore, no better place to take Rome's pulse than at the table where food and wine are as much about passion, verve and history as mere sustenance. Not even the tourist throngs can dilute the indomitable spirit of Rome and it's not hard to find authentic local eateries.

Generally, the restaurants around Stazione Termini are to be avoided if you want to pay reasonable prices for good quality Italian food, although there are exceptions and it is the best area for ethnic food. Rome is not big on international cuisine, but appreciation of world food is increasing and you can find a few restaurants specialising in Indian, Chinese, African, Japanese and Mexican cooking.

Oysters from the Riccioli Café (p160)

For an altogether more rewarding experience head either to the centre or the university enclave of San Lorenzo. An up-and-coming area to the east of Termini, it boasts a number of highly regarded restaurants and an inviting, vivacious buzz.

The *centro storico* (historic centre) is teeming with places to satisfy all tastes and most pockets. It's difficult to find genuinely bargain prices around Piazza Navone or Campo de' Fiori but you may very well decide that the stunning backdrop is worth a few extra euros. Trastevere is always a favourite area, both with locals and visitors, offering an excellent selection of rustic-style trattorie where it still doesn't cost the earth to sit at an outside table.

The neighbourhoods around Monti provide local *and* ethnic eats while for hard-core Roman cuisine the two best areas are the Ghetto, where Roman-Jewish cuisine abounds, and Testaccio, near the former abattoir, the spiritual home of offal and the more grisly side of *cucina romana*.

Self Catering

Rome has no shortage of *alimentari* (delicatessens) selling wide selections of Italian and imported cheeses, salami, olives, bread and other gourmet delights. Only a few of the more notable outlets are listed in this section. If you're looking for food of other nationalities, try the Ghetto area (centred around Via di Portico di Ottavia; Map pp311–13) for shops stocking kosher food and delicious pastries, or the area around Piazza Vittorio Emanuele II (Map pp314–16) for Middle Eastern, Asian and African food stores. There is also a growing number of supermarkets. Three of the easiest to get to from the centre are Conad (Map pp314–16; Stazione Termini), Standa (Map p317–19; Viale di Trastevere) and Standa (Map p311–13; Via Cola di Rienzo 173).

The following are some of Rome's better-known gastronomic establishments. See the boxed text (p153) for details about the daily fresh-food markets in Rome.

CASTRONI Map pp308–10

☎ 06 687 43 83; Via Cola di Rienzo 196; metro Ottaviano

This historic shop provides succour to many expats in Rome. Stocking a wide range of gourmet foods, packaged and fresh, it's famous for its selection of otherwise impossible to find reminders of home. Desperate Aussies will find Vegemite, Brits baked beans, Worcester sauce and salad cream. Don't, however, expect to pay the same as you would at home: the mark-ups are considerable.

EMPORIUM NATURAE Map pp304–5

☎ 06 372 53 94; Viale delle Milizie 9a; metro Ottaviano

Situated within a stone's throw of the Ottaviano metro stop, Emporium Naturae is a well-stocked health food supermarket. The shelves are lined with organically produced stock, from wholemeal bread to organic fruit and veg. There's also a comprehensive selection of herbal cures and remedies, or if you're having back trouble, a futon with orthopaedic mattress.

FRANCHI Map pp308–10

☎ 06 687 46 51; Via Cola di Rienzo 198; metro Ottaviano

Still in the Vatican area, Franchi's is a feast to the eye. From the street you look in on counters straining under the weight of wine and cheese, cured meats and vegetables conserved in oil. Step inside and you enter an Aladdin's cave of delectable deli treats. Why not try the gourmet truffles? They'll only cost €22 per 100g!

IL CANESTRO Map pp317–19

☎ 06 574 28 00; Via Luca della Robbia 47; bus or tram to Via Marmorata

In the offal-dominated area of Testaccio, near the market, Il Canestro has a large selection of health foods, as well as fresh fruit and vegetables and takeaway food. What's more, as if in defiance of local traditions, there is a vegetarian restaurant attached to the shop.

L'ALBERO DEL PANE Map pp311–13

☎ 06 686 50 16; Via Santa Maria del Pianto 19; tram to Piazza B Cairoli

This well-stocked health-food shop runs decidedly counter to the culinary traditions that reign in Rome's Jewish Ghetto. Rather than fish and meat which sustain most of the area's restaurants, here you can find organic lemonade, natural cosmetics and an impressive range of healthy seeds. Products are sold either packaged or fresh and the service is friendly and helpful.

RUGGERI Map pp311–13

Via dei Giubbonari; bus to Corso Vittorio Emanuele II

Vegetarians shouldn't be put off by the hams hanging in the doorway of this vibrant deli. Inside is everything from tea leaves to gift-wrapped pasta. However, it wouldn't be a proper *alimentari* if it wasn't packed to the gills with hams and cheeses of every sort. Diligent assistants cut, chop and scoop with skill.

VOLPETTI Map pp317–19

☎ 06 574 23 52; www.volpetti.com (Italian only); Via Marmorata 47; bus or tram to Via Marmorata

The best selection of Italian cheeses are in this pioneering gourmet deli, a showcase for some of the finest foods in Italy. If you're feeling peckish, you won't leave without an armful of bounty. Oils, vinegar, wine, grappa and packaged pasta make good presents and you can organise international shipping through their website.

To Market, to Market

Despite the gradual intrusion of the supermarket, Rome's fresh-produce markets survive as treasured reminders of a more traditional way of life. There's generally a dazzling array of fresh fruit and veg, some meat and fish stalls, the usual deli fare and also stalls selling clothing, shoes or bric-a-brac. They're always lively and can warrant a visit just for the sheer pleasure of it.

The daily market in Campo de' Fiori (Map pp311–13) is certainly the most picturesque, but also the most expensive. Prices are graded corresponding to the shopper's accent, so the Roman-speaker pays one sum, the Italian-speaker another and the non-Italian yet another.

Trastevere locals shop at the excellent Piazza San Cosimato market (Map pp317–19), a traditional neighbourhood market adjacent to one of the best food-shopping streets in Rome, Via Natale del Grande.

The covered Piazza dell' Unità market (Map pp308–10), near the Vatican, is another good place to shop. The Ponte Milvio market (Map pp302–3), north of the city centre, caters for well-heeled shoppers.

The covered market at Via Lamarmora (Map p314–16; site of the recently relocated Piazza Vittorio Emanuele II Food Market) is one of the cheapest markets in the city and the place to find exotic ingredients alongside the usual fare, as it's in the most cosmopolitan area of Rome. Great bargains can be found on Saturday afternoon when the market is closing.

The Testaccio market on Piazza Testaccio (Map pp317–19) is the most Roman of all the city's markets. It is noted for its excellent quality and good prices.

Food markets operate from around 7am to around 1.30pm, Monday to Saturday.

Tipping

Bills usually include *pane e coperto* (basically, a cover charge), which ranges from €1 to an outrageous €5 per person. Service may or may not be added to your bill. Additional tipping is at your discretion; Italians often don't bother leaving anything but tourists are expected to leave anything from 5% in a pizzeria to 10% in a more upmarket restaurant. At the very least you'll be expected to round up the bill.

Opening Hours & Meal Times

Restaurants usually open for lunch from 12.30pm to 3pm although many are not keen to take orders after about 2.15pm. In the evening, business lasts from 7.30pm in tourist areas, 8pm in other less central quarters, to about 11pm. However, particularly in the family-run trattorie, these times can vary, often for no other reason than a whim of the owner. What is less open to the vagaries of chance is the fact that should you arrive at a popular restaurant or pizzeria between 8.30pm and 9pm, you will be queuing for a table.

Leisurely afternoon outside a Roman café

Where opening hours are listed with each eatery, it indicates that they vary from the usual opening times. Where incomplete or no opening hours appear with a review, assume that the standard hours apply.

Many restaurants close on Mondays and for at least two weeks in August.

Booking Tables

Booking a table is generally not necessary in a simple trattoria or pizzeria and is often not even possible. However, to secure a table at a mid- to top-range restaurant, especially for the 8.30pm to 9.30pm window, booking is a good idea and sometimes necessary. Either that or arrive early.

How Much?

As a general rule of thumb, for a three-course meal and wine expect to pay around €13 per person in a pizzeria, €20 at a simple trattoria, up to €40 at a mid-range restaurant and around €60 or more at Rome's top eating places. Eating only a pasta dish and salad and drinking the house wine can keep the bill down, while ordering meat or fish will push the price up substantially.

Where to Eat...

If you're not sure how to distinguish a *ristorante* from a *rosticceria*, or an *enoteca* from an *osteria*, check out Where To Eat & Drink in the Food & Drink chapter (p39).

Numerous restaurants offer tourist menus, with an average price of €15 excluding drinks. The food is usually reasonable but choices will be limited.

It is worth saying, however, that in Rome price is not always an indicator of quality. In fact, many of the best meals can be had in the smaller, often cheaper, Mamma-style trattorie.

Also, never assume a restaurant accepts credit cards. Most of the top-end eateries do but it's always worth checking beforehand.

In this chapter Cheap Eats are defined as those where you can eat for €15 or less.

ANCIENT ROME

Although the streets around the Colosseum are packed to the gills with overpriced, overfull tourist traps, this area does have a number of good neighbourhood eateries. Packed into the charming streets between Via Nazionale and Via Cavour, you'll find many small trattorie offering traditional fare at reasonable prices. Stroll around Via del Boschetto, Via dei Serpenti, Via Panisperna, Via Urbana and Via Madonna de' Monti and you're bound to find something to whet your appetite.

Top Five Around Ancient Rome

- La Cicala e La Formica (below)
- Da Ricci (p156)
- Pasqualino (right)
- Il Guru (below)
- Mexico al 104 (p156)

IL GURU   Map pp314–16   *Indian*
☎ 06 474 41 10; Via del Cimarra 4-6; meals €25;
🕑 7.30pm-midnight; metro Cavour

Tucked away down a tiny Roman side street is a little piece of India. Decorated with traditional elephants, buddhas and silk drapes, Il Guru is the perfect place to give your palate a break from pasta and pizza. The menu offers no real novelties, but the tandoori dishes, curries (of every strength) and great vegetarian choices seem especially exotic given the very Italian setting. The friendly proprietor will steer you clear of curries that are too hot to handle.

LA CICALA E LA FORMICA
Map pp314–16   *Ristorante*
☎ 06 481 74 90; Via Leonina 17; meals about €20;
🕑 Mon-Sat; metro Cavour

A charming little restaurant, La Cicala e La Formica serves up wonderful food with a smile. The modest menu does not try to set records of culinary innovation; rather it veers towards the traditional. However, taste the food and you'll be glad it does. As an antipasto the bruschetta with lard is a nice twist on an old favourite, while the *carpaccio di pescespada*, painfully thin slices of raw swordfish, tastes strongly of the sea as it dissolves on the tongue.

OSTERIA GLI ANGELETTI
Map p314–16   *Trattoria*
☎ 06 474 33 74; Via dell'Angeletto 3; meals about €20; closed Dec; metro Cavour

Just off Via Cavour in the cobbled Via dell' Angeletto, Osteria Gli Angeletti continues to attract the crowds. Although it's unlikely to win any culinary awards, the food is good and the outdoor seating on atmospheric Piazza Madonna dei Monti a lovely setting for dinner. The menu is comprehensive and caters well for vegetarians, with a cluster of fail-safe pasta dishes to satisfy the fussiest of eaters. Starters include flavoursome marinated anchovies served with chillies or pear and Parmesan salad, while of the pasta dishes the spaghetti with pancetta and balsamic vinegar was interesting, if not totally successful.

PASQUALINO
Map pp320–1   *Trattoria*
☎ 06 700 45 76; Via dei SS Quattro Coronati 66;
mains €7-12; 🕑 Tue-Sun; metro Colosseo

The restaurants and bars opposite the Colosseum are overpriced and best avoided. However, if you wander eastwards into the grid of streets behind you'll find a number of options. One of the most appealing, despite the multilingual menu, is Pasqualino, an authentic neighbourhood trattoria frequented by locals. Decent staples – antipasto, pasta, grilled fish and meat – are served by a squadron of spirited, orange-clad and inquisitive waiters who dart around cluttered tables between old photographs and paintings depicting local scenes. The pasta with seafood in a creamy tomato sauce is excellent and the fish is usually first class.

Cheap Eats

AL GIUBILEO   Map pp314–16   *Pizzeria*
☎ 06 48 59 29; Via del Boschetto 44; pizzas €6-7;
🕑 Tue-Sun; bus to Via Nazionale

This place is unusual in that it does Roman *and* Neapolitan pizzas, both of which are pretty good. Waiters dash around this high-tempo pizzeria punching orders into computer handsets, pizza is piled onto wooden slabs and hungry punters dig in. If doughy discs don't ring your bell, there are plenty of pasta dishes and bruschette on the menu. The *gnocchi alla sorrentina* is said to be particularly good.

BAIRES Map pp314–16 *Argentinian*
☎ 06 692 02 164; Via Cavour 315; set menus €11-14; metro Cavour

Argentinian food is renowned for its steaks, usually the size of South America, and that's exactly what you'll find at this fun and funky chain restaurant. The menu is full of meat any which way – spare ribs, sausages, steaks – and flavoursome vegetable and pulse-based soups. Knock it all back with the excellent organic house wine or an ice-cold beer. It's a good place for a rowdy, hungry group.

DA RICCI Map pp314–16 *Pizzeria*
☎ 06 488 11 07; Via Genova 32; meals about €10; ☺ Tue-Sun; bus to Via Nazionale, metro Repubblica

Also known as Est! Est!! Est!!!, this highly popular pizzeria is reputed to be the oldest in Rome. It started up as a wine shop in 1905 and has been run by the same family ever since. The pizzas turned out here are the deep-crust Neapolitan version and, along with the calzoni, are much appreciated by the boisterous students and workers who gather here. There are some who say this is the best pizza in town. The salads and home-made desserts are pretty decent as well.

MEXICO AL 104 Map pp314–16 *Mexican*
☎ 06 474 27 72; Via Urbana 104; set menus €15; ☺ Tue-Sun; metro Cavour

It would be quite easy to miss this small restaurant, so heavy is the ivy foliage which covers every inch of the building's facade. Acapulco it's not, but it's the closest you'll get in the centre of Rome and one of the very few Mexican restaurants in town. There are no surprises on the menu, but the tacos, burritos, *chimichanga*, *flautas*, tamales or enchiladas are better than your standard Tex-Mex fare.

WANTED IL POSTO RICERCATO
Map pp314–16 *Pizzeria*
☎ 06 474 22 05; Via Leonina 90; pizzas about €9; ☺ 11.30-2am daily except Mon; metro Cavour

You won't find many locals eating at this modest pizzeria not a stone's throw from the Cavour metro station. However, take a seat, choose from the place-mat menu and enjoy what are, in fact, surprisingly good pizzas. Cooked in a traditional wood oven, they are Roman thin and have that lovely charcoal aftertaste which every good pizza should have. There are also the usual pasta and meat dishes on offer.

CENTRO STORICO

This area, comprising Piazza Navona, Campo de' Fiori, the Pantheon, Via del Corso and the Ghetto, has a place for everyone. Clearly, however, proximity to some of the city's top attractions affects prices and it's not uncommon for the setting to cost as much as the food. But perhaps you'll decide that to eat in a 17th-century *palazzo* fronting a picture-postcard piazza is worth a few extra euros.

As a general rule of thumb, the areas around Piazza Navona, Campo de' Fiori and the Pantheon are trendy, busy and relatively expensive. The food remains predominantly Roman classic but you will find a number of modern restaurants making innovations on traditional themes. The Ghetto, on the other hand, is not the place for new takes on old recipes. You'll want to come here for Jewish-Roman cooking, prepared today as it's always been. Fried salted cod, artichokes in batter and intestines feature heavily.

Top Five in the Centro Storico
- La Rosetta (p159)
- Albistrò (below)
- Filetti di Baccalà (p162)
- Pizzeria da Baffetto (p163)
- Sergio alla Grotta (p160)

ALBISTRÒ
Map pp311–13 *International*
☎ 06 686 52 74; Via dei Banchi Vecchi 140a; mains €6.50-17.50; ☺ Thu-Tue; bus to Corso Vittorio Emanuele II

This charming little bistro has been winning plaudits ever since the Swiss owner started serving her own brand of international cuisine. Borrowing from her Helvetic culinary heritage, she has added regional Italian and oriental tastes to produce dishes ranging from fish curry and couscous to zucchini and trout flan in carrot sauce. If that doesn't appeal, how about a steak in balsamic vinegar? However, the menu changes with the season so these might not be on offer when you visit. No matter, the quality is consistently high whatever the dish. The pretty interior features a tiny open courtyard. At weekends booking is essential.

BOCCONDIVINO

Map pp308–10   *Ristorante*

☎ 06 683 08 626; Piazza Campo Marzio 6; meals €45;
✎ Mon-Sat; bus to Piazza San Silvestro

The idea of paying as much attention to a restaurant's decor as to its food would have most old-school Roman restaurateurs choking on their *pajate* (veal intestines). Boccondivino bucks this tradition, bringing style and a successful brand of modern cuisine to Rome's historic core. Thoroughly stylish – with salvaged Roman columns flanking the entrance and a snazzy modern interior – the 'Divine Mouthful' specialises in traditional Italian fare for lunch and Mediterranean fusion by night. Menus are seasonal, but expect innovative versions of *carpaccio* (raw beef), risotto and steak served by smooth staff.

CAMPONESCHI

Map pp311–13   *Ristorante*

☎ 06 687 49 27; Piazza Farnese 50; meals €60;
✎ evenings Mon-Sat ; bus or tram to Largo Argentina

A favoured haunt of politicians, diplomats and the glitterati, Camponeschi sits on one of Rome's (or if you believe Goethe, one of the world's) most beautiful squares, Piazza Farnese. As befits the clientele, the atmosphere is spiked with a matter-of-fact elitism while the food is a fail-safe fusion of French and Mediterranean. Menu classics include tagliatelle in a partridge sauce and lobster with black truffle.

CUL DE SAC Map pp311–13   *Enoteca*

☎ 06 688 01 094; Piazza Pasquino 73; meals from €15; bus to Corso Vittorio Emanuele II

Just off the southern end of Piazza Navona, Cul De Sac started life as a wine bar but has recently developed a reputation for its earthy food. Soups, pasta, pâté, dips (the *baba ganoush* made with eggplant and garlic is delicious) and a bountiful selection of cheeses and cured meats ensure that most palates are catered to. The narrow wood-panelled dining room, lined with bottles of wine, is cosy in winter but there are also outdoor tables in summer.

DA GIGGETTO Map pp311–13   *Trattoria*

☎ 06 686 11 05; Via del Portico di Ottavia 21-22; meals €35-40; ✎ Tue-Sun; tram to Piazza B Cairoli

For a typical taste of Roman-Jewish cooking head to Da Giggetto, one of the Ghetto's emblematic eateries. A labyrinthine restaurant, it specialises in the likes of *carciofi alla giudia*

(deep-fried artichokes) and *baccalà* (salted cod) served by scatty waiters in old-fashioned clobber. The location, next to the 1st-century Portico d'Ottavia, can't be beaten, especially if you get a footpath table.

DA GINO Map pp308–10   *Trattoria*

☎ 06 687 34 34; Vicolo Rosini 4; meals about €24; ✎ Mon-Sat; bus to Via del Corso

As a restaurant guide, you could do worse than follow those great experts of the city's culinary landscape, the politicians and journalists. In Rome, many go to Da Gino, a popular trattoria of the old school. Menu classics include home-made fettuccine cooked with peas and *guanciale* (bacon made from pig's cheek) or the *coniglio al vino bianco* (rabbit cooked in white wine).

DITIRAMBO Map pp311–13   *Trattoria*

☎ 06 687 16 26; Piazza della Cancelleria 72; mains €8-13; ✎ Tue-Sun; bus to Corso Vittorio Emanuele II

For traditional – and largely organic – Italian fare with innovative twists, you won't find better than this funky little trattoria which oozes rustic charm and manages to keep its personality despite the tourists. The owners take particular pride in using high-quality ingredients in signature dishes such as Gorgonzola and pear soufflé and salmon puff pastry with orange marinated zucchini. The home-made bread and pasta add to its charms.

EDY Map pp304–5   *Ristorante*

☎ 06 360 01 738; Vicolo del Babuino 4; mains from €15; ✎ Mon-Sat; metro Spagna

Providing value in an area not renowned for it, Edy is a classic Roman trattoria with a candle-lit interior, warm and welcoming staff, and a chef who's constantly popping out to see how his creations are going down. With a regular clientele of discerning locals and shopkeepers from upmarket Via del Babuino, Edy's speciality is a splendid *spaghetti al cartoccio* (a silver-foil parcel of pasta and seafood).

EL TOULÀ Map pp308–10   *Ristorante*

☎ 06 687 34 98; Via della Lupa 29; lunch menus €35-40, à la carte €57-70; bus to Via del Corso

El Toulà is an upmarket restaurant of the old school that specialises in dishes from northern Italy's Veneto region. The decor resembles that of an elegant salon and complements perfectly the conservative offerings of the menu. Typical dishes when we visited included salt cod whipped with milk and oil and Venetian-style fish soup with croutons. But it's not all seafood; try, for example, the home-made *tagliolini* with spring vegetables and basil.

'GUSTO

Map pp308–10   *Pizzeria/Ristorante*

☎ 06 322 62 73; Piazza Augusto Imperatore 9; lunch buffets €8, full evening meals about €40; bus to Via del Corso

A popular lunch stop for Rome's busy and beautiful, 'Gusto has brought a touch of Terence Conran to Rome. It's a huge place, with exposed brick walls and a converted warehouse feel. An original concept in Roman dining, it offers several possibilities for eating: substantial bar snacks, a pizzeria serving Neapolitan-type pizzas (with a thicker crust than the Roman variety) or a more formal restaurant on the first floor. The lunch-time salad buffet is a great fill-up and the ideal pit stop between shops. There's also a bookshop-cookshop, a wine shop and a cigar room. The eating-bar areas are closed on Monday.

HOSTARIA GIULIO

Map pp311–13   *Trattoria*

☎ 06 688 06 466; Via della Barchetta 19; meals about €25; ☽ Mon-Sat; bus to Corso Vittorio Emanuele II

Roman writer Alberto Moravia was a regular at this laid-back family-run trattoria. Hidden away in a tiny street between Via Monserrato and Via Giulia, it serves decent, if unspectacular, traditional food at very reasonable prices. The gnocchi, a home-made speciality, are feather light, while the grilled calamari are tender and tasty. The building dates from the 16th century, the dining room has a vaulted ceiling and it's decorated cheerfully, with plenty of outdoor tables in summer.

IL BACARO

Map pp308–10   *Ristorante*

☎ 06 686 41 10; Via degli Spagnoli 27; mains €13-16; ☽ Mon-Sat; bus to Corso del Rinascimento

Just around the corner from the Pantheon, Il Bacaro is not much bigger than a postage stamp. But secure a table and you'll find its food out of the top drawer, with outstanding risotto and pasta dishes, beefy mains, rich desserts and a well-chosen wine list. Summer seating is under a vine-covered pergola and booking is recommended year-round.

IL CONVIVIO DI TROIANO

Map pp308–10   *Ristorante*

☎ 06 686 94 32; Vicolo dei Soldati 31; meals around €70; ☽ Mon evening, Tue-Sat; bus to Corso del Rinascimento

For some of the finest dining in Italy, book yourself into the Michelin-starred Il Convivio, run with aplomb by the three Troiano brothers. The setting is a 16th-century building, elegantly decorated and intimately laid out. The inspired menus encompass fish, vegetables, meat and game and take advantage of what looks best at the market; whatever you choose will be memorable, and you can wash it down with any of 20,000 bottles from the wine cellar. Atmosphere is a little formal.

IL PRIMOLI Map pp308–10   *Ristorante*

☎ 06 681 35 112; Via dei Soldati 22-23; mains €13-18; ☽ evenings Mon-Sat; bus to Corso del Rinascimento

With its deep banquettes, hardwood floor and minimalist white walls, Il Primoli would look perfectly in place in any major capital. But the food is contemporary Italian. Pasta choices range from traditional to innovative and veal, lamb and beef feature among the mains. The waiters can at times be a little in-your-face.

L'ANGOLETTO

Map pp311–13   *Ristorante*

☎ 06 686 80 19; Piazza Rondanini 55; mains €11-20; ☽ Mon-Sat; bus to Corso del Rinascimento

Appropriately named, L'Angeletto (the little corner) sits in the corner of yet another picturesque square. Dripping in ivy, it is the perfect example of what an idyllic Roman restaurant should look like. Traditional in style, it has a faithful clientele and relies on its long-standing reputation for good food rather than creativity or innovation. The *spaghetti alle vongole* (with clams, olive oil, garlic and chilli) is delicious and the mussel soup tastes satisfyingly of the sea.

L'ORSO 80 Map pp308–10   *Trattoria*

☎ 06 686 49 04; Via dell'Orso 33; meals about €35; ☽ Tue-Sun; bus to Corso del Rinascimento

If you're the sort that gets so hungry you have difficulty choosing from the menu, L'Orso is the place for you. The antipasto spread is legendary – mozzarella, risotto balls, prosciutto, roasted vegetables, meatballs, beans, salads, marinated mushrooms. Tuck in until you can take no more. If you're still hungry, the pasta dishes are not great but the char-grilled meats

Designer tableware shows sleek Italian style

or wood-fired pizza are excellent. Celebrities like their antipasti the same as the rest of us – just look at the signed photos of Tom and Nicole in happier times, Brad Pitt and others on the walls.

LA CARBONARA

Map pp311–13   *Ristorante*
☎ 06 686 47 83; Campo de' Fiori 23; meals about €35;
☼ Wed-Mon, closed 3 weeks in August; bus to Corso Vittorio Emanuele II

As a spot to watch the world go by while dining, you could do a lot worse than La Carbonara. Dominating one side of Campo de' Fiori, Rome's most happening square, it is a historic rather than modern restaurant which serves consistently good traditional Roman fare at surprisingly honest prices. As the name might suggest, it is known for its *spaghetti alla carbonara* (spaghetti with bacon, egg and Parmesan).

LA ROSETTA Map pp311–13   *Ristorante*
☎ 06 686 10 02; Via della Rosetta 8-9; full meals about €115; ☼ Mon-Fri, evenings only Sat; bus to Via del Corso

Regarded by many as the best seafood restaurant in Rome, La Rosetta offers fashionable dining at memorable prices. Ruling the stylish roost is one of Italy's top chefs, Massimo Riccioli, who proposes a house speciality of spaghetti with scampi and zucchini flowers or innovative combos like shrimp, grapefruit and raspberry

salad. The mixed antipasto also provides a wonderful opportunity to sample many of his specialities. Booking is essential and if possible avoid the cramped outside seating.

LA TAVERNA DEGLI AMICI

Map pp311–13   *Trattoria*
☎ 06 699 20 637; Piazza Margana; mains €18;
☼ Tue-Sun; bus to Piazza Venezia

The proximity to nearby Piazza Venezia does nothing to dent the tranquillity of ivy-draped Piazza Margana on the edge of the Ghetto. Occupying a corner of this oasis of calm is the charming and highly regarded La Taverna with its much coveted terrace seating. Lunch time sees an influx of locals (especially politicians from the nearby Democratici di Sinistra headquarters), so service can be very slow. The menu, however, is small but perfectly formed with a backbone of meaty Roman classics, innovative vegetarian options and sturdy house wines.

LE CORNACCHIE

Map pp311–13   *Vegetarian*
☎ 06 681 34 544; Piazza Rondanini; menus €10-20; bus to Corso del Rinascimento

Run by the same operators as Margutta Vegetariano (see p159), this smart, if a little subdued, restaurant is just a hop and skip from the Pantheon. It serves a terrific buffet lunch of pasta or main vegie dish, dessert, water and coffee while in the evening the wood stove is fired up for some wonderfully inventive pizzas.

LE PAIN QUOTIDIEN

Map pp308–10   *French*
☎ 06 688 07 727; Via Tomacelli 18; meals about €18;
☼ Tue-Sun; bus to Via del Corso

Bringing a touch of Paris to the centre of Rome, Le Pain Quotidien (Daily Bread) offers a selection of baguettes, *tartines* and quiches. The mixed quiche and salad is excellent although you can't help but feel you're paying more for the faux-rustic decor than for the food, good though it is. Frequented by a young, well-to-do crowd, both foreign and local, it's a fun, table-sharing type of place where beer is drunk from the bottle and queues are the norm.

MARGUTTA VEGETARIANO

Map pp304–5   *Vegetarian*
☎ 06 678 60 33; Via Margutta 118; meals from €20;
☼ Mon-Sat; metro Spagna or Flaminio

A world away from the soy and salad penury of other vegetarian joints, this historic eatery

159

is decked in modern art and has stylish table settings and a jazzy soundtrack. The innovative menu occasionally misses the mark but most dishes – like artichoke hearts with potato cubes and smoked provolone cheese – are sensational. There's a full bar, impressive wine list and friendly bilingual staff. There's also another branch of the same operation called Le Cornacchie (see p159) near the Pantheon.

OLIPHANT Map pp308–10   *Tex-Mex*
☎ 06 686 14 16; Via della Coppelle 31; meals about €20; bus to Corso del Rinascimento

Hailed as the first 'Tex-Mex' theme restaurant in Rome, Oliphant is still going strong. The decor is the usual explosion of Americana, complete with jukebox and printed place mats which provide a riveting pictorial history of a cowboy's equipment. The menu includes all the old favourites, so if you want a meat fix go Tex with hot dogs or buffalo wings, or opt for Mex for tortillas and enchiladas. For dessert, the brownies and cheesecake tempt. To wash everything down there is a good range of beers.

OSTERIA DELL'INGEGNO
Map pp311–13   *Ristorante*
☎ 06 678 06 62; Piazza di Pietra 45; mains €12.50-20; Mon-Sat; bus to Via del Corso

The designer decor and modern cuisine give this place a thoroughly modern feel despite its position opposite Hadrian's Temple. The cuisine is central Italian with an international twist although the menu changes monthly to incorporate the freshest seasonal ingredients. Signature dishes include warm buffalo ricotta cheese with grilled seasonal vegetables and *farfalle* with leeks and saffron. The emphasis is on vegetarian but turkey, veal and Angus beef do feature among the seconds. There's also an excellent wine list.

PIPERNO Map pp308–10   *Ristorante*
☎ 06 688 06 629; Via Monte de' Cenci 9; meals about €40; Tue-Sat, noon-3pm Sun; tram to Via Arenula

One of the bastions of traditional Roman-Jewish cuisine, Piperno has turned the practice of deep-frying into an art form. The house speciality is a mixed platter of deep-fried, crunchy on the outside, soft on the inside, fillets of *baccalà*, stuffed zucchini flowers, vegetables and mozzarella cheese. If that doesn't appeal then try the offal, another Roman staple. The atmosphere is formal without being stuffy and perfect for family occasions, although eating *palle del nonno* ('grandpa's balls', ricotta and

chocolate puffs) might make some feel uneasy. Booking is essential on Sundays.

RICCIOLI CAFÉ Map pp311–13   *Café*
☎ 06 682 10 313; Piazza delle Coppelle 10a; meals €20; 12.30pm-12.30am Mon-Thu, until 1.30am Fri & Sat; bus to Corso del Rinascimento

A sleek bar of stainless steel and neon, this relative newcomer stylishly sets out to satisfy a range of tastes. If you want a plain old cuppa, they'll do you one; some sushi and sashimi, no problem; oysters and cocktails, of course, right away. However, the feel is trendy and you'll probably feel more at home with a martini than an Earl Grey.

RISTORANTE MONSERRATO
Map pp311–13   *Ristorante*
☎ 06 687 33 86; Via del Monserrato 96; full meals about €39; Tue-Sun; bus to Corso Vittorio Emanuele II

Within a stone's throw of Piazza Farnese, this unassuming neighbourhood eatery does great things with fish and seafood. The *spaghetti alle vongole* and *risotto con scampi* are among Rome's most outstanding. Shady outdoor tables and a superb wine list (with excellent whites from northeastern Italy) encourage long, relaxed summer lunches. Some reports do, however, grumble that the service is not as friendly as it might be.

SERGIO ALLA GROTTA
Map pp311–13   *Trattoria*
☎ 06 686 42 93; Via delle Grotte 27; meals about €20; Mon-Sat; bus or tram to Largo Argentina

Tucked away behind Campo de' Fiori, Sergio is the very picture of a Roman trattoria – red and white chequered tablecloths, bustling waiters, steaming plates of pasta being whisked here and there; not a frill in sight. And it is this lack of airs and graces that pulls in a clientele which counts as many office workers as street cleaners among its ranks. The food is Roman classic and the portions are massive. If you don't fancy pasta, the steaks are grilled with skill and the pizzas prepared in a wood oven.

SORA MARGHERITA Map pp311–13 *Trattoria*
☎ 06 686 40 02; Piazza delle Cinque Scole 30; full meals €20; noon-3pm Mon-Fri; tram to Via Arenula

For a true, no-holds-barred Roman eating experience head to Sora Margherita. This spot is so popular it doesn't even need a sign above its door; locals queue – and customarily cut in – for

Eating – Centro Storico

cheap and scrumptious pasta, Roman and Jewish dishes served on Formica table tops. Service is prompt and you're expected to be likewise. Thursday's gnocchi are legendary.

ST TEODORO Map pp320–1 *Ristorante*
☎ 06 678 09 33; Piazza dei Fienili 49-50; meals about €50; ☽ Mon-Sat; bus to Teatro di Marcello

Of a summer evening Rome's well-to-do can be found dining alfresco on the terrace at this, one of the jewels in Rome's culinary crown. Although a recent refurbishment has done little to lift the decor or atmosphere the food is fabulous, taking in pasta (prepared daily by the owner's mother), exquisite seafood creations, desserts to remember and a wine list for connoisseurs. A menu stalwart is the *tonarelli St Teodoro*, incredibly light pasta with a sauce of juicy prawns, zucchini and cherry tomatoes.

THIEN KIM Map pp311–13 *Vietnamese*
☎ 06 683 07 832; Via Giulia 201; full meals from €24; ☽ evenings only Mon-Sat; tram to Via Arenula

Oriental cooking is not well represented in Rome, so this discreet restaurant just over the river from Trastevere deserves plaudits for its pioneering efforts. The cuisine is an Italian take on Vietnamese cooking, with tasty dishes that are lighter and more strongly flavoured than other eastern concoctions served elsewhere in the city.

UKIYO Map pp314–16 *Japanese*
☎ 06 678 60 93; Via di Propoganda 22; meals €25; ☽ Thu-Tue; metro Spagna

For the authentic flavours of classical Japanese food, head for this ever-popular restaurant near Piazza di Spagna. Divided into separate rooms to preserve the atmosphere and ritual of Japanese dining, it offers a wide range of dishes covering sushi, sashimi, tempura and *yakitori* (grilled chicken). For the truly curious there is a €62 *menu degustazione* (tasting menu), which includes 11 different portions. Designed for four people, this option must be booked at least two days in advance. To wash it all down there is sake, beer and Italian wine.

VECCHIA ROMA Map pp311–13 *Ristorante*
☎ 06 686 46 04; Piazza Campitelli 18; meals €45; ☽ Thu-Tue; bus to Teatro di Marcello

Ideal for a romantic tête-à-tête, the candle-lit terrace here is one of the prettiest in Rome and an enchanting spot for winter dining. The Pan-Italian menu changes with the season, offering a huge range of tasty salads

in summer, a hundred-and-one things to do with polenta in winter, and lots of decent pastas and risottos year round. Service is genteel and friendly.

YOTVATA Map pp308–10 *Trattoria*
☎ 06 681 34 481; Piazza Cenci 70; meals about €18; ☽ Mon-Thu & Sun, lunch only Fri; tram to Via Arenula

All of the diners seem to know one another at this large and family-run kosher dairy (no meat but plenty of fish) trattoria, in a Ghetto blind spot. Settle into a cosy little snug and sample some honest-to-goodness Roman-Jewish fare, from the ubiquitous *carciofo alla giudia* (deep-fried artichokes) to spaghetti with tomato and fish sauce.

Cheap Eats
BELLA NAPOLI
Map pp311–13 *Pasticceria*
Corso Vittorio Emanuele II 246; bus to Corso Vittorio Emanuele II

Naples is justifiably famous for its cakes and pastries, and none is more famous than the *sfogliatelle*. Consisting of a shell of filo pastry filled with ricotta cheese, they are delicious – especially when eaten fresh from the oven. This Neapolitan bar-*pasticceria* on busy Corso Vittorio serves them better than most. With a cappuccino or even an espresso they slip down a treat.

BENITO Map pp311–13 *Tavola Calda*
☎ 06 686 15 08; Via dei Falegnami 14; pasta dishes €4.50; ☽ Mon-Sat; tram to Via Arenula

On the other side of Via Arenula at the start of the Jewish Ghetto is one of Rome's most popular lunch spots. Business is breezy and brisk here as the lunch-time punters pile in for their daily fill-up. The daily choice of two pasta dishes and a range of meats and vegetables is written up on the blackboard outside enabling you to rattle off your order and keep up with the frenetic pace. This is not the place if a long, leisurely lunch is what you're after.

BERNASCONI Map pp311–13 *Café*
Piazza B Cairoli 16; tram to Piazza B Cairoli

For a quick breakfast on the hop, this unassuming café is perfect as there's always a tempting selection of cakes and pastries. Particularly good are the *cornetti alla crema*, croissants filled not with cream *(panna)* but with a thick, creamy custard.

BRUSCHETTERIA DEGLI ANGELI

Map pp311–13   *Pub/Ristorante*

☎ 06 688 05 789; Piazza B Cairoli 2A; meals about €15; ☺ Mon-Sat & evenings Sun; tram to Via Arenula

Half pub, half restaurant, this place concentrates on one of Italy's most exported and simple specialities, bruschetta. Thick slabs of toasted bread come with a range of toppings from the classic tomato, basil and olive oil to zucchini flowers and mozzarella to truffles in season. There's also pasta, steaks and a good range of seldom-seen Italian beers.

FILETTI DI BACCALÀ

Map pp311–13   *Trattoria*

☎ 06 686 40 18; Largo dei Librari 88; meals about €13; ☺ 6.30-10.30pm Mon-Sat; bus or tram to Largo Argentina

If you thought the Brits had the monopoly on cod in batter, think again. On a tiny piazza strewn with scooters, the sign above the door says it all, and this restaurant (officially Dar Filettaro a Santa Barbara) is now unofficially named after the deep-fried *baccalà* (salted cod) in which it specialises. It's the Roman equivalent of your favourite fish and chipper, and the 'fish sticks' are accompanied by deep-fried vegies, other antipasti and various salads. Note the early opening hours.

FORNO DI CAMPO DE' FIORI

Map pp311–13   *Pizza a Taglio*

☎ 06 688 06 662; Campo de' Fiori 22; ☺ 7am-1.30pm & 5.30-8.30pm Mon-Wed, Fri & Sat , 7am-1.30pm Thu; bus or tram to Largo Argentina

Ideally placed for a quick, on-the-hop bite, this takeaway bakery draws people from all over the city. Aficionados head straight for the *pizza bianca*, which has no topping bar a drizzling of extra virgin olive oil and crunchy grains of sea salt, thus proving the maxim that less is more. The *pizza rossa* with a thin layer of tomato paste is just as good. Buy it by the metre.

GELATERIA DELLA PALMA

Map pp311–13   *Gelateria*

☎ 06 688 06 752; Via della Maddalena 20; ☺ 8-1am; bus to Via del Corso

Like an ice-cream version of Willy Wonka's chocolate factory, this modern *gelateria* believes in customer choice, offering up to 100 different flavours. The house specialities are extra creamy (and rich) mousse *gelati* and the *meringata* varieties infused with bits of meringue.

GELATERIA GIOLITTI

Map pp308–10   *Gelateria*

☎ 06 699 12 43; Via degli Uffici del Vicario 40; ☺ 7-2am; bus to Corso del Rinascimento

Overpriced and overrated, Giolitti continues to trade on its reputation as Rome's finest ice-cream purveyor. In its heyday it regularly delivered tubs of Pope John Paul II's favourite flavour, *marrons glacé* (candied chestnut), to his summer residence. However, although it's not what it was, it's still not bad and from the 70-odd flavours on offer you should be able to find something to suit your tastes.

INSALATA RICCA

Map pp311–13   *Trattoria*

☎ 06 856 88 036; Largo dei Chiavari 85; meals about €13; ☺ daily; bus to Corso Vittorio Emanuele II

This is the place for a quick, meal-in-itself salad or a bruschetta followed by a speedy plate of pasta. There is nothing characterful about this chain restaurant, with the feel distinctly fast-food, but it is good value and it's popularity with young Romans has spawned a number of new branches. There is another one nearby at **Piazza Pasquino 72** (Map pp311–13; ☎ 06 683 07 881) and at **Via FP Calboli 50/52** (Map pp304–5; ☎ 06 375 13 941).

Alfresco dining

Eating – Centro Storico

LA DOLCEROMA

Map pp311–13   *Pasticceria*

Via del Portico d'Ottavia 20; ☺ **8am-1.30pm & 3.30-8pm Tue-Sun; tram to Piazza B Cairoli**

The Ghetto is something of a treasure-trove for cake lovers with a number of ravishing *pasticceria*. One such is La Dolceroma (meaning Sweet Rome), between the Teatro di Marcello and Via Arenula. It specialises in Austrian cakes and pastries but also has American treats such as cheesecake, brownies and chocolate-chip cookies.

M & M VOLPETTI

Map pp308–10   *Rosticceria*

Via della Scrofa 31; bus to Corso del Rinascimento

Near Piazza Navona, this is an upmarket sandwich bar/deli/*rosticceria* where you can buy gourmet lunch snacks (and takeaway dinners) for above-average prices. The quality is high and business brisk as locals descend for their lunch-time *panini* and tourists peruse the tempting array of sandwich fillings.

OSTERIA BASSETTI

Map pp311–13   *Osteria*

Via del Governo Vecchio 18; full meals about €15; ☺ **Mon-Sat evenings; bus to Corso del Rinascimento**

The lack of a name hasn't stopped this trattoria from earning a reputation as one of the top low-cost eats in town. In fact, locals often pass by on their way home to pick up dinner. The decoration consists of a few dusty old prints and an AS Roma football calendar, but you don't come here for the ambience, you come here to eat. The kitchen serves up huge portions of Roman staples, such as the delicious *spaghetti alla carbonara* which is as good as anybody's in Rome.

PALADINI

Map pp311–13   *Rosticceria*

☎ **06 688 06 662; Via del Governo Vecchio 29;** ☺ **7am-1.30pm & 5.30-8pm Mon-Wed, Fri & Sat, 7am-1.30pm Thu; bus to Corso Vittorio Emanuele II**

There's no sign, the staff are miserable, the waits are long, and there's nowhere to sit; welcome to Rome's best grocery store-cum-sandwich bar, where you can fill focaccias or piping-hot *pizza bianca* with cured meats, cheese, artichokes and more. It's positively chaotic at lunchtime but it really is worth going out of your way for one of its doorstoppers.

PIZZERIA CORALLO

Map pp311–13   *Pizzeria*

☎ **06 683 07 703; Via del Corallo 10; pizzas about €7; bus to Corso Vittorio Emanuele II**

One of three pizzerie in and around Via del Governo Vecchio, Corallo serves thin Roman pizzas as well as pasta dishes. The food is good without being outstanding, but the area is lively and ideal for aimless postdinner wandering.

Top Five Shopping Pit Stops

As you break off from the arduous task of flexing your plastic you might want to replenish your reserves at one of these fine establishments:

- 'Gusto (p158)
- Al 34 (p165)
- Mario (p165)
- Edy (p157)
- Margutta Vegetariano (p159)

PIZZERIA DA BAFFETTO

Map pp311–13   *Pizzeria*

☎ **06 686 16 17; Via del Governo Vecchio 11; pizzas €8;** ☺ **7pm-1am daily; bus to Corso Vittorio Emanuele II**

One of Rome's trendiest pizzerie, da Baffetto was a famous meeting point for '60s radicals and now teems with loud Romans and timid tourists. The pizzas, considered among the best in town, are thin and crispy with charred edges and simple toppings. If you want to avoid the almost constant queues or sharing a table, arrive very early or very late.

PIZZERIA LA MONTECARLO

Map pp311–13   *Pizzeria*

☎ **06 686 18 77; Vicolo Savelli 11-13; pizzas €4-6.50; bus to Corso Vittorio Emanuele II**

The photos of celebrities that line the walls at La Montecarlo testify to the popularity of this classical Roman pizzeria. Just off Via del Governo Vecchio, it offers no innovations, but rather the usual, tried-and-tested selection of pizza toppings. It can get very busy here, especially at weekends, so don't be surprised if you end up queuing.

QUINTO BOTTEGA DEL GELATO

Map pp311–13   *Gelateria*

☎ **06 686 56 57; Via di Tor Millina 15; bus to Corso del Rinascimento**

Although it's only the size of a telephone box, this self-styled 'ice-cream boutique' does milkshakes, smoothies and fruit salad as well as dozens of *gelato* flavours. Decorated with an eclectic mix of Red Indian knives, bananas and photos of second-rate city celebrities, it's almost worth popping in just for a look. In fact, the decor is considerably more striking than the ice cream.

TRATTORIA PIZZERIA DA FRANCESCO

Map pp311–13   *Trattoria/Pizzeria*
☎ 06 686 40 09; Piazza del Fico 29; mains €6-7; ⏲ daily except Tue lunch; bus to Corso Vittorio Emanuele II

Traditional, atmospheric and friendly, this is the classic eat-up and ship-out pizzeria for which you'll have to queue unless you rock up early. Pizzas are tasty and typical, beer is on tap, and music comes by way of folksy guitar-strumming buskers. Lone diners can be given the run-around although the waiters are friendly enough. There's also bruschette, pastas and fried brains.

TRE SCALINI Map pp311–13   *Gelateria*
☎ 06 688 01 996; Piazza Navona 30; ⏲ 8-1.30am Thu-Tue; bus to Corso del Rinascimento

If you're going to have an ice cream on Piazza Navona, try Tre Scalini. This joint's famous creation is a rich ball of chocolate *gelato*, filled with huge chunks of pure chocolate, squashed flat and served with peaks of whipped cream. In comparison, Bernini's achievements in the square fade into insignificance.

ZÌ FENIZIA Map pp311–13   *Pizza a Taglio*
Via di Santa Maria del Pianto 64; ⏲ 8am-8pm Sun-Thu, 8am-3pm Fri, closed Jewish holidays; tram to Via Arenula

Although no longer Rome's only kosher pizzeria, Zì Fenizia remains the best known. Named after a legendary character who cooked for the Ghetto during the lean times following WWII, it makes outstanding pizza and although there's no cheese on this kosher variety, you don't miss it as the tasty toppings compensate. This is *pizza a taglio* (pizza by the slice) *par excellence*.

EAST OF VIA DEL CORSO

Stretching from San Lorenzo to Via Veneto, Piazza di Spagna and the Trevi Fountain, this swath of Rome swings from the historic elegance of the days of la dolce vita to the modern chaos of Stazione Termini.

Starting in the east, San Lorenzo is a vibrant up-and-coming area where you'll find a number of slick restaurants sitting shoulder to shoulder with cheap and chirpy pizzerie. Not so in the cosmopolitan streets surrounding Termini, where the emphasis is often on the speed of service rather than the quality of the food. However, there are some great ethnic eats at very decent prices as well as the usual ton of trattorie, some of which are very good.

Piazza di Spagna, Via Veneto and the Barberini areas are a step up in the world. Much frequented by wealthy Romans as well as hungry tourists, you'll find a mix of formal, old-school restaurants and younger, hipper vegetarian bistros, of cheap eateries and expensive cafés.

AFRICA

Map pp314–16   *Ethiopian & Eritrean*
☎ 06 494 10 77; Via Gaeta 26-28; mains €6-10; ⏲ Tue-Sun; metro Castro Pretorio

The area around Termini is the closest thing to a multicultural zone in Rome and this laid-back and cheerful restaurant caters to local expats and curious Romans. Use your fingers to dig into deliciously spicy fare like falafel and *sambusas* (a cross between a spring roll and a samosa), and scoop up meat and vegetables with soft, spongy *injera* bread before finishing off with sweet halva and spicy tea.

AGATA E ROMEO

Map pp314–16   *Ristorante*
☎ 06 446 61 15; Via Carlo Alberto 45; meals €75; ⏲ Mon-Fri, closed 2 weeks in Jan & Aug; metro Vittorio Emanuele

Run by Agata and Romeo, the husband and wife team who lend their names to the title, this intimate and elegant restaurant is the best fine-dining option on this side of town. The innovative menu combines tradition with unbounded creativity, and highlights include beans studded with mussels and Agata's legendary *millefoglie* (puff pastry filled with almonds and cream).

AL 34 Map pp308–10   *Ristorante*

☎ 06 679 50 91; Via Mario de' Fiori 34; full meals about €30; 🕙 Tue-Sun; metro Spagna

After a hard day's shopping on Via Condotti, rest your legs and treat your taste buds with lunch or dinner at this exceedingly popular eatery, where hearty Roman and regional dishes – the spaghetti with clams is exceptional – are served in a narrow, vaulted interior lined with scarlet wallpaper. For those with a really large appetite, a *menu degustazione* is available. Service can be slapdash but you still need to book.

ARANCIA BLU

Map pp314–16   *Vegetarian*

☎ 06 445 41 05; Via dei Latini 55-65; meals around €30; 🕙 evenings only; bus to Via Tiburtina

This well-known San Lorenzo restaurant has been flying the flag for good-quality vegetarian cooking for a number of years. Although it tries a little too hard to be upmarket and sophisticated with its slightly smarmy service and an elaborate *nouvelle* menu, the Mediterranean dishes hit more than they miss. Particularly good is the *spaghetti alla chitarra con tartufo nero e pecorino*, thick spaghetti with black truffle and spicy cheese. The soft lighting and wood ceilings are attractive and the wine list is inviting.

BISTRÒ Map pp314–16   *Ristorante*

☎ 06 447 02 868; Via Palestro 40; meals €50; 🕙 noon-2am Mon-Sat; metro Termini

An elegant barrel-vaulted restaurant, Bistrò provides a welcome break from the tourist-oriented trattorie that populate the Termini area. The menu, overseen by Sicilian Emanuele Vizzini, proposes a huge range of dishes with seafood featuring strongly. Some of the pastas, however, are a bit disappointing although seconds and desserts offer better value. There is a comprehensive list of Italian and foreign wines and service is cordial, if a bit slow. Reservations are preferred.

COLLINE EMILIANE

Map pp314–16   *Trattoria*

☎ 06 481 75 38; Via degli Avignonesi 22; meals about €25; 🕙 Sat-Thu; metro Barberini

Tucked away in a cheerless little street, this humble trattoria comes to Rome bearing gifts from the Emilia-Romagna province – think *parmigiano reggiano* (Parmesan), *aceto balsamico* (balsamic vinegar), *bolognese* and Parma ham just for starters. The food is exceptionally good – from *tortelli di zucca*

(pumpkin pasta) to *gimabonnetto* (roast veal with roast potatoes) – and, in itself, this place is the perfect winter warmer.

GRAN CAFFÈ LA CAFFETTIERA

Map pp308–10   *Café*

☎ 06 321 33 44; Via Margutta 61a; 🕙 lunch & dinner until 9pm Tue-Sun, until late Thu-Sat; bus to Piazza San Silvestro, metro Spagna

This huge old-fashioned tearoom with Art-Nouveau woodwork and fresco-adorned ceilings occupies what was once the Teatro Alibert. Offering a range of eating and drinking options, it serves delicious light meals such as rice timbale with vegetables and cheese, or buffalo mozzarella with salad. Dinner from Thursday to Saturday is served in the piano bar.

IL DITO E LA LUNA

Map pp302–3   *Ristorante*

☎ 06 494 07 26; Via dei Sabelli 49-51; meals about €35; 🕙 evenings Mon-Sat; bus to Via Tiburtina

In the student-dominated San Lorenzo district, this bistro is a cut above your ordinary trattoria and serves a Sicily-inspired menu which changes seasonally. Interesting dishes include fresh anchovies marinated in orange juice, a savoury tart made with onions and melted Parmesan, *caponata* (a sort of Sicilian ratatouille), and fish cooked in a potato crust. The restaurant accepts debit cards, but not credit cards.

MARIO Map pp308–10   *Ristorante*

☎ 06 678 38 18; Via delle Vite 55; meals €30; 🕙 Mon-Sat; metro Spagna

Right in the heart of serious shopping territory, Mario pulls in the weary shoppers at lunch and the beautiful people at dinner. Specialising in filling Tuscan food, there is a good selection of thick broths – the *ribollita*, bread soup, is excellent – grilled meat and game. According to some the service is dreadful, others say it's wonderful.

NATURIST CLUB – L'ISOLA

Map pp308–10   *Vegetarian*

☎ 06 679 25 09; Via delle Vite 14, 4th fl; full meals from €20; 🕙 Mon-Sat; metro Spagna

Also trading under the snappy name Centro Macrobiotico Italiano, this simple and jolly vegetarian haven leads a double life: at lunch it's a semi-self-service vegetarian eatery serving wholegrain risottos and vegie pies; by night it offers à la carte dining with speciality fish dishes. The decor is cheerful with red chairs surrounding candle-lit tables. Nudity is not strictly required.

OSTERIA MARGUTTA

Map pp308–10 *Trattoria*
☎ 06 323 10 25; Via Margutta 82; full meals €40;
☽ Mon-Sat; metro Spagna

Osteria Margutta presents one of Rome's prettiest fronts with blue flowers and ivy almost drowning the quaint entrance. As colourful as it is discreet, this place has an artsy, theatrical decor. Plaques on the chairs testify to the famous thespian bums that have sat on them, with Meryl Streep's being a recent addition. Service is warm, the wine list terrific, and the food a combination of classic and regional dishes. Tuesdays and Fridays mean seafood.

OTELLO ALLA CONCORDIA

Map pp308–10 *Trattoria*
☎ 06 679 11 78; Via della Croce 81; mains €15;
☽ Mon-Sat; metro Spagna

This local favourite is set inside the courtyard of an 18th-century *palazzo*, where you can dine in the shadow of its pergola whatever the season (preferable to the poky dining room). The Caporicci family have built up a loyal following over the last 50 years with Roman staples such as *saltimbocca* (veal with ham), cannelloni and *parmigiana* (meat

or veg cooked in a tomato sauce). A colourful extra is the daily fountain of fruit.

TRAM TRAM Map pp302–3 *Ristorante*
☎ 06 49 04 16; Via dei Reti 44; meals €25;
☽ Tue-Sun; bus to Via Tiburtina

You'll understand how Tram Tram got its name when you hear the trams rumbling past but don't mind them, as this trendy San Lorenzo haunt is a buzzing place to eat. The cuisine is Puglian which means plenty of vegetables, fish and seafood. A perennial favourite is the *orecchiette alla 'ncapriata di fave*, ear-shaped pasta with broad beans. The wine list has been carefully selected to complement the menu.

TRATTORIA DA BRUNO

Map pp314–16 *Trattoria*
Via Varese 29; full meals about €18; ☽ daily; metro Termini

This modest trattoria makes no claims to innovation, preferring to keep to what it knows best, which is classical Roman cooking. One of the better places in an area not known for its attention to culinary detail, its walls are covered with pictures and from the ceiling hangs a curious wood construction that looks suspiciously like a medieval instrument of torture. The home-made gnocchi served on Thursdays are tasty and light.

TULLIO Map pp314–16 *Ristorante*
☎ 06 475 85 64; Via di San Nicola da Tolentino 26; meals €40; ☽ Mon-Sat; metro Barberini

Tullio brings a taste of Tuscany to the heart of Rome. A simple place, it opened in the days of la dolce vita and attracted a faithful clientele of politicians, journalists and artists. Little has changed and it is still a good place to get stuck into Tuscan staples like *bistecca alla fiorentina* (Florentine steak) and *biscotti* (almond biscuits) dipped in sweet *vin santo*.

Cheap Eats
ANTICO FORNO

Map pp314–16 *Pizza a Taglio*
☎ 06 679 28 66; Via delle Muratte 8; ☽ 9am-9pm daily; bus to Via del Corso

Bang opposite the Trevi Fountain, this takeaway does a roaring trade in fountain-side snacks. The pizza and *panini* are surprisingly good and reasonably priced given the area. If you want to return, follow tradition and throw a coin into the fountain.

Enjoying lunch at an outdoor café on Campo de' Fiori

FORMULA 1 Map pp302–3 *Pizzeria*

☎ 06 445 38 66; Via degli Equi 13; pizzas from €4;
Ⓨ Mon-Sat; bus to Via Tiburtina

A worthy pit stop for pizza fans, this historic San Lorenzo joint is as authentic as any short-term visitor could handle. It's always packed with local students and slumming uptowners so you'll probably have to queue (and even then be pretty pushy). Place mats double as menus and you can order tasty snacks like bruschette and stuffed zucchini flowers as well as classic thin-crust pizzas from rascally waiters as they speed by.

HOSTARIA ANGELO

Map pp314–16 *Trattoria*
Via Principe Amedeo 104; pastas from €5; metro Termini

This traditional Roman trattoria is one of many that populate the streets immediately surrounding Termini train station. If it's elegant candle-lit dining you're after, try elsewhere. But if you want a straightforward, honest plate of pasta this is just the place. As befits the menu of standard Italian fare, the decor is basic and the atmosphere jovially relaxed.

INDIAN MAMMA FAST FOOD

Map pp314–16 *Indian*
☎ 06 447 03 096; Via Magenta 41; set menus €5;
metro Termini

This recent addition to the area's ethnic food scene has already won rave reviews from travellers. Despite the unlikely neon and high-stool bar feel, this small takeaway does a brisk business in all your favourite Indian nibbles. And with the set menu including a drink, it's difficult to think of a cheaper place to fill up before hitting (or leaving) town.

LE MASCHERE

Map pp314–16 *Pizzeria*
☎ 06 445 38 05; Via degli Umbri 8; pizzas from €4;
bus to Via Tiburtina

This is another San Lorenzo pizzeria favoured by the student population. All the pizzas are prepared as they should be in a wood oven and whisked out to feed the hungry hordes. You can take away or eat on-site. The street seats fill very quickly in the hotter summer months.

MOKA Map pp314–16 *Snack Bar*

☎ 06 474 22 11; Via Giovanni Giolitti 34; metro Termini

Brilliant for train travellers (and night owls), Moka, next to platform 24 at Stazione Termini, offers surprisingly tasty ready-made food – pastas, salads and snacks – and is open 24 hours a day.

PANELLA L'ARTE DEL PANE

Map pp314–16 *Pasticceria*
☎ 06 487 23 44; Via Merulana 54; metro Vittorio Emanuele

For self-caterers, Panella has a tempting variety of pastries and breads. And to fill that freshly baked *panino* try the nearby market on Via Lamarmora or the numerous Indian and oriental shops in the area.

PIZZERIA IL LEONCINO

Map pp308–10 *Pizzeria*
☎ 06 687 63 06; Via del Leoncino 28; pizzas from €4;
Ⓨ Thu-Tue, closed Sat lunch; bus to Via del Corso

It's cheap, it's hectic and it's not full of tourists. Best of all, it serves delicious *pizza alla romana* (with thin and crispy crusts), fast, for lunch *and* dinner. It's a *centro storico* institution and the beer flows from the bottle and the tap. Bring cash as credit cards are not accepted.

PIZZERIA L'ECONOMIA

Map pp314–16 *Pizzeria*
Via Tiburtina 44; pizzas from €4; bus to Via Tiburtina

Another San Lorenzo favourite that attracts a student crowd, Pizzeria l'Economia stands by its name, serving local fare and good pizzas at budget prices. Take away or eat in.

SAN CRISPINO

Map pp314–16 *Gelateria*
☎ 06 679 39 24; Via della Panetteria 42; Ⓨ noon-12.30am daily (to 1.30am Fri & Sat); metro Barberini

Roman ice-cream cognoscenti say you've never tasted real *gelato* until you've been to San Crispino. The fruit-flavoured sorbets change according to season but it's the cream-based flavours – ginger, whisky and pistachio to name a few – that are the real winners. The cinnamon is divine.

TRASTEVERE

Trastevere has dozens of good restaurants for all tastes and wallets. Just wander the streets and you'll find something that appeals. In the maze of tiny streets there are any number of pizzerie and cheap trattorie. The area is beautiful at night and most establishments have outside tables. It is also very popular, so arrive before 8.30pm unless you want to queue for a table.

ALBERTO CIARLA

Map pp317–19 *Ristorante*

☎ 06 581 86 68; Piazza San Cosimato 40; meals €55; ⏰ evenings Mon-Sat; bus or tram to Viale Trastevere

Trastevere might not be on the sea but that's not a problem for the masters who cook here. If sensational seafood turns you on, you won't find better than this celebrity restaurateur's den. The decor is garish but it fades into irrelevance as soon as the first morsel passes your lips; five *menu degustazione* complement the à la carte fare which includes platters of raw, smoked and marinated fish, accompanied by wines from throughout Italy and beyond.

Top Five in Trastevere

- **Alle Fratte di Trastevere** (below)
- **Paris** (p169)
- **Alberto Ciarla** (above)
- **Da Augusto** (right)
- **Pizzeria da Vittorio** (p171)

ALLE FRATTE DI TRASTEVERE

Map pp317–19 *Trattoria*

☎ 06 583 57 75; Via delle Fratte di Trastevere 50; meals €25; ⏰ Thu-Tue; bus or tram to Viale Trastevere

If *all* you're looking for is an authentic trattoria with delicious, hearty food and a warm welcome then you can now give up the search; this, for our money, is the best in Rome. Join local businesspeople, priests and grateful tourists for generously portioned Roman fare amid chirpy decor and with bilingual service.

ATM SUSHI BAR

Map pp308–10 *Japanese*

☎ 06 683 07 053; Via della Penitenza 7; full meals from €24; ⏰ 8pm-1am Tue-Sun; bus to Piazza Trilussa

The excellent Japanese ATM is in a quiet backstreet, beyond the crowds which fill Trastevere's narrow medieval streets. Chill out amid the minimalist decor, soft lighting and relaxed music, and chow down on excellent sushi, sashimi, *nori* (seaweed) rolls, tempura and other Japanese classics.

CASETTA DI TRASTEVERE

Map pp317–19 *Trattoria*

☎ 06 580 01 58; Piazza de' Renzi 31a; full meals about €25; ⏰ Tue-Sun; bus or tram to Viale Trastevere

A neighbourhood trattoria in the local mould, Casetta di Trastevere serves up steaming plates of no-nonsense hearty fare, including a number of lovely legume-based dishes. Try, for example, the *crema di fave con crostini* (broad bean puree with croutons) or steaming bowls of *pasta e fagioli* (thick borlotti bean soup). In the summer months the outdoor tables cram up and service can get slow, but there are worse places to wait for your food.

DA AUGUSTO

Map pp317–19 *Trattoria*

☎ 06 580 37 98; Piazza de' Renzi 15; full meals €20; ⏰ Mon-Fri & lunch only Sat, closed Aug; bus or tram to Viale Trastevere

One of Trastevere's favourite mamma's kitchens, Da Augusto comes complete with all the accoutrements – paper tablecloths and down-to-earth snarling Roman wits. Enjoy your home-made fettuccine pasta or *stracciatella* (clear broth with egg and Parmesan) at one of the rickety tables that spill out onto the piazza in summer. The opening hours should only be taken as an approximate guide as every so often, and without notice, Augusto decides to close on other days of the week.

DA LUCIA Map pp317–19 *Trattoria*

☎ 06 580 36 01; Vicolo del Mattonato 2; meals about €18; ⏰ Tue-Sun; bus or tram to Viale Trastevere

Step back in time and pause for eats beneath the fluttering linen and knickers of the neighbourhood at this terrific trattoria. Much frequented by hungry locals, it serves up a cavalcade of Roman specialities including *trippa all romana* (tripe with tomato sauce) and *pollo con peperoni* (chicken with capsicum), as well as a tasty array of antipasti.

FERRARA Map p308–10 *Ristorante*

☎ 06 580 37 69; Via del Moro 1a; full meals €52; ⏰ 8pm-midnight Mon & Wed-Sun, also 1-3.30pm Sun; bus to Piazza Trilussa

This former *enoteca* (wine bar) is spread over three elegant, whitewashed levels. Predictably, *vino* is the speciality and when the encyclopaedic list beats you, seek guidance from the friendly and expert waiters, who talk about Italian wines like personal friends. The trendy Italian food will please whether you're in the mood for a snack or a banquet. Classic dishes include *orecchiette* (ear-shaped pasta) with zucchini and ginger-scented prawns, and warm rabbit salad with spicy couscous.

IL CONTE DI MONTECRISTO

Map pp308–10   *Ristorante*

☎ 06 581 31 89; Vicolo del Bologna 87-89; meals €20; ☽ Tue-Sun; bus to Piazza Trilussa

This atmospheric restaurant is hidden away in a tiny lane behind the noise and buzz of the busier Trastevere streets. Start with delicious zucchini flowers which are stuffed with mozzarella and anchovies, and then char-grilled rather than fried. Follow them with fabulous lamb, either oven roasted or grilled chops, called *scottaditto* (literally 'finger-burners').

LA BOTTICELLA

Map pp317–19   *Trattoria*

☎ 06 581 47 38; Vicolo del Leopardo 39a; meals about €25; ☽ 4pm-midnight Mon-Tue & Thu-Sat; bus to Piazza Trilussa

Discreetly positioned in a *vicolo* (alley) parallel to Via della Scala, La Botticella offers real neigbourhood dining. In summer you'll eat outside beneath the strung-up washing as the locals converse and argue right over you. It's great. Not surprisingly, they excel in Roman staples, such as the excellent *spaghetti all'amatriciana*, as well as tripe (ox or lamb) and *fritto alla botticella*, a tempura-like dish of deep-fried vegetables, including strangely delicious apple slices.

LA TANA DI NOANTRI

Map pp317–19   *Trattoria/Pizzeria*

☎ 06 580 64 04; Via della Paglia 1; pizzas from €7, pastas from €8; ☽ Wed-Mon; bus to Piazza Trilussa

A great location, good Sardinian fare and friendly service make this a year-round hit. It's cosy and welcoming in winter, while shaded outdoor tables set up in the small courtyard opposite the restaurant make an excellent spot to watch the passing parade in summer. Kids can tuck into a pizza while parents enjoy rustic, more sophisticated fare. Particularly good are the antipasti, meat and fish dishes although portions can be on the small side.

PARIS Map pp317–19   *Ristorante*

☎ 06 581 53 78; Piazza San Calisto 7; full meals €45; ☽ Tue-Sat & lunch Sun; bus or tram to Viale Trastevere

A restaurant of the old school, Paris remains the best place outside the Ghetto to sample true Roman-Jewish cuisine. The delicate *fritto misto con baccalà* (deep-fried vegetables with salt cod) is memorable, as are simpler dishes such as the *pasta e ceci* (a thick chickpea soup in which the pasta is cooked) and fresh grilled fish.

On Tuesdays and Fridays the *minestra di arzilla ai broccoli* (skate soup with broccoli) is unique.

RIPA 12 Map pp317–19   *Ristorante*

☎ 06 580 90 93; Via di San Francesco a Ripa 12; mains from €12; ☽ Mon-Sat; bus or tram to Viale Trastevere

In the heart of Rome's most original area, you'll find this anomaly – a Calabrian family restaurant. Credited by some with the invention of *carpaccio di spigola* (very fine slices of marinated raw sea bass), the menu is heavily slanted towards fish and seafood. The food is usually excellent although the service can sometimes be indifferent. There are some tables on the street but, unless you want your fish smoked by traffic fumes, you'll do better sitting inside.

SURYA MAHAL Map pp308–10   *Indian*

☎ 06 589 45 54; Piazza Trilussa 50; full meals €25; bus to Piazza Trilussa

For the unlikely but winning combination of Indian food and Trastevere atmosphere, head to Surya Mahal. Hidden away behind the grandiose fountain that stands over Piazza Trilussa is the shaded garden terrace of this fine Indian restaurant. Set menus – vegetarian, meat or fish – while not particularly original, do provide an opportunity to try almost everything.

Cheap Eats
BAR SAN CALISTO

Map pp317–19   *Gelateria*

☎ 06 583 58 69; Piazza San Calisto; ☽ 6-1.30am Mon-Sat; bus or tram to Viale Trastevere

There's nothing fancy about this neighbourhood bar which is precisely its appeal. That and the fantastic ice cream it serves. The chocolate *gelato* – soft and creamy and almost like a mousse – is rated highly by experts while the coffee flavour's not bad if you prefer something less sweet.

DA CORRADO Map pp317–19   *Trattoria*

Via della Pelliccia ; pastas from €5; ☽ Mon-Sat, closed Aug; bus to Piazza Trilussa

They don't come much more basic than this canteen, a favourite of Trastevere's shopkeepers. At lunch it fills quickly with hungry workers keen to choose from the two or three pasta or meat dailies. The service is gruffly friendly and the food filling and simple. Ideal if you're after a quick, no-frills bite in a genuine workaday eatery, but for a long lingering lunch with fine wine and designer tableware, go elsewhere.

DANIELA ORECCHIA

Map pp317–19   *Pasticceria*
☎ 06 581 00 60; Vicolo del Cinque 40; bus to Piazza Trilussa

To partake in that very Italian of habits, the late night *cornetto*, Daniela Orecchia is the place to go. It bakes *cornetti caldi* (hot croissants) from 7pm until 2am every night. They are all good, but for an old classic try one with chocolate and cream *(panna)*.

FORNO LA RENELLA

Map pp317–19   *Pizza a Taglio*
☎ 06 581 72 65; Via del Moro 15-16; 9am-9pm daily; bus to Piazza Trilussa

For sliced pizza worth crossing rivers for, check out the bakery that's been producing magnificent bread for decades. When the embers in the wood-fired ovens die down, the white caps turn their hand to slabs of thick, doughy pizza with simple and delicious toppings like potato and rosemary. To help you choose there is a list of seasonal ingredients on a board outside.

FRONTONI

Map pp317–19   *Pizza a Taglio*
Viale di Trastevere; 10am-1am Mon-Sat, 5pm-midnight Sun; bus or tram to Viale Trastevere

Among the city's more famous sandwich outlets, Frontoni is a deli delight. It makes its *panini* with both *pizza bianca* and bread and provides an enormous range of fillings. It also has good *pizza a taglio* – the ham and fig topping being a tasty novelty – and hot pasta dishes available for takeaway. There is also a restaurant upstairs.

LA FONTE DELLA SALUTE

Map pp317–19   *Gelateria*
☎ 06 589 74 71; Via Cardinal Marmaggi 2-6; 10am-1.30am daily, until 2am Fri & Sat; bus or tram to Viale Trastevere

While La Fonte della Salute may not be 'the fountain of health' it purports to be – although the soy- and yoghurt-based *gelati* do seem to support its claim – the fruit flavours are so delicious they're bound to lift your spirits anyway. Scoops are more generous here than at some of the more central places.

OMBRE ROSSE

Map pp317–19   *Pub*
☎ 06 588 41 55; Piazza Sant'Egidio 12; panini €4.50, pastas €7; Mon-Sat 7am-2.30am Mon-Sat, 5pm-2.30am Sun; bus or tram to Piazza Sonnino

This is a wonderful place to sit and watch the world stroll by while sipping on a cappuccino or beer or crunching into a fresh salad. In fact, the salads are particularly good and on a hot day make a wonderful lunch. The atmosphere, as befits Trastevere, is laid-back and the waiters are young and attractive. What's more, the cinema Pasquino (see p198), which shows films in English, is right next door.

OSTERIA DER BELLI

Map pp317–19   *Trattoria*
☎ 06 580 37 82; Piazza Sant'Apollonia 9-11; mains from €7; Tue-Sun; bus or tram to Piazza Sonnino

Right in the heart of the Trastevere action, just off central Piazza Santa Maria, is Osteria Der Belli. A solid trattoria with a great antipasto selection and large helpings of pasta, its main courses are nothing special (don't order the fish except on Tuesday or Friday). However, the pizzas are good and the location is fantastic for people watching.

PANATTONI

Map pp317–19   *Pizzeria*
☎ 06 580 09 19; Viale di Trastevere 53; pizzas from €4.50; 7pm-2am Thu-Tue, closed Aug; bus or tram to Viale Trastevere

This lively streetside pizzeria is known locally as L'Obitorio (the morgue) on account of its marble slab tables. Open late and always crowded, it serves good, if not amazing, thin-crust pizzas. The service can occasionally be slow and surly but don't take it personally, the waiters are not singling you out as a foreigner, they're stroppy with everyone.

PASTICCERIA TRASTEVERE

Map pp317–19   *Pasticceria*
Via Natale del Grande 49-50; bus or tram to Viale Trastevere

The sweet of tooth are particularly well served in Trastevere and this place, not yards from the area's main thoroughfare, is a consistently good bet for pastries of assorted sizes and flavours, delicious cakes and biscuits. The service is friendly and the assistants willingly help you choose.

PIZZERIA DA VITTORIO

Map pp317–19   *Pizzeria*

☎ 06 580 03 53; Via di San Cosimato 14; pizzas from
€5; ⏱ Tue-Sun; bus or tram to Viale Trastevere

Roman or Neapolitan? The great pizza debate
will run for as long as there's flour to make the
dough. Here, however, you'll find the thicker
Neapolitan-style version. Arrive after 9pm and
you'll be queuing for an outside table, but
the pizzas are worth it and the atmosphere
is fun. There are all the regular pizzas plus a
few house specials such as the *Vittorio* (fresh
tomato, basil, mozzarella and Parmesan) and
the *Imperiale* (fresh tomatoes, lettuce, cured
ham and olives).

PIZZERIA POPI-POPI

Map pp317–19   *Pizzeria*

☎ 06 589 51 67; Via delle Fratte di Trastevere 45;
pizzas from €4.15; ⏱ Fri-Wed; bus or tram to Viale
Trastevere

A popular haunt among the young of
Rome – hardly surprising since its pizzas are
good, big and cheap – this place boasts a
cavernous interior decorously draped in garlands of hanging garlic. The outdoor tables
that spill onto the square opposite are a summer bonus.

PIZZERIA SAN CALISTO

Map pp317–19   *Pizzeria*

☎ 06 581 82 56; Piazza San Calisto 9a; pizzas from
€4.20; ⏱ Tue-Sun; bus or tram to Viale Trastevere

Cosy by comparison to other pizzerie – as
long as you avoid the basement – this place
provides good value and friendly service, two
things you might not expect on such a busy
tourist thoroughfare. There's a lengthy list of
bruschette and crostini, and more than 30
toppings for pizzas so big they hang off the
edge of your plate.

SACCHETTI Map pp317–19   *Pasticceria*

Piazza San Cosimato 61; bus or tram to Viale Trastevere

A local favourite with shoppers and stallholders at Piazza San Cosimato market,
Sacchetti serves a fabulous array of sweet
nibbles. From elegantly wrapped trays of
individual pastries to your more everyday
cake requirements, the grumpy proprietors
have got the lot. Gems include a chestnut
and cream confection called *monte bianco*
and, on a hot day, the *granita di caffè con
panna*, a slushy coffee-flavoured ice concoc-
tion topped with cream.

VALZANI Map pp317–19   *Pasticceria*

Via del Moro 37; ⏱ 10am-8.30pm Wed-Sun; bus or
tram to Piazza Sonnino

Look in the window of this humble pastry
shop and try not to enter. If you like chocolate
of any kind, you'll find it difficult, so tempting
are the cakes on display. The proprietors speak
English and will happily discuss your needs before making their informed suggestions. The
speciality of the house is the legendary *torta
sacher*, favourite cake of Roman film director
Nanni Moretti.

SOUTHERN ROME

Testaccio, a traditional working-class
area, has been reinvented as Rome's top
nightlife district. It's therefore popular
with the young crowd who pile in to eat at
one of the various trattorie before hitting
the pubs and clubs. A bit off the beaten
track, it's worth making the effort to get
here to experience a part of Rome largely
ignored by tourists. But, be warned, this
is offal country where the so-called *quinto
quarto* (the fifth quarter, or the insides
of the animal) features heavily on many
menus.

Top Five in Southern Rome

- Cecchino dal 1887 (below)
- Trattoria da Bucatino (p172)
- Pizzeria Remo (p172)
- Shawerma (p172)
- Volpetti Più (p173)

CECCHINO DAL 1887

Map pp317–19   *Ristorante*

☎ 06 574 63 18; Via di Monte Testaccio 30; meals
€55; ⏱ Tue-Sat, closed Aug; bus or tram to Via
Marmorata

When travel magazines want to feature a traditional Roman diner, they usually rock up to
this historic eatery. Situated within a cow's tail
of the city's former abattoir, it's no surprise to
discover that offal dominates the menu – from
calf's head to pig's trotters and sweetbreads.
Specialities include *rigatoni con pajata* (pasta
with veal intestines) and *coda alla vaccinara*
(braised oxtail), although there's more standard, seasonal fare if you can't stomach Roman
soul food. The well-stocked wine cellar is an
added bonus.

DA FELICE Map pp317–19 *Trattoria*
☎ 06 574 68 00; Via Mastro Giorgio 29; meals from €16; ⏱ Mon-Sat; bus or tram to Via Marmorata

Lunch time for the shoppers and stallholders at nearby Testaccio market often means a plate of pasta at Da Felice. For an outsider, it's not so simple as the cantankerous old owner sticks *'riservato'* signs on all the tables and personally vets every customer. If he doesn't like the look of you, you don't get in. But make it into this hallowed trattoria – a Roma football scarf will help your cause – and you'll enjoy true Roman fare, great pasta and lots of meat and offal.

IL CANESTRO Map pp317–19 *Vegetarian*
☎ 06 574 28 00; Via Luca della Robbia 47; meals about €20; ⏱ Mon-Sat; bus or tram to Via Marmorata

Testaccio is offal country, so it's all the more pleasing to come across this restaurant bravely flying the flag of vegetarian cooking. The atmosphere is informal and if you like the food (solid if unspectacular), you can always buy the ingredients at the attached shop.

SHAWERMA Map pp320–1 *Egyptian*
☎ 06 700 81 01; Via Ostilia 24; meals €25; ⏱ Tue-Sun; bus or tram to Via Labicana, metro Colosseo

A novelty in Rome, Shawerma is perhaps the only place in the city where you can eat a kebab, drink a lager and watch a belly dancer

Waiters navigate the outdoor tables crowding Piazza Navona

all at the same time. Half pub, half informal eatery, the house specialities are vegetable couscous, vegetable *tajine*, kebabs, *tabouli* and falafels. Come Friday and Saturday nights for the belly dancing.

TRATTORIA DA BUCATINO
Map pp317–19 *Trattoria*
☎ 06 574 68 86; Via Luca della Robbia 84; meals €18; ⏱ Tue-Sun; bus or tram to Via Marmorata

A popular Testaccio eating place, da Bucatino is decorated with an eclectic collection of photos, paintings, empty chianti bottles and a mounted boar's head. The antipasto buffet is excellent and includes a delicious seafood salad. There's also a good variety of pasta dishes, which are served in colossal quantities, and the meat and fish dishes are chalked up daily depending on what the chef's got to hand. The desserts also exceed normal trattoria standards.

Cheap Eats
AUGUSTARELLO
Map pp317–19 *Trattoria*
☎ 06 574 65 85; Via G Branca 98; mains from €6.70; ⏱ Mon-Sat; bus or tram to Via Marmorata

Vegetarians please note that this is not the place for you, as the food here is offal. Specialising in sweetbreads and oxtail, variety isn't a strongpoint either as virtually every dish (other than the pasta) has some correlation to the innards of an animal. Still, if that's your thing, the cheerful folk at this old-fashioned trattoria will be happy to see you.

PIZZERIA REMO Map pp317–19 *Pizzeria*
☎ 06 574 62 70; Piazza Santa Maria Liberatrice 44; pizzas about €5; ⏱ 6.30pm-12.30am Mon-Sat; bus or tram to Via Marmorata

Whether or not the Roman pizza here is the best in town is debatable. What's not is that you won't find a noisier, more popular pizzeria. The pizzas are huge and come with a very thin crust as the city recipe dictates. Place your order by ticking your choices on a sheet of paper the waiter gives you. Expect to queue if you arrive after 8.30pm.

VOLPETTI PIÙ
Map pp317–19 *Tavola Calda*
Via A Volta 8; ⏱ Mon-Sat; bus or tram to Via Marmorata

It is worth making a special trip to Testaccio to eat lunch at this fantastic *tavola calda* (snack bar). The pizza by the slice is extraordinarily good and there are plenty of pasta, vegetable and meat dishes. A house speciality is rice salad which comes in different guises – choose from rice and chickpea salad, black rice and grilled vegetables or rice and fish salad.

The Perfect Pizza

Rome and Naples have been vying for pizza supremacy for centuries. Yet the two products could scarcely be more different. Pizzas in Naples have a soft doughy base while your true Roman pizza usually has a very thin crust.

Neapolitans regard their version as the authentic one, but the fact is it may very well have been the Roman legionnaires who first introduced the pizza to the peninsula. Pizza historians claim that back in the old days of empire the canny soldiers imported a flat unleavened bread. This, they say, was the first focaccia, served in Rome about 1000 years ago. They also note that Virgil mentions something sounding suspiciously like a pizza in his epic the *Aeneid*.

What is not in dispute is that it was a Neapolitan, Raffaele Esposito, who created the *margherita* as we know it. The great man truly excelled himself when, in honour of a visit by King Umberto I and his wife Queen Margherita in 1889, he created his masterpiece. The queen was said to have been mighty taken by the novelty, especially as its colours reflected those of Italy's new flag – the tomatoes gave red, mozzarella white and basil green.

Today, the division of taste is split on predictably geographic lines. Ask a Roman and you'll hear that it's a thin, flaky crust that you want. A Neapolitan will argue that no true pizza is prepared with a rolling pin. Any dough preparation will be done strictly by hand.

Both will, however, agree that a real pizza must be prepared in a wood oven and served as the cheese starts to boil and the crust to char.

Whichever pizza crust you prefer, you can find both in the capital. Do a bit of research, and *buon appetito*!

NORTHERN ROME

The area around Villa Borghese, although pleasant enough for a wander, offers few options for great eats. Northern Rome is predominantly a business district and many of the restaurants are geared for working lunches. They tend to quieten down considerably in the evening.

PAPÀ BACCUS   Map pp306–7   *Ristorante*

☎ 06 427 42 808; Via Toscana 36; meals €45;

☺ Mon-Fri, evenings only Sat; bus to Via Boncompagni

In the heart of Rome's upmarket business quarter, Papà Baccus is a fine place to savour the food and wine of *cucina toscana*. A smart and formal restaurant, it sources most of its ingredients from Tuscany itself, and Chianina beef is one of its draw cards. There's plenty besides, including *panzanella* (a delicious summery starter of stale, soaked bread with mixed salad, herbs and oil). Smoking and nonsmoking. Reservations are preferred.

VATICAN CITY

Most establishments around St Peter's and the Vatican are geared towards tourists and can be overpriced for fairly mediocre food. The streetside cafés and restaurants on Via delle Conciliazione are best avoided. If you head north into the Borgo and beyond it through Piazza del Risorgimento, or northeast towards the Tiber, you'll find better options.

DA CESARE   Map pp308–10   *Ristorante*

☎ 06 686 12 27; Via Crescenzio 13; meals €40;

☺ Tue-Sat & Sun lunch; bus to Piazza Cavour

Wood panelling and sombre fabrics lend Da Cesare a clubby feel and an air of grandeur. It is, however, not as stuffy as it might appear and is especially popular in the autumn and winter, when the menu offers game, truffles, porcini mushrooms and wonderful soups made from lentils, chickpeas, borlotti and cannellini beans. The seafood suggestions should not, though, be dismissed out of hand.

Top Five Around Vatican City

- **Siciliainbocca** (p174)
- **Cacio e Pepe** (p174)
- **Osteria dell'Angelo** (p174)
- **Da Cesare** (above)
- **Antonini** (p174)

IL MOZZICONE   Map pp308–10   *Trattoria*

☎ 06 686 15 00; Borgo Pio 180; mains from €7;

☺ Mon-Sat; metro Ottaviano

It's difficult not to feel a wonderful sense of wellbeing as you sit at one of Mozzicone's streetside tables glowing in the captivating atmosphere.

The menu is unexceptional but has all the usual suspects at reasonable prices. Try the *fettuccine al ragù* or the *spaghetti all'amatriciana*, and follow it with *saltimbocca alla romana* (veal with ham), *scamorza* (grilled cheese) and *trippa alla romana* (tripe with tomato sauce).

SICILIAINBOCCA

Map pp304–5 *Trattoria*

☎ 06 373 58 400; Via Emilio Faá di Bruno 26; meals about €40; Mon-Sat; metro Ottaviano

Tangelo walls, cheerful ceramics and the sunny demeanour of the lemon-clad staff here mean you can enjoy the soul and sensibility of the south whatever the season. It's a great place to sample Sicilian specialities like *caponata* (browned vegetables, anchovies and capers), and the island's legendary desserts such as *cannoli* (fried pastry tubes filled with ricotta) accompanied by *pantelleria*, the great muscatel.

Cheap Eats

ANTONINI Map pp304–5 *Pasticceria*

Via Sabotino 21-29; bus to Piazza Giuseppe Mazzini

Sweet tooths will also be satisfied west of the Tiber. Antonini, near Piazza Giuseppe Mazzini in Prati, is considered one of Rome's top *pasticcerie*. With a counter approximately 25 yards long, chances are that you'll find something to tickle your fancy, be it a fruit-topped tart or a cake drowning in chocolate.

CACIO E PEPE Map pp304–5 *Trattoria*

☎ 06 321 72 68; Via Avezzana 11; meals about €15; Mon-Sat; bus to Piazza Giuseppe Mazzini

It's difficult to imagine a smaller place than Cacio e Pepe. Situated between Piazza Giuseppe Mazzini and the Tiber, it's not much more than a hole in the wall, but for its homemade pasta it's well worth the squeeze. The *spaghetti alla carbonara* and namesake *al cacio e pepe* (spaghetti with cheese and pepper) are sublime. In summer, tables spill onto the street, and in winter hungry Romans will sit outside, wrapped in overcoats and scarves, rather than wait for a table indoors.

L'ISOLA DELLA PIZZA

Map pp304–5 *Pizzeria*

☎ 06 397 33 483; Via degli Scipioni 43-47; pizzas €6-7, mains from €8; Thu-Tue; metro Ottaviano

Despite its name (pizza island), this bright and breezy place also serves a decent array of antipasti and beautifully grilled meat. But it's the pizza – rigorously thin-crust Roman – that pulls in the punters, along with the huge calzone which in themselves constitute a filling meal. The decor is cheerful, with pride of place going to a 1950 Guzzetto motorbike.

OSTERIA DELL'ANGELO

Map pp304–5 *Trattoria*

☎ 06 38 92 18; Via G Bettolo 24; meals €20-30; lunch & dinner Tues & Fri, dinner only Mon, Wed & Sat; metro Ottaviano

Just a few minutes' walk from the Vatican, this is a hugely popular neighbourhood trattoria with solid wooden furniture, photographs of the owner's sporting heroes, a sociable atmosphere and robust versions of Roman favourites like *tonnarelli cacio e pepe* (pasta with cheese and pepper), tripe and braised oxtail. Evening menus are set at €22. To get there, walk along Via Leone IV from Piazza del Risorgimento.

RUSCHENA Map pp308–10 *Pasticceria*

Lungotevere Mellini 1; bus to Piazza Cavour

Another candy cove in the Prati area near Piazza Cavour, Ruschena sells excellent cakes, biscuits and pastries, especially the bite-sized *mignons* (sweet pastries).

> ## Top Five Ice-Cream Parlours
> - **San Crispino** (p167)
> - **Bar San Calisto** (p169)
> - **Tre Scalini** (p164)
> - **La Fonte della Salute** (p170)
> - **Gelateria Giolitti** (p162)

Entertainment

Entertainment

Entertainment in Rome is not what it was. No longer do Rome's great and good don their togas and head to the Colosseum to catch a bout or two of gladiatorial combat. But that doesn't mean modern-day Romans don't know how to have fun. While the nightlife may not have the cutting-edge feel of London or Berlin, there is something unique about partying in such a fabulously beautiful city.

Much of the activity is in the *centro storico* (historic centre). Campo de' Fiori is especially popular with young revellers and it's here that you'll find the major drinking going on. The alleyways around Piazza Navona also have some trendy late-night hang-outs, ranging from elegant wine bars to English-style pubs. Trastevere, itself a perfect place for just wandering aimlessly, is another pub-heavy area where locals and tourists mingle merrily. To get away from the tourist scene, head for San Lorenzo, east of Stazione Termini, where the atmosphere is young, fun and increasingly trendy. There are plenty of good restaurants

Relaxed afternoon outside Bar del Fico (p177)

(see p151) and the numerous pubs are frequented by the city's student population. Alternatively, and for a clubbier feel, try Testaccio which thumps to a harder beat.

Roman entertainment is not all about bars, pubs and clubs. The city's cultural calendar is well established and proposes a host of unforgettable events, particularly in the summer when much of the theatre, cinema, opera and music moves outdoors. Many performances take place in parks, gardens and church courtyards, with classical ruins and Renaissance villas providing atmospheric backdrops. Autumn is also full of cultural activity with specialised festivals dedicated to dance, drama and jazz.

The most comprehensive listings guide in Rome is *Roma C'è* (€1) published every Wednesday, complete with a small, but perfectly informed, English-language section. Two other useful guides are *Metro*, a Thursday supplement to *Il Messaggero*, and *Trovaroma*, which comes with *La Repubblica* (also on Thursdays). Both papers also carry daily cinema, theatre and concert listings.

Wanted in Rome (€0.77) is an English-language news magazine that contains listings and reviews of festivals, exhibitions, dance shows, classical music events, operas and cinema releases. It is published every other Wednesday.

Useful websites for listings include www.romace.it (Italian only), www.romaturismo.com and www.comune.roma.it.

Summer Fun

Every summer Romans pour out of the city, headed for the sea. Those who remain are treated to the annual Estate Romana Festival which transforms much of the city into one enormous stage. Supported by the city authorities, it sponsors hundreds of events ranging from organised skateboarding sessions to opera under the stars to book fairs for kids. For once there really is something for everyone. It runs every year from June to September with details available online at www.estateromana.comune.roma.it.

DRINKING

You've really got three drinking options in Rome: traditional Italian-style bars/cafés (where all ages are welcome), *enoteche* (wine bars) or *birrerie* (pubs). If you're after beer in large quantities surrounded by like-minded individuals (usually non-Italians), the pub is the obvious choice; for a relaxed glass of whatever while you watch the world go by, head for a café; for a carefully selected wine served at precisely the right temperature with a plate of salami and olives, you'll want a wine bar.

Ancient Rome

Supping a pint with the Colosseum in the background can't be bad.

EDOARDO II Map pp317–19
☎ 06 699 42 419; Vicolo Margana 14; ☼ 8pm-12.30am; bus to Piazza Venezia

This gay bar, just off Piazza Venezia, offers amusing decor (it's done up like a medieval torture chamber) and a mixed clientele (mostly dressed in black). There's no dancing, it's just a bar, but a good cruising spot nonetheless. Two nights a week there is cabaret.

THE SHAMROCK Map pp320–21
☎ 06 679 17 29; Via Capo d'Africa 26d; ☼ 11am-2am; metro Colosseo

It's thirsty work visiting the nearby Colosseum and this Irish pub provides the perfect antidote. Popular with an international crowd, it has Guinness on tap, darts and pay TV for those unmissable footy games. There are also occasional Celtic music jam sessions.

Centro Storico

Most of the action is concentrated around the two major squares – Campo de' Fiori and Piazza Navona. But walk down the narrow alleys and you're sure to find somewhere to quench that thirst, be it an elegant, ivy-clad café or a heaving, sweaty pub.

ANTICA ENOTECA Map pp308–10
☎ 06 679 08 96; Via della Croce 76b; ☼ 10am-1am; metro Spagna

A local institution in the Piazza di Spagna area, this bar serves everything from salads to whisky to afternoon tea. Frequented by shopkeepers and shoppers alike, it's a great place to rest your weary legs, and wallet, and enjoy a soothing drink in the wood-panelled interior or at a table outside. There's a cold buffet at the impressive, polished wood-and-brass counter and a good selection of wines. There's also a restaurant at the back if you need something more substantial.

BABINGTON'S TEA ROOMS Map pp308–10
☎ 06 678 60 27; Piazza di Spagna 23; ☼ 9am-8.15pm Wed-Mon; metro Spagna

This 19th-century tearoom has been brewing its overpriced tea since two English spinsters decided to bring a touch of Blighty to the Italian capital. However, don't expect a steaming mug of strong brew, it's very much cups and saucers and crowds of curious tourists.

Top Five Drinking Dens

- **Rive Gauche 2** An Irish pub on a grand scale, full of happy young drinkers (p188)
- **Sloppy Sam's** Beer by the bottle at this vibrant Campo bar (p187)
- **Bar del Fico** Sip your aperitif with Rome's bohemian set (see below)
- **Jonathan's Angels** Great for a beer and what a loo! (p187)
- **Café della Scala** Industrial-strength cocktails in Trastevere (p189)

BAR DEL FICO Map pp311–13
☎ 06 686 52 05; Piazza del Fico 26; ☼ 8am-2am Mon-Sat; bus to Corso Vittorio Emanuele II

While Bar della Pace attracts the sharp dressers, Bar del Fico, just around the corner, pulls in the bohemian crew. Gas heaters allow you to sit outside even in winter, and the place is packed all hours with people passing the time of day playing chess, playing cards, reading the newspaper or simply chatting.

BAR DELLA PACE Map pp311–13
☎ 06 686 12 16; Via della Pace 5; ☼ 9am-2am; bus to Corso Vittorio Emanuele II

The 'in' café of the 'it' crowd looks exactly as you'd have a Roman café look – ivy streaming down the facade, tables arranged in front, sharply dressed beauties sipping from glasses tinkling with ice. The prices correspond, but as a place for an early-evening aperitif in summer or a leisurely nightcap in winter it takes some beating.

BAR VEZIO Map pp311–13

☎ 06 678 60 36; Via dei Delfini 23; ⏱ 7am-8.30pm
Mon-Sat; bus to Largo di Torre Argentina

From the outside this seems a bar like thousands of others but go inside and you'll discover why it's not. A veritable temple to communism, the walls are papered with photos of communist politicians (past and present), communist rallying cries, red flags and posters of Che. If it's communist, it's here, on the walls.

BARONATO QUATTRO BELLEZZE

Map pp308–10

☎ 06 687 28 65; Via di Panico 23; ⏱ 8pm-2am
Tue-Sun; bus to Corso Vittorio Emanuele II

Hidden away between Via dei Coronari and Corso Vittorio Emanuele II, Baronato is quirky and original. Late on Thursday nights, drag-queen owner Dominot likes to don a gown and wig and perform Piaf songs to piano accompaniment. A menu of mainly Tunisian meals and snacks will sustain you through your cocktail tipples, *vin chaud* (hot wine) or *amaro* (bitter liqueur). Reserve a table for the Piaf show.

BARTARUGA Map pp311–13

☎ 06 689 22 99; Piazza Mattei 9; ⏱ 3pm-2am; tram
to Via Arenula

Looking onto a tiny square in the Ghetto, Bartaruga is named – in a fashion – after the Fontana delle Tartarughe outside. A combined cocktail bar, tearoom and pub, it's decked out in bright colours with Oriental furniture, velvet cushions and a Turkish harem feel. It's the type of place where you can spend hours either sipping tea or scoffing wine.

BEVITORIA NAVONA Map pp311–13

☎ 06 688 01 022; Piazza Navona 72; ⏱ 11am-midnight (1am in summer); bus to Corso del Rinascimento

For a cooling white or a warming mulled wine, this Piazza Navona wine bar is one of the more reasonably priced in this touristy area. You can get a glass of wine at the bar from around €3.50 – although expect to pay much higher prices if you sit outside. The cellar is also worth a quick glance – ask the owner – as it houses some remains of Domitian's stadium (see p52), on top of which Piazza Navona was built.

CAFFÈ FARNESE Map pp311–13

☎ 06 688 02 125; Via dei Baullari 106; ⏱ 7am-2am;
bus to Corso Vittorio Emanuele II

This popular café near Campo de' Fiori serves everything from ice cream to snacks, from croissants to coffee. Outdoor tables look onto the beautiful Piazza Farnese.

CAFFÈ GRECO Map pp308–10

☎ 06 679 17 00; Via Condotti 86; ⏱ 8am-9pm;
metro Spagna

Everyone who was anyone in the world of 19th-century literature and music supped at this historic café. Goethe and Wagner, Byron, Shelley and Baudelaire were all regulars during their time here. Nowadays, the tourist clientele is less exclusive but considerably more lucrative.

The Fiddler's Elbow Irish pub (p188)

ENOTECA PICCOLO Map pp311–13

☎ 06 688 01 746; Via del Governo Vecchio 75;
⏱ noon-3.30pm & 7pm-1am Tue-Sun; bus to Corso
Vittorio Emanuele II

A dinky wine bar in a nice part of town, the Piccolo has a good, if not exhaustive, selection of Italian wines, Cognac and fruit juices. Snacks, either savoury or sweet, are also available.

JOHN BULL Map pp311–13

☎ 06 687 15 37; Corso Vittorio Emanuele II 107a;
⏱ 11-2am; bus to Corso Vittorio Emanuele II

This well-known pub near Largo di Torre Argentina gets very crowded, particularly on Friday and Saturday nights. Styled after the English model, it's a pints-and-crisps place rather than a wine-and-olives bar.

(Continued on page 187)

1 One of the world's great public spaces, Piazza San Pietro, with Bernini's immense oval of columns representing the 'motherly arms of the church' (p128) 2 Enjoying the view from the terrace of the gardens at Pincio (p100)
3 Comprising most of Vatican City, the Giardini del Vaticano are 24 hectares of formal parkland (p131)
4 View from Piazzale Giuseppe Garibaldi over central Rome (p111)

179

1 Wine bottles stylishly arranged in an Art-Nouveau display case 2 Cool down from the Roman summer heat with a scoop (or two) of delicious gelati from a gelateria 3 Food as art. Colourful sandwich fillings brighten up the window of a Roman snack shop 4 Soaking up the ambience of the Ombre Rosse pub (p170)

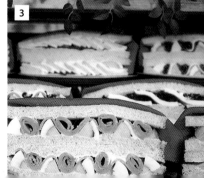

1 The traditional Jewish-Roman Da Giggetto (p157) *2* Staff work at a frantic pace at the popular Gelateria Giolitti (p162) *3* The colourful interior of Osteria Margutta (p166) *4* Romans pioneered the art of alfresco dining

1 Hanging out at The Drunken Ship, Campo de' Fiori (p187) 2 Wind down after a long day with some good wine and a chat at Rosati (p188) 3 Catch Italian and international acts at Alexanderplatz, Rome's top jazz and blues club (p195) 4 Staff get ready to serve Rome's thirsty locals and visitors at Sacchetti (p171)

1 Choose a drink from the wide selection of wine and beer on offer at Vineria (also known as Da Giorgio) (p187) 2 Romans are passionate about their football. Smoke erupts from flares as one of Rome's two teams, AS Roma, plays against Ajax Amsterdam at the Stadio Olimpico in Viale del Foro Italico (p199) 3 The colourful decor of L'Alibi (p192)

1 All the brand basics and more can be found at La Rinascente department store (p207)
2 Footwear to tempt passers-by; the window display at Fausto Santini (p212) 3 Home of breathtaking jewellery at breathtaking prices, Bulgari is located on Rome's most prestigious shopping strip, Via Condotti (p212)
4 A mecca for shopping lovers, you'll never fail to find unusual gifts and eclectic treasures in one of Rome's boutique stores

1 Antipasto in the raw; vegies on display at the Piazza San Cosimato market in Trastevere (p153) *2* Flowers add a splash of colour to the daily market on Campo de' Fiori (p153) *3* Suede jackets for sale at the covered Via Sannio market (p217) *4* Buyers rummage through a stall at the ever-crowded Porta Portese flea market (p218)

1 Two sculpted torsos frame a fountain in the terraced gardens of the Villa d'Este, Tivoli (p244) 2 A moated castle outside the ruined port city of Ostia Antica (p244) 3 The remarkable tumoli (great mounds of earth with carved stone bases), in which the Etruscans entombed their dead (p247) 4 The well-preserved remains of a Roman theatre built by Agrippa at Ostia Antica (p245)

(Continued from page 179)

JONATHAN'S ANGELS Map pp311–13
☎ 06 689 34 26; Via della Fossa 18;
⏰ 5pm-2.30am Tue-Sun, 8pm-2am Mon; bus to Corso Vittorio Emanuele II

A kitsch temple to everything that glitters or glows, Jonathan's has the most amazing loo in Rome – worth a peer if not a pee. The owner, an ex-circus acrobat, has styled this place very much in his own image and for a late-night tipple it is certainly an experience.

L'ANGOLO DIVINO Map pp311–13
☎ 06 686 44 13; Via dei Balestrari 12;
⏰ 10am-2.30pm & 5.30pm-1am Mon-Sat; bus to Corso Vittorio Emanuele II

A charming wine bar with wooden beams and terracotta floors, Divino sits off one end of Campo de' Fiori. For many years it was a simple *vini e oli* (wine and oil) outlet but now serves a variety of interesting dishes, including at least one hot dish daily and an excellent selection of cheeses to compliment its changing selection of wines by the glass.

MAD JACK'S Map pp311–13
☎ 06 688 08 223; Via Arenula 20; ⏰ 11-1am Mon-Sat; tram to Via Arenula

Near Largo di Torre Argentina, Mad Jack's is a very popular Irish-style pub. The Guinness logo is everywhere and the atmosphere suitably beer-orientated. To add to the buzz, MTV booms out of the various televisions dotted around the place.

MISCELLANEA Map pp311–13
☎ 06 679 32 35; Via delle Paste 110a; ⏰ 12pm-3am; bus to Via del Corso

A historic meeting point for foreign students, this is one of Rome's longest-running American-style bars. With a relaxed and welcoming atmosphere, it's a great place to enjoy an early drink – happy hour is between 5pm and 8pm everyday. It is also possible to watch American TV here.

SLOPPY SAM'S Map ppp311–13
☎ 06 688 02 637; Campo de' Fiori 10; ⏰ 4pm-2am Mon-Fri, 10pm-2am Sat & Sun; bus to Corso Vittorio Emanuele II

A cross between an Italian bar and an English pub, with several beers on tap, Sloppy Sam's is a friendly and relaxed place that attracts both a young international and a Roman crowd. Happy hour runs from 4pm to 8pm daily, adding to the already vivacious atmosphere.

TAVERNA DEL CAMPO Map pp311–13
☎ 06 687 44 02; Campo de' Fiori 16; ⏰ noon-3pm & 7.30pm-midnight Tue-Sun; bus to Corso Vittorio Emanuele II

Right next door to the Vineria (see below), Taverna del Campo is where the market folk and locals sip during the day, and where the fashionable set come to drink at night. Crowds from both places tend to spill out onto Campo de' Fiori in summer and it's always buzzing until the small hours.

THE DRUNKEN SHIP Map pp311–13
☎ 06 683 00 535; Campo de' Fiori 20; ⏰ 5pm-2am; bus to Corso Vittorio Emanuele II

Another bar on Campo de' Fiori that pulls in the crowds. There's a daily happy hour between 7pm and 9pm and on Wednesday a 'power hour' from 9pm to 10pm. During this 60-minute frenzy you're invited to drink as much beer as you can for €5.

TRINITY COLLEGE Map pp311–13
☎ 06 678 64 72; Via del Collegio Romano 6;
⏰ noon-3am; bus to Via del Corso

Just off the central shopping strip of Via del Corso, Trinity College has a good selection of international beers and great food. It gets packed to overflowing at the weekend and groups of single men might have trouble getting past the bouncers.

VINERIA Map pp311–13
☎ 06 688 03 268; Campo de' Fiori;
⏰ 9am-1am Mon-Sat, 5pm-1am Sun; bus to Corso Vittorio Emanuele II

Also known as Da Giorgio, Vineria has a wide selection of wine and beers and was once the gathering place of the Roman literati. Today it is less glamorous but still a good place to drink (it's cheaper if you stand at the bar) and has some light snacks.

East of Via del Corso

There are plenty of pubs and bars dotted around this area but the highest concentration is in the student quarter of San Lorenzo, east of Stazione Termini. Otherwise, try the streets around Piazza Santa Maria Maggiore.

CAFÉ RENAULT Map pp314–16
☎ 06 478 24 452; Via Nazionale 183; ⏰ 8-1am Mon-Sat; bus to Via Nazionale

There's not much in the way of nightlife

in this neck of the woods but this stylish black, glass and chrome bar provides one option. There are plenty of reminders of the building's former function as a Renault car dealership, but they'll need to rev up the atmosphere before this trendy place really takes off.

CAVOUR 313 Map pp314–16
☎ 06 678 54 96; Via Cavour 313; ✇ 10am-2.30pm & 7.30pm-12.30am Mon-Sat; metro Cavour

One of the oldest wine bars in Rome, Cavour 313 has an extensive cellar of about 1200 bottles. Unusually for an Italian bar, this includes Australian and Californian wines. There are also snacks – the cheeseboard is superb – and light meals if you're feeling a bit peckish.

DRUID'S DEN Map pp314–16
☎ 06 488 02 58; Via San Martino ai Monti 28; ✇ 6pm-1.30am; bus to Via Cavour

With a name like Druid's Den, this couldn't be anything other than a smoky Irish nook of a pub. Laid-back and warm, there is sometimes live music.

FIDDLER'S ELBOW Map pp314–16
☎ 06 487 21 10; Via dell'Olmata 43; ✇ 5pm-1.15am; bus to Via Cavour

The Fiddler's Elbow, near Piazza Santa Maria Maggiore, was one of the first Irish pubs to hit Rome. Its Guinness, darts and chips formula is still very popular and it boasts more than 180 labels of whisky and rum.

HANGAR Map pp314–16
☎ 06 488 13 97; Via in Selci 69; ✇ 10.30pm-2am Wed-Mon; bus to Via Cavour

This is Rome's oldest gay bar. Just off Largo Venosta in the Esquiline area, it's run by an American and has a varied clientele, both international and Italian, of all ages but with a significant portion of gym bunnies.

IL POSTO DELLE FRAGOLE Map pp314–16
☎ 06 478 24 868; Via Carlo Botta 51; admission €3; ✇ 5pm-2am Wed-Sun; metro Vittorio Emanuele

Scandinavia recently arrived in Rome in the form of this Swedish pub. With an ample selection of beer and wine, you can also eat here, watch a film, check out an exhibition or enjoy one of the frequent live concerts with everything from folk and blues to ethnic music.

JULIUS CAESAR Map pp314–16
☎ 06 446 15 65; Via Castelfidardo 49; ✇ 4.30pm-2am; metro Termini

What would Rome be without at least one pub named after its most famous forefather? This large pub near Stazione Termini has over 40 different beers and is popular with backpackers staying in the area's numerous hostels and hotels.

L'APEIRON Map pp314–16
☎ 06 482 88 20; Via dei Quattro Cantoni 5; ✇ 10.30pm-3am Mon-Sat; bus to Via Cavour

A well-known gay bar, L'Apeiron is just off Piazza San Martino ai Monti. You can choose to hang out in one of several distinct lounge and bar areas or in the basement video and dark room. There's also a maze where hands roam free.

MARCONI Map pp314–16
☎ 06 48 66 36; Via Santa Prassede 9; ✇ noon-1.30am; bus to Via Cavour

An old-style *birreria*, Marconi features eclectic pub food – Irish breakfasts, English fish and chips and Hungarian goulash – relaxing music, and lighting that's kept to an intimate minimum.

MAX'S BAR Map pp314–16
☎ 06 702 01 599; Via Achille Grandi 3a; ✇ 10.30pm-3.30am Mon-Fri, until 5am Sat & Sun; bus to Via Cavour

An institution in gay Rome, Max's is an informal place – the ordinary man's bar – with little attitude and great music. It's frequented by young, old and everything in between.

RIVE GAUCHE 2 Map pp302–3
☎ 06 445 67 22; Via dei Sibelli 43; ✇ 7pm-2am; bus to Via Tiburtina

One of the most popular pubs in San Lorenzo, Rive Gauche 2 is nearly always full of students, foreigners and assorted friends. A vibrant and animated spot, it offers little in the way of entertainment other than drinking, but creates a buzz that's genuinely infectious. However, be warned: it's a big place, gets very full and has only one tiny loo.

ROSATI Map pp304–5
☎ 06 322 58 59; Piazza del Popolo 5; ✇ 7.30am-11.30pm; metro Flaminio

A well-known meeting place and an elegant spot for a coffee, tea, snack or *gelato*. The cocktails are great and you can look out over the lovely piazza for the rest of the day. While it's not the cheapest bar in town, the cakes are magnificent. Its equally well-known rival opposite, **Canova** (Map p304–5; ☎ 06 361 22 31; Piazza del Popolo 16; ☻ 8am-midnight), is less sophisticated.

SKYLINE Map pp302–3
☎ 06 444 14 17; Via degli Aurunci 26; admission with Arci membership; ☻ 10.30pm-3am Tue-Sun; bus to Via Tiburtina
An American-style gay bar in San Lorenzo, Skyline is best known for its big darkroom and Sunday screenings of gay films (in the original language) that never got a national or international release.

TRIMANI Map pp314–16
☎ 06 446 96 61; Via Cernaia 37; ☻ 9.30am-1.30pm & 3.30-7.30pm Mon-Sat; metro Termini
Rome's biggest wine bar, Trimani has a vast selection of Italian regional wines and regularly hosts wine-tasting courses, for which you'll need to book ahead. They also serve excellent soups, pasta and *torta rustica* (quiche).

Trastevere
This picturesque part of town is riddled with pubs, bars and cafés. For years, Trastevere was *the* place for that quintessential Roman night out but as the crowds poured in, so the trendsetters moved on and there are those who claim it's losing ground to San Lorenzo. However, its charm remains and the fun seekers continue to come.

ARTÙ Map pp317–19
☎ 06 588 03 98; Largo Fumasoni Biondi 5; ☻ 6pm-2am Tue-Sun; tram to Viale Trastevere
A diminutive, dark-panelled bar with stained-glass windows and an easy air, Artù is popular with expats and is particularly convenient for a sip and snack on the way to or from the Pasquino cinema (see p198). It's in a tiny square between Piazza Sant'Egidio and Piazza Santa Maria in Trastevere.

BUON PASTORE CENTRE Map pp308–10
☎ 06 686 42 01; cnr Via San Francesco di Sales & Via della Lungara; ☻ 7pm-midnight Tue-Sat; bus to Piazza Trilussa
A lesbian centre just beyond the heaving throngs of Trastevere central, Buon Patore has a café and a women-only restaurant called Le Sorellastre.

CAFÉ DELLA SCALA Map pp317–19
☎ 06 580 37 63; Via della Scala 4; ☻ 4pm-2am; tram to Viale Trastevere
This small, laid-back café does mean cocktails. With measures poured by eye, waiters usually err on the side of generosity and the effects can be quite marvellous. Centrally located, it's a great place to watch the passing parade or view the frequent art exhibitions.

FERRARA Map pp308–10
☎ 06 580 37 69; Via del Moro 1a; ☻ 8pm-midnight Mon & Wed-Sat, 1-3.30pm & 8pm-midnight Sun; bus to Piazza Trilussa
For serious wine buffs, Ferrara boasts an exhaustive list of regional Italian wines and great food. Experts will feel at home with the wine list which comes in two encyclopaedic volumes – one for reds and one for whites. Amateurs may need help. Booking is advisable.

FRIENDS ART CAFÉ Map pp308–10
☎ 06 581 61 11; Piazza Trilussa 34; ☻ 7am-2am daily except Sun afternoon; bus to Piazza Trilussa
It's all stainless steel and attitude at this fashionable drinking spot. Full of young Romans dressed to the nines, it's not the place to bumble into wearing your shorts and flip-flops – looks count at Friends.

IL CANTINIERE DI SANTA DOROTEA
Map pp308–10
☎ 06 581 90 25; Via di Santa Dorotea 9; ☻ 7pm-2am Mon-Sat; bus to Piazza Trilussa
Nearby, at this friendly wine bar, there's a lengthy selection of wine by the glass (or beer if you prefer) and a good-value menu. The vaulted ceilings and exposed bricks give the place a cellar feel. Sit outside in the summer and you'll be alarmed at how much traffic passes.

LA SCALA Map pp308–10
☎ 06 580 37 63; Piazza della Scala 60; ☻ 12.30pm-2am; bus to Piazza Trilussa
This is not a world-famous opera house doing a few drinks on the side, but a loud and brassy pizzeria-cum-bar. When the pizza boys finish, the DJ takes over, spinning everything from house to pop.

MOLLY MALONE Map pp317–19
☎ 06 583 30 904; Via dell'Arco di San Calisto 17; tram to Viale Trastevere
Where would Trastevere be without its own Irish pub? Thankfully, we'll never know as Molly

Malone fits the bill. The decor is standard Irish, harps are everywhere and the atmosphere is lively.

STARDUST LIVE JAZZ BAR Map pp317–19
☎ 06 583 20 875; Vicolo dei Renzi 4; ☽ 3pm-2am Mon-Sat, noon-2am Sun; tram to Piazza Sonnino
A cross between a bar and a pub, Stardust often has live jazz music and jam sessions and on Sunday there are bagels and American coffee for brunch. It's a real neighbourhood place that tends to close only when the last customers fall out the door. There are more than 23 varieties of crepes on the menu.

Southern Rome
Heading out of the centre, southern Rome, and in particular Testaccio, is the heartland of clubbing country (see opposite). Simple pubs and bars do exist but are mostly frequented as a warm-up to the numerous clubs and discos.

COMING OUT Map pp320–1
☎ 06 700 98 71; Via San Giovanni in Laterano 8; ☽ 7pm-2.30am; metro Colosseo
With a name like this, Coming Out couldn't be anything but a gay and lesbian bar. Opened in 2003, it hosts gigs by emerging talent, and for wannabe crooners there is karaoke from Wednesday to Sunday.

FOUR XXXX Map pp317–19
☎ 06 575 72 96; Via Galvani 29; ☽ noon-4pm Mon-Fri, 6pm-2am Sat & Sun; bus or tram to Via Marmorata
A mix of Caribbean, Mexican and old Roman, this pub has moved on since its Australian early days. Head upstairs for a Latin night of tequila and colour, downstairs for the music (predominantly jazz and soul).

Vatican City
As befits the holy *raison d'être* of the Vatican, drinking joints are few and far between.

TASTEVIN Map pp304–5
☎ 06 320 80 56; Via Ciro Menotti 16; ☽ 1-3.30pm & 8pm-midnight Mon-Sat; bus to Piazza Mazzini
Tucked in between two mechanics' shops, Tastevin is a wine bar *par excellence*. With more than 1000 wines in the cellar, all rigorously Italian or French, this is the place where experts come to bone up on the latest trends. The food is good too. You can nibble on

cheeses and salamis, tuck into a daily hot dish or chomp on a choice of salads.

CLUBBING
Club snobs will have a tough time of it in Rome, but although the city's venues are not at the cutting edge of the clubbing movement that doesn't mean there isn't plenty of choice. The scene comprises everything from seriously expensive, seriously tasteless celebrity hangouts to heaving warehouse floors packed with energetic dancers.

Most places open around 10.30pm or 11pm and continue through to about 4am (although at the time of writing the government was talking about introducing a universal 3am closing time). Admission charges clearly vary, but expect to pay anywhere between €5 and €25, which may or may not include a drink. Saturday night is the best club night in Rome so expect to queue.

The best clubbing in town is in Testaccio, near the Piramide metro stop on Linea B.

ALIEN Map pp306–7
☎ 06 841 22 12; Via Velletri 13; ☽ 11pm-4am Tue-Sun; bus to Piazza Fiume
An old favourite, Alien has recently had a complete make-over. Drapes, carpets and incense add an ethnic feel while laser lights sear across the main dance floor. The music is a mix of house, techno and hip-hop, although one of the two dance areas also features '70s and '80s revivals. Alien goes gay on Saturday.

ALPHEUS Map pp302–3
☎ 06 541 39 58; Via del Commercio 271b; ☽ 10pm-4am Tue-Sun; metro Piramide
It's a fair way from the centre, but this huge three-room dance club is where it happens for gays and lesbians on Friday nights when hosts are the 'Muccassassina' DJ crew from the Mario Mieli gang (see p266). There is an Arabic restaurant should you require sustenance. Women get in free until midnight.

ANIMA Map pp311–13
☎ 06 686 40 121; Via di Santa Maria dell'Anima 57; ☽ 11pm-4am Tue-Sun; bus to Corso Vittorio Emanuele II
You'll hear plenty of good funk, soul, house and jungle at this hip food-and-club bar, although you'll hardly get room to dance to it. The decor is very postmodern, the food sushi,

the young crowd expensively dressed and the cocktails mighty fine.

BLACK OUT ROCK CLUB Map p320–1

☎ 06 704 96 791; Via Saturnia 18; admission €8;
🕒 11pm-4am Thu-Sat; bus to Piazza Tuscolo

One of Rome's most popular rock clubs, Black Out provides a postindustrial backdrop to the many national and international bands that pass through. The music ranges from heavy metal to ska with Saturday night's Rock Arena throwing up a mix of punk and pop.

BLUECHEESE – EX BOCCIODROMO
Map pp317–19

☎ 06 572 88 312; Via di Monte Testaccio; 🕒 11pm-4am Thu-Sat; bus or tram to Via Marmorata

The best of a string of clubs along this Testaccio strip, Ex Bocciodromo has two rooms (one outdoor dance floor) where the best local and some international DJs serve up juicy slabs of deep house, funk, electronica and sexy soul in a party atmosphere.

Top Five Clubs

- **Ex Bocciodromo** The hottest DJs with the latest sounds (see above)
- **Goa** Glamorous and showy, Goa keeps up appearances (see opposite)
- **Villaggio Globale** The only rule is to enjoy (p193)
- **Caffè Latino** Latin rhythms and shaking hips (see below)
- **Black Out Rock Club** Rock comes to town (see above)

BUSH Map pp317–19

☎ 06 572 88 691; Via Galvani 46; 🕒 10pm-4am Tue-Sat; bus or tram to Via Marmorata

House music in a modern setting is the recipe that has served Bush well. An established venue on the Testaccio club scene, it attracts top DJs and a faithful following. On Sundays you can have one of the resident shiatsu masseurs knead your aching muscles, while on Tuesday night Bush goes gay with cube dancers and drag queens.

CAFFÈ LATINO Map pp317–19

☎ 06 574 40 20; Via di Monte Testaccio 96; admission free Mon, €6-10 Tue-Sun; 🕒 10.30pm-3am Tue-Sun; bus or tram to Via Marmorata

Romans love Latin American rhythms and this is the place to hear them. Dancers samba to

the live music before DJs take over, spinning Latin, acid jazz and funk. You'll also find cabaret and film screenings here.

EX MAGAZZINI Map pp302–3

☎ 06 575 80 40; Via Magazzini Generali 8;
🕒 10pm-4am Tue-Sun; bus to Via Ostiense

A huge disco bar in a converted warehouse, this place is *molto* trendy. It's full of boys and girls bumping and grinding to everything from pop to breakbeat downstairs while models and media types flirt and frolic in the lounge above. Expect queues and occasional live performances.

GILDA Map pp314–16

☎ 06 678 48 38; Via Mario de' Fiori 97; 🕒 11.30pm-5am; metro Spagna

You'll need a jacket to get into this up-market VIP hangout. For many years this has been the place for the glamour pusses, partying politicians and aspiring types to be seen. If you have the money and want to see how Rome's beautiful people let down their expensive hair, this is your place.

GOA Map pp302–3

☎ 06 574 82 77; Via Libetta 13; 🕒 11pm-3am; metro Garbatella

Some way out from central Rome, Goa remains one of the capital's top clubs. Decked out in an ethnic-industrial style (read slinky couches and colourful wrought iron), it regularly hosts the best Italian DJs. Be warned though, the bouncers rule – if they don't like the look of you, you don't get in. One Sunday a month Goa goes gay with 'Gorgeous Goa' and 'Venus Rising'.

IL CONTROLOCALE Map pp320–1

☎ 06 700 89 44; Via dei Santissimi Quattro Coronati 103; 🕒 10.30pm-3am; metro Colosseo

Not far from the Colosseum, Il Controlocale showcases a variety of live music, from Italian folk to blues, on its distinctly red stage. There's an unplugged jam session on Monday.

JACKIE O Map pp306–7

☎ 06 428 85 457; Via Boncompagni 11; 🕒 9pm-4am Wed-Sat; bus to Via Boncompagni

A celebrated disco for the stars, Jackie O is a routine stop for the trawling paparazzi. Politicians, stars of the small (and big) screen and moneyed aristocrats all feel at home at this top-end party joint. For their wellbeing there is also an awesomely expensive restaurant.

L'ALIBI Map pp317–19

☎ 06 574 34 48; Via di Monte Testaccio 40;
⏰ 11.45am-5am Wed-Sun; bus or tram to Via
Marmorata

What was for years Rome's premier gay venue now attracts a mixed crowd, especially in summer, which is perhaps why it's lost much of its edge. Never mind, there's still plenty of good music across two levels – including old house and disco – and a great roof terrace.

LA MAISON Map pp311–13

☎ 06 683 33 12; Vicolo dei Granari 4; ⏰ 11pm-4am
Tue-Sun; bus to Corso Vittorio Emanuele II

Banquettes, chandeliers and terrific sounds – from deep house to funk – make this the perfect *centro storico* spot for late-night action. The mainly local crowd is flirty, thirty-something and *very* good-looking.

LOCALE Map pp311–13

☎ 06 687 90 75; Via del Fico 3; ⏰ 10pm-4am
Tue-Sun; bus to Corso Vittorio Emanuele II

One of the best places in the centre for live music, Locale stages concerts by local and international bands. Much frequented by city celebs, the atmosphere is informal and ideally suited for a cocktail or two. Expect to queue on Friday and Saturday nights.

NO STRESS BRASIL Map pp302–3

☎ 06 583 35 015; Via degli Stradivari;
⏰ 8.30pm-3.30am; tram to Viale Trastevere

The name says it all – this colourful and bubbly restaurant-cum-disco has live music every night with Brazilian bands and dancers getting everyone in a samba frenzy before DJs take over and drive them all home, so to speak. The karaoke on Monday, Tuesday and Wednesday nights never fails to excite.

PIPER Map pp304–5

☎ 06 841 44 59; Via Tagliamento 9; ⏰ 10.30am-
4.30am Sat & Sun; tram to Viale Regina Margherita

This historic disco has been around for decades but reinvents itself regularly and still manages to draw a young crowd. Its gay night 'Stomp' is on Saturday and there's live music on Thursday.

SHELTER DISCOPUB Map pp317–19

Via dei Vascellari 35; ⏰ 9pm-3am; tram to Viale
Trastevere

Gay men and women come together at this friendly Trastevere pub where the vibe is laid-back and the action gentle.

TESTACCIO VILLAGE Map pp317–19

Via di Monte Testaccio; ⏰ 7pm-2am Jun-Sep; bus or
tram to Via Marmorata

In summer, this stretch of open street is transformed into an outdoor entertainment complex with bars, several dance areas and live music in the form of rock, pop, ethnic and jazz. The music is mostly performed by local artists (with the occasional international name).

THE GROOVE Map pp311–13

☎ 06 687 24 27; Vicolo Savelli 10; bus to Corso
Vittorio Emanuele II

This place stages bands on the make and fashionable DJs. In the heart of tourist country, it attracts both young foreigners and Italians.

Gay & Lesbian Nightlife

Gay and lesbian nightlife in the capital is emerging from the somewhat secretive world it has occupied up until now. Although Rome is not as open as San Francisco or Sydney, attitudes are changing, and for the better.

Many gay bars are springing up in suburban areas, especially on and near Via Casilina, and it's becoming increasingly common for the larger clubs to host regular gay and lesbian nights. Details are provided in gay publications and through local gay organisations (see p266).

Most gay venues (bars and clubs) require you to have an annual Arci-Gay membership card. These cost €10 and are available from any venue that requests them. They are valid throughout Italy for one year from the date of issue. Gay and lesbian venues are included in the main listings above.

For a cleansing sweat there are several gay saunas in central Rome. Most open from 2pm or 3pm until very late daily and admission costs around €14 with an Arci-Gay card (which you can buy at the saunas), with discounts for students. You could try:

- **Sauna Mediterraneo** (Map p320–1; ☎ 06 772 05 934; Via Villari 3)
- **Europa Multiclub** (Map p314–16; ☎ 06 482 36 50; Via Aureliana 40)
- **Apollion** (Map p314–16; ☎ 06 482 53 89; Via Mecenate 59a)

Rome also boasts a gay beach, *Il Buco*, 9km south of Lido di Ostia. To get there take the Lido di Ostia train from Porta San Paolo station (right next to Piramide station on Metro Linea B). From there a bus will take you past all the expensive bathing clubs to the *spiaggia libera* (free beach). Ask for directions on the bus.

Entertainment – Clubbing

Centri Sociali

Italy's alternative music venues, the *centri sociali* (social centres), are increasingly becoming mainstream, moving away from their roots as centres of anti-establishment counter-culture. They survive today, but the politics are somewhat watered down and the entertainment considerably slicker.

There are about 30 *centri sociali* in and around Rome – many in the outskirts in disused factories, garages or industrial estates.

The biggest and best-known centres are **Forte Prenestino** (☎ 06 218 07 855; Via F. Delpino Centocelle), east of the city centre, and **Villaggio Globale** (below) in Testaccio. The daily newspaper *Il Manifesto* and the weekly *Roma C'è* usually carry listings of events.

VILLAGGIO GLOBALE Map pp317–19

☎ 06 573 00 39; Lungotevere Testaccio; bus or tram to Via Marmorata

A multipurpose entertainment village, Villaggio Globale is one of Rome's *centri sociali* (social centres). Founded by the squatters who moved into the city's former slaughterhouse, it now advertises a wealth of opportunities. Just to name a few, you can dance, catch a big band, learn to play the drums, eat African food and take a course in cinematography.

ZARAGOZANA Map pp311–13

☎ 06 687 58 67; Vicolo delle Grotte 3; ☽ 10pm-6am; tram to Via Arenula

Grotte by (street) name and grotty by nature, this place is expensive and uncouth and you'll love it. It's the only central place that stays open this late and if you've made it this far into the night, you're obviously in the mood to party. You have to become a member but don't chuck your card on the way home because, whether you intend to or not, you'll probably end up back here again.

MUSIC

Tickets & Reservations

Tickets for musical events are widely available throughout the city. Prices range from €6 for entry to a live music jazz joint to about €40 and upwards for a major classical performance.

For classical music try the **Accademia di Santa Cecilia** (Map pp308–10; ☎ 06 688 01 044; www.santacecilia.it, Italian only; Via della Conciliazione 4) or the **Auditorium Parco Della Musica** (Map p194; ☎ 06 802 42 350; www.auditoriumroma.com, Italian only; Viale Pietro de Coubertin).

Tickets to many concerts, classical or rock, are also available at major record outlets, including **Messagerie Musicali** (Map p210; ☎ 06 679 81 97; Via del Corso 123) and **Ricordi Media Store** (Map pp314–16; ☎ 06 679 80 22; Via Cesare Battisti 120d).

The **Orbis agency** (Map pp314–16; ☎ 06 482 74 03; Piazza dell'Esquilino 37) sells tickets for rock and pop events.

CLASSICAL & OPERA

The opening of the long-awaited Auditorium has excited classical music fans throughout the capital with critics hailing it as the best concert hall in Europe (see p194). It certainly provides Rome with a spectacular music venue and a shot of adventurous modern architecture, something mostly lacking in this historic city.

Free concerts are often held in many of Rome's churches, especially at Easter and around Christmas and New Year, with seats available on a first-come-first-served basis. The programs are generally excellent. Sant'Ignazio in Loyola is a popular venue for choral masses as are the Pantheon and San Giovanni in Laterano. San Paolo Fuori-le-Mura hosts an important choral mass on 25 January and a *Te Deum* (hymn) is sung at the Gesù on 31 December. Details are published in daily newspapers, *Roma C'è* or *Trovaroma*.

Classical Festival

Concert a Villa Giulia (☎ 06 688 01 044; ☽ Jun & Jul) The Accademia di Santa Cecilia orchestra performs a series of concerts in the beautiful Villa Giulia (Map pp304–5)

ACCADEMIA DI SANTA CECILIA

Map pp308–10

☎ 06 688 01 044; Via della Conciliazione 4; bus to Piazza Pia

The year-round program features world-class performers together with the highly regarded Santa Cecilia orchestra (directed, at least until 2005, by Myung-Whun Chung). Short festivals dedicated to a single composer are a feature of the autumn calendar. The orchestra is now permanently based in the new Auditorium

Parco della Musica (see below). In June the orchestra and its guest stars move to the beautiful gardens of Villa Giulia (Map pp304–5) for its summer concert series.

ASSOCIAZIONE MUSICALE ROMANA
Map pp308–10
☎ 06 393 66 322; Via dei Banchi Vecchi 61; bus to Corso Vittorio Emanuele II
The Associazione organises recitals and concerts in various locations throughout the year as well as two prestigious events: an international organ festival in September (in the Basilica di San Giovanni de' Fiorentini) and an international harpsichord festival in spring.

Alexanderplatz jazz club (p195)

AUDITORIUM PARCO DELLA MUSICA
Map pp302–3
☎ 06 802 42 350; www.auditoriumroma.com, Italian only; Viale Pietro de Coubertin; tram to Via Flaminio
Opened in December 2002, Rome's magnificent new €140m auditorium is one of the most advanced and spectacular venues in the world. Designed by the Genovese architect Renzo Piano (who also designed the Pompidou Centre in Paris), it comprises three separate theatres around an open-air arena and is used for symphonic music, chamber music, opera, contemporary, theatre and ballet performances. The largest theatre has

2756 seats making it the largest concert hall in Europe, and has been baptised 'Sala Santa Cecilia' after the patron saint of music and the orchestra that is based here.

Guided visits depart at 11am, 2pm and 6pm Monday to Friday, 10.30am and 6.30pm Saturday and Sunday. They last one hour and cost €9.

ISTITUZIONE UNIVERSITARIA DEI CONCERTI
Map pp314–16
☎ 06 361 00 51; www.concertiiuc.it, Italian only; Piazzale Aldo Moro 5; metro Castro Pretorio
From October to May, the recitals and chamber music concerts held in the Aula Magna of La Sapienza university range from classical to contemporary; it could be Mozart or Beethoven one week and Miles Davis the next.

TEATRO OLIMPICO
Map pp302–3
☎ 06 320 17 52, 06 326 59 91; www.teatroolimpico.it; Piazza Gentile da Fabriano 17; bus or tram to Piazza Manzini
The Accademia Filarmonica Romana holds its season here (see p197). The academy was founded in 1821 and its members have included Rossini, Donizetti and Verdi. The program mainly features chamber music, with some contemporary concerts and multimedia events.

TEATRO GHIONE
Map pp308–10
☎ 06 637 22 94; www.ghione.it, Italian only; Via delle Fornaci 37; bus to Via Gregorio VII
This historic theatre near St Peter's offers a varied program of recitals often featuring major international opera stars. Further details are available online.

JAZZ
In the summer, all true jazz aficionados head to Umbria Jazz in Perugia (see p252), which hosts some of the best live international and Italian acts. Umbria Jazz now also holds a winter event in Orvieto (see p250) and an Easter edition (featuring gospel and soul music) in Terni. For more information contact ☎ 075 573 24 32 or check out the website at www.umbriajazz.com.

There are also plenty of opportunities to hear jazz without leaving the capital, with two annual festivals and a host of great jazz venues around the city.

Entertainment – Music

ALEXANDERPLATZ Map pp302–3

☎ 06 397 42 171; Via Ostia 9; admission with membership €6.50; ⏱ 9pm-3am; metro Ottaviano

Rome's leading jazz and blues club, this is where you can catch top international and Italian musicians doing their stuff most nights. You'll need to book a table if you want dinner, while the music starts around 10.30pm. From July to September, the club moves outside to the grounds of the Renaissance Villa Celimontana (Map pp320–1) for the Villa Celimontana Jazz festival.

Jazz Festivals

Roma Jazz Festival (☎ 06 543 96 361; ⏱ Oct & Nov) Top international jazz performers come to Rome to do their thing, with main concerts taking place at the Auditorium Massimo in EUR and smaller fringe events at venues such as Alexanderplatz and Big Mama

Villa Celimontana Jazz (☎ 06 589 78 07; ⏱ Jun-Sep) The city's most atmospheric jazz festival, under the stars in the grounds of the Renaissance Villa Celimontana

BIG MAMA Map pp317–19

☎ 06 581 25 51; Vicolo di San Francesco a Ripa 18; admission with membership €6; ⏱ 9pm-1.30am Tue-Sun; bus to Piazza Trilussa

A well-established Trastevere club, Big Mama has branded itself the 'home of the blues', although it's just as good for jazz, funk and rock. It has weekly residencies from well-known Italian musicians and songwriters, as well as many international artists stopping by on tour.

FOLKSTUDIO Map pp314–16

☎ 06 487 10 630; Via Frangipane 42; metro Cavour

Near Via Cavour, Folkstudio is a Roman music-scene institution, providing a stage for folk, jazz and world music as well as young artists just starting out.

FONCLEA Map pp308–10

☎ 06 689 63 02; Via Crescenzio 82a; ⏱ noon-3pm & 7.30pm-2am; bus to Piazza del Risorgimento

Don't let the English country pub decor put you off – this is a great little venue for jazz, soul, funk and rock music (often cover bands) most nights. The Italian and Mexican food is reasonable.

LA PALMA

☎ 06 435 99 029; Via Giuseppe Mirri 35; ⏱ 8.30pm-12.30am; bus to Via Tiburtina

Insiders reckon this club is equal to Alexanderplatz as a top jazz venue. It's a bit of a hike out from the centre but worth it for the top-quality music by Italian and international artists. Monday and Friday are jazz nights, the rest of the week is given over to electronic music.

NEW ORLEANS CAFÉ Map pp314–16

☎ 06 420 14 785; Via XX Settembre 52; metro Repubblica

A city-centre bar in a not particularly lively part of town, New Orleans is a good bet for live jazz. Concerts are regular and performances well supported. If there's no concert on, however, the atmosphere can be stilted.

ROCK

Italy's rock map seems largely to bypass Rome. Most top international acts stop off at Milan or Bologna but depressingly fail to venture further south. When they do, it's usually as part of a summer festival or to play at the free May Day concert held every year on 1 May in Piazza di Porta San Giovanni.

However, smaller-scale rock concerts are held throughout the year and are advertised on posters plastered around the city. The city's *centri sociali* (see p193) host major and emerging Italian talent, while for bigger fish the three biggest venues are listed below. For information and bookings, see local listings publications or contact Orbis (Map pp314–16; ☎ 06 482 74 03; Piazza dell'Esquilino 37), an agency near Stazione Termini.

Major concerts are held at Palazzo dello Sport (☎ 06 592 50 06; Viale dell'Umanesimo, EUR), Stadio Flaminio (Map pp302–3; ☎ 06 323 65 39; Viale Tiziano) and Stadio Olimpico (Map pp302–3; ☎ 06 3 68 51; Viale del Foro Italico).

THEATRE

Theatre in Rome tends to the traditional and productions are often more melodramatic than dramatic. As audiences are generally keen to participate it can be fun, especially if you choose to watch the audience as much as the stage.

In summer, in keeping with city habits, many theatre productions move outdoors.

Check magazines or the daily press for details.

English theatre in Rome is thriving, thanks to the large numbers of expat and bilingual thespians resident in the city. These are usually weekly fixtures or short seasons, and details (even theatres) can change at short notice. Call for information or check *Wanted in Rome* or *Roma C'é* for details.

In summer the **Miracle Players** (☎ 06 446 98 67; www.miracleplayers.org) perform classic English theatre pieces such as *Everyman* and *Julius Caesar*, usually in abridged form, near the Roman Forum and other atmospheric open-air locations. The performances are of a high standard and are usually free.

Theatre Festivals

Rome's main festival season runs from June to November.

Cosmophonies (www.cosmophonies.com, Italian only; ☙ Jun-Jul) A short season of theatre, music and dance in the Roman theatre at Ostia Antica (p244)

Romaeuropa Festival (www.romaeuropa.net; ☙ Oct & Nov) Autumn kicks in with great theatre, dance and opera from around the world

Tickets & Reservations

Tickets & Reservations

Ticket prices range from about €8 for the smaller, experimental theatres to €20 and upwards for big-budget productions at the grander venues. To reserve a ticket either contact the theatre direct or, where possible, log onto its website. Alternatively, try a ticketing venue such as **Orbis** (Map pp314–16; ☎ 06 482 74 03; Piazza dell'Esquilino 37) near Stazione Termini, where you'll have to pay a small booking fee. Many hotels can also help you with ticket reservations.

Further theatrical information can be found online at www.tuttoteatro.com (Italian only).

There are more than 80 theatres dotted across town, many of them worth visiting as much for their architecture and decoration as for their productions. The ones listed here include the biggest and best known in Rome.

ANFITEATRO DELLA QUERCIA DEL TASSO Map pp317–19

☎ 06 575 08 27; Gianicolo; bus or tram to Viale Trastevere

Classical Greek and Latin works and 18th-century Italian comedies are perfectly suited to this ancient amphitheatre. They are performed from July to September each year, with afternoon performances for children.

ARTE DEL TEATRO STUDIO Map pp314–16

☎ 06 488 56 08, 06 444 13 75; Via Urbana 107; metro Cavour

The Ford Entertainment English Theatre of Rome is an international theatre company that performs a mix of contemporary one-act plays and full-length dramas in English every Friday at the Arte del Teatro Studio.

TEATRO AGORA Map pp308–10

☎ 06 687 41 67; Via della Penitenza 33; bus to Piazza Trilussa

English-language theatre is presented periodically, and in short runs, by the International Theatre at Agora in Trastevere. French and Spanish productions are also staged here.

TEATRO ARGENTINA Map pp311–13

☎ 06 688 04 601; www.teatrodiroma.net; Largo di Torre Argentina 52; bus to Largo di Torre Argentina

This state-funded theatre is the official home of the Teatro di Roma and stages major theatre and dance productions. Book early for the dance productions, which often sell out.

TEATRO DELL'OROLOGIO Map pp311–13

☎ 06 683 08 735; Via dei Filippini 17a; bus to Corso Vittorio Emanuele II

Comprising four separate stages, the fare on offer here is modern and experimental including works by contemporary Italian playwrights.

TEATRO QUIRINO Map pp311–13

☎ 06 679 45 85; www.teatroquirino.it, Italian only; Via Mario Minghetti 1; bus to Via del Corso

Within a stone's throw of the Trevi Fountain, this traditional theatre is for the purists, relying heavily on well-known works by well-known playwrights.

TEATRO SISTINA Map pp314–16

☎ 06 482 68 41; www.ilsistina.com, Italian only; Via Sistina 129; metro Barberini

This is the place to tap your toes to the tunes. Big-budget theatre spectaculars and musicals are the staples of the Sistina's ever-conservative, ever-popular repertoire.

TEATRO VALLE Map pp311–13
☎ 06 688 03 794; Via del Teatro Valle 23a; bus to Largo di Torre Argentina

This perfectly proportioned theatre is like a mini opera house, with three levels of private boxes. The variable program occasionally includes contemporary English-language works with subtitles or translated into Italian. You can also catch the occasional Italian singer.

TEATRO VASCELLO Map pp317–19
☎ 06 588 10 21; Via Giacinto Carini 72, Monteverde; bus to Via Carini

A little way out of the centre, this is an independent theatre which stages interesting fringe work, including dance performances. They also stage workshops and conferences.

DANCE

Dance is generally something Italians prefer to do rather than watch. But there is an active dance scene in Rome and many of the world's best companies tour Italy, although quality home-grown companies are few and far between. See the daily papers and listings press for details.

TEATRO DELL'OPERA Map pp314–16
☎ 06 481 60 255, toll free 800 01 66 65; www.opera.roma.it; Piazza Beniamino Gigli; metro Repubblica

Rome's principal opera stage also hosts a number of ballets in its season which runs from December to June. These productions are generally only worth seeing if there are important guest stars – the opera's *corps de ballet* has been in a somewhat sorry state for a number of years. The cheapest seats cost around €10.50, the most expensive €59.50.

TEATRO OLIMPICO Map pp302–3
☎ 06 320 17 52, 06 326 59 91; www.teatroolimpico.it, Italian only; Piazza Gentile da Fabriano 17; bus or tram to Piazza Manzini

In the northern suburbs, Rome's leading dance stage often hosts world-class dance troupes, ranging from classical ballet to dance theatre, from ethnic dance to avant-garde performances. Momix, Moses Pendleton, Daniel Erzalow, Pina Bausch, Jiri Kylian and Lindsay Kemp are among the many choreographers

and companies to have performed in recent years.

Dance Festival

Invito alla Danza (☎ 06 442 92 323; 🕐 Jul & Aug) A long-established modern dance festival in the beautiful grounds of Villa Massimo (Map pp302–3)

CINEMA

Italians, and Romans are no exception, love the cinema. Film buffs can therefore take delight in Rome's 80-odd cinemas, some of which are multiscreen. Unfortunately, unless you speak Italian your choices are going to be severely limited as nearly all foreign films are dubbed over; those shown in the original language with Italian subtitles are indicated in listings by *versione originale* or 'VO' after the title.

Tickets & Reservations

Tickets cost between €4.50 and €8. Afternoon and early-evening screenings are generally cheaper. Check the listings press or daily papers for schedules and ticket prices.

The following listings are cinemas which regularly show films in English.

ALCAZAR Map pp317–19
☎ 06 588 00 99; Via Merry del Val 14; tram to Viale Trastevere

Alcazar is an anomaly among Roman cinemas – it shows films without an interval. On Monday you can see films in English or with English subtitles. Smokers will appreciate the smoking section.

THE METROPOLITAN Map pp304–5
☎ 06 320 09 33; Via del Corso 7; metro Flaminio

This modern multiplex not two metres from Piazza del Popolo occasionally shows films in the original language. Releases are strictly of the blockbuster variety.

NUOVO SACHER Map pp317–19
☎ 06 581 81 16; Largo Ascianghi 1; tram to Viale Trastevere

Owned by Roman film director Nanni Moretti, this is the place to catch the latest European art-house flick. Originally designed to support home-made film talent, it shows films in their original language (English, French, Swedish etc) on Monday and Tuesday.

PASQUINO Map pp317–19

☎ 06 580 36 22; Piazza Sant'Egidio 10; tram to Viale Trastevere

Right in the heart of Trastevere, this Roman cinematic institution is the best bet if you want to see films in English. Labelling itself a multiscreen (there are three), it runs a program that changes daily, comprising everything from blockbusters to art-house flicks.

QUIRINETTA Map pp314–16

☎ 06 679 00 12; Via Minghetti 4; bus to Via del Corso

Opposite the Teatro Quirino (see p196), this rather run-down, single-screen cinema offers an unimaginative selection of Hollywood releases in English.

WARNER VILLAGE MODERNO

Map pp314–16

☎ 06 477 79 202; Piazza della Repubblica; metro Repubblica

Hidden behind the columns that circle Piazza Repubblica, the Warner Village Moderno multiplex has five cinemas showing Hollywood blockbusters (both in English and dubbed into Italian) and major-release Italian films.

OPERA

Opera and Italy go together like Pavarotti and Verdi, like Ferrari and red. Rome's main opera house, Teatro dell'Opera, is often considered a poor cousin to Milan's La Scala or Naples' San Carlo, mainly due to a lack of consistent artistic direction and poor management. However, there are some top-class productions and tickets are not impossible to come by. What's more, *Cavalleria Rusticana* by Mascagnai and Puccini's *Tosca* had their world premieres here. Rossini's operas *Il Barbiere di Siviglia* and *La Cenerentola* also premiered in Rome, at Teatro Argentina (see p196).

In summer, opera is performed outdoors and at the time of writing the Terme di Caracalla (see p114) were once again being used for the summer season after a lay-off of six years. The Stadio Olimpico football stadium had been used as an interim venue, but somehow just didn't quite generate the same captivating atmosphere.

Many of the summer festivals include opera performances in their programs. Check magazines for current events.

Tickets & Reservations

The opera season at the Teatro dell'Opera starts in December and continues until June. Tickets are expensive: the cheapest upper balcony seats (not recommended for vertigo sufferers) start at around €20 and prices go up to €119. First-night performances cost more.

For reservations contact the theatre direct or go online at www.opera.roma.it.

TEATRO DELL'OPERA Map pp314–16

☎ 06 481 60 255, toll free 800 01 66 65; Piazza Beniamino Gigli; metro Repubblica

The functional Fascist-era exterior of Rome's opera house doesn't prepare you for the elegance of the capital's premier opera house. Its 19th-century interior is all plush red velvet and gilt. Neither Milan nor Naples can boast a summer venue as incredible as the Terme di Caracalla.

SPORT
FOOTBALL

Rome has two teams, AS Roma and Lazio. Both have enjoyed a short run of success recently: Lazio won the championship in 2000, Roma the following year. They both play at the **Stadio Olimpico** (Map pp302–3; ☎ 06 3 68 51; Viale del Foro Italico), where you should head for tickets. Prices range from around €15 to €62. Alternatively, try an authorised ticket venue such as **Orbis** (Map pp314–16; ☎ 06 482 74 03; Piazza dell'Esquilino 37).

Lazio souvenir socks for sale on the Piazza Navona

BASKETBALL

The second most popular spectator sport in Rome is basketball. The arrival of several star players from the United States and from the former Yugoslavia has spiced up the Italian league. The season runs over the winter months and matches are played at the **Palazzo dello Sport** (☎ 06 592 50 06; Viale dell'Umanesimo) in EUR.

Rome's Mega-Venues

- **Stadio Olimpico** Football, opera and rock (see left)
- **Auditorium Parco della Musica** Spectacular setting for classical sounds (p193)
- **Stadio Flaminio** Rugby and rock (see below)
- **Palazzo dello Sport** Basketball and biggish bands (see below left)

TENNIS

The world's top players arrive in Rome in May for the Italian International Tennis Championships. Matches are played on the clay courts at the **Foro Italico** (Map pp302–3; ☎ 06 321 90 64; Via dei Gladiatori 31). Tickets can be bought at the Foro Italico each day of the tournament, except for the final days which are sold out weeks in advance.

ATHLETICS

The Golden Gala athletics meet takes place in June at the **Stadio Olimpico** (Map pp302–3; ☎ 06 3 68 51; Viale del Foro Italico). It's organised by the **Federazione Italiana di Atletica Leggera** (☎ 06 3 65 81 for information).

RUGBY UNION

If the national football team is considered a dangerous predator, Italy's rugby braves are by comparison minnows. But interest in rugby is growing – thanks largely to Italy's plucky performance in the Six Nations Championship in 2003. In only their third year in the tournament they managed not to come last, finishing ahead of the Welsh.

The team play home international games at Rome's **Stadio Flaminio** (Map pp302–3; ☎ 06 323 65 39; Viale Tiziano).

OUTDOOR ACTIVITIES
CYCLING

Cycling is especially popular in provincial areas. Second only to the Tour de France, the Giro d'Italia is *the* event on Europe's summer cycling calendar. Unusually for a major sporting event, it's free for spectators – simply find out where and when the tour is passing and plonk yourself by the side of the road to watch.

RUNNING

Good places to jog include Circo Massimo, Villa Borghese, Villa Ada and Villa Doria Pamphilj. But for those aspiring to more than just a gentle jog the Rome Marathon, which starts and finishes at the Colosseum, takes place in late March. If you think you're up to 42km on cobblestones, you should register well in advance with **Italia Marathon Club** (☎ 06 406 50 64, 06 445 66 26).

HORSE RIDING

Prices at the exclusive Il Galoppatoio equestrian club in **Villa Borghese** (Map pp302–3; ☎ 06 322 67 97; Via del Galoppatoio 25) make horse riding a costly pursuit. For a minimum of 10 lessons you'll be forking out something in the region of €400 when the requisite annual membership is added to the cost of the lessons and insurance.

The annual Piazza di Siena equestrian show-jumping competition is held in May in **Villa Borghese**. Call ☎ 06 322 53 57 for ticket details.

HEALTH & FITNESS

SWIMMING

Rome's public swimming pools are generally well outside the city centre and can be difficult to reach on public transport (indications are given in the boxed text opposite). Admission will cost around €10, with an additional annual membership fee (usually about €5) payable on the first visit.

Bear in mind that these pools usually close for part of August (some close for the whole month) and opening hours and days vary. Some pools also require a doctor's certificate before you are allowed to swim; call first to check.

There are also several privately run pools, including pools run by upmarket hotels where you can swim and lounge – at a price.

Splashing About in Rome

Depending on how much you want to spend, you can choose to do your laps in public or privately run pools.

Viale dei Consoli (☎ 06 769 00 627) Off Via Tuscolana southeast of the city; take Metro Linea A to Numidio Quadrato then follow Via San Curione to Viale dei Consoli

Via Bravetta (☎ 06 661 60 985) Past Villa Doria Pamphilj park; take bus No 98 from Via Paola at the end of Corso Vittorio Emanuele II

Piscina delle Rose (☎ 06 592 67 17; Viale America 20; admission per half-/full day €8/10; ⏱ 9 am-7pm Jun-Sep) Metro Linea B to EUR Palasport

Cavalieri Hilton Hotel (Map pp302–3; ☎ 06 3 50 91; Via Cadlolo 101, Monte Mario; admission Mon-Fri €40, Sat & Sun €65, under-18s half-price) Bus to Piazzale Medaglie D'Oro

Parco dei Principi (Map pp306–7; ☎ 06 85 44 21; Via G Frescobaldi 5; admission Mon-Fri €35, Sat & Sun €45; ⏱ 10am-6pm May-Sep) Take bus No 910 from Stazione Termini or No 52 from Piazza San Silvestro

---

Shopping

Shopping

Romans love shopping. You only have to wander down flashy Via del Corso on a Saturday afternoon to see how much. And they're extremely good at it too. To witness an Italian shopping is to witness a maestro in action. Brushing aside the surly affectations, or occasionally even polite approaches of the shop assistant, they'll hone in mercilessly on what they want, dismissing second-rate substitutes with disdain, until they find exactly what they came for. Only then will they buy. It's a serious drama involving deadly intent, passion and considerable cunning.

As a visitor you'll never be expected to demonstrate local levels of expertise but enthusiastic amateurs are welcomed with open doors. You shouldn't therefore feel bad if you find that Rome's shop windows are competing with its monuments for your attention – you'll simply be slipping into local habits. Just make sure there's plenty of time in your itinerary to allow you to indulge in this national pastime.

Italy is renowned for its top-quality designer clothes, shoes and leather accessories and you'll find no shortage of choice as you wander the busy streets. All of the big designer names are represented in Rome and even if your budget doesn't allow for an Armani suit, a Prada handbag or a pair of Gucci loafers, you can still have fun looking.

Mannequin in La Rinascente department store window (p207)

If you confine your expeditions to the main shopping districts, you'll find a concentration of clothing and accessories shops that, apart from the designer outlets, sell ridiculous tat at inflated prices. Get into the side streets, root around the more out-of-the-way shopping areas and you'll discover a side of Rome often hidden even from its residents. In this chapter we cover the main places to shop and things to buy, as well as the more off-beat side to shopping in Rome.

Where to Go for What

Whether it's the latest designer gear or more modest threads you're after, Rome has a street to suit your every shopping need:

- **Via Condotti** For the big guns of the fashion biz, head to Rome's most prestigious shopping street
- **Via del Corso** Join the crowds and search the flagship chain stores
- **Via Nazionale** Mid-range clothes and shoe shops line this major thoroughfare
- **Via del Governo Vecchio** Stroll this laid-back street and browse in the colourful second-hand clothes shops
- **Via del Babuino** Art comes at a price in the shop galleries on this picturesque street

Shopping Areas

For top of the range designers, head for the area between Piazza di Spagna and Via del Corso (Map p210) and in particular Via Condotti, Via Frattina, Via della Vite and Via Borgognona. Here you'll find most of the main designer shops for clothing, shoes, leather goods and other accessories, with a fair sprinkling of more affordable shops for those looking to avoid eye-popping prices.

Moving down a euro or two, Via Nazionale (Map pp314–16), Via del Corso (Map p210) and Via dei Giubbonari (Map pp311–13) are good for mid-range clothing stores while second-hand clothes can be found along Via del Governo Vecchio (Map pp311–13), a winding street that runs from a small square just off Piazza Navona towards the river.

The main areas to find the best antique shops are around Via Giulia, Via dei Coronari and Via del Babuino (Map pp314–16). Even if you're just window shopping, there are some fascinating places to browse. If you're looking for an unusual gift, try Via Margutta (Map p210), where the shops often resemble galleries and the prices exhibit no mercy.

Across the river, near the Vatican (Map pp308–10), Via Cola di Rienzo harbours a number of clothing and shoe shops, as well as some excellent fine food outlets. Trastevere (Map pp317–19), just across the river from the *centro storico* (historic centre), offers lots of interesting little boutiques and knick-knack shops tucked away down narrow medieval streets and lanes.

Survive the Sales

Rome's sales are not for the faint-hearted as bargain-hungry shoppers will often stop at nothing to satiate their desires. To help you navigate the jungle of sales time in Rome, and not lose your sanity in the process, try following these simple rules:

- **Get there early** – queues start at the crack of dawn so you'll need to move with the larks
- **Know what you want from where** – a lightning strike to the shelves is good, dawdling bad
- **Give no quarter and ask for none** – if you happen to get there first, it's yours – end of story
- **Have a back-up plan** – if your number one choice bag's gone, switch to plan B
- **Keep cool** – this is bare-knuckle shopping so expect a few elbows and shoves
- **Enjoy**

Romans have also begun to embrace the concept of one-stop shopping with a number of department stores and *centri commerciali* (large shopping centres) popping up all over the place, although most are on the outskirts of the city.

If you can time your visit to coincide with the sales *(saldi)*, you'll pick up some great bargains, although you'll need to be up for some bare-knuckle shopping (see the boxed text above). Winter sales run from early January to mid-February and the summer sales from July to early September.

Most shops accept credit cards and many accept travellers cheques. See p273 for information on value-added tax refunds, known in Italy as IVA (Imposta di Valore Aggiunto). It's also important to remember that you are required by Italian law to ask for a *ricevuta* (receipt) for your purchases.

Opening Hours

Shops are usually open from 9.30am to 1pm and 3.30pm to 7.30pm (in winter) or 4pm to 8pm (in summer) Monday to Saturday, although a small boutique might not open until 10am and afternoon hours might be shortened. However, most of the larger shops and department stores in the centre are now open from 9.30am to 7.30pm. Many shops are closed on Monday morning.

Where opening hours are listed, it indicates they vary from the standard opening times.

ANCIENT ROME

FABIO PICCIONI Map pp314–16 *Jewellery*
☎ 06 474 16 97; Via del Boschetto 148;
🕑 11am-8.30pm; metro Cavour

Not far from the Colosseum and almost hidden in the ivy, this snug treasure-trove is the domain of artisan Fabio Piccioni. A walking exhibit of his own designs, he recycles old trinkets to create exquisite handcrafted jewellery which, if he doesn't sell, he simply wears himself. Credit cards are not accepted.

MEL GIANNINO STOPPANI LIBRERIE PER RAGAZZI
Map pp314–16 *Books (Children)*
☎ 06 699 41 045; Piazza Santi Apostoli 59-65;
🕑 9.30am-7.30pm Mon-Sat, 10am-1pm & 4-7.30pm Sun; bus to Piazza Venezia

The best children's bookshop in Rome stocks mainly Italian books but has a corner devoted to French, Spanish, German and English books. Decorated in cheerful colours, it is well equipped for kids' (and parents') needs with a play area and a bathroom.

RICORDI MEDIA STORE
Map pp314–16 *Music*
☎ 06 679 80 22; Via Cesare Battisti 120d;
🕑 10am-8pm daily; bus to Piazza Venezia

One of Rome's biggest music stores, Ricordi is well stocked with all sorts of music, music videos and original-language films. In the shop next door there's a large selection of classical music, musical instruments, scores and books. Ricordi also has outlets in Via del Corso, Viale Giulio Cesare and Piazza Indipendenza.

RINASCITA Map pp311–13 *Music*
☎ 06 699 22 436; Via delle Botteghe Oscure 5;
🕑 10am-8pm Mon-Fri, 10am-2pm & 4pm-8pm Sat; bus to Largo di Torre Argentina

World and contemporary are the watchwords at this trendy music store (adjacent to the bookshop of the same name) but there's also a good selection of jazz, soul, blues and classical.

UNITED COLORS OF BENETTON
Map pp314–16 *Clothing*
☎ 06 699 24 010; Via Cesare Battisti 129; bus to Piazza Venezia

One of the many Benetton outlets in the capital, this branch near Piazza Venezia is as popular as ever for its staples such as wool and wool-mix jumpers in a kaleidoscope of colours, T-shirts, shirts, trousers and jackets at accessible prices. You can find further branches near the **Vatican** (Map pp308–10; Via Cola di Rienzo) and on **Via del Corso** (Map p210; Via del Corso 422).

CENTRO STORICO

AI MONASTERI Map pp311–13 *Cosmetics*
☎ 06 688 02 783; Corso del Rinascimento 72; bus to Corso del Rinascimento

If you've ever wondered what monks do when they're not meditating, the answer lies in this impressive wood-panelled shop. It's full of herbal essences, spirits, soaps, balms, deodorants, anti-wrinkle creams, bubble-bath and various liqueurs, all rigorously made by the brothers around Italy.

ALBERTA GLOVES
Map pp311–13 *Accessories*
☎ 06 678 57 53; Corso Vittorio Emanuele II 18a; bus to Corso Vittorio Emanuele II

Long, arm-length silk gloves for that very special evening, nifty driving gloves for the motorists – there's a glove for every occasion at this handy shop. Gentlemen will also find a good range of braces available. Prices start at around €20.

A knight's armour for sale in a Roman antiques store

AL SOGNO Map pp311–13 *Toys*
☎ 06 686 41 98; Piazza Navona 53; ◷ 9.30am-8pm Mon-Fri, 10pm-8pm Sun; bus to Corso del Rinascimento

Toys to dream about litter this expensive wonderland. The mezzanine floor of this stunning toyshop strains under the weight of dolls and stuffed animals of every shape and size. Even the fluffy sharks are cute. Go in with a child and your wallet is finished!

AMATI & AMATI Map pp308–10 *Gifts*
☎ 06 686 43 19; Via dei Pianellari 21; bus to Corso del Rinascimento

An ideal shop if you're searching for that Ali Baba look. It's full of unusual imported objects and homeware, including small pieces of furniture from Morocco, fez-shaped lamps, clothing, original jewellery and funky accessories.

ANTICHITÀ TANCA Map pp311–13 *Antiques*
☎ 06 687 52 72; Salita de' Crescenzi 12; ◷ closed Sat afternoon; bus to Corso del Rinascimento

Antichità Tanca, near the Pantheon, has a fascinating atmosphere. In addition to a wide range of antique prints it has an excellent selection of bronze, silver and chinaware, as well as crystal, jewellery and paintings dating from the 18th century to the turn of the 20th century.

BARTOLUCCI Map pp311–13 *Toys*
☎ 06 691 90 894; Via dei Pastini 98; bus to Largo di Torre Argentina

A temple to the art of wood carving, this fantastic toy shop has a huge collection of clocks, cars, planes and Pinocchios, all flawlessly hand-carved in pine wood. It's the perfect place to pick up a gift.

BAULLÀ Map pp311–13 *Clothing*
☎ 06 686 76 70; Via dei Baullari 37; ◷ 4-7.30pm Mon, 9.30am-7.30pm Tue-Sat; bus to Corso Vittorio Emanuele II

This gem of a shop between Campo de' Fiori and Piazza Farnese sells good-quality knits, original coats and jackets, skirts, tops, bags, scarves and accessories. In the summer it's one of the few places where you'll find espadrilles for sale.

BERTÈ Map pp311–13 *Toys*
☎ 06 687 50 11; Piazza Navona; bus to Corso del Rinascimento

The patriarch of the family who run this fabulous toy shop bears a striking resemblance to Pinocchio's Geppetto. So it's rather appropriate that the toys here include beautifully made wooden dolls and puppets, finely crafted scooters in wood and metal, and high-quality educational games.

BORINI Map pp311–13 *Shoes*
☎ 06 687 56 70; Via dei Pettinari 86-87; tram to Via Arenula

Originally a shoe repair shop, Borini's is now crowded with girls looking for fancy footwear at affordable prices. High heels, loafers, lace-ups and boots – there is an eclectic range which includes something for most tastes.

CARO VINILE...CARO CINEMA
Map pp311–13 *Music*
☎ 06 687 40 05; Piazza Paradiso 42; ◷ 4pm-7.30pm daily; bus to Corso Vittorio Emanuele II

The name says it all (Dear Vinyl...Dear Cinema). A buff's paradise, this place is ideal for those timeless Bogie posters or an early Fab Four recording. There are rare discs from the 1960s, a special section of Beatles memorabilia and film posters and photos.

Clothing sizes

Measurements approximate only, try before you buy

Women's Clothing

Aust/UK	8	10	12	14	16	18
Europe	36	38	40	42	44	46
Japan	5	7	9	11	13	15
USA	6	8	10	12	14	16

Women's Shoes

Aust/USA	5	6	7	8	9	10
Europe	35	36	37	38	39	40
France only	35	36	38	39	40	42
Japan	22	23	24	25	26	27
UK	3½	4½	5½	6½	7½	8½

Men's Clothing

Aust	92	96	100	104	108	112
Europe	46	48	50	52	54	56
Japan	S		M	M		L
UK/USA	35	36	37	38	39	40

Men's Shirts (Collar Sizes)

Aust/Japan	38	39	40	41	42	43
Europe	38	39	40	41	42	43
UK/USA	15	15½	16	16½	17	17½

Men's Shoes

Aust/ UK	7	8	9	10	11	12
Europe	41	42	43	44½	46	47
Japan	26	27	27½	28	29	30
USA	7½	8½	9½	10½	11½	12½

CASAMARIA Map pp311–13 *Cosmetics*
☎ 06 683 30 74; Via della Scrofa 71; bus to Corso del Rinascimento
Tucked away in the labyrinthine streets that surround Piazza Navona, Casamaria is a roomy and well-stocked *profumerie* with leading cosmetic brands at good prices.

CENCI Map pp308–10 *Clothing*
☎ 06 699 06 81; Via Campo Marzio 1-7; bus to Via del Corso
This Roman institution near the Pantheon stocks a big selection of top Italian and international labels for men, women and children. It's a good bet if you prefer classic fashions on the conservative side of English country squire. Think waxed jackets and green wellies.

CITTÀ DEL SOLE Map pp311–13 *Toys*
☎ 06 688 03 805; Via della Scrofa 65; bus to Corso del Rinascimento
This shop is a parent's dream – imaginative and well-made toys that are educational and creative. With very few electronic gadgets in sight, this is the place to remember the toys you played with as a kid and then stock up for Christmas.

COMICS BAZAR Map pp308–10 *Antiques*
☎ 06 68 80 29 23; Via dei Banchi Vecchi 127-8;
⏱ 9am-8pm Mon-Sat; bus to Corso Vittorio Emanuele II
Not far from Campo de' Fiori is Comics Bazar, a veritable warehouse of antiques. It's crammed with objects, lamps and furniture dating from the late 19th century to the 1940s, including a large selection of Viennese furniture by Thonet.

CONTEMPORANEA
Map pp311–13 *Homeware*
☎ 06 6880 45 33; Via dei Banchi Vecchi 143; bus to Corso Vittorio Emanuele II
Designs at this modish furniture shop are not for those who like their armchairs comfy and their fabrics to match. They are kooky, original – think a mix of '70s retro and heavy baroque – and fabulously expensive: the work of some of Italy and Europe's top avant-garde designers.

C.U.C.I.N.A. Map p210 *Homeware*
☎ 06 679 12 75; Via Mario de' Fiori 65; metro Spagna
Once upon a time, this place was seriously avant-garde, selling groovy chrome this and innovative modular that. The stainless steel look has become ubiquitous, but you can still find good-quality kitchenware that's as beautiful as it is convenient.

DANIELA ROSATI Map pp308–10 *Gifts*
☎ 06 68 80 20 53; Via della Stelletta 27; bus to Corso del Rinascimento
Near the Pantheon, Daniela Rosati specialises in lovely hand-printed paper. Here you can buy photo albums bound in the paper of your choice, dinky little leather notebooks and handy storage boxes.

Home Wonders

- **Contemporanea** Futuristic designs for the bold at heart (left)
- **De Sanctis** Well-heeled cutlery and ceramics (below)
- **Spazio Sette** Frescoes and forks at the palazzo (p209)
- **Artemide** Light fittings made sexy (p211)
- **La Chiave** Incense and ethnic decor (p207)

DE SANCTIS Map pp311–13 *Homeware*
☎ 06 6880 68 10; Piazza Navona 82-84; bus to Corso del Rinascimento
De Sanctis has been supplying well-to-do Romans with fashionable utensils since 1890. Today it offers a good selection of Alessi products (including replacement parts) and other designer kitchenware and tableware. Its Italian ceramics, including the colourful work of the Sicilian ceramicist De Simone, are interesting.

DISTANÉS
Map pp311–13 *Second-Hand Clothing*
☎ 06 683 33 63; Via della Chiesa Nuova 17;
⏱ standard hours plus 10.30pm-midnight spring & autumn; bus to Corso Vittorio Emanuele II
If you're after a blast from the sartorial past, head down to this cheerful den. It specialises in remainders (or reminders), second-hand clothes and accessories from the 1960s and '70s. This is mix and match party time.

ETHIC Map pp311–13 *Clothing*
☎ 06 6830 10 63; Piazza Cairoli 11-12; tram to Via Arenula
Trendy as its name, Ethic, just off Via dei Giubbonari, describes itself as a multiconcept store. This means that it sells hip decor and groovy clothes (fake-fur trimmed coats, jackets and separates in daring fabrics and finishes). It's extremely popular with young lady Romans.

FELTRINELLI

Map pp311–13   *Books (Italian)*

☎ 06 688 03 248; Largo di Torre Argentina 5a; bus to Largo di Torre Argentina

One of the ubiquitous chain, this is a well-organised bookshop with a wide range of books on art, photography, cinema and history, as well as an extensive selection of Italian literature and travel guides. Other Feltrinelli bookshops are at Via del Babuino 39 and Via VE Orlando 84, next to **Feltrinelli International** (Map pp314–16), the branch that specialises in English and other foreign language titles.

FRANCESCO BIASIA

Map pp311–13   *Accessories*

☎ 06 686 50 98; Via di Torre Argentina 7; bus to Largo di Torre Argentina

Bag ladies of the world rejoice: various Biasia boutiques have opened around Rome. Incredibly soft leather wallets, funky patent leather bags in jewel-like colours, practical black evening bags, leopard-skin and fake fur handbags now available at unbeatable prices. There is another store at **Via Due Macelli 62**, near Piazza di Spagna.

Bags Away

- **Prada** Less is everything as long as it's black (p214)
- **Mandarina Duck** Why use leather when rubber will do? (p214)
- **Francesco Biasia** Fake fur means fun (above)
- **Carry-On** Classic styles, brown leather (p212)
- **Furla** A bag for all seasons (p213)

GALLERIA DI ORDITI E TRAME

Map pp311–13   *Accessories*

☎ 06 689 33 72; Via del Teatro Valle 54; bus to Corso Vittorio Emanuele II

A collection of colourful cotton accessories adorns the shelves of this rather expensive little shop. There are funky handmade hats, knitted scarves, gloves, bags and jolly clothes. Credit cards are not accepted.

HAUSMANN & CO

Map p210   *Jewellery*

☎ 06 687 15 01; Via del Corso 406; bus to Via del Corso

Watchmakers since 1794, Hausmann & Co today spend rather more time selling watches than making them. However, the expertise remains and this is a convenient place to peruse the top international brands.

HERDER BUCHHANDLUNG

Map pp311–13   *Books (German)*

☎ 06 679 46 28; Piazza Montecitorio 117; bus to Via del Corso

Directly opposite the Palazzo di Montecitorio (Italian parliament building) is not perhaps the most likely spot for a German bookshop but it's particularly good for theological and philosophical works (in German). You can also pick up lighter fare, including Harry Potter (in English).

INTIMISSIMI Map p210   *Lingerie*

Via del Corso 167; bus to Via del Corso

Italy's favourite high street lingerie chain, Intimissimi sells a range of good quality underwear, primarily for the ladies, at less than designer prices.

LA CHIAVE Map pp311–13   *Gifts*

☎ 06 683 08 848; Largo delle Stimmate 28; bus to Largo di Torre Argentina

La Chiave is a laid-back shop full of everything from feather-light paper lampshades to heavy dark wood furniture. The stock, much of which is imported, includes the standard range of ethnic drapes, jewellery and joss sticks but the atmosphere is friendly and browsing is never a problem.

LA PROCURE

Map pp311–13   *Books (French)*

☎ 06 6830 75 98; Piazza San Luigi dei Francesi 23; bus to Corso del Rinascimento

French-speakers will find a good selection of literature, fiction, non-fiction, general interest and children's books here. Afterwards, you might like to pop into the church next door to see the paintings by Caravaggio.

LA RINASCENTE

Map pp308–10   *Department Store*

☎ 06 679 76 91; Largo Chigi 20; ☼ 9am-9pm Mon-Sat, 10.30am-8 pm Sun; bus to Via del Corso

La Rinascente sells a good range of reasonable quality clothing, accessories and big-name cosmetics. Styles are fashionable without ever being cutting edge and service can be brusque. The store at **Piazza Fiume** (Map pp306–7; ☎ 06 841 60 81; ☼ 9am-9pm Mon-Sat, 10.30am-8pm Sun) also stocks homeware.

Shopping – Centro Storico

LEI Map pp311–13 — *Clothing*

☎ 06 687 54 32; Via dei Giubbonari 103; tram to Via Arenula

Near Campo de' Fiori, Lei is the place to go for a pretty dress or an elegant party outfit. Most of the stock is by French designers, although they do have some local names.

LEONE LIMENTANI

Map pp308–10 — *Homeware*

☎ 06 688 06 686; Via Portico d'Ottavia 47 (basement); tram to Via Arenula

This warehouse-style shop has an unbelievable choice of kitchen and tableware. High-priced fine porcelain and crystal sit alongside bargain basement items. It also stocks plenty of Alessi and a good selection of quality pots and pans.

LIBRERIA BABELE

Map pp308–10 — *Books (Gay & Lesbian)*

☎ 06 687 66 28; Via dei Banchi Vecchi 116; bus to Corso Vittorio Emanuele II

Well-known and well-loved, Babele is an exclusively gay and lesbian bookshop that has a well-stocked English section. The staff are extremely friendly and helpful and it is a good first stop for information about Rome's gay scene. Forthcoming gay and lesbian events are listed on the shop's noticeboard.

LIBRERIA DEL VIAGGIATORE

Map pp311–13 — *Books (Italian)*

☎ 06 688 01 048; Via del Pellegrino 78; bus to Corso Vittorio Emanuele II

A veritable mine of travel literature, this charming bookshop has most countries covered. Crammed with guides and travel literature in various languages, it also has a huge range of maps, including hiking maps. Some books are available in English and French.

LIBRERIA SORGENTE

Map pp311–13 — *Books (Spanish)*

☎ 06 6880 69 50; Piazza Navona 90; bus to Corso del Rinascimento

Squeezed between the restaurants that border Piazza Navona and stuck behind a newsagent's kiosk, Sorgente has a wide range of books and some videos in Spanish. It also stocks some Portuguese-language books.

LOCO Map pp311–13 — *Shoes*

☎ 06 688 08 216; Via dei Baullari 22; bus to Corso Vittorio Emanuele II

Just off Campo de' Fiori, Loco is ideally situated for pulling in the youth it courts. A trendy and street-styled shoe shop, it sells the latest foot fashion – at the time of writing this happened to be boxing boots and Converse.

MATEROZZOLI

Map p210 — *Cosmetics*

☎ 06 688 92 686; Piazza San Lorenzo in Lucina 5; bus to Via del Corso

Ladies and gents can attend all their grooming needs at this charming Roman landmark. Materozzoli stocks a selection of rare perfumes, particularly from France and England, as well as cosmetics and exquisite beauty accessories.

MERCATO DELLE STAMPE

Map p210 — *Market*

Largo della Fontanella di Borghese; 🕙 8am-sunset Mon-Sat; bus to Piazza Augusto Imperatore

This market is well worth a look if you're interested in antique prints and second-hand books, as it's devoted exclusively to just that. Early music scores, architectural engravings, chromolithographs of fruit and flowers and views of Rome are among the stunning objects up for grabs. The cheap reproductions make fun souvenirs.

MESSAGERIE MUSICALI

Map p210 — *Music*

☎ 06 679 81 97; Via del Corso 123; bus to Via del Corso

Rome's largest music store has three levels of everything from Italian golden oldies to the most recent chart 'offerings' (and lots of fluff in between). You can also pick up magazines in English, concert tickets and a range of Lonely Planet titles (in Italian only).

MONDELLO OTTICA

Map pp311–13 — *Accessories*

☎ 06 686 19 55; Via del Pellegrino 97-8; bus to Corso Vittorio Emanuele II

Specs and sunnies have never looked this good – this is *the* place for the grooviest, quirkiest eyewear in town, with frames by leading European and international designers including Anne et Valentin, l.a.Eyeworks, Cutler and Gross, and the Belgian designer Theo. Prescription glasses can be ready the same day.

MORESCO OTTICA

Map pp311–13 *Accessories*
☎ 06 688 05 079; Via dei Falegnami 23a; tram to Via Arenula

Moresco is excellent for discount glasses. This tiny shop stocks frames by all the major labels – Gucci, Chanel, Persol, Web and Luxottica to name a few – and the friendly proprietor can organise prescriptions in a couple of hours.

NARDECCHIA Map pp311–13 *Antiques*
☎ 06 686 93 18; Piazza Navona 25; bus to Corso del Rinascimento

This Roman landmark is only marginally less famous than the piazza it's on, and you'll find antique prints, including 18th-century etchings of Rome by Giovanni Battista Piranesi, and more inexpensive 19th-century views of the city.

OFFICINA PROFUMO FARMACEUTICA DI SANTA MARIA NOVELLA

Map pp311–13 *Cosmetics*
☎ 06 687 96 08; Corso del Rinascimento 47; bus to Corso del Rinascimento

Prize for the snappiest shop title in Rome goes to this central scent shop. Many of the lotions and cosmetics are based on original recipes handed down by the Dominican monks of Santa Maria Novella in Florence, with some dating back to the 17th century.

PASSAMANERIE CROCIANELLI

Map p210 *Homeware*
☎ 06 687 35 92; Via dei Prefetti 37-40; bus to Corso del Rinascimento

This is the place to come for a tassel or two. A traditional *passamanerie* (furnisher of ribbon, braided cord and colourful tassels used as trimmings for furnishings) Crocianelli has bundles of fringes and cords piled from floor to ceiling.

SCHOSTAL Map p210 *Clothing*
☎ 06 679 12 40; Via del Corso 158; bus to Via del Corso

This old-fashioned outfitters has been selling sensible clothes from its elegant shop since 1870. For the gentlemen there are shirts, socks and underpants; for the ladies knitwear and lingerie.

SPAZIO SETTE Map pp311–13 *Homeware*
☎ 06 688 04 261; Via dei Barbieri 7; bus to Largo di Torre Argentina

Spread over three floors of a Renaissance palazzo, this is one of Rome's premier homeware stores. If you can tear your attention away from the frescoed ceiling at the entrance, you'll find three levels of quality designer furniture, kitchenware, tableware and gifts.

STILO FETTI Map pp311–13 *Gifts*
☎ 06 678 96 62; Via degli Orfani 82; bus to Largo di Torre Argentina

Sleek leather briefcases, natty desktop toys and top of the range fountain pens, modern and antique, are the reasons you'll come here. Afterwards you can write your postcards from the Pantheon.

STOCKMARKET

Map pp308–10 *Homeware*
☎ 06 686 42 38; Via dei Banchi Vecchi 51; bus to Corso Vittorio Emanuele II

A colourful trove of everything you could possibly want, or not, for the house. Purple plastic beanbags may not be to all tastes but don't worry, what about a placemat in the shape of a cat, or a ceramic centrepiece for your dining room? There's also plenty of useful stuff too, all at affordable prices.

T'STORE Map p210 *Clothing*
☎ 06 322 60 55; Via del Corso 477-478; metro Spagna

All steel grey, white and glass shelves T'Store is the younger line of Trussardi, and sells jeans, sportswear, chunky knits, jackets, casual trousers and more.

TAD Map p210 *Homeware*
☎ 06 360 01 679; Via di San Giacomo 5; metro Flaminio

With its lime-green walls and impressive stock of ethnic furniture, silk screens, vases, textiles and linens, Tad affects a certain style and you'll invariably leave with something.

TEBRO Map p210 *Lingerie*
☎ 06 687 34 41; Via dei Prefetti 46-54; bus to Corso del Rinascimento

An upmarket department store tending to your sartorial night needs, Tebro has been selling pyjamas since 1870. Well stocked with underwear and nightwear for men, women and children, it also carries bed and table linen, bath towels and the like.

AROUND VIA DEL CORSO

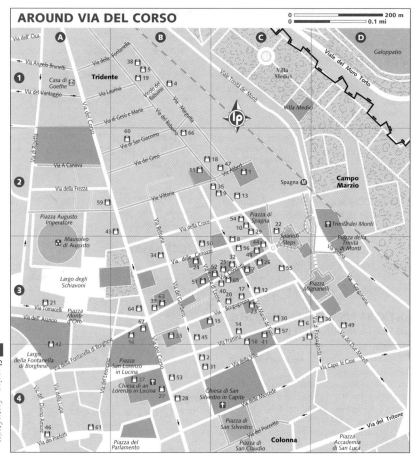

TEMPI MODERNI

Map pp311–13   *Jewellery*
☎ 06 687 70 07; Via del Governo Vecchio 108; bus to Corso Vittorio Emanuele II

Vintage costume jewellery dating from the last century (with an emphasis on Art Nouveau and Art Deco) is the speciality here: 19th-century resin brooches, Bakelite from the '20s and '30s and costume jewellery by couturiers such as Chanel, Dior and Balenciaga.

TOD'S Map p210   *Shoes*
☎ 06 678 68 28; Via della Fontanella di Borghese 56; bus to Via del Corso

Perhaps it's the practical rubber studs on the back of the heel (to reduce driving scuffs) that makes these men's and women's loafers so popular. The shoes are classic and costly, but aficionados swear they're the most comfortable you'll ever buy.

TRONCARELLI

Map pp311–13   *Accessories*
☎ 06 687 93 20; Via della Cuccagna 15; bus to Corso del Rinascimento

The heyday of the hat shop is a thing of the past, but still folk of a certain class require their headgear and this is where to find it. Just off Piazza Navona, Troncarelli stocks top-brand hats for men and women, including bowlers, top hats, Panama hats, Borsalino hats and straw hats.

VESTITI USATI CINZIA

Map pp311–13   *Second-Hand Clothing*
☎ 06 686 17 91; Via del Governo Vecchio 45; bus to Corso Vittorio Emanuele II

One of Rome's most popular second-hand clothes stores, Cinzia sells once-loved clothes looking for new owners. A good place to snap up a bargain leather jacket or vintage skirt.

YAKY Map pp311–13   *Antiques*
☎ 06 688 07 724; Via Santa Maria del Pianto 55; tram to Via Arenula

If you're in the market for antique Chinese furniture, head for Yaky in the Ghetto area. It has a range of objects including beautiful rocking chairs, stunning wooden cabinets and lacquered bowls.

EAST OF VIA DEL CORSO

ALINARI Map p210   *Antiques/Books*
☎ 06 679 29 23; Via Alibert 16a; metro Spagna

The Alinari brothers were famous late-19th-century Florentine photographers, and the prints (mostly views of Rome) and books on sale here are reproduced from the archives of their work. The archives contain more than a million glass plate negatives.

ANDREW'S TIES

Map p210   *Accessories*
☎ 06 679 74 17; Via del Gambero 29; metro Spagna

Italy is famous for its silk ties and there are shops for all tastes and budgets. Andrew's sells printed, woven and embossed silk ties as well as the wool and cashmere variety, priced from €16 upwards. You'll also be able to pick up a matching shirt.

ANGLO-AMERICAN BOOKSHOP

Map p210   *Books (English)*
☎ 06 678 96 57; Via della Vite 102; metro Spagna

Well-known to Rome's English-speaking community, this well-stocked shop has an excellent range of literature, travel guides, reference books and maps. It also has a pretty good kids' selection.

ANIMALIER E OLTRE

Map p210   *Antiques*
☎ 06 320 82 82; Via Margutta 47; metro Spagna

Difficult to define, this antique/curio shop stocks rustic furniture from northern Europe and North America, bric-a-brac and a huge selection of animal-shaped antiques (including reproductions of French 19th-century *animalier* sculptures). Among other things, you'll find an exquisitely made porcelain kangaroo.

ARTEMIDE Map p210   *Homeware*
☎ 06 3600 18 02; Via Margutta 107; metro Flaminio

The sexy designer lamps on sale here are simply but effectively displayed in individual alcoves set into the white walls. For cutting-edge minimalist light fittings and kooky lamps, this is your place. Prices match the style.

BENY Map pp314–16   *Accessories*
☎ 06 679 58 69; Via Nazionale 164; bus to Via Nazionale

Easy to miss despite the outlandish designs gracing some of their silks, Beny is a tiny emporium selling designer ties and scarves. Noteworthy is a selection reproducing patterns created in the 1950s by the eclectic Italian designer Piero Fornasetti. Prices start at €10.

BRIGHENTI

Map p210 *Lingerie*

☎ 06 679 14 84; Via Frattina 7-10; metro Spagna

Luxurious lingerie and sensational, too-good-to-get-wet swimming costumes are what keeps generations of Italian women – including television and film stars – coming back to Brighenti.

BRIONI Map pp314–16 *Clothing*

☎ 06 485 855; Via Barberini 79-81; metro Barberini

Brioni, Rome's most elegant tailor, has a license to cut, sew and stitch. As creator of costumes for the James Bond films, Brioni has dressed some of the world's most perfect bodies. It also makes ready-to-wear fashions for mortal men and women. A suit will set you back around €2000.

BULGARI Map p210 *Jewellery*

☎ 06 679 38 76; Via Condotti 10; ☉ 3-7.30pm Mon, 10am-7.30pm Tue-Sat; metro Spagna

It's only right that this prestigious jeweller's should grace Rome's top shopping strip. If the breathtaking prices mean you're just window shopping, you can admire the precious and unique jewellery displayed as if in a museum.

CARRY-ON

Map pp307–7 *Accessories*

☎ 06 4890 41 94; Via Veneto 165; metro Barberini

If it's slinky, chic and in leather you'll find it at Carry-On. For the gents there are tan brown briefcases by The Bridge, slippers to relax into and even dinky little boxes for your golf tees. For the ladies, a host of handbags, suede coats and more of those dinky little boxes for your golf tees.

Shoe Fever

- **Fausto Santini** Quixotic and quirky designs for the dandy (right)
- **Sergio Rossi** Sexy styles to impress (p216)
- **Tod's** Shoes have never been so comfy (p211)
- **Loco** Funky footwear for the fashionable (p208)
- **Borini** Loafers, lace-ups, heels and boots (p205)

DE BACH Map p210 *Shoes*

☎ 06 678 33 84; Via del Babuino 123; metro Spagna

This slinky little shop, squeezed in between the big name outlets, sells sexy sandals and stylish women's shoes. The grey, concertina-like display unit enhances the design and colour of the shoes.

DISFUNZIONI MUSICALI

Map pp302–3 *Music*

☎ 06 446 19 84; Via degli Etruschi 4-14; bus to Via Tiburtina

In the heart of San Lorenzo, Rome's university area, this music store is the best for alternative, indie, rare, bootlegged and underground sounds. There's also a good range of second-hand vinyl and CDs, local and international, from opera to rock.

ECONOMY BOOK & VIDEO CENTER

Map pp314–16 *Books (English)*

☎ 06 474 68 77; Via Torino 136; metro Repubblica

The name says it all. This unpretentious shop has a reasonable selection of books, as well as second-hand paperbacks. There's also a haphazard collection of videos to buy or rent.

EMPORIO ARMANI

Map p210 *Clothing*

☎ 06 3600 21 97; Via del Babuino 140; metro Spagna

Roll up for Giorgio Armani's range of elegant ready-to-wear suits and separates for men and women. His clothes are renowned for exceptional fabrics and cuts, along with incredibly subtle and considered palates. These are the clothes for celebrities *not* trying make a statement.

ETRO Map p210 *Clothing*

☎ 06 678 82 57; Via del Babuino 102; metro Spagna

Etro uses fine printed fabrics including some stunning paisley prints to create exclusive clothing and accessories at exclusive prices. A printed T-shirt will, for example, cost you around €87.

FAUSTO SANTINI Map p210 *Shoes*

☎ 06 678 41 14; Via Frattina 120; metro Spagna

Italy's most original shoemaker is famous for his quixotic, colourful designs and no hipster's wardrobe is complete without a pair of his peppermint-coloured patent leather mules. There are good men's brogues too. For bargains and previous seasons, check out the outlet store at **Via Cavour 106** (Map pp314–16; ☎ 06 488 09 34), near the Basilica di Santa Maria Maggiore.

FELTRINELLI INTERNATIONAL

Map pp314–16 *Books (English)*

☎ 06 482 78 78; Via Orlando 84; metro Repubblica

A branch of the ubiquitous chain, Feltrinelli International has the best selection of books in English – go down the stairs at the back of the shop to the basement floor. There are also books in Spanish, French, German and Portuguese.

FENDISSIME Map p210 _Clothing_
☎ 06 69 66 61; Via della Fontanella Borghese 56a; bus to Via del Corso

Erring on the groovy side of classic, the clothes and accessories at Fendissime bear all the hallmark quality of the family name – Fendi. In fact, it is the third generation of the family who run Fendissime.

FLOS ARTELUCE
Map p210 _Homeware_
☎ 06 320 76 31; Via del Babuino 84-85; metro Spagna

This shop is more like a museum of lighting fixtures than a retail outlet. The 'exhibits' at Flos are minimalist, in chrome, steel and simple shades such as black and white.

FRANCO MARIA RICCI
Map p210 _Books (Italian)_
☎ 06 679 34 66; Via del Babuino 49; metro Spagna

A historic name in the world of Italian design, Franco Maria Ricci still produces and sells splendidly illustrated books on art and culture, published in-house, as well as the celebrated _FMR_ art and design magazine.

FRATELLI ROSSETTI
Map p210 _Shoes_
☎ 06 678 26 76; Via Borgognona 5a; metro Spagna

No one does leather better than the Italians, as this classy outlet for shoes, bags and leather jackets demonstrates. Designs are classic and quality assured.

FURLA Map p210 _Leather_
☎ 06 692 00 363; Piazza di Spagna 22; ☺ 9am-7pm; metro Spagna

Next to the Spanish Steps, this is one of many Furla outlets selling high-quality leather bags and accessories, including wallets, belts, sunglasses, watches and costume jewellery at prices that won't burn a hole in your old wallet. There are various other outlets including those at **Via del Corso 481** and **Via Tomacelli 136**.

IL TUCANO Map pp314–16 _Homeware_
☎ 06 679 75 47; Piazza dei Crociferi 10; bus to Largo di Torre Argentina

Just around the corner from the Trevi Fountain, Il Tucano has everything from home furnishings and haberdashery to kids' toys. Everything is displayed in the shop windows and the staff retrieve your selection from the storeroom. Credit cards are not accepted.

IO SONO UN AUTARCHICO
Map pp314–16 _Homeware_
☎ 06 228 66 48; Via del Boschetto 92; metro Cavour

Named after a Nanni Moretti film, this tiny shop in the atmospheric Monti part of town is full of interesting homeware even if the high turnover means that its stock changes continually.

Leather goods from Mandarina Duck (p214)

LA CICOGNA
Map p210 _Children's Clothing_
☎ 06 678 69 77; Via Frattina 138; metro Spagna

If the adults are shopping at Armani and D&G, why can't the kids go to La Cicogna? Stocking a selection of fashionable children's clothes by top designers, it also has its own prestigious label.

LA CORONA Map p210 _Accessories_
☎ 06 679 01 64; Via del Gambero; metro Spagna

Next door to Andrew's Ties (p210), this tiny tie emporium has a good selection of tastefully designed and affordable neckwear. You can also pick up kids' ties for €16.

LA PERLA Map p210 *Lingerie*
☎ 06 699 41 933; Via Condotti 78; metro Spagna

Diamonds may be a girl's best friend, but a set of lingerie from La Perla can't be far behind. Luxury has never felt as good as the lace-trimmed silk bras and delicious negligées with matching dressing gowns; stiletto-heeled house slippers finish the set. Guaranteed to make you feel a million dollars and cost you almost as much.

LE GALLINELLE
Map pp314–16 *Second-Hand Clothing*
☎ 06 488 10 17; Via del Boschetto 76; metro Cavour

The only thing that remains of this former butcher's shop are the meat hooks which now hold up good-quality second-hand garb, as well as interesting clothing made from vintage fabrics.

LILIA LEONI Map p210 *Antiques*
☎ 06 678 32 10; Via Belsiana 86; metro Spagna

Among the unusual objects and furniture are collectable Murano drinking glasses and Art Nouveau (known as 'Liberty' in Italy) garden furniture, as well as pieces dating from the early 1900s to the 1950s.

MAC Map p210 *Cosmetics*
☎ 06 679 21 65; Via del Babuino 124; metro Spagna

You've bought the dress, you've got the shoes, so why not treat yourself to that long-promised make-up spree? Maestros of the facial arts, MAC are well positioned to help you out.

MANDARINA DUCK
Map p210 *Accessories*
☎ 06 699 40 320; Via di Propaganda 1; metro Spagna

Italy's most contemporary accessories and luggage company, Mandarina Duck is the designers' designer and produces ergonomic bags and luggage in the state-of-the-art technology fabrics. All the pieces have the signature yellow duck logo, collected religiously by design junkies.

MAS Map pp314–16 *Department Store*
☎ 06 446 80 78; Via dello Statuto 11; ⌚ 9am-7pm Mon-Sat; metro Vittorio Emanuele

A bargain-hunter's paradise, this place is cheap as chips and sells everything from cheese graters and umbrellas to army pants and (some pretty good) leather jackets. But to get to the bargains, you'll need to wade through plenty of tat.

Designer Delirium

You can seriously improve your wardrobe and whip your wallet at these designer addresses:

- **Dolce e Gabbana** (Map p210; ☎ 06 679 22 94; Piazza di Spagna 94-95)
- **Ermenegildo Zegna** (Map p210; ☎ 06 678 91 43; Via Borgognona 7e)
- **Fendi** (Map p210; ☎ 06 69 66 61; Via Borgognona 36-40)
- **Ferre** (Map p210; ☎ 06 679 74 45; Via Borgognona 6)
- **Gianni Versace** Men: (Map p210; ☎ 06 679 50 37; Via Borgognona 24-25) Women: (Map p210; ☎ 06 678 05 21; Via Bocca di Leone 26)
- **Giorgio Armani Boutique** (Map p210; ☎ 06 699 14 60; Via Condotti 77)
- **Gucci** (Map pp210; ☎ 06 678 93 40; Via Condotti 8)
- **Krizia** (Map p210; ☎ 06 679 37 72; Piazza di Spagna 87)
- **Laura Biagiotti** (Map p210; ☎ 06 679 12 05; Via Borgognona 43-44)
- **Missoni** (Map p210; ☎ 06 679 25 55; Piazza di Spagna 78)
- **Prada** (Map p210; ☎ 06 679 08 97; Via Condotti 92-95)
- **Roccobarocco** (Map p210; ☎ 06 679 79 14; Via Bocca di Leone 65a)
- **Salvatore Ferragamo** Men: (Map p210; ☎ 06 678 11 30; Via Condotti 66) Women: (Map p210; ☎ 06 679 15 65; Via Condotti 73-74)
- **Trussardi** (Map p210; ☎ 06 678 02 80; Via Condotti 49-50)
- **Valentino** (Map p210; ☎ 06 678 36 56; Via Condotti 13)

MAURIZIO GROSSI
Map p210 *Homeware*
☎ 06 360 01 935; Via Margutta 109;
⌚ 10am-7.30pm; metro Flaminio

They'll make very heavy gifts but you can rest assured of an impact. The repro marble busts at this shop-cum-gallery are decidedly in tune with the city's artistic heritage – it's difficult to imagine anything more Roman than a bust or mosaic. As a novelty, check out the cleverly deceptive bowls of sculpted figs and apricots.

MAX & CO Map p210 *Clothing*
☎ 06 678 79 46; Via Condotti 46; metro Spagna

Trendy tops and bottoms, coats, leather jackets and accessories are the name of the game at this, the home of MaxMara's youth range.

Perfectly located, it's popular with Rome's young dandies.

MAXMARA Map pp314–16 *Clothing*
☎ 06 679 36 38; Via Frattina 28; metro Spagna
One of Italy's top labels, MaxMara is well known for its ready-to-wear clothes at reasonably affordable prices. Trademark items include jackets, trousers, suits and superb winter coats in luxurious cashmere blends. You'll find other branches of this label at **Via Condotti 17** (Map p210) and **Via Nazionale 28** (Map pp314–16).

MEL BOOKSTORE
Map pp314–16 *Books (Italian)*
☎ 064885405; ViaNazionale 254-255; metro Repubblica
Mel Bookstore, near Piazza della Repubblica, is a combination bookshop, music store and coffee shop spread out across three levels. It has a wide selection of literature, fiction, reference books, dictionaries, school books and travel guides as well as a range of half-price books. It also has some books in English and French.

Shoppers at Città del Sole (p206)

MOSCHINO JEANS
Map p210 *Clothing*
☎ 06 6920 04 15; Via Belsiana 53-57; metro Spagna
Another popular haunt of the capital's fashion-conscious youth, this is home to Moschino's diffusion/sportswear range. Provocative T-shirts are among the hallmarks of this iconoclastic Italian designer.

OTTICA SPIEZIA
Map pp304–5 *Accessories*
☎ 06 361 05 93; Via del Babuino 199; metro Flaminio
Italy's most visual film director Federico Fellini was the star customer of this tiny opticians just off Piazza del Popolo. Not surprisingly it's crammed with stylish, high-quality frames and sunglasses.

PALAZZO DELLE ESPOSIZIONI
Map pp314–16 *Gifts*
☎ 06 482 80 01; access from Via Milano 9a; bus to Via Nazionale
Looking for something special? Try the gift shop inside the Palazzo delle Esposizioni, one of Rome's main exhibitions spaces. Accessible from the building's side entrance, the shop has a range of unusual design objects, gadgets and homeware. There's also a bookshop that specialises in art, design and photography books.

POLLICINA Map p210 *Jewellery*
☎ 06 322 41 32; Via Margutta 61c; metro Spagna
Coloured crystals, beads and coral are the main materials used in the kooky designs at this artistic jewellery shop. Not for those after subtle touches of glamour – the trinkets here are big and bold.

PRÉNATAL
Map pp314–15 *Children's Clothing*
☎ 06 488 14 03; Via Nazionale 45; bus to Via Nazionale
One of a number of children's clothing chain stores in Italy, Prénatal has its own range of affordable, good-quality clothing for kids aged up to 11, as well as for expecting mothers. It also stocks prams and pushchairs.

QUEER Map pp314–16 *Books (Gay & Lesbian)*
☎ 06 474 06 91; Via del Boschetto 25; bus to Via Nazionale
A gay bookshop just off Via Nazionale, Queer sells books in Italian and English as well as videos and gifts. It also happens to be a great place to check out the latest news on the gay scene.

RED & BLUE Map p210 *Shoes*
☎ 06 678 07 50; Via dei Due Macelli 67; metro Spagna
An all-purpose shoe, bag and clothing store, the range at Red & Blue includes lots of Tod's products (sometimes at better prices),

Burberry coats and a selection of other top-quality gear.

SERGIO ROSSI Map p210 *Shoes*
☎ 06 678 32 45; Piazza di Spagna 97-100; metro Spagna

With heels or without, the Sergio Rossi touch is clear from the classic styles and sky-high prices at this, his flagship showroom. Gaze in the windows at glamorous day and evening shoes created by this top Italian designer. Matching handbags are also there to tempt you.

SERMONETA
Map p210 *Accessories*
☎ 06 679 19 60, Piazza di Spagna 61; metro Spagna

To pamper your hands, head for Sermoneta, the prime place in Rome for gloves. It stocks a kaleidoscopic range of coloured and textured leather and suede gloves with linings ranging from silk to cashmere. There are two other Sermoneta shops on Piazza di Spagna, one stocking ties and scarves and the other handbags and luggage.

SINGLE Map pp314–16 *Gifts*
☎ 06 679 07 13; Via Francesco Crispi 47; metro Barberini

Near Via Sistina, Single has a good selection of designer objects, including unusual watches, Alessi kitchenware and expensive fountain pens. It's an ideal place to pick up a little something for a working loved one.

SIRAGUSA Map p210 *Jewellery*
☎ 06 679 70 85; Via delle Carrozze 64; metro Spagna

The hallmark of the jewellery at Siragusa is the innovative use of antique materials. They create exceptionally beautiful and unusual jewellery by setting antique coins and gems in gold.

SISLEY Map p210 *Clothing*
☎ 06 699 41 787; Via Frattina 19a; metro Spagna

Fashionable clothes at high street prices are what you'll find at Sisley. Jeans, T-shirts, sweaters and sneakers are the staples that feed the trendy, but not painfully so, clientele.

STEFANEL Map p210 *Clothing*
☎ 06 679 26 67; Via Frattina 31-32; metro Spagna

Aimed at the fashionable young, Stefanel is another mid-range option for reasonably priced casual gear. If you can't find what you're after at Sisley, try Stefanel, or vice versa.

UNDERGROUND
Map pp314–16 *Market*
☎ 06 360 05 345; Ludovisi underground car park; Via Francesco Crispi 96; ☾ 3-8pm Sat & 10.30am-7.30pm Sun 2nd weekend of the month, closed July & Aug; metro Barberini

Located between Via Sistina and Via Veneto, this monthly market has over 150 stalls selling antiques and collectables. There's a section for hand-made goods and another stocked with clothes and toys for children.

Coin department store (p217)

UPIM Map pp314–16 *Department Store*
☎ 06 678 33 36; Via del Tritone 172 and Via Nazionale 211; metro Barberini/bus to Via Nazionale

A budget department store selling everything from clothing and household goods to toys and school stationery. The quality can be patchy and the choice limited, but it's often convenient.

VALENTINO Map p210 *Clothing*
☎ 06 3600 19 06; Via del Babuino 61; metro Flaminio

There's nothing cheap about Valentino, the ageing king of Roman designers. Here you'll find his *slightly* more affordable range, aimed at a younger market than his couture collections.

NORTHERN ROME

BORGO PARIOLI

Map pp307–7   *Market*

☎ 06 855 27 73; Via Tirso 14; ⌚ 9am-8pm Sat & Sun 1st three weekends of the month; tram to Viale Regina Margherita

Venture into the 'burbs north of the centre for this market and you'll find original jewellery and accessories from the 1950s onwards – such as brooches, cigarette cases and watches – all in mint condition (although not always at bargain prices). If you're after something for the house, you can also pick up silverware, paintings, antique lamps and old gramophones.

LIBRERIA L'ARGONAUTA

Map pp306–7   *Books (Italian)*

☎ 06 854 34 43; Via Reggio Emilia 89; bus to Via Nizza

A beautiful little travel bookshop, L'Argonauta stocks many Lonely Planet titles and other travel guides. The friendly and helpful staff will happily help you or let you browse in peace. An elegant touch is the grand piano on the shop floor.

PONTE MILVIO Map pp302–3   *Market*

⌚ 9am-sunset 1st Sun of the month, closed Aug; bus to Ponte Milvio

Even farther north, the Ponte Milvio market specialises in antiques and bric-a-brac and is held on the Lungotevere Capoprati, which extends along the Tiber from the Ponte Milvio to the Ponte Duca d'Aosta.

SOUTHERN ROME

COIN Map pp320–1   *Department Store*

☎ 06 708 00 91; Piazzale Appio 7; metro San Giovanni

A quality Italian department store, COIN stocks clothing and accessories, cosmetics, children's clothes and a good range of homeware. Don't expect much in the way of polite, attentive service, however. Another branch exists at **Via di Cola di Rienzo 173** (Map p0304–5; ☎ 06 360 04 298; bus to Piazza del Risorgimento).

VIA SANNIO Map pp320–1   *Market*

⌚ 8am-1pm Mon-Sat; metro San Giovanni

There is a covered market selling new and second-hand clothing and shoes in Via Sannio, near Porta San Giovanni and the Basilica di San Giovanni in Laterano. If you're looking for leather jackets or second-hand cashmere at bargain prices, this is your place.

TRASTEVERE

BIBLI BOOKSHOP

Map pp317–19   *Books (Italian)*

☎ 06 588 40 97; Via dei Fienaroli 28; ⌚ until midnight daily; tram to Viale Trastevere

Near Piazza Santa Maria, Bibli is a bookshop-cum-café-cum-Internet café, as well as an occasional venue for poetry readings. It's a great place to meet for a chat; the Sunday brunch is also worth checking out. See p267.

THE CORNER BOOKSHOP

Map pp317–19   *Books (English)*

☎ 06 583 69 42; Via del Moro 45; bus to Piazza Trilussa

This tiny bookshop is stuffed to the gills with English-language books and travel guides. The selection of contemporary novels, best-sellers and non-fiction is ample and piles of books cover every available space.

GRACE GALLERY

Map pp317–19   *Gifts*

☎ 06 581 04 02; Via del Moro 40; bus to Piazza Trilussa

American photographer Nancy Robinson has spent four years snapping her way around Italy and the results are displayed here. As well as many photos of Rome, in colour and black and white, there are numerous shots of Vesuvius and the Bay of Naples.

Out of Town Malls & Megastores

Most shopping centres open at least six days a week from 9.30am to 8pm, sometimes later. For a taste of genuine Roman shopping you could try:

- **Auchan** (☎ 06 432 071; Via Alberto Pollio 50; metro B Tiburtina & a 20-minute walk)
- **Cinecittà Due** (☎ 06 722 09 10; Via P Togliatti 2; metro A Subaugusta)
- **I Granai** (☎ 06 519 55 890; Via Mario Rigamonti 100, EUR; metro EUR Palasport)

GUAYTAMELLI Map pp317–19   *Gifts*

☎ 06 588 07 04; Via del Moro 59; bus to Piazza Trilussa

For dinky desktop accessories or sundials, Guaytamelli is a feast. It specialises in all sorts of elegant adult toys – there are hand-crafted compasses, hourglasses and free-standing globes, all based on 16th- to 18th-century designs.

LA CRAVATTA SU MISURA

Map pp317–19 *Accessories*

☎ 06 581 66 76; Via Santa Cecilia 12; tram to Viale Trastevere

For the man who already has everything, how about a made-to-measure tie? Only the finest Italian silks and English wools are used in this tiny *bottega* (shop). Choose your fabric, the width and length of the tie and, at a push, it can be ready for you in just a few hours.

LIBRERIA DELLE DONNE: AL TEMPO RITROVATO

Map pp317–19 *Books (Lesbian)*

☎ 06 581 77 24; Via dei Fienaroli 31d; tram to Viale Trastevere

Well known on the lesbian scene, Libreria delle Donne is a women's bookshop with a well stocked lesbian section, including lots of material in English. The shop's notice board is packed with information and details of events.

LUMIERES Map pp317–19 *Antiques*

☎ 06 580 36 14; Vicolo del Cinque 48; bus to Piazza Trilussa

Deep in the heart of Trastevere glows Lumieres, a decidedly unpretentious light shop. Crammed into the tiny space is a large collection of lamps, from Art Nouveau and Art Deco to the 1950s.

OFFICINA DELLA CARTA

Map pp317–19 *Gifts*

☎ 06 589 55 57; Via Benedetta 26b; bus to Piazza Trilussa

Florence is more famous than Rome for hand-printed papers, but this tiny workshop makes beautiful storage boxes, photo albums, recipe books, notepads, photo frames and diaries – all of which make terrific gifts.

PANDORA Map pp317–19 *Gifts*

☎ 06 581 71 45; Piazza Santa Maria; tram to Viale Trastevere

Head for the purple decorated doors. Here you'll find unusual costume jewellery from around the world but, in particular, gorgeous necklaces made from Murano glass. The shop also sells ceramics, some glassware, photo frames and scarves.

PORTA PORTESE

Map pp317–19 *Market*

🕑 7am-1pm Sun; tram to Viale Trastevere

Rome's biggest and best-known flea market is held in the area extending south from the Porta Portese, an ancient Roman gate on the River Tiber, to Piazza Ippolito Nievo, in the streets parallel to Viale Trastevere. With thousands of stalls pushing everything from bags to bikes and clothes to furniture, bargaining is most definitely the order of the day. It gets incredibly crowded so watch out for pickpockets.

VATICAN CITY

ANGELO DI NEPI Map pp308–10 *Clothing*

☎ 06 322 48 00; Via Cola di Rienzo 267a; bus to Piazza del Risorgimento

If you want to add a dash of colour to your wardrobe, head to this independent boutique, which sells beautifully made skirts, trousers, tops and scarves in stunning fabrics, including bright and often embroidered Indian silks.

GRANDI FIRME Map pp308–10 *Accessories*

☎ 06 397 23 169; Via Germanico 8; bus to Piazza del Risorgimento

Designer quality at knock-down prices can't be bad and that's what you'll find here, close to the Vatican Museums. An unassuming outlet, it sells designer bags, luggage, ties, belts, scarves, umbrellas, shoes and similar items.

L'ALLEGRETTO Map pp304–5 *Music*

☎ 06 320 82 24; Via Oslavia 44; bus to Piazza Mazzini

Music fans would do well to venture off the beaten track to L'Allegretto where the extensive selection of opera and classical music is second to none. Jazz and pop tastes are also catered to and, upstairs, there's a decent choice of videos and DVDs.

ONYX Map pp308–10 *Clothing*

☎ 06 360 06 073; Via Cola di Rienzo 225-229; bus to Piazza del Risorgimento

Trendy tracksuits and trainers draw the street smart to Onyx. It's a good-value shop popular with the hip young things who buy gold lamé shirts, leather jackets and furry handbags.

Sleeping

Sleeping

Accommodation in Rome has never looked so good. Ranging from small, family-run *pensioni* and humble B&Bs to opulent five-star palaces, the city is positively gleaming in the aftermath of the 2000 Jubilee spruce-up. Many hotels are looking better than ever, both inside and out.

Most of the budget *pensioni* and larger hotels which cater for tour groups are located in the not-so-beautiful area around Stazione Termini (Map pp314–16). The area southwest (to the left as you leave the platforms) can be noisy and unpleasant. Pickpockets are active in this area and women alone may find it unsafe at night, although the city authorities have achieved some success in cleaning it up in recent years. To the northeast of Termini you can find accommodation in a quieter and more pleasant residential area, and in the streets around Via Nazionale, a busy traffic thoroughfare and shopping area, there are several decent hotels.

But to experience the best the city has to offer, the *centro storico* is the place to head for. Prices are higher, but it's here that you'll experience Rome as it's portrayed in the postcards. The area around the Vatican (Map pp308–10) is much less chaotic, but beautiful all the same. Both of these areas are only a short bus or metro ride away from Termini. If you come by car, be warned that there is a terrible lack of on-site parking facilities in the city centre, although your hotel should be able to direct you to a private garage. As for street parking, good luck!

The one constant, whatever the price range or period, is the need to book ahead. Turn up without a reservation and you'll probably find yourself shunted from one hotel to another as operators phone around looking for vacancies. Relying on the people at the train station who claim to be tourism officials and offer to find you a room won't help much either. Chances are they'll lead you to a seedy dump which will end up costing way more than the official rates.

The accommodation listed here is divided into two categories: mid-range and up, and cheap sleeps. The cheap sleeps charge anywhere up to €100 for a double (€50 for a single). Hotels accept credit cards and travellers cheques unless otherwise indicated; for those in the cheap sleeps category, it's always best to check in advance. All listings are in alphabetical order.

Styles of Accommodation

Following the improvements that were forced on the city's hotels by the Jubilee, Rome now has a good selection of accommodation options. The major categories are bed & breakfast (B&B), hostels, *pensioni* (guesthouses), hotels, religious institutions and student digs.

BED & BREAKFAST

The latest trend, the B&B, has taken off in a big way thanks to the influx of pilgrims during the Jubilee and the over-demand for really good budget accommodation. There are now more than 850 private B&B operators listed in Rome.

The bonus of B&B accommodation is that Italian houses are invariably spotlessly clean. The drawback is that you are staying in someone's home, and will probably be expected to operate within the family's timetable. As keys are not always provided, a hotel would be more suitable for those who expect to be coming in late at night. However, many of the new B&B establishments are really what was once known as *pensioni*, often run by young Italians who have travelled and speak English.

The tourist office publishes a full list of B&Bs, with prices. Lists of authorised private B&B operators in and around Rome can be obtained from the tourist information offices and are also available online at www.romaturismo.it. Private B&B operators are also listed in *Wanted in Rome* (see p222), although not all of these are registered (and therefore insured) by the city authorities.

The following are agencies specialising in B&B accommodation:

Bed & Breakfast Italia (Map pp308–10; ☎ 06 688 01 513; www.bbitalia.it; Corso Vittorio Emanuele II 282) is the longest-established B&B network. It has accommodation throughout Rome in three categories: 2 Crowns singles/doubles €37/30.50 per person, 3 Crowns singles/

doubles with bathroom €50.60/43.40 per person, 4 Crowns luxurious singles/doubles with bathroom €66.60/57.80 per person. You can view apartments and book online.

The **Bed & Breakfast Association of Rome** (Map pp302–3; ☎ 06 553 02 248; www.b-b.rm.it; Via A Pacinotti 73) offers a similar service and can also arrange high-quality, fully furnished apartment rentals for brief periods, usually a minimum of three nights.

A useful online accommodation agency which has a large number of very good B&Bs or *affittacamere* (virtually the same thing but without the breakfast) on its books is **Cross Pollinate** (www.cross-pollinate.com). This website allows you to view pictures and maps of the accommodation (most of which is in the city centre) and tells you if the place is already booked. A credit-card deposit reserves the room and you'll have a confirmation in 24 hours.

HOSTELS

The Italian youth hostels association, **Associazione Italiana Alberghi per la Gioventù** (AIG; Map pp314–16; ☎ 06 487 11 52; Via Cavour 44), has details on all youth hostels in Italy and assists with bookings to stay at universities in summer. You can also join HI (Hostelling International) here.

A valid HI card is required in all associated youth hostels in Italy. You can get this in your home country or at the Ostello Foro Italico youth hostel (see p236) in Rome. In the latter case you either pay the full cost of €16/12 for over/under 21 years old, or collect a stamp on each of the first six nights you spend in the hostel. With six stamps you are considered a full member; HI is on the Internet at www.iyhf.org.

PENSIONI & HOTELS

Rome has a wide range of *pensioni* and hotels catering to all wallets, although prices have risen considerably in recent years – especially as the Jubilee and conversion to the euro were greeted by all and sundry as a good excuse for hefty price hikes.

Traditionally, a *pensione* was more personal and smaller than a hotel, often occupying one or two floors in a building housing other, similar establishments. However, the distinction is becoming blurred and most former *pensioni* now class themselves as hotels.

The one- to five-star hotel rating relates to facilities only: it's no indication of value, comfort, atmosphere or friendliness. Many hotels have been recently revamped (and new ones opened), but standards can still trail behind international levels. Even the top five-star hotels won't usually offer facilities you might expect elsewhere. Rooms in converted *palazzi* are often small (albeit luxurious); there are seldom gyms and pools. Deluxe and top-end hotels provide minibar, air-conditioning, television, fine linen, 24-hour room service and private bath with hairdryer. Facilities are more basic in mid-range places: you won't always find a hairdryer, minibar, room service or even air-conditioning. The only guarantee at budget places is a bed and a roof.

Breakfast in cheaper accommodation is rarely worth a bleary eye so, if you have the option, save a few bob and pop into a bar for a coffee and *cornetto* (croissant) as the Romans do.

RELIGIOUS INSTITUTIONS

A good budget bet are the numerous religious institutions which offer accommodation. To stay in one, you usually apply to the nearest Catholic archdiocese in your home town, although some institutions (including those listed here) will consider independent requests. It is wise to book well in advance.

Bear in mind that all religious institutions have strict curfews and the accommodation, while clean, is of the basic, no-frills variety. Breakfast is included in the price and almost all rooms have private bathrooms unless stated otherwise.

STUDENT ACCOMMODATION

Students planning to study in Italy can usually organise accommodation through the school or university they will be attending. Options include a room with an Italian family, or a share arrangement with other students in an independent apartment. Some Italian universities operate a *casa dello studente*, which houses Italian students throughout the school year and lets rooms to others during the summer break (July to the end of September).

It can be very difficult to organise a room in one of these institutions. The best idea is to go through your own university or contact the Italian university directly.

Sleeping

Price Ranges

It is very difficult to be precise when outlining price ranges as not only do rates fluctuate madly between periods but also between hotels in the same category. But as an approximate guide, for a double in a one-star hotel you can expect to pay from €40 to €100; in a two-star €50 to €130; in a three-star €80 to €230; in a four-star €150 to €400; and in a five-star from €450 upwards. A double in a B&B will cost €40 to €100.

What this effectively means is that there are bargains to be had. Many hotels offer considerable discounts for low-season visits, long stays or for weekend breaks. Check out hotel websites for the latest information.

It should also be noted that single travellers are not particularly well served, with single rooms often disproportionately expensive compared to double or triple rooms.

Checking In & Out

Hotels usually require you to check out on the day of departure between 10am and noon. Later than this and you run the risk of being charged for a further night; check with individual hotels for specific regulations. As to check-in times, there are no hard and fast rules, but if you're going to arrive late in the day, it's probably best to mention this when you book your room.

Many hostels will not accept prior reservations for dorm beds, so arrive after 10am and it's first come, first served. Check-out times are often earlier in hostels, typically around 9am.

Reservations

It is always a good idea to book ahead, especially if you're coming in high season or for a major religious festival (in particular Christmas or Easter). Many hotels will request a faxed confirmation of your reservation together with a credit-card number as deposit. However, a request for a credit-card number does not always mean the hotel will accept payment by plastic, so to avoid embarrassing scenes at check-out it's not a bad idea to check in advance. If you don't have a credit card, you'll often be asked to send a money order to cover the first night's stay.

Many hotels now, however, are encouraging guests to book directly over the Internet which saves the hassle of international faxes and money orders.

You should also note when reserving your room that in some, not all, hotels a *camera doppia* (double room) means two twin beds, while for a double bed you should ask for a *camera matrimoniale*.

For further details on reservation services see p263.

Longer-term Rentals

Apartments near the centre of Rome are expensive; you can expect to pay around €900 per month for a studio apartment or a small one-bedroom place. On top of this there are bills for electricity (which is quite expensive in Italy) and gas. There's usually also a *condominio* (building maintenance charge) of between €25 and €155, depending on the size and location of the apartment. However, for a longer stay they can often work out cheaper than a hotel.

A room in a shared apartment will cost around €500 per month, plus bills. You'll usually be asked to pay a deposit equal to one or two months' rent and the first month in advance.

Several of the English-language bookshops in Rome have notice boards where people looking for accommodation or offering a room on a short- or long-term basis place their messages. Try the **Economy Book & Video Center** (Map pp314–16; Via Torino 136), near Via Nazionale, or the **Corner Bookshop** (Map pp317–19; Via del Moro 48 in Trastevere), between Piazza Santa Maria in Trastevere and Piazza Trilussa. Internet cafés around town also have notice boards.

Another good way to find a shared apartment is to buy *Wanted in Rome* (published fortnightly on Wednesday) or *Porta Portese* (published twice-weekly on Tuesday and Friday) at newsstands. Online resources include the official tourist board website, www.romaturismo.com, and www.wantedinrome.com.

There are many estate agencies specialising in short-term rentals in Rome, which charge a fee for their services. You will also be asked for a deposit of up to one month's rent. They are listed in the telephone directory under *Agenzie immobiliari*.

Sleeping

ANCIENT ROME

The accommodation in this area, the classical core of Rome, veers towards the top end. However, to sip on your early morning cappuccino against a backdrop of the Colosseum and the Imperial Forum is a pleasure that you won't enjoy every day of the year. These three hotels have all been chosen on the basis of their charm as well as comfort and perfectly complement the timeless surroundings in which they stand.

HOTEL CELIO Map pp320–1 *Hotel*
☎ 06 704 95 333; www.hotelcelio.com; Via dei Santissimi Quattro Coronati 35c; high season s/d €210/290, low season €110/160; metro Colosseo; P

Enter Hotel Celio and you step into a world apart. The mosaic floors, heavy baroque furnishings, repro frescoes – they all add up to an original and entertaining place, decorated with an artist's vision in mind. In fact, the medium-sized rooms, complete with mod cons and large-screen TVs, are all named after artists and Roman emperors. There are also various suites available, from €330, and a private garage for guest parking.

Signpost

If you're staying in Ancient Rome, you'll find the closest sights on p70, the nearest eateries on p155 and shops on p204.

HOTEL FORUM Map pp314–16 *Hotel*
☎ 06 679 24 46; www.hotelforum.com; Via Tor de' Conti 25; high season s/d €225/320, low season €145/220; metro Cavour

The best asset of this former convent-turned-hotel is its delightful roof-garden restaurant with stunning views over the nearby Forum and Palatine. Over breakfast you can watch Rome come to life, or dine at night against one of Rome's more-impressive backdrops. Antique furniture abounds in the wood-panelled lobby lounge area and rooms are well appointed and comfortably large.

HOTEL NERVA Map pp314–16 *Hotel*
☎ 06 678 18 35; www.hotelnerva.com; Via Tor de' Conti 3; high season s/d €160/220, low season €100/130; metro Cavour

Tucked in behind the Forum, Hotel Nerva is a discreet establishment run by a friendly,

The aptly named Hotel Forum

almost English-speaking manager. Although the carpeted rooms aren't huge, they are comfortable and elegantly fit in all the mod cons. Considerable discounts are available out of season and if you pay in cash. There are also two rooms (a single and a double) with facilities for disabled people.

CENTRO STORICO

This area comprises the heart of Rome. Piazza Navona, Campo de' Fiori, the Pantheon, Ghetto and Via del Corso all buzz until late at night, offering visitors a wonderful glimpse of Rome at play. The atmospheric squares, streetside cafés and ivy-clad *palazzi* fulfil many expectations of what Rome should be like, so it's not surprising that most hotels fall within the upper price range. There are a few budget choices hidden away, but even these are at the top end of their price category.

ALBERGO ABRUZZI
Map pp311–13 *Hotel*
☎ 06 679 20 21; fax 06 697 88 076; Piazza della Rotonda 69; high season s/d €150/195, low season €125/175; bus to Largo di Torre Argentina

Winning the prize for position is Albergo Abruzzi, directly opposite the Pantheon, but it can be very noisy until late at night when the square finally clears. The rooms are basic but well equipped and have air-con. The chatty management make this a perennial favourite.

ALBERGO DELLA LUNETTA

Map pp311–13   *Hotel*

☎ 06 686 10 80; fax 06 689 20 28; Piazza Paradiso 68; s/d €55/85, with bathroom €65/110; bus to Corso Vittorio Emanuele II

A charming rabbit warren of a hotel, this popular *pensione* near Campo de' Fiori is of the old school, where cleanliness counts for more than modern gadgetry. Rooms are consequently spotless, almost monastic in their simplicity and much frequented by young foreign students who stay for months at a time. And at these prices, that's not surprising.

Top Five Views

- **Hotel Forum** Looks over the nearby Imperial Forum and Palatine Hill. Classical Rome has never looked so good (p223)
- **Hotel Fontana** Open your bedroom curtains to admire the magnificent Trevi Fountain (right)
- **Hotel Eden** View the city spread out before you from the vantage point of this grand old luxury hotel (p229)
- **Hotel Scalinata di Spagna** From the top of the Spanish Steps, enjoy the evocative spread of Roman rooftops (p230)
- **Albergo Abruzzi** Wake up to the Pantheon silently looming over vibrant Piazza della Rotonda (p223)

ALBERGO DEL SOLE

Map pp311–13   *Hotel*

☎ 06 688 06 873; www.soealbiscione.it; Via del Biscione 76; s/d €65/95, with bathroom €83/125; bus to Corso Vittorio Emanuele II; [P]

Occupying a crumbling *palazzo* near Campo de' Fiori, this characterful hotel claims to be the oldest in Rome. Dating from 1462, it has low wood-beamed ceilings and comfortable rooms, some with antique furniture. The reasonable prices do not include breakfast. The roof terrace (open to guests until 11pm) is a decided bonus, as are the garage facilities for €23 per day. Credit cards are not accepted.

CASA HOWARD Map pp314–16   *Hotel*

☎ 06 699 24 555; www.casahoward.com; Via Capo le Case 18; high season s/d €160/190, low season €120/160; metro Spagna

Decorated by someone with a keen eye for style, Casa Howard is a model of elegance. Fine fabrics abound and the paintings perfectly suit the individual colour schemes in the five rooms. Two of the rooms have en suite bathrooms while the others have their own private bathroom in a separate room next door; there is also a Turkish bath available for those in the mood. The same people also have a further 10 rooms at **Via Sistina 149** (s/d from €150/200).

GREGORIANA Map pp314–16   *Hotel*

☎ 06 679 42 69; fax 06 678 42 58; Via Gregoriana 18; s/d incl room-service breakfast €124/250; metro Spagna

This fashionable hotel has long attracted an A-list clientele: Naomi Campbell, Claudia Schiffer and, more recently, Italy's favourite Australian, Megan Gale, have all stayed here. Its rooms are not numbered but are instead adorned with letters by the 1930s French fashion illustrator Erté. A haven from the shopping frenzies outside, it offers discretion at reasonable prices.

HOTEL CAMPO DE' FIORI

Map pp311–13   *Hotel*

☎ 06 688 06 865; www.hotelcampodefiori.com; Via del Biscione 6; d €100, with shower/bathroom €120/150; bus to Corso Vittorio Emanuele II

The narrow entrance lined with mirrors and columns is a disconcerting introduction to this peculiar six-storey (no lift) establishment. However, it's in a great location, just off Campo de' Fiori, and the garish room decor could, at a push, claim a certain kitsch appeal. Prices include breakfast and discounts are negotiable out of season. It also has nine mini-apartments, which can sleep up to five people. They cost from €120 per day.

HOTEL FONTANA

Map pp314–16   *Hotel*

☎ 06 678 61 13; www.hotelfontana-trevi.com; Piazza di Trevi 96; s/d €180/260; metro Barberini

If you fancy a late-night dip in the Trevi Fountain, the Fontana is your place. Standing bang opposite the legendary and very busy fountain, it has some rooms with *the* view, but they have their drawbacks – the noise from the crowds lasts late into the night.

HOTEL FORTE Map pp308–10   *Hotel*

☎ 06 320 76 25; www.hotelforte.com; Via Margutta 61; high season s/d €160/230, low season €113/140; metro Spagna

Housed in a lovely 17th-century *palazzo*, a haunt of artists and antiquarians, Hotel Forte offers a warm welcome and bright, decent-sized rooms. The decor is a mix-match of ancient and modern and veers pleasantly from the tasteful to the kitsch. The management will help with reservations for museums, restaurants, city tours and, if necessary, baby-sitting. Rates include breakfast.

HOTEL MANFREDI Map pp308–10 *Hotel*
☎ 06 320 76 76; www.hmanfredi.com; Via Margutta 61; high season s/d €205/270, low season €150/190; metro Spagna

Shopaholics are well placed at this quiet hotel. There are plenty of antique shops on your doorstep while the designer boutiques of Via Condotti are not two minutes' walk away. Rooms are heavily decorated and comfortable with all the mod cons incorporated. The hotel staff are amiable and professional. Rates include an American-style buffet breakfast.

The reception area of Hotel d'Este (p229)

HOTEL MARGUTTA Map pp304–5 *Hotel*
☎ 06 322 36 74; fax 06 320 03 95; Via Laurina 34; s/d €88/99, d with shared/private terrace €124/135; metro Spagna

Hotel Margutta is a good choice if you want to save your euros for the shops. Rooms are a little poky but are never less than spotlessly clean. The three rooms with terrace are forever in demand, often booked up months ahead. Some of the ground-floor rooms have wheelchair access.

HOTEL MIMOSA Map pp311–13 *Hotel*
☎ 06 688 01 753; www.hotelmimosa.net; Via di Santa Chiara 61; high season s/d €77/93, with bathroom €88/108, low season €50/70, with bathroom €70/79; bus to Corso Vittorio Emanuele II

A popular choice, you'll need to book ahead to guarantee a room at this modest hotel. The corridors are mined with dangerous steps and some rooms are a bit cramped, but all of them are clean and, because of their prime location, often taken. Payment by cash is preferred although you might be able to pay by card with prior arrangement.

HOTEL POMEZIA
Map pp311–13 *Hotel*
☎ /fax 06 686 13 71; www.hotelpomezia.it; Via di Torre Chiavari 13; high season s/d €105/125, low season €60/90; bus to Largo di Torre Argentina

Close to Campo de' Fiori, Hotel Pomezia is a good lower mid-range choice. The no-frills rooms are basic but the location is great and the welcome friendly. There is also one room equipped for disabled travellers. Prices include breakfast.

HOTEL PONTE SISTO
Map pp311–13 *Hotel*
☎ 06 686 31 00; www.hotelpontesisto.it; Via dei Pettinari 64; s/d €150/310, ste €340-420; bus to Corso Vittorio Emanuele II; [P]

An extensive renovation has turned this hotel, close to Campo de' Fiori and the lovely Via Giulia, into a city-centre delight; several of the elegant rooms have their own terraces with unrivalled Roman rooftop views. The parking is also a considerable bonus in an area where street parking is almost impossible.

HOTEL PORTOGHESI
Map pp308–10 *Hotel*
☎ 06 686 42 31; www.hotelportoghesiroma.com; Via dei Portoghesi 1; s/d €145/185, ste from €205; bus to Via di Monte Brianzo

The international flags sign the way to this 150-year-old hotel north of Piazza Navona. Situated in a quiet street in the busy heart of town, Hotel

Sleeping – Centro Storico

Signpost

If you're staying in the *centro storico* (historic centre), you'll find the closest sights on p82, the nearest eateries on p156 and shops on p204.

Portoghesi offers rooms that are discreetly furnished and comfortable. Prices include breakfast on the wonderful roof terrace. The hotel does not accept Amex or Diners Club cards.

HOTEL PRIMAVERA

Map pp311–13   *Hotel*

☎ 06 688 03 109; fax 06 686 92 65; Piazza di San Pantaleo 3; high season s/d €95/125, d without bathroom €95; bus to Corso Vittorio Emanuele II

Hotel Primavera is a good option for serious sightseers as buses pass Corso Vittorio Emanuele II regularly and much of the city centre is within easy walking distance. Rooms are clean and comfortable, although possibly a bit floral for some tastes, and all have air-con and double glazing. Booking is recommended and one night's deposit is requested. Credit cards are not accepted.

HOTEL RAPHAÈL Map pp311–13   *Hotel*

☎ 06 68 28 31; www.raphaelhotel.com; Largo Febo 2; high season s/d €290/420, low season €260/390, ste from €530; bus to Corso del Rinascimento

This ivy-clad hotel is the picture of Roman elegance. A former hangout of disgraced prime minister Craxi, it offers luxury with class – from the Picasso ceramics in reception to the stunning views from the roof-terrace restaurant. There's also a gym and sauna and three rooms are equipped for disabled people. Special weekend rates are available.

HOTEL SANTA CHIARA

Map pp311–13   *Hotel*

☎ 06 687 29 79; www.albergosantachiara.com; Via di Santa Chiara 21; s/d €143/212; bus to Largo di Torre Argentina

Situated behind the Pantheon and within a stone's throw of Bernini's *Elefantino*, Hotel Santa Chiara presents guests with marble columns and Venetian chandeliers in its public areas. Guestrooms, however, are furnished with more-modest modern trappings. Some rooms also have small balconies overlooking the street, although those around the internal courtyard are quieter.

HOTEL TEATRO DI POMPEO

Map pp311–13   *Hotel*

☎ 06 683 00 170; www.hotelteatrodipompeo.it; Largo del Pallaro 8; high season s/d €150/190, low season €130/170; bus to Corso Vittorio Emanuele II

Apart from the quiet, comfortable rooms, guests can enjoy a touch of real Roman magic

It's a Bellboy's Life

The Americans tip best. Roberto Proietti doesn't even hesitate before answering. 'The English are generous, most of our guests are, but the Americans are definitely the best. An American once gave me €50.' An exception to the €20 to €30 that he considers his daily average.

Roberto, 39, is a bellboy at the **Sheraton Golf Hotel** (☎ 06 65 85 88; www.sheraton.com; Viale Parco de Medici 167; s/d from €140/165) in the city's southern suburbs. With its 385 rooms and 18-hole golf course it's a popular venue for business conferences and is busy year-round.

'A lot of football teams come here,' explains Roberto. 'Among others we've had Arsenal, Chelsea and the Argentinian national team. They like the golf course.'

He reels these teams off with a professional indifference which he then loses altogether. 'I delivered a message to James Brown once,' he reveals with the excitement of a genuine fan. You mean, the real James Brown? Living in America and all that? 'He was a lovely man. He was very little and had the most massive heels on. Still I couldn't see him very well as he came in because he was surrounded by massive bodyguards.

'And, of course, there was Fidel Castro. He stayed when he came to meet the Pope in 1996. I shook his hand. It was amazing to see him, he seemed so big with his beard and enormous cigar.'

But not every day is so eventful. Roberto's average working day generally starts early.

'If I'm working the morning, I come in at 7am, ready for the 7.30am shift. There are three shifts to cover 24 hours: 7.30am to 3.30pm, 3.30pm to 11.30pm and 11.30pm to 7.30am. There are five of us to cover these, two each for the day and one for the night.

'We carry mobile phones so that reception can always call us when clients check in or out. When they arrive we carry their bags to their room, give them a short welcome speech and explain how everything in the room works. Then when they leave we'll help them with their luggage.'

Roberto reckons on about 20 check-outs a day.

'We also have to deliver messages to rooms and on the night shift, at about 3am, pass by every room checking for breakfast requests on the doors. It takes about 25 minutes to cover the whole hotel.

'The night shift can be a bit boring,' Roberto confides. But, after 10 years on the job, he's earned the right to the two day shifts. This, he says, means he has more time to help his wife and two young children.

'The food is definitely one of the good things. We pay €8 a month and then eat the same food as the clients. My worst memory? We got hit by armed robbers once. They got away with all the money and jewellery and have never been found.'

here. Part of the hotel is built over the remains of Pompey's Theatre which dates back to 55 BC and it's here, in the grottolike dining room, that breakfast is served. It's difficult to imagine a more atmospheric place to take your morning cappuccino.

MINERVA Map pp311–13 *Hotel*
☎ 06 69 52 01; www.hotel-invest.com; Piazza della Minerva 69; high season s/d €410/570, low season €326/410; bus to Largo di Torre Argentina

Bernini's *Elefantino* statue near the Pantheon trumpets the presence of the grand old Minerva, one of Rome's top hotels. Occupying a 17th-century *palazzo*, it was given a thorough postmodern restyling by Paolo Portoghesi in the late 1980s. One of his additions was a magnificent Art Deco–style, coloured-glass ceiling in the lobby. There are nonsmoking rooms and one room for disabled travellers as well as a restaurant and gym.

RESIDENZA FARNESE
Map pp311–13 *Hotel*
☎ 06 688 91 388; residenzafarnese@libero.it; Via del Mascherone 59; s/d €144/170; bus to Corso Vittorio Emanuele II

Occupying a former 17th-century monastery, this smart outfit resembles a colonial club more than a traditional hotel. Furnished with tiles rather than carpet, the bar and billiard table merely add to this slightly formal impression. Some of its rooms are huge, while others are tiny but no two are the same. The friendly management can help with tickets to cultural and sporting events.

SUORE DI SANTA BRIGIDA
Map pp311–13 *Religious Institution*
☎ 06 688 92 596; brigida@mclink.it; Piazza Farnese 96; s/d per person €95/85; bus 116 to Via Monserrato

Rome's best convent hotel occupies the house where the Swedish St Brigid died in 1373. The rooms are simple and you *are* dossing down with nuns, but the sisters are very friendly and you can't get a much better location. The 11pm curfew might bother some people; the church bells others. The entrance is at Via Monserrato 54.

Cheap Sleeps

CASA KOLBE Map pp320–1 *Hotel*
☎ 06 679 88 66; fax 06 699 41 550; Via di San Teodoro 44; s/d €62/80, breakfast €6; bus to Via dei Cerchi

Tour groups tend to take over this former Fran-

ciscan monastery, opposite the Palatine, but it's a comfortable place – when the weather's not extreme – with a large sheltered garden in a quiet but central area of the city. Rooms are spartan but try and get one around the courtyard. The hotel named after a former resident, a Polish monk who was killed in Auschwitz.

EAST OF VIA DEL CORSO

Some of the hotels in this area count among Italy's grandest, occupying the most prestigious addresses in the country. Others, particularly those near Stazione Termini, would never boast of their postcode, but nonetheless offer comfort, often combined with style. From the luxury celebrity haunts above the Spanish Steps to the budget hostels of the Esquiline, there really is something for everyone in this area. As a general rule of thumb, places nearer the station are cheaper than those in the more attractive central areas.

58 LE REAL B&B Map pp314–16 *B&B*
☎ 06 482 35 66; www.58viacavour.it; Via Cavour 58; high season s/d €100/180, low season from €50/70; metro Termini

Clean and spacious rooms in a lovely apartment with panoramic views and a sun-terrace. Guests appreciate the friendly management and free access to fridge with juices, yoghurt and water.

CARLITO'S WAY Map pp314–16 *Hotel*
☎ 06 444 03 84; www.rome-hotel-carlitosway.com; Via Villafranca 10; high season s/d €125/135, low season €87/92; metro Castro Pretorio

Improbably named after an Al Pacino film, this quiet and comfortable hotel is run by the same people as the highly popular Hotel Des Artistes. Almost a carbon copy of its better-known sister hotel, it offers understatement and a laid-back efficiency. The reception is down the road at Via Villafranca 20.

DAPHNE B&B Map pp314–16 *B&B*
☎ 06 478 23 529; www.daphne-rome.com; Via degli Avignonesi 20; high season d/tr €110/135, low season from €68/81; metro Barberini

This cosy, clean, convenient and well-equipped place has been described as a 'home sweet home' by a number of travellers. Guests have enthused over the warm, kind, informative and helpful owners who have nevertheless respected their privacy.

HASSLER VILLA MEDICI

Map pp314–16 *Hotel*

☎ 06 69 93 40; www.hotelhasslerroma.com; Piazza della Trinità dei Monti 6; s €435, d €589-781; metro Spagna

Rome's grand old luxury hotel is, and has long been, a favourite of royalty and the American A-list. Guests have included the royal families of Sweden, Greece and England, John F Kennedy and Elizabeth Taylor. The atmosphere is discreetly glamorous and, although the standard rooms aren't huge, features such as the rooftop restaurant (with stupendous views) and courtyard bar are ample compensation. Special weekend and 'romance' packages are available at certain times of the year, so check online.

HOTEL ADVENTURE

Map pp314–16 *Hotel*

☎ 06 446 90 26; www.hoteladventure.com; Via Palestro 88; d €93-160; metro Termini

Pretty in pink, or at least pink, the reception of Hotel Adventure resembles a kitsch lighting showroom complete with chandeliers and reproduction antique furniture. However, the rooms are immaculate and very safe, with video cameras and security doors monitoring those who enter and exit each floor. All rooms have air-con and TV. The rooms looking onto the internal courtyard are quieter than those facing the street.

HOTEL ARTEMIDE Map pp314–16 *Hotel*

☎ 06 48 99 11; www.venere.it/roma/artemide; Via Nazionale 22; high season s/d €235/325, low season €216/300; bus to Via Nazionale

Hotel Artemide is an elegant four-star oasis of calm after the incessant traffic of Via Nazionale. Rooms are well equipped with one twin room, including facilities for disabled people. Nice extras include free breakfast, mineral water, soft drinks and daily newspapers. There are substantial discounts in low season – it's worth asking.

HOTEL CARAVAGGIO

Map pp314–16 *Hotel*

☎ 06 48 59 15; ht.caravaggio@flashnet.it; Via Palermo 73-75; s/d €123/180; bus to Via Nazionale

Just off Via Nazionale and a 10-minute walk from Stazione Termini, this pleasant three-star hotel offers considerable discounts out of season. The rooms are small but beautifully furnished and all have at least one antique piece. What's more, those facing Via Palermo all have mosaic floors. Room services include TV, minibar and air-con. The hotel also has a Jacuzzi.

HOTEL COLUMBIA Map pp314–16 *Hotel*

☎ 06 474 42 89; www.hotelcolumbia.com; Via del Viminale 15; high season s/d incl breakfast €189/208, low season incl breakfast €104/138; metro Termini or Repubblica

The tasteful, tranquil Columbia is an anomaly in a part of town renowned for characterless hotels. It's good for both business and leisure travellers; rooms are bright and compact, all have data plugs and some have beautiful Murano-crystal chandeliers. There's also a pleasant breakfast terrace with views over the surrounding rooftops.

HOTEL CONTILIA Map pp314–16 *Hotel*

☎ 06 446 68 87; www.hotelcontilia.com; Via Principe Amedeo 81; high season s/d €135/168, low season €55/65; metro Termini

An elegant hotel in a not-so-chic area, Hotel Contilia is great value in low season but becomes more expensive in the busy months. The rooms are decorated in various colours, ranging from orange to green, and if not huge are a decent enough size. They all have satellite TV and independent air-con.

HOTEL DE RUSSIE Map pp304–5 *Hotel*

☎ 06 32 88 81; www.roccofortehotels.com; Via del Babuino 9; high season s/d €510/1050, low season from €418/572; metro Flaminio

Increasingly popular with Hollywood's visiting superstars – Cruise, Di Caprio, Diaz and Spielberg have all stayed here – the Hotel de Russie is perhaps the most beautiful in Rome, with decor that is at once sumptuous, minimal and tasteful. No expense has been spared – from the massive mosaic-tiled bathrooms to the finest linen, exquisite terraced gardens and luxurious spa.

HOTEL DES ARTISTES

Map pp314–16 *Hotel*

☎ 06 445 43 65; www.hoteldesartistes.com; Via Villafranca 20; high season s/d €149/159, low season €99/109; metro Castro Pretorio

Run by a young and helpful couple, the non-smoking Hotel Des Artistes has been winning rave reviews for its welcoming hospitality. The elegantly decorated, air-conditioned rooms, fitted in gold and wood, boast satellite TV, computer line and direct-dial telephone as well as all the other three-star trappings; the lovely roof garden is a distinct bonus. There are also cheaper rooms available without a bathroom or breakfast (s/d from €52/59).

HOTEL D'ESTE Map pp314–16   *Hotel*
☎ 06 446 56 07; www.hotel-deste.com; Via Carlo Alberto 6; high season s/d €129/165, low season €37/41; metro Vittorio Emanuele

Mosaic lovers would find this calm hotel convenient for its proximity to Piazza Santa Maria Maggiore and nearby churches. Prices are at the upper end of mid-range – although they drop substantially in the off-season – and the rooms are attractively furnished. Friendly staff work hard to please.

HOTEL DINA Map pp314–16   *Hotel*
☎ 06 474 06 94; fax 06 489 03 614; Via Principe Amedeo 62; high season s/d €75/115, low season €33/43; metro Termini

Friendly Hotel Dina boasts what so many hotels across Rome cannot: a large lift. This saves the considerable hassle of squeezing bodies around bags, or worse still making two journeys. Rooms are fitted with the standard hotel clobber, although two are equipped for disabled people, with open showers and hand rails – unusual for hotels in this price range. Breakfast is an extra €3.

HOTEL D'INGHILTERRA
Map pp308–10   *Hotel*
☎ 06 699 81 204; www.hoteldinghilterraroma.it; Via Bocca di Leone 14; high season s/d €325/798, low season €250/335; metro Spagna

A favourite of Liszt, Mendelssohn and Hemingway, the Hotel d'Inghilterra has been offering exclusive Roman hospitality since 1850. Today, the wood-panelled corridors reverberate to the echoes of the past, while the overall decor is an elegant chaos of dowdy, tasteful and opulent. The rooms on the 5th floor are smaller, with sloping roofs and exposed wooden beams, but have their own private balconies.

HOTEL EDEN Map pp314–16   *Hotel*
☎ 06 47 81 21; www.hotel-eden.it; Via Ludovisi 49; high season s/d €675/1040, low season from €478/676; metro Barberini

One of the most glamorous hotels in Rome – despite losing some of its thunder to de Russie – the Eden is situated on a hilltop close to Villa Borghese so most rooms have splendid views over Rome. Guest quarters are spacious and graceful and there's a marvellous rooftop restaurant and bar.

HOTEL ERCOLI Map pp306–7   *Hotel*
☎ 06 474 54 54; www.hotelercoli.com; Via Collina 48; high season s/d with bathroom €75/105, low season €52/75; metro Termini & bus to Via Piave

This comfortable hotel is about a 10-minute walk from Stazione Termini. Its characterful rooms are at the upper end of the budget scale and have a bath, TV, telephone and hairdryer.

Signpost
If you're staying East of Via del Corso, you'll find the closest sights on p96, the nearest eateries on p164 and shops on p211.

HOTEL ES Map pp314–16   *Hotel*
☎ 06 44 48 41; www.eshotel.it; Via Filippo Turati 171; high season s/d €418/572, low season from €398/539; metro Vittorio Emanuele

A model for the 21st century – and a *Wallpaper* magazine cover waiting to happen – this stunning new designer hotel is the only central Roman construction built from scratch in recent years. It looks like a multistorey car park from the outside but within it's a five-star minimalist oasis with swathes of space, luminous reception desks, a spectacular polychromatic inner atrium and what *will* be the legendary 'seventh floor', a sophisticated and fun space with bars, restaurants and balconies. Comfort and style in equal measures.

HOTEL FLORIDIA Map pp308–10   *Hotel*
☎ 06 445 46 95; www.sebraeli.it; Via Montebello 43; s/d with bathroom €166/207, low season €47/62; metro Castro Pretorio

The hospitality on offer at Hotel Floridia is efficient and professional. Rooms come fitted with requisite minibar and air-con and, although comfortable enough, are impersonal. However, for a quick stay the comforts more than compensate for the lack of charm. Breakfast is included in the price.

HOTEL GABRIELLA Map pp314–16   *Hotel*
☎ 06 445 01 20; www.gabriellahotel.it; Via Palestro 88; high season s/d €115/135, low season €70/90; metro Termini

A friendly, family-run place, this unassuming hotel offers well-fitted rooms complete with

Sleeping – East of Via del Corso

air-con and mod cons. Fabric furnishings follow a blue colour scheme so as not to clash with the mosaic tiling in the bathroom. Security is assured by the swipe-card locks.

HOTEL IGEA Map pp314–16 *Hotel*
☎ 06 446 69 11; Via Principe Amedeo 97; high season s/d €90/140, low season €50/80; metro Termini
The fancy entrance promises a comfort which the rooms don't quite live up to. However, they are a good size and with air-con, double-glazed windows and satellite TV, quite comfy enough. Prices also include breakfast. The management can organise sightseeing tours on request.

HOTEL JULIA Map pp314–16 *Hotel*
☎ 06 488 16 37; info@hoteljulia.it; Via Rasella 29; s with shower €110, d with bath €165; metro Barberini
Close to busy Piazza Barberini, Hotel Julia is just off Via delle Quattro Fontane. Situated on a tranquil cobbled street it offers simple, unfussy rooms with the usual array of extras: satellite TV, air-con, minibar, hairdryer and safe.

HOTEL LOCARNO Map pp304–5 *Hotel*
☎ 06 361 08 41; www.hotellocarno.com; Via della Penna 22; high season s/d €120/310, low season €90/130; metro Flaminio
Central to lots of sights, shopping and restaurants, these are some of the friendliest lodgings in Rome. Some of the rooms feel a little *too* lived-in although there are also gleaming new suites. Bonuses include an attractive Art-Deco lounge bar, filling breakfasts and free use of bicycles. One room is equipped for disabled travellers.

HOTEL OCEANIA Map pp314–16 *Hotel*
☎ 06 482 46 96; www.hoteloceania.it; Via Firenze 38; high season s/d €105/150, low season €79/135; metro Repubblica
In a quiet 19th-century *palazzo*, this discreet hotel stands out for the unbeatable hospitality offered by the owners. The decor is simple and inviting and it wins extra points for the thoughtful extras – English newspapers for guests to read and modem plugs for those with computers. There are only nine rooms, so book early.

HOTEL PALLADIUM PALACE
Map pp314–16 *Hotel*
☎ 06 446 69 18; www.hotelpalladiumpalace.it; Via Gioberti 36; high season s/d €186/284, low season €71/82; metro Termini
This large and comfortable hotel offers individually decorated rooms. Some have parquet

floors, others carpet or marble tiles and fittings are in wood and gold. However, with the exception of the cosy pastel-coloured basement breakfast room, the feel of the place is somewhat impersonal. There are four rooms for disabled travellers, a bar and a roof garden with sauna.

HOTEL PIEMONTE Map pp314–16 *Hotel*
☎ 06 445 22 40; www.hotelpiemonte.com; Via Vicenza 34; s/d €110/150; metro Termini
A stone's throw from Stazione Termini, Hotel Piemonte has relaxing cream-coloured rooms. There's double glazing to keep out the hubbub from the busy streets and rooms on the ground floor have bars across the windows as an added security measure. One room has disabled access. Breakfast is included in the price.

HOTEL RIMINI Map pp314–16 *Hotel*
☎ 06 446 19 91; www.hotelrimini.it; Via Marghera 17; high season s/d €105/160, low season €95/120; metro Termini
Despite the grouchy doorman-cum-receptionist guarding the grand-looking mirrored and wood-panelled entrance of the Rimini, you'll find decent enough rooms. Furnished with heavy wooden furniture, they're comfortable and clean. The Internet café (€1.10 for half an hour) and the left-luggage facility next door are added bonuses.

HOTEL SCALINATA DI SPAGNA
Map pp314–16 *Hotel*
☎ 06 679 30 06; www.hotelscalinata.com; Piazza della Trinità di Monti 17; high season s/d €300/350, low season €150/200; metro Spagna
Boasting one of Rome's premier addresses, the friendly and informal Hotel Scalinata di Spagna is superbly located at the top of the Spanish Steps. The panoramic views of Rome's rooftops are wonderfully evocative and to admire them over breakfast is a rare pleasure. The hotel is very popular, so book well in advance and try to get one of the rooms that lead onto the terrace.

HOTEL SEILER Map pp314–16 *Hotel*
☎ 06 488 02 04; www.hotelseiler.com; Via Firenze 48; high season s/d €99/130, low season €47/75; metro Repubblica
The star attraction at the Hotel Seiler (pronounced sailor) is room 405, known as *la camera degli angeletti* for its ceiling fresco of angels dating from 1885. The other rooms are

less spectacular but perfectly comfortable, although some of the corridors could do with a good lick of paint. There are also family rooms for five people (more if necessary) for €26 to €32 per person.

HOTEL SWEET HOME

Map pp314–16 *Hotel*

☎ 06 488 09 54; www.hotelsweethome.it, Italian only; Via Principe Amedeo 47; high season s/d €52/72, with bathroom €93/103; metro Termini

Situated within a stone's throw of Termini, Hotel Sweet Home is handy if you have an early train to catch. The management can be a little brusque but rooms are decent enough, especially those facing away from the street which are larger and quieter.

HOTEL VENEZIA Map pp314–16 *Hotel*

☎ 06 445 71 01; www.hotelvenezia.com; Via Varese 18; high season s/d €189/208, low season €104/138; metro Termini

In an area decidedly short of class, this hotel is an oasis of style and calm – the nicest place to stay in the area. The reception area is beautifully furnished with antiques and attractive fabrics, while rooms are of a decent size and tastefully furnished. Rooms on the top floor are smaller but each has its own balcony. The multilingual staff make charming hosts.

RESIDENZA CELLINI Map pp314–16 *Hotel*

☎ 06 478 25 204; www.residenzacellini.it; Via Modena 5; d €145-180, jr ste €165-205; metro Repubblica

Hidden away in a fairly nondescript building near Piazza della Repubblica is this gem of a place. With only six vast rooms the atmosphere is one of discreet elegance and the service is never less than courteous and efficient. The entire hotel has been decorated with an eye to detail – the owner personally designed the mosaic tiles in the bathroom – and is a beautiful mix of antique furniture and modern fittings, all rigorously chosen to fit in. Fresh flowers adorn the bright corridor which literally glows in the early evening sun. This is the perfect hideaway for a romantic break.

Cheap Sleeps

ALBERGO SANDRA

Map pp314–16 *Pensione*

☎ 06 445 26 12; fax 06 446 08 46; Via Villafranca 10; s/d €50/60, with bathroom €60/85; metro Castro Pretorio

Run by a house-proud Italian mamma and her English-speaking son, this 3rd-floor *pensione*

(between Via Vicenza and Via San Martino della Battaglia) offers rooms that vary in shape and size. Some are huge, others smaller and one looks suspiciously like an ex-kitchen with a shower plonked in the corner. Still, of a morning you won't have to stumble far out of bed.

BEEHIVE Map pp314–16 *Hostel*

☎ 06 447 04 553; www.the-beehive.com; Via Marg022 8; dm €18, d with/without bathroom per person €40/30; metro Termini

The place for the discerning budget traveller, with clean, attractive rooms and use of the kitchen. Book ahead as walk-ins are not accepted and party animals positively discouraged.

FAWLTY TOWERS Map pp314–16 *Pensione*

☎ 06 445 03 74; www.fawltytowers.org; Via Magenta 39; dm with/without shower €24/19, s/d €39/66, with bathroom €47/82; metro Termini

One of Rome's most-popular budget options, Fawlty Towers is run by the people at Enjoy Rome (see p275). Some of the orange rooms have air-con, while extras for everyone include a sunny terrace, satellite TV, communal fridge and microwave. To reserve a dorm bed, call in (either in person or by phone) at 9pm the night before you wish to stay; they'll hold the bed until around 10am the following morning.

HOSTEL BEAUTIFUL

Map pp314–16 *Hostel*

☎ 06 446 58 90; www.hostelbeautiful.com; Via Napoleone III 35; dm €20-25; metro Termini

A recent and very welcome addition to Rome's budget accommodation, Hostel Beautiful is a clean and friendly place, just around the corner from the main train station. There are 40 beds in rooms of four, six or eight and in addition to the communal kitchen there is a lively common room. There is no curfew but you'll have to leave a deposit for a key. Internet access is provided free for 15 minutes.

HOTEL ASCOT Map pp314–16 *Hotel*

☎ 06 474 16 75; web.cheapnet.it/hotel.ascot, Italian only; Via Montebello 22; high season s/d with bathroom €55/80, low season €40/60; metro Termini

This quiet and friendly family-run hotel provides a haven from the bustling and often seedy street life outside. The 21 rooms are simply furnished and half have a TV while 10 have air-con at an extra €10 per day. For no extra cost ask for No 28, which still has its original parquet floor.

HOTEL CASTELFIDARDO

Map pp314–16 *Pensione*

☎ 06 446 46 38; castelfidardo@italmarket.it; Via Castelfidardo 31; s/d €44/64, with bathroom €55/74; metro Termini or Castro Pretorio

Situated off Piazza dell'Indipendenza, this is one of Rome's better one-star *pensione*. It has clean and pleasant rooms and the English-speaking staff are friendly and helpful.

HOTEL CERVIA Map pp314–16 *Pensione*

☎ 06 49 10 57; www.hotelcerviaroma.com; Via Palestro 55; s/d €35/55, with bathroom €55/80; metro Castro Pretorio

Not all rooms in this 19th-century building are enormous, but the high-vaulted ceilings give an airy feel and, at these prices, they're something of a bargain. Children are also welcome; free cots are provided for kids under two. A continental breakfast is available for €2.50.

HOTEL CONTINENTALE

Map pp314–16 *Hotel*

☎ 06 445 03 82; www.hotel-continentale.com; Via Palestro 49; high season s/d €70/90, low season €40/72; metro Castro Pretorio

There are several good mid-range hotels at this address. On the ground floor, Hotel Continentale has clean, unassuming white rooms with air-con and small private bathrooms. The owners and staff are friendly and speak several languages, including English and French.

HOTEL DOLOMITI Map pp314–16 *Hotel*

☎ 06 495 72 56; www.hotel-dolomiti.it; Via San Martino della Battaglia 11; high season s/d €67/93, low season €55/75; metro Castro Pretorio

One of two hotels in the same building run by the same friendly family, Hotel Dolomiti offers airy rooms, all with private bathroom, minibar, TV, telephone, air-con, double glazing, safe and hairdryer. Breakfast is served in a delightful marble-panelled bar-breakfast area. There are also some rooms without a bathroom with doubles starting at €55. Given its three-star trimmings, this place is a bargain.

HOTEL ELIDE Map pp314–16 *Hotel*

☎ 06 474 13 67; fax 06 489 04 318; Via Firenze 50; s/d €54/78, d with bathroom €88; metro Repubblica

Run by a family from Naples, this cosy hotel offers comfortable, uncluttered rooms. The best is No 18 with an elaborate gilded ceil-

ing. Prices, which include breakfast, drop by around €25 from December to March. Payment is by cash only.

HOTEL GALATEA Map pp314–16 *Hotel*

☎ 06 474 30 70; fax 06 48 66 70; Via Genova 24; s/d from €41/56, with bathroom from €51/67; bus to Via Nazionale

Hotel Galatea is entered through the grand entrance of an old palace. Frequently full of excitable school groups, it has something of the medieval about it with heavy drapes, solid wooden furniture and cast-iron light fittings hanging from the ceiling. The staff claim to speak six European languages.

HOTEL LACHEA Map pp314–16 *Hotel*

☎ 06 495 72 56; www.hotel-dolomiti.it; Via San Martino della Battaglia 11; high season s/d €67/93, low season €55/75; metro Castro Pretorio

Recently renovated Hotel Lachea is the second of the two hotels in the same building run by the same family. The spacious rooms are fitted with cherry-wood furnishings which lend an air of elegance. Some, overlooking the main road, have balconies, but all have double glazing which drastically reduces the noise. The owners speak English, French and Spanish.

HOTEL POSITANO Map pp314–16 *Hotel*

☎ 06 49 03 60; www.hotelpositano.it; Via Palestro 49; high season s/d €75/100, low season 35/40, without shower from €20/35; metro to Castro Pretorio

Next to the Hotel Continentale, this is a particularly good choice for families as they don't charge for children under six. The rooms have private bathrooms plus all the mod cons. There are also some five-/six-bed dorm rooms for €20 per person, although some readers have complained that these are cramped enough to embarrass a sardine. All credit cards are accepted.

HOTEL TIZI Map pp306–7 *Hotel*

☎ 06 482 01 28; fax 06 474 32 66; Via Collina 48; s/d €42/52, d with bathroom €62; metro Termini & bus to Via Piave

Hotel Tizi makes no claims to luxury, rather it offers a warm welcome and a charmingly ramshackle atmosphere with chandeliers and antique furniture dotted around the place. Rooms are simple and, if a little worn around the edges, clean and spacious. There are discounts out of season and for longer stays. Payment is by cash only.

PAPA GERMANO Map pp314–16 *Hotel*

☎ 06 48 69 19; www.hotelpapagermano.it; Via Calatafimi 14a; dm €16-22, s €28-40, d with bathroom €52-85; metro Termini

A good budget bet, this hotel enjoys a bubbly atmosphere thanks to the efforts of English- and French-speaking management. It offers various sleeping options, from a dormitory bed to a double room complete with cloying green and pink-rose wallpaper. There are free city maps and guide books available on loan. At the time of writing, a breakfast bar was also being added.

PENSIONE GIAMAICA

Map pp314–16 *Pensione*

☎ 06 49 01 21; md0991@mclink.it; Via Magenta 13; high season s/d without bathroom €38/54, low season €30/38, breakfast €2.50; metro Termini

Pensione Giamaica is a slightly scruffy, laid-back lodge that offers a warm welcome and clean, basic rooms. Each room has its own basin and the communal bathrooms are fine, although floodings are possible as not all the showers come with a fitted curtain. There's no curfew and the owners will provide front-door keys for those planning to come in late.

PENSIONE PANDA

Map pp308–10 *Pensione*

☎ 06 678 01 79; www.pensionepanda.com; Via della Croce 35; s/d from €41/62, with bathroom from €62/88; bus to Via del Corso, metro Spagna

You know you're on to something special when regular guests yelp when they hear the words 'guidebook' and 'research'. This is one of the best *pensioni* in Rome; it's cheap, close to the Spanish Steps, has pretty rooms with arched ceilings, and hospitable English-speaking staff.

PENSIONE RESTIVO

Map pp314–16 *Pensione*

☎ /fax 06 445 26 29; Via Palestro 55; high season s/d €40/62, low season €30/45, d with bathroom €85-93; metro Castro Pretorio

The atmosphere is homely and the hospitality motherly at this modest, but immaculate, *pensione*. Former guests have been known to send gifts and thank-you letters to the owners, who display them with considerable pride. Breakfast is not included, but there's usually a cup of coffee on offer before you set off. Bookings are only taken in the morning and there is a midnight curfew.

POP INN HOSTEL

Map pp314–16 *Hostel*

☎ 06 495 98 87; www.popinnhostel.com; Via Marsala 80; dm s/d €20/25; metro Termini

Situated right by Termini train station, this place is clean, comfortable and run by friendly and helpful management. For a place as cheap as this one is, it's also several steps above the usual hostel conditions.

The lobby in designer Hotel Es (p229)

SANDY HOSTEL Map pp314–16 *Hostel*

☎ 06 488 45 85; www.sandyhostel.com; Via Cavour 136; dm per person €12-18; metro Cavour

It can be something of a sweat to reach this backpackers' crash pad on the 5th floor as there's no lift. Once you get there, you'll find space is tight, so any ideas of a cooling repose are out. Beds, the cheapest in the area, are in dorms for between three and five people (eight in summer). Reservations are not accepted and payment is by cash only. There's no curfew but there is a lockout between 11.30am and 2.30pm.

YWCA Map pp314–16 *Hostel*

☎ 06 488 04 60; fax 06 487 10 28; Via Cesare Balbo 4; s/d €37/62, with bathroom €47/74, tr/quads per person €26; bus to Via Cavour

The YWCA is a good option for budget travellers – women, men and couples. This is the ideal place for early risers with a serious sightseeing agenda, but is probably best avoided by night owls as there's a midnight curfew. From Via

Cavour, turn right into Via A Depretis at Piazza dell' Esquilino. Via Cesare Balbo is the second street on the right. Payment is by cash only and breakfast is included.

TRASTEVERE

Until recently, Trastevere, the most characteristic of all Rome's central quarters, had very little accommodation. However, as the popularity of this lively area full of restaurants, pubs, cafés and increasingly tourists grew, so the city's hoteliers caught on. There are now a number of hotels, many of which are in restored *palazzi* tucked away down picturesque side streets. But, if you want to get away from it all at the end of the day, you're probably better off elsewhere.

DOMUS TIBERINA Map pp317–19 *Hotel*
☎ /fax 06 580 30 33; www.hotelseiler.com; Via in Piscinula 37; s/d €95/130; tram to Viale di Trastevere
This place has a marvellous position at the non-noisy end of Trastevere and is very close to the lovely Ponte Cestio that leads across the river to Teatro Marcello. Rooms are cosy, if twee.

> ## Signpost
> If you're staying in Trastevere, you'll find the closest sights on p108, the nearest eateries on p167 and shops on p217.

HOTEL CISTERNA Map pp317–19 *Hotel*
☎ 06 581 72 12; fax 06 581 00 91; Via della Cisterna 7-9; s/d €90/140; bus or tram to Piazza Sonnino
Hotel Cisterna is located in a quiet, pretty street around the corner from the busy Piazza Santa Maria in Trastevere, and close to all the best restaurants, cafés and night spots in the area. The rooms are unexceptional but comfortable and clean. Some of the rooms are much larger and airier than others.

HOTEL SANTA MARIA
Map pp317–19 *Hotel*
☎ 06 589 46 26; www.htlsantamaria.com; Vicolo del Piede 2; high season s/d/ste €155/207/259, low season €124/145/181; bus to Piazza Trilussa
This gorgeous place is a recently renovated, former 17th-century cloister and its 19 rooms, all with spanking new en suite bathrooms, telephone and TV, are built around a

delightful courtyard garden. It's a beautiful haven enclosed behind a protective fence in the heart of a popular area.

> ## Top Five Hotels
> - **Residenza Cellini** A romantic hideaway where the wonderful rooms are complemented by the attentive personal service (p231)
> - **Hotel de Russie** The minimalist luxury is perfect for resting your weary bones after a hard day's filming/sightseeing/shopping (p228)
> - **Hotel Bramante** Within a stone's throw of St Peter's Basilica, the timeless elegance of this historic hotel matches the charm of the surrounding streets (p236)
> - **Hotel Teatro di Pompeo** Where else can you sip your morning cappuccino in an ancient Roman theatre? (p226)
> - **Hotel Des Artistes** A haven of modestly priced class in the streets surrounding Stazione Termini (p228)

TRASTEVERE HOUSE
Map pp317–19 *B&B*
☎ /fax 06 588 37 74; trastevere.hotelinroma.com; Vicolo del Buco 7; high season s/d €60/90, with bathroom €120/130, low season s/d €40/60, with bathroom from €65/75; tram to Viale di Trastevere
This quaint little building has pretty, comfortable rooms in the heart of the old Roman quarter. Within walking distance of all the sights and close to the neighbourhood's numerous restaurants and active nightlife, the hotel nevertheless offers peace and quiet.

VILLA DELLA FONTE
Map pp317–19 *Hotel*
☎ 06 580 37 97; fax 06 580 37 96; Via della Fonte d'olio 8; s/d €95/145; tram to Viale di Trastevere
Just a jump from popular Piazza Santa Maria in Trastevere, this fully renovated building offers five charming and pristine little rooms, all with modern conveniences, including Internet access for personal computers. There's a lovely sunny garden terrace for breakfast or just dozing.

Cheap Sleeps
LA FORESTERIA ORSA MAGGIORE
Map pp308–10 *Guesthouse*
☎ 06 684 01 724; www.casainternazionaledelledonne.org; Via di San Francesco di Sales 1a; s with/without

bathroom €57/47, d/tr without bathroom per person €31/29, 8-bed dm without bathroom €21; bus to Piazza Trilussa

For women only, this lovely guest house in a beautifully restored, 16th-century convent offers 35 beds in single or multiple rooms which mostly face an internal garden, providing a peaceful stay in the most elegant surroundings. It's run by the Casa Internazionale delle Donne (International Women's House), which has its headquarters here. There is a communal room with TV, newspapers and a library. Breakfast (included in the price) and other meals are served in the beautiful garden restaurant which offers regional, ethnic and international cuisine and is usually packed full of lively women, both local and not-so. Special rates for group bookings (minimum eight women) for a stay exceeding one week.

HOTEL CARMEL Map pp317–19 *Hotel*
☎ 06 580 99 21; hotelcarmel@hotmail.com; Via Mameli 11; s/d with bathroom €70/90; bus or tram to Viale di Trastevere

Particularly good value for the price, Carmel counts a beautifully shady roof terrace and proximity to the nightlife of Trastevere among its attractions. Rooms are clean and simple and breakfast is included.

HOTEL TRASTEVERE
Map pp317–19 *Hotel*
☎ 06 581 47 13; hoteltrastevere@tiscalinet.it; Via Luciano Manara 24a-25; s/d €77/98; tram to Viale Trastevere

One of Rome's better deals, this friendly hotel overlooks Piazza San Cosimato. All nine immaculate rooms have bathrooms (with hairdryers) and TV, and most of them look out over the morning market in the square. Attractive frescoes decorate the reception and breakfast areas. They also have apartments sleeping four in the same building for €154.

SOUTHERN ROME
To enjoy the refined air of one of Rome's most sought-after residential areas, head to the Aventine. You're not so far from the

Signpost
If you're staying in southern Rome, you'll find the closest sights on p111, the nearest eateries on p171 and shops on p217.

sights of the centre, while you couldn't be better placed for escaping to the tranquil pleasures of Via Appia Antica. On the other hand, the anything-but-peaceful nightlife of Testaccio is also within easy distance.

AVENTINO – SANT'ANSELMO HOTELS
Map pp317–19 *Hotel*
☎ 06 574 35 47; www.aventinohotels.com; Piazza Sant'Anselmo 2; high season s/d €109/166, low season from €42/78; bus to Via Marmorata, metro Circo Massimo

The perfect place if you want olde worlde charm, affordable luxury and quieter surroundings, these five separate Art-Nouveau villas – each with gardens and courtyards – are situated on the largely residential and affluent Aventine Hill, but still close to the historic centre. They're ideal if you have a car, as street parking is fairly easy to find, and there are some facilities for disabled people.

NORTHERN ROME
Villa Borghese, one of central Rome's beautiful parks, is the centrepiece of this well-to-do area, which fills with office workers during the day but quietens considerably at night. Stretching further north, Via Salaria and Via Nomentana both lead out of the city, whilst the Foro Italico is dominated by the spectacular Stadio Olimpico.

Signpost
If you're staying in northern Rome, you'll find the closest sights on p122, the nearest eateries on p173 and shops on p217.

HOTEL VILLA BORGHESE
Map pp306–7 *Hotel*
☎ 06 853 00 919; hotel.villaborghese@tiscalinet.it; Via Pinciana 31; high season s/d €146/190, low season €113/157; bus to Via Pinciana

Overlooking the park of the same name, Hotel Villa Borghese is a good choice for lovers of literature as Roman writer Alberto Moravia was born and lived here. Rooms in this attractive and comfortable Art-Nouveau building range from the smallish to the grand, some have carpet, some parquet; all have the requisite mod cons. There's also an attractive garden that doubles as a summer breakfast area.

PARCO DEI PRINCIPI

Map pp306–7   *Hotel*

☎ 06 85 44 21; www.parcodeiprincipi.com; Via G Frescobaldi 5; high season s/d €400/620, low season from €380/540; bus to Via G Paisiello

This is a gorgeous place any time, but in summer it's particularly good, as it has a swimming pool with poolside waiters to serve you iced drinks in the garden and something from the barbeque. The rooms have all been redecorated and have marvellous views across the park. From the top floor you can see as far as St Peter's.

Cheap Sleeps
DOMUS AURELIA DELLE SUORE ORSOLINE

Map pp302–3   *Religious Institution*

☎ 06 63 67 84; fax 06 393 76 480; Via Aurelia 218; s/d/tr €40/62/80; metro Baldo degli Ubaldi then bus No 46 to Via Aurelia

This place is about 1km west of St Peter's Basilica. Get off the bus after it has done a steep ascent and made a sharp left turn. Prices include breakfast.

OSTELLO FORO ITALICO

Map pp302–3   *Hostel*

☎ 06 323 62 79; www.hostelbooking.com; Viale delle Olimpiadi 61; segregated dm incl breakfast & showers €16; metro Ottaviano, then bus No 32 to Foro Italico

Rome's only official youth hostel is nothing flash. It has a bar, self-service restaurant and a garden but no kitchen and bookings must be made one month in advance; otherwise you have to turn up at 10am. However, you cannot enter the dorm until 2pm and there is a midnight curfew. It's also a long way from the action.

VATICAN CITY

Although there aren't many bargains in this area, it is comparatively quiet and still close to the main sights. It is also well connected with the rest of the city. Bookings are an absolute necessity because rooms

Signpost

If you're staying in the Vatican City, you'll find the closest sights on p127, the nearest eateries on p173 and shops on p218.

are often filled with people attending conferences at the Vatican. In some cases car parking is possible, either in the street or in a nearby garage.

HOTEL ADRIATIC Map pp308–10   *Hotel*

☎ 06 688 08 080; www.adriatichotel.com; Via Vitelleschi 25; high season s/d €80/105, low season €60/80; metro Ottaviano & tram to Piazza del Risorgimento

Should the owner's ambitious plans for the large terrace come to fruition, then Hotel Adriatic will be able to boast what many higher-ranked establishments can not – a swimming pool. In the meantime, the carpeted rooms come with satellite TV and hairdryer and the five junior suites (€100 to €130) each have their own private balcony. Breakfast is not included.

HOTEL AMALIA Map pp304–5   *Hotel*

☎ 06 397 23 356; www.hotelamalia.com; Via Germanico 66; s/d €130/185; metro Ottaviano

Ideal for the Vatican and spread over five floors, Hotel Amalia offers tastefully decorated, spacious rooms with all the mod cons, including air-con. A particularly good bargain in low season when prices drop by 30%, it also has some cheaper rooms with a shared bathroom from €55. Prices include breakfast.

HOTEL BRAMANTE Map pp308–10   *Hotel*

☎ 06 688 06 426; www.hotelbramante.com; Vicolo delle Palline 24; s/d €140/197; metro Ottaviano & tram to Piazza del Risorgimento

Fashions change but class remains and this charming hotel is nothing if not classy. Tucked away behind St Peter's in a restored 16th-century building, it's a testament to the art of interior decoration. The antique furniture complements the wooden-beamed ceilings and the details are all so exactly right. It's an absolute gem.

HOTEL COLUMBUS Map pp308–10   *Hotel*

☎ 06 686 54 35; www.hotelcolumbus.net; Via della Conciliazione 33; high season s/d €200/330, low season from €100/150; bus to Piazza Pio XII

Any closer to St Peter's Basilica and you'd be bunking up with the pope. This magnificent 15th-century Renaissance palace is quiet and surprisingly homely given its history and proportions. Splendid public rooms have frescoes by Pinturicchio, and the guestrooms are modern and cosy. There's a pretty roof terrace and a delightful restaurant in the old refectory.

HOTEL FLORIDA Map p308–10 *Hotel*

☎ 06 324 18 72; fax 06 324 18 57; Via Cola di Rienzo 243; s/d €40/75, with bathroom €85/113; metro Ottaviano & tram to Piazza del Risorgimento; **P**

In this small and quiet lodging on the 2nd floor, the red carpet leads to decent-sized rooms which come with air-con included in the price (except for the rooms with a shared bathroom); breakfast, however, is not included. Discounts are available out of season and if you pay in cash. Car parking can also be arranged in a nearby garage for €15 per day.

Sleep like Caesar at Hotel Celio (p223)

HOTEL MELLINI Map pp308–10 *Hotel*

☎ 06 32 47 71; www.hotelmellini.com; Via Muzio Clementi 81; s €280, d €320-350; bus to Piazza Cavour

Situated between the Lepanto and Flaminio metro stops, Hotel Mellini has excellent facilities for disabled people, including an external lift for access from the street. Rooms are a good size and you can always relax on the roof terrace overlooking the Palazzo della Giustizia while nibbling on a little something served from the snack bar. The 5th and 6th floors are reserved for nonsmokers.

RESIDENZA DEI QUIRITI

Map pp304–5 *Hotel*

☎ 06 360 05 389; quiriti@tiscalinet.it; Via Germanico 198; high season s/d €100/125, low season €60/75; metro Ottaviano

One of a number of accommodation options in the same building, Residenza dei Quiriti is within a stone's throw of the Vatican. Situated on the 4th floor, it offers elegantly appointed rooms – ignore the fake columns which line the corridor – and a welcoming air of calm. Rooms come with air-con and all mod cons.

Cheap Sleeps

COLORS HOTEL & HOSTEL

Map pp308–10 *Hostel*

☎ 06 687 40 30; www.colorshotel.com; Via Boezio 31; dm from €18, s/d €40/65; metro Ottaviano & tram to Piazza del Risorgimento

This sunny hotel-cum-hostel is run by the folk from Enjoy Rome (see p275). It offers both dorm beds and colourful private rooms, some with private showers/toilets. It also boasts a fully equipped kitchen, laundry facilities and Internet access (€3 per hour). There is no curfew and no lock-out period.

HOTEL JOLI Map pp308–10 *Hotel*

☎ 06 324 18 93; fax 06 360 06 637; Via Cola di Rienzo 243; s/d €67/100; metro Ottaviano & tram to Piazza del Risorgimento

Families with children will like this laid-back place where the owners' kids cheerfully run around. Situated on the 6th floor, rooms have ceiling fans and some boast views of the nearby dome of St Peter's Basilica. The breakfast room doubles as a TV lounge. Book well in advance.

HOTEL LADY Map pp304–5 *Pensione*

☎ 06 324 21 12; fax 06 324 34 46; Via Germanico 198; high season s/d €72/88, d with bathroom €124, low season s/d from €36/58, with bathroom from €67/78; metro Lepanto

They don't speak much English, but the Roman couple who run this peaceful *pensione* always provide a warm welcome. Furnished with rustic antiques, the pleasant rooms – two of which have original beamed ceilings – have stunning wooden doors and the (mostly) shared bathrooms are modern and clean.

PADRI TRINITARI

Map pp308–10 *Religious Institution*

☎ 06 638 38 88; fax 06 393 66 795; Piazza Santa Maria alle Fornaci 27; s/d/tr €47/78/104; bus No 64 to Via di Porta Fabbrica

The accommodation here is of the no-frills, basic type. But it's very close to St Peter's and there is one room equipped for disabled people. Breakfast is included.

PENSIONE NAUTILUS

Map pp304–5 *Hotel*

☎ 06 324 21 18; Via Germanico 198; high season s/d €52/77, with bathroom €77/93; metro Ottaviano

On the 2nd floor, the unassuming Pensione Nautilus is a homely hotel, furnished in an old-fashioned style with heavy dark-wood furniture made to last. Rooms offer the bare essentials but are clean and perfectly adequate, although some of the 'bathrooms' are in fact just a shower stall in the corner of the bedroom. There is a small lounge/TV area. Payment is by cash only.

PENSIONE OTTAVIANO

Map pp308–10 *Hostel*

☎ 06 397 38 138; www.pensioneottaviano.com; Via Ottaviano 6; high season dm per person €18-20, d/tr €70/81; metro Ottaviano & tram to Piazza del Risorgimento

Doss Down with the Romantics

If you fancy staying in the building where the poet John Keats died, contact the Landmark Trust in the UK. Established as a charity in 1965, the trust restores and conserves a host of architectural marvels in the UK, as well as several in Italy including the 3rd-floor apartment where Keats died in Piazza di Spagna, Rome.

For further information, contact the **Landmark Trust** (☎ 01628-825 925; Shottesbrooke Maidenhead, Berkshire SL6 3SW, UK).

Well placed for the Vatican, this friendly hostel near Piazza del Risorgimento offers beds in dormitories, doubles or triples, while the TV in the reception area beams out the BBC World Service for travellers suffering from English-language deprivation. There's no curfew or lock out, the staff speak English and email access is free between 3pm and 11pm, although you'll need to sign up for it.

PENSIONE PARADISE

Map pp304–5 *Pensione*

☎ 06 360 04 331; www.pensioneparadise.com; Viale Giulio Cesare 47; high season s/d with bathroom €52/88, s/tr with shared bathroom €42/112; metro Lepanto

This modest lodging offers clean as a pin, no-frills rooms at decent rates. Depending on the season they are either coolly shaded from the sun or a bit on the dark side, but the owner is friendly and extends a warm welcome in Italian or English.

SUORE DOROTEE

Map pp308–10 *Religious Institution*

☎ 06 688 03 349; fax 06 688 03 311; Via del Gianicolo 4a; half board per person €65; bus no 64 to Lungotevere in Sassia

The sisters are located in a sea of tranquil green off a steep, winding road that leads up from the Lungotevere to the top of the Gianicolo Hill. Rooms are of the convent standard – basic, clean and functional.

Excursions

Excursions

Rome demands so much of your time and concentration that most visitors forget the city is part of the Lazio region and counts Tuscany and Umbria among its close neighbours. There's plenty on offer within a few hours of the city.

ROMAN REMINDERS

Declared a *regione* in 1934, the Lazio area has been an extension of Rome since ancient Roman times. Through the ages, the rich built their villas in the Lazio countryside and many towns developed as the fiefs of noble Roman families. Even today Romans build their weekend and holiday homes in the picturesque areas of the region.

Not far from Rome there are some hilltop towns worth visiting, including **Anagni** (p242), known for the remarkable frescoes in its cathedral, and the **Castelli Romani** (p242) in the hills just past Rome's outskirts. Nearby is the terraced town of **Palestrina** (p243), offering spectacular views from its ancient Roman sanctuary.

The ruins of Villa Adriana (Hadrian's Villa), near **Tivoli** (p244), and of the ancient-Roman port at **Ostia Antica** (p244) are both easily accessible from Rome, as is the medieval town of **Viterbo** (p245) to the north.

ETRUSCAN ESCAPES

A tour of Etruria, the ancient land of the Etruscans which extended into northern Lazio, is highly recommended. Visits to the tombs and museums at **Cerveteri** (p247) and **Tarquinia** (p248) provide an insight into Etruscan civilisation. If you have the time, a few days touring here should constitute one of your most fascinating experiences in Italy. A useful guidebook to the area, *The Etruscans*, is published by the Istituto Geografico de Agostini and has a map. If you really want to lose yourself in a poetic journey, read DH Lawrence's 'Etruscan Places' in *DH Lawrence and Italy*.

Shadows of visitors on ancient mosaics in Ostia Antica (p244)

THE LAKES & COAST

In the heat of the summer, tired and overheated visitors can head for the lakes north of Rome, including **Bracciano** (p249) and **Bolsena** (p249). The lake shores never seem to get as crowded as Lazio's beaches and their hilly, leafy environment makes them more attractive swimming destinations.

Beaches close to Rome include Fregene, the Lido di Ostia and the long stretch of dune-lined beach between Ostia and Anzio. However, they really aren't terribly inviting and the water tends to be heavily polluted. You'll need to go further south to **Sperlonga** (p250) to find cleaner and more attractive spots for a swim.

UMBRIAN UTOPIA

Heading further afield, you can do no better than a foray into two of the most attractive towns in Umbria. **Orvieto** (p250) warrants an overnight stay, as does lively **Perugia** (p252).

ANAGNI

Anagni, known as the 'city of the popes' because it was the birthplace and seat of several pontiffs during the Middle Ages, is of particular interest for its 11th-century Lombard-Romanesque **cathedral**. Its pavement, and that of its crypt, were laid in the Middle Ages by Cosmati marble workers. The crypt has an extraordinary series of vibrant, restored frescoes, painted by Benedictine monks in the 13th century. Depicting a wide range of subjects, they are considered to be a major example of medieval painting at the crucial stage of its transition from the Byzantine tradition to the achievements of Giotto.

Transport

Distance from Rome 65km

Direction Southeast

Travel Time 40 mins by car

Car Take the A1

Bus Change at Colle Ferro; COTRAL buses for Colle Ferro leave from the Anagnina stop on the Metro Linea A approximately every half-hour. From here take the bus to Anagni.

Train Take the Frosinone train (FM6) from Stazione Termini (leaving approximately every hour) and get off at Anagni-Fiuggi.

CASTELLI ROMANI

Just past the periphery of Rome are the Colli Albani (Alban Hills) and the 13 towns of the Castelli Romani. A summer resort area for wealthy Romans since the days of the Roman Empire, its towns were mainly founded by popes and patrician families. **Castelgandolfo** and **Frascati** are perhaps the best known; the former is the summer residence of the pope and the latter is famous for its crisp white wine. The other towns are Monte Porzio Catone, Montecompatri, Rocca Priora, Colonna, Rocca di Papa, Grottaferrata, Marino, Albano Laziale, Ariccia, Genzano and Nemi.

The area has numerous villas, including the spectacular 16th-century **Villa Aldobrandini**, designed by Giacomo della Porta and built by Carlo Maderno, which has a beautiful garden. Just outside Frascati is the site of the ancient city of **Tusculum**. Imposing and impregnable, Tusculum remained independent until 380 BC, when it came under Roman domination. Today scant evidence of the city remains. There is a small amphitheatre, the remains of a villa and a stretch of ancient Roman road leading up to the city.

At Grottaferrata there's a 15th-century *abbazia* (**abbey**), founded in the 11th century and home to a congregation of Greek monks. There is also a museum.

Nemi is worth a visit to see the pretty **Lago di Nemi** in a volcanic crater. In ancient times there was an important sanctuary beside the lake, where the goddess Diana was worshipped. Today very little remains of this massive temple complex but it is possible to see the niche walls of what was once an arcade portico. New excavations at the site have just started.

Transport

Distance from Rome 30km

Direction Southeast

Travel Time 30 mins

Car It is best to tour this area by car; you can see most of the more interesting sights on an easy day trip from Rome.

Bus Most of the towns of the Castelli Romani are accessible by COTRAL bus from Rome's Anagnina station on Metro Linea A. Access between them, though, is well-nigh impossible.

Train Trains (FM4 line) leave from Stazione Termini for Frascati, Castelgandolfo and Albano Laziale, from where you can catch a bus to Nemi.

The incongruous-looking building at the edge of the lake, near the ruins of the temple, has an interesting story attached to it. It was built by Mussolini to house two ancient Roman boats (one 73m, the other 71m long), which were recovered from the bottom of the lake when it was partly drained between 1927 and 1932. The official story is that retreating German troops burned the ships on 1 June 1944. Locals tell a different story, but you'll have to go there to find out!

Sights & Information

Abbey (☎ 06 945 93 09; Viale San Nilo, Grottaferrata; admission free; ✆ 8.30am-noon & 4.30-6pm Tue-Sat, 8.30-10am & 4.30-6pm Sun)

Tourist Office (☎ 06 942 03 31; Piazzale Marconi 1, Frascati; ✆ 8am-2pm Mon-Sat, plus 3.30-6.30pm Tue-Fri)

Villa Aldobrandini Frascati (☎ 06 942 03 31; admission by permit available from the tourist office)

Eating & Sleeping

B&B Accommodation (☎ 06 76 81 70; www.promonetonline.it/b&b)

Trattoria la Sirena del Lago (☎ 06 936 80 20; Via del Plebiscito 26, Nemi) Right on the edge of a cliff overlooking the lake, this delightful trattoria offers simple but excellent meals.

PALESTRINA

Palestrina is one of the many neglected places of interest around Rome. A pretty, sleepy place, the town is dominated by the massive **Santuario della Fortuna Primigenia**. Built by the ancient Romans on a series of terraces on the slope of Monte Ginestro, the sanctuary was topped by a circular temple with a statue of Fortuna Primigenia, the ancient goddess believed to determine the destiny of children, on the top. On a clear day the view from the sanctuary is sensational.

The 17th-century **Palazzo Colonna Barberini** was built on the sanctuary site and is now home to the **Museo Nazionale Archeologico Prenestino**. Situated at the highest point of town, the museum houses an important collection of Roman artefacts and is one of Lazio's best. Exhibits include Etruscan remains from the area, and Roman tablets, artefacts and statues. Of particular interest is the spectacular **Nile mosaic**, a masterpiece of Hellenistic art, which came from the most sacred part of the temple (where the cathedral with its Romanesque belfry now stands). It depicts the Nile in flood from Ethiopia to Alexandria.

Apart from its historical and archaeological importance, Palestrina is also renowned for being the birthplace of the 16th-century choral composer, Giovanni Pierluigi da Palestrina. Considered one of the all-time greatest composers of liturgical music, Pierluigi's former home, the **Casa di Palestrina**, is now a museum and important music library. Craft-lovers can purchase locally produced beaten copper work in the shape of shells and 'Palestrina point' embroidery.

Transport

Distance from Rome 35km

Direction East

Travel Time 45 mins

Car Take Via Prenestina (S155).

Bus COTRAL bus (€2; 30 mins; every half-hour) from the Anagnina stop on Metro Linea A. At Palestrina, you can either walk uphill to the Santuario or take the small local bus.

Sights & Information

Museo Nazionale Archeologico Prenestino (☎ 06 953 81 00; Piazzadella Cortina; admission €4.15; ✆ 9am-8pm, shorter hrs in winter)

Tourist Office (☎ 06 957 31 76; Piazza Santa Maria degli Angeli 2; ✆ 9.30am-1pm & 3.30-5.30pm)

Casa di Palestrina (admission €4.15; ✆ 9.30am-12.30pm Tue-Sun)

Detour: Antonello Colonna

If you're driving, you might like to do as many Italians do and detour to Labico, to lunch at **Antonello Colonna** (☎ 06 951 00 32; Via Roma 89), one of Lazio's best restaurants. It's definitely not cheap, but it's run (and named after) one of the top chefs in the country.

TIVOLI

Set on a hill by the Aniene river, Tivoli was a resort town of the Romans and became popular as a summer playground for the rich during the Renaissance. While the majority of tourists are attracted by the terraced gardens and fountains of the **Villa d'Este**, the ruins of the spectacular **Villa Adriana**, built by the Roman Emperor Hadrian, are far more interesting.

Emperor Hadrian's summer residence, Villa Adriana, was built between AD 118 and 134. It was one of the largest and most sumptuous villas in the Roman Empire. A model near the entrance gives you some idea of the scale of the massive complex, which you'll need several hours to explore.

Hadrian travelled widely and was a keen architect, and parts of the villa were inspired by buildings he had seen around the world. The massive **Pecile**, through which you enter, was a reproduction of a building in Athens. The **Canopo** is a copy of the sanctuary of Serapis near Alexandria, with a long canal of water, originally surrounded by Egyptian statues, representing the Nile. Highlights of the excavations include the fish pond encircled by an underground gallery, where Hadrian took his summer walks, and the emperor's private retreat, the **Teatro Marittimo**, on an island which could be reached only by a retractable bridge over an artificial pool. There are also nymphaeums, temples and barracks, and a museum displaying the latest discoveries from ongoing excavations. Archaeologists have found features such as a heated bench with steam pipes under the sand and a network of subterranean service passages for horses and carts.

There's a sense of faded splendour about Villa d'Este. This former Benedictine convent was transformed by Lucrezia Borgia's son, Ippolito d'Este, into a sumptuous pleasure palace with a breathtaking formal garden full of elaborate fountains and pools in 1550. From 1865 to 1886 the villa was home to Franz Liszt and inspired his composition *Fountains of the Villa d'Este*.

The Mannerist frescoes in the villa are worth a fleeting glance but it's the garden you come for – terraces with water-spouting gargoyles, shady pathways and spectacular fountains powered solely by gravitational force. One fountain once played the organ, another imitated the call of birds. Don't miss the Rometta fountain, which has reproductions of the landmarks of Rome.

Sights & Information

Tourist Office (☎ 0774 31 12 49; Largo Garibaldi; 8.30am-2.30pm & 3-6pm Tue-Thu, 8.30am-2.30pm Fri-Sat)

Villa Adriana (☎ 0774 53 02 03; admission €6.50; 9am-1hr before sunset)

Villa d'Este (☎ 0774 31 20 70; Piazza Trento; admission €6.50; 8.30am-6.45pm Tue-Sun Apr-Sep, 8.30am-4pm Tue-Sun Oct-Mar)

Transport

Distance from Rome 30km

Direction East

Travel Time 30 mins-1hr

Car Take the Rome-L'Aquila autostrada (A24).

Bus COTRAL buses depart from Ponte Mammolo station on Metro Linea B at least every 20 minutes, stopping at Villa Adriana along the way. Local bus No 4 goes to Villa Adriana from Tivoli's Piazza Garibaldi.

Train Trains depart from Tiburtina (FM2 line); the journey takes 40 mins-1hr.

OSTIA ANTICA

The Romans founded this port city at the mouth of the River Tiber in the 4th century BC and it became a strategically important centre for defence and trade, populated by merchants, sailors and slaves. The ruins of the city provide a fascinating contrast to the ruins at Pompeii, which was a resort town for the wealthy classes. Barbarian invasions and the outbreak of malaria led to the city's eventual abandonment, and it slowly became buried – up to 2nd-floor level – under river silt, which explains the excellent state of preservation of the remains. Pope Gregory IV re-established the town in the 9th century AD.

The **ruins** are quite spread out and you will need a few hours to see them all. The clearly discernible remains of restaurants, laundries, shops, houses and public meeting places give a good impression of everyday life in a working Roman town. The main thoroughfare, the **Decumanus Maximus**, runs over 1km from the city's entrance (the Porta Romana) to the Porta Marina, which originally led to the sea. Behind the restored **theatre**, built by Agrippa and later enlarged to hold 3000 people, is the **Piazzale delle Corporazioni**, the offices of Ostia's merchant guilds, which display well-preserved mosaics depicting the different interests of each business.

The 2nd-century **Casa di Diana** is a pristine example of ancient Rome's high-density housing, built when space was minimal. Nearby the **Thermopolium** bears a striking resemblance to a modern bar.

Ostia had several baths complexes, including the **Baths of the Forum**, which were also equipped with a roomful of stone toilets – the *forica* – still pretty much intact.

Continue along the Via dei Dipinti in order to reach the **museum**, which houses statuary and sarcophagi excavated on-site.

Sights & Information

Ruins (☎ 06 563 58 099; Viale dei Romagnoli 717; admission €4.20; ☾ 9am-7pm Tue-Sun Feb-Oct, 9am-5pm Tue-Sun Nov-Mar)

Museum (☎ 06 565 00 22; admission €4.20; ☾ 9am-4pm, till 4.30pm in summer, 1.30pm in winter)

Transport

Distance from Rome 25km

Direction Southwest

Travel Time 30-40 mins

Car Take Via del Mare, a fast superstrada that runs parallel to Via Ostiense.

Train Metro Linea B to Piramide or Magliana, then the Ostia Lido train from Stazione Porta San Paolo (next to the Metro station). Trains leave about every 30 minutes.

VITERBO

Founded by the Etruscans and eventually taken over by Rome, Viterbo developed into an important medieval centre, and in the 13th century became the residence of the popes.

Papal elections were held in the town's Gothic Palazzo Papale and stories abound about the antics of impatient townspeople anxious for a decision. In 1271, when the college of cardinals had failed to elect a new pope after three years of deliberation, the Viterbesi locked them in a turreted hall of the palazzo, removed its roof and put the cardinals on a starvation diet. Only then did they manage to elect Gregory X.

Although badly damaged by bombing during WWII, Viterbo remains Lazio's best-preserved medieval town and is a pleasant base for exploring northern Lazio. For travellers with less time, Viterbo is an easy day trip from Rome.

Apart from its historical appeal, Viterbo is famous for its therapeutic hot springs. The best known is the sulphurous Bulicame pool, mentioned by Dante in his *Divine Comedy*.

The main square, Piazza del Plebiscito, is enclosed by 15th- and 16th-century palaces, the most imposing of which is the **Palazzo dei Priori**, with an elegant 17th-century fountain in its courtyard. Many rooms are decorated with frescoes, notably the Sala Reggia, which is decorated with a late-Renaissance fresco depicting the myths and history of Viterbo.

The 12th-century **cathedral** was rebuilt in the 14th century to a Gothic design, although the interior has just been restored to its original Romanesque simplicity.

Transport

Distance from Rome 65km

Direction Northwest

Travel Time 1½ hrs

Car Take Via Cassia (S2).

Bus Several buses leave Rome daily from the Saxa Rubra station on the Ferrovia Roma–Nord train line. The intercity bus station is at Riello, a few kilometres northwest of Viterbo, but buses also stop at the Porta Romana and Porta Fiorentina entrances to the city. If you find yourself at Riello, catch city bus No 11 into Viterbo.

Train Direct, if slow, FS trains depart hourly from Rome's Ostiense, Trastevere and San Pietro stations (FM3 line), stopping at both Porta Romana (closer to the sights) and Porta Fiorentina.

Also on the piazza is the **Palazzo Papale**, built in the 13th century with the aim of enticing the popes away from Rome. Its beautiful, graceful loggia (colonnade) is in the early Gothic style. The part facing the valley collapsed in the 14th century but the bases of some of the columns remain. The hall, the **Sala del Conclave**, in which papal conclaves were held, is at the top of the steps. Admission is included with your ticket to the cathedral museum and opening times are the same as the cathedral's.

Nearby, Romanesque **Chiesa di Santa Maria Nuova** was restored after bomb damage in WWII. The cloisters, which are believed to date from an earlier period, are worth a visit.

Via San Pellegrino takes you through the medieval quarter into **Piazza San Pellegrino**. The extremely well-preserved buildings that enclose this tiny piazza comprise the finest group of medieval buildings in Italy.

At the old northern entrance to the town is the **Chiesa di San Francesco**, a Gothic building that was restored after suffering serious bomb damage during WWII. The church contains the tombs of two popes: Clement IV (died 1268) and Adrian V (died 1276). Both are lavishly decorated, notably that of Adrian, which features Cosmati work, a mosaic technique used in the 12th and 13th centuries.

There's no shortage of museums in town. The **Museo della Macchina di Santa Rosa** documents the history of the festival that takes place on 3 September each year, when the Viterbesi parade a 30m-high tower around the town.

The **Museo Civico** is housed in the restored convent of the church of Santa Maria della Verità, just outside the Porta della Verità, on the eastern side of town. Among the works in the museum are Iron-Age Etruscan artefacts, a lovely Pietà by Sebastiano del Piombo and a Roman sarcophagus which is said to be the tomb of Galiana, a beautiful and virtuous woman murdered by a Roman baron after she refused his advances.

Detour: Thermal Springs

Viterbo's thermal springs are about 3km west of town. They were used by both the Etruscans and the Romans, and the latter built large bath complexes of which virtually nothing remains. Travellers wanting to take a cure or relax in the hot sulphur baths will find the **Terme dei Papi** (☎ 0761 35 01; Strada Bagni 12; ☷ daily year-round; pool open Wed-Mon only) the easiest to reach. Take city bus No 2 from the bus station in Piazza Martiri d'Ungheria, near-ish the APT tourist office. Admission to the pool fed by the thermal springs costs €12.90 per day; specialist and therapeutic mud and water treatments cost much more and must be booked in advance.

Sights & Information

Cathedral (☎ 0761 32 54 62; Piazza San Lorenzo; admission €2.60; ☷ 9am-12.30pm & 3.30-6pm)

Chiesa di San Francesco (Piazza San Francesco; admission free; ☷ 8am-noon & 3.30-7pm)

Chiesa di Santa Maria Nuova (Piazza Santa Maria Nuova)

Museo Civico (☎ 0761 34 82 75; Piazza Crispi; admission €3.10; ☷ 9am-7pm Tue-Sun)

Museo della Macchina di Santa Rosa (☎ 0761 34 51 57; Via San Pellegrino; admission €1.05; ☷ 10am-1pm & 4-8pm Wed-Sun)

Palazzo dei Priori (Piazza del Plebiscito; admission free; ☷ 9am-1pm & 2-7pm)

Province of Viterbo Tourist Information (☎ 0761 29 10 03; www.apt.viterbo.it; Piazza dell'Oratorio 2)

Sala del Concave (Palazzo Papale; included in cathedral admission; ☷ 9am-12.30pm & 3.30-6pm)

Tourist Office (☎ 0761 30 47 95; infoviterbo@apt.viterbo.it; Piazza San Carluccio; ☷ 9am-1pm Mon-Sat, sporadic afternoon openings)

Eating

Il Labirinto (☎ 0761 30 70 26; Via San Lorenzo 46; pizzas €6.20, pasta €6.20, mains €4.65-8.25) Typical Roman pasta dishes are good here, but the pizzas and excellent desserts also draw the crowds.

Il Richiastro (☎ 0761 22 80 09; Via della Marrocca 18; mains €25.30) Hearty food based on ancient Roman recipes; outside tables in summer.

Sleeping

Hotel Roma (☎ 0761 22 72 74; fax 0761 30 55 07; Via della Cava 26; s/d without bathroom €40/57, with bathroom €41/60; P) One step up from budget accommodation.

Hotel Tuscia (☎ 0761 34 44 00; fax 0761 34 59 76; Via Cairoli 41; s/d up to €55/86) Comfortable accommodation.

CERVETERI

Cerveteri, ancient Caere, was one of the most important commercial centres in the Mediterranean from the 7th to the 5th century BC. In 358 BC the city was annexed to Rome and the inhabitants granted Roman citizenship. This colonisation of the city resulted in the absorption of the Etruscan culture into Roman culture and its eventual disappearance.

After the fall of the Empire, the spread of malaria and repeated Saracen invasions caused further decline. In the 13th century there was a mass exodus from the city to the nearby town of Ceri, and Caere became Caere Vetus ('Old Caere'), from which its current name derives. The first tentative archaeological explorations in the area began in the 19th century.

The main attraction here is the atmospheric **Necropoli di Banditaccia** and its remarkable *tumoli* – mounds of earth with carved stone bases – in which the Etruscans entombed their dead. The *tumoli* are laid out in the form of a town, with streets, squares and terraces. The best example is the 4th-century-BC **Tomba dei Rilievi**, decorated with painted reliefs of household items.

Treasures taken from the tombs can be seen in the Vatican Museums and Villa Giulia in Rome, and also at the **Museo Nazionale di Cerveteri** in the town centre.

To get to the main necropolis area, take the (infrequent) local bus from the main square. Otherwise it is a pleasant 2km walk west from the town.

Transport

Distance from Rome 35km

Direction Northeast

Travel Time 40 mins by car; 1¼ hrs by bus

Car Take either Via Aurelia (S1) or the Civitavecchia autostrada (A12) and come off at the Cerveteri-Ladispoli exit.

Bus COTRAL bus leaves from outside the Lepanto stop on Metro Linea A every half-hour. A regional ticket (BIRG; €4.50) covers the return bus journey, public transport in Cerveteri and the metro and buses in Rome.

Train Trains depart from Termini and Ostiense (FM5 line) and take about 30-45 mins.

Sights & Information

Museo Nazionale di Cerveteri (☎ 06 994 13 54; Piazza S Maria; admission free; ☾ 9am-7pm Tue-Sun)

Necropoli di Banditaccia (☎ 06 994 00 01; Via del Necropoli; admission €4.20; ☾ 9am-7pm Tue-Sun summer, 9am-4pm Tue-Sun winter)

Tourist Office (☎ 06 995 51 971; Piazza Risorgimento 19)

Eating

Antica Locanda Le Ginestre (☎ 06 994 06 72; Piazza Santa Maria 5) Many Romans make the trip to Cerveteri just to eat at this delightful place.

Etruscan Mysteries

Much of the fascination of the Etruscans comes from the fact that so much about this civilisation remains unknown. The jury is still out as to whether the Etruscans were native to Italy, or whether they migrated from somewhere in Asia Minor. They did, however, leave a wealth of archaeological remains and had an enormous influence on Roman culture.

The boundaries of Etruria were the River Arno in the north, the Tiber in the south and the Mediterranean Sea. Many of the major sites are in Tuscany but some, most notably Tarquinia, Cerveteri, Veio, Viterbo and Tuscania, are in Lazio. Among the surviving architectural treasures are the foundations of temples and the alluring Etruscan cemeteries.

The grandest tombs resembled houses, even down to their arrangement in 'streets'. The wealthy dead were buried in spectacular portrait sarcophagi; the walls were painted with happy scenes of the afterlife, which resembled the best aspects of this existence (the Etruscans obviously looked forward to an eternity of parties and hunting). They also packed suitable goods to ensure a pleasant afterlife, including bucchero tableware, engraved mirrors and gold jewellery.

The Etruscans also excelled in bronzework, surviving examples of which include the Capitoline Wolf (originally minus the twins) and the Mars of Todi, now in the Vatican Museums.

The deep-seated ambivalence the Romans felt towards the Etruscans is reflected in their legends. Of the three Etruscan kings who ruled Rome, Servius Tullius is credited with building the first walls and organising the political and military systems, while the last, Tarquinius Superbus, was expelled from Rome after his son raped a nobleman's wife.

The Romans did adopt many Etruscan civil and religious customs, including the study of the flight of birds and the entrails of sacrificed victims to determine the will of the gods, and the *fasces*, an axe inserted into a bundle of rods which symbolised the State's powers of corporal and capital punishment. The *fasces* was also adopted as a symbol by Mussolini.

TARQUINIA

Believed to have been founded in the 12th century BC, and home of the Tarquin kings who ruled Rome before the creation of the Roman Republic, Tarquinia was an important economic and political centre of the Etruscan League. The town has a small medieval centre with a good Etruscan museum but the major attractions here are the **painted tombs** of the burial grounds.

The 15th-century Palazzo Vitelleschi houses the **Museo Nazionale Tarquiniese**, a significant collection of Etruscan treasures, including frescoes that were removed from the tombs. There is a beautiful terracotta frieze of winged horses, taken from the Ara della Regina temple. Numerous sarcophagi found in the tombs are also on display.

The famous painted tombs are at the **necropolis**, a 15- to 20-minute walk away (get directions from the museum). Almost 6000 tombs have been excavated, of which 60 are painted, but only a handful are open to the public. Excavation of the tombs started in the 15th century and continues today. Unfortunately, exposure to air and human interference has led to serious deterioration in many tombs and they are now enclosed and maintained at constant temperatures. The painted tombs can be seen only through glass partitions.

If you have time, wander through the pleasant medieval town; several churches are worth a look.

Transport

Distance from Rome 70km

Direction Northwest

Travel Time 1½ hrs

Car Take the autostrada for Civitavecchia then Via Aurelia (S1).

Bus COTRAL buses leave from outside the Lepanto stop on Metro Linea A approximately every hour.

Train Trains depart from Termini and Ostiense (FM5 line) and take about 1¼-1½ hrs.

Detour: Tarxuna

If you have a car, you can get to the remains of the Etruscan acropolis of Tarxuna, on the crest of Civita Hill near Tarquinia. There is little evidence of the ancient city, apart from a few limestone blocks that once formed part of the city walls, since the Etruscans generally used wood to build their temples and houses. However, a large temple, the **Ara della Regina**, has been excavated.

People waiting on Piazza Cavour in Tarquinia

Sights & Information

Museo Nazionale Tarquiniese (☎ 0766 85 60 36; Piazza Cavour; admission including the necropolis €6.20; 🕒 9am-7pm Tue-Sun)

Necropolis (☎ 0766 85 63 08; 🕒 9am-1hr before sunset Tue-Sun)

Tourist Office (☎ 0766 85 63 84; info@tarquinia@apt.it; Piazza Cavour 1; 🕒 8am-2pm Mon-Sat)

Sleeping

Hotel all'Olivo (☎ 0766 85 73 18; info@hotel -allolivo.it; Via Togliatti 13-15; s/d €52/78) A 10-minute walk downhill from the medieval centre; prices include breakfast.

Hotel San Marco (☎ 0766 84 22 34; Piazza Cavour 10; s/d €52/67) Pleasant rooms in the medieval section of town, near the museum.

LAGO DI BRACCIANO

Pretty Lago di Bracciano is easily accessible by public transport. Visit the **Castello Orsini-Odelscalchi** in the medieval town of Bracciano or head straight to the lake for a swim. On the northern edge of the lake is the picturesque town of **Trevignano Romano**, with its lovely waterfront and modest beach.

Sights & Information

Castello Orsini-Odelscalchi (☎ 06 998 04 348; Piazza Castello, Bracciano; admission free; 🕒 10am-noon & 3-5pm Tue-Sun)

www.lakebracciano.com

www.trevignanoromano.it

Eating

La Tavernetta (☎ 06 999 90 26; Via Garibaldi 62, Trevignano Romano; meals from €15.50) This rustic, family-run restaurant serves simple but tasty fare.

Trattoria del Castello (☎ 06 998 04 339; Piazza Castello, Bracciano) This has excellent food; try the *funghi porcini*.

Vino e Camino (☎ 06 998 03 433; Piazza Mazzini 11, Bracciano; mains €20-30) A wine bar with good wine and food.

Transport

Distance from Rome 40km

Direction Northwest

Travel Time 1hr

Car Take Via Braccianense (S493) for Bracciano, or Via Cassia (S2) and then follow the signs to Trevignano Romano.

Bus COTRAL buses depart roughly every hour from outside the Lepanto metro station.

Train Trains from Rome's Ostiense, Trastevere and San Pietro stations bound for Viterbo (FM3 line) stop at Bracciano.

LAGO DI BOLSENA

This elliptical lake, close to Viterbo, is a good day trip from Rome. The town of Bolsena was the scene of a miracle in 1263 – a doubting priest was convinced of transubstantiation when blood dripped from the host he was holding during a mass. To commemorate the event Pope Urban IV founded the festival of Corpus Domini and each June the townspeople hold a 3km procession and decorate the town with flowers.

Of interest in the medieval quarter are the 11th-century **Chiesa di Santa Cristina** and the **catacombs** beneath it. Just before the entrance to the catacombs is the **altare del miracolo**, where the miracle occurred. The catacombs contain tombs that are still sealed.

Castello Monaldeschi in the medieval quarter has an interesting history. The original structure dates from between the 13th and 16th centuries. However, it was pulled down by the locals in 1815 to prevent it from being taken by Luciano Bonaparte. It now houses a museum and a tourist office.

Detour: Montefiascone

If you're touring the area by car, it's worth heading on via the S2 to Montefiascone, which is noted for its white wine, Est, Est, Est. Local history has it that on his travels a monk wrote 'est' (it is) to indicate the places where the wine was good. On arriving at Montefiascone he was so overcome by the quality of the wine that he exclaimed 'Est! Est! Est!'. Visit the cathedral and the nearby Romanesque church of Sant' Andrea.

Sights & Information

Castello Monaldeschi (☎ 0761 79 86 30;
🕓 9.30am-1.30pm & 4-8pm Tue-Fri in summer,
9.30am-1.30pm Tue-Fri in winter, 10am-1pm & 3-6pm
Sat & Sun year-round)

Tourist Office (☎ 0761 79 99 23; Castello Monaldeschi)

Sleeping

Hotel Eden (☎ 0761 79 90 15; fax 0761 79 60 56; Via
Cassia; s/d €46.50/62) This hotel is by the lake.

Villaggio Camping Lido (☎ 0761 79 92 58; sites per
adult/child/tent €7.75/4.15/5.15) This large camp site
1.5km from Bolsena has a bar, restaurant and bungalow
facilities.

Transport

Distance from Rome 100km

Direction North

Travel Time 1½ hrs

Car Take Via Cassia (S2) to Viterbo and follow the
signs from the Riello bus station.

Bus In summer COTRAL runs a direct service from the
Saxa Rubra stop on Ferrovia Roma-Nord, otherwise
change at Viterbo. Buses for Bolsena from Viterbo
depart from the town's Riello bus station (Sunday
there's only one; departs 9am, returns around 6pm).

Train From Rome's Ostiense, Trastevere or San Pietro
stations (FM3 line) to Viterbo, then the bus to Bolsena.

SPERLONGA

The small coastal town of Sperlonga is a good destination for a weekend break, with two long,
sandy beaches on either side of a rocky promontory jutting into the sea. The town is divided
into two parts. Medieval Sperlonga Alta is on top of the promontory and, with its whitewashed
buildings, seems more Greek than Italian. Modern Sperlonga Bassa is at sea level.

Other than the beach, the main attraction is the **Grotta di Tiberio**, a cave with a circular pool
used by the emperor Tiberius. The remains of his villa are in front of the cave. Statues found
in the cave are housed in the nearby museum.

Sights & Information

Grotta di Tiberio (admission €2.60; 🕓 9am-7pm
summer, 9am-4pm winter)

Eating & Sleeping

Agli Archi (☎ 0771 5 43 00; Via Ottaviano 17; full meals
€45) This restaurant specialises in fish and there are a lot of
dishes to choose from.

Albergo Major (☎ 0771 54 92 44; Via Romita I4; low
season s/d €56.80/67.15, high season half-board per
person €77.50) Prices include access to sun lounges and
umbrellas on the private beach area.

Lido da Rocco (☎ 0771 5 44 93; Via Spiaggia Angelo 22)
Great for snacks on the beach.

Transport

Distance from Rome 120km

Direction Southeast

Travel Time 1½ hrs

Car Take Via Pontina (S148) from EUR going south
and follow signs to Terracina. From Terracina it's a
short drive on the S213.

Train & Bus Take a diretto regional train (not the
Intercity) from Stazione Termini towards Naples
and get off at Fondi. From here take the connecting
COTRAL bus (or a taxi) to Sperlonga. The return bus
leaves from the main piazza at the top of the hill in
the centre of Sperlonga Alta.

ORVIETO

Tourists are drawn to Orvieto by the magnificent cathedral, one of Italy's finest Gothic buildings. The town rests on top of a craggy cliff and although medieval Orvieto is the magnet,
Etruscan tombs and the city's underground chambers testify to the area's antiquity.

Trains pull in at Orvieto Scalo and from here you can catch bus No 1 up to the old town
or board the cable car to take you up the steep hill to **Piazza Cahen**. But call in first at the small
ATC tourist office near the station, where you can get maps and the CartaOrvieto Unica card,
which allows you limited free parking or bus and cable car transport. From the cable car and

bus station at the top of the hill, walk straight along Corso Cavour, turning left into Via del Duomo to reach the cathedral. There's plenty of parking space in Piazza Cahen and in several designated areas outside the old city walls.

A century-old cable car connects Piazza Cahen with the train station; carriages leave every 15 minutes from 7.15am to 8.30pm daily (€0.65 or €0.85 including the bus from Piazza Cahen to Piazza del Duomo). Bus No 1 also runs up to the old town from the train station (€0.65). Once in Orvieto, the easiest way to see the city

Transport

Distance from Rome 80km

Direction North

Travel Time 1½ hrs

Car The city is on the A1.

Bus SIRA runs a daily service to and from Rome.

Train Hourly trains depart from Rome's Stazione Termini.

is on foot, although ATC bus A connects Piazza Cahen with Piazza del Duomo and bus B runs to Piazza della Repubblica.

Little can prepare you for the visual feast that is the **cathedral**. Pope Urban IV ordered that the cathedral be built, following the Miracle of Bolsena in 1263. Started in 1290, this remarkable edifice was originally planned in the Romanesque style but, as work proceeded and architects changed, Gothic features were incorporated into the structure. The black and white marble banding of the main body of the church is overshadowed by the rich rainbow colours of the facade. A harmonious blend of mosaic and sculpture, plain stone and dazzling colour, it has been likened to a giant outdoor altar screen.

The building took 30 years to plan and three centuries to complete. It was probably started by Perugia's Fra Bevignate and continued over the years by Lorenzo Maitani (responsible for Florence's cathedral), Andrea Pisano, his son Nino Pisano, Andrea Orcagna and Michele Sammichelli.

The **facade** appears almost unrelated to the main body of the church. The three huge doorways are separated by fluted columns and the gables are decorated with mosaics that come to life in the light of the setting sun. The great bronze doors, the work of Emilio Greco, were added in the 1960s.

Inside, Luca Signorelli's fresco cycle *The Last Judgement* shimmers with life. Look for it to the right of the altar in the **Cappella di San Brizio**. Signorelli began work on the series in 1499, and Michelangelo is said to have taken inspiration from it. Indeed, to some, Michelangelo's masterpiece runs a close second to Signorelli's work. The **Cappella del Corporale** houses the blood-stained altar linen of the miracle, preserved in a silver reliquary decorated by artists of the Sienese school. The walls feature frescoes depicting the miracle, painted by Ugolino di Prete Ilario.

Next to the cathedral is the **Museo dell'Opera del Duomo**, which has been closed for restoration. Check at the tourist office to see if it has reopened. **Museo di Emilio Greco** displays a collection of modern pieces donated by the creator of the cathedral's bronze doors. Around the corner in the Palazzo Papale, you can see Etruscan antiquities in the **Museo Archeologico Nazionale**. The **Museo Claudio Faina e Civico**, opposite the cathedral, houses artefacts found near Piazza Cahen in tombs dating back to the 6th century BC. There are guided tours at 11am and 4pm (3pm October to March) and an interactive trip for kids.

You can also head northwest along Via del Duomo to Corso Cavour to **Torre del Moro**. Climb all 250 steps for sweeping views of the city. Back on ground level, continue west to **Piazza della Repubblica**, to the 12th-century **Chiesa di Sant'Andrea** and its curious decagonal bell tower. The piazza, once Orvieto's Roman forum, is at the heart of what remains of the medieval city.

North of Corso Cavour, the 12th-century Romanesque-Gothic **Palazzo del Popolo** presides over the piazza of the same name. At the northwestern end of town is the 11th-century **Chiesa di San Giovenale** on the Piazza Giovenale, its interior brightened by 13th- and 14th-century frescoes.

Standing watch at the town's easternmost tip is the 14th-century **La Rocca**, part of which is now a public garden. To the north of the fortress is the **Pozzo di San Patrizio** (St Patrick's Well), which was sunk in 1527 on the orders of Pope Clement VII. More than 60m deep, it is lined by two spiral staircases for water-bearing mules.

Excursions – Orvieto

For a trip back in time, **Orvieto Underground** is a fascinating tour of the city's underground caves. These were still in use well into last century; the cool air meant that food could be safely stored before the advent of the fridge. They even doubled up as air-raid shelters in WWII. Tours (with English-speaking guides) leave from in front of the tourist office on Piazza del Duomo at 11am, 12.15pm, 4pm and 5.15pm.

Sights & Information

Cappella del Corporale (admission free; ☸ 7.30am-12.45pm & 2.30-7.15pm in summer, shorter hrs in winter, closed during Mass)

Cappella di San Brizio (admission €3; ☸ 10am-12.45pm year-round, plus 2.30-7.15pm Apr-Sep, 2.30-6.15pm Mar & Oct, 2.30-5.15pm Mon-Sat, 2.30-5.45pm Sun Nov-Feb, closed during Mass)

Cathedral (☎ 0763 34 11 67; Piazza del Duomo; admission free; ☸ 7.30am-12.45pm year-round, plus 2.30-7.15pm Apr-Sep, 2.30-6.15pm Mar & Oct, 2.30-5.15pm Nov-Feb)

Chiesa di San Giovenale (Piazza Giovenale; admission free; ☸ 8am-12.30pm & 3.30-6pm)

Chiesa di Sant'Andrea (Piazza della Repubblica; admission free; ☸ 8.30am-12.30pm & 3.30-7.30pm)

Museo Archeologico Nazionale (☎ /fax 0763 34 10 39; Palazzo Papale, Piazza del Duomo; admission €2; ☸ 8.30am-7.30pm)

Museo Claudio Faina e Civico (☎ 0763 34 15 11; www.museofaina.it; Piazza del Duomo 29; adult/concession €4.50/3; ☸ 9.30am-6pm Apr-Sep, 10am-5pm Tue-Sun Oct-Mar)

Museo dell'Opera del Duomo (☎ 0763 34 24 77; Palazzo Soliano, Piazza del Duomo)

Museo di Emilio Greco (☎ 0763 34 46 05; fax 0763 34 46 64; Palazzo Soliano, Piazza del Duomo; adult/child €2.50/1.50; ☸ 10.30am-1pm & 2-6.30pm Tue-Sun Apr-Sep, 10.30am-1pm & 2-5.30pm Tue-Sun Oct-Mar)

Orvieto Underground (☎ 0763 34 48 91; speleotecnici@libero.it; Parco delle Grotte; admission €5.50; ☸ 11am-6pm)

Pozzo di San Patrizio (☎ 0763 34 37 68; fax 0763 34 46 64; Viale Sangallo; adult/concession €3.50/2.50; ☸ 10am-6.45pm Apr-Sep, 10am-5.45pm Oct-Mar)

Torre del Moro (☎ 0763 34 45 67; Corso Cavour; adult/child €2.60/1.85; ☸ 10am-8pm May-Aug, 10am-7pm Mar, Apr, Sep & Oct, 10.30am-1pm & 2.30-5pm Nov-Feb)

Tourist Office (☎ 0763 34 17 72; info@iat.orvieto.tr.it; Piazza del Duomo 24; ☸ 8.15am-1.50pm & 4-7pm Mon-Fri, 10am-1pm & 4-7pm Sat, 10am-noon & 4-6pm Sun & hols)

Eating

Cantina Foresi (☎ /fax 0763 3 46 11; itforesi@tin.it; Piazza del Duomo 2) Delicious, cheap snacks made with the finest local products.

Hosteria Nonnamelia (☎ 0763 34 24 02; Via del Duomo 25) Excellent lunch dishes served on beautifully carved wooden tables.

L'Asino d'Oro (☎ 0763 34 44 06; Vicolo del Popolo 9; mains around €7.75; ☸ Tue-Sun Apr–mid-Oct) Despite the modest appearance of this restaurant, the food here is superb.

Osteria dell'Angelo (☎ 0763 34 18 05; Piazza XIX Marzo; meals €40; ☸ Tue-Sun) This elegant restaurant was judged by local food writers to be one of the best in Umbria.

Ristorante Zeppelin (☎ 0763 34 14 47; Via G Garibaldi 28; mains from €24; ☸ closed Sun evening) Traditional Umbrian food served in a cool 1920s atmosphere.

Sleeping

Corso (☎ /fax 0763 34 20 20; hotelcorso@libero.it; Corso Cavour 343; s €41-59, d €62-80) Attractive three-star hotel with 16 bright rooms.

Hotel Duomo (☎ 0763 34 18 87; hotelduomo@tiscalinet.it; Vicolo di Maurizio 7; s €55-70, d €80-100) Duomo is rather swish; the rooms are very comfortable and Internet and fax access is available.

Hotel Posta (☎ 0763 34 19 09; fax 0763 34 09 09; Via L Signorelli 18; s/d without bathroom €31/44, with bathroom €37/56, breakfast €6) The rooms in this ramshackle but impressive 16th-century building are simple but have a quirky edge.

Hotel Virgilio (☎ 0763 34 18 82; fax 0763 34 37 97; Piazza del Duomo 5; s/d with bathroom €62/85) Has an unrivalled position, clean, bright basic rooms and welcoming communal areas.

Valentina (☎ /fax 0763 34 16 07; valentina.z@tiscalinet.it; Via Vivaria 7; per person per night, including breakfast €60) Try this place for a room with a view; you'll want to stay for weeks.

PERUGIA

One of Italy's best-preserved medieval hill towns, Perugia has a lively and bloody past. The Umbrii tribe inhabited the surrounding area but it was the Etruscans who founded the city, which reached its zenith in the 6th century BC.

It fell to the Romans in 310 BC and was given the name Perusia. During the Middle Ages the city was racked by the internal feuding of the Baglioni and Oddi families and violent wars against its neighbours; in the mid-13th century it was home to the Flagellants, a curious sect who whipped themselves as a religious penance. In 1538 the city was incorporated into the Papal States under Pope Paul III, remaining under papal control for almost three centuries.

Perugia has a strong artistic and cultural tradition. Its university, founded in the 13th century, is one of the oldest in the world. In the 15th century it was home to fresco painters Bernardino Pinturicchio and his master Pietro Vannucci (known as Il Perugino, who was to teach Raphael), and also attracted the great Tuscan masters Fra Angelico and Piero della Francesca.

Transport

Distance from Rome 135km

Direction North

Travel Time 1½-2½ hrs

Car Take the A1 north from Rome, leaving it at the Orte exit and follow the sign for Perugia.

Bus The Perugia-Rome service is operated by Sulga (www.sulga.it, Italian only); there are roughly five buses daily in each direction.

Train There are nine daily direct services to Rome (including two fast Eurostar services), but otherwise change at Terontola or Foligno. The main train station, Stazione Fontivegge, is a few kilometres west of the city centre but easily accessible by frequent buses from Piazza Italia.

The imposing entrance to the cathedral in Perugia

AROUND PIAZZA IV NOVEMBRE

The imposing facades identify Piazza IV Novembre as the old city's main square. The austere **cathedral** was started in 1345 and completed in 1430. The magnificent 16th-century doorway, facing the Fontana Maggiore in the square, is by Galeazzo Alessi. On 30 July, you can witness the annual unveiling of the city's prized relic: the Virgin Mary's wedding ring, usually locked inside 15 boxes.

Fra Bevignate designed the **Fontana Maggiore** (Great Fountain) in 1278, but it was left to Nicola and Giovanni Pisano to execute the plan. The bas-relief statues represent scenes from the Old Testament and the 12 months of the year. A female figure on the upper basin (facing Corso Vannucci) bears fruit representing fertility, the city's symbol.

Most eye-catching of all in the square is the 13th-century Palazzo dei Priori. The longtime seat of secular power in Perugia, it still houses the municipal offices. Annexed to these is the **Galleria Nazionale dell'Umbria**, a collection of paintings by Umbrian artists, including Pinturicchio and Il Perugino.

The vaulted **Sala dei Notari** (Notaries' Hall), on the first floor of the palazzo, was built in 1296 for the city council. Its walls are decorated with colourful frescoes. To reach it, climb the flight of steps from Piazza IV Novembre.

In the Corso Vannucci side of the palazzo is the **Collegio della Mercanzia** (Merchants' Guild). This was the seat of the city's powerful Renaissance-era merchants who formed one of several *arti* (guilds) that still exist today. Reflecting their one-time prestige is the impressive early-15th-century carved-wood panelling inside.

A few doors up in the same building is the **Collegio del Cambio** (Exchange Guild), constructed in 1450 and decorated with magnificent frescoes by Perugino.

WEST OF CORSO VANNUCCI

Head west along Via dei Priori to reach Piazza San Francesco. The 15th-century **Oratorio di San Bernardino** has a facade decorated with bas-reliefs by the early Renaissance sculptor Agostino di Duccio. Next to it is the ruined **Chiesa di San Francesco al Prato**, destroyed over the centuries by various natural disasters. It is an atmospheric location for concerts.

TOWARDS THE UNIVERSITÀ PER STRANIERI

You can venture down into the 3rd-century-BC **Pozzo Etrusco** (Etruscan Well). From here take Via del Sole to the **Cappella di San Severo**, decorated with Raphael's 'Trinity with Saints' (thought by many to be his first fresco) and frescoes by Perugino.

From the cappella, walk back to Piazza Michelotti and turn north into the small Piazza Rossi Scotti, from where you can enjoy a lovely view. Take the steps down to Piazza Fortebraccio and the **Università per Stranieri**, housed in the Baroque Palazzo Gallenga. To the southeast is the **Arco d'Augusto**, one of the ancient city gates.

Excursions – Perugia

The Thermopolium, an ancient bar at Ostia Antica (p245)

AROUND CORSO GIUSEPPE GARIBALDI

North along Corso Giuseppe Garibaldi is the **Chiesa di Sant'Agostino**, with a beautiful 16th-century choir by sculptor and architect Baccio d'Agnolo. Further north along the same thoroughfare, Via del Tempio branches off to the Romanesque **Chiesa di Sant'Angelo**, said to stand on the site of an ancient temple. Corso Giuseppe Garibaldi continues through the 14th-century wall by way of the **Porta Sant'Angelo**. A 10-minute walk south of the gate along Via Zefferino Faina takes you to the former Chiesa di San Francesco delle Donne and the headquarters of the **Giuditta Brozzetti fabric company**, where you can buy hand-woven linens.

SOUTH OF THE CENTRE

At the southern end of Corso Vannucci are the tiny **Giardini Carducci**, with lovely views of the countryside. The gardens stand atop a once-massive 16th-century fortress, now known as the **Rocca Paolina**, which was built by Pope Paul III. The ruins remain a symbol of defiance against oppression for Perugia's people. A series of *scala mobili* (escalators) run through the Rocca so that you can wander through the ancient medieval streets.

Along Corso Cavour, the early-14th-century **Chiesa di San Domenico** is the city's largest church. Sadly, its Romanesque interior, lightened by the immense stained-glass windows, was replaced by austere Gothic fittings in the 16th century. Pope Benedict XI, who died after eating poisoned figs in 1325, lies buried here. The adjoining convent is the home of the **Museo Archeologico Nazionale dell'Umbria**, which has an excellent collection of Etruscan pieces and a section on prehistory.

Continuing along Corso Cavour, you come to the **Porta San Pietro**. Keep going along Borgo XX Giugno to reach the 10th-century **Chiesa di San Pietro**, entered through a frescoed doorway in the first courtyard. The interior is an incredible mix of gilt and marble and contains a Pietà by Perugino.

Sights & Information

Cappella di San Severo (☎ 075 573 38 64; Piazza Raffaello; admission including Pozzo Etrusco €1.80; ☺ 10.30am-1.30pm & 2.30-6.30pm Apr-Sep, 10.30am-1.30pm, plus 2.30-4.30pm Mon-Fri & 2.30-5.30pm Sat & Sun Oct-Mar)

Cathedral (☎ 075 572 38 32; Piazza IV Novembre; admission free; ☺ 8am-noon & 4pm-sunset)

Chiesa di San Domenico (☎ 075 573 16 35; Piazza Giordano Bruno; admission free; ☺ 8am-noon & 4pm-sunset)

Chiesa di San Pietro (☎ 075 3 47 70; Borgo XX Giugno; admission free; ☺ 8am-noon & 4pm-sunset)

Chiesa di Sant'Agostino (Piazza Lupattelli; admission free; ☺ 8am-noon & 4pm-sunset)

Chiesa di Sant'Angelo (☎ 075 57 22 64; Via Sant'Angelo; admission free; ☺ 9.30am-noon & 3.30pm-sunset)

Collegio del Cambio (☎ 075 572 85 99; Corso Vannucci 25; admission €2.60; ☺ 9am-12.30pm & 2.30-5.30pm Tue-Sun, 9am-12.30pm Sun Mar-Oct; 8am-2pm Tue-Sat, 9am-12.30pm Sun & hols Nov-Feb)

Collegio della Mercanzia (☎ 075 573 03 66; Corso Vannucci 15; admission €1.05; ☺ 9am-1pm & 2.30-5.30pm Mon-Sat, 9am-1pm Sun & hols Mar-Oct; 8am-2pm Tue, Thu & Fri, 8am-4.30pm Wed & Sat, 9am-1pm Sun & hols Nov-Feb)

Galleria Nazionale dell'Umbria (☎ /fax 075 572 10 09, bookings & information ☎ 199 10 13 30; www.gallerianazionaledellumbria.it, Italian only; Corso Vannucci 19; adult/18-25 year old/EU citizen under 18 or over 65 €6.50/3.25/free; ☺ 8.30am-7.30pm)

Giuditta Brozzetti fabric company (☎ 075 4 02 36; www.brozzetti.com; Via T Berardi 5; ☺ 9am-1pm & 3-6pm Mon-Fri)

Museo Archeologico Nazionale dell'Umbria (☎ 075 57 27 14; Piazza Giordano Bruno 10; admission €2.05, free to EU citizens under 18 & over 65; ☺ 8.30am-7.30pm Tue-Sun, 2.30-7.30pm Mon)

Pozzo Etrusco (☎ 075 573 36 69; Piazza Danti 18; adult/child €1.80/1.05, includes Cappella di San Severo; ☺ 10.30am-1.30pm & 2.30-6.30pm Apr-Sep, 10.30am-1.30pm daily, plus 2.30-4.30pm Mon-Fri & 2.30-5.30pm Sat & Sun Oct-Mar)

Sala dei Notari (☎ 075 577 23 39; Palazzo dei Priori, Piazza IV Novembre 3; admission free; ☺ 9am-1pm & 3-7pm Tue-Sun year-round, plus Mon Jun-Sep)

Tourist Office (☎ 075 572 33 27; Palazzo dei Priori, Piazza IV Novembre 3; ☺ 8.30am-1.30pm & 3.30-6.30pm Mon-Sat, 9am-1pm Sun)

Eating

Caffè di Perugia (Via Mazzini 10) Judged one of the best cafés in Italy by the prestigious Italian *Gambero Rosso* guide.

Osteria del Bartolo (☎ 075 573 15 61; Via del Bartolo 30; meals €40-60) This elegant place specialises in Umbrian dishes, but with its own creative input.

Osteria del Gambero (☎ 075 573 54 61; Via Baldeschi 17; mains €30) One of the best restaurants in town, with a great atmosphere and excellent wines.

Ristorante Victoria (☎ 075 572 59 00; Piazza IV Novembre 7) Intimate little restaurant, serving local and national dishes.

Sandri (Corso Vannucci 32) One of the city's finest cafés.

Sleeping

Albergo Anna (☎ /fax 075 573 63 04; www.alber goanna.it; Via dei Priori 48; without bathroom s €26-30, d €42-46, with bathroom s €36.15, d €50-62)

A quirky little pensione on the 2nd floor of a 17th-century town house.

Hotel Fortuna (☎ 075 572 28 45; fortuna@umbria hotels.com; Via Luigi Bonazzi 19; without bathroom s €35-68, with bathroom s €40-72, d €55-133) Very comfortable; there's even the odd fresco.

Hotel la Rosetta (☎ /fax 075 572 08 41; www.perugiaonline.com/larosetta; Piazza Italia 19; s €77.50, d €117.50-168) One of Perugia's better hotels with exquisite individually designed rooms.

Hotel Rosalba (☎ 075 572 82 85; Piazza del Circo 7; s/d with bathroom €50/65) Beautifully decorated with all mod cons. Highly recommended.

Primavera Mini Hotel (☎ 075 572 16 57; www.primav eraminihotel.com; Via Vincioli 8; s/d €41/57) A quiet, cosy hotel in the centre of Perugia with spectacular views.

Directory

Directory

TRANSPORT
AIRLINES

Italy's national carrier is **Alitalia** (www.alitalia.it), which operates direct flights between Rome and most European cities. Many of Alitalia's intercontinental flights (and intercontinental flights by other carriers) fly via Milan, connecting with domestic services to Rome, though there are a limited number of direct flights to Rome.

Regular domestic flights connect Rome to all major Italian airports. The majority of these are operated by Alitalia and its subsidiary airlines.

Other domestic airlines include **Air One** (Map p306–7; ☎ 06 47 87 61; www.air-one.it; Via Sardegna 14) for flights between Rome, Milan, Turin, Bologna, Naples, Bari, Reggio Calabria and Crotone; and **Meridiana** (Map p314–16; ☎ 06 47 80 41; www.meridiana.it; Via Barberini 67) for flights to Milan, Catania, Verona and Sardinia.

Airlines with direct connections to Rome include British Airways, American Airlines, Emirates Airlines, Qantas Airways, Lufthansa Airlines, Singapore Airlines and Malaysia Airlines. No-frills airlines operating within Europe that fly into Rome include: Go, Easy Jet, Ryan Air and Virgin Express.

Most airlines have counters in the departure hall at Fiumicino. Many of the head offices are now based at or near the airport. Most of their ticket offices are in the area around Via Veneto and Via Barberini, northwest of Stazione Termini, including:

Alitalia (☎ 06 6 56 41; www.alitalia.it; Via Bissolati 11)

Air France (☎ 06 48 79 11; www.airfrance.it; Via Sardegna 40)

British Airways (☎ 147 81 22 66; www.british airways.com; Via Bissolati 54)

Air Canada (☎ 06 659 13 00; www.aircanada.ca; Via C Veneziani 58)

Delta Air Lines (☎ 1800 221 12 12; www.delta.com; Via Sardegna 40)

Lufthansa Airlines (☎ 06 656 84 004; www.lufthansa.com; Via di San Basilio 41)

Qantas Airways (☎ 06 529 22 87; www.qantas.com.au; Via Bissolati 54)

Singapore Airlines (☎ 06 47 85 51; www.singaporeair.com; Via Barberini 11)

TWA (☎ 1800 221 20 00; www.twa.com; Via Barberini 67)

AIRPORTS

Rome's main airport is **Leonardo da Vinci** (FCO; ☎ 06 659 55 571, 06 54 65 91; www.adr.it) commonly referred to as Fiumicino. Left luggage facilities are available in the international arrivals area on the ground floor. Open 24 hours a day, it costs €2.15 per item per day; luggage over 160cm long is an extra €2.15 per day. Make sure you have your passport handy as a photocopy will be made when you leave your luggage.

Rome's smaller second airport, **Ciampino** (CIA; ☎ 06 794 94 225; www.adr.it) is used by many low-cost airlines and charter flights.

Airport Transfers
FIUMICINO

Rome's main airport is 30km southwest of Rome and is well-connected to the city centre.

The Leonardo Express, the direct Fiumicino-Stazione Termini train (follow the signs to the train station from the airport arrivals hall), costs €8.80. It arrives at and leaves from platform 27 at **Stazione Termini** (Map p314–16) and takes about 30 minutes. The first direct train leaves the airport for Termini at 6.37am, then runs half-hourly until the last train at 11.37pm. From Termini to the airport, trains start at 5.51am and run half-hourly until the last train at 10.51pm.

Another slower train from Fiumicino stops at Trastevere, Ostiense and Tiburtina stations. From the airport, it runs about every 20 minutes from 6.27am to 11.27pm (look for the destination Orte or Fara Sabina) and from Tiburtina from 5.04am until 10.34 pm. It costs €4.70 and takes 30 minutes to/from Ostiense and 45 minutes to/from Tiburtina. On Sundays and public holidays there is approximately one train every hour. This train does not stop at Termini.

Tickets for both trains can be bought from vending machines in the main airport arrivals hall (make sure you have some small notes as these machines rarely have much change) or from the ticket offices, tobacconists or vending machines in the train stations.

From midnight to 5am an hourly bus runs from Stazione Tiburtina via Stazione Termini to the airport. The same bus departs for the city from outside the arrivals hall. Tickets cost €4.65. Don't hang around Tiburtina at night – it's not safe.

Fiumicino airport is connected to the city by an autostrada. Follow the signs for Rome out of the complex and exit from the autostrada at EUR, following the target sign for the centre. From there, Via Cristoforo Colombo will take you directly into the centre.

Official white or yellow taxis leave from outside the arrivals hall. They are expensive: a taxi to the centre of Rome will cost between €35 and €45 plus surcharges for luggage, at night and on public holidays. Unofficial operators abound and ask for ridiculous sums.

Several private companies run limousine services which work out to be the same price as a taxi but are usually a lot more comfortable. **Airport Connection Services** (☎ 06 338 32 21; www.airportconnection.it) has two deals: a minivan shuttle service for €25 per person (minimum two people); or a chauffeur-driven Mercedes for €39. **Airport Shuttle** (☎ 06 420 14 507; www.airportshuttle.it) offers transfers to/from Fiumicino in a minivan for €28.50 for one or two passengers, €34 for three, and €45.50 for four. Each additional passenger costs €5.50. A 30% surcharge is added between 10pm and 7am. Both services can be booked for airport pick-ups and drop-offs.

CIAMPINO

Getting to/from Ciampino airport, 15km southeast of the city centre, is not simple and is time-consuming and uncomfortable by public transport (COTRAL bus and metro). Buses run infrequently, finish early and do not connect well with the metro.

Several charter firms, such as Ryan Air and Easy Jet now charter their own buses to Ciampino, which leave from Via Magenta outside Stazione Termini two hours before each scheduled flight and from Ciampino soon after the arrival of a flight. You can buy tickets, which cost around €8, from the Hotel Royal Santina, Via Marsala 22, opposite the bus stop, or at Ciampino airport.

Otherwise take the **COTRAL bus** (€1.30; buy your ticket from a *tabacchi* inside the airport) to the Metro A stop Anagnina (about 30 minutes), then take the metro (€0.77) to Stazione

Termini. If you miss the bus and it's after 11pm, you'll have to take a taxi (around €39 plus surcharges for luggage).

With Airport Shuttle – see Fiumicino (p258) – to/from Ciampino costs €39.50 for one to two people with €5.50 for each additional person.

BICYCLE

If you ignore the fact that Rome was built on seven hills and that most Roman drivers are not used to seeing bicycles on the roads, it can be fun to pedal around the city streets – especially on Sundays when much of the city centre is closed to traffic.

Rome City Council has published a useful brochure, *Exploring By Bike*, available from the Tourist Information kiosks, which offers some suggestions for cycling around town.

On Sundays you can hire bikes at Via Appia Antica, when the ancient road is closed to traffic, and cycle around the catacombs and Roman ruins.

Uneven cobblestones are the most common hazard, followed by potholes and very slippery roads when it rains.

Rental

Daily rental rates range from €5.50 to €18. You will usually need a credit card and identity document which can sometimes be left in lieu of a cash deposit. Reliable operators include:

Bici e Baci (Map p314–16; ☎ 06 482 84 43; Via del Viminale 5)

Happy Rent (Map p314–16; ☎ 06 481 81 85; Via Farini 3) Baby seats are available for bicycles.

Treno e Scooter (Map p314–16; ☎ 06 489 05 823; Stazione Termini) On the northeastern side of the bus terminus at Piazza dei Cinquecento, these guys include chains and locks with hire; show a train ticket and you get a 20% discount on the first day's rental. A cash or credit-card deposit is required.

Public Transport

On Sundays you are permitted to take your bike on the Metro Linea B and the connecting Lido di Ostia train. You'll have to stamp two tickets though – one for you and one for the bike – before you get on the train (front carriage only).

To take a bike on regional trains you have to pay a supplement of €3.50, while on some Intercity and Eurocity/Euronight services it costs an extra €5 for national routes and €12 for international journeys.

BUS

See the boxed text (below) for details on tickets. Many of the main bus routes terminate in Piazza dei Cinquecento in front of Stazione Termini where there's an information booth, on stand C in the centre of the square.

Another central point for the main bus routes is Largo di Torre Argentina, near Piazza Navona (Map p311–13). Buses generally run from about 5.30am to midnight, with limited services throughout the night on some routes. If you're planning on using the buses and trams a lot, pick up a free transport map from the information kiosk at Termini or from any tourist information booth.

Useful routes include:

No 46 Piazza Venezia to St Peter's and Via Aurelia

No 64 Stazione Termini to St Peter's

No 40 Stazione Termini to St Peter's (express route with fewer stops than No 64)

55N Night bus (same route as Metro Linea A)

40N Night bus (same route as Metro Linea B)

Long distance national and international buses arrive at and depart from the terminal at Stazione Tiburtina.

CAR & MOTORCYCLE
Driving

Negotiating Roman traffic by car is difficult enough, but you may be taking your life in your hands if you ride a motorcycle or moped in the city. The rule is to look straight ahead to watch the vehicles in front and hope that the vehicles behind are watching you!

Most of the historic centre is closed to normal traffic. Monday to Friday, from 6.30am to 6pm and Saturday from 2pm to 6pm you are not allowed to drive in the centre of Rome unless you are a resident or have special permission.

All 22 streets accessing the so-called 'Limited Traffic Zone' have been equipped with electronic access detection devices. If you are planning to stay here, contact the hotel management who will fax authorities with your number plate details so you can avoid a fine. For further information visit www.sta.roma.it (Italian only) or call ☎ 06 571 18 333 (8am-6pm Mon-Fri, 2pm-6pm Sat).

Major mandatory road rules in Italy may seem familiar: drive on the right hand side of

Tickets Please!

ATAC (☎ 800 43 17 84; www.atac.roma.it; ☺ 8am-6pm Mon-Fri) is the city's public transport company, operating the buses, trams, metro and suburban railway network. The same ticket is valid for all modes of transport.

At the time of writing, prices were as follows: *un biglietto della metro* (single ticket) €0.77 for 75 minutes' travel (but this includes only one metro ride); *biglietto giornaliero* (daily tickets) €3.10; *biglietto settimanale* (weekly tickets) €12.40; and *abbonamento mensile* (monthly passes) €26. There is talk of a price increase.

Travel to destinations in Lazio can usually be done with a *biglietto integrato regionale giornaliero*, a ticket valid for one day's travel on COTRAL buses and Trenitalia (previously Ferrovie dello Stato; State Railway) trains (within specified zones in the Lazio region) and all public transport in Rome. These tickets range in price depending on the number of zones travelled. You can purchase them from all metro, bus and train stations.

Purchase a ticket *before* you get on the bus or train and then validate it in the yellow machine as you enter. On the metro, tickets must be validated as you go through the electronic barriers before you descend to the platform. If changing from bus to metro, the ticket should be validated a second time. The standard fine for travelling without a validated ticket is €52 and, although inspections are rare, they are increasing in frequency and severity. The usual refrain that you 'didn't know' is unlikely to wash these days. Tickets can be bought in Piazza dei Cinquecento, at tobacconists and newsstands and from vending machines at main bus stops.

the road and overtake on the left; wear seat belts (including rear seat belts if fitted); drive with your headlights on outside built-up areas; and carry a warning triangle to be used in the event of a breakdown. The blood alcohol limit is 0.05%.

Speed limits, unless otherwise indicated by local signs, are: 130km/h (in rain 110 km/h) on autostradas; 110km/h (in rain 90 km/h) on all main, non-urban roads; 90km/h on secondary, non-urban roads; and 50km/h in built-up areas.

Tolls apply on most of the main autostradas. You pick up a ticket as you enter and pay as you exit (the amount depends on the distance travelled).

Speeding fines follow EU standards and are proportionate with the number of kilometres that you are caught driving over the speed limit (to €260). The penalty for driving through a red light is €137.

At the time of writing the authorities were about to introduce new licences for small cylinder scooters. To ride a moped under 50cc you should be aged 14 years or over and you may not carry passengers or use the autostradas. The speed limit for a moped is 40km/h.

To ride a motorcycle or scooter up to 125cc, you must be at least 16 years old and have a licence (a car licence will do). Helmets are compulsory. The days of the Italian scooter rider with free-flowing locks came to an abrupt end in 2000 when police started to issue hefty fines.

For motorcycles over 125cc you need a motorcycle licence. You will be able to enter restricted traffic areas in Italian cities without any problems and Italian traffic police generally turn a blind eye to motorcycles parked on footpaths.

The cost of *benzine senza piombo* (unleaded petrol) in Italy is high, around €1.05 per litre, while *gasolio* (diesel) is cheaper at €0.87. If you are driving a car which uses LPG, you will need to buy a special guide to service stations that have *gasauto* (or 'GPL'). By law these must be located in nonresidential areas and they are usually in the country or on the outskirts of cities, and at some autostrada service stations (although not all).

Rental
CAR
There's no point renting a car to tour the city but it could be useful if you are travelling to destinations outside Rome. It is cheaper to arrange car rental before leaving your own country through a fly/drive deal. Most major firms, including Hertz, Avis and Budget, will arrange this, and you simply pick up the vehicle at a nominated point upon arrival or on a specified day.

You will need to be aged 21 years or over (23 years or above for some companies) and possess a valid driving licence. You will find the deal far easier to organise if you have a credit card. No matter where you rent, make sure you understand what is included in the price (unlimited kilometres, tax, insurance, collision damage waiver etc) and what your liabilities are. In some cases you are liable for penalties of between €260 and €520 if the car is stolen.

Average prices stand at around €65 per day. Major rental companies include:

AVIS
24-hr booking (☎ 800 86 30 63; www.avis.com)
Ciampino airport (☎ 06 793 40 195)
Fiumicino airport (☎ 06 650 11 531)
Stazione Termini (☎ 06 481 43 73)

EUROPCAR
Central booking (☎ 800 01 44 10; www.europcar.com)
Ciampino airport (☎ 06 793 40 387)
Fiumicino airport (☎ 06 650 10 287)
Stazione Termini (☎ 06 488 28 54)

MAGGIORE NATIONAL
Central booking (☎ 848 86 70 67; www.maggiore.it)
Ciampino airport (☎ 06 793 40 368)
Fiumicino airport (☎ 06 650 10 678)
Stazione Termini (☎ 06 488 00 49)

HERTZ
Central booking (☎ 02 69 68 24; www.hertz.com)
Ciampino airport (☎ 06 650 10 256)
Fiumicino airport (☎ 06 592 27 42)
Stazione Termini (☎ 06 474 03 89)

MOTORCYCLE & MOPED
For renting a motorcycle you'll usually need a credit card and identity document which can sometimes be left in lieu of a cash deposit. Average per day prices range from €105 for a 600cc motorcycle to €26 to €67 for 50cc-125cc scooters and mopeds. Agencies include:

Bici e Baci (Map pp314–16; ☎ 06 482 84 43; Via del Viminale 5) This invitingly named outfit – Bikes and Kisses – has a wide range of mopeds and motorbikes to choose from. All major credit cards are accepted.

Happy Rent (Map pp314–16; ☎ 06 481 81 85; Via Farini 3) Off Via Cavour between Stazione Termini & Piazza Esquilino. The helpful crew here will happily set you in the right direction offering tourist advice and discounts.

Treno e Scooter (Map pp314–16; ☎ 06 489 05 823; Stazione Termini) You'll find these guys on the northeastern side of the bus terminus at Piazza dei Cinquecento. Chains, locks, helmet and goggles are included in the price and breakdown assistance is provided during office hours. If you show a train ticket you get a 20% discount on the first day's rental. A cash or credit-card deposit is required.

Parking

Parking in Rome is no fun at all, especially now that traffic police are getting very tough on illegally parked cars. At best you'll get a heavy fine (around €105), at worst a wheel clamp or your car towed away. In the event that your car goes missing, always check first with the **traffic police** (☎ 06 6 76 91). You'll have to pay about €95 to get it back, plus a hefty fine.

To bring order to where chaos reigned before, the authorities have introduced a pay parking system around the periphery of Rome's city centre. Blue lines denote roadside spaces which can be yours for the price of a ticket from the nearest meter or a scratch ticket from tobacconists. Between 8am and 8pm (11pm in some parts of town) parking costs €1 per hour.

The major parking area closest to the city centre is at **Villa Borghese** (Map pp306–7); entry is from Piazzale Brasile at the top of Via Veneto. There is also a supervised car park at Stazione Termini. Expect to pay between €1.15-2.50 for the first three to four hours.

Other car parks are at Piazzale dei Partigiani, just outside **Stazione Ostiense** (Map pp302–3; take the metro into the centre from nearby Piramide metro station); at Stazione Tiburtina (from where you can also catch the metro into town); and at St Peter's train station.

METRO

The Metropolitana (metro) has two lines, Linea A and Linea B which traverse the city in an X-shape. Both pass through Stazione Termini, the only point at which you can change from one line to the other.

It operates from 5.30am to 11.30pm (one hour later on Saturday) and trains run approximately every 5 to 10 minutes. See Map p322 for routes around the city. See the boxed text on p260 for details on tickets.

Stations on Linea B are wheelchair accessible except for Circo Massimo, Colosseo and Cavour.

TAXI

Hailing a cab, as in whistling and waving your arm, doesn't work in Rome. You must either telephone for one or wait at a taxi rank.

To call one, try: **Cooperativa Radio Taxi Romana** (☎ 06 35 70), **La Capitale** (☎ 06 49 94) or **Samarcanda** (☎ 06 55 51), all of which are reliable operators. If you phone for a taxi, the driver will turn on the meter immediately and you will pay the cost of travel from wherever the driver receives the call.

Taxi ranks are at the airports, Stazione Termini, Largo Argentina, the Pantheon, Corso Rinascimento-Piazza Navona, Piazza di Spagna, Lorgo Goldoni, Piazza del Popolo, Piazza Venezia, the Colosseum, Piazza GG Belli in Trastevere and near the Vatican at Piazza Pio XII and Piazza Risorgimento.

Make sure your taxi is licensed (it'll be white or yellow) and metered and always go with the metered fare, never an arranged price. Daytime trips within the centre of Rome can cost anywhere from €5 to €15. If you pay any more, you can be pretty certain you're being taken for a ride.

At the time of writing, the official rates were as follows: minimum charge €2.33 (7am-10pm), €3.36 (Sundays and holidays), €4.91 (10pm-7am) with increments of €0.78 in town, €1.29 out of town (defined as outside Rome's ring road – the GRA) at every click of the meter. There are also surcharges for luggage (€1.03 for every large bag or suitcase) and travel to and from the airport.

TRAIN

Almost all trains arrive at and depart from **Stazione Termini** (Map pp314–16). There are regular connections to other European countries, all the major cities in Italy and many smaller towns.

Rome's second train station is Stazione Tiburtina. There are eight other train stations scattered throughout Rome. Some northbound trains depart from or stop at Stazione Ostiense and Stazione Trastevere.

For train information (Italian only), ring ☎ 89 20 21 or go to the information office at the train station, where English is spoken. The office opens from 7am to 9.45pm but be aware that there are always lengthy queues. If you are doing a reasonable amount of travelling, it is worth buying a train timetable. There are several available, including the official Trenitalia (previously Ferrovie dello Stato; FS) timetables, which can be purchased at newsstands in or near train stations for around €3. Alternatively, train information is available online at www.trenitalia.com.

Remember to validate your train ticket in one of the yellow machines on the station platforms. If you don't, you may be forced to pay a fine on the train.

Apart from connections to the airports, Rome's overground rail network is useful only if you are heading out of town to the Castelli Romani, the beaches at Lido di Ostia or the ruins at Ostia Antica. See Excursions (p239).

There is a left luggage office available at Termini on the lower ground floor under platform 24. Open from 7am to midnight, it costs €3.10 for the first five hours then €0.52 per hour for each additional hour (€13 for 24 hours).

TRAM

There is a small network of trams in Rome. Especially useful to tourists are routes :

No 8 Largo di Torre Argentina to Trastevere (and on to Stazione Trastevere for trains to the airport).

No 30B Porta San Paolo to Villa Borghese via the Colosseum, San Giovanni and San Lorenzo.

PRACTICALITIES

ACCOMMODATION

Rome has a vast number of accommodation options but it is always best to book. There is a **free hotel reservation service** at Stazione Termini (☎ 06 699 10 00; opposite platform 21; ☯ 7.30am to 9pm) or as an alternative try the private tourist office **Enjoy Rome**. See Tourist Offices (p275).

Accommodation listed in the Sleeping chapter of this book has been divided into two categories: mid-range and up, and cheap sleeps. Cheap sleeps charge anywhere up to €100 for a double. Within these categories all listings are in alphabetical order. For further details on styles of accommodation, price ranges, checking in and out, reservation procedures and longer-term rentals refer to the Sleeping chapter (p219).

Peak periods include spring and autumn and although Rome does not have a low season as such you'll pay considerably less for your room in July and August and from November to March (excluding the Christmas/New Year period).

Useful websites include: www.romaturismo.it (click on Tour Operators), which has the list and prices of all officially recognised accommodation; www.ostellionline.org, for hostel information; www.wantedinrome.com for private and agency properties for longer term rentals; and www.cross-pollinate.com for *affitacamere* (B&B, without the breakfast).

For further details refer to the Sleeping chapter (p219).

BUSINESS
Hours

Shops generally open from 9am to 1pm and 3.30pm to 7.30pm (or 4pm to 8pm) Monday to Friday. Most food shops close on Thursday afternoon and some also on Saturday afternoon, while other shops tend to remain closed on Monday morning. Many department stores and most larger supermarkets, however, now have continuous opening from 9am to 7.30pm Monday to Saturday. Some even open from 9am to 1pm (or longer) on Sunday.

Banks open 8.30am to 1.30pm and 2.45pm to 4.30pm Monday to Friday, though hours can vary. Some banks in the city centre also open Saturday morning. It is always possible to find an exchange office open in major tourist areas.

For post office and pharmacy hours see under Post (p271) and Pharmacies (p271).

Bars (in the Italian sense, ie coffee and sandwich places) and cafés generally open 7.30am to 8pm, though some stay open after 8pm and turn into pub-style drinking and meeting places. Discos and clubs open around 10pm but often there'll be no-one there until around midnight. Restaurants open midday to 3pm and 7.30pm to 11pm (later in summer). Restaurants and bars are required to close for one day each week; which day it is varies between establishments. For further details see the Eating chapter (p151).

The opening hours of museums, galleries and archaeological sites vary, although there is a trend towards continuous opening from 9.30am to 7pm. Increasingly, the major national museums and galleries remain open until 10pm during the summer. Most of Rome's museums are closed on Monday.

Centres

A GSM mobile phone and a good laptop computer will probably be all you need to do business in Rome. However, some of the better hotels in the city have business centres or secretarial assistance for guests.

Executive Services Business Centres (Map pp306–7; ☎ 06 852 37 250; www.executivenetwork.it; Via Savoia 78) can provide secretarial services, meeting rooms with video conferencing facilities, company addresses, voice mailboxes, translators and interpreters and other services.

World Translation Centre (Map pp314–6; ☎ 06 488 10 39; www.wtcsrl.com; Via Merulana 259) can provide sworn translations for legal and corporate needs.

CHILDREN

Italians – Romans are no exception – love children but although there are often discounts available for them, there are few special amenities. Restaurants, however, will usually be happy to provide *seggioloni* (high chairs) and you can often ask for a *mezzo porzione* (child's portion).

Many of the larger hotels provide child-minding facilities and most of the others can arrange baby-sitters. If you want to find your own English-speaking baby-sitter, try **Angels** (Map pp314–16; ☎ 06 678 28 77, mobile 0338 667 97 18; staffinitaly@yahoo.co.uk). They charge €8 to €10 an hour plus an agency fee of €16.

All city transport is free for children under 1m tall and major car-rental firms will rent out children's safety seats subject to prior reservation.

Museums, galleries and archaeological sites are free for those aged under 18. For further details see Neighbourhoods (p69).

Information about current events for children can be found in *Roma C'è* (see under the heading Children's Corner in the English section) and in *Trovaroma*, the Thursday supplement to *La Repubblica*, under Città dei Ragazzi. For more general information on how to keep the kids amused, see Lonely Planet's *Travel with Children*, or log on at www.travelwithyourkids.com or www.familytravelnetwork.com.

CLIMATE

Rome's climate is generally mild but you will be likely to strike unpleasantly hot weather in July and August, and briskly cold weather from December to February when icy winds blow in from northern Europe. Spring and autumn are without doubt the best times to visit, with generally sunny skies and mild temperatures, although late autumn (November) can be rainy.

The main tourist season starts at Easter and runs until October; peak periods are in spring and autumn, when the tour buses pour in and tourists are herded around like cattle. In July and August temperatures can soar to around 37°C and humidity is often close to 100% in Rome during those months. There are some advantages: Romans desert the city for the beaches and mountains, which means very light traffic and a less-crowded city centre. In summer there are also numerous outdoor festivals and concerts. If you must visit in summer, try to hit the sights early, take a long lunch and

a nap, and then head out again around 6pm to take advantage of the cooler evening.

While November is noted for heavy rain and December to February can bring icy weather, Rome is hardly Moscow! In fact, the city is less overrun with tourists and there are some fun events around Christmas time, including free concerts of sacred music in churches and the traditional Christmas market held in Piazza Navona.

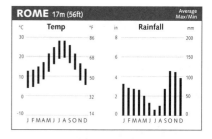

COURSES

Holiday courses are a booming section of the Italian tourist industry, covering subjects such as painting, art, sculpture, wine, food and photography. In Rome, cooking and language courses are particularly popular.

Cooking

Well known cookery writer Diane Seed, author of *The Top One Hundred Pasta Sauces* and *Diane Seed's Rome for All Seasons*, runs cooking courses four or five times a year from her kitchen in the Doria Pamphilj palace. Week-long courses cost from around €680. For information call ☎ 06 679 71 03 or email her at dianeseed@compuserve.com. Subjects covered include the Italian art of shopping and olive oil tasting.

Language

What better place than Rome to learn the language? Courses can cost anything from about €325 for a 40 hour, two week course to more than €1300 for a longer 6 month course. Some schools also offer accommodation packages. Reputable schools include:

Berlitz (Map p311–13; ☎ 06 683 40 00, 06 688 06 951; www.berlitz.com; Via di Torre Argentina 21)

Centro Linguistico Italiano Dante Alighieri (Map p302–3; ☎ 06 442 31 400; www.clidante.it; Piazza Bologna 1)

Centro Studi Flaminio (Map pp304–5; ☎ 06 361 09 03 or 06 361 08 96; Via Flaminia 21)

Italiaidea (Map pp311–13; ☎ 06 683 07 620; italiaidea@italisidea.com; Piazza della Cancelleria 85)

Torre di Babele Centro di Lingua e Cultura Italiana (Map pp314–16; ☎ 06 700 84 34; www.torredibabele.com; Via Bixio 74)

CUSTOMS

There is no limit on the amount of euros brought into the country. Goods brought in and exported within the EU incur no additional taxes, provided duty has been paid somewhere within the EU and the goods are for personal consumption.

Duty-free sales within the EU no longer exist. Visitors coming into Italy from non-EU countries can import, duty free: 1L of spirits, 2L wine, 60mL perfume, 250mL eau de toilette, 200 cigarettes and other goods up to a total of €175.50; anything over this limit must be declared on arrival and the appropriate duty paid. On leaving the EU, non-EU citizens can reclaim any Value Added Tax (VAT) on expensive purchases.

DISABLED TRAVELLERS

Rome is not an easy city for disabled travellers and getting around can be a problem for those in a wheelchair. For example, although many buildings have lifts, they are not always wide enough to accommodate a wheelchair.

Public transport is, however, improving. On Metro Linea B all stations have disabled facilities except for Circo Massimo, Colosseo and Cavour; Rome's newer trams are generally accessible; and there are wheelchair-accessible buses on several busy routes. No 590 follows the route of Metro Linea A and is specially equipped for disabled passengers and wheelchairs. For information on transport for disabled passengers, check out www.atac.roma.it or call ☎ 800 43 17 84 (8am-9pm Mon-Fri).

Some taxis are equipped to carry passengers in wheelchairs. It is advisable to book a taxi by phone and tell the operator that you need a taxi for a *sedia a rotelle* (wheelchair). See the Taxi section (p262).

Airline companies should be able to arrange assistance at airports if you notify them of your needs in advance. If you are travelling by train from Stazione Termini to Fiumicino airport or elsewhere, call ☎ 06 488 17 26 beforehand.

Many of the city's main museums have been overhauled in recent years so things are looking better for disabled travellers than ever before. Tourists in wheelchairs will find access ramps, toilets and spacious lifts in the Vatican and Capitoline Museums, the Galleria Borghese, the Galleria Nazionale d'Arte Moderna, the Palazzo delle Esposizioni and Palazzo Massimo.

Organisations

The best point of reference for disabled travellers is **Consorzio Cooperative Integrate** (COIN; ☎ 06 712 90 11; www.coinsociale.it; Via Enrico Giglioli 54) which can provide information about services for the disabled in Rome (including transport and museum access). It operates a telephone help line ☎ 06 712 90 11 from 9am to 5pm Monday to Friday and publishes a multilingual guide, *Roma Accessibile*. The guide is available from public offices and by mail order; some tourist offices might also have copies.

Tourist offices can provide information about museum access and transport for disabled travellers. The Italian State Tourist Office in your country may be able to provide advice on tour operators which organise holidays for the disabled. It may also carry a small brochure, *Services for Disabled People*, published by the Italian railways, which details facilities at stations and on trains.

The Italian travel agency, **CIT** (Map pp314–16; ☎ 06 462 03 11; Piazza della Repubblica 65), can advise on hotels with special facilities, such as ramps and so on. It can also request that wheelchair ramps be provided on arrival if you book train travel through CIT.

DISCOUNT CARDS

Discounts (usually half the normal fee) for galleries and sites are available to EU-citizens aged between 18 and 25 (you will need to produce proof of your age). An ISIC (International Student Identity Card) is no longer sufficient at many sites as prices are based on age – a passport or driving licence is preferable. It will still prove useful for cheap flights, theatre and cinema discounts. For nonstudent travellers who are under 25, there is the International Youth Travel Card (IYTC; www.istc.org) which offers the same benefits. Similar cards are available to teachers (ITIC).

A Euro<26 card (www.euro26.org) is universally acceptable and is available to everyone aged under 26.

In Rome, the **Centro Turistico Studentesco e Giovanile** (CTS; Map pp314–16; ☎ 06 687 26 72; Corso Vittorio Emanuele II 297) issues ISIC, ITIC and Euro<26 cards.

EU citizens aged over 65 are often entitled to discounted or free admission to museums and monuments. Your travel documents are adequate identification.

Discounts are also available on public transport but usually only for monthly passes (not daily or weekly tickets). The minimum qualifying age is 65 years.

For rail travel on Trenitalia (the state railway service), seniors (people over 60 in this case) can get a 20% reduction on full fares by purchasing an annual seniors' pass called the *Carta Argento* for €20.66. You can purchase these at major train stations.

ELECTRICITY

The electric current in Italy is 220V, 50Hz, but make a point of checking with the hotel management because some places, especially older buildings, may still use 125V. Power points have two or three holes and do not have their own switches; plugs have two or three round pins. You may have to buy an adaptor at an electrical shop to use your laptop or electric shaver.

EMBASSIES & CONSULATES

Australia (Map pp306–7; ☎ 06 85 27 21; www.australian -embassy.it; Via Alessandria 215, Rome 00198; ☼ consular section 8.30am-12pm & 1.30-4.15pm Mon-Fri)

Austria (Map pp306–7; ☎ 06 844 01 41; www.austria.it; Via Pergolesi 3, Rome 00198); Consulate (Map pp306–7; ☎ 06 855 29 66; Viale Liegi 32, Rome 00198; ☼ 9am-12pm Mon-Fri)

Canada (Map p302–3; ☎ 06 44 59 81; www.canada.it; Via G B de Rossi 27, Rome 00198); Consulate (Map pp306–7; ☎ 06 44 59 81; Via Zara 30, Rome 00198; ☼ 8.30am-12.30pm & 1.30-4pm Mon-Fri)

France (Map pp311–13; ☎ 06 68 60 11; www.france -italia.it; Piazza Farnese, Rome 00186); Consulate (Map pp311–13; ☎ 06 688 02 152; Via Giulia 251; ☼ 9am-12.30pm Mon-Fri)

Germany (Map pp314–16; ☎ 06 49 21 31; www.deutsc hebotschaft.rom; Via San Martino della Battaglia 4, Rome 00185; ☼ consular section 9am-12pm Mon-Fri)

Ireland (Map pp311–13; ☎ 06 697 91 21; Piazza Campitelli 3, Rome 00186; ☼ 10am-12.30pm & 3-4.30pm Mon-Fri)

Netherlands (Map pp306–7; ☎ 06 322 11 41; www.olanda.it; Via M Mercati 8, Rome 00197; ☼ 9am-12pm Mon-Fri)

New Zealand (Map pp306–7; ☎ 06 441 71 71; www.nzembassy.com; Via Zara 28, Rome 00198; ☼ consular section 9.30am-12pm)

Switzerland (Map p302–3; ☎ 06 80 95 71; www.eda.admin.ch/roma; Via Barnarba Oriani 61 Rome, 00197; ☼ consular section 9am-12pm Mon-Fri)

UK (Map pp306–7; ☎ 06 482 54 41; www.britain.it; Via XX Settembre 80a, Rome 00187; ☼ consular section 9.15am-12.45pm Mon-Fri)

USA (Map pp314–16; ☎ 06 4 67 41; www.usembassy.it; Via Vittorio Veneto 119a-121, Rome 00187; ☼ consular section 8.30am-12.30pm Mon-Fri)

EMERGENCIES

Police	☎ 113
Ambulance	☎ 118
Fire	☎ 115

GAY & LESBIAN TRAVELLERS

Homosexuality is legal in Italy and the legal age of consent is 16. It's well tolerated in Rome, as active participation in Gay Pride 2003 demonstrated, although you'll have to put up with periodic antigay vitriol from the Vatican. A few years ago the gay capitals of Italy were Milan and Bologna but Rome is now giving both cities some strong competition. See the boxed text (p192).

On a political level, Italy is still a long way behind most Western countries in making gay rights a major issue, as the shadow of the disapproving Church looms large. Despite this, the year 2000 was a watershed for gay Rome, when the city hosted World Pride, a week-long festival of parties and events, bang in the middle of the Roman Catholic Jubilee year.

In Rome, the main cultural and political organisation is the **Circolo Mario Mieli di Cultura Omosessuale** (Map pp302–3; ☎ 06 541 39 85; www.mariomieli.org (Italian only); Via Efeso 2a) off Via Ostiense near the Basilica di San Paolo. It organises debates, cultural events and social functions, as well as free AIDS/HIV testing and a care centre. It also orchestrates Rome Pride, which takes place in June every year. The free monthly magazine *AUT* (predominantly in Italian) is available from gay bookshops and organisations.

Other useful sources of information include: *Pride* (€3.10), a national monthly magazine, the international gay guide *Spartacus* and online www.gay.it/guida/Lazio/Roma (Italian only), which features listings for Rome and the Lazio region.

The national organisation for lesbians is **Coordinamento Lesbiche Italiano** (CLI), also known as the

Directory – Practicalities

Buon Pastore Centre (Map p308–10; ☎ 06 686 42 01; cli_network@iol.it; cnr of Via San Francesco di Sales and Via della Lungara; Trastevere). The weekly political meetings of the Centro Femminista Separatista are held here, as well as conferences and literary evenings. There is also a women-only restaurant, Le Sorellastre, and hostel, La Foresteria Orsa Maggiore (p234).

Zipper Travel Association (Map pp314–16; ☎ 06 488 27 30, Via Castelfidardo 18), northeast of Stazione Termini, specialises in customised travel for gays and lesbians.

HOLIDAYS

Most Romans tend to take their annual holidays in August, deserting the steamy, tourist-laden city for the cooler seaside or mountains. This means that many businesses and shops close down for at least a part of the month, particularly during the week around *Ferragosto* (Feast of the Assumption) on 15 August. During this period the city is left to the tourists, who may experience frustration when they find that many restaurants, clothing and food shops are closed until early September.

Italy's public holidays are:

Epiphany 6 January

Easter Monday March/April

Liberation Day 25 April

Labour Day 1 May

Republic Day 2 June

Feast of Sts Peter and Paul 29 June (Rome only)

Feast of the Assumption 15 August

All Saints' Day 1 November

Feast of the Immaculate Conception 8 December

Christmas Day 25 December

Feast of Santo Stefano 26 December

For further details of Rome's holiday calendar see (p9).

INTERNET ACCESS

If you are bringing your laptop to Rome and want access to the Internet you will need to have a server that operates in Italy. **AOL** (www.aol.com), **CompuServe** (www.compuserve.com) and **IBM Net** (www.ibm.net) have dial-in codes in Rome and Milan as well as slower-access numbers in other towns. It's best to download a list of the dial-in numbers before you leave home. If you access your Internet email account at home through a smaller ISP or your office or school network, your best option is either to open an account with a global ISP, such as those mentioned above, or rely on Internet cafés and other public access points to collect your mail.

If you do intend to rely on Internet cafés, you'll need to carry three pieces of information with you to enable you to access your Internet mail account: your incoming (POP or IMAP) mail server name, your account name and your password. Your ISP or network supervisor will be able to give you these. Armed with this information, you should be able to access your Internet mail account from any net-connected machine in the world, provided it runs some kind of email software (remember that Netscape and Internet Explorer both have mail modules). It pays to become familiar with the process for doing this before you leave home.

Keep in mind that the telephone socket in Rome will probably be different from the one at home, so ensure that you have at least a US RJ-11 telephone adapter that works with your modem. Most electronics shops in Rome sell adapters that convert from RJ-11 to the local three-pinned plug variety; more modern phone lines take the RJ-11 jack directly. Consider bringing an extension cord and a female-to-female RJ-11 adapter to make life easier. Also make sure you've got the right AC adapter for your computer, which enables you to plug it in anywhere without frying the innards. For further information on travelling with a portable computer, see www.teleadapt.com.

Some Italian servers can provide short-term accounts for local Internet access while several ISPs offer free Internet connections: check out **Tiscalinet** (www.tiscalinet.it, Italian only), **kataweb** (www.kataweb.com); and **Libero** (www.libero.it, Italian only).

Rome has dozens of Internet cafés where you can surf the Net and send emails. Some places also provide email accounts. Costs vary but are usually between €3 and €10 an hour, with hefty discounts or bonus hours if you take out a subscription.

Easy Internet Café (Map p314–16; ☎ 06 429 03 388; Piazza Barberini 2) Computer credit at an hourly rate; you can use as little as €1 worth of time.

Netgate (Map pp308–10; ☎ 06 689 34 45; Piazza Firenze 25; including an email account €4/hr, students €3; ☺ 10.30am-9pm) There are two other locations: near St Peter's Basilica at **Borgo Santo Spirito 17-18** (Map pp308–10; ☎ 06 681 34 082) and in the underground Forum shopping area at **Stazione Termini** (Map p314–16; ☎ 06 874 06 008).

Rimaweb Internet Point (Map pp311–13; ☎ 06 688 91 356; Via del Portico d'Ottavia 2a; €1.55 per 15 mins; ⏱ 9.30am-7.30pm Mon-Fri & 11am-7pm Sat & Sun)

Bibli Bookshop (Map pp317–19; ☎ 06 588 40 97; Via dei Fienaroli 28; €4/6 per half/full hr including an email account; ⏱ 5.30pm-midnight Mon, 11am-midnight Tue-Sun) Popular with English-speaking residents as it also a café and cultural centre.

New Internet Point (Map pp317–19; ☎ 06 583 33 316; globalservice@mclink.it; Piazza Sonnino 27; €5.16/hr; ⏱ 8am-midnight) Staff are helpful and speak English.

Splashnet (Map p314–16; ☎ 06 493 82 073; €3.10/hr or 10 mins free if you're doing your laundry)

Internet Café (Map p302–3; ☎ 06 445 49 53; Via Marrucini 12; €4.15/31 per 1/10 hrs; ⏱ 9-2am Mon-Fri, 5pm-2am Sat & Sun)

Internet Café (Map pp314–16; ☎ 06 478 23 051; Via Cavour 213; €3.10/hr; ⏱ 9-1am)

LEGAL MATTERS

For many Italians, finding ways to get around the law (any law) is a way of life. Few people pay attention to speed limits, most motorcyclists and many drivers don't stop at red lights although a new points penalty system introduced at the time of writing was beginning to curb some of the worst excesses. No-one bats an eyelid about littering or dogs pooping in the middle of the footpath – even though many municipal governments have introduced laws against these things.

The voting age in Italy is 18, the age of consent 16 (homosexual and heterosexual) and you can drive at 18.

Italy has some anti-terrorism laws which could make life very difficult if you happen to be detained by the police, for any alleged offence. You can be held for 48 hours without a magistrate being informed and you can be interrogated without the presence of a lawyer. It's difficult to obtain bail and you can be held legally for up to three years without a trial.

Drugs

Although Italy's drug laws are relatively lenient, drugs are seriously frowned upon, in part due to a massive heroin problem. Although a 'few' grams of cannabis or marijuana are permissible for personal use, there is nothing to say how much a few grams is and it's better to avoid the risks altogether given the fact that the police can hold you for as long as it takes to analyse your case. If the police further decide that you are a pusher you could end up in prison.

Police

If you run into trouble in Italy, you're likely to end up dealing with either the *polizia* (police) or the *carabinieri* (military police). The *polizia*, in navy, are a civil force and take their orders from the Ministry of the Interior, while the *carabinieri*, in dark-blue with a red stripe, fall under the Ministry of Defence.

The **police headquarters** (☎ 46 86; Via San Vitale 15) is called the *questura*. The **Ufficio Stranieri** (Foreigners' Bureau; Map pp314–16; ☎ 46 86 29 87) is around the corner at Via Genova 2. It opens 24 hours a day and thefts can be reported here. You need to go here if you want to apply for a *permesso di soggiorno* (see p276).

The local police station is called the *commissariato*. Most areas of Rome have either a *commissariato* or a *carabinieri caserma* (barracks); sometimes both.

Other varieties of police in Italy include the *vigili urbani* (traffic police), with whom you will have to deal if you get a parking ticket or if your car is towed away; and the *guardia di finanza* (fiscal police) who are responsible for fighting tax evasion and drug smuggling. You could be stopped by them if you leave a shop without a receipt for your purchase – although it's a long shot.

MAPS

Lonely Planet's fold-out *Rome City Map* is perfect for sightseeing. It is plastic-coated, virtually indestructible and indicates all the major landmarks, museums and shops. There's also a street index.

Editrice Lozzi publishes a street map and bus guide entitled *Roma* (€3), available at just about any newsstand. It lists all major streets, with map references, as well as bus/tram routes. The slightly more expensive *Roma Today* (€5.50) version offers three maps in one – on the back is a map of the province of Rome and there's also an enlarged plan of the city centre. Lozzi also publishes an excellent Roma Metro-Bus map (€5.50). You can find these maps in bookshops, news and magazine outlets and at Stazione Termini.

The free city map, *Charta Roma*, has a reasonable map of the city centre with major monuments and sights indicated. It also details the city's public transport routes, including buses, trams and the metro. Information is in English and Italian. Pick it up at tourist offices or at the ATAC booth in Piazza dei Cinquecento, in front of Stazione Termini (Map pp314–16).

If you're driving, the best road maps are published by the Touring Club Italia, available at all good bookshops.

For maps of Ancient Rome, Lozzi also publishes the very good *Archaeo Map* (€5), a plan of the Roman Forum, Palatine and Colosseum and *Roma Antiqua*. The smaller *Ancient Rome* (€2), published by Electa, is a good introduction and is available at most museums and bookshops associated with Rome's museums.

MEDICAL SERVICES

Italy has a public health system which is legally bound to provide emergency care to everyone. This is not so for non-emergency cases. EU nationals are entitled to free medical care with an E111 form, which they should get from their home local health authority. They will also require limitless patience as the bureaucratic system is most charitably described as Byzantine.

Non-EU citizens should ensure they are covered by medical insurance.

Clinics

If you need an ambulance call ☎ 118. For emergency treatment, go straight to the *pronto soccorso* (casualty) section of a *ospedale* (public hospital), where it's also possible to receive emergency dental treatment. You are likely to find doctors who speak English, or a volunteer translator service. Rome's major hospitals are:

Ospedale Bambino Gesù (Map pp308–10; ☎ 06 685 92 351; Piazza Sant' Onofrio) Paediatric hospital on the Giancolo.

Ospedale Fatebenefratelli (Map pp317–19; ☎ 06 683 71; Piazza Fatebenefratelli, Isola Tiberina)

Ospedale Nuova Regina Margherita (Map pp317–19; ☎ 06 581 06 58; Via Morosini 30, Trastevere)

Ospedale San Camillo (Map pp302–3; ☎ 06 587 01; Circonvallazione Gianicolense 87) Free clinic.

Ospedale San Gallicano (Map pp317–19; ☎ 06 588 23 90; Via San Gallicano) For skin problems and venereal diseases.

Ospedale San Giacomo (Map pp304–5; ☎ 06 362 61; Via Canova 29, off Via del Corso near Piazza del Popolo)

Ospedale San Giovanni (Map pp320–1; ☎ 06 770 51; Via Amba Aradam 8, near Piazza San Giovanni in Laterano)

Ospedale Santo Spirito (Map pp308–10; ☎ 06 683 51; Lungotevere in Sassia 1)

Policlinico Umberto I (Map pp314–16; ☎ 06 499 71; Via del Policlinico 155, near Stazione Termini)

METRIC SYSTEM

Many travellers will have to cope with the change from pounds to kilograms, miles to kilometres and gallons to litres. A standard conversion table can be found in the Quick Reference displayed on the inside front cover of this book.

Basic terms for weight include *un etto* (100g) and *un chilo* (1kg). Half a kilo corresponds to about six *panini* while 100g represents prosciutto for a picnic for four. Note that Italians generally indicate decimals with commas and thousands with points.

MONEY

On 1 January 2002 the euro became the currency of cash transactions in all of Italy and throughout the EU (except for the three foot-draggers: Denmark, Sweden and the UK). The euro is divided into 100 cents. Coin denominations are one, two, five, 10, 20 and 50 cents, €1 and €2. The notes are €5, €10, €20, €50, €100, €200 and €500.

After a fairly uncertain start the euro has taken hold and at the time of writing was doing very well against the US dollar, thus signalling a major departure for an Italian currency; the lira was notoriously weak and its massive denominations were a nightmare for visitors to get to grips with.

Exchange rates are given in the Quick Reference displayed on the inside front cover of this book and a guide to costs can be found on p16.

ATMs

Credit cards can be used in *bancomat* (ATMs) displaying the appropriate sign, provided you have a PIN.

You can also obtain cash advances over the counter in many banks – Visa and MasterCard are among the most widely recognised.

It is possible to use your own ATM debit card in machines throughout Italy to obtain money from your own bank account. This is without doubt the simplest way to handle your money while travelling.

Italian ATMs are notoriously fickle. If an ATM rejects your card, don't despair or start wasting money on international calls to your bank.

Try a few more ATMs displaying your credit card's logo before assuming that the problem lies with your card rather than the local system.

Currency & Exchange Rates

A good website for keeping abreast of exchange rates is www.oanda.com. See the Quick Reference on the inside front cover of this book for a list of exchange rates.

Credit Cards

Credit and debit cards enable you to get money after hours and on weekends, and the exchange rate is better than that offered for travellers cheques or cash exchanges.

Major credit cards, such as Visa, MasterCard, Eurocard, Cirrus and Euro Cheques cards, are accepted throughout Italy. *Pensioni*, smaller trattorie and pizzerie still tend to accept cash only.

If your credit card is lost, stolen or swallowed by an ATM, telephone toll-free to have an immediate stop put on its use. For **MasterCard** the number in Italy is ☎ 800 87 08 66, or make a reverse-charges call to St Louis in the USA on ☎ 314 275 66 90; for **Visa**, phone ☎ 800 81 90 14 in Italy. If, by chance, you have a credit card issued in Italy call ☎ 800 82 20 56 to have it blocked.

American Express is also widely accepted throughout Italy (although it's not as common as Visa or MasterCard). Amex's full-service offices (such as those in Rome and Milan) will issue customers with new cards, usually within 24 hours and sometimes immediately, if yours has been lost or stolen. Some Amex offices also have ATMs that you can use to obtain cash advances if you have made the necessary arrangements in your own country.

The toll-free emergency number to report a lost or stolen Amex card varies according to where the card was issued. Check with **Amex** in your country or contact the office in Rome on ☎ 06 7 22 82, which itself has a 24-hour cardholders' service.

Changing Money

You can change money in banks, at the post office or in a *cambio* (exchange office). Banks are generally the most reliable and tend to offer the best rates. Commission fluctuates and depends on whether you are changing cash or cheques.

While the post office charges a flat rate of €0.60 per cash transaction, banks charge at least €1.55. Travellers cheques attract higher fees. Exchange booths often advertise 'no commission' but the rate of exchange is usually inferior.

The desire to save on such fees by making occasional large transactions should be balanced against a healthy fear of pickpockets.

Receipts

Tightening of laws on the payment of taxes means that the onus is on the buyer to ask for and retain receipts for all goods and services. This applies to everything. Although it rarely happens, you could be asked by an officer of the *guardia di finanza* (fiscal police) to produce the receipt immediately after you leave a shop. If you don't have it, you may be obliged to pay a fine of up to €155.

Travellers Cheques

These are a safe way to carry money and are easily cashed at banks and exchange offices in Rome and throughout Italy. Always keep the bank receipt (listing the cheque numbers) separate from the cheques and keep a list of the numbers of those you have cashed – this will reduce problems in the event of loss or theft. Check the conditions applying to such circumstances before buying the cheques.

If you buy your travellers cheques in euros, there should be no commission charge when cashing them. Most hard currencies are widely accepted, although you may have occasional trouble with the New Zealand dollar. Buying cheques in a third currency (such as US dollars if you are not coming from the USA) means you pay commission when you buy the cheques and again when cashing them in Italy. Get most of the cheques in fairly large denominations to save on per-cheque exchange charges.

Travellers using the better-known cheques, such as Visa, American Express (Amex) and Thomas Cook, will have little trouble in Rome. Amex, in particular, has offices in all the major Italian cities and agents in many smaller cities. If you lose your **Amex** cheques while in Rome, you can call a 24-hour toll-free number (☎ 800 87 20 00). For **Thomas Cook** or **MasterCard** cheques call ☎ 800 87 20 50 and for Visa cheques call ☎ 800 87 41 55.

Take along your passport when you go to cash travellers cheques.

NEWSPAPERS & MAGAZINES
English Language

In Rome it's relatively easy to find English-language publications, albeit at a slightly higher price than you'd pay at home. The *International Herald Tribune* is available Monday to Saturday. It has a four-page supplement, *Italy Daily*, specifically on Italian news.

British daily papers, including the *Guardian*, the *Times*, the *Daily Telegraph*, the *Independent* and the *Financial Times* as well as various tabloids, are sent from London. They are available from newsstands towards lunchtime on the day of publication. British Sunday papers are usually available on the following Monday.

US newspapers *USA Today*, the *Wall Street Journal Europe* and the *New York Times* are also available, as are *Time*, *Newsweek* and the *Economist*.

The major German, French and Spanish dailies and some Scandinavian papers can also be found fairly easily. If you can't find any foreign papers try one of the larger central newsstands on Via del Corso, Piazza Navona, Via Veneto, Largo di Torre Argentina or at Stazione Termini.

Wanted in Rome (€0.77) is a fortnightly English-language news and listings magazine aimed at Rome's foreign residents. It contains informative articles about Italian politics and bureaucracy, city news, history and culture, plus arts and entertainment listings and reviews. It also has hundreds of classified ads that are useful for those seeking accommodation or jobs.

Italian Language

Italian newspapers can be frustrating, even for fluent Italian readers. The articles tend to be long-winded and the point, if indeed there is one, is usually buried in the final paragraphs. The domestic politics section, which normally occupies the first four or five pages of the newspaper, is difficult to follow even for the most dedicated reader and if you miss an instalment it's almost impossible to catch up on events.

Il Messaggero is the most popular broadsheet in Rome. It is especially good for news about Rome itself and the Vatican, and has a weekly listings supplement, *Metro*.

Milan-based *Corriere della Sera* is the country's leading daily and has the best foreign news pages and the most comprehensive and comprehensible political coverage. Rome-based *La Repubblica* is its major competitor. Its Thursday supplement, *Trovaroma*, provides entertainment listings. The church paper *L'Osservatore Romano* is published daily in Italian (with weekly editions in English and other foreign languages) and is the official voice of the Vatican. There are several other daily papers. Most Italian daily newspapers cost €0.90

(or €1.20 if a supplement is included) and are available from all newsstands.

Porta Portese (€1) is a weekly newspaper full of classified ads of every description. If you're looking for a flat or a second-hand synthesiser, this is a good place to start. Rome's best listings guide *Roma C'é* (€1) comes out every Wednesday. There is a small section in English towards the end.

PHARMACIES

Farmacie (pharmacies) usually open 9am to 12.30pm and 3.30pm to 7.30pm Monday to Friday, and Saturday mornings. They open on Sunday at night and for emergencies on a rotation basis. Night pharmacies are listed in the daily newspapers (usually at the back near the cinema listings). When a pharmacy is closed, it is required by law to post on the door a list of others open nearby.

There is a **24-hour pharmacy** (Map pp314–16; ☎ 06 488 00 19; Piazza dei Cinquecento 51) just outside Stazione Termini. Within the station, a pharmacy on the lower-ground floor opens 7.30am to 10pm daily.

The **Farmacia del Vaticano** (Map pp308–10; ☎ 06 698 83 422), just inside the Porta Sant' Anna, sells certain drugs that are not available in Italian pharmacies, and will also fill prescriptions from some other countries, which Italian pharmacies cannot do.

If you take a regular medication, make sure you bring an adequate supply. Also make sure you note the drug's generic name (rather than the brand name) in case you need a prescription written in Italian.

POST

Italy's postal system is notoriously unreliable. The most efficient service to use is *posta prioritaria* (priority mail).

Francobolli (stamps) are available at post offices and authorised tobacconists (look for the official *tabacchi* sign: a big 'T', usually white on black). Since letters often need to be weighed, what you get at the tobacconist's for international air mail will occasionally be an approximation of the proper rate. Tobacconists keep regular shop hours.

Rome's **main post office** (Piazza San Silvestro 18-20) opens 8.30am to 6pm Monday to Friday, 8.30am to 2pm Saturday and 9am until 2pm on Sunday.

There are local post offices in every district of the city. They usually open 8.30am to 1.50pm Monday to Friday and 8.30am to 11.50pm on Saturday. All post offices close two hours earlier than normal on the last business day of each month.

Rates

The cost of sending a letter air mail (*via aerea*) will depend on its weight, the destination and the method of postage. The ordinary postal rates for letters up to 20g are divided into three zones: Zone 1 (Europe and the Mediterranean Basin) €0.41; Zone 2 (other countries in Africa, Asia and America) €0.52; and Zone 3 (the Pacific including Australia, Japan and New Zealand) €0.52. It can take up to two weeks for mail to arrive in the UK or USA, while a letter to Australia will take between two and three weeks. Postcards can take even longer to arrive. If you're worried about arriving home before your postcards, put them in an envelope and send them as letters.

For *posta prioritaria* (priority mail), letters up to 20g cost Zone 1 €0.62 and Zone 2 and 3 €0.77. This service guarantees to deliver letters within Europe in three days and to the rest of the world within four to eight days. Letters weighing 21g to 100g cost €1.24 within Europe, €1.55 to Africa, Asia and the Americas and €1.81 to Australia and New Zealand.

For more important items, you could use *raccomandata* (registered mail) – €2.17 on top of the normal cost of the letter – or *assicurato* (insured mail), the cost of which depends on the value of the object being sent (€5.16 for objects up to the value of €51.65 in Zone 1).

Urgent mail can be sent by *postacelere* (also known as CAI Post), the Italian post office's courier service.

Information about postal services and rates can be obtained on ☎ 800 22 26 66 or online at www.poste.it (Italian only).

Receiving Mail

Poste restante (general delivery) is known as *fermo posta* in Italy. Mail to Rome should be addressed as follows:

John SMITH,
Fermo Posta,
00100, Roma,
Italy

You will need to pick up your letters in person.

American Express card or travellers cheque holders can use the free client mail-holding service at American Express offices. You can obtain a list of these online at http://travel.am ericanexpress.com or from any **American Express office** (try Piazza di Spagna 38; ☎ 06 6 76 41). In all cases, take your passport when you go to pick up mail.

Vatican Post

Many people, both Romans and tourists, choose to use the Vatican postal system instead of the Italian one. Rates are similar but many consider the service considerably better. There is a post office in **Piazza di San Pietro** (Map pp308–10) next to the information office and another one inside the Vatican Museums. These post offices don't accept poste restante mail.

RADIO

There are three state-owned stations: RAI-1 (1332kHz AM or 89.7MHz FM), RAI-2 (846kHz AM or 91.7MHz FM) and RAI-3 (93.7MHz FM). They combine classical and light music with news broadcasts and discussion programs. RAI-2 broadcasts news in English every day from 1am to 5am at three minutes past the hour.

Popular commercial radio stations in Rome include: Radio Centro Suono (101.3MHz FM); the Naples-based Radio Kiss Kiss (97.25MHz FM); and Radio Città Futura (97.7MHz FM), which broadcasts a listing of the day's events in Rome at 10am daily.

You can pick up the BBC World Service on medium wave at 648kHz, short wave at 6.195MHz, 9.410MHz, 12.095MHz and 15.575MHz, and on long wave at 198kHz, depending on where you are and the time of day. Voice of America (VOA) can usually be found on short wave at 15.205MHz.

Vatican Radio (1530kHz AM, 93.3MHz FM and 105MHz FM) broadcasts the news in English at 7am, 8.30am, 6.15pm and 9.50pm. The reports usually include a run-down on what the pope is up to on any particular day.

SAFETY

Rome is not a dangerous city but pickpockets and bag-snatchers are active. The best way to avoid being robbed is to wear a money belt under your clothing. You should keep all important items, such as money, passport, other papers and tickets, in your money belt at all times. If you are carrying a bag or camera, ensure that you wear the strap across your body and have the bag on the side away from the road to deter thieves who snatch items while on motorcycles and scooters. Since the aim of young motorcycle bandits is often fun rather than gain you are just as likely to find yourself relieved of your sunglasses – or worse, of an earring. A favourite method is to knock your front mirror and then, when you put your hand out to adjust it, to snatch your watch.

You should also watch out for groups of dishevelled-looking women and children. They generally work in groups of four or five and carry paper or cardboard, which they use to distract your attention while they swarm around and rifle through your pockets and bag. Never underestimate their skill – they are lightning fast and very adept. A city rumour has it that former sprinter Ben Johnson had his wallet pinched and was then outrun by his fleeing assailant. Their favourite haunts are in and near major train stations, at tourist sights (such as the Colosseum) and in shopping areas. If you notice that you have been targeted by a group, either take evasive action, such as crossing the street, or shout '*Va via!*' ('Go away!') in a loud, angry voice.

Pickpockets often hang out on crowded buses (the No 64 bus, which runs from Stazione Termini to the Vatican, is notorious) and in crowded areas such as markets. There is only one way to deter pickpockets: simply *do not* carry any money or valuables in your pockets and be very careful about your bags. Be cautious, even in hotels, and don't leave valuables lying around.

Parked cars, particularly those with foreign number plates or rental company stickers, are also prime targets for thieves. Try removing or covering the stickers and leave a local newspaper on the seat to make it look like a local car. Never leave valuables in your car – in fact, try not to leave anything on display if you can help it and certainly not overnight. It is a good idea to pay extra to leave your car in supervised car parks.

When driving in town you also need to beware of snatch thieves when you pull up at traffic lights. Keep the doors locked and, if you have the windows open, ensure that there is nothing valuable on the dashboard or on the back seats.

Unfortunately, some Italians practise a more insidious form of theft: short-changing. Numerous travellers have reported losing money this way. Take the time to acquaint yourself with euro denominations. When paying for something, keep an eye on the notes you hand over and then count your change carefully. One popular dodge occurs when you hand over a banknote, receive some change and, while the person who sold you the goods hesitates, you hurry off without checking it. If you'd stayed for another five seconds, the rest of the change probably would have been handed over without any fuss.

In case of theft or loss, always report the incident to the police within 24 hours and ask for a statement, otherwise your travel insurance company won't pay out.

TAXES & REFUNDS

A value-added tax of around 19%, known as IVA (Imposta di Valore Aggiunto), is slapped onto just about everything in Italy. If you are a non-EU resident and you spend more than €335 on a purchase, you can claim a refund when you leave. The refund only applies to purchases from affiliated retail outlets which display a 'tax free for tourists' sign. You have to complete a form at the point of sale, then get it stamped by Italian customs as you leave. At major airports you can then get an immediate cash refund; otherwise it will be refunded to your credit card. For information, pick up a pamphlet on the scheme from participating stores.

TELEPHONE

The area code for Rome is 06; the international code for Italy is 39. The area code is followed by anything from four to eight digits. Area codes, including the 0, are an integral part of all telephone numbers in Italy. Mobile phone numbers begin with a three-digit prefix such as 330. Toll-free (free-phone) numbers are known as *numeri verdi* and usually start with 800. National call rate numbers start with 848 or 199. To call Italy from abroad dial ☎ 39 and then the area code, including the 0. For directory inquiries, dial ☎ 12.

Public Phones

The state-run Telecom Italia is the largest telecommunications organisation in Italy and its silver public pay phones are liberally scattered about town. The most common accept only *schede telefoniche* (telephone cards), although you will still find some that accept cards and coins. Some card phones accept credit cards.

Telecom pay phones can be found in the streets, train stations and some stores as well as in Telecom offices. Where these offices are staffed, it is possible to make international calls and pay at the desk afterwards. You can buy phonecards at post offices (usually a fixed euro rate of €5/10/20), tobacconists and newsstands. You must break the top left-hand corner of the card before you can use it.

Public phones operated by the private telecommunications companies Infostrada and Albacom can be found in airports and stations. These phones accept Infostrada or Albacom phonecards (available from post offices, tobacconists and newspaper stands). The rates are slightly cheaper than Telecom's for long-distance and international calls.

There are cut-price call centres all over Italy. These are run by various companies and the rates are lower than Telecom payphones for international calls. You simply place your call from a private booth inside the centre and pay for it when you've finished. Not all phone centres accept credit cards.

Domestic Calls

Rates, particularly for long-distance calls, are among the highest in Europe. The cheapest time for domestic calls is from 11pm to 8am and all of Sunday. A local call from a public phone will cost €0.10 for three to six minutes, depending on the time of day you call. Peak call times are 8am to 6.30pm Monday to Friday and 8am to 1pm on Saturday. Rates for long-distance calls within Italy depend on the time of day and the distance involved. At the worst, one minute will cost about €0.20 in peak periods.

International Calls

If you need to call overseas, beware of the cost – calls to most European countries cost about €0.50 per minute (closer to €1 from a public phone). Travellers from countries that offer direct dialling services paid for at home-country rates (such as AT&T in the USA and Telstra in Australia) should take advantage of them.

Direct international calls can easily be made from public telephones by using a phonecard. Off-peak times are between 11pm and 8am and all of Sunday. Dial ☎ 00 to get out of Italy, then the relevant country and area codes, followed by the telephone number. It is, however, worth noting that the cheap international rates advertised on cards at most public payphones are ludicrously expensive.

To make a reverse charges (collect) international call from a public telephone, dial ☎ 170. For European countries dial ☎ 15. All operators speak English.

Easier, and often cheaper, is using the Country Direct service for your country. You dial the number and request a reverse charges call through the operator in your country.

Numbers for this service include:

Australia (Telstra)	☎ 172-10 61
Australia (Optus)	☎ 172-11 61
Canada	☎ 172-10 01
France	☎ 172-00 33
New Zealand	☎ 172-10 64
UK (BT)	☎ 172-00 44
UK (BT Chargecard Operator)	☎ 172-01 44
USA (AT&T)	☎ 172-10 11
USA (IDB)	☎ 172-17 77
USA (MCI)	☎ 172-10 22
USA (Sprint)	☎ 172-18 77

For international directory inquiries telephone ☎ 176.

Mobile Phones

Italy uses GSM 900/1800, which is compatible with the rest of Europe and Australia but not with North American GSM 1900 or the totally different system in Japan (although some GSM 1900/900 phones do work here). If you have a GSM phone, check with your service provider about using it in Italy and beware of calls being routed internationally (very expensive for a 'local' call).

Italy has one of the highest levels of mobile phone penetration in Europe, and there are several companies through which you can get a temporary or prepaid account if you already own a GSM, dual- or tri-band cellular phone. You will usually need your passport to open an account.

Both TIM (Telecom Italia Mobile) and Omnitel offer *prepagato* (prepaid) accounts for GSM phones (frequency 900mHz), whereby you can buy a SIM card (€51.65) for either network which gives you €25.80 worth of calls. You can then top up the account with multiples of €25.80 (plus a €5.15 service fee) as required. There are TIM and Omnitel retail outlets throughout Rome. Calls on these plans cost around €0.10 per minute.

The dual-band operator Wind works on frequencies of 900mHz and 1800mHz and also offers prepaid accounts. You don't pay for Wind's SIM card but calls are more expensive than Telecom and Omnitel – around €0.25 per minute for the first three minutes, then €0.10 per minute. There are Wind retail outlets in Rome.

Check with your mobile service provider in your home country to ascertain whether your handset allows use of another SIM card.

TELEVISION

Italian television is compellingly awful. There are an inordinate number of interminable quiz shows and variety programs with troupes of scantily clad women prancing and thrusting across the set. The home-bred soap operas are generally so dreadful that it's sometimes embarrassing to watch, but they attract a huge following. So, too, do the many imported soaps, mainly from the USA, all of which are dubbed into Italian. Current-release films transfer to the small screen relatively quickly in Italy but they are always dubbed.

The state-run channels are RAI-1, RAI-2 and RAI-3. The main commercial stations are Canale 5, Italia 1, Rete 4 and newcomer La7. The French-language TV channel, Antenne 2, can sometimes be received on Channel 10.

Most of Rome's mid- to top-range hotels, as well as many bars and restaurants, have satellite TV and can receive BBC World, Sky Channel, CNN and NBC Superchannel.

TIME

Italy is in a single time zone, one hour ahead of GMT. Countries such as France, Germany and Spain are in the same zone. Greece and Israel are one hour ahead, the UK one hour behind. When it's noon in Rome, it's 3am in San Francisco; 6am in New York; 11am in London; 7pm in Perth; 9pm in Sydney and 11pm in Auckland.

Daylight-saving time, when clocks are moved forward one hour, starts on the last Sunday in March. Clocks are put back an hour on the last Sunday in October.

Italy operates on a 24-hour clock, so 6pm is 18.00.

TIPPING

You are not expected to tip but it's common (in bars, for example) to leave a small amount:

€0.10 or €0.20. If there is no service charge, the customer might consider leaving up to a 10% tip (see Eating, p151, for more details). Tipping taxi drivers is not common practice but you should tip the porter at higher-class hotels.

TOILETS

Public toilets are not exactly widespread in Rome (it is estimated that there are less than 40 of them in the whole city) although the situation has improved slightly as some of the 'portaloos' brought in for the Jubilee year have remained. Most people use the toilets in bars and cafés – although you might need to buy a coffee first.

At Stazione Termini there are two sets of public toilets on the lower-ground level that charge €0.60. The toilets on the Via Giolitti side also have showers (€7.80). There are also toilets at **Piazza di Spagna** (Map pp308–10; 10am-7.40pm) and **Piazza di San Silvestro** (Map pp308–10; 10am-7.40pm).

TOURIST OFFICES

There's a **multilingual tourist infoline** (☎ 06 360 04 399) which operates from 9am to 7pm daily. Otherwise tourist information offices are helpful and numerous:

Rome Tourism Board (Map pp314–16; ☎ 06 48 89 91; www.romaturismo.com; Via Parigi 5; 9am-7pm Mon-Sat) Information on accommodation, itineraries, activities, maps and guides to monuments, within Rome and Lazio.

Enjoy Rome (Map pp314–16; ☎ 06 445 18 43; www.enjoyrome.com; Via Marghera 8; 8.30am-7pm Mon-Fri, till 2pm Sat) A privately run tourist office just north-east of the train station with an excellent Rome City Guide.

Stazione Termini (Map pp314–16; ☎ 06 489 06 300; end of Platform 4; 8am-9pm)

As well as an information point at Fiumicino (Terminal B, Arrivals) there are 11 official Tourist Information kiosks dotted around the city, all of which open 9.30am-7.30pm daily:

Castel Sant'Angelo (Map p308–10; Piazza Pia)

Fontana di Trevi (Map p311–13; Via Marco Minghetti)

Piazza dei Cinquecento (Map pp314–16; outside Stazione Termini)

Piazza Navona (Map pp311–13; Piazza delle Cinque Lune)

Piazza San Giovanni in Laterano (Map pp320–1; opposite the basilica)

Piazza Santa Maria Maggiore (Map pp314–16; Via dell'Olmata)

Stazione Termini (Map pp314–16; Galleria Gommata)

Trastevere (Map pp317–19; Piazza Sonnino)

Via dei Fori Imperiali (Map pp314–16; near Largo Ricci)

Via del Corso (Map pp308–10; Largo Goldoni)

Via Nazionale (Map pp314–16; next to the Palazzo delle Esposizioni)

In the Vatican City, **Centro Servizi Pellegrini e Turisti** (Map pp308–10; ☎ 06 698 84 466; Piazza San Pietro; ◐ 9am-5pm Mon-Sat), left of the basilica, has general information about St Peter's and the Vatican.

Internet Resources

Useful information is also available online at:

Lonely Planet (www.lonelyplanet.com) A page is dedicated to Rome and there's a guide to the Vatican as well.

Rome municipal government (www.romaturismo.it) It provides a good overview of current and forthcoming major events.

Rome Tourist Board (www.romaturismo.it, click on Tour Operators) Listings and prices of all officially recognised accommodation options in Rome.

The Vatican (www.vatican.va) The official site which details everything from the history of the Swiss Guards to the laws of the Vatican State.

VISAS

Italy is among the 15 countries that have signed the Schengen Convention, an agreement whereby all EU member countries (except the UK and Ireland), Iceland and Norway agreed to abolish checks at common borders. Legal residents of one Schengen country do not require a visa for another Schengen country. Citizens of the UK and Ireland are also exempt from visa requirements for Schengen countries. Nationals of Australia, Canada, Israel, Japan, New Zealand, Switzerland and the USA, do not require visas for tourist visits of up to 90 days to any Schengen country.

The standard tourist visa is valid for up to 90 days. A Schengen visa that has been issued by one Schengen country is generally valid for travel in other Schengen countries. Individual Schengen countries may, however, impose additional restrictions on certain nationalities. It is therefore worth checking visa regulations with the consulate of each country you plan to visit.

It's now mandatory that you apply for a Schengen visa in your country of residence.

You can apply for no more than two Schengen visas in any 12-month period and they are not renewable inside Italy. If you are going to visit more than one Schengen country, you are supposed to apply for the visa at a consulate of your main destination country or the first country you intend to visit.

EU citizens do not require any permits to live or work in Italy. They are, however, required to register with a police station if they take up residence and obtain a *permesso di soggiorno*.

Permesso di Soggiorno

If you plan to stay at the same address for more than one week you are obliged to report to the police station to receive a *permesso di soggiorno* (permit to remain in the country). Tourists staying in hotels are not required to do this.

A *permesso di soggiorno* only becomes a necessity if you plan to study, work (legally) or live in Italy. Obtaining one is never a pleasant experience. It involves enduring long queues and the potential frustration of finally arriving at the counter to find that you don't have all the necessary documents.

The exact requirements, such as specific documents and *marche da bollo* (official stamps), can change from year to year. In general, you will need: a valid passport, containing a visa stamp indicating your date of entry into Italy; a special visa issued in your own country if you are planning to study; four passport-style photographs; and proof of your ability to support yourself financially.

It is best to obtain precise information on what is required. Sometimes there is a list posted at the police station, otherwise you will need to go to the information counter.

The main Rome *questura*, in Via Genova, is notorious for delays and best avoided if possible. You can also apply at the *ufficio stranieri* (foreigners' bureau) of the police station closest to where you are staying.

Study Visas

Non-EU citizens who want to study at a university or language school in Italy must have a study visa. These visas can be obtained from your nearest Italian embassy or consulate. You will normally require confirmation of your enrolment, proof of payment of fees and the adequate funds to support yourself before a visa is issued. The visa will then cover only the period of the enrolment. This type of visa is renewable within Italy but, again, only with confirmation of ongoing enrolment and proof that you are able to support yourself (bank statements are preferred).

WOMEN TRAVELLERS

Rome is not a dangerous city for women but those travelling alone should use their common sense. Avoid walking alone in dark streets, and look for hotels that are central (unsafe areas are noted throughout this book). Women should also avoid hitchhiking alone.

Many will often find themselves plagued by unwanted attention from men – usually stares, whistles and the occasional *'ciao bella'*. Usually this is more annoying than threatening. Lone women will also find it difficult to remain alone – Italian men harass you as you walk down the street, drink a coffee or read in the park. The best defence is generally to ignore them but if that doesn't work, politely tell them that you're waiting for your *fidanzato* (boyfriend) or *marito* (husband) and walk away. If all else fails, go to the *carabinieri*.

Wandering hands can also be a problem, particularly on crowded public transport. If you feel someone start touching you, make a fuss. A loud *'Che schifo!'* ('How disgusting!') usually works.

The *Handbook for Women Travellers* by M and G Goss is a good read for women who travel solo.

WORK

It is illegal for non-EU citizens to work in Italy without a work permit but trying to obtain one can be time consuming. EU citizens are allowed to work in Italy but they still need to obtain a *permesso di soggiorno* (p276) from the main *questura*. New immigration laws require foreign workers to be 'legalised' through their employers, which can apply even to cleaners and baby-sitters. The employers then pay pension and health insurance contributions. This doesn't mean that unofficial work can't still be found.

Jobs are advertised in *Porta Portese* and in *Wanted in Rome* (www.wantedinrome.com). You could also look in *Il Messaggero* and the *Herald Tribune* for job ads, and on the bulletin boards of English-language bookshops. See Shopping (p201).

Work Permits

Non-EU citizens wishing to work in Italy will need to obtain a *permesso di lavoro* (work permit). If you intend to work for an Italian company, the company must organise the *permesso* and forward it to the Italian consulate in your country – only then will you be issued an appropriate visa.

If non-EU citizens intend to work for a non-Italian company or will be paid in foreign currency or wish to go freelance, they must organise the visa and *permesso* in their country of residence through an Italian consulate. This process can take many months.

In any case it's advisable to seek detailed information from an Italian embassy or consulate on the exact requirements before attempting to organise a legitimate job in Italy. Many foreigners, however, don't bother with such formalities, preferring to work undeclared in areas such as teaching English, bar work and seasonal jobs.

Working Holiday

The best options, once you're in the country, are restaurant, bar and nightclub work during the tourist season. Baby-sitting is also a good possibility; as is au pair work, organised before you come to Italy. Two useful guides are *The Au Pair and Nanny's Guide to Working Abroad* (Vacation Work Publications; 1997), by S Griffith and S Legg, and *Work Your Way Around the World* (Globe Pequot Pr; 2001) by S Griffith. You may be able to pick up a summer job accompanying a family on their annual beach holiday – you could look in *Wanted in Rome* (www.wantedinrome.com) or even place an advertisement.

Teaching English

The easiest source of work for foreigners is teaching English, but even with full qualifications an American, Australian, Canadian or New Zealander might find it difficult to secure a permanent position. Most of the larger, more reputable schools will hire only people with work permits, but their attitude can become more flexible if demand for teachers is high and they come across someone with good qualifications. The more professional schools will require a TEFL (Teaching English as a Foreign Language) certificate. It is advisable to apply for work early in the year, in order to be considered for positions available in October (language school years correspond roughly to the Italian school year which is late September to the end of June).

Numerous schools hire people without work permits or qualifications but the pay is usually low (around €10 per hour). It is more lucrative to advertise your services and pick up private students (although rates vary wildly, ranging from as low as €15 up to €26 per hour). The average rate is around €20.

Most people get started by placing advertisements in shop windows and on university notice boards, or in a local publication, such as *Wanted in Rome* or *Porta Portese*.

International Organisations

Several international organisations are based in Rome, including the Food and Agriculture Organization of the United Nations and the UN World Food Program. However, unless you've got very specific skills, they are hard to get into. Foreign embassies sometimes require administrative or domestic staff and prefer to employ their own nationals.

Tour Guiding

If you've got strong vocal chords, plenty of stamina and an encyclopaedic knowledge of Rome's ancient ruins (or willingness to learn about it) then tour guiding could be a good option. There are plenty of companies that run 'promotional' tours of the Roman Forum and Colosseum – designed as a sweetener to get tourists to sign up for another paid tour – and they sometimes need more tour leaders. Try out a tour and go from there.

Volunteer

Volunteer work in Rome is fairly thin on the ground for foreigners, especially for those who don't speak Italian. However, volunteers are always sought at the **Torre Argentina Cat Sanctuary** (☎ 06 687 21 33; www.romancats.de) which looks after a resident population of the capital's strays.

Alternatively, you could consult Vacation Work's *International Directory of Voluntary Work* by Louise Whetter and Victoria Pybus.

Language

Language

It's true – anyone can speak another language. Don't worry if you haven't studied languages before or that you studied a language at school for years and can't remember any of it. It doesn't even matter if you failed English grammar. After all, that's never affected your ability to speak English! And this is the key to picking up a language in another country: you just need to start speaking.

Learn a few key phrases before you go. Write them on pieces of paper and stick them on the fridge, by the bed or even on the computer – anywhere that you'll see them often.

You'll find that locals appreciate travellers trying their language, no matter how muddled you may think you sound. So don't just stand there, say something! If you want to learn more Italian than we've included here, pick up a copy of Lonely Planet's comprehensive but user-friendly *Italian phrasebook*.

PRONUNCIATION

c	as the 'k' in 'kit' before **a**, **o** and **u**; as the 'ch' in 'choose' before **e** and **i**
ch	as the 'k' in 'kit'
g	as the 'g' in 'get' before **a**, **o**, **u** and **h**; as the 'j' in 'jet' before **e** and **i**
gli	as the 'lli' in 'million'
gn	as the 'ny' in 'canyon'
h	always silent
r	a rolled 'rr' sound
sc	as the 'sh' in 'sheep' before **e** and **i**; as 'sk' before **a**, **o**, **u** and **h**
z	as the 'ts' in 'lights', except at the beginning of a word, when it's as the 'ds' in 'suds'

SOCIAL
Meeting People

Hello.
Buon giorno.
Goodbye.
Arrivederci.
Please.
Per favore.
Thank you (very much).
(Mille) Grazie.
Yes/No.
Sì/No.
Do you speak English?
Parla inglese?
Do you understand (me)?
(Mi) capisce?
Yes, I understand.
Sì, capisco.

No, I don't understand.
No, non capisco.

Could you please ...?
Potrebbe ...?
  repeat that — ripeterlo
  speak more slowly — parlare più lentamente
  write it down — scriverlo

Going Out

What's on ...?
Che c'è in programma ...?
  locally — in zona
  this weekend — questo fine settimana
  today — oggi
  tonight — stasera

Where are the ...?
Dove sono ...?
  clubs — dei clubs
  gay venues — dei locali gay
  places to eat — posti dove mangiare
  pubs — dei pub

Is there a local entertainment guide?
C'è una guida agli spettacoli in questa città?

PRACTICAL
Question Words

Who? — Chi?
What? — Che?
When? — Quando?
Where? — Dove?
How? — Come?

Numbers & Amounts

1	uno
2	due
3	tre
4	quattro
5	cinque
6	sei
7	sette
8	otto
9	nove
10	dieci
11	undici
12	dodici
13	tredici
14	quattordici
15	quindici
16	sedici
17	diciasette
18	diciotto
19	dicianove
20	venti
21	ventuno
22	ventidue
30	trenta
40	quaranta
50	cinquanta
60	sessanta
70	settanta
80	ottanta
90	novanta
100	cento
1000	mille

Days

Monday	lunedì
Tuesday	martedì
Wednesday	mercoledì
Thursday	giovedì
Friday	venerdì
Saturday	sabato
Sunday	domenica

Accommodation

I'm looking for a ...
Cerco ...

guesthouse	una pensione
hotel	un albergo
youth hostel	un ostello per la gioventù

Do you have any rooms available?
Ha camere libere?

I'd like (a) ...
Vorrei ...

single room	una camera singola
double room	una camera matrimoniale
room with two beds	una camera doppia

with a bathroom	con bagno

How much is it ...?	Quanto costa ...?
per night	per la notte
per person	per ciascuno

Banking

I'd like to ...
Vorrei ...

cash a cheque	riscuotere un assegno
change money	cambiare denaro
change some travellers cheques	cambiare degli assegni di viaggio

Where's the nearest ...?
Dov'è il ... più vicino?

automatic teller machine	bancomat
foreign exchange office	cambio

Post

Where is the post office?
Dov'è la posta?

I want to send a ...
Voglio spedire ...

fax	un fax
parcel	un pachetto
postcard	una cartolina

I want to buy ...
Voglio comprare ...

an aerogram	un aerogramma
an envelope	una busta
a stamp	un francobollo

Phones & Mobile Phones

I want to buy a phone card.
Voglio comprare una scheda telefonica.
I want to make ...
Voglio fare ...

a call (to ...)	una chiamata (a ...)
reverse-charge/ collect call	una chiamata a carico del destinatario

Where can I find a/an ...?
Dove si trova ...
I'd like a/an ...
Vorrei ...

adaptor plug	un addattatore
charger for my phone	un caricabatterie
mobile/cell phone for hire	un cellulare da noleggiare
prepaid mobile/ cell phone	un cellulare prepagato
SIM card for your network	un SIM card per vostra rete telefonica

Internet

Where's the local Internet cafe?
Dove si trova l'Internet point?

I'd like to ...
Vorrei ...

| check my email | controllare le mie email |
| get online | collegarmi a Internet |

Shopping

| I'd like to buy ... | Vorrei comprare ... |
| How much is it? | Quanto costa? |

more	più
less	meno
smaller	più piccolo/a (m/f)
bigger	più grande

Do you accept ...?	Accettate ...?
credit cards	carte di credito
travellers cheques	assegni per viaggiatori

Transport

What time does the ... leave?
A che ora parte ...?

bus	l'autobus
plane	l'aereo
train	il treno

What time's the ... bus?
A che ora passa ... autobus?

first	il primo
last	l'ultimo
next	il prossimo

Are you free? (taxi)
È libero questo taxi?
Please put the meter on.
Usa il tassametro, per favore.
How much is it to ...?
Quant'è per ...?
Please take me to (this address).
Mi porti a (questo indirizzo), per favore.

FOOD

breakfast	prima colazione
lunch	pranzo
dinner	cena
a restaurant	un ristorante
a grocery store	un alimentari

I'd like the set lunch.
Vorrei il menù turistico.
Is service included in the bill?
È compreso il servizio?
What is this?
(Che) cos'è?
I'm a vegetarian.
Sono vegetariano/a.
I'm allergic to nuts.
Sono allergico/a alle noci.

I don't eat ...	Non mangio ...
meat	carne
chicken	pollo
fish	pesce

For more detailed information on food and dining out, see the Eating chapter, pp151-174.

EMERGENCIES

It's an emergency!
È un'emergenza!
Could you please help me/us?
Mi/Ci può aiutare, per favore?
Call the police/a doctor/an ambulance!
Chiami la polizia/un medico/ un'ambulanza!
Where's the police station?
Dov'è la questura?

HEALTH

Where's the nearest ...?
Dov'è ... più vicino?

chemist (night)	la farmacia (di turno)
dentist	il dentista
doctor	il medico
hospital	l'ospedale

I need a doctor (who speaks English).
Ho bisogno di un medico (che parli inglese).

Symptoms

I have (a) ...
Ho ...

diarrhoea	la diarrea
fever	la febbre
headache	mal di testa
pain	un dolore

Glossary

abbonamento mensile – monthly pass for public transport

ACI – Automobile Club Italiano (Italian Automobile Association)

aeroporto – airport

affitacamere – rooms for rent in private houses

albergo, alberghi (pl) – hotel (up to five stars)

alimentari – grocery shop

amaro – Italian liqueur (literally: 'bitter')

ambasciata – embassy

ambulanza – ambulance

APT – Azienda di Promozione Turistica (provincial tourist office)

autostazione – bus station/terminal

autostrada, autostrade (pl) – motorway, highway

baldacchino – canopy of fabric or stone over an altar, shrine or throne in a Christian church

benzina – petrol

benzina senza piombo – unleaded petrol

biblioteca, biblioteche (pl) – library

biglietteria – box or ticket office

biglietto – ticket

birreria – brewery or pub

borgo, borghi (pl) – walled village

bottega – shop

calcio – football (soccer)

campanile – a bell tower, usually free-standing

cappella – chapel

carabinieri – police with military and civil duties

carnevale – carnival period between Epiphany and Lent

carta d'identità – identity card

cartoleria – stationery shop

casa – house, home

caserma (dei carabinieri) – (carabinieri) barracks

castello – castle

catacomba – catacomb; underground tomb complex

cattedrale – cathedral

centro – city centre

centro commerciali – large shopping centres

centro sociale – social club

centro storico – historic centre, old city

chiesa, chiese (pl) – church

chilo – kilogram

chiostro – cloister; covered walkway, usually enclosed by columns, around a quadrangle

ciborio – goblet-shaped lidded vessel used to hold consecrated hosts for Holy Communion

cimitero – cemetery

circo – circus; chariot racetrack

CIT – Compagnia Italiana di Turismo (Italy's national travel agency)

collina – hill (*colle* in place names)

colonna – column

commissariato (di polizia) – police station

comune – equivalent to a municipality or county; town or city council; historically, a commune (self-governing town or city)

cordonata – stepped ramp

corso – main street

CTS – Centro Turistico Studentesco e Giovanile (Centre for Student and Youth Tourists)

cupola – dome

deposito bagagli – left luggage

digestivo – after-dinner liqueur

enoteca – specialist wine shop/bar

(un) etto – 100 grams

EUR – Esposizione Universale di Roma, a Fascist-era cultural complex south of the city centre

fermoposta – poste restante

ferragosto – Feast of the Assumption; more often refers to the major August (summer) holiday period

ferrovia – train station

festa – feast day; holiday

fidanzato/a (m/f) – fiancé, fiancée; also used colloquially for boyfriend/girlfriend

fiume – river

fontana – fountain

fornaio – bakery

fortezza – fort

forum, fora (pl) – public square

francobolli – stamps

FS – Ferrovie dello Stato; Italian State Railway

gabinetto – toilet, WC

gasolio – diesel

gelateria – ice-cream parlour

Ghetto – Jewish quarter

giunta – group of councillors

guardia di finanza – fiscal/finance police

IAT – Informazioni e Assistenza ai Turisti (local tourist office)

insula – multistorey apartment block

isola – island

IVA – Imposta di Valore Aggiunto (value-added tax)

lago – lake

largo – (small) square

lavanderia – laundrette

lavasecco – dry-cleaning

libreria – bookshop

lido – beach

lingua originale – original language

locanda – inn, small hotel

loggia – covered area on the side of a building, porch

lungolago – road along lake edge

lungomare – seafront road or promenade

marche da bollo – official stamps for tax or other payments

Language

mercato – market
merceria – haberdashery shop
Metropolitana (Metro) – suburban underground train system
mezzo porzione – half or child's portion
monte – mountain
motorino – moped
(le) mura – city wall
museo, musei (pl) – museum

necropoli – 'city of the dead' above-ground tomb complex, often Etruscan
numeri verdi – toll-free numbers

orto botanico – botanical gardens
ostello – hostel

palazzo, palazzi (pl) – mansion, palace, large building of any type (including an apartment block)
panetteria – bakery
parco – park
passeggiata – traditional evening stroll
pasticceria – cake/pastry shop
pellicola – roll of film
peristilio –peristyle or garden courtyard
permesso di lavoro – work permit
permesso di soggiorno – permit to stay in Italy for a nominated period
pescheria – fish shop or market
piazza, piazze (pl) – square
piazzale – (large) open square
pietà – literally pity or compassion; sculpture, drawing or painting of the dead Christ supported by the Madonna
pinacoteca – art gallery
piscina – pool
ponte – bridge
porta – city gate
portico – covered walkway, usually attached to the outside of buildings
posta – post office
posta prioritaria – priority mail
prepagato – prepaid phone account
presepio – model Nativity scene
profumeria – perfumery
pronto soccorso – first aid; (riparto di) pronto soccorso is a casualty/emergency ward

questura – police station

raccomandata – registered (eg mail, letter)
regioni – administrative regions in Italy, such as Lazio
ricevuta – receipt
Risorgimento – late-19th-century movement led by Garibaldi and others to create a united, independent Italian state

sala – room in a museum or a gallery
saldi – sales (ie with price reductions)
salumeria – delicatessen
scala – staircase
scalinata – staircase
sedia a rotelle – wheelchair
seggliolono – child's high chair
senza piombo – unleaded (petrol)
servizio – service charge in restaurants
sindaco – mayor
stazione – station
stazione di servizio – petrol or service station
supplemento – supplement, payable on a fast train

tabaccheria – tobacconist's shop
TCI – Touring Club Italiano
teatro – theatre
tempio – temple
terme – baths, hot springs
tesserae – small square tiles of stone, glass etc used in mosaics
titilus – a private house used for clandestine Christian worship
torre – tower
torta rustica – quiche
tumoli – mounds of earth with carved stone bases used by the Etruscans to entomb their dead

ufficio postale – post office
ufficio stranieri – foreigners' bureau (in police station)

via – street, road
via aerea – air mail
vicolo – alley, alleyway
vigili urbani – municipal police
Viterbesi – people of the Viterbo region

Behind the Scenes

THE LONELY PLANET STORY

The story begins with a classic travel adventure: Tony and Maureen Wheeler's 1972 journey across Europe and Asia to Australia. There was no useful information about the overland trail then, so Tony and Maureen published the first Lonely Planet guidebook to meet a growing need.

From a kitchen table, Lonely Planet has grown to become the largest independent travel publisher in the world, with offices in Melbourne (Australia), Oakland (USA), London (UK) and Paris (France).

Today Lonely Planet guidebooks cover the globe. There is an ever-growing list of books and information in a variety of media. Some things haven't changed. The main aim is still to make it possible for adventurous travellers to get out there – to explore and better understand the world.

At Lonely Planet we believe travellers can make a positive contribution to the countries they visit – if they respect their host communities and spend their money wisely. Since 1986 a percentage of the income from each book has been donated to aid projects and human rights campaigns, and, more recently, to wildlife conservation.

THIS BOOK

This edition was written by Duncan Garwood and Kristin Kimball with a contribution from Richard Watkins (History). The Food & Drink chapter was based on Lonely Planet's *World Food Italy* by Matthew Evans and the Excursions chapter was based on the research of Wendy Owen. The previous edition (2nd) was written and updated by Sally Webb. Helen Gillman, Stefano Cavedoni and Sally wrote the first edition. This edition was commissioned in Lonely Planet's UK office and produced by:

Commissioning Editor Michala Green
Coordinating Editor Tegan Murray
Coordinating Cartographer Natasha Velleley
Layout Designer Dianne Zammit
Editors & Proofreaders Meg Worby, David Andrew & Julia Taylor
Cartographer Andrew Smith
Cover Designer Wendy Wright
Series Designer Nic Lehman
Series Design Concept Nic Lehman & Andrew Weatherill
Layout Manager Adriana Mammarella
Managing Cartographer Mark Griffiths
Managing Editor Bruce Evans
Mapping Development Paul Piaia
Project Manager Glenn van der Knijff
Language Editor Quentin Frayne
Regional Publishing Manager Katrina Browning
Series Publishing Manager Gabrielle Green
Series Development Team Dani Valent, Ed Pickard, Fiona Christie, James Ellis, Janine Eberle, Kate Cody, Michele Posner, Roz Hopkins, Simone Egger, Anna Bolger, Dave McClymont, Erin Corrigan, Howard Ralley, Jenny Blake, Rachel Peart, Leonie Mugavin, Nadine Fogale
Thanks to Steven Cann, Indra Kilfoyle & Kate McDonald

Cover photographs Main stairway in the Musei del Vaticano, Greg Elms/Lonely Planet Images (top); Piazza Venezia, warden directing heavy traffic, Stephen Studd/Getty Images (bottom); Lunchtime at La Foccacia on the Via della Pace 11, Martin Moos/Lonely Planet Images (back)

Internal photographs by Martin Moos/Lonely Planet Images except for the following: p61 (#2), p182 (#4), p185 (#1, 3), p186 (#3) Sally Webb/Lonely Planet Images; p2 (#5), p84 Glenn Beanland/Lonely Planet Images; p17, p179 (#1) John Hay/Lonely Planet Images; p44, p199 Neil Setchfield/Lonely Planet Images; p26 Richard Meier & Partners; p179 (#3) Jenny Jones/Lonely Planet Images; p186 (#1) Geoff Stringer/Lonely Planet Images; p253 Tony Wheeler/Lonely Planet Images. All images are the copyright of the photographers unless otherwise indicated. Many of the images in this guide are available for licensing from Lonely Planet Images: www.lonelyplanetimages.com.

ACKNOWLEDGMENTS

Many thanks to the following for the use of their content: ATAC S.p.A. Rome Metro Map © 2001; © Richard Meier & Partners (image26).

THANKS
DUNCAN GARWOOD

Lots of people helped me on this job. A big thank you to Michala Green for giving me the commission and then patiently answering all my ridiculous questions; Rebecca Lennox for so generously giving me the time off and Richard McKenna for his pointers. Christian Bayliss was brilliant, advising me on the very latest on the Rome scene.

Thanks also to Roberto Proietti who generously gave me some of his time, and proved a wonderfully generous interviewee; to Carlo Biancheri for his restaurant advice; and to fellow author Kristin and Kelly for their lively company.

Finally, grazie di cuore to Lidia for so calmly looking after our beautiful baby boy Ben and to Ma and Pa Salvati for taking such good care of them both.

KRISTIN KIMBALL

Reverent thanks to the immortal artists of the Eternal City for never disappointing. Thanks and much love to Sister Kelly Elizabeth for piloting the Vespa. May there be many occasions to laugh so hard over coffee so good. Thanks to Mark, once again, for being home.

OUR READERS

Many thanks to the travellers who used the last edition and wrote to us with helpful hints, useful advice and interesting anecdotes. Your names follow: Daryl Achilles, Ron Alexander, Zubeir Alvi, Carol

Andrews, Steve Bailey, Jonathan Barrett, Tony Bellette, Ashley Benjamin, Daniel Bleakin, Jane Bobko, Cameron Bush, Christian Byhahn, Jackie Carter, Flaminia Chapman, Cindy Chittenden, Lila Cohen, Ron Corbett, Sheila Corbett, Sue Craven, Steve Cummins, Bronwyn Curnow, Luke Das-Gupta, Adrian de Almeida, David Deutscher, Anne Dillon, Robert Dillon, Jim Dingwall, Majorie Douglass, Silvia Duerrsperger, Mitch Dushay, James Farquhar, Elizabeth Finch, Matt Goben, Chantal Haillez, Jennifer Hansen, Mubashir Hasan, Emily Heilbrun, Megan Heim, Adrian Hervey, Janet Houston, Amina Hussain, Diana James, Mark Jital, Falko Kernchen, Sonia Knox, Louise Kyme, Emma Laney, Alex Lang, Lena Liacopoulou, Jo Linsdell, Andrew Lyons, Sean Lyons, Daniela Madelaine, Stephanie Mazur, Emily McKenzie-Kay, Paul McKernan, Bert Meissgeyer, Sarah Mills, Amy Morale, Paul Murtagh, Shahak Nagiel, Robin O'Donoghue, Gustavo Orlando-Zon, Hrafnkell Oskarsson, Perry Oza, Sue Phillips, Cécile Pommeron, J Redmond, Tony Richmond, Carmen Salazar, Mark Sammut, Annette Satterfiled, Herbert Schurian, Tanja Schwaegerl, Harvey Schwartz, Trisha Simmons, Halouani Slim, Deborah Sloan, Clyde and Elva Slonaker, Graham Smithard, Sanne Tieke, Julia Tobey, Juha Valimaki, Josh van Wagoner, Philip Vandenbroeck, Erik Vloeberghs, Roz Webb, Gerry White, Annette Wiesner, Fiona Wilson, Danielle Wolbers, Helen Yau.

SEND US YOUR FEEDBACK

We love to hear from travellers – your comments keep us on our toes and help make our books better. Our well-travelled team reads every word on what you loved or loathed about this book. Although we cannot reply individually to postal submissions, we always guarantee that your feedback goes straight to the appropriate authors, in time for the next edition. Each person who sends us information is thanked in the next edition – and the most useful submissions are rewarded with a free book.

To send us your updates – and find out about LP events, newsletters and travel news – visit our award-winning website: www.lonelyplanet.com.

Note: We may edit, reproduce and incorporate your comments in Lonely Planet products such as guidebooks, websites and digital products, so let us know if you don't want your comments reproduced or your name acknowledged. For a copy of our privacy policy, email privacy@lonelyplanet.com.au.

Notes

Notes

Notes

Notes

Notes

Index

See also separate indexes for Eating (p298), Shopping (p299) and Sleeping (p300).

Index

000 map pages
000 photographs

000 map pages
000 photographs

LEGEND
ROUTES

Tollway		One Way Street
Freeway		Unsealed Road
Primary Road		Mall/Steps
Secondary Road		Tunnel
Tertiary Road		Walking Tour
Lane		Walking Tour Detour
Under Construction		Walking Path

TRANSPORT

Ferry	Rail
Metro	Rail (Underground)
Monorail	Tram
Bus Route	Cable Car, Funicular

HYDROGRAPHY

River, Creek	Canal
Intermittent River	Water
Swamp	Lake (Dry)

BOUNDARIES

International	Regional, Suburb
State, Provincial	Ancient Wall

AREA FEATURES

Airport	Cemetery, Christian
Area of Interest	Cemetery, Other
Beach, Desert	Land
Building, Featured	Mall
Building, Information	Market
Building, Other	Park
Building, Transport	Sports
Campus	Urban

POPULATION

✪ **CAPITAL (NATIONAL)**	◉ CAPITAL (STATE)
● **Large City**	● Medium City
○ Small City	○ Town, Village

SYMBOLS

SIGHTS/ACTIVITIES	EATING	INFORMATION
Beach	Eating	Bank, ATM
Buddhist	**DRINKING**	Embassy/Consulate
Castle, Fortress	Drinking	Hospital, Medical
Christian	Café	Information
Confucian	**ENTERTAINMENT**	Internet Facilities
Hindu	Entertainment	Parking Area
Islamic	**SHOPPING**	Petrol Station
Jewish	Shopping	Police Station
Monument	**SLEEPING**	Post Office, GPO
Museum, Gallery	Sleeping	Telephone
Picnic Area	Camping	Toilets
Point of Interest	**TRANSPORT**	**GEOGRAPHIC**
Ruin	Airport, Airfield	Lighthouse
Shinto	Border Crossing	Lookout
Sikh	Bus Station	Mountain
Skiing	Cycling, Bicycle Path	National Park
Taoist	General Transport	Pass, Canyon
Winery, Vineyard	Taxi Rank	River Flow
Zoo, Bird Sanctuary	Trail Head	Waterfall

NOTE: Not all symbols displayed above appear in this guide.

Map Section

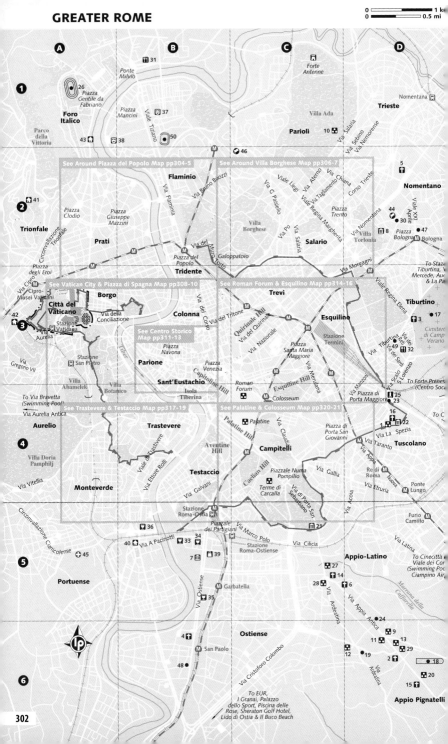

GREATER ROME

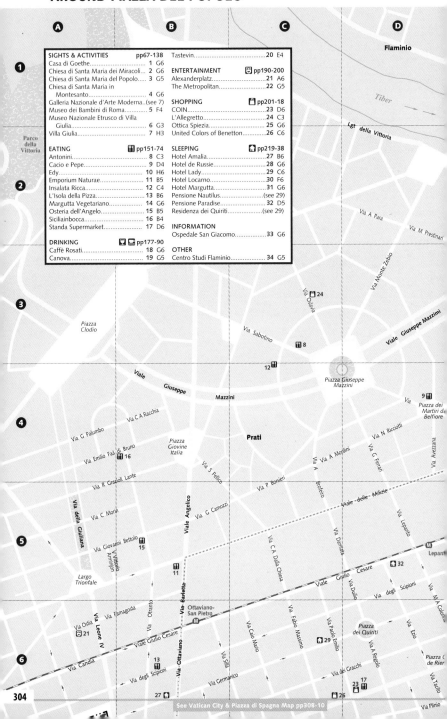

See Vatican City & Piazza di Spagna Map pp308-10

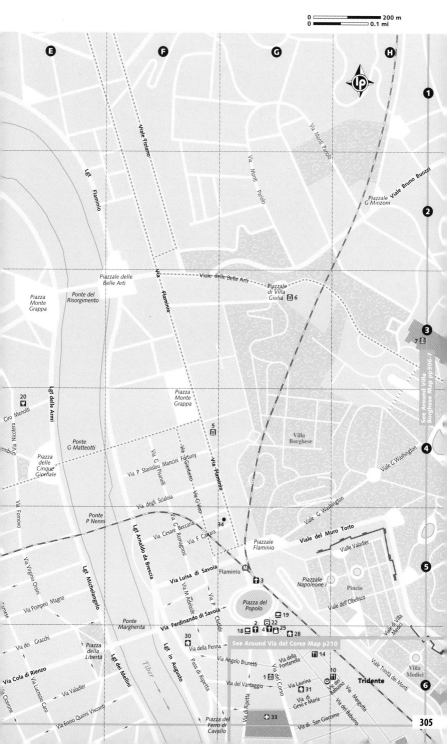

0 — 200 m
0 — 0.1 mi

E F G H

1
2
3
4
5
6

Viale Triziano

Via Monti Parioli

Via Monti Parioli

Viale Bruno Buozzi

Piazzale G Minzoni

Lgt Flaminio

Piazzale delle Belle Arti

Ponte del Risorgimento

Viale delle Belle Arti

Piazzale di Villa Giulia 🏛 6

Piazza Monte Grappa

7 🏛

See Around Villa Borghese Map pp306-7

Lgt delle Armi

20 🏛

Ciro Menotti

Via Nicotera

Piazza Monte Grappa

5 🏛

Villa Borghese

Piazza delle Cinque Giornate

Ponte G Matteotti

Via P Stanislao Mancini Fortuny

Via G Pisarelli

Via Ganterou

Via G Mico

Via Flaminia

Viale G Washington

Via Fornovo

Via degli Scialoia

Ponte P Nenni

Lgt Arnaldo da Brescia

Via Cesare Beccaria

Via F Cavara

34

Viale del Muro Torto

Viale Valadier

Piazzale Flaminio

Via Virginio Orsini

Via Luisa di Savoia

Via M Adelaide

Via P Adelaide

Flaminio

🚇 3

Piazzale Napoleone I

Pincio

Lgt Michelangelo

Ponte Margherita

Via Ferdinando di Savoia

Via Cialdie

Piazza del Popolo

19 🏛

Viale dell'Obelisco

Via Pompeo Magno

Via dei Gracchi

Piazza della Libertà

Lgt dei Mellini

Tiber

30 🏛

Via della Penna

18 🏛 2 22 🏛 4 🏛 25 28 🏛

Viale di Villa Medici

Via Cola di Rienzo

Via Lucrezio Caro

Via Valadier

Lgt in Augusto

Pass di Ripetta

See Around Via del Corso Map p210

🏛 14

Villa Medici

Via Cicerone

Via Ennio Quirini Visconti

Via Angelo Brunetti

Via della Fontanella

10 🏛

Viale Trinità dei Monti

Piazza del Ferro di Cavallo

Via di Ripetta

🏥 33

1 🏛 Via del Corso

Via del Vantaggio

Via Laurina

Via di Gesù e Maria

Via del Babuino

Via Margutta

Via di San Giacomo

Tridente

AROUND VILLA BORGHESE

A   **B**   **C**   **D**

1

Via G Antonelli

Parioli

Viale dei Parioli

Via A Stoppani

Via F Siacci

Viale Romania

Villa Ada

Via Panama

Piazza Cuba

Piazza Ungheria

Viale   Bruno   Buozzi

Via Liegi

Via M

Mercati

2 22

Via G D'Arezzo

19

Via U Aldrovandi

Viale G Rossini

Via Cavalieri

V G Carissimi

Piazza G Verdi

3

See Around Piazza del Popolo Map pp304-5

Via Ulisse Aldrovandi

Viale del   Giardino   del   Zoologica

Via S Mercaddante

Via N Porpora

Via G Paisiello

1

Piazza Giardino Zoologico

Via G Frescobaldi

16

20

Via Pergolesi

Largo N Spinelli

Viale dell'Uccelliera

Viale dei Due Mascheroni

Piazzale di Daini

4

Giardino del Lago

3

Largo Aqua Felix

Villa Borghese

Via G Vasariio

Piazza San Borghese **4**

15

Via Po

Viale Pietro Canonica

Viale dei

Piazza di Sienna

Piazza le dei Cavalli Marini

Cavalli Marini

Via Pinciana

Via Tevere

Via Isonzo

Via

Piazza le di Canestre

5

Viale delle Magnolie

Via Wolfango Goethe

Viale San Paolo del Brasile

Viale del Museo Borghese

Piazzale Sienkiewicz

V G Puccini

Via Teresa

Via Anier

Villa Borghese

2

Galoppatio

Via Campania

Via Lucania

See Around Via del Corso Map p210

Via Pinciana

Corso d'Italia

Via Puglie

Villa Medici

Viale del Galoppatio

Viale del Muro Torto

Porta Pinciana

Piazzale Brasile

Largo Federico Fellini

Via Campania

Via Sardegna

6 **6**

Via Toscana

Via Piemonte

Via Abruzzi

Via Romagna

Via Pugle

6

5

Campo Marzio

Via Lazio

11

17

Via Vittorio Veneto

Via Marche

Via Sicilia

8

Via Boncompagni

Piaz Sallu

0 ——— 200 m
0 ——— 0.1 mi

SIGHTS & ACTIVITIES pp67-138

Bioparco	1 B3
Il Galoppatio Equestrian Club	2 A5
Museo Canonica	3 B4
Museo e Galleria Borghese	4 C4
Villa Medici	5 A6

EATING 🍴 pp151-74

Papà Baccus	6 C6

DRINKING 🍸 pp177-90

Alien	7 E5
Jackie O	8 C6
Piper	9 E3

SHOPPING 🛍 pp201-18

Borgo Parioli Market	10 E2
Carry-On	11 B6
La Rinascente	12 E5
Liberia L'Argonauta	13 F5

SLEEPING 🏠 pp219-38

Hotel Ercoli	(see 14)
Hotel Tizi	14 E6
Hotel Villa Borghese	15 D4
Parco dei Principi	16 C3

TRANSPORT pp258-63

Air One	17 B6

INFORMATION

Australian Embassy & Consulate	18 G4
Austrian Consulate	19 D2
Austrian Embassy	20 C3
Canadian Consulate	21 H4
Dutch Embassy & Consulate	22 B2
New Zealand Consulate	23 G4
UK Embassy	24 E6

OTHER

Executive Services Business Centres	25 E4

See Roman Forum & Esquilino Map pp314-16

A B C D

1
2
3
4
5
6

See Around Piazza del Popolo Map pp304-5

Via degli Scipioni
Via Germanico
Via Caio Mario
Via Fabio Massimo
Via Paolo Emilia
Via Reglia
Via Plinio

77
Via Vespasiano
Via Ottaviano
98
Via dei Gracchi
Via della Unità
93
83
34
39
Via Catullo
Via Boezio
86
Viale B di
Michelangelo
Piazza del Risorgimento
Via Catone
73
54
Via Cola di Rienzo
Via Terenzio
Via Cassiodoro

Viale della Zitella

Via di Porta Angelica
Borgo Angelico
Via Stefano Porcari
Via P Leto
Via Varrone
63
Via Properzio
Via Tibullo
Via Crescenzio

28
Via della Posta
Via della Tipografia
Via del Pellegrino
Via del Mascherino
Via del Falco
Piazza Americo Capponi
Via Cancelleri
Via Alberico II
Via Plauto
Vittorio
Via Vitelleschi
Via Ombrellari
88
Via S Pallavicini
Via P
Della Valle
Via Adriana

Giardini del Vaticano

Via del Belvedere
109
Largo San Martino
Piazza della Città Leonina
Borgo Pio
Vic delle Palline
Vic del Orfeo
45
Largo di Porta Castello
89
Borgo
Borgo
Via P
Castello

Borgo

24
Cittá del Vaticano
Piazza San Pietro
Piazza Pio XII
Piazza Rusticucci
Via dei Corridori
Borgo Sant'Angelo
Piazza Pia
Piazza Giovanni XXIII
Lgt Vaticano
67
107

25
Largo Colonnato
Via della Conciliazione
Ponte Sant'Angelo

Piazza dei P Romani
101
Via Paolo VI
Via del Sant'Uffizio
Via Pfeiffer
90
Largo I Gregore
Borgo
Santo Spirito
Via San Pio X
Ponte Vittorio Emanuele II
Piazza Paoli
Lgt della Altovit
Ponte

Piazza Santa Marta
103
Largo degli Alicorni
Lgt in Sassia
Piazza della Oro
5
Piazza P Paoli
Largo Tassoni
Ponte

Via Aurelia
Piazza di Sant'Uffizio
105
Piazza della Rovere
Ponte Principe Amedeo
Lgt Fiorentini
84
Vic delle Palle

Piazzale Gregorio VII
Largo Porta Cavalleggeri
Galleria Principe Amedeo Savoia Aosta
Piazza della Rovere
Vic delle

Via Sergio I
Via di Porta Cavalleggeri
Via A De Gasperi
71
Via del Gianicolo
Vic Sant'Onofrio
Via di Sant'Onofrio
Vic del Cefalo
Via dei Bressani
Lgt D Sangallo

Via del Crocifisso
97
Piazza Santa Maria alle Fornaci
Via Nicolò III
Via del Largo Stazione di San Pietro
Via D Silveri
Salita di Sant'Onofrio
Via di Sant'Onofrio

Via Clivo
Via di Monte del Gallo
Via del Gallo
Monte del Gallo
Piazza di Sant'Onofrio
104

Monte di Gallo
San Pietro
Via G Massori
Viale delle Mura Aurelie
delle Fornaci
Ponte G Mazzini

87
Via di Monte del Gallo
Via Innocenzo III
Via degli Orti d'Alibert
Via delle Mantelate

Rampa Ceriala
Via A Ceriani
Via Clemente Alessandrino
Lgt Gianicolense
108
Via di Lungar

Vic dei Vicario
68
Via di San Francesco di Sales
96
70
32
Via della Penitenza
Villa Orto Botanico

1
Piazzale Anita Garibaldi
Via dei Riari

Via della Cava Aurelia

Villa Abamelek
13
Piazzale Giuseppe Garibaldi
Parco Gianicolense
17
Gianicolo Hill

See Trastevere & Testaccio Map pp317-19

CENTRO STORICO (pp312-13)

A B C D

1

Palazzo
Gabrielli

Piazzella di
San Simeone

Via dei Tre Archi
Via dei Coronari

Piazza Tor
Sanguigna

Piazza Sant'
Apollinare

Piazza
di Sant'
Agostino
Via di San Agostino

Via dei
Loronesi

Piazza delle
V Lune

Largo
Febo

Via di Santa Maria dell'Anima

Corso del Rinascimento

Via del Salvatore

2

Piazza dell'
Orologio ● 52

Via di Tor Millina

Piazza
Navona

Via di Teatro
Pace

Via de Cupis

Via degli Staderari

Piazza San
Cesarini

Piazza della
Chiesa Nuova

Corso Vittorio Emanuele II

Piazza
Pasquino

Via
Pasquino

Via dei
Canestrari

Via dei Sediari

3

Parione

Piazza dei
Massimi

Piazza di San
Pantaleo

Largo del
Teatro Valle

Via dei Banchi Vecchi

Piazza
Ricci

Piazza della
Cancelleria

Piazza di
Sant'Andrea
della Valle

Corso Vittori

Piazza
Vidoni

4

Regola

Via Giulia

Via del Pellegrino

Via dei
Cappelli

Via di Montoro

Piazza
Campo
de' Fiori

Piazza
Pollarola

Piazza
Paradiso

Via del Sudari

Piazza del
Biscione

Largo del
Pallaro

5

Piazza
Farnese

Via San Girolamo della Carità

Via dei Farnesi

Via del Mascherone

Piazza della
Quercia

Via Arco del Monte

Piazza dei
Satiri

Piazza del
Monte di Pietà

Piazza
Trinità
Pelegrini

6

Lgt dei Tebaldi

Tiber

Lgt della Farnesina

Piazza SV
Pallotti

Via dei Pettinari

Via del Conservatorio

Ministero di
Giustizia e Giustizia
● 5

Campo
Marzio

Sallustiano

Piazza
Sallustio

Piazza di
Spagna

Piazza
della Trinità
di Monti

Piazza
Mignanelli

Piazza
Accademia
di San Luca

Trevi

Barberini

Piazza
Barberini

Piazza
San Bernardo

Piazza
San Bernardo

Piazza
Orlando

Piazza della
Repubblica

Repubblica

Giardino del
Quirinale

Quirinal

Quirinale Hill

Piazza
Scanderberg

Piazza di
Trevi

Piazza del
Quirinale

Montecarlo

Villa
Colonna

Piazza
B Gigli

Piazza dell'
Esquilino

Piazza dei
SS Apostoli

Piazza
Santissimi
Apostoli

Largo
Magnanapoli

Largo
Angelicum

Piazza
Viminale

Ministero
dell'
Interno

Piazza della
Madonna
Venezia di Loreto

Foro Trajano

Piazza
Madonna
dei Monti

Piazza Suburra

Largo
Visconti
Venosta

Cavour

Piazza
Zingari

Piazza
San Marti
ai Mont

Monti

Piazza del
Campidoglio

Capitoline Hill

Largo C Ricci

Largo
Romolo
e Remo

Piazza San
Francesco
di Paola

Piazza di
San Pietro
in Vincoli

Largo D
Polveriera

Parco Opj

Piazza della
Consolazione

Largo G
Agnesi

Esquiline Hill   Colle Oppio

Campitelli

Orti
Farnesiani

Colosseo

Viale della Domus Aurea

Colosseum

Piazza del
Coloseo

314

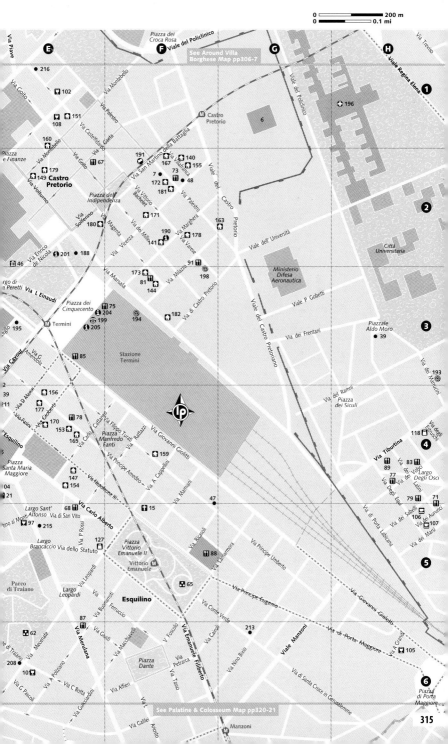

ROMAN FORUM & ESQUILINO (pp314-15)

316

A   B   C   D

1

Aurelio

Trastevere

Villa
Abamelek

See Vatican City & Piazza
di Spagna Map pp308-10

Via della Cava Aurelia

Via delle Mura Aurelie

Passeggiata del Gianicolo

Via delle Nuova Fornaci

Via

Aurelia

Antica

Villa
Aurelio

Via di Porta San Pancrazio

Via San Pietro
in Montorio

● Garibaldi
18

Via Garibaldi

Via di San Pancrazio

Piazzale
Porta San
Pancrazio

● 25
13

2

Via di San Pancrazio

Via Merca ntini

V G Bruzzesi

Viale delle Mura Gia

Via G Medici

Via Trenta Aprile

Via Trenta Aprile

Largo G
Cocchi

Via F Daverio

Viale Nicola Fabrizi

Piazza
F Cucchi

Via A Algardi

Via Fratelli Bonnet

Via P Roselli

Via di Villa Pamphilj

Via Basilio Bricci

Via dei Quattro Venti

Largo
L Miceli

Via Giacinto Carini

Via di Calandrelli

Villa
Sciarra

Via Dandolo

3

Via Vitellia

Via Fonteiana

Via Bolognesi

Via O Regnoli

Via del Vascello

Via Ni Serri

Gianicolensi

Vic Cosmo de Torres

Via A Busiri Vici

Via FS Sprovieri

78

Via G Rossetti

V U Bassi

4

Via R Giovagnoli

Piazza
Pilo
Rosolino

Via M Quadrio

Scalea U Bassi

Via Monreale

Via A Colautti

Via F Torre

Via G B Nicolini

Via Felice Cavallotti

Via Alessandro Poerio

Via F Brunetti

Francesco da Ir Ongaro

5

Monteverde

Via di Villa Pamphilj

Via S Calandrelli

Viale di Quattro Venti

Via Antonio Cesari

Giulio Barrili

Via Francesco
D Guerazzi

Via Anton

Piazzale
Quattro
Venti

Via Pisacane

6

Via G Cuocizzelli

Via Alessandro Poerio

Via di Ponziano

Via G Cavalcanti

Via G Parrasio

8

319

PALATINE & COLOSSEUM

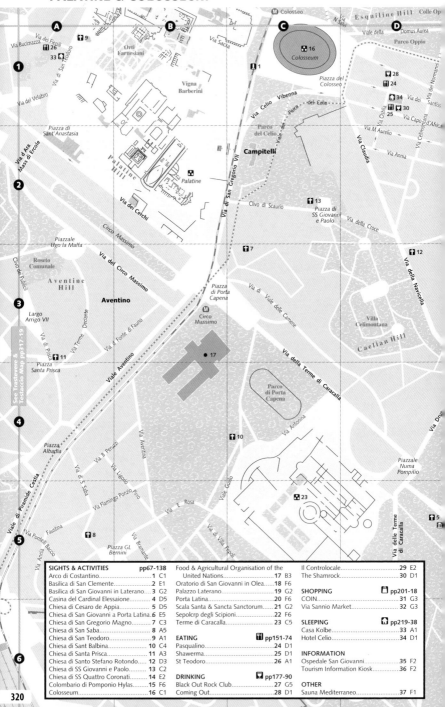